Charles Dickens

HIS TRAGEDY AND TRIUMPH

BY EDGAR JOHNSON

FICTION

Unweave a Rainbow:
A Sentimental Fantasy

The Praying Mantis

BIOGRAPHY

One Mighty Torrent:
The Drama of Biography

The Heart of Charles Dickens:
His Letters to Angela Burdett Coutts

ANTHOLOGIES

A Treasury of Satire

A Treasury of Biography

DICKENS IN MIDDLE AGE
Engraved by George E. Perine from a Photograph

Charles Dickens

HIS TRAGEDY AND TRIUMPH

By Edgar Johnson

VOLUME TWO

SIMON AND SCHUSTER

1952

Appreciation is expressed to the following for their courtesy in granting permission to reproduce various pictures from their collections in the photographic sections of these volumes:

New York Public Library Picture Collection: pictures 3, 4, 15, 16, 17, 18, 19, 21, 22, 23, 27, 44, 47, 52, 57, 60, 62, 63, 64, 65, 66, 67, 68, 79, 80, 85; Frontispiece, Vol. Two

Dickens House, Doughty Street, London: pictures 11, 20, 25, 43, 53, 59

National Portrait Gallery, London: picture 24

Courtesy of Major Philip Dickens and Dickens House, Doughty Street, London: picture 30

Courtesy of Leigh B. Block: picture 31

Courtesy of Leslie C. Staples: picture 37

Carlyle House, Cheyne Row, Chelsea, London: pictures 40, 41

Reproduced by courtesy of Sir Michael Culme-Seymour: picture 50

Central Office of Information, London: picture 72

William M. Elkins Collection, Philadelphia: picture 84

MANUFACTURED IN THE UNITED STATES OF AMERICA
BY AMERICAN BOOK—STRATFORD PRESS, INC., N. Y.

Contents

List of Illustrations

VOLUME TWO

Frontispiece: Dickens in Middle Age

REPRODUCTIONS OF ORIGINAL "PHIZ" DRAWINGS FOR DICKENS'S WORKS

ILLUSTRATION SECTION: DICKENS'S LIFE FROM 1850 TO 1870
(immediately following this listing)

[VII]

[45] DICKENS, 1850-1852. Photograph by J. Mayall, engraved by Linton

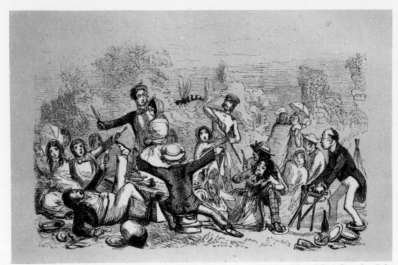

[46] AWFUL APPEARANCE OF A "WOPPS" at a picnic, Shanklin Sands, Isle of Wight. Cartoon by John Leech, in Punch, August 25, 1849

[47] MARK LEMON, the Dickens children's "Uncle Porpoise," Editor of Punch

[48] WILLIAM HENRY WILLS, Sub-Editor of Household Words. A drawing in the possession of Punch

[49] ROCKINGHAM CASTLE, home of the Watsons and the original of Chesney Wold in *Bleak House*

[50] THE HONORABLE MRS. RICHARD WATSON. Portrait at Rockingham Castle

[51] THE HONORABLE MR. RICHARD WATSON. Portrait at Rockingham Castle

[52] Edward Lytton Bulwer Lytton, Baron Lytton

[53] Knebworth, Hertfordshire, Garden Front. The home of Lord Lytton

[54] DICKENS, 1856. From the portrait by Ary Scheffer

[55] MRS. HENRY LOUIS WINTER (Maria Beadnell)

[56] TAVISTOCK HOUSE, Dickens's home, 1851-1860, where he wrote *Bleak House* and *Little Dorrit*. Photograph by Catherine Weed Barnes Ward

[57] WILKIE COLLINS, favorite companion of Dickens's middle years

[58] CLARKSON STANFIELD, R.A., "Dear Old Stanny," scene-painter of *The Lighthouse* and *The Frozen Deep*

[59] Scene from the performance of *The Lighthouse* at Camp-den House, July 10, 1855

[60] William Makepeace Thack-eray. Painted by Alonzo Chappell from a drawing by Samuel Laurence

[61] John Forster in middle age, his "Podsnap" period. Engraving by C. H. Jeens

[62] CHARLES CULLI-
FORD BOZ DICKENS, age
fifteen. Drawing by
George Richmond

[63] SYDNEY SMITH
HALDIMAND DICKENS.
From a painting by Mar-
cus Stone, R.A.

[64] EDWARD BULWER
LYTTON DICKENS,
"Plorn." From a paint-
ing by Marcus Stone

[65] HENRY FIELDING
and FRANCIS JEFFREY
DICKENS

[66] WALTER LANDOR
DICKENS

[67] MARY DICKENS,
"Mamey."
From a Miniature

[68] KATE MACREADY
DICKENS (Mrs. Peru-
gini). From a portrait
by Marcus Stone, R. A.

A GALLERY OF DICKENS'S CHILDREN

[69] DICKENS, 1859. From the portrait by W. P. Frith, R.A.

[70] *Right*, FROM WHOM WE HAVE GREAT EXPECTATIONS, 1861. Photographic caricature

[71] DICKENS, 1861. From a pencil drawing by Rudolph Lehmann

[72] GAD'S HILL PLACE, entrance front, Dickens's home, 1857-1870, where he wrote *A Tale of Two Cities, Great Expectations, Our Mutual Friend,* and *Edwin Drood,* and where he died. Photograph by J. Dixon-Scott

[73] DICKENS READING to Mamey and Katey, circa 1865. Photograph by R. H. Mason

[74] GAD'S HILL PLACE from the garden. Photograph by Catherine Weed Barnes Ward

[75] THE BRITISH LION IN AMERICA, 1868. From the *Daily Joker*, New York

[76] DICKENS AS PEDESTRIAN, 1868. From the Boston *Daily Advertiser*

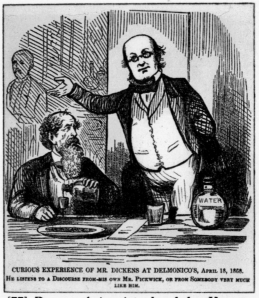

CURIOUS EXPERIENCE OF MR. DICKENS AT DELMONICO'S, APRIL 18, 1868. HE LISTENS TO A DISCOURSE FROM HIS OWN MR. PICKWICK, OR FROM SOMEBODY VERY MUCH LIKE HIM.

[77] DICKENS being introduced by HORACE GREELEY at the New York newspaper dinner

[78] DICKENS, 1868. From the photograph by Ben Gurney

[79] DICKENS IN HIS STUDY at Gad's Hill. From a pen-and-ink sketch by W. Steinhaus

[80] Above, CHARLES DICKENS exhausted after a reading. Pen-and-ink sketch by Harry Furniss

[81] Left, DICKENS, FEBRUARY, 1870. Caricature sketch by Spy (Leslie Ward)

[82] Jasper's Gate House, Rochester, with the parish church on the right, used as one of the settings in *Edwin Drood*

[83] The Swiss Chalet, in which the last lines of *Edwin Drood* were written. Photograph by Catherine Weed Barnes Ward

[84] "The Empty Chair," Gad's Hill, June 7, 1870. Painting by Sir Luke Fildes on the day of Dickens's death

[85] Charles Dickens after Death. Drawing by Sir J. E. Millais, R.A.

[86] Westminster Abbey, the Poet's Corner. Dickens's grave at lower right. Pen-and-ink drawing by Arthur Moreland

PART SEVEN

At Grips with Himself

1846–1853

A NOTE ON THE NOTES

The bulk of these references, indicated by numbers in roman type, give the sources of the statements and quotations in the text. The numbers in italics, however, mark notes containing supplementary information or discussion.

CHAPTER ONE

Difficulties with Dombey

ALTHOUGH Dickens was no longer editor, he did not completely sever all connection with the *Daily News*. His friend Forster sat in the editorial chair, elated with his new dignity and big with plans for improving the paper;[1] it had been Dickens's own creation and in the main still represented his reform liberalism. Both personal loyalty and principle suggested that he should act as if it had always been his intention merely to give the new paper a start and then step out.[2] Six more of his brightly colored Italian travel letters consequently appeared at intervals in its pages. (Near the end of May, illustrated with four wood-block vignettes by Samuel Palmer and with five added chapters, these were published in book form by Bradbury and Evans under the title of *Pictures from Italy*.) Before his resignation Dickens also contributed a letter describing the work of the Ragged Schools; and after it, in March, he wrote three letters on capital punishment.[3]

These letters, probably representing the gist of his abandoned article for the *Edinburgh Review*, contain some penetrating observations on the psychology of murder. On crimes of gain, sudden rage, or despairing affection (as when a parent kills a starving child), Dickens insisted that the punishment of death had no restraining influence at all. On those of vengeance or the craving for notoriety, he argued, the death penalty often served as an added stimulus. By threatening the murderer's own life it suggested to distorted minds that his crime was fair enough if he was ready to risk the punishment. Let his victim not feel too sure of being safe in the protection of the gallows; the murderer would have his revenge though he were hanged for it! And over certain morbid imaginations, the publicity of the trial and the tense

climax before an assembled multitude exercised a horrible fascination.[4]

Nor could it be claimed that the death penalty diminished crime.
Out of a hundred and sixty-seven convicts under sentence of death,
an officiating clergyman found only three who had never seen an execution. Statistics in all countries showed that murders decreased after
every period in which the number of death sentences was reduced.[5]
Further, the many recorded examples of the death penalty having
been inflicted upon people afterward proved innocent should make
"men of finite judgment" hesitate to inflict "an infinite and irrepa-
rable punishment." [6] In conclusion, Dickens said, "I beg to be understood as advocating the total abolition of the Punishment of Death,
as a general principle, for the advantage of society, for the prevention
of crime, and without the least reference to, or tenderness for any individual malefactor whatsoever." [7]

Dickens's argument was formulated entirely in terms of social welfare, not at all in tenderness for the condemned killer. Many people,
however, like Thomas Babington Macaulay, continued to regard the
movement for abolishing the death penalty as rooted in nothing more
than a misapplied sentimentality about murderers. Dickens became
convinced that the reform was too far in advance of popular feeling
and comprehension to be practicable, and he had no desire to waste
his energies agitating for remote ends when immediate goods might
be attained. The major evil, as he saw it, was the psychological effect
of the horrible drama of hanging before a brutalized and gloating mob.
Without changing his personal view, he consequently modified his
public position in the course of the next few years to the demand that
executions be confined to the interior of the jail.

During the time of these last contributions to the *Daily News* Dickens was restless and uncertain of his future movements. He even dal-
lied with the idea of qualifying as a paid London magistrate and
wrote a member of the Government to inquire about his chances of
receiving an appointment. But the reply was discouraging; and, besides, the idea for another book was beginning to simmer in his mind,
bringing its usual feelings of excitement and vague dissatisfaction.[8] By
April he had arranged with Bradbury and Evans to write a novel in
twenty monthly parts. "I don't think," he told Forster, "I *could* shut
out the paper sufficiently, here, to write well." [9] In the end, he re-

turned to the idea of subletting Devonshire Terrace and going abroad again.

"Now, I need not tell you," he wrote Mme. De la Rue, "that *I* want to go to Genoa! But Mrs. Dickens, who was never very well there, cannot be got to contemplate the Peschiere, though I have beset her in all kinds of ways." (Very probably, too, Kate's distaste for being once more near the De la Rues was not diminished by knowing that the ethereal young Christiana Thompson might also be in that part of the world.) "Therefore," Dickens went on, "I think I should take a middle course for the present, and, coming as near you as I could, pitch my tent somewhere on the Lake of Geneva, say at Lausanne, whence I should run over to Genoa immediately." [10]

Meanwhile Dickens continued to receive applications for posts on the *Daily News*—including one from Edgar Allan Poe, who wished to become its American correspondent [11]—to all of which he replied that he was no longer connected with its management. He also presided at the first annual dinner of the General Theatrical Fund, an organization founded seven years previously to help aged or invalid actors not eligible for aid under the Drury Lane and Covent Garden funds.

Both of these latter pension funds were richly endowed, but the two theaters to which they were limited had almost ceased to present legitimate drama. Covent Garden had become a scene of political meetings. "You might play the bottle conjuror with its dramatic company," Dickens said in his speech, "and put them all into a pint bottle." [12] Drury Lane was so exclusively devoted to opera and ballet "that the statue of Shakespeare over the door" only served "emphatically to point out his grave." [13] In affectionate gratitude, Dickens pleaded, the public should ensure that when old actors "passed for the last time from behind that glittering row of lights," they did not "pass away into gloom and darkness," [14] but retired into the cheerfulness and light of a contented home.

The end of May saw a round of friendly farewell dinners. "Nothing is ever so good as it is thought," remarked Lord Melbourne at one of these. "And nothing so bad," Dickens rejoined. [15] There was a dinner with Macready on the 28th and with Forster on the 30th. [16] All Dickens's preparations were made for a year abroad: [17] Devonshire Terrace rented to Sir James Duke for £300, Roche hired again as courier. [18]

On the last day of the month his ménage started on its journey—
Dickens himself, Kate, Georgina, the six children, ranging from nine-
year-old Charley to the seven-months-old baby Alfred, plump beaming Roche, the faithful Anne, two other female servants, and the little
white dog Timber. Forster accompanied them as far as Ramsgate,
where they embarked for Ostend.[19]

The sunny Rhine journey by river steamboat was picturesque but
uneventful. At Mainz there came on board a German wine merchant,
one Josef Valckenberg, a native of Worms, who spoke to Kate. "Your
countryman Mr. Dickens is travelling this way just now, our papers
say. Do you know him, or have you passed him anywhere?" Introduc-
tions took place, and Dickens apologized for his ignorance of German.
"Oh dear! that needn't trouble you," Herr Valckenberg replied; even
in so small a town as Worms there were at least forty who spoke English and many more who read Dickens's works in the original.[20]

In translation as well, Dickens was popular throughout all Germany. As early as 1837–8, *Pickwick Papers* had been a great success,
and *Nicholas Nickleby* and *Oliver Twist* appeared on the very heels
of their English publication. Dickens had given Dr. Künzel biographical details for inclusion in the Brockhaus *Conversations-Lexikon* in
1838 and was so warmly gratified by the high esteem in which he was
held in Germany as to exclaim that next to his own people he respected and treasured the Germans. In 1841 *Pickwick* had been the
second in Bernhard Tauchnitz's well-known series; in 1843 Tauchnitz
had agreed to pay Dickens a fee for being supplied with corrected
proofs; by 1846 no fewer than ten of Dickens's books were in Tauchnitz editions.[21]

Arriving at Strasbourg on the 7th of June, the family went on by
rail the following day to Basle, and thence in three coaches to Lausanne.[22] At one of the inns on the road a *voiturier* complained that the
food was bad. The landlord exclaimed, " 'Scélérat! Mécréant! Je vous
boaxerai!' to which the voiturier replied, 'Aha! Comment dites-vous?
Voulez-vous boaxer? Eh? Voulez-vous? Ah! Boaxez-moi donc!' " with
violent gestures showing that this new verb was based on the English
verb "to box." "If they used it once," Dickens commented, "they used
it at least a hundred times, and goaded each other to madness with it
always." [23]

Putting up at the Hotel Gibbon, a large ugly structure fronting the

Lake of Geneva, Dickens at once began hunting for a house.[24] Ten
minutes' walk from the hotel, on the sloping shore, he found Rosemont, a little doll's house like a bandbox, with stone colonnades supporting a balcony, all overwhelmed in a cluster of roses that might
"smother the whole establishment of the Daily News." [25] The whole
house, Dickens said, might have been put bodily into the *sala* of the
Palazzo Peschiere,[26] but there were enough bedrooms to provide one
to spare, a hall, dining room, and two drawing rooms with mirrors and
shining inlaid floors, one furnished in red velvet, the other in green.
Six French windows under the balcony looked across the blue waters
toward the prodigious mountain gorges rising to the Simplon Pass.[27]
The surrounding countryside was delightful with cornfields, neat pas-
tures, green lanes, deep glens, and "branchy places," [28] as well as "hills
to climb up, leading to the great heights above the town; or to stagger
down, leading to the lake." [29]

Rosemont was taken at £10 a month for the first six months and £8
thereafter.[30] A school was promptly found for Charley between Lausanne and Ouchy.*[31]* Within three days Dickens had settled in a study
"something larger than a Plate Warmer," [32] from which he could walk
out on the long broad balcony and see the Castle of Chillon glittering
in the sunlight.[33] He now began planning the opening numbers of his
novel and trying "to look the little Christmas Volume in its small red
face." [34] But until his box of books came with the blue ink in which
he always wrote and the bronze desk ornaments he had to have before
his imagination would flow, he could not get started. Instead, he devoted himself to clearing away a number of other obligations—correspondence, some material he had promised Lord John Russell about
the Ragged Schools, half a simplified story of the New Testament that
he was writing for his own children,*[35]* advice for Miss Coutts upon
her charitable activities.

Of these last, the most recent was a home that she intended to establish for the rehabilitation of fallen women. Before leaving London,
Dickens had outlined a plan for the working of this institution, and
during the summer they corresponded about it. The Governors of the
London prisons, Dickens wrote, should be empowered to send any
woman who so desired straight to the home when her term expired.
"I would put in the power of any penitent creature to knock at the
door, and say for God's sake, take me in." [36]

Once there, a woman or girl should understand that her purpose was to cease a way of life miserable to *herself*. "Never mind society while she is at that pass. Society has used her ill and turned away from her, and she cannot be expected to take much heed of its rights or wrongs." For a number of months she should be placed on probation, receiving stated credits for work and good conduct, and demerits for each outbreak of ill-temper, disrespect, or bad language. Before even mingling with the established residents of the institution she should pass such a probation.[37]

"Her pride, emulation, her sense of shame, her heart, her reason, and her interest, are all appealed to at once, and if she pass through this trial, she *must* . . . rise somewhat in her own self-respect" and advance in forming "habits of firmness and self-restraint." "It is a part of this system, even to put at last, some temptation within their reach, as enabling them to go out, putting them in possession of some money, and the like; for it is clear that unless they are used to some temptation and used to resist it, within the walls, their capacity of resisting it without, cannot be considered as fairly tested." [38]

The training of the institution would emphasize order, punctuality, cleanliness, and the household duties of washing, mending, and cooking. It would be understood, however, by all that its object was not a monotonous round of occupation and self-denial for their own sakes, but the restoration of a way of life and a character that could end in achieving happy homes of their own.[39] The Government was to be sounded on the possibility of helping to send reformed women to the Colonies, where they might be married.[40] Dickens believed that if the institution were run on a well-devised system, one-half its inmates might be reclaimed from the start, and ultimately a much larger proportion.[41]

Miss Coutts had doubts about the desirability of suggesting marriage as a goal, and qualms about deliberately subjecting the inmates of the home to temptations. Dickens replied that he did not propose to hold out the hope of marriage as an immediate end, merely as a possible consequence of an altered life. Not even the sincerest penitence could stand the wear and tear of the world without the hope of finally recovering something like what one had lost. As for temptation, did not every merchant and banker expose their employees to it daily? Therefore was it not a Christian act, he asked, to say to these poor women, "Test for yourselves the reality of . . . your power of resisting temptation, while you are *here,* and before you are in the world outside, to fall before it!" [42]

*　　*　　*　　*　　*

With the arrival of his big box, Dickens settled to his desk in good earnest. Unpacking, he told Forster, "I took hold of a book, and said to 'Them,'—'Now, whatever passage my thumb rests on, I shall take as having reference to my work.' It was TRISTRAM SHANDY, and opened at these words, 'What a work it is likely to turn out! Let us begin it!' " [43] Shortly thereafter, on the 28th, he was able to write Forster the exciting announcement—

"BEGAN DOMBEY!

I performed this feat yesterday—only wrote the first slip— but there it is, and it is a plunge straight over head and ears into the story." [44]

During the first week's writing, however, his efforts were impeded by a spell of sultry weather and a plague of flies worse than the mosquitoes at Albaro.[45] "The overhanging roofs of the houses, and the quantity of wood employed in their construction (where they use tile and brick in Italy), render them perfect forcing-houses. The walls and floors, hot to the hand all the night through, interfere with sleep . . ." As for the flies, "They cover everything eatable, fall into everything drinkable, stagger into the wet ink of newly-written words and make tracks on the writing paper, clog their legs in the lather on your chin while you are shaving in the morning, and drive you frantic at any time there is daylight if you fall asleep." [46]

In spite of these impediments he nevertheless managed to get his opening chapter written and the second started.[47] He also had an "odd shadowy undefined idea" of connecting his Christmas story with a great battlefield: "Shapeless visions of the repose and peace pervading it in after-time; with the corn and grass growing over the slain, and people singing at the plough; are . . . perpetually floating before me . . ." [48] Its title would be *The Battle of Life.* He hoped by the end of November to have finished this Christmas book and four numbers of *Dombey,* and then to move to Paris at "the very point in the story when the life and crowd of that extraordinary place will come vividly to my assistance in writing." [49]

The idea behind *Dombey and Son* Dickens considered "interesting and new." At first, however, he refrained from telling Forster anything about it, for fear of spoiling the effect of the first number for him. Meanwhile he poured out directions for Forster to give Browne about the illustrations. "The class man to a T" for Mr. Dombey, he said, was "Sir A—— E——, of D——'s." (Forster suppressed the names to these initials.) But this pictorial identification was probably a disguise; when the book began to appear there were readers who were sure they recognized the character as Thomas Chapman, in whose Leadenhall Street business Dickens's young brother Augustus was employed. "Great pains will be necessary," he went on, "with Miss Tox. The Toodle family should not be too much caricatured, because of Polly. I should like Browne to think of Susan Nipper, who will not be wanted for the first number. What a brilliant thing to be telling you all these names so familiarly, when you know nothing about 'em! I quite enjoy it." [50]

Next week, in a letter dated July 25th, he grew more communicative about the story and its theme. Mr. Dombey, in the frigid dynastic pride of his great mercantile position, was to repel the love of his daughter and concentrate all his hopes on the frail little boy whom he designed to make his successor. But the tenderness of the child would turn toward the despised sister, and even when he was dying he would cling to her, keeping "the stern affection of his father at a distance." "The death of the boy is a death-blow, of course, to all the father's schemes and cherished hopes; and 'Dombey and Son,' as Miss Tox will say . . . 'is a Daughter after all.' " [51]

"From that time, I purpose changing his feeling of indifference and uneasiness towards his daughter into a positive hatred. For he will always remember how the boy had his arm round her neck when he was dying, and whispered to her, and would take things only from her hand, and never thought of him. . . . So I mean to carry the story on . . . through the decay and downfall of the house, and the bankruptcy of Dombey, and all the rest of it; when his only staff and treasure, and his unknown Good Genius always, will be this rejected daughter, who will come out better than any son at last, and whose love for him, when discovered and understood, will be his bitterest reproach. For the struggle with himself, which goes on in all such obstinate natures, will have ended then; and the sense of his injustice, which you may be sure has never quitted him, will have at last a gentler office than that of only making him more harshly unjust." [52]

Distractions continued, however, to draw him from his desk. There was more social life at Lausanne than there had been at Genoa. A resident English colony mingled with summer visitors from England in a round of dinner parties and pleasant excursions. Dickens dined with William Haldimand, a former member of Parliament who lived nearby with his sister Mrs. Marcet, the well-known author of *Conversations on Chemistry, Conversations on Political Economy*, and other books. At their table he met William de Cerjat, a Swiss gentleman, and his English wife, and the Honorable Mr. and Mrs. Richard Watson of Rockingham Castle in Northamptonshire.[53] Watson, "a thorough good liberal" who had been in Parliament at the time of the Reform Bill, entertained Dickens with stories about Lord Grey [54] that revived his memories of how he had disliked that unattractive statesman's personality.

Current political events in England also roused him to indignant excitement. Though the Corn Laws had been repealed, an angry rebellion against Peel led by Disraeli and Lord John Manners had driven him out of office. "I little thought," Dickens wrote, "that I should ever live to praise Peel. But d'Israeli and that Dunghill Lord have so disgusted me, that I feel inclined to champion him . . . It must come in my opinion as Cobden told them in the House, to a coalition between Peel and Lord John." This would make a strong government, Dickens thought, "and as governments go, a pretty good one." [55]

Another piece of news, at almost the same time, Dickens found more personally startling. A fellow clerk with his brother Augustus in Thomas Chapman's business establishment was a man named Thomas Powell—not the Powell whom Dickens had chosen as subeditor of the *Daily News*, but a minor writer and dramatist who paid his own publishing expenses. Though a man of thirty-five, Powell had shown a friendly interest in Augustus, established through him an acquaintance with Dickens, and dined on several occasions at Devonshire Terrace.[56] It now came out that by a series of forgeries Powell had defrauded his employers of around £10,000.[57] The facts reached Dickens in a letter from Chapman himself.

It was very considerate and friendly, Dickens replied, for Chapman to tell him personally about this painful breach of confidence. "Accept my thanks for this proof of your regard among many others, and with this, the assurance of my friendship and esteem." He had been horrified, he went on, by the whole story, all the more because, though he had no intimate knowledge of the culprit, he had believed him to have a great respect and regard for Chapman. To be sure, he had often wondered how Powell met his publishing costs. "But whenever I have sounded Augustus on the subject . . . he always hinted at a rich uncle, and some unknown share in some unknown business, which of course I could not gainsay. He told the tale as it was told to him, and had every reason to believe it. Indeed I suppose you and your partners laboured under the like delusion?" [58]

Streams of English visitors steadily passing through Lausanne made it hard for Dickens to concentrate on his writing. In July, Henry Hallam the historian visited Mr. Haldimand. "Heavens!" Dickens wrote, "how Hallam did talk yesterday! I don't think I ever saw him so tremendous. Very good-natured and pleasant, in his way, but Good Heavens! how he did talk." [59] Ainsworth and his daughters made an appearance on their way to Geneva,[60] and "we walked about all day, talking of our old days at Kensal Lodge." [61] Toward the end of August, after a day of incessant mountain rain, when Dickens was walking up and down "racking my brain about Dombeys and Battles of Lives," Tennyson turned up, very travel-stained, so that Dickens had to lay aside his work again while he entertained the poet with "Rhine wine, and cigars innumerable." [62] Nassau Senior the economist, the engineer Isambard Brunel, and Lord Vernon the Dante scholar, were also among the numerous other visitors.[63] With all these "invasions, past and to come, of people coming through here," Dickens felt reluctantly obliged to refuse an invitation from Charles Lever, the Irish novelist, to visit him at the château he was renting at Bregenz, Austria.[64]

Among the newcomers settling down for a while in Lausanne were the T. J. Thompsons, who took a house there for eight months. Dickens was much disappointed in Christiana. "She seems (between ourselves)," he wrote Mitton, "to have a devil of a whimpering, pouting temper . . ." [65] And to M. De la Rue: "She is a mere spoiled child, I think, and doesn't turn out half as well as I expected. Matrimony has improved him, and certainly has not improved her." [66] Dickens's brother Frederick was by this time impatiently eager to marry her younger sister Anna, although his income was insufficient for the support of a family and she was fully two years too young to be married. Frederick was working himself up to a mood of bitter resentment at Mr. Weller's consequent opposition.[67] Dickens was beginning to wish he had never met the fair Christiana and her family.[68]

The interest which Dickens never ceased to feel in public institutions took him within the first six weeks of his arrival to those of Lausanne. Mr. Haldimand was President of the Blind Institution,[69] and the Director was a brilliant young German named Hertzel,[70] who had taught one of the deaf, dumb, and blind inmates to speak by getting him to play with his tongue upon his teeth and palate and connecting the performance with words in the finger-language—a feat previously thought quite impossible. His pupil, a youth of eighteen, was very fond of cigars, and Dickens arranged a supply of them for him. "I don't know whether he thinks I grow them, or make them, or produce them by winking, or what. But it gives him a notion that the world in general belongs to me." [71] Before Dickens left Rosemont, the young man had learned to say, "M. Dickens m'a donné les cigares," and voiced his gratitude by repeating these words for a half hour on end.[72]

The jail at Lausanne had until a short time before been conducted according to the silent system, in which the prisoners were not allowed to speak; but its physician, M. Verdeil, had observed so many cases of mental affections, terrible fits, and madness attaining to such alarming heights among them that he had formed a party that brought about its abolition. His conclusions interestingly substantiated many of those Dickens himself had arrived at in *American Notes*. Though the Swiss prisoners were well fed and cared for, Dickens observed, their sentences were too long for that monotonous and hopeless life, and they generally broke down after two or three years. "One delusion," he noted, was common to many of them: "Under the impression that there is something destructive put into their food 'pour les guérir de crime' (says M. Verdeil), they refuse to eat!" [73]

In addition to these investigations, there were regattas, children's fetes, and excursions to Chamonix and the Castle of Chillon. What a sight was the ponderous Roche riding through the Col de Balme "on a very small mule up a road exactly like the broken stairs of Rochester Castle, with a brandy bottle slung over his shoulder, a small pie in his hat, a roast fowl looking out of his pocket, and a mountain staff of six feet long carried crosswise on the saddle"! At the Mer de Glace, when it seemed that they must have reached the top of the world, there suddenly came a cold air blowing, and past a ridge of snow startlingly towered, unseen till then, "the vast range of Mont Blanc, with attendant mountains diminished by its majestic side into mere dwarfs, tapering up into innumerable rude Gothic pinnacles." Dickens wished to cross the intervening chasms and precipices to what was called " 'The Garden:' a green spot covered with wild flowers . . . but I could find no Englishman at the hotels who was similarly disposed, and the Brave *wouldn't go*. No Sir! He gave in point blank (having been horribly blown in a climbing excursion the day before) and couldn't stand it. He is too heavy for such work, unquestionably." [74]

Chillon rekindled all Dickens's horror at the barbarity of the Middle Ages. "The insupportable solitude and dreariness of the white walls," he wrote Forster, "the sluggish moat and drawbridge, and the lonely ramparts, I never saw the like of. But there is a courtyard inside; surrounded by prisons, oubliettes, and old chambers of torture; so terrifically sad, that death itself is not more sorrowful. And oh! a wicked old Grand Duke's bedchamber upstairs in the tower, with a secret staircase . . . ; and Bonnivard's dungeon; and a horrible trap whence prisoners were cast out into the lake; and a stake all burnt and crackled up . . . Great God, the greatest mystery in all the earth, to me, is how or why the world was tolerated by its creator through the good old times, and wasn't dashed to fragments.[75]

Early in September occurred a trip to the convent of the Great St. Bernard, which included Haldimand, the Cerjats, and the Watsons, as well as Dickens, Kate, and Georgina. "I wish to God," Dickens exclaimed to Forster, "you could have seen that place. A great hollow on the top of a range of dreadful mountains, fenced in by riven rocks of every shape and colour: and in the midst a black lake, with phantom clouds perpetually stalking over it." The air was so fine that it was hard to breathe, there was no vegetation, everything was iron-bound and frozen up. And beside the convent, "in a little outhouse with a grated iron door," were "the bodies of people found in the snow . . . standing up, in corners and against walls; some erect and horribly human, with distinct expressions on the faces; . . . some tumbled down altogether, and presenting a heap of skulls and fibrous dust." [76]

Dramatic as was the scene of the convent, the holy fathers, in Dickens's opinion, were humbugs, "a lazy set of fellows . . . employing servants to clear the road," and growing rich at innkeeping. "Trashy French sentiment and the dogs (of which there are only three remaining) have done it all." To be sure, they made no charge for their hospitality, "but you are shown to a box in the chapel, where everybody puts in more than could, with any show of face, be charged for the entertainment." As for the self-sacrifice of living up there, it was an "infinitely more exciting life than any other convent can offer; with constant change and company through the whole summer." [77]

*   *   *   *   *

Throughout all these amusements Dickens did not neglect *Dombey and Son*. In the excitement of writing again, he found, he had made his first number six pages too long. He wondered if he should not transfer the chaper introducing the Wooden Midshipman and its inhabitants to the second number, writing a shorter one to take its place.[78] The small chapter gave unexpected difficulty: "I have been hideously idle all the week," he wrote Forster on August 14th, "and have done nothing but this trifling interloper; but hope to begin again on Monday—ding—dong." [79] (It was the chapter giving the first glimpse of Miss Tox's neighbor, Major Bagstock.) Forster, however, thought it would weaken the opening to defer the appearance of Walter Gay and Captain Cuttle, and persuaded Dickens to solve the problem by making cuts in the number instead.[80]

While he was working at the second number, his enthusiasm was stimulated by the interest of his circle of friends at Lausanne. "I read them the first number, last night 'was a' week, with unrelateable success; and old Mrs. Marcet, who is devilish 'cute, guessed directly (but I didn't tell her she was right) that Paul would die. They were all so apprehensive that it was a great pleasure to read it, and I shall leave here, if all goes well, in a brilliant shower of sparks struck out of them by the promised reading of the Christmas book." [81]

The enjoyment of his audience gave Dickens a novel idea: "a great deal of money might possibly be made (if it were not infra dig) by one's having Readings of one's own books. It would be an *odd* thing." And jestingly he suggested that Forster had better step around and engage Miss Kelly's theater or the St. James's.[82] It was the first facetious whisper of a course that would lead to disaster in his later life.

Despite his delight in the story, Dickens found the task of writing uphill work. "Invention, thank God, seems the easiest thing in the world; and I seem to have such a preposterous sense of the ridiculous, after this long rest, as to be constantly requiring to restrain myself from launching into extravagances in the height of my enjoyment. But the difficulty of going at what I call a rapid pace is prodigious: it is almost an impossibility. I suppose this is partly the effect of two years' ease, and partly of the absence of streets . . ." London, indeed, seemed to him to be a magic lantern in which his imaginative vision renewed itself; he could work furiously for a little while, he declared, in a retired place like Broadstairs, and then needed to plunge himself into the metropolis again. Even in Genoa, where he had written only *The Chimes*, he had felt the deprivation, "but Lord! I had two miles of streets at least, lighted at night, to walk about in; and a great theatre to repair to, every night." [83]

The strain of getting *The Battle of Life* under way at the same time also troubled him. It was the first time he had tried to start two stories at once. "I cancelled the beginning of a first scene—which I have never done before—and, with a notion in my head, ran wildly about and about it, and could not get the idea into any natural socket." [84] The difficulty of doing both, "coupled with that craving for streets," so put him off that he even considered abandoning the Christmas book. Then, suddenly, the opening came right, and he worked heatedly from nine-thirty to six, and felt better, though the effort left him with a headache.[85]

A week later, however, he was once more plunged in gloom. "I fear there may be NO CHRISTMAS BOOK!" [86] He had bogged down again, and worried lest he would so wear himself out that he would be unable to resume *Dombey* with the necessary freshness and spirit. "If I had nothing but the Christmas book to do, I WOULD do it; but I get horrified and distressed beyond conception at the prospect of being jaded when I come to the other . . . I am sick, giddy, and capriciously despondent. I have bad nights; am full of disquietude and anxiety; and am constantly haunted by the idea that I am wasting the marrow of the larger book, and ought to be at rest." [87]

Anxiously he tried to determine what was impeding him. Was it purely the effort of beginning two books at the same time? Was it trying to write in such a quiet place, with no stimulating noise and bustle? Was it that constant change was indispensable to him when he was at work? [88] Or was it that there was "something in a Swiss valley" that disagreed with him? "Certainly, whenever I live in Switzerland again, it shall be on a hill-top. Something of the *goitre* and *crétin* influence seems to settle on my spirits sometimes, on the lower ground." [89] "There is an idea here, too, that people are occasionally made sluggish and despondent in their spirits by this great mass of still water, Lake Leman." [90] And yet he liked Lausanne enormously, and the little society of friends he had made there.

Desperately, in late September he decided on the expedient of going to Geneva for a week to see if change of scene would stimulate him. He would make a final effort there, and if it failed abandon the Christmas book as a bad job. [91] He arrived in Geneva with a bloodshot eye and a pain across the brow so bad that he thought he must have himself cupped. [92] But within a few days he felt better. "The sight of the rushing Rhone seemed to stir my blood again," he wrote; and "My eye is recovering its old hue of beautiful white, tinged with celestial blue." [93] He got in three good days' work, which encouraged him to hope that with application he might finish the little book, even at Lausanne, by the 20th of October. Then he would return to Geneva and have three weeks there to work on *Dombey and Son* before setting out for Paris on November 10th. [94]

Hammering away morning, noon, and night, Dickens actually completed *The Battle of Life* on October 17th, although during the last week he kept dreaming that it was "a series of chambers impossible to be got to rights or got out of, through which I wandered drearily all night." [95] But two days' rest and a bottle of hock at dinner with Dr. Elliotson set him up again, and he reported buoyantly to Forster, "I feel in Dombeian spirits already." Meanwhile the first number of *Dombey* had exceeded all Dickens's hopes. "The Dombey sale is BRILLIANT! I had put before me thirty thousand as the limit of the most extreme success, saying that if we should reach that I should be more than satisfied and more than happy; you will judge how happy I am!" [96]

Despite the difficulty he had had in working at Lausanne, as the time for his departure drew near Dickens was sorry to be leaving. Though he made friends everywhere, nowhere abroad had he found a more congenial circle that that composed by Haldimand, the Cerjats, and the Watsons, all of whom became his lifelong friends. "I don't believe there are many dots on the map of the world where we shall have left such affectionate remembrances behind us . . . . It was quite miserable this last night, when we left them at Haldimand's." [97] And for Switzerland and the Swiss, too, he had from the first conceived a warm esteem.

Nothing was more unjust, he said, than to call them "the Americans of the Continent." [98] The allegation that they were rude or churlish was entirely unfounded. "They have not the sweetness and grace of the Italians, or the agreeable manners of the better specimens of French peasantry, but they are admirably educated (the schools of this canton are extraordinarily good, in every little village), and always prepared to give a civil and pleasant answer. . . . I never saw . . . people who did their work so truly *with a will*. And in point of cleanliness, order, and punctuality to the moment, they are unrivalled." [99]

In August there had been a great fete at Lausanne to celebrate the first anniversary of the New Constitution. The "old party" were very bitter about what they had chosen to call a revolution, though it had been nothing, Dickens said, but a change of government. "Thirty-six thousand people, in this small canton, petition against the Jesuits— God knows with good reason. The Government chose to call them a 'mob.' So, to prove that they were not, they turned the Government out. I honour them for it. They are a genuine people, these Swiss. There is better metal in them than in all the stars and stripes of all the fustian banners of the so-called, and falsely called, U-nited States. They are a thorn in the sides of European despots, and a good wholesome people to live near Jesuit-ridden Kings on the brighter side of the mountains." [100]

The sight of the Swiss intensified Dickens's feelings about what he called "Catholicity Symptoms." [101] In the valley of the Simplon, he told Forster, where "this Protestant canton ends and a Catholic canton begins, you might separate two perfectly distinct and different conditions of humanity by drawing a line with your stick in the dust on the ground. On the Protestant side, neatness; cheerfulness; industry; education; continual aspiration, at least, after better things. On the Catholic side, dirt, disease, ignorance, squalor, and misery. I have so constantly observed the like of this, since I first came abroad, that I have a sad misgiving that the religion of Ireland lies as deep at the root of all its sorrows, even as English misgovernment and Tory villany." [102]

When the October revolution occurred in Geneva, consequently, Dickens refused to believe "the lies . . . afloat against the radicals" that were circulated by the Sardinian consul and other representatives of the Catholic powers.[103] "Apart from this, you have no conception of the preposterous, insolent little aristocracy of Geneva: the most ridiculous caricature the fancy can suggest of what we know in England. . . . Really, their talk about 'the people' and 'the masses,' and the necessity they would shortly be under of shooting a few of them as an example for the rest, was the kind of monstrosity one might have heard at Genoa." [104] Consequently, though it was "a horribly ungentlemanly thing to say here," Dickens concluded, "I *do* say it without the least reserve—but my sympathy is all with the radicals." [105]

And back in Geneva again, less than a fortnight after the revolution, aside from a large smashed mirror at the Hôtel de l'Écu, a few holes made by cannon balls, and two broken bridges, Dickens could see no signs of disorder.[106] "The people are all at work. The little streets are rife with every sight and sound of industry; the place is as quiet by ten o'clock as Lincoln's Inn Fields . . ." [107] Dickens believed there was "no other country on earth . . . in which a violent change could have been effected . . . in the same proud, independent, gallant style. Not one halfpennyworth of property was lost, stolen, or strayed. Not one atom of party malice survived the smoke of the last gun. Nothing is expressed in the government addresses to the citizens but a regard for the general happiness, and injunctions to forget all animosities." [108]

The third number of *Dombey* was duly finished at Geneva. "I hope you will like Mrs. Pipchin's establishment," he wrote Forster. "It is from the life, and I was there—I don't suppose I was eight years old; but I . . . certainly understood it as well, as I do now. We should be devilish sharp in what we do to children." [109] Mrs. Pipchin was in fact a fusion of the old woman who kept the dame-school at Chatham and Mrs. Roylance, of the Bayham Street days. "Mrs. Roylance, Mrs. Wigchin, Mrs. Tipchin, Mrs. Alchin, Mrs. Somchin, Mrs. Pipchin," read Dickens's notes.[110] "I thought of that passage in my small life, at Geneva." [111]

The recurrent complaints about the difficulty he found in writing that marked his stay in Switzerland are warning signals of an inner disquietude the nature of which Dickens had so far failed to recognize. Instead he invented a half-dozen reasons to explain his struggles: living in a valley, the dampness of Lake Leman, too much peace and quiet, a craving for constant change, a need for the stimulation of London, the lack of streets to walk in. Only on rare occasions in the past had he spent a morning looking at an empty page; no such endless wrestling to get his ideas on paper had troubled his earlier days in Doughty Street, when he could write at a side table in a sitting room filled with chatter, or dash off a number of *Barnaby Rudge* in three days at a lonely inn in the Trossachs.

A sharp observer might have traced the change from the time of Dickens's restless desire to get away from England during the composition of *Martin Chuzzlewit*—almost, indeed, from the time of his return from America. There are suggestive hints in his sudden infatuation for Christiana Weller, and in the stamping fury that sent him out of the offices of Chapman and Hall determined to pay them off. At Genoa and during all his stay in Italy, Dickens wrote only *The Chimes*, began to talk about his dependence on crowded streets, and had friction with Kate over Mme. De la Rue. The entire *Daily News* episode was characterized by caprice of action and touchy irritability.

Now, in Switzerland, surrounded by a circle of congenial friends, Dickens had achieved the triumph of *Dombey* (and its writing was as brilliant as its success with the public) but had done so only through the most desperate and repeated contention with unidentified obstacles. Despite his lively enjoyment in observing the world around him, despite the vitality with which he could fling himself into every amusement, despite the will power that victoriously smashed its way through this disorientation of his accustomed fluency, there was a progressive underlying disturbance at work. What it was Dickens as yet showed no signs of trying to analyze. But in the course of the following year, almost by intuition, he revived an old device for distracting himself from restlessness or unhappiness, and his writing went with more ease. Over and over again, from then on, he would fling himself with desperate intensity into the same distraction. It was to have fateful consequences for his entire future.

CHAPTER TWO

The "Want of Something"

DURING the three months Dickens spent in Paris his writing went no more easily. He had left Geneva on November 16th in a train of three carriages, one "a villainous old swing" full of young Dickenses. "The children as good as usual, and even Skittles jolly to the last. That name has long superseded Sampson Brass, by the bye. I call him so, from something skittle-playing and public-housey in his countenance." [1] Arriving at Paris with his "tons of luggage, other tons of servants, and other tons of children," Dickens put up at the Hôtel Brighton.[2] It was extravagant to stay at a hotel, so the first delay to his work was in finding a residence. "The agonies of house-hunting," he wrote, "were frightfully severe. It was one paroxysm for four mortal days." [3]

The following week, however, saw them all in 48 Rue de Courcelles, Faubourg Saint-Honoré. "The premises are in my belief," Dickens wrote Forster, "the most ridiculous, extraordinary, unparalleled, and preposterous in the whole world; being something between a baby-house, a 'shades,' a haunted castle, and a mad kind of clock. They belong to a Marquis Castellane, and you will be ready to die of laughing when you go over them." The bedrooms were as small as a nest of opera boxes. "The dining-room," Dickens continued, "is a sort of cavern, painted (ceiling and all) to represent a grove, with unaccountable bits of looking-glass sticking in among the branches of the trees." [4] This was the invention of Henry Bulwer,[5] "who when he had executed it (he used to live here), got frightened at what he had done, as well he might, and went away." [6] "There is a gleam of reason in the drawing-room. But it is approached through a series of small

[607]

chambers, like the joints in a telescope, which are hung with inscrutable drapery." [7]

As soon as he was settled in the Rue de Courcelles, Dickens tried
to get to work on the fourth number of *Dombey*. It was an intensely
cold winter: they burned five pounds' worth of firewood in a single
week and three fires were needed on the ground floor.[8] Nevertheless,
Dickens wrote, "The water in the bed-room jugs freezes into solid
masses, . . . bursts the jugs with reports like small cannon, and rolls
out on the tables and wash-stands, hard as granite." [9] And, despite his
hopes of being inspired by the bustle of Paris, he found himself out
of writing sorts, "with a vile touch of biliousness," he said, "that makes
my eyes feel as if they were yellow bullets." [10]

This time he thought it was the strange surroundings that put him
off. He couldn't begin; "took a violent dislike to my study, and came
down into the drawing-room; couldn't find a corner that would answer my purpose; fell into a black contemplation of the waning
month; sat six hours at a stretch," and wrote only six lines. He tried
rearranging all the tables and chairs, cleared off his correspondence,
then started again, "and went about it and about, and dodged at it,
like a bird with a lump of sugar." [11] But in spite of all these efforts,
and the fierce energy with which he paced the streets, he turned out
only five printed pages, and began to fear he should be behindhand.

His observations of the French gave him no such esteem for them
as he had formed for the Swiss people. "The night after his arrival,"
Forster reports, "he took a 'colossal' walk about the city, of which the
brilliancy and brightness almost frightened him." [12] But he thought
it "a wicked and detestable place, though wonderfully attractive."
Strolling on the illuminated boulevard with Georgina, he saw "a man
fall upon another, close before us, and try to tear the cloak off his
back. After a short struggle, the thief fled (there were thousands of
people walking about), and was captured just on the other side of the
road." [13]

"The Parisian workpeople and smaller shopkeepers are more like
(and unlike) Americans than I could have supposed possible. To the
American indifference and carelessness, they add a procrastination
and want of the least heed about keeping a promise or being exact,
which is certainly not surpassed in Naples. They have the American
semi-sentimental independence too, and none of the American vigour

or purpose. If they ever get free trade in France . . . these parts of the population must, for years and years, be ruined. They couldn't get the means of existence, in competition with the English workmen. . . . They are fit for nothing but soldiering—and so far, I believe, the successors in the policy of your friend Napoleon have reason on their side." [14]

Agricultural and industrial depression gripped the country, there was diplomatic tension between France and England, the Monarchy was nervously drawing to its inglorious close. When Dickens dined at the British Embassy with Lord Normanby, the Ambassador, he found that nobleman as "good-natured as ever, but not so gay . . . having an anxious haggard way with him, as if his responsibilities were more than he had bargained for." [15] Dickens was struck by the sight of King Louis Philippe returning from the country, huddled far back in a carriage dashing hurriedly through the Champs Élysées, closely surrounded by horse guards and preceded by the Préfet de Police, "turning his head incessantly from side to side, like a figure in a Dutch clock, and scrutinizing everybody and everything, as if he suspected all the twigs in all the trees in the long avenue." [16]

Suddenly Dickens found his writing going better, and by the middle of December he was able to dash over to London to settle the form for a new cheap edition of his books and help the Keeleys stage *The Battle of Life* at the Lyceum Theatre. The cheap edition was printed in double columns, without illustrations, in weekly numbers at three halfpence each, and dedicated "to the English people, in whose approval, if the books be true in spirit, they will live, and out of whose memory, if they be false, they will very soon die." [17] The dramatic version of *The Battle of Life* was to open on the 21st, just two days after its publication in book form. [18]

The little volume had illustrations by Doyle and Leech, and in November Forster had made Dickens "jump for joy" with the news that he had also arranged with Maclise and Stanfield to supply additional plates. [19] But in the actual book Dickens did not care much for any of the pictures except the landscapes by Stanfield. Leech had gone badly astray by portraying in one scene a character who was not there at all; in his first horror Dickens wanted to have the printing stopped, and decided not to only when he thought "of the pain this might give to our kind-hearted Leech." [20]

The story itself is one of sickly sacrificial sentimentality, in which a younger sister pretends to elope with another man in order to bring about a marriage between her fiancé and her elder sister, whose unspoken love for him the girl has divined. Lord Jeffrey praised this piece of confectionery, but Thackeray thought it "a wretched affair," [21] and Dickens's old foe the *Times* slated it even more brutally than it had *The Cricket on the Hearth*.[22] Dickens was responsible, the *Times* said, for "the deluge of trash" that glutted the Christmas book market, and this was "*the very worst*" of the lot, without "one spark of originality, of truth, of probability, of nature, of beauty." [23] The feeble little book deserves small praise but hardly calls for such ferocity. Dickens accidentally saw a reference to the review. "Another touch of the blunt razor," he commented, "on B.'s nervous system." [24] Nevertheless the book sold well—twenty-three thousand copies on its first day of publication, and by the end of January far more than any of its predecessors.

At the Lyceum Dickens found the "confounded *dramatization* . . . in a state so horrible" that he was almost disheartened about it. Mistakes in copying had confused the actors' parts "into the densest and most insufferable nonsense," [25] and although liberal sums had been spent on the scenery all the actors except the Keeleys were so bad that they had no idea of the play. In desperation, Dickens summoned the entire company to Lincoln's Inn Fields and, despite a frightful cold, read the script to them to show how it should go. Forster provided seventy-six ham sandwiches by way of refreshment, and sent the forty-two that remained uneaten to be distributed to the poor. His strict injunctions to the servant, Dickens said, "to find out very poor women and institute close enquiry into their life, conduct, and behaviour before leaving any sandwiches for them, was sublime." [26] Through strenuous rehearsals, protracted until two in the morning, while perspiration streamed down the actors' faces, Dickens whipped the production into shape. Its first-night reception was one of "immense enthusiasm, with uproar and shouting for me." [27]

* * * * *

Christmas saw Dickens back with his family in Paris, ready to start the fifth number, in which Paul would die. Beginning, as usual by now, was hard: he felt "most abominably dull and stupid," [28] he wrote; and a few days later still, "Inimitable very mouldy. . . . Hardly able to work." [29] Soon, however, the familiar magic flowered, and Dickens half began to think the artfulness of Captain Cuttle and the fading life of little Paul "the only reality . . . and to mistake all the realities for shortlived shadows." [30] On the 14th of January, the last brief chapter of the number was finished. "Between ourselves," Dickens wrote Miss Coutts, "—Paul is dead. He died on Friday night about 10 o'clock, and as I had no hope of getting to sleep afterwards, I went out, and walked about Paris until breakfast time next morning." [31]

"Paul's death has amazed Paris," [32] Dickens later reported; and it drowned English readers in a grief they had not known since the death of Little Nell. "Oh, my dear dear Dickens!" wrote Jeffrey from Edinburgh, "What a No. 5 you have given us! I have so cried and sobbed over it last night, and again this morning; and felt my heart purified by those tears . . ." [33] And Thackeray, whose second number of *Vanity Fair* had just appeared, felt deeply discouraged. Hastening to *Punch's* printing office, and entering Mark Lemon's room, he dashed a copy of *Dombey* on the table with startling vehemence and exclaimed, "There's no writing against such power as this—One has no chance! Read that chapter describing young Paul's death: it is unsurpassed— it is stupendous!" [34]

After pacing the Paris streets all night, Dickens went directly to the office of the *malle-poste*, where Forster was arriving at eight o'clock for a fortnight's holiday.[35] Dickens had been delighted to hear in October that Forster was resigning from the *Daily News*, and this visit had been arranged toward the end of November. "That, being what you are, you had only one course to take and have taken it, I no more doubt than that the Old Bailey is not Westminster Abbey. . . . You were bound to leave; and now you *have* left, you will come to Paris, and there, and at home again, we'll have, please God, the old kind of evenings and the old life again, as it used to be before those daily nooses caught us by the legs . . ." [36]

With "dreadful insatiability" [37] the two men plunged into a delirium of sightseeing and entertainment: the Louvre, Versailles, Saint-Cloud; prisons, hospitals, and the Morgue; the Bibliothèque Royale, the Opéra, the Conservatoire; all the theaters.[38] At the Gymnase, Rose Chéri expired with heart-rending pathos in *Clarissa Harlowe*; at the Variétés *Gentil Bernard* was "a little picture of Watteau"; a melo-

drama called *The French Revolution* at the Cirque was spectacular
with battles and had mob scenes that were "positively awful"; and
there were revivals of Molière's *Don Juan* and Hugo's *Lucretia Borgia*.
Dickens was amused also by portrayals of English life in some of the
other plays: a Prime Minister who ruins himself in railway speculation
and alludes frequently to "Vishmingster" and "Regeenstreet," and
a Lord Mayor of London wearing a stage-coachman's waistcoat, the
Order of the Garter, and a broad-brimmed hat like a dustman's.[39]

Dickens now spoke French fluently, though with a heavy English
accent, and the two friends consorted with a circle of theatrical and
literary celebrities—supped with Dumas and Eugène Sue, met Gau-
tier, and saw a great deal of Scribe. Dickens renewed an acquaintance
with Lamartine, whom he had met at Albaro, and paid a visit of
homage to Chateaubriand, the aged and ailing author of *Atala* and
Mémoires d'Outre-Tombe.[40] The greatest figure of them all, however,
in Dickens's eyes, was Victor Hugo, at this time just beginning to
write his epic novel of the poor, *Les Misérables*, but already a European figure of advanced opinions whose views embraced a league of
nations and the reorganization of Europe as a union of republics.

Hugo's apartment in the Place Royale, crammed full of "old
armour and old tapestry, and old coffers, and grim old chairs and
tables, and old canopies of state from old palaces, and old golden lions
going to play at skittles with ponderous old golden balls," looked,
Dickens said, "like an old curiosity shop, or the property-room of some
gloomy, vast, old theatre." [41] And even more striking was Hugo himself, talking of his childhood in Spain, laughing at the actors who had
murdered his tragedy at the Odéon, sympathizing with Dumas' dramatic venture, and paying felicitous compliments to Dickens,[42] all
the while looking "like a genius as he is, every inch of him." [43]

Returning to England at the end of January, Forster took back with
him young Charley Dickens, now just turned ten years of age.[44] The
boy was to be enrolled at Eton, where Miss Coutts had asked to be
allowed the privilege of providing for his schooling, and to prepare
for entrance there was placed in charge of Dr. Major, the Headmaster
of King's College School.[45] His father immediately set himself to
writing the next number of *Dombey*, making his head ache with the
difficulties of transferring all the interest of the story now to Florence
Dombey.[46] No sooner was this installment sent to the printer than

Dickens discovered to his horror that it was two pages short, and decided that he must hurry to London himself to supply the deficiency.[47]

Consequently he saw Charley while he was there, took him to dine at Hampstead, and to Sunday dinner at Gore House. There was an empty seat beside the youngster's at the table. "It is only the Prince," explained Lady Blessington; "he is always late." Shortly "a sallow, rather sullen, heavy-looking man" came in, kissed her hand, and took the place. He paid little attention to the rest of the company, but talked pleasantly to the boy about his school and his recent stay in Paris. This was Prince Louis Napoleon, still moodily "biding his time" until events should make him ruler of France.[48]

Hardly had Dickens reached Paris again when Charley was taken ill with scarlet fever.[49] Dickens quickly cut short his stay abroad and returned to London. Devonshire Terrace was still occupied by Sir James Duke, so, leaving the other children with Georgina in Paris, he and Kate stayed at the Victoria Hotel, Euston Square, while looking for a temporary residence.[50] Charley was under the care of his grandmother, Mrs. Hogarth, in Albany Street, but it was some time before the anxious father could be allowed to see him, and more than a month before the other members of the family could do so.

When Dickens paid his first visit, an elderly charwoman employed there was much astonished. "Lawk ma'am!" she exclaimed. "Is the young gentleman upstairs the son of the man that put together *Dombey*?" Though she could not read, she attended on the first Monday of every month a tea held by subscription at a snuff-shop above which she lodged, where the landlord read the month's number aloud. She had not imagined it possible that a single man *could* have put together that work. "Lawk ma'am! I thought that three or four men must have put together *Dombey!*" [51]

Charley's illness and the troubles of finding, and settling into, a house at 1 Chester Place rendered Dickens almost desperate about his next monthly number. "What could I do," he cried, "house-hunting at first," and then "beleaguered" "by furniture that must be altered, and things that must be put away?" It was already the 9th of March, and "So far from having 'got through my agonies' . . . ," he wrote to Georgina, who was still with the children in Paris, "I have not yet begun them." In consequence, "My wretchedness, just now, is inconceivable." [52]

Other distractions, relentlessly pressed upon him. William Hall had just died, and Dickens, who had ceased to feel any bitterness toward his former publishers and who had really liked the well-intentioned little man, felt that he should pay him the respect of going to the funeral.[53] And on April 18th Kate was brought to bed of their seventh child, a son. The boy was christened Sydney Smith Haldimand, the last of these names after William Haldimand, who became one of his godfathers. Kate had such a painfully difficult delivery that the specialist hastily and wildly sent for told Dickens he had seen but one such case in his experience. "But thank God she is as well today as ever she has been at such a time," Dickens wrote Macready, "and sends all sorts of love to you." [54]

Somehow or other, nevertheless, Dickens managed to get through that month's "convulsions of Dombey," [55] as he called them, only, near the beginning of the next month, to have his arm severely mauled by the bite of a horse, who made a sudden attack on him in the stable, and tore off his coat sleeve and shirt sleeve, "I believe," Dickens explained, "under the impression that I had gone into his stall to steal his corn, which upon my honor I had no intention of doing." [56] Unstrung by the shock, he discovered that he felt "hideously queer" when he got up each morning and suffered distressingly with "a low dull nervousness." [57] To recover from these symptoms, he took Kate, now "in a brilliant state" [58] again, down to Brighton for the latter part of May. Although he had been too shaken even to start his number before he left town, he picked up heart and went at it so furiously that by the 23rd it was very nearly done.

* * * * *

Returning to London, Dickens found himself shortly involved in a quarrel that had broken out between Thackeray and Forster.[59] In April, Thackeray had started a series of parodies called *Punch's Prize Novelists,* of which the first, "George de Barnwell," was an annihilating imitation of Bulwer Lytton's pompous literary style. Forster was a friend of Lytton's and he had smarted also at pictorial caricatures of himself that he knew Thackeray had passed around among their acquaintances. Talking with a young journalist named Tom Taylor, Forster loudly and violently said that Thackeray was "false as hell." Taylor, laughing immoderately, assumed that this outburst was merely a comic pretense of spleen, and repeated it to Thackeray as a good joke.[60] But Thackeray promptly took umbrage. At a large party at the Procters' he publicly refused to shake hands with Forster.[61]

The latter immediately asked Dickens to demand an explanation. Forster did not remember having used the words objected to, although he granted that in the heat of the moment he might have. But could Thackeray, he retorted, deny having given him equal reason for offense both by word and pictorial jibe? [62] Dickens supported Forster, remarking that he had even better reason than Forster to know the force of the allusion to Thackeray's caustic little sketches.[63]

Remorsefully Thackeray admitted that he too had been at fault. He understood "how a man of Forster's emphatic way of talking . . . chafed by ridicule," could have exploded as he did. "He consigned me to Hell for making caricatures of him: roasting me as I own & I'm sorry for it, to have done him." [64] Summarizing the whole affair, Thackeray wrote, "Forster ought not to have used the words: Taylor ought not to have told them: and I ought not to have taken them up." [65] Forster too expressed his regret, and the quarrel was buried in a reconciliation dinner at Greenwich.

But either Thackeray or Bradbury and Evans (who were the publishers of *Punch*) prudently decided that it might be better not to include Dickens in the series of parodies, as had been originally planned. Thackeray was convinced that people were jealous of his growing reputation. "Jerrold hates me," he wrote, "Ainsworth hates me, Dickens mistrusts me, Forster says I am false as hell, and Bulwer curses me—" "There are no end of quarrels in this wicked Vanity Fair, and my feet are perpetually in hot water." [66] The literary triumph of *Vanity Fair*, he thought, had done it all. "There is no use denying the matter or blinking it now. I am become a sort of great man in my way—all but at the top of the tree: indeed there if the truth were known and having a great fight up there with Dickens." [67]

Certainly Thackeray was acutely conscious of rivalry with Dickens. *Mrs. Perkins's Ball*, his Christmas book for that year, was "a great success—the greatest I have had—very nearly as great as Dickens. That is Perkins 500 Dickens 25000 only that difference!" [68] He was bowled over by the pure brilliance of some of Dickens's achievements, but on the whole critical of his literary art, which he regarded as a mere caricature of reality. As for Dickens, no writer more warmly and generously praised his contemporaries than he did, or depreciated them so little. But he was disagreeably impressed by what seemed to him a flippant cynicism in Thackeray's attitude and seldom read him, though he spoke well of his books whenever he mentioned them. "I am saving up the perusal of Vanity Fair," he wrote Thackeray a year later, "until I shall have done Dombey . . ." [69]

Concerning the parodies, Dickens made in the same letter a jocose personal complaint. "It is curious, about Punch," he wrote Thackeray, "that I was so strongly impressed by the absurdity and injustice of my being left out of those imitations, that I several times said at home here I would write to you and urge the merits of the case." Nevertheless he felt obliged to admit candidly that he did not admire the design; it seemed to him that literary men lessened their dignity with the public and made enemies among themselves sneering at each other. He himself, he told Thackeray, always hoped by his own conduct to leave their position in England higher than he had found it. [70]

The two men remained on cordial terms with each other. Thackeray dined at Devonshire Terrace and his two little girls were invited to shining children's parties there. When Dombey and Son was finished Dickens gave "a solemn dinner . . . to celebrate the conclusion" of that "immortal book." "It couldn't be done without you," Dickens wrote Thackeray. "Therefore book it, cher citoyen!" [71] But there was a faint cloud of mutual suspicion between them which cast potential shadows over their future relationship.

* * * * *

Meanwhile the restlessness that fretted Dickens's work at his desk had burst out in another plan for amateur dramatics. The amiable but perennially indigent Leigh Hunt was again in financial straits. He should, Dickens said, "have received long ago, but has not yet, some enduring return from his country for all he has undergone and all the good he has done." [72] The same company that acted two years previously would therefore present Every Man in His Humour and The Merry Wives of Windsor in London and then later in Manchester and Liverpool for Hunt's benefit. It would be a deserved mark of sympathy and help to its recipient. "And we know, from himself, that it would be most gratifying to his own feelings." [73]

Dickens was soon deep in gathering together his cast. New members included George H. Lewes, Dudley Costello, and the artist Augustus Egg, as well as Dickens's old friend Cruikshank.[74] T. J. Thompson, who had surrendered his role in *Every Man* at the time of his marriage, wrote plaintively to ask if he was now quite out of the revived enterprise. Dickens replied that unfortunately all the good parts in *The Merry Wives* were allotted, but that there would certainly be an opening in the other play and probably a good one in *Comfortable Lodgings*, the farce that would be given with it.[75] Ultimately, Thompson played his old role of Wellbred.

Like Dickens, perhaps, Thompson had his reasons for feeling restless and needing distraction. "Tell Madame," Dickens had written De la Rue in March, "that the Thompsons are not happy, and that he screws and pinches her (I don't mean with his fingers) most villainously, I am told, in respect of creature comforts. My brother Fred is transported to madness with love of Mrs. Thompson's sister, and from him . . . . I hear odd stories, which I pretend to doubt, but don't very much." [76]

Barely had rehearsals started at Miss Kelly's than, with a concern for unrewarded merit unusual in governments, Lord John Russell's administration granted Hunt a pension of £200. But it took more than such a piece of inconsiderate generosity to frustrate Dickens's desire to give a play. Hunt's debts still remained to be discharged; and the aging dramatist John Poole, author of successful farces like *Paul Pry* and *Turning the Tables*, was now desperately poor. Though the London performances were consequently given up, and *The Merry Wives* eliminated from the scheme, the amateurs, under Dickens's leadership, found themselves going ahead with the provincial representations of *Every Man in His Humour*.[77]

There were the usual managerial problems. One actor was disgruntled at his part having only twelve words; a second couldn't remember his at all; a third, in his nervousness, had "a restless, stupid movement of his hands." Another, though "hurt by his own sense of not doing well," clutched his part tenaciously; "and three weary times we dragged through it last night." Still another was "too innately conceited" to be taught, although "I would as soon laugh at a kitchen poker." One unfortunate was inaudible; "and as regularly as I stop him . . . exclaims (with a face of agony) that 'he'll speak out loud on the night,' as if anybody ever did without doing it always!" [78]

Dickens coaxed, bullied, drilled; taught them graceful movement, proper inflection, natural gesture; wore everybody out and kept everybody in good humor; and resumed operations next day with the energy of a cheerful dynamo.

At the end of June, fairly well satisfied, Dickens went to Broadstairs for a few weeks' vacation. Here there was a dark gray sea with a howling banshee of a wind rattling the windows as if it were late autumn rather than midsummer. All the children proceeded to get whooping cough and wandered disconsolately about the beach choking incessantly.[79] The only amusement was a wild beast show, in which a young woman in shining scaly armor pretended to fall asleep reclining on the principal lion, while a keeper who spoke through his nose exclaimed: [80] "Beold the abazick power of woobbud!" [81]

Meanwhile Dickens was kept busy writing "100 letters a day, about these plays": [82] to Nathan the theatrical costumer; to Lemon about securing the services of Wilson the wig man, making a final choice of the afterpieces, assigning the actors to them, and letting the committees in Manchester and Liverpool know the names of the professional actresses who would play the feminine parts; to the committees, discussing the scale of prices to be charged; to Jerrold, Cruikshank, and Thompson, making arrangements with them about the parts they would take in the farces; to all the actors, appointing nightly rehearsals at Miss Kelly's for the entire week preceding their journey north. For these Dickens returned to London on the 16th of July. The performances at Manchester and Liverpool were scheduled for the 26th and 28th respectively.

In both cities Dickens made hotel reservations for his entire cast as well as those wives and feminine relations who were accompanying them, and took a large general sitting room for the use of the company.[83] At the railway station he tore wildly up and down the platform in a perspiration, with a great box of papers under his arms, talking to everyone, gloriously excited, and almost got left behind.[84] Both nights were brilliant successes; their receipts were £440 12s. the first night and £463 8s. 6d. the second.[85]

Back in Broadstairs, where the children were almost recovered from their whooping cough, Dickens vigorously settled himself to make up the accounts of the trip, and wrote all the members of the cast to send their share of the expenses to Lemon.[86] "Business arising out of the

late blaze of triumph," he complained happily, "worse than ever." [87]
The costs of the production proved so great, however, that there was
a clear profit of only four hundred guineas instead of the five hundred
Dickens had confidently expected. It occurred to him that the additional sum might be earned by publishing a comic story of the adven-
ture, told as a new "Piljians Projiss" by Mrs. Gamp, and illustrated
by the artist-members of the company. But the artists, less docile than
Phiz, failed to do their part, and Dickens therefore wrote only a fragmentary few pages.[88]

No sooner were the last business details tidied up than his restlessness returned again. "I am at a great loss for means of blowing my
superfluous steam off, now that the play is over—but that is always my
misfortune—and find myself compelled to tear up and down, between
this and London, by express trains." [89] In London he saw *Cymbeline*; [90] in Broadstairs lamed Frank Stone by walking him seventeen
miles [91] and received a visit from Hans Christian Andersen,[92] whom
he had met at Lady Blessington's that June; at Canterbury bought a
copy of Cruikshank's *The Bottle*.[93]

The artist, once a hilarious climber of lampposts and wallower in
gutters, had now become a fanatical teetotaler and was using his etch-
ing needle to depict the horrors of alcoholism. He carried his mania
even into social intercourse; dining with Dickens, he snatched a glass
of wine from a lady's hand, intending to throw it on the floor. "How
dare you," exclaimed Dickens furiously, "touch Mrs. Ward's glass?
. . . What do you mean? Because someone you know was a drunkard
for forty years, surely it is not for you to object to an innocent glass
of sherry!" [94] And Douglas Jerrold once said soothingly, "Yes, George,
I know, water is a *very* good thing—*except on the brain!*" [95]

Cruikshank's plates, however, Dickens thought almost Hogarthian
in their power. He objected, nevertheless, that they were wrong in
their philosophy: "the drinking should have begun in sorrow, poverty,
or ignorance—the three things in which, in its awful aspect, it *does*
begin. The design would then have been a double-handled sword—
but too 'radical' for good old George, I suppose." [96]

*   *   *   *   *

Meanwhile, no distractions of fierce walks or racing about in express trains could allay Dickens's sharp unrest, despite the fact that

with *Dombey and Son* he had reached a place in his career beyond which he was never to feel financial uneasiness again. In the previous six months his earnings had been £2,000 more than his expenses; and now, after drawing £100 monthly, he had another clear £2,220. This was exhilarating, but he still complained of the difficulty of working: "Deep slowness," he recorded, "in the inimitable's brain." [97]

Even Broadstairs he found unsuitable to work in now. The noise of street musicians seemed to him to be growing so much worse as almost to drive him out of his mind. "Unless it pours of rain, I cannot write half-an-hour without the most excruciating organs, fiddles, bells, or glee-singers. There is a violin of the most torturing kind under the window now (time, ten in the morning) and an Italian box of music on the steps—both in full blast." [98]

Although *Dombey* was by this time more than half done and was more successful every day, Dickens groaned again, as he had the preceding year, at the toil of doing a Christmas book at the same time. He felt "seedy"; the longer book took so much out of him that he began "to have serious doubts" if it was "wise to go on with the Christmas book." "On the other hand, I am very loath to lose the money. And still more so to leave any gap at Christmas firesides which I ought to fill. In short I am (forgive the expression) BLOWED if I know what to do." [99] In the end, instead of struggling to write it, as he had done at Lausanne and Geneva, Dickens did hold over the little book for a year.

His own difficulties were not the only ones Dickens had to deal with. His brother Fred's love affair with Anna Weller was going badly. Anna's father disliked Fred and would not receive him in his house, but every week-end the young man miserably traveled the hundred and twenty miles to Birmingham, where he imposed himself on the grudging hospitality of a son-in-law of Mr. Weller's. [100] Anna had violent tempers with her family, and Fred felt resentful and ill-used. [101] But Mr. Weller objected unanswerably to the marriage that she was still too young and Fred's Treasury salary too small. [102] Fred chafed at the injustice of having so little money, spent more than he could afford on each week's journey, and took a high line about how willing he would be to struggle against all difficulties if he were only married. [103]

Dickens pitied Fred's unhappiness but pointed out that Mr.

Weller's position had sense, and tried to establish an understanding between them about waiting, and seeing Anna at reasonable intervals.[104] But he had himself, by now, deep objections to an alliance with the Weller family. There was, he thought, "an 'impracticability' in that blood which cannot be reconciled with happiness"; "breeding, Education, and the weakest parents on this globe" had made Anna's own character one "which can never come right." These "deliberate opinions," he told Fred, he felt it necessary that he should not disguise, and Fred should ask himself if this infatuation did not make him more unhappy than he would be "in any other attachment under precisely the same worldly circumstances." [105]

Throughout this same period, Dickens was tremendously busied in helping Miss Coutts with her reform home for women, now being inaugurated at Urania Cottage in Shepherd's Bush.[106] Dickens chose the house, on Acton Road.[107] He selected the Matron from a series of candidates whom he interviewed.[108] He took great pains to find out all he could about the nature and history of the women admitted, "to give the Matron some useful foreknowledge of them." He insisted that there must be cheerful variety in their lives in the home: "On the cheerfulness and kindness all our hopes rest." [109] Through Edward Chapman he ordered books for them to read, and arranged with his old friend the composer Hullah for them to have lessons in part-singing.[110]

Their religious instruction, he said, should be based on the New Testament, not on the censorious thundering of the more vengeful parts of the Old. The unfortunates they were dealing with would be well enough aware of their degraded past lives so that it would be a blind mistake even to refer to them. All rules framed solely in the abstract should yield to a gentle consideration for the best way of helping these women not to fall back into their old ways. The great point to be remembered always was that they were "to be *Tempted* to virtue." [111] The same warm-spirited wisdom runs through all the principles and procedures Dickens laid down.

His own spirits, however, continued to be very unsettled, and perhaps contributed to a chilling off of his relations with Forster that lasted through October and into November. Both men confided in Macready, but the latter's diary does not say what the quarrel was about. Forster told him that their long and intimate friendship "was likely to terminate." Trying to move Dickens, Macready found him "more stiff" than he thought right, though Macready felt forced to admit that Dickens had "great excuse." "They have both faults with their good qualities, but they have been *too* familiar." [112] Not until the middle of December were they on cordial terms again.

* * * * *

Meanwhile, on December 1st, Dickens had presided at a soirée of the Leeds Mechanics' Institute. Despite a disastrous cold, he made an eloquent speech defending education for the masses against those who feared putting the power of knowledge into their hands. "Reflect," he said, "whether ignorance be not power, and a very dreadful power . . . for every kind of wrong and evil? Powerful to take its enemies to its heart, and strike its best friends down—powerful to fill the prisons, the hospitals, and the graves—powerful for blind violence, prejudice, and error . . ." Far from undermining the social structure and setting class against class, popular education, "unlike that Babel tower that would have taken heaven by storm," would "end in sweet accord and harmony among all classes . . ." [113]

The wintry London to which Dickens returned was in a "hideous state of mud and darkness. Everybody is laid up with the Influenza except all the disagreeable people." At the theater "a most extraordinary effect was produced by the whole audience being in a paroxysm of sniffling. . . . I am in a dreadful state of mental imbecility myself, and am pursuing Dombey under difficulties." [114] With the terrified and broken-hearted flight of Florence from her father's house, Dickens had reached one of the crises of the story. Lord Jeffrey, writing from Edinburgh, positively refused to believe that Mr. Dombey's second wife could have become the mistress of the villainous Carker, and this gave Dickens an idea for an ingenious twist in the plot. "What do you think," he asked Forster, "of a kind of inverted Maid's Tragedy, and a tremendous scene of her undeceiving Carker, and giving him to know that she never meant that?"[115]

As the climax of the novel drew near—Mr. Dombey's ruin and his reconciliation with Florence—and Dickens's imagination kindled to the ending, he made fewer plaints about his difficulties in writing. Nevertheless, he was glad after Christmas to take a holiday run to Scotland, where he visited friends in Edinburgh and presided at the first anniversary of the Glasgow Athenaeum. On the railway journey from Edinburgh to Glasgow Kate was suddenly taken ill and had a miscarriage. When the train reached Glasgow, she was hurriedly conveyed to the home of Sheriff Alison, where they were staying, put to bed, and a famous doctor called in to her. At the meeting, however, nobody missed her, and one of the newspapers reported her presence in a description so fulsome that Dickens was sure Alison's beautiful seventeen-year-old daughter must have been taken for Kate. "The Inimitable did wonders. His grace, elegance, and eloquence enchanted all beholders." [116]

Kate recovered sufficiently to return to Edinburgh with Dickens on the 30th of December. There she was taken violently ill again and another famous doctor called in. He declared that she would not be fit to travel back to London for another three days.[117] Meanwhile, Dickens passed his time sightseeing, going to Abbotsford, and visiting friends. "I am sorry to report the Scott Monument a failure. It is like the spire of a Gothic church taken off and stuck in the ground." [118] From Jeffrey he learned that the dramatist James Sheridan Knowles, author of *Virginius* and *The Hunchback*, had just declared himself bankrupt.[119] This news rekindled all Dickens's restless ardor for amateur dramatics, and he returned to London fired with determination to run another benefit.

There was already a project on foot to purchase Shakespeare's house at Stratford-on-Avon for the nation. Why not combine this, Dickens thought, with an endowment for a perpetual curatorship of the house, and make Knowles the first incumbent of the post? The amateur group should be revived to raise money for these purposes.[120] In December, indeed, for recreation, they had met at Miss Kelly's theater and rehearsed Ben Jonson's *The Alchemist* several times, but had dropped that play although Forster thought Dickens splendid as Sir Epicure Mammon.[121] Now, despite the fact that he had the last three numbers of *Dombey* still to do, Dickens eagerly called the company together again.[122]

Their meetings did not go so smoothly as Dickens had hoped. The company disagreed about the choice of a play, and, in a vain endeavor to achieve agreement, successively rehearsed Beaumont and Fletcher's *Beggar's Bush*, Goldsmith's *Good-Natured Man*, Jerrold's *Rent Day*, and Bulwer Lytton's *Money*.[123] Dickens grew disgusted at the unpleasant atmosphere of these nightly rehearsals and voiced his annoyance in a sharp note to each member of the cast. "I was mistaken," he wrote, "in supposing there to be an universal feeling of common consideration among us . . . which would prevent any of us from inconveniencing and utterly disregarding the rest"; he therefore reluctantly abandoned his share in the design.[124]

In the midst of these little contentions had come the news of the Revolution in France. Dickens was wildly enthusiastic. "Vive la République!" he wrote Forster. "Vive le Peuple! Plus de Royauté!" [125] To M. De la Rue he was less effervescent, but quite as decided: "The aristocratic feeling of England is against it, of course. All the intelligence, and liberality, I should say, are with it, tooth and nail. If the Queen should be marked in her attentions to old Papa Philippe . . . there will be great discontent and dissatisfaction expressed, throughout the country." [126] Dickens thought Lamartine, the right-wing leader, "one of the best fellows in the world," and had "lively hopes of that great people establishing a noble republic." [127]

There were, however, no sharp repercussions of foreign disorders in England. Though the gates of the Green Park and Constitution Hill were closed and the iron shutters of Apsley House bolted when the Chartist procession presented its petition in April, the populace showed no disposition to violence and the middle class was solidly behind the Government. "The popular victory over the Corn Laws two years back," summarizes G. M. Trevelyan, "and the far-spreading tide of new prosperity and well-being removed all fear of revolutionary contagion." [128]

*   *   *   *   *

Turning his back on these public excitements, Dickens went to Brighton in March to finish *Dombey*.[129] When the proofs were already returned to Bradbury and Evans, it struck him that he had forgotten to say a final word about Florence's dog, Diogenes. "Will you put him in the last little chapter?" he asked Forster. "After the word 'favourite' in reference to Miss Tox, you can add, 'except with Diogenes, who is growing old and wilful.' Or, on the last page of all, after 'and with them two children: boy and girl' . . . you might say 'and an old dog is generally in their company,' or to that effect. Just what you think best." [130]

Shortly after, Forster's *Life of Goldsmith* was published, and Dickens read it with loyal approbation. "I think the Goldsmith very great indeed . . . ," he wrote his friend. "As a picture of the time, I think it impossible to give it too much praise." It was a noble achievement in its tracing of Goldsmith's life and its "dignified assertion of him without any sobs, whines, or convulsions of any sort." And above all, it was admirable in its statement of "the case of the literary man." "The gratitude of every man who is content to rest his station and claims quietly on literature, and to make no feint of living on anything else, is your due for evermore." [131]

In some way, probably with no great resistance on Dickens's part, he had been brought to take charge again of the dramatic amateurs. The town council of Stratford was buying the Shakespeare House, but funds for endowing the curatorship were still to be raised.[132] Dickens was soon buoyantly arranging all the details and dominating and cajoling his company as before.

Another pattern was establishing itself in his life. Increasingly he felt an "unhappy loss or want of something" which he was to lament a few years later. In his youthful days of misery over Maria Beadnell he had discovered that he could dull his heartache by an intensity of absorption in his labors on the *Mirror of Parliament*; and during the most desperate height of his unhappiness he had directed the acting of *Clari* in Bentinck Street. And now, in the course of this last year, when his work itself had grown strangely difficult to him, he had found that by playing at the drama as hard as if it were work he drained off some of his distressing restlessness. The congenial turmoils of the Leigh Hunt benefit proved an anodyne that eased him of inward tension. More and more often, whenever he felt unsettled or distressed, he was to resort to the same relief. But, like all drugs, it built up ultimately only a more desperate need and afterwards plunged him only into deeper misery.

CHAPTER THREE

The World of Dombeyism

CRITICISM: *Dombey and Son*

THE period of *Dombey and Son* represents a turning point both in Dickens's life and in his literary art. He had recovered the control of half his copyrights, and the continuing sale of earlier books combined with the splendid profits of *Dombey* made him prosperous beyond all further worry.[1] Despite his large family and lavish scale of living, his cheerfully improvident father and irresponsible brothers, and his own generous charities, from this time on Dickens always had several thousand pounds invested or in the bank.[2] And yet he was not at peace within himself. A deep inward dissatisfaction made his work laborious to him and drove him for relief to those stage excitements that enabled him to forget himself in the representation of some character quite different from his own.

His discontent had roots in personal emotion, but it was reflected too in his changing outlook on society. He expressed no consciousness of the reasons for his own restlessness, but he became steadily more analytical of the causes underlying the world's evils. His earliest books had assailed the debtors' prisons, the new Poor Law, the Yorkshire schools, and the slum breeding-grounds of disease and crime as if they were isolated abuses, dreadful but disconnected. Responsibility for them lay at the hands of individual knaves and dullards—ignorant parish officials, bullying magistrates, greedy usurers, brutal schoolmasters, lordly wastrels, dishonest lawyers, a misgoverning aristocracy. Even in *The Old Curiosity Shop* and *Barnaby Rudge* Dickens's warnings of labor violence and mob revolt endangering the social order implied no great complicity in society itself—hardly more, in fact, than

[626]

a blind unawareness of the cruelties on which he strove to open men's eyes.

Somewhat later, *A Christmas Carol* had made Scrooge symbolize a whole social class and an entire economic philosophy. But Scrooge remained in his own person a mean and grasping old skinflint. The grotesque crew of commentators in *The Chimes*—the statistical Filer, Sir Joseph Bowley, "the Poor Man's Friend," and Alderman Cute—represented a savage showing-up of the hard-hearted economic rationalizations that supported business rapacity. The respectable businessman himself, however, Dickens had portrayed only in such figures as old Fezziwig, the Cheeryble Brothers, and Mr. Pickwick, benevolent old boys beaming through their spectacles in a warm mist of generous feeling. And from the beginning Dickens had had readers who wondered how Mr. Pickwick ever made enough money to retire on and who found the Cheerybles as fantastic as Scrooge.

What was the businessman really like, the City merchant, the rich banker, the prosperous middle-class citizen, subscribing his guineas to the proper charities, and behaving with complete rectitude according to conventional lights? By the time of *Dombey and Son* Dickens had heard him and scores of his fellows at hospital banquets expressing sentiments at which "any moderately intelligent dustman would have blushed through his cindery bloom." [3] Had they in their counting-houses no responsibility for the slums and the cholera and the starved laborer and the maimed factory child? What of the share the solid member of society had in allowing and fostering evils of which he was often smugly unaware? What, in short, of Mr. Dombey?

The troubled concern Dickens felt over these problems of modern society is reflected in the very period setting of *Dombey and Son*. The scene of *Pickwick* was almost contemporary with the time in which it was written,[4] and *Oliver Twist* if anything anticipated criticisms of the workhouse that were barely beginning to be made. But the books between *Pickwick* and *Dombey* remained in the *Pickwick* period or reverted to still earlier times, precisely during the years when the rapid changes of industrialism were making the world Dickens portrayed one of the past. *Nicholas Nickleby, The Old Curiosity Shop,* and *Martin Chuzzlewit* (except for its American episodes) are full of the old stage-coach days that were fast dying out, and drenched in the atmosphere of an old England and an old London. With *Dombey and Son,* however,

Dickens leaps forward into the age of railway travel and jerry-built suburbs and company shares: little Paul is weaned while Euston Station is being constructed, old Sol Gills makes a comfortable fortune out of his investments, and most of the action takes place in the bustling forties.

The book vividly describes the building of the London and Birmingham Railway: "Houses were knocked down; streets broken through and stopped; deep pits and trenches dug in the ground; enormous heaps of earth and clay thrown up; buildings that were undermined and shaken, propped by great beams. Here, a chaos of carts, overthrown and jumbled together, lay topsy-turvy at the bottom of a steep unnatural hill; there, confused treasurers of iron soaked and rusted in something that had accidentally become a pond. Everywhere were bridges that led nowhere . . . and piles of scaffolding, and wildernesses of brick, and giant forms of cranes, and tripods straddling above nothing. . . . Boiling water hissed and heaved within dilapidated walls; whence, also, the glare and roar of flames came issuing forth; and mounds of ashes blocked up rights of way, and wholly changed the law and custom of the neighbourhood." [5]

No less sharply noted are the effects on the outskirts of the city surrounding the construction, the new taverns called the "Railway Arms" and the "Excavators' House of Call" among the mud and ashes, the "frowsy fields, and cowhouses, and dunghills, and dustheaps, and ditches, and gardens, and summer-houses, and carpet-beating grounds," with "little tumuli of oyster shells in the oyster season, and of lobster shells in the lobster season, and of broken crockery and faded cabbage leaves in all seasons." [6] And farther out still, on the deserted great North Road, are places that were once rural but are now "only blighted country, and not town," with "a few tall chimneys belching smoke all day and night," and brickfields, tumble-down fences, and dusty nettles among a scrap or two of hedge.[7]

It is through this new world of change and speed and desolation and machinery that Mr. Dombey after the death of Paul takes his railway journey to Leamington. "Through the hollow, on the height, by the heath, by the orchard, by the park, by the garden, over the canal, across the river, where the sheep are feeding, where the mill is going, where the barge is floating, where the dead are lying, where the factory is smoking . . . away, with a shriek, and a roar, and a rattle, and no trace to leave behind but dust and vapour . . . Louder and louder yet, it shrieks and cries as it comes tearing on resistless to the goal: and now its way, still like the way of Death, is strewn with ashes thickly. Everything around is blackened. There are dark pools of water, muddy lanes, and miserable habitations far below. There are jagged walls and falling houses close at hand, and through the battered roofs and broken windows, wretched rooms are seen, where want and fever hide themselves in many wretched shapes, while smoke and crowded gables, and distorted chimneys, and deformity of brick and mortar penning up deformity of mind and body, choke the murky distance. As Mr. Dombey looks out of his carriage window, it is never in his thoughts that the monster who has brought him there has let the light of day in on these things: not made or caused them." [8]

Mr. Dombey himself is even more significant than the railroad showing up the horrors he and his kind have long suffered to exist hidden in obscurity. With him, Dickens has left behind those merchants like the Cheerybles, crude but kindly, eating with their knives, living in quarters above their place of business, and, like old Fezziwig, having their employees dwell with them in a relation of genial master and apprentice. Although Dombey's House is engaged in maritime commerce with England's colonial empire rather than with manufacturing industry, he represents the merchant-prince involved in close relations with bankers and industralists and laying claims to an impressive magnificence. He displays a stiff propriety of manners, resides with bleak pomposity "in a tall, dark, dreadfully genteel street" [9] between Portland Place and Bryanston Square, rides to his offices on a smart pacer, and maintains a frigid detachment from all his employees. His associates—not friends, he has none—are wealthy East India directors and bank directors who boast with proud humility of their poor little hothouses for pineapples and delightedly profess themselves unable to afford the opera. [10]

These slashing details brilliantly surpass anything of the kind that H. G. Wells was later to do in *Tono-Bungay* or Sinclair Lewis in *Babbitt,* and they are a portent of Dickens's altered judgment of the mercantile middle class. He no longer erects their virtues in opposition to a dissolute aristocracy represented by Sir Mulberry Hawk and Lord Frederick Verisopht or the dishonest trickery of upper-class governors like Mr. Gregsbury, M.P., and the icily egoistic Sir John Chester.

Now he sees the broad group of businessmen as selfish, smug, and cold-hearted in their professional dealings, and realizes that they are as venally indifferent to the consequences of their behavior on social welfare and as harshly unsympathetic toward the poor as the most idly irresponsible of the aristocracy with whom they are beginning to intermingle and marry.

* * * * *

Dickens described the theme of *Dombey and Son* as pride, but Mr. Dombey's pride, though a dark and omnipresent strand in the story, is not its dominant principle. That principle is the callous inhumanity of an economic doctrine that strips Mr. Dombey's relations with everyone to an assertion of monetary power. He wants no ties of affection between his infant son and Polly Toodle, the wet nurse whom he engages for the child. "When you go away from here, you will have concluded what is a mere matter of bargain and sale, hiring and letting: and will stay away." [11] He is affronted to learn that Miss Tox, the poor toady on his grandeur, has dared to lift eyes of personal admiration to him and to dream that he might raise her to his side as his wife. It never enters his mind that he cannot hire the obedience of his subordinates to any of his commands, or that Mr. Carker, his Manager, even while he does his great chief's bidding, can resent being employed in degrading and humiliating ways. He believes that he can buy the respect and obedience of an aristocratic wife whose pride and beauty are to reflect luster on his greatness. Even his love for his son, though sincere and strong, is engendered in the doctrine that the wealth and pre-eminence of the House of Dombey and Son must go on forever.

The attitudes that Mr. Dombey displays toward those with whom he comes into immediate contact are also his attitudes toward society as a whole, and toward the welfare of society. "I am far from being friendly," he explains coldly, "to what is called by persons of levelling sentiments, general education. But it is necessary that the inferior classes should continue to be taught to know their position, and to conduct themselves properly. So far I approve of schools." [12] Fundamentally, however, Mr. Dombey agrees with his companion Major Bagstock, who distrusts all education for the poor: "Take advice from plain old Joe, and never educate that sort of people, Sir," says the Major. "Damme, Sir, it never does! It always fails!" [13]

Mr. Dombey is the living symbol of the nineteenth-century theory of business enterprise and its social philosophy. Not even the Lancashire industralists who bitterly resisted the regulation of child labor and defied the law demanding the fencing-in of dangerous machinery exemplified a more relentless devotion to their own profits and power. Many factory owners, indeed, were decent enough men, devoted to their families, kind to those with whom they came in direct contact, and desirous of doing right by their workers. But they were helpless against ruthless competition and blinded by the belief that any protective interference with the operations of laissez-faire economics would be disastrous. Richard Oastler, the humane reformer who spent years trying to get the working man's day cut down to ten hours, explained the principles of competitive business to Dr. Thomas Chalmers: "Take advantage of another's poverty or ignorance, forcing or coaxing him to sell cheap; and when he is a buyer, using the same means to make him buy dear . . . get money any how, even at the cost of life and limb to those employed in his aggrandisement . . ." [14]

The entire complex development of *Dombey and Son* orchestrates these themes of callous indifference and social evil into a vast symphonic structure in which all the groups and individuals brought into contact with Mr. Dombey and his affairs are organically related. The group at the Wooden Midshipman, old Sol Gills, his bright, high-spirited nephew Walter Gay, simple-minded Captain Cuttle, the wooden-headed Bunsby; Polly Toodle and her apple-cheeked family; sharp-tongued Susan Nipper; poor, foolish, kind-hearted Mr. Toots; Cousin Feenix, with his willful legs and wandering speech—all display the warm humanity banished from the cold heart of Mr. Dombey. Even Miss Tox, toady though she is, reveals a disinterested loyalty and devotion ignored and despised by the object of her adulation. These characters surround with a glowing counterpoint the icy dissonances of Mr. Dombey's world.

The contrasts are developed with consummate artistry. Little Paul Dombey's christening is rendered entirely in glacial imagery: the freezing library with all the books in "cold, hard, slippery uniforms," Mr. Dombey taking Mr. Chick's hand "as if it were a fish, or seaweed, or some such clammy substance," [15] the chill and earthy church, the cold

collation afterwards, "set forth in a cold pomp of glass and silver," the
champagne "so bitter cold" as to force "a little scream from Miss Tox,"
the veal that strikes "a sensation of cold lead to Mr. Chick's extrem-
ities," Mr. Dombey as unmoved as if he were "hung up for sale at a
Russian fair as a specimen of a frozen gentleman." [16]

From this silent, icy celebration the very next chapter plunges into
the warm clamor of Polly Toodle's visit to her family in Stagg's Gardens with her "honest apple face . . . the centre of a bunch of smaller
pippins, all laying their rosy cheeks close to it," [17] and all growing noisy,
vehement, disheveled, and flushed with delight. Even the calmer
scenes of everyday domesticity in the Toodle household are as different from those in the Dombey mansion as these two festive occasions.
Mr. Toodle home from firing his locomotive engine recharges himself with innumerable pint mugs of tea solidified with great masses of
bread and butter, with both of which he regales his expectant circle
of children in small spoonfuls and large bites: snacks that "had such
a relish in the mouths of these young Toodles, that, after partaking
of the same, they performed private dances of ecstasy among themselves, and stood on one leg a-piece, and hopped, and indulged in other
saltatory tokens of gladness." [18]

In the fierce sequence of climactic events centering around the
flight of Edith, Mr. Dombey's second wife, with his treacherous Manager, Mr. Carker, Dickens designedly emphasizes the same contrasts.
Again they occupy successive chapters, the heavy blow with which the
marble-hearted father almost fells his daughter to the marble floor,
her cry of desolation as she runs from that loveless and pitiless house,
understanding at last that she has "no father upon earth"; [19] and then
Captain Cuttle, trembling and "pale in the very knobs of his face,"
soothing the weeping girl with murmured endearments of "Heart's
Delight," and "my pretty," as he tenderly raises her from the
ground; [20] the freezing rancor of Mr. Dombey's gloomy board, and
the little dinner the Captain prepares at the parlor fire.

There is a wonderful radiance in the Captain bustling about this
meal, his coat off and his glazed hat on his head, making the egg sauce,
basting the fowl, heating the gravy, boiling some potatoes, keeping his
eye on the sausages "hissing and bubbling in a most musical manner,"
and at last removing his hat, putting on his coat, and wheeling up the
table before Florence's sofa. "My lady lass," he begs her, "cheer up,

and try to eat a deal. Stand by, my deary! Liver wing it is. Sarse it is. Sassage it is. And potato!" [21]

No less heart-warming is the Captain's endeavor to bestow on Florence the tin canister containing his savings of £14 2s. for any purchases she needs to make, his request to the shop girl to "sing out" if any more is required, his casually "consulting his big watch as a deep means of dazzling the establishment, and impressing it with a sense of property," and his disappointment when Florence does not use his money. "It ain't o' no use to *me*," he says. "I wonder I haven't chucked it away afore now." [22] What an illustration of the ludicrous forms goodness of heart can take without ceasing to be real goodness! No speech was ever more absurd, and yet no gentleman ever said anything more truly imbued with delicacy and generosity.

Captain Cuttle, together with Mr. Toots, is among the great portraits of the book, both irresistibly ridiculous and both at the same time possessed of a true dignity shining through all their absurdity. Poor Toots, with his "It's of no consequence whatsoever," his vapid chuckle, the trousers and waistcoats that are masterpieces of Burgess and Company, and his hopeless devotion to Florence, rises to heights of noble selflessness. And even when Captain Cuttle is scrambling quotations like a parody on T. S. Eliot and rambling through chains of dim association suggestive of Joyce's Molly Bloom, there is a heart of tender sanity in his nonsense. "If you're in arnest, you see, my lad," he comforts Toots, "you're a object of clemency, and clemency is the brightest jewel in the crown of a Briton's head, for which you'll overhaul the constitution as laid down in Rule Britannia, and, when found, *that* is the charter as them garden angels was a singing of, so many times over. Stand by!" [23]

Seen with no such gentle satire as the Captain and Toots, certain other characters represent disguised forms of Mr. Dombey's own cold egoism. Mrs. Skewton, Edith Dombey's mother, with her specious cult of the "heart," is a hypocritical parody of the sympathies that flow so sincerely in chuckle-headed Mr. Toots and the acidulous Susan Nipper; underneath the languishing phrases she is completely selfish and venal. Major Bagstock, "leering and choking, like an over-fed Mephistopheles," [24] covers a toadying malignance in a blustering pretense of blunt-spoken friendship.

The name of Dombey, the Major tells its owner, is one "that a man is proud to recognise. There is nothing adulatory in Joseph Bagstock, Sir. His Royal Highness the Duke of York observed on more than one occasion, 'there is no adulation in Joey. He is a plain old soldier is Joe. He is tough to a fault is Joseph'; but it's a great name, Sir. By the Lord, it's a great name!" [25] And Mrs. Skewton, reclining in her wheeled chair like Cleopatra in her gilded barge, wants to know what "we live for *but* sympathy! What else is so extremely charming! Without that gleam of sunshine on our cold cold earth, how could we possibly bear it? . . . . I would have my world all heart; and Faith is so excessively charming that I won't allow you to disturb it . . ." [26]

As a part of her patter Cleopatra dotes upon the Middle Ages. "Those darling bygone times, Mr. Carker," she gushes, "with their delicious fortresses, and their dear old dungeons, and their delightful places of torture . . . and everything that makes life truly charming! How dreadfully we have degenerated!" There is no such Faith today, she goes on, as there was in the days of Queen Bess, "which were so extremely golden. Dear creature! She was all Heart!" And then there was her father, so bluff, so English, "with his dear little peepy eyes, and his benevolent chin!" [27] How appropriate that this creature of masks and attitudes should have detachable hair and a painted rosy complexion, and that when these are removed the little that is real of her should be put to bed "like a horrible doll." [28]

Grim parallels to Cleopatra and Edith Dombey are two figures from that dark lower world on which Mr. Dombey looked down from his railway carriage on the way to Leamington. But "Good Mrs. Brown" and her daughter, Alice Marwood, are linked to Mrs. Skewton and Edith by more than Dickens's desire for an artificial symmetry of plot. They symbolize the fatal mingling in society of those evils that creep from high to low like the greed-engendered cholera coiling from the slums into lordly homes. There is a deeper significance than mere accident in Alice Marwood's being the illegitimate daughter to an elder brother of Edith's father, and in her being seduced and abandoned by Carker, Mr. Dombey's Manager, as Edith has been bought in matrimony by Mr. Dombey himself. When the two mothers and their daughters meet by chance on the downs, Edith is fearfully struck by their dark resemblance to each other, and Mrs. Skewton guiltily jabbers her belief that Mrs. Brown is a good mother, "full of what's her name—and all that," "all affection and et cetera." [29] "No great lady,"

Alice has previously said with bitter irony, ever thought of selling her daughter, "and that shows that the only instances of mothers bringing up their daughters wrong, and evil coming of it, are among such miserable folks as us." [30] And looking after Edith, she exclaims, "You're a handsome woman; but good looks won't save us. And you're a proud woman; but pride won't save us." [31]

* * * * *

On every level in the world of *Dombey and Son,* although not in every breast, the same forces are at work. From the stately mansions of the aristocracy on Brook Street and the pineries of Mr. Dombey's banker-associates down to the rag-filled hovel of Good Mrs. Brown, competitive greed and indifference to the welfare of others create a cynical economic system that spawns all the vices and cruelties of society. And of that system—it might even be called Dombeyism—Mr. Dombey is the symbolic embodiment. He is not, of course, directly and personally responsible for all the wrongs Dickens paints; and, despite grave defects of character, he is not even inherently vicious. He too has been shaped by the forces he now embodies. "When I thought so much of all the causes that had made me what I was," Edith says of Mr. Dombey, "I needed to allow more for the causes that had made him what he was." [32] But Dickens has also come to understand that, whatever the individual blame for the evils he is fighting, a statistically large proportion of them must be laid at the door of Dombeyism.

That is why even society's charities and generosities so often fail of their stated objects. They are not really directed toward human welfare, but are instruments of ostentation and keeping the poor in their place. So of the Charitable Grinders' School, to which Mr. Dombey nominated Polly Toodle's son Rob. Beaten daily by his master, "a superannuated old Grinder of savage disposition, who had been appointed schoolmaster because he didn't know anything, and wasn't fit for anything," [33] what wonder that Rob turns out a liar and a sneak? "But they never taught honour at the Grinders' School, where the system that prevailed was particularly strong in the engendering of hypocrisy. Insomuch, that many of the friends and masters of past Grinders said, if this were what came of education for the common people, let us have none. Some more rational said, let us have a better one. But the governing powers of the Grinders' Company were always ready for *them*, by picking out a few boys who had turned out well, in spite of the system, and roundly asserting that they could only have turned out well because of it. Which settled the business . . ." [34]

It is this emphasis on abstract forces that explains the diminished role of the villains in *Dombey and Son*. Though contemptible enough personally, they are not demonic creators of evil like Ralph Nickleby, Fagin, Quilp, Sir John Chester, and Jonas Chuzzlewit. They batten, not on the weakness of innocent victims, but on the vices of the powerful. Major Bagstock, "rough and tough old Joey," that hypocrite of truculence, exploits Mr. Dombey's snobbery and pride; but Mr. Dombey already had them, ripe for sycophancy. Mr. Carker, with his feline smile and those glittering teeth whose symbolic falseness Dickens is constantly suggesting without ever stating directly, flatters the demand for absolute abasement that Mr. Dombey was already making of all those about him. In a sense, Mr. Dombey may be said to have tempted and corrupted Carker rather than the reverse. Both the Manager and the blue-faced Major merely smooth a way that everything in Mr. Dombey's background and character predetermines he shall travel.

This way is hinted as early as the second page of the book and implicit in its very title. The three words "Dombey and Son," we are told, "convey the one idea of Mr. Dombey's life. The earth was made for Dombey and Son to trade in, and the sun and moon were made to give them light. Rivers and seas were formed to float their ships; rainbows gave them promise of fair weather; winds blew for or against their enterprises; stars and planets circled in their orbits, to preserve inviolate a system of which they were the centre." [35] His feeling about his first wife's death is hardly more than a sense of "something gone from among his plate and furniture, and other household possessions, which was well worth the having, and could not be lost without sincere regret." [36] He thinks of himself and his wealth as all-powerful. "The kind of foreign help which people usually seek for their children, I can afford to despise; being above it, I hope." [37] When his second wife asks if he believes he "can degrade, or bend or break" *her* "to submission and obedience," Mr. Dombey smiles, as if he had been asked "whether he thought he could raise ten thousand pounds." [38] Such is the nature of the man whom Carker maliciously describes as "the slave

The Dombey Family

of his own greatness . . . yoked to his own triumphal car like a beast of burden." [39]

Given these elements in Mr. Dombey, it is natural that he should regard his daughter with indifference and bring whatever affection is in his chill nature to the son who may carry on his name and business. "He had never conceived an aversion to her: it had not been

worth his while or in his humour." [40] But when he sees her fear of
him and feels his exclusion from the tenderness between her and her
dying mother, he cannot avoid knowing that it is a reproach to him.
Later still, as he realizes that all the tenderness of his cherished son
and heir is bestowed on his despised daughter, and observes in a moment of farewell the contrast between the limp and careless hand his
boy gives him and the sorrowful face he turns to Florence, it is a bitter
pang to the father's proud heart.[41] With what fateful steps it follows
that as she reaps the love his riches cannot command his indifference
should turn to jealous dislike! And that when Paul dies, he should
see in her "the successful rival of his son, in health and life" and find
it "gall to him to look upon her in her beauty and her promise"? [42]

In the course of the fierce duel between Mr. Dombey and his obdurate second wife, his resentment of his daughter deepens. While
his bourgeois pride dashes itself in vain against the barriers of her aristocratic pride, who is it that wins his wife as she had won his boy,
"whose least word did what his utmost means could not! Who was
it who, unaided by his love, regard or notice, thrived and grew beautiful when those so aided died! Who could it be, but the same child at
whom he had often glanced uneasily in her motherless infancy, with
a kind of dread, lest he might come to hate her; and of whom his foreboding was fulfilled, for he DID hate her in his heart." [43]

All this is handled with enormous skill and power. That the cancerous growth of Mr. Dombey's bitterness is delineated with absolute
fidelity has never been denied. But there are readers who have not
been convinced of his later change of heart. Their skepticism, however, ignores both the repeated psychological preparations Dickens
makes for it in the book and the complex involutions of emotion in
human beings. Is there anyone who has not often known, even as he
sullenly persisted in a course of injustice, that his behavior was indefensible, and half longed to make the very change that he stubbornly
resisted making? Does no one ever turn with unavailing remorse and
belated affection to the memory of those he has wronged, and wish
that he could make amends and win the love he has thrown away?

These emotions have struggled in Mr. Dombey from the very beginning. He has never been utterly without tender emotion, even for
his daughter. Seeing her clasped in her mother's arms, he has felt
an uneasiness that troubled his peace. On a later night he looks from

his door upon his two children going to bed, and in the time thereafter his memory is haunted by the image of her small figure toiling
up the stairs, singing to the baby brother in her arms." [44] Leaving his
boy at Brighton with Florence, and bending down to kiss him
good-by, his sight dimmed "by something that for a moment blurred
the little face," he has a twinge of feeling about his injustice that
makes his mental vision, "for that short time," Dickens tells us, "the
clearer perhaps." [45]

Numerous impulses of contrition like these reach a culmination on
the evening Mr. Dombey returns from Paris with his bride and, pretending to sleep, secretly watches Florence bent over her work from
which she occasionally raises to him pathetic speaking eyes. "Some
passing thought that he had had a happy home within his reach—had
had a household spirit bending at his feet—had overlooked it in his
stiff-necked arrogance, and wandered away and lost himself," [46] en-
genders a gentler feeling toward her. "As he looked, she became
blended with the child he had loved" and "he saw her for an instant
by a clearer and a brighter light, not bending over that child's pillow
as his rival . . . but as the spirit of his home . . ." [47] Almost about to
call her to him, he hears Edith's footstep on the stairs, and the moment is lost. Florence becomes a weapon in his struggle with his wife,
and his softening hardens once again to resentment.

But after the flight of Edith and Florence, the bankruptcy of his
business, and the loss of his fortune, as he sits alone in his desolate
house, there is not one of these things that does not return to his
memory. Again he sees the small childish figure singing on the stair,
again he hears her heartbroken cry at the blow he struck her, and
knows that if he had not thrown it away he would always have had her
love, even now, in his fall, and "that of all around him, she alone had
never changed. His boy had faded into dust, his proud wife had sunk
into a polluted creature, his flatterer and friend been transformed into
the worst of villains; his riches had melted away," but "she alone had
turned the same gentle look upon him always. . . . She had never
changed to him—nor had he ever changed to her—and she was lost."
In his anguish, "Oh, how much better than this," he cries in his heart,
"that he had loved her as he had his boy, and lost her as he had his
boy, and laid them in their early grave together!" [48]

Even in Mr. Dombey's remorse, though, with a marvelous touch of psychological insight, Dickens shows him still his old self. If he had "heard her voice in the adjoining room," Dickens writes, "he would not have gone to her. If he could have seen her in the street, and she had done no more than look at him as she had been used to look, he would have passed on with his old cold unforgiving face, and not addressed her, or relaxed it, though his heart should have broken soon afterwards." [49] In their superb penetration these few vivid words, for all their brevity, are equivalent to paragraphs of intricate psychological analysis.

His misery is resolved only by the unhoped-for return of Florence, imploring his forgiveness instead of proffering the forgiveness he could never have forced himself to beg. "I was frightened when I went away, and could not think." [50] Although the mercy is undeserved, no reader who has understood the entire delineation of Florence's character could doubt it any more than he could disbelieve the behavior of Mr. Dombey. What wonder that the broken man exclaims, in a passion of grief, "Oh my God, forgive me, for I need it very much!" [51]

* * * * *

Throughout all this personal drama of pride, heartache, and bankruptcy, Dickens has never lost sight nor allowed the reader to lose sight of the social bearings of his theme. On the crash of Dombey and Son, "The world was very busy now, in sooth," he writes, "and had a deal to say. It was an innocently credulous and a much ill-used world. It was a world in which there was no other sort of bankruptcy whatever. There were no conspicuous people in it, trading far and wide on rotten banks of religion, patriotism, virtue, honour. There was no amount worth mentioning of mere paper in circulation, on which anybody lived pretty handsomely, promising to pay great sums of goodness with no effects. There were no shortcomings anywhere, in anything but money. The world was very angry indeed; and the people especially, who in a worse world, might have been supposed to be bankrupt traders themselves in shows and pretences, were observed to be mightily indignant." [52]

Two-thirds of the way through the book, Dickens had sounded his own deeper indignation in a powerful outburst. "Hear the magistrate or judge admonish the unnatural outcasts of society; unnatural in brutish habits, unnatural in want of decency, unnatural in losing and

confounding all distinctions between good and evil," Dickens exclaims; and then go "down into their dens, lying within the echoes of
our carriage wheels," and look "upon the world of odious sights," at
which "dainty delicacy, living in the next street . . . lisps 'I don't believe it!' Breathe the polluted air," he bids us: "And then, calling up
some ghastly child, with stunted form and wicked face, hold forth on
its unnatural sinfulness, and lament its being, so early, far away from
Heaven—but think a little of its having been conceived, and born
and bred, in Hell!

"Those who study the physical sciences," he goes on, ". . . tell us
that if the noxious particles that rise from vitiated air were palpable
to the sight, we should see them lowering in a dense black cloud above
such haunts, and rolling slowly on to corrupt the better portions of a
town. But if the moral pestilence that rises with them, and in the
eternal laws of outraged Nature, is inseparable from them, could be
made discernible too, how terrible the revelation! . . . Then should
we stand appalled to know, that where we generate disease to strike
our children down and entail itself on unborn generations, there also
we breed, by the same certain process, infancy that knows no innocence, youth without modesty or shame, maturity that is mature in
nothing but in suffering and guilt, blasted old age that is a scandal
on the form we bear. Unnatural humanity! When we shall gather
grapes from thorns, and figs from thistles; when fields of grain shall
spring up from the offal in the bye-ways of our wicked cities, and roses
bloom in the fat churchyards that they cherish, then we may look for
natural humanity and find it growing from such seed." [53]

In its faithfulness to the literal truths of human character and in its
portrayal of their social consequences, *Dombey and Son* is a realistic
development and elaboration of the themes fabulously set forth in
A Christmas Carol. Like Scrooge, Mr. Dombey is symbolic, but he
is also the mercantile reality of which Scrooge is a pantomime caricature. The picturesque glimpses in the *Carol* of humble courage and
generosity, of evil and suffering, like brightly lighted scenes in a fairy
tale, give way to fully detailed pictures of life on a dozen levels, from
Mrs. Brown's slum to Portland Place, all suggested in their relation to
each other. All the flashing intuitions of the *Carol* and *The Chimes*
are richly worked out in the intellectual and emotional comprehension
of *Dombey and Son*.

Though not, like them, an economic fantasy but a realistic study of contemporary society, it shares with them a curious strain of symbolism and symbolic imagery. To please his son and heir Mr. Dombey relieves the distress of Walter Gay's uncle, but then gratifies his own dislike of the courageous, high-spirited Walter by sending him forth on the voyage of the ominously named *Son and Heir*. Walter Gay survives, but the ship is lost—almost at the same time as the child who was always wondering what the waves were saying and who was in a way its namesake. The cold depths of the mahogany board at which Mr. Dombey sits just before his ill-fated marriage reflect vessels of dead-sea fruit riding there at anchor.[54] Beneath the picture that resembles Edith in Mr. Carker's dining parlor, there swings a chafing and imprisoned bird in "a pendant gilded hoop within the cage, like a great wedding-ring." [55] At Mr. Dombey's table a "long plateau of precious metal frosted . . . whereon frosted Cupids offered scentless flowers" [56] separates him from his second wife. Constantly Mr. Dombey's house and the meals there are described in terms of cold "and that unnecessary article in Mr. Dombey's banquets—ice." [57] And when his daughter takes her wounded heart to the Wooden Midshipman and its guardian, "A wandering princess and a good monster in a story-book," Dickens writes, "might have sat by the fireside and talked as Captain Cuttle and Florence thought—and not have looked very much unlike them." [58]

Such images—and there are many more of them—show that Dickens's creative powers were not working in naturalistic terms alone. With a surface observation almost as detailed as Balzac's and often far more brilliant, underneath there are always depths in which his vision pierces to something closely resembling myth and its mysterious power. These bold liberties with the canons of realism are no less exemplified by Dickens's melodrama at its best. It is as irrelevant to criticize some of the scenes between Edith Dombey and Carker by saying that people do not talk like that as to complain that Mirabell and Millamant converse in a shower of epigrams or that Iago distills his hate into a concentration of poisoned words. Drenched in theatricality, the interview in which Carker gives Edith Mr. Dombey's ultimatum is also tightly knit, loaded in every word with bitter suggestion and emotional intensity, and dramatically effective throughout every coil of its intricate subtlety.

The total achievement of *Dombey and Son* makes it one of Dickens's great books. With a creative vitality hardly surpassed by any of the books between it and *Pickwick*, it leaves all its predecessors far behind in structural logic, intellectual power, and social insight. His writing until now is the work of a brilliantly inspired youthful writer; *Dombey* is the first masterpiece of Dickens's maturity. Readers may prefer individual scenes in *Nickleby*, *Oliver*, or *Martin Chuzzlewit* to individual scenes in *Dombey*—although it is debatable that they contain anything really better than Captain Cuttle and Mr. Toots—but no one could say critically that they are better books. The problem of building a unified plot around a central theme so imperfectly tackled in *Chuzzlewit* is triumphantly solved in *Dombey*. None of Dickens's later books exhibit the loose improvisation with which he had begun; their elaboration is not that of planlessness but of a vast cathedral. And with *Dombey*, above all, Dickens has achieved a form by means of which he can convey the more detailed and philosophic social criticism that was to animate his work in the future.

CHAPTER FOUR

A Haunted Man

THE first outline of *Dombey and Son* that Dickens sent Forster contained no hint of one element in the story that swelled into unforeseen prominence: the friction between Mr. Dombey and his wife. It was not altogether chance that what was to have been a study of vainglory became at least in part a delineation of marital unhappiness. Poor, jealous, plaintive, amenable Kate, to be sure, was no Edith Dombey. But Dickens, though he did not share Mr. Dombey's freezing heartlessness, had enough of his rigid self-will. Even Dickens's difficulty in concentrating on his work is perhaps reflected in Mr. Dombey's neglect of the business enterprise that was his life's pride. Gradually Dickens had come to feel himself haunted by a specter of his own unhappiness. Throughout the five months following the completion of *Dombey* he managed to keep up his spirits by the violent stimulations of stage directing and acting. Then, as soon as they were over, he subsided again into outcries of misery.

He had galvanized himself and his company of amateurs into a frenzy of action. They would not only raise the money for the Shakespeare House curatorship; they would force the Government, as he authoritatively wrote one correspondent, "to make Knowles the first custodian." [1] This time it was quickly decided to alternate between *Every Man in His Humour* and *The Merry Wives of Windsor*, together with an assortment of farces. [2] Dickens willingly accepted a proposal from Mary Cowden Clarke that she should play Mistress Quickly opposite Mark Lemon's Falstaff. [3] Although she would be the only amateur actress in the group, it was fitting that the compiler of the great Shakespeare *Concordance* be connected with the enterprise. Soon Dickens was deep in the excitements of production. He sent copies of *The Merry Wives of Windsor* and *Love, Law, and Physic* to members of his company.[4] He discussed with Peter Cunningham, the treasurer of the Shakespeare Society, what theater should be engaged.[5] He dispatched advertisements to the newspapers.[6] He decided the overtures to be played: before *The Merry Wives* "something Shakespearian," before *Animal Magnetism* something light, "like Fra Diavolo," and "jolly little Polkas and Quadrilles between the pieces." [7]

Busy though Dickens was, he made a point of asking Forster to arrange an evening at Lincoln's Inn Fields with Ralph Waldo Emerson, who had just returned to England from revolutionary Paris. A fourth member of their party was Thomas Carlyle, whom Forster greeted loudly as "My Prophet!" Carlyle was feeling in one of his wild-Orson, savage-Isaiah moods, and fulminated about the lewdness of the London streets, whoredom, and the wickedness of civilization. Chastity in the male sex, he said, was a thing of the past; and Dickens, seeing that their prim-minded American visitor was shocked, mischievously endorsed the judgment. Emerson protested that in America bridegrooms approached marriage as virgin as their brides. Incontinence, Dickens piled it on, was taken for granted in England; if his own son were "particularly chaste" (Charley was at this time twelve years of age) he would be alarmed about his health. All this Emerson solemnly confided to his journal.[8]

Dickens was now calling rehearsals almost every day at Miss Kelly's, both *The Merry Wives* and *Every Man in His Humour*, as well as the farces to be given with them. He sat to one side at a little table near the front of the stage, constantly leaping up to show the performers how some piece of business needed to be done or the expression with which their lines should be read. His own roles he carried off with a fine dash. "In *Love, Law, and Physic*," said Mrs. Cowden Clarke, "he used to tuck me under his arm with the free-and-easy familiarity of a lawyer patronizing an actress whom he chances to find his fellow-traveller in a stage coach. . . . It is something to remember, having been tucked under the arm by Charles Dickens, and had one's hand hugged against his side! One thinks better of one's hand ever after." [9]

The "protracted agonies of management" kept Dickens, "like Falstaff," he said, " 'in a state of continual dissolution and thaw.' " [10] John Leech was so shaky in his words as the Marquis in *Animal Magnetism* that he put out all the other players. Dickens told him he must either get them perfectly or drop out.[11] Leech obediently bestirred himself: Dickens was soon able to report him positively "limp with being brilliant." The entire company was worked to death. "Stone is affected with congestion of the kidneys, which he attributes to being forced to do the same thing twenty times when he forgets it once. Beads break out all over Forster's head, and *boil* there, visibly and audibly." [12]

The final rehearsals were held at the Theatre Royal, Haymarket, where Dickens had determined the plays should be performed. As the crucial dates drew near he was swamped in final details—allotting press tickets, checking over how completely the house was sold out, seeing to the numbering of the seats.[13] Even the printing of the tickets he kept under his own eye, designing a special form with a stub to be returned to the holder, and decreeing that red pasteboard should be used for the pit, green for the lower boxes, and yellow for the upper.[14]

On May 15th *The Merry Wives of Windsor* and *Animal Magnetism* filled the theater with a gathering in full evening dress.[15] Two nights later, at *Every Man in His Humour* and *Love, Law, and Physic*, a no less numerous assemblage included the Queen and the Prince Consort. Both performances were brilliantly successful. Carlyle, to be sure, was astringent about Shakespeare's comedy: "A poor play," he said, as the curtain went down, "but *plaudite, plaudite!*" [16] Most of the audience, however, were enthusiastic. Bulging Mark Lemon was a hilarious Falstaff. Dickens covered himself with glory as Shallow, adopting a senile stoop and feeble step into which he infused "a certain attempted smartness of carriage," and inventing "a kind of impeded sibilation" of utterance, as if through the loss of teeth. He gave the part a wonderful mingling of assumed virility and shaky decrepitude.[17]

The London performances barely over, demands poured in for appearances in Liverpool and Birmingham.[18] Stratford and Leamington were also eager, but Dickens learned in a quick trip to Birmingham that the committee there were afraid performances so near by would cut down the size of their own audiences. He consequently decided not to include the smaller towns.[19] Manchester, however, was fitted in, and saw the first of the provincial performances on Saturday, June 3rd. There were flowers for Kate, Georgina, and the ladies of the troupe at the Manchester Hotel; [20] and the theater echoed to wild enthusiasm, with "the storm of plaudits . . . loudest when Dickens was recognized." [21] Thence the company went on to Liverpool and Birmingham on the 5th and 6th.

At railway stations Dickens flashed the free pass the railway authorities had bestowed upon his entire party. As the train sang along the tracks he entertained them with countless stories. At one stop he leaped out to get food at the refreshment room for one of them who had complained of hunger, and came back with a plate of buns, crying, "For Heaven's sake, somebody eat some of these buns; I was in hopes I saw Miss Novello eye them with greedy joy." Throughout these journeys, said Mrs. Cowden Clarke, "there was a positive sparkle . . . of holiday sunshine about him; he seemed to radiate brightness and enjoyment." [22]

Every Man in His Humour roused such a furore in Birmingham that there were insistent pleas for a return engagement to play *The Merry Wives* as well. As an addition to the bill, Dickens determined on "the screaming afterpiece of *Past Two O'Clock in the Morning,*" which he had originally acted in Montreal. Mrs. Cowden Clarke dined at Devonshire Terrace on the evening he and Mark Lemon cut it down to proper size for this purpose. On another such evening she sat out in the garden after dinner while the children played on the lawn, and was amused to see one of the little boys in eager conference with his father, the light of the setting sun on the childish upturned face while Dickens looked smilingly down. "The little fellow gave me so many excellent reasons why he should not go to bed so soon," Dickens explained, "that I yielded the point and let him sit up half an hour later." [23]

By this time Edinburgh and Glasgow also were clamorous to have the company come north. The proprietor of the Glasgow theater, however, demanded an extortionate share of the receipts for its use. They had never paid, Dickens exclaimed indignantly, more than a flat £50 for one night at a provincial theater.[24] "It is quite clear, I take it, that we are at the mercy of this Mr. Alexander, and must make . . . the best terms we can." But under no circumstances should these involve anything but a fixed sum agreed upon in advance. "Also I would recommend that he be as far as possible disconnected from the proceedings of the night." Wilmott, Macready's stage director, would come down and make all the stage arrangements a few days before-hand.[25]

On the second railway journey to Birmingham, Dickens asked Mrs. Cowden Clarke to hear him repeat his part of Sobbington in *Past Two O'Clock in the Morning*. Nobody, she thought, could ever forget "the convulsive writhes and spasmodic draw-up of his feet on the rungs of the chair, and the tightly-held coverlet round his shivering body just out of bed as he watched in an ecstasy of impatience the in-vasion of his chamber by that horribly intrusive Stranger." Lemon, too, as the Stranger, was exquisitely comic, and the two men were hand in glove in inventing liberties that lifted the farce to heights of absurdity.[26]

Between the second Birmingham engagement, on June 27th, and the Scottish engagements there was an interval of a few weeks during which Dickens tyrannically rehearsed his company in a new farce, *Used Up*, to alternate with the others.[27] In this piece Cruikshank had the part of a blacksmith. Mrs. Cruikshank became ill, and he had to give it up. Suddenly Mrs. Cruikshank was well again, and he wanted it back. "O questa femina maladetta!" Dickens exclaimed to George Lewes. "O Impressario sfortunato!—ma sempre dolce, tranquilissimo, cristianissimo, exempio di pazienza! . . . In una parola—Carlo." [28]

On July 17th *The Merry Wives* was played at Edinburgh with *Love, Law, and Physic* and *Past Two O'Clock in the Morning*. The follow-ing night, at Glasgow, it was given with *Animal Magnetism*. Two nights later there was a second Glasgow performance, at half prices, announcement of which had been carefully deferred, to prevent its injuring the sale of tickets for the earlier performance.[29] On this occasion *Used Up* was the farce, with Dickens acting Sir Charles Coldstream.[30] The hit of the piece, however, was made by Mark Lemon as one of Sir Charles's fop friends. During rehearsal Lemon startled the company by inventing for this part a ridiculous little laugh, exquisitely inane and disproportioned to the huge bulk of man from which it came, a "squeaking hysterical giggle closing in a sud-denly checked gasp." Dickens was so delighted that "a dozen times a day, until the night of the performance," he would make Lemon repeat this "incomparably droll new laugh," which transformed his small part into an important one and brought down the house every time it was uttered.[31]

After the last night at Glasgow the company held a champagne supper to celebrate the triumphal conclusion of their tour. Dickens was in the most tearing spirits, asking again and again for Lemon's "fopling-laugh," or suddenly calling out to Augustus Egg, as he often did during the suppers of the group, "Augustus!" and then, when Egg looked up, exclaiming half seriously, half playfully, "God bless you, Augustus!" [32] Observing that Mrs. Cowden Clarke took no wine, he said, "Do as I do; have a little champagne put into your glass and fill it up with water; you'll find it a refreshing draught. I tell you this as a useful secret for keeping cool on such festive occasions, and speak to you *as man to man*." [33]

The entire series of performances had been highly successful, the gross receipts coming to £2,551 0s. 8d. In the end, to be sure, the Government had granted Knowles a pension, so that it proved unnecessary to establish him in the curatorship of the Shakespeare House, and the profits of the theatricals were placed directly in his hands.[34] The enterprise had been no less noteworthy as a source of enjoyment to the performers. "What enthusiastic hurrahs at the rise of the curtain, and as each character in succession made his appearance on the stage!" Mrs. Cowden Clarke summarized, "What times those were! What rapturous audiences a-tiptoe with expectation . . ." [35]

* * * * *

Proportional to the exaltation of those glittering nights, however, for Dickens, was the depression that followed. The ghost had returned. How insupportable was Devonshire Terrace "after that canvas farm wherein I was so happy." What was a humdrum dinner at five-thirty "compared with *that* soup, and the hundreds of pairs of eyes that watched its disappearance?" Why did he have seven children, "not engaged at sixpence a-night apiece, and dismissable for ever, if they tumble down, not taken on for an indefinite time at a vast expense, and never,—no never, never,—wearing lighted candles round their heads" like the fairies in *The Merry Wives*? [36]

As usual, he burlesqued his feelings. Of course he loved his children, but what father of seven would not feel sometimes weighed down by these responsibilities "taken on for an indefinite time at a vast expense?" "I have no energy whatever, I am very miserable. I loathe domestic hearths. I yearn to be a vagabond. Why can't I marry

Mary!" [37] Mary was the farmer's daughter in *Used Up*, with whom Sir Charles Coldstream is in love, a fetching little charmer in pink muslin and a ribboned apron: but the name may also have held some nostalgic echo of the Mary of a vanished happy past "in those chambers three storeys high." [38]

Other family troubles deepened the unhappiness of his mood. His sister Fanny had long been in delicate health, and in November, 1846, had broken down during an attempt to sing at a party in Manchester. Medical examination revealed her to be suffering from tuberculosis. The doctor advised that the truth be kept from her and her husband, Henry Burnett; and Dickens, deeply grieved, insisted on her being brought to London to be looked over by Dr. Elliotson. For a time there seemed room for hope, but in the course of the following year her illness grew worse. By May of 1848 she coughed incessantly and could obtain rest only by the use of morphine.[39] She was brought to London again, to be examined by Sir James Clark, an authority on pulmonary diseases. From him Dickens learned that she could not possibly live many more weeks. In the purer air of Hornsey, a suburban village north of London, quarters were found for the dying woman and her husband.[40]

One day in early July she felt better and her coughing almost ceased. Only two nights before, she had been planning for "after Christmas," but now, in the midst of this seeming improvement she suddenly realized that her state was hopeless. Dickens was with her throughout a painful hour of despair and struggle; then she resigned herself, and voiced some wishes about her funeral and burial. Dickens asked if she had any other care or anxiety in the world. "She said No, none. It was hard to die at such a time of life, but she had no alarm. . . . Burnett had always been very good to her; they had never quarrelled; she was sorry to think of his going back to such a lonely home . . ." The sad words must have twisted in Dickens's heart as he recalled the disharmonies of his own home. She was distressed, Fanny went on, about the children she would leave motherless, especially the little crippled child whose fragile health had suggested Paul Dombey to her brother's imagination; and she "spoke about an invention she had heard of that she would like to have tried, for the deformed child's back . . ." Coming out of her sickroom into the bright summer day, Dickens was wrung with grief and pity.[41]

Throughout the latter part of July, he visited his sister daily.[42] Then, as she still lingered on, he allowed Kate, who was pregnant once again, to persuade him to join her and the children at Broadstairs, where she might "grumble 'unbeknown' to all, but our hoarse old monster-friend, the sea here." [43] At Broadstairs he continued to feel "used up" and forlorn.[44] Any day might bring the fatal summons to Fanny's deathbed. Walking moodily on the shore, he tried to plan his Christmas book,[45] or, giving that up, stretched out on the sands reading Bulwer Lytton's *Harold*.[46]

On the 9th of August, he took the boys up to school at the end of their vacation.[47] Returning to Margate and walking along the road where he was expecting Kate to meet him in their pony chaise, he was startled to see an excited crowd, Kate in its midst, and John, the groom, swathed in bandages. At the top of a steep hill the pony had bolted. John, in a panic, had leaped out, leaving Kate alone to take care of herself. "He says he was thrown out, but it cannot be." [48] The reins tangled in the wheels, the pony galloped madly downhill, Kate "astounding the whole Isle of Thanet with her screams. However, she kept her seat, and the pony, plunging over a steep bank, broke the shafts and tumbled down," [49] "a mere bundle of legs, with a head tucked up somewhere inside." [50] The chaise remained standing on the bank with Kate frightened but unhurt. John, all cuts and bruises, was put to bed "plastered all over like Mr. Squeers, 'a brown-paper parcel chock-full of nothing but groans.' " [51] Unsympathetic in their indignation, the women servants exclaimed, "How could he go and leave a unprotected female in the shay!" [52]

With the close of the month Dickens received word that Fanny's death was only a matter of days. He hurried back to town and out to Hornsey. He found her in one of the paroxysms now constantly recurrent. "No words," he wrote Kate, "can express the terrible aspect of suffering and suffocation—the appalling noise in her throat—and the agonizing look around," followed repeatedly by a lethargy of exhaustion. "Sleep seems quite gone, until the time arrives for waking no more." [53] On the 2nd of September Fanny was dead,[54] and on the 8th her body was lowered into a grave at Highgate Cemetery.[55]

During these agonizing last days, Fred's engagement to Anna Weller continued to be a source of disturbance. "I must do my duty," Dickens wrote his brother, "by protesting against this connexion as fatal and hopeless. . . . I do in my soul believe that the step you are about to take, is as disastrous and ill-advised a one as ever was taken in the like direction by mortal man." What made it even worse, Dickens now learned that Fred was in debt and looked to him for financial aid. "I never supposed it possible that you would contemplate marriage, on your income, with such fetters on your limbs." Dickens had intended to set them up in housekeeping by furnishing their home for them. But with all the claims of his children heavy upon him, he did not feel that he could fling money "into the unfathomable sea of such a marriage with debt upon its breast." [56]

Fred responded angrily. "I shall never justify the mean opinion you have of me," Dickens replied, "when you suppose it possible that such a thing as your letter of Friday, can move me in the least." [57] Nevertheless, in a way that Dickens thought "unworthy of an independent spirit," Fred pressed for the sum of £80 to clear his immediate embarrassments. "If I were asked to pay it to do you some good, or procure you some advance in life," Dickens commented, "that would be another thing." Before making up his mind, he demanded a complete accounting of Fred's debts, to whom they were owed and for what, including a statement of what would still remain unpaid, "and how you would propose to clear that off, and exactly what effect these arrangements would have on your intentions as to marriage." In his "present absence of enlightenment on these heads," he refused to "make the least approach to a promise" that he would advance the money.[58] In the end Dickens probably gave him some assistance, for not long afterward we find Fred confidently asking for further aid.

Dickens had by this time gone back to Devonshire Terrace for the winter.[59] While still at Broadstairs, however, he had been grieved by the serious illness of Roche, "the Brave courier" of his Italian and Swiss sojourns. The stout, bustling, cheerful creature was discovered to have heart disease. "Roche was very ill last night," Dickens had written Forster, "and looks like one with his face turned to the other world, this morning." [60] During the fall his condition grew worse. He should have hospital care, Dickens thought, not be left alone in his poor lodgings. Dickens promptly sought the aid of Miss Coutts.

"Brompton Hospital," he wrote her, ". . . is under an old obligation to me, and they are very ready and willing to take him in; but the bed he is to occupy (if he should live to go there) is not likely to be vacant for the next two or three months." Could she not, therefore, use her influence to have Roche admitted to St. George's Hospital at once? "I have the deepest interest in the matter. He is a most faithful, affectionate, and devoted man. He is dreadfully changed from a fine handsome fellow, in a very short time." [61]

Roche was accordingly admitted to St. George's, and for a time the change and care did him good. "My dear Roche," Dickens wrote him in French, "I am charmed to receive such good news of you, and I hope . . . that you will soon regain your strength, to journey, for the winter, to a milder climate than that of England. Before two years have gone by, we must (the Brave and I) take a trip to Spain." The whole family asked about him continually. "While awaiting that trip to Spain I spoke of, you will have to become excessively robust and ruddy. Courage then, my friend!" [62] But the trip to Spain never took place. Before the end of the following year Roche was dead.

* * * * *

During almost the whole of 1848 Dickens undertook no new work of fiction. It is a far cry from the days when he had exuberantly begun another long novel while its predecessor was still in full career. Between spring and fall his entire literary output amounted to no more than nine short articles—totaling some fourteen thousand words—all appearing in the *Examiner*. Small enough as the six months' work of any man of letters, for one as copiously productive as Dickens had been in the great period from 1836 to 1844, it represents for the four years that follow a striking shrinkage interrupted only by the great effort of *Dombey and Son*.

Several of these articles, however, strongly underline Dickens's views on social problems. "Ignorance and Crime" uses the Metropolitan Police statistics of 1847 to point out the connection between illiteracy and crime. Out of 61,000 offenders of all kinds, 22,000 were totally illiterate and only a few hundred had more "than the mere ability to blunder over a book like a little child." Society must pull up by the roots, Dickens insists, the comfortable belief "that a parrot acquaintance with the Church Catechism and the Commandments is enough shoe-leather for poor pilgrims by the Slough of Despond, sufficient armour against the Giants Slay-Good and Despair, and a sort of Parliamentary train for third-class passengers to the beautiful

Gate of the City." "Side by side with Crime, Disease, and Misery in England, Ignorance is always brooding, and is always certain to be found." Schools of Industry, where useful knowledge is reinforced by "the sublime lessons of the New Testament . . . deep as the lowest depth of Society, and leaving none of its dregs untouched, are the only means of removing the scandal and the danger that beset us in this nineteenth century of our Lord." [63]

In a review of Cruikshank's *The Drunkard's Children*, a sequel to *The Bottle*, Dickens protests against the notion that alcoholism is caused by an injudicious nip of gin after dinner starting once decent families on a downhill rush to destruction. He does not deny that personal faults and crimes are involved. But drunkenness "as a national horror" grows from social causes not remedied by "the government that forms the people, with all *its* faults and vices." "Foul smells, disgusting habitations, bad workshops and workshop customs, want of light, air, and water, the absence of all easy means of decency and health" are the main physical causes, and consequent upon these, "mental weariness . . . the want of wholesome relaxation, the craving for *some* stimulus and excitement," finally, ignorance and the lack of rational training. [64]

These were the things that should come first, not African civilization, foreign missions, introducing improved agriculture in Fernando Po, and abolishing the slave trade, laudable as those other goals undoubtedly were. Let England begin, Dickens says in an article on "The Niger Expedition," with her own savages at home, before turning her eyes abroad. "To your tents, O Israel! but see that they are your own tents! Set *them* in order; leave nothing to be done *there*; and outpost will convey your lesson to outpost, until the naked armies of King Obi and King Boy are reached and taught." [65]

Dickens never falls into the insular complacency of lauding English ways and occidental civilization generally as free from those shortcomings and superstitions that afflict other more benighted parts of the world. Often he seizes upon a foreign delusion to point out its analogues at home. Visiting a Chinese junk, for example, moored in the West India Docks, he describes the mimic eye in the vessel's prow by which she was supposed to find her way, the red rags fastened on mast, rudder, and cables to ensure her safety at sea, and the eighteen-armed idol Chin-Tee, with joss-sticks and incense burning before its niche. "It is pleasant, coming back from China by the Blackwall railway," Dickens then adds ironically, "to think that WE trust no red rags in storms, and burn no joss-sticks before idols; that WE never grope our way by the aid of conventional eyes which have no sight in them . . . The ignorant crew of the *Keying* refused to enter on the ship's books, until 'a considerable amount of silvered paper, tinfoil, and joss-sticks' had been laid in . . . ; but OUR seamen—far less our bishops, priests, and deacons—never stand out upon points of silvered paper and tinfoil, or the lighting up of joss-sticks upon altars!" [66]

The attitudes defined by these articles come to weigh more and more heavily in determining the very choice of dominant themes in almost all Dickens's later books. Even in *David Copperfield*, where their influence is least striking, the cruel, gloomy religion of the Murdstones, the depressing toil in the warehouse, the sardonic passages on aristocracy and blood, and the involved precedents and predatory formulas of the Courts of Doctors' Commons all emphasize society's callousness to human welfare and its worship of blind eyes and brutal idols. From then on, Dickens's attacks are constant and relentless. In *Bleak House* they unify the portrayal of the Courts of Chancery, the slum tenements of Tom-all-Alone's, Mrs. Jellyby's neglect of her home for the natives of Borioboola-Gha, and the Parliamentary satire on Coodle and Doodle. They make of *Hard Times* one concentrated onslaught. In *Little Dorrit* they run through the elaborate parallels between the Marshalsea, Mrs. Clennam's grim imprisoning theology, Bleeding Heart Yard, and the life of the upper classes, with their reverence for that greasy golden calf, the great financier-swindler Merdle. They dominate the rendition of the Veneerings and Podsnaps who represent the voice of society in *Our Mutual Friend*, and whose only values in the gray world of nineteenth-century London are the dustheaps that symbolize their material ambitions. Throughout these novels Dickens develops consistently the social criticism—already implicit, to be sure, in *A Christmas Carol* and *Dombey and Son*—to which his *Examiner* articles bear witness.

Social criticism, however, dwindles to a minor strand in *The Haunted Man*, the major theme of which had its roots in Dickens's relation to his own past. Its portrayal of unhappy memories haunting the present may, indeed, have been partly responsible for the fact that he had found himself unable to deal with it the preceding autumn and had been putting it off for an entire year. But now he could delay no longer if it was to be ready for Christmas, and he set himself to write despite those difficulties and groans of tribulation that had come to afflict his efforts at composition.

The first stage, he wrote Mrs. Watson, on October 5th, was "sitting frowning horribly at a quire of paper," and falling into a state of irascibility "which utterly confounds and scares the House. The young family peep at me through the bannisters as I go along the hall; and Kate and Georgina quail (almost) as I stalk by them." [67] Once again he must "hermetically seal" himself up in his room all morning, "and wander about the streets full of faces at night." [68] "Grinding" away at it, even though he was now in London and could not blame Genoa's lack of crowded streets to plunge in, or the sluggish waters of Lake Leman, or the street musicians of Broadstairs, he nevertheless found the story obstinately intractable. "The Haunted Man won't do something I want him to do," [69] he complained to Miss Coutts. Perhaps a little fresh air would help. "I think of taking him down to Brighton next week for ten days or so, and putting an end to him." [70] Then, just two days before departure, the snarls untangled and the rest of the story was written without too much trouble at the Bedford Hotel. "I finished last night," he reported on December 1st, "having been crying my eyes out over it . . . these last three days." [71]

The Haunted Man was published, with illustrations by Tenniel, Leech, Clarkson Stanfield, and Frank Stone, on December 19th, and sold eighteen thousand copies before evening of that day.[72] Toward the end of the year a dramatic version by Mark Lemon was produced with considerable success at the Adelphi Theatre. Dickens gave some aid in the writing and rehearsal of the play, though his feelings about the dramatization of a novelist's works remained unaltered.[73] "But in the accursed state of the law on this subject," he explained to his father-in-law George Hogarth, "I have no power to prevent it; and therefore I think it best to have at least one Theatre where it is done in a less Beastly manner than at others, and where I can impress *something* (however little) on the actors." [74]

Even in its narrative form, however, *The Haunted Man* is a weak performance. Its pallidness is slightly, but not much, relieved by the slapdash caricature of Little Moloch, the Tetterbys' baby, a fractious blight on the existence of its young brother, who staggers around all day under its weight, never catching more than "meek glimpses of things in general from behind its skirts, or over its limp flapping bonnet." [75] The Tetterbys are a cruder variation on the Cratchit family, and Milly Swidger, the redeeming angel of the story, a mature but still more syrupy version of Dot Peerybingle. Redlaw, the distinguished chemist, is a dimmer Scrooge, without the latter's vivid and almost hilarious misanthropy, the brooding victim of a gray melancholy pervading the present from an unhappy past.

Yet, feeble though the tale is, it is significant because it reflects the inward preoccupations with which Dickens was struggling. Like Redlaw, he himself is a famous and outwardly successful man. In the imaginative laboratory of his art, as in Redlaw's test tubes and retorts, there are hosts of spectral shapes like those glass vessels with their chemicals, all subject to his power to uncombine and recombine.[76] But like Redlaw he has known wrongs and sufferings from under the burden of which he cannot escape, until he asks himself whether the years bring anything but "More figures in the lengthening sum of recollection that we work and work at to our torment . . ." [77] Does he indulge his griefs, ever evoking these phantoms of past and present despondency? It matters not; bidden or unbidden, they come.[78]

In the first scene with the Spectre, all of Redlaw's feelings about his life are, with slight modifications, what Dickens still felt about his own. "I am he, neglected in my youth, and miserably poor, who strove and suffered, and still strove and suffered, until I hewed out knowledge from the mine where it was buried . . ." "No mother's self-denying love, no father's counsel aided *me*." [79] It was unjust to Dickens's mother, but so he had always felt since the days in the blacking warehouse. "My parents," Redlaw says, "at the best, were of that sort whose care soon ends, and whose duty is soon done; who cast their offspring loose, early, as birds do theirs; and, if they do well, claim the credit; and, if ill, the pity." [80]

Like Dickens too, Redlaw, although not so recently, has lost a beloved sister, who lived long enough to see him become famous. He had also had a sweetheart to whom he had given his earliest and deepest devotion. "I was too poor to bind its object to my fortune then, by any thread of promise or entreaty. . . . But, more than ever I had striven in my life, I strove to climb!" [81] The parallels, of course, are not made exact or complete; Redlaw's beloved, unlike Maria Beadnell,

is won by the man whom he has regarded as his best friend, and Redlaw remains unmarried in his empty bachelor chambers.

His experiences have not made him hard-hearted or uncharitable.
He sympathizes with the sufferings of others, and hastens to relieve
misfortunes the instant they become known to him.[82] But would not
both he and they be happier and better if they could lose their unfortunate weight of memories darkening every hour? [83] Thus reflects
Redlaw, taciturn, "shadowed by habitual reserve," a haunted figure,
though still well-knit, with "his sunken brilliant eye" and "his grizzled
hair." [84] Thus, too, Dickens, so deeply reserved about his inmost feelings despite the social buoyancy and frankness of manner that seemed
to reveal his every thought, and despite the demonic vitality that could
fling itself with such gusto into every enjoyment. Even in physique
he was no longer the almost girlishly beautiful figure he had been, but
a mature man, coming to think of himself as middle-aged, with lines
beneath the eyes, a glance that could be hard and unyielding, and
hair beginning to recede above the brow.

The Ghost grants Redlaw's desire to lose his memory of wrong and
sorrow, and with it bestows the power to pass on the gift to all those
whom he approaches. Then Redlaw discovers, to his horror, that with
the memory of unhappiness depart all tenderer memories as well, together with the softening influence on the heart that grief may bring.
All those he touches grow callous, surly, bitter, and brutal. The struggling news dealer Tetterby and his devoted wife regret their marriage;
he notices with distaste that she is fat and aging, she that he is com-
mon-looking, small, beginning to stoop, and getting bald.[85] Redlaw's
servant resents his aged father, and the old man grows selfish and
querulous.[86]

In anguish, Redlaw prays to have the gift reversed. "In the material
world," he cries, "as I have long taught . . . no step or atom in the
wondrous structure could be lost, without a blank being made in the
great universe. I know, now, that it is the same with good and evil,
happiness and sorrow, in the memories of men." [87] Only Milly, his
servant's wife, resists the spell, because sorrow has but made her the
more zealous to serve others and love them; and she is the instrument
by which his fatal gift is destroyed. In deeper understanding, Redlaw
realizes that not oblivion, and not a corrosive brooding, but the puri-
fying and strengthening influences of memory are the sources of self-

conquest and peace of mind. Instead of praying for forgetfulness, one should more wisely pray, "Lord, keep my memory green." [88]

Dickens knew this in his mind, but was unable to make himself feel it is in his heart. Doubtless that is why the story seems so sentimental, mawkish, and overmoralistic, and the characters insufficiently realized for the emotion they are intended to convey. Its artistic deficiencies, however, only underline the sharpness of the inner tensions Dickens was striving to subdue. There is a personal and persistent discord that has not been resolved by this endeavor to exorcise it into acceptance. Neither the intellectual comprehension of a psychological problem nor the attempt to impose its solution by an act of will can produce a successful work of art. It must be felt in the very deepest fibers of its creator's being.

But Dickens, although he tried to believe otherwise and tried to feel otherwise, was full of self-justification in his present frustrations and steeped in self-pity for his past sufferings. In his domestic frictions he might admit in the abstract that he had faults, but he did not really think himself in any signficant way to blame, and his only resource was to dash off on a trip or a further bout of theatricals or some other distraction. In his fragment of childhood autobiography, begun not long before or after *The Haunted Man* was conceived,[89] he had said, "I do not write resentfully or angrily: for I know how all these things have worked together to make me what I am." [90] It was true that he knew that, but it was not true that his bitterness was gone. His parents, he wrote in that very fragment, "could hardly have been" more satisfied if, instead of being a "poor little labouring hind" in the blacking warehouse, he "had been twenty years of age, distinguished at a grammar-school, and going to Cambridge." [91] And as for his mother, "I never afterwards forgot, I never shall forget, I never can forget, that my mother was warm for my being sent back." [92] Those are not the accents of absolution.

It might perhaps be only through a complete ventilation of his entire past and its conflicts, only by committing it to paper and as it were casting it out of himself, that he could lay its unhappy ghost. Some such feeling probably suggested the idea of writing his autobiography, but after struggling with it for a time Dickens found it too painful and gave it up. The part dealing with his childhood, through the blacking-warehouse days and up to the time he was a scholar at Wellington

House Academy, he did give Forster to read. But as he came to the humiliations of his heartbroken love for Maria Beadnell he found he could not bear to allow anyone else to read, could not bear even to go on. He gave them to the fire. Only in the disguised form of *David Copperfield*, with many changes and omissions which are as significant as what he tells, could he make confessional to the world.

CHAPTER FIVE

"Myself into the Shadowy World"

D URING all the later part of 1848 Dickens's thoughts were turning more and more often to the form his next book should take. Forster suggested that it be written in the first person, and Dickens at once seized eagerly on this idea. The decision to fuse some of his own youthful experiences with those of his hero, and to make the story of David Copperfield at least in part his own story, would enable him at the same time to reveal and conceal the dark unhealed wounds that he could not expose without disguise, to analyze, to assess, and to assuage. Surely if in his own heart he confronted it all, the burden would fall from him and leave him free. Shortly after the New Year, still revolving the problem in his mind, he took it with him to Norwich and Yarmouth on a brief holiday jaunt before settling down to work.

Preceding his departure there had been two festivities at Devonshire Terrace, a dinner on January 3rd to celebrate the "christening" of The Haunted Man and a Twelfth-Night birthday party for Charley and the children, with a magic lantern and conjuring,[1] to which "some children of larger growth" were invited. [2] For this occasion little Mamey and her sister Katey had taught Dickens the polka that he might dance it with them. In the middle of the previous night he suddenly found himself afraid he had forgotten the step, and, leaping out of bed in the wintry dark, began practicing on the cold floor. On the evening itself, only Captain Marryat and possibly Mrs. Macready equaled Dickens in vigor and vivacity [3] To Macready, who was once again touring in America, Dickens described how they drank his health, "then dashed into a Sir Roger de Coverley—then into a reel—" and how, "for two mortal hours," he himself and Mrs. Macready "danced without ceasing—breathing Willie, prostrating Nina, reducing to 'tarnal smash' (as we say in our country) all the other couples one by one. With shame and grief I own that at last I—I—gave in, when she was fresh and active still." [4]

The following day he started off for Norwich, with Leech and Lemon for companions. After visiting the Cathedral they rode out to Stanfield Hall, recently the scene of a frightful murder,[5] a grim place with "a murderous look that seemed to invite such a crime." [6] Norwich was disappointingly dull, "all save its place of execution, which we found fit for a gigantic scoundrel's exit." [7] Dickens bought a bright Norwich scarf as a gift for Kate, and then with his two friends went on to Yarmouth, whence they took a twenty-three-mile walk down the coast to Lowestoft and back.[8] "Yarmouth, Sir," he wrote Forster, was the success of the trip, "the strangest place in the wide world: one hundred and forty-six miles of hill-less country between it and London. . . . I shall certainly try my hand at it." [9] That spongy and soppy place, with its great dull waste of pebbled beach, was in fact to become the home of the Peggottys and Mrs. Gummidge and Little Em'ly.

Back in London, Dickens still did not begin his book. Kate was near her time for their eighth child, and she had had a hard time at the birth of Sydney twenty-one months ago. Dickens consequently would not risk going to Manchester to present a testimonial silver tea and coffee service to his old schoolmaster, William Giles, although he was a member of the committee of former pupils who were making the gift.[10] He had learned all the facts about the use of chloroform during a childbirth, and had promised Kate, who was also apprehensive, that she should have it.[11]

The baby was born on January 15th. As they had feared, the birth was not a normal one, and Dickens kept his word. "The doctors were dead against it, but I stood my ground, and (thank God) triumphantly. It spared her all pain (she had no sensation, but of a great display of sky-rockets) and saved the child all mutilation. It enabled the doctors to do, as they afterwards very readily said, in ten minutes, what might otherwise have taken them an hour and a half; the shock to her nervous system was reduced to nothing; and she was, to all intents and purposes, *well* the next day." Administered by someone expert in its use, Dickens was convinced, despite the conservatism of the medical profession, that chloroform was as safe as it was miraculous and merciful. A fortnight later Kate was "eating mutton-chops in the drawing room," and the baby—a boy, who was to be christened Henry Fielding Dickens—was so thriving as to look, Dickens said, like "what the Persian Princes might have called a 'moon-faced' monster." [12]

Meanwhile little Harry Burnett, his sister Fanny's crippled son, had just died, and the father wrote to ask Dickens if the child might be buried in his mother's grave at Highgate. "If you wish him to be beside his dear Mother," Dickens replied, "why, let it be so, I can only say do what will console you most, and what you think she would have liked. You have a brave fine boy to rear up still, and God send that he may be a source of happiness to you." [13]

Dickens's father had also been exceedingly unwell. Going out to Lewisham, where his parents now lived, Dickens found his father in bed looking weak and low, and worrying conscientiously about "that eternal *Daily News*." (John Dickens was still discharging his old duties on the paper his son had founded.) "I quieted his mind by saying that I should write to Dilke, and tell that potentate how he was going on." [14]

Three articles Dickens contributed to the *Examiner* around this time show how little the treatment of pauper children had changed since the time of *Oliver Twist*. Cholera had broken out at a baby farm in Tooting where one Drouet boarded fourteen hundred children. Soon the parish churchyard was too small for the piles of infant coffins. Bitterly calling his first article "The Paradise at Tooting," [15] Dickens pointed out that these small cholera patients had been left without medical care, four in a bed, in foul, damp rooms.[16] The potatoes at their table were black and diseased,[17] and their whole diet so inadequate that they had climbed secretly over palings to pick out scraps from the tubs of hogwash.[18] Their bodies were emaciated and covered with boils and sores.[19] The guardians of the poor for the Holborn Union had paid only the most cursory attention to adverse criticism; one of them recommended that boys who complained should be horsewhipped. In short, the establishment "was brutally conducted, vilely kept, preposterously inspected, dishonestly defended, a disgrace to a Christian community, and a stain upon a civilized land." [20]

There followed, as Dickens noted, the usual defensive flourishing of foolscap and red tape, the "official gabble . . . about responsibility, and non-responsibility, and divided responsibility, and powers, and sections, and chapters," [21] calculated to crush the remedy "in a mill of words." Public indignation nevertheless led to Drouet's being indicted for manslaughter. But the judge before whom the case was tried directed an acquittal.[22] There was no evidence, he said, that the victims had been strong enough, even before they were placed in Drouet's care, to have recovered from the epidemic. "Drouet was 'affected to tears' as he left the dock." [23] Despite this fantastic verdict, however, the publicity, as Dickens hoped, aided in the breaking up of the child-farming system.

By the middle of February, Dickens had taken Kate down to Brighton, where she could enjoy the sea air and he could be thinking out the plan of his novel and casting about in his mind for a title. Here they were joined in their lodgings by Leech and his wife. Hardly were the two families settled in than both their landlord and his daughter went violently insane.[24] "If you could have heard the cursing and crying of the two; could have seen the physician and nurse quoited out into the passage by the madman . . . ; could have seen Leech and me flying to the doctor's rescue; could have seen our wives pulling us back; could have seen the M. D. faint with fear; could have seen three other M. D.'s come to his aid; with an atmosphere of Mrs. Gamps, straitwaistcoats, struggling friends and servants . . . you would have said it was quite worthy of me, and quite in keeping with my usual proceedings." [25]

At the Bedford Hotel, to which the lodgers moved, Dickens returned to his former cogitations. "A sea-fog to-day," he wrote Forster, "but yesterday inexpressibly delicious. My mind running, like a high sea, on names—not satisfied yet, though." [26] As always, he could not get started until the novel was named. At first he thought of *Mag's Diversions*, with various subtitles in which the hero began as "Mr. Thomas Mag," [27] then became "David Mag of Copperfield House," and finally "David Copperfield." [28] The title still went through a number of experimental changes, including *The Copperfield Disclosures*, *The Copperfield Records*, *The Copperfield Survey of the World as It Rolled*, and *Copperfield Complete*, before it settled down to the ultimate choice, of which the full form was *The Personal History, Experi-*

*ence, and Observations of David Copperfield the Younger, of Blun-
derstone Rookery, which he never meant to be published on any
account.*[29] Once the hero's name had become David Copperfield,
however, that never altered. Dickens was much startled when Forster
pointed out to him that the initials were his own reversed, and exclaimed that it was "just in keeping with the fates and chances that
were always befalling him. 'Why else,' he said 'should, I so obstinately
have kept to that name when once it turned up?' "[30]

In London again before the end of February, Dickens wrote the
first two chapers. The opening number was to appear in May, but as
late as the 19th of April he was finding it hard to keep the story
going.[31] "My hand is out," he said, "in the matter of Copperfield.
Today and yesterday I have done nothing. Though I know what I
want to do, I am lumbering on like a stage-waggon. I can't even dine
at the Temple today, I feel it so important to stick at it this evening,
and make some head. I am quite aground . . . and the long Copper-
fieldian perspective looks snowy and thick, this fine morning."[32]
Nevertheless, before the deadline Dickens managed to complete the
difficulty Yarmouth chapter, with its dewy lyricism and exquisite
touches of humor, and its chill transition back to Mr. Murdstone pet-
rifying all the tenderness of the Rookery parlor.[33]

The number was an instantaneous and unmistakable success.
Thackeray, whose own semi-autobiographic *Pendennis* had already got
under way in yellow-covered installments, was warmly generous in his
praise. "Get David Copperfield," he wrote his friend Brookfield; "by
Jingo it's beautiful—it beats the yellow chap of this month hollow—"[34] And to Mrs. Brookfield: "Have you read Dickens?—O it is
charming. Bravo Dickens. It has some of his very prettiest touches—
those inimitable Dickens touches w^h make such a great man of him."
Then, with a touch of that rivalry which always lurked at the back
of Thackeray's mind, he adds: "And the reading of the book has done
another author a great deal of good. In the first place it pleases the
other Author to see that Dickens who has long left off alluding to his
the O A's works has been copying the O A, and greatly simplifying
his style and foregoing the use of fine words. By this the public will
be the gainer and David Copperfield will be improved by taking a lesson from Vanity Fair."[35]

Thackeray came to a dinner at Devonshire Terrace on May 12th,

shortly after this initial triumph, among a group of guests which included Phiz, Jerrold, Mr. and Mrs. Tagart, and the Carlyles.[36] Jane
Carlyle, in a letter, was acid about the magnificence of the table, over-
loaded with "pyramids of figs raisins oranges" and candles rising out of
"quantities of *artificial* flowers"; at Lady Ashburton's dinner parties
"there were just *four cowslips* in china pots—four silver shells containing sweets, and a silver filigree temple in the middle!" She also noted
the presence of "old Rogers, who ought to have been buried long ago,
so old and ill-natured he is grown," and Mrs. Gaskell, whose recently
published *Mary Barton* Dickens greatly admired, "a natural unassum-
ing woman," Jane wrote, "whom they have been doing their best to
spoil by making a lioness of her." [37] Carlyle was feeling in a more
genial mood, and laughingly replied to an inquiry about his health
in the words of Mrs. Gummidge, "I am a lone lorn creetur' and every-
think goes contrairy with me." [38]

Other guests of this year included Lord Jeffrey and his family, Sheriff Gordon, Lord Robertson, and more of Dickens's Edinburgh
friends; artists such as Eastlake, Frith, and Charles and Edwin Landseer; the actors Webster, Harley, and Mr. and Mrs. Keeley; old intimates like Mitton, T. J. Thompson, and his trusted medical adviser
Frank Beard; and numbers of friends made during the American
visit, among them Prescott, Hillard, and Bancroft, now the American
Minister to the Court of St. James's.[39] One June evening Dickens was
a guest of Professor Owen at Richmond, where he heard the great scientist describe a huge telescope built by a clergyman who was an enthusiastic amateur astronomer. With it he hoped to see farther into
heaven—Owen was going to say "than Lord Rosse," when Dickens
interrupted dryly, "than his professional studies had enabled him to
penetrate." [40]

*   *   *   *   *

David Copperfield now progressed with rapidity and ease.[41] On
May 4th the second chapter of the June number was sent to Browne
(who illustrated it with pictures of the friendly waiter drinking
David's ale for him and of Mr. Mell tootling dismally on his flute); [42]
the very next afternoon the final chapter of the number was dispatched to Bradbury and Evans.[43] Of the third number, "Copperfield
half done," he wrote Forster on June 6th. "I feel, thank God, quite
confident in the story. I have a move in it ready for this month: an-

other for the next; and another for the next." [44] At the beginning of July, Dickens fell on his left side, where he sometimes had an inflamed kidney, and had to be cupped and blistered. The injury delayed his getting off the first chapter of the number, but by the 10th it was completed.[45] This was the section in which he used his blacking-warehouse experiences. "I really think I have done it ingeniously," he told Forster, "and with a very complicated interweaving of truth and fiction. Vous verrez. I am going on like a house afire in point of health, and ditto ditto in point of number." [46]

He was now at the Albion Hotel at Broadstairs, which he thought beat "all watering places into what the Americans call 'sky-blue fits.'" [47] He had intended to take his family to Folkestone from August to October, but changed his mind on hearing that there was neither satisfactory house-room nor bathing there.[48] With Leech, who planned to spend the summer near them, he accordingly ran down to the Isle of Wight, where he rented Winterbourne, "a delightful and beautiful house" at Bonchurch belonging to James White, a literary clergyman friend, and Leech took a neighboring cottage.[49] There was, Dickens added in a note to Kate, "a waterfall on the grounds, which I have arranged with a carpenter to convert into a perpetual shower-bath." [50] To Beard he wrote that the fall was one hundred and fifty feet, and to Bradbury that it was five hundred.[51]

Coming off the ferry from Portsmouth at Ryde, the Dickens family ran into Thackeray, who was just leaving. "I met on the pier as I was running for the dear life," he wrote, "the great Dickens with his wife his children his Miss Hogarth all looking abominably coarse vulgar and happy and bound to Bonchurch where they have taken one of White's houses for the summer—" [52]

At first Dickens found everything enchanting, although he had some trouble getting into the swing of his work. "From the tops of the highest downs there are views which are only to be equalled on the Genoese shore of the Mediterranean . . . The waterfall acts wonderfully, and the sea-bathing is delicious. Best of all, the place is certainly cold rather than hot, in the summer time." [53] Forming a club called the Sea Serpents, with a banner portraying a curling serpent cut out of yards of bronze-green calico, Dickens organized picnics to Cook's Castle.[54] Here he boiled potatoes, and "Uncle Porpoise," as the children called Mark Lemon, ran races on the downs with an equally

stout London physician, Dr. Lankester.[55] Sometimes the youngsters
played with a flaming-haired little boy named Algernon Charles in
Lady Jane Swinburne's garden while the grownups drank tea.[56] There
were also merry evenings with James White and others, at which they
drank gin punch, enjoyed games, or watched Dickens give wonderful
exhibitions of conjuring as "the unparalleled necromancer Rhia
Rhama Rhoos." [57] A constant succession of guests further enlivened
the summer: Dickens's friend Talfourd, recently elevated to the
bench, Frank Stone and Egg, Jerrold, Browne, Letitia and her husband Henry Austin.[58]

A friend who did not come to Bonchurch was also much in Dickens's mind at this time. Giuseppe Mazzini, the Italian revolutionist,
had dined at Devonshire Terrace and, one Sunday evening, taken
Dickens to see the school he had established at Clerkenwell for Italian organ-boys. Dickens had eagerly welcomed the proclamation of
the Roman Republic. He followed the siege of the city by Oudinet's
army, his mind divided between detestation of Louis Napoleon and
the French and "admiration of Mazzini and his friends." [59] With the
fall of Rome he was anxious until he learned that Mazzini had escaped
back to England. The public appeal issued that September for the
Italian political refugees was of Dickens's authorship.

These exiles, he wrote, were "the good citizens who, when Rome
was abandoned by her Monarch . . . arose to give her law, tranquillity
and order . . . They are the brave besieged who held Rome with a
courage and devotion worthy of her ancient glories . . ." Their enforced capitulation "to a foreign army forty thousand strong" was "an
ineffaceable stain upon the honour and name of France." Now that
their noble cause was lost, England was almost the only free land in
which they could be safe. "Haunted by them, and the world's enemies," they came to England "forlorn and penniless"; and England
should be "worthy of its love of freedom, and its high renown" by
coming to their aid.[60]

In the course of August, Dickens's enthusiasm for Bonchurch gave
way to a note of discomfort. Even in his first letter to Forster he made
one reservation: "I have been, and am, trying to work this morning,
but I can't make anything of it, and am going out to think." [61]
Around a fortnight later, "I have made it a rule," he reported, "that
the Inimitable is invisible, until two every day. I shall have half the

number done, please God, tomorrow. I have not worked quickly here yet, but I don't know what I *may* do." [62] Then came the feeling that his health required a different air. He would have to climb daily to the top of the downs. "It makes a great difference in the climate to get a blow there and come down." But he fell prey to an obstinate cough, was "stethoscoped" and ordered rubbings for his chest.[63] By the end of the month his disturbance boiled over in a long bill of complaints:

"Before I think of beginning my next number, I perhaps cannot do better than give you an imperfect description of the results of the climate of Bonchurch after a few weeks' residence. The first salubrious effect of which the Patient becomes conscious is an almost continual feeling of sickness, accompanied with great prostration of strength, so that his legs tremble under him, and his arms quiver when he wants to take hold of any object. An extraordinary disposition to sleep (except at night, when his rest, in the event of his having any, is broken by incessant dreams) is always present . . . and if he have anything to do requiring thought and attention, this overpowers him to such a degree that he can only do it in snatches: lying down on beds in the fitful intervals. Extreme depression of mind, and a disposition to shed tears from morning to night . . . When he brushes his hair in the morning, he is so weak that he is obliged to sit upon a chair to do it. He is incapable of reading, at all times. And his bilious system is so utterly overthrown, that a ball of boiling fat appears to be always behind the top of the bridge of his nose, simmering between his haggard eyes." His cough was so "constant, deep, and monotonous" that " 'The faithful watch-dog's honest bark' " was nothing in comparison. "It's a mortal mistake!—That's the plain fact. Of all the places I ever have been in, I have never been in one so difficult to exist in, pleasantly. Naples is hot and dirty, New York feverish, Washington bilious, Genoa exciting, Paris rainy—but Bonchurch, smashing. I am quite convinced that I should die here, in a year. It's not hot, it's not close, I don't know what it is, but the prostration of it is *awful*." [64]

The hyperbole of this outburst did not mean that Dickens was joking. Something in this climate—which had now become too mild—he did find seriously enervating; a visit to him early in September convinced Forster of his discomfort.[65] By the middle of that month he was almost frantic to pull up stakes and get back to the "brisk and bracing" air of Broadstairs.[66] Only a few days before Dickens was to leave, however, Leech was knocked down while in bathing by a bad blow from a great wave, and developed congestion of the brain. "He is in bed, and had twenty of his namesakes on his temples this morning." [67] Dickens and Beard sat up with him all night putting ice to his head.[68] Dickens would not start, he wrote, "while I can be of any service to him and his good little wife." [69] Leech became worse, restless with pain, and unable to get any sleep.

Dickens suggested trying to mesmerize him into a magnetic slumber, and the husband and wife anxiously begged him to try it. By this time Leech was throwing himself ceaselessly about: "He was like a ship in distress in a sea of bedclothes." [70] An hour and a half passed before he could be tranquillized enough to be put to sleep, but then he fell into a quiet rest, and awoke much better. "I talked to the astounded little Mrs. Leech across him, when he was asleep, as if he had been a truss of hay. . . . What do you think of my setting up in the magnetic line, with a large brass plate? 'Terms, twenty-five guineas per nap.' " [71] It did not prove necessary to repeat the magnetism.[72] Nevertheless, Dickens remained at Bonchurch several days longer, stretching out nightly on a little sofa in the Leeches' sitting room, until he was satisfied that his friend was beyond further danger.[73]

At his old watering place he was delighted to receive good reports of Leech's improvement,[74] and immediately felt better himself despite a spell of bad weather. "Such a night and day of rain I should think the oldest inhabitant never saw! and yet, in the old formiliar Broadstairs, I somehow or other don't mind much. The change has done Mamey a world of good, and I have begun to sleep again." [75] But he still had trouble working, and, "mowed down by a fit of laziness," went to Canterbury for a day's outing, then returned. "I write, as my friend Mr. Micawber says, 'with a sickly mask of mirth,' but I am rather behind time, and have been hammering away all day, until I don't know whether this is my head that is oppressing my shoulders, or a pumpkin stuffed with lead." [76]

His half-yearly accounts, which Evans had brought him in September, showed that the first three numbers of *Copperfield* had not done quite so well as *Dombey*, but Dickens was not discouraged. Back numbers continued to go off, and the current numbers were selling a steady twenty-five thousand. Bradbury and Evans, receiving nothing but the highest opinions of the story, felt very confident about it.[77] Nevertheless, Dickens began to think again of what he called "the dim design" [78] of a weekly periodical as a regular addition to his novel earnings. Now it seemed clear to him that he must set it going in the spring: "I have already been busy, at odd half-hours, in shadowing forth a name and an idea." [79] Meanwhile he plugged away at his sixth and seventh numbers.

* * * * *

Back in London in mid-October,[80] Dickens received annoying news of Thomas Powell, once the friend of his brother Augustus and clerk of Thomas Chapman, Augustus's employer. Out of pity for his wife and family, the firm had forgiven his defalcations.[81] The ingratiating forger had subsequently passed forged checks among a number of Croydon tradesmen and been haled before a magistrate, but escaped prosecution by getting himself certified insane and committed to a lunatic asylum at Hoxton. Released from there, he made his way to New York, where he promptly cashed a letter of credit for £250 forged in the name of a partner in the Chapman firm. Some flaw in the legal proof of his guilt, however, led once more to his release. Presenting himself to the New York newspapers as a literary man who had mingled with the great of London, he published in the *Evening Post* a biographical and critical sketch of Dickens.[82] Among other false statements so numerous as to make it, Dickens exclaimed, "from beginning to end, one intact and complete Lie," [83] the sketch stated that Mr. Dombey was a literal and therefore libelous portrait of Thomas Chapman.

Outraged, Dickens at once sent off a letter to Lewis Gaylord Clark, containing a full account of Powell's career and leaving Clark at liberty to use it as he liked. This account appeared in the New York *Tribune*. Powell retaliated by jailing the publisher of the letter and suing Dickens for libel, claiming $10,000 damages.[84] Dickens thereupon obtained from Chapman's firm a letter testifying to Powell's thefts from them as "too painfully true," and copies of the correspondence dealing with the fraudulent letter of credit he had presented in New York. To this he added the London *Times* account of the proceedings before the Croydon magistrates and a letter from Dr. Southwood Smith, who had certified Powell for the asylum. All these Dickens had printed in a four-page pamphlet, of which he sent copies to New York and to various newspapers.[85]

Powell's case of course collapsed, although in some strange way he still managed to escape punishment and continued to move in New York literary circles. As usual in Dickens's brushes with the law, however, he found himself out of pocket for his legal defense. "When I find that I am obliged to smart to that extent," he wrote Clark, "for saving your fellow citizens from a Swindler, I began to think your law must be as bad as ours—I can't think worse of it." [86]

During November work on *David Copperfield* was interrupted and delayed by Dickens witnessing the execution of Mr. and Mrs. Manning, which he made the occasion of two letters to the *Times* protesting against public hangings. In the first he expressed his horror of "the wickedness and levity of the immense crowd" in Horsemonger Lane—"thieves, low prostitutes, ruffians and vagabonds," "boys and girls"—fighting, whistling, joking brutally, letting out cries and howls, showing no touch of pity or awed emotion when "the two miserable creatures who attracted all this ghastly sight about them were turned quivering into the air." [87] In the second he emphasized his argument that such sights had only a hardening and debasing influence on their spectators, and that from the moment a murderer was convicted he should be kept from curious visitors and reporters serving up his sayings and doings in the Sunday papers, and executed privately within the prison walls.[88] These two letters caused an enormous sensation and engulfed Dickens in "a roaring sea of correspondence." [89] It was not, however, until 1868 that the reform he suggested was effected.

Unhappily, the letters also brought about an estrangement between Dickens and Douglas Jerrold, who bitterly resented Dickens's compromising in the slightest degree on the principle of abolishing capital punishment.[90] For a number of months they did not see each other, but then it fell out that each was dining, with his own separate party, in the Strangers' room of the Garrick Club. "Our chairs were almost back to back," Dickens told Jerrold's son, years later. "I said not a word (I am sorry to remember) and did not look that way." But before long, Jerrold "openly wheeled his chair round, stretched out both his hands . . . and said aloud, with a bright and loving face that I can see as I write to you: 'For God's sake, let us be friends again! Life's not long enough for this!'" [91]

Continuing *David Copperfield,* Dickens brought his hero to the point where he was finishing school and about to enter upon a profession. Rejecting a notion of making him a special pleader, he considered having him enter a banking house,[92] then rejected that too. "Banking business impracticable on account of the confinement: which would stop the story, I foresee. I have taken, for the present at all events, the proctor. I am wonderfully in harness, and nothing galls or frets." [93] The 20th of November saw his month's work completed: "Copperfield done after two days very hard work indeed; and I think a smashing number. His first dissipation I hope will be found worthy of attention, as a piece of grotesque truth." [94]

Finishing this number freed Dickens for a long-planned visit to his Lausanne friends, the Richard Watsons, at their ancestral home of Rockingham Castle in Northamptonshire. Dating from the thirteenth century, the structure surrounded a great court entered by an archway between two bastion towers with curtain walls. Dickens described it to Forster in a high-spirited parody of a recent American travel volume whose author had been much impressed by the magnificent hospitality of large country houses, especially by a guest's clothes always being pressed and put away whenever he took them off and his washbasin being immediately cleaned even though he might use it twenty times a day.[95] "Picture to yourself, my dear F," Dickens wrote gaily, "a large old castle, approached by an ancient keep, portcullis, &c, &c, filled with company, waited on by six-and-twenty servants; the slops (and wine-glasses) continually being emptied; and my clothes (with myself in them) always being carried off to all sorts of places; and you will have a faint idea of the mansion in which I am at present staying." [96]

Dickens tremendously enjoyed this holiday. He flirted playfully with Miss Mary Boyle, a niece of Mrs. Watson's, a tiny, blue-eyed lady two years his senior, she flirted back, and he wrote her a burlesque of Gray's "Elegy" in which he punningly declared himself mortally smitten by her charms.[97] On the last night of his visit there were private theatricals, conjuring by Dickens, and country dances in the great hall lasting until three in the morning. Dickens and Miss Boyle played Sir Peter and Lady Teazle in some scenes from *The School for Scandal* and the scene of the lunatic on the wall making passionate declarations of love to Mrs. Nickleby. "To see all the household," he concluded his American parody, "headed by an enormously fat house-keeper, occupying the back benches last night, laughing and applaud-ing without any restraint; and to see a blushing sleek-headed footman produce, for the watch-trick, a silver watch of the most portentous di-mensions, amidst the rapturous delight of his brethren and sisterhood; was a very pleasant spectacle, even to a conscientious republican like yourself or me, who cannot but contemplate the parent country with feelings of pride in our land which (as was well observed by the Hon-ourable Elias Deeze, of Hartford, Conn.) is truly the land of the free." [98]

He signalized his return to London by writing Mrs. Watson a letter of mock despair. "Plunged in the deepest gloom," his thoughts were being driven "to madness. On the way here I was a terror to my com-panions, and I am at present a blight and mildew on my home." Un-der his elaborate signature he added a postscript: "I am in such an incapable state, that after executing the foregoing usual flourish I swooned, and remained for some time insensible. Ha, ha, ha! Why was I ever restored to consciousness!!!" [99] But the first two or three weeks of every month, as he explained to another correspondent, he was "the Slave of the Lamp called Copperfield," [100] and he was soon driving ahead cheerfully enough.

As he neared the end of his number he received a curious and touch-ing communication. This was from a chiropodist and manicurist named Mrs. Seymour Hill, a tiny dwarf, whom he had seen trotting around on short legs in the neighborhood of Devonshire Terrace, and whose grotesque oddity of physique he had used for Miss Mowcher in his story, never imagining it would meet her eyes.[101] But she had seen it, and been bitterly hurt. "I have suffered long and much," she wrote, "from my personal deformities but never before at the hands of a Man so highly gifted as Charles Dickens . . ." What made the injury worse was that the character was clearly intended to be odious. "Now you have made my nights sleepless and my daily work tear-full." [102]

Dickens was moved to remorse. He was unfeignedly sorry, he replied, to have given her a moment's distress. It was true that he had partly had her in mind, but a great portion of the character was based on someone quite different, and even in appearance Miss Mowcher re-sembled almost as much still another person, unknown to him, whom he had passed in the streets. "Pray consider all these things and do not make yourself unhappy." He was so pained by her distress that to prevent her passing "another of those sleepless nights" he would alter the entire design of the character from his original intention "and oblige the Reader to hold it in a pleasant remembrance." [103] This offer Mrs. Hill accepted, and in the later numbers of the novel Dickens faithfully kept his promise.

At the end of the month he confronted "the first page of Copperfield No. 10, now staring at me," he said, "with what I may literally call a blank aspect," [104] and began mournfully considering little Em'ly's flight with Steerforth. It made him think of all those lost creatures of the streets of whom he knew so many in connection with the aid he gave Miss Coutts in her Home for them at Shepherd's Bush. "In all you suggest with so much feeling," he wrote his friend Cerjat, "about their return to virtue being cut off, I concur with a sore heart. I have been turning it over in my mind for some time, and hope, in the history of Little Em'ly (who *must* fall—there is no hope for her), to put it before the thoughts of people in a new and pathetic way, and perhaps to do some good." [105]

The second half of *Copperfield*, in spite of many additional labors and numerous other activities, went along smoothly and confidently. Only a few days after Dickens had sent proof sheets of the tenth number to Lord Jeffrey he learned of his old friend's death. "Poor dear Jeffrey! I bought a Times at the station yesterday morning, and was so stunned by the announcement, that I felt it in that wounded part of me . . . I had a letter from him in extraordinary good spirits within this week or two—he was better, he said, than he had been for a long time . . . I say nothing of his wonderful abilities and great career, but he was a most affectionate and devoted friend to me . . ." [106]

In February, Dickens was portraying David's infatuation for Dora. "I begin to have my doubts of being able to join you," he wrote Forster, "for Copperfield runs high, and must be done to-morrow. But I'll do it if possible, and strain every nerve. Some beautiful comic love, I hope, in the number." [107] In March, he went away to Brighton for a while "to pursue Copperfield in peace." [108] "Such weather here!" he exclaimed to Henry Austin. "So bright and beautiful! and here I sit, glowering over Copperfield all day—though God forbid I should represent there being any hardship in *that*." [109] Although Dora, he knew, was to die, he had not quite made up his mind when it should happen. "Undecided about Dora," he wrote Forster in May, "but MUST decide to-day." [110]

The approach of summer saw Dickens so pressed with work that he looked forward to a visit to the sea. "I hope to go down to that old image of Eternity that I love so much, and finish . . . to its hoarse murmur. May it be as good a book as I hope it will be, for your children's children to read." [111] Dickens made a short trip to Paris in June, and then in August went to Broadstairs, where he expected to remain "until the end of October, as I don't want to come back to London until I shall have finished Copperfield." [112] Here he was rejoiced to learn that James White, his landlord at Winterbourne, would be joining him. "You will find it the healthiest and freshest of places; and there are Canterbury, and all varieties of what Leigh Hunt calls 'greenery' within a few minutes' railway ride." [113]

At Broadstairs the end of the story was written with rising excitement. "I have been hard at work these three days, and have still Dora to kill. But with good luck, I may do it to-morrow. . . . Am eschewing all sorts of things that present themselves to my fancy—coming in such crowds!" [114] "I have been tremendously at work these two days; eight hours at a stretch yesterday, and six hours and a half today, with the Ham and Steerforth chapter, which has completely knocked me over— utterly defeated me!" [115] "I shall soon be sitting down to my final wrestle with Copperfield. . . . I am looking very hard at a blank quire of paper, and trying to persuade myself that I am going to begin Nos. 19 and 20 in earnest." [116] Finally, on October 21st, there comes word of its conclusion: "I am within three pages of the shore; and am strangely divided, as usual in such cases, between sorrow and joy. Oh, my dear Forster, if I were to say half of what Copperfield makes me feel to-night, how strangely, even to you, I should be turned inside out! I seem to be sending some part of myself into the Shadowy World." [117]

[678] CHARLES DICKENS

CHAPTER SIX

His Favorite Child

CRITICISM: *David Copperfield*

O F all Dickens's novels, *David Copperfield* is the most enchanting. Few novelists have ever captured more poignantly the feeling of childhood, the brightness and magic and terror of the world as seen through the eyes of a child and colored by his dawning emotions. Dickens renders all the vividness and flavor of those early days when the grass is unbelievably green and fruit "riper and richer than fruit has ever been since." [1] He mirrors the tenderness of reposing safely in the assurance of maternal love, the heart-quaking mystery of a sudden harshness or frightening anger in grownups, the disjointed strangeness of a universe discovered to contain such wonders as geese and crocodiles and graveyards and cathedrals. *David* has, too, the savagery and brutality of boyhood, its boyish hero-worship, and its luminous blur of shining aspiration. And, following on these, come the widening though still confused horizons of adolescence and its endeavors to grasp the world, the problems of embarking upon a career, the tremulous silliness and ecstasy of youthful love.

All these things have their roots in Dickens's personal experience, and derive their depths from the intensity of his feeling about his own childhood and days of youth. Above all, they are steeped in his childhood unhappiness and sense of rejection, and in the misery and heartbreak of his love for Maria Beadnell. The elements in his own past that Dickens uses and those he does not tell at all, the way he weaves them in with imagined episodes, and the nature of the invented material, are all deeply revealing. Both the suppressions and the fantasy are profoundly indicative of the wounds that were still unhealed after a quarter of a century. In addition to its delight as a story, *David Copperfield* is thus of cardinal significance to the psychologist and the biographer.

Not every deviation from the literal facts of Dickens's own career, of course, is emotionally meaningful. Some are determined by the necessities of adjustment to other fictional elements in the narrative that are remote from personal implication. Although Dickens's experiences as a shorthand writer in Doctors' Commons certainly suggested starting David toward becoming a proctor there, the fact does not mean that Dickens ever really aspired to membership in that genteel legal fraternity. He needed a comfortable profession for Betsey Trotwood to settle David in, and rejected banking as an alternative because he wanted David to have no fixed hours of work. Banking in turn may have entered Dickens's mind because it was the occupation of Mr. Beadnell, but it does not follow that Dickens ever seriously desired to be a banker or thought of it at all except in the boyish way in which a youngster wishes he might become a man of wealth.

Doctor Strong's school at Canterbury, on the other hand, with its red-brick walls and great stone urns and clerkly rooks pacing the grass of the quiet courtyard, is the embodiment of all that passionate desire for education with which the little laboring hind in the blacking warehouse had so desperately wept as he felt crushed within his breast all his "early hopes of growing up to be a learned and distinguished man." [2] The gentle, erudite old Doctor and the well-ordered teaching, the grave serenity of the building and the "noble games" [3] in its green close—so different from the red-faced and ferocious Creakle and the dirty desolation of Salem House Academy or their prototypes Mr. Jones and the inky schoolroom at Wellington House—were the visions of what Dickens had longed for and never had. Though he had achieved things greater than being "distinguished at a grammar-school, and going to Cambridge," [4] he could not help dreaming of the happier boyhood and better education that had not been. Perhaps, too, since this story of a boy who becomes a reporter and then a famous novelist was bound to be identified by readers with Dickens himself, he was unable to resist the temptation to portray his schooling as fuller and less fragmentary than it was.

Other changes in the facts came from still more aching depths. The most distressing things in that buried past he found it unbearable, even in a fictional confession, to reveal in their literal and painful truth. No reader might know with certainty that these things had indeed happened to Charles Dickens, but it did not matter: he *could not* lay them bare without disguise. To deal with them at all was like constricting a tortured nerve. Only by indirection and circumvention was he able to approach those dreadful and secret places in his heart. And even in doing that much he shrank as one might from tearing off a hideous and half-healed scar.

In this way one may understand the succession of surrogate parents who move through David Copperfield's story, from the youthful mother and the faithful servant Peggotty, to the dark and wrathful stepfather Mr. Murdstone and his inexorable sister, Mr. and Mrs. Micawber, with whom the orphaned boy lives in London, and the fairy godmother, Miss Betsey Trotwood, and the wandering-witted but gentle Mr. Dick. They are all dissolutions and refusions of Dickens's own actual parents or of facets of his feelings about them, separated from each other and for the most part not related to David at all, so that without filial disloyalty David may feel toward them in the different ways Dickens did toward his father and mother. Each of these people symbolizes one sharply differentiated aspect of Dickens's merged and contradictory sentiments about John and Elizabeth Dickens.

David's pretty young mother—that "loving baby," [5] as Miss Betsey calls her—laughing and singing in her soft voice, dancing in the parlor, and winding her bright curls around her finger, is the mother everyone has in early childhood, the divine, angelic mother, all tenderness and beauty, dwelling with her child in the Eden of infancy. The mother, too, that every child loses, with the realization that he is not the only center of her world, and that Dickens lost in the bewildered unhappiness of the Bayham Street days if she had not begun fading away before. That mother died for Dickens, beyond all hope of recovery, in the crisis of his misery at the blacking warehouse, when she was warm for his being sent back to that place of despair.

The devoted Peggotty, with her bursting hugs and her needle-pricked forefinger, is also a mother-image, although she may have traces too of Mary Weller, the servant of the Chatham days. She is the hard-working mother who presides over the kitchen and the pantry, bakes the pastries, mends the clothes from a bright-lidded sewing box, and has such puzzling alternations of crossness and affection. Although she is not so idealized as the dream-mother of infancy, she is more firmly set in a reality that will not altogether melt away with the years.

There is no father-image in the earlier part of *David Copperfield* corresponding either to David's mother or to Peggotty. David's father has died before his son was born, and Dickens's fictional self has no all-powerful father to hoist him onto tables for the piping of comic songs or to take him on those wordily cheerful rambles Dickens knew as a boy. Dickens loved his father, but years of rescuing him from the troubles into which his feckless irresponsibility stumbled had almost entirely destroyed any reverential estimate of a father as one to look up to. The first appearance of a father for David is in the shape of the rival for his mother's love, the darkly ominous Mr. Murdstone, who becomes David's stepfather and tyrant.

This fictional alteration of the autobiographic facts enables Dickens to transform the jealousy a boy feels of the tie between his parents to the resentment of a stepfather. It renders that feeling still more justifiable by delineating Mr. Murdstone in colors of gloomy cruelty. It is Mr. Murdstone, too, who is responsible for David's heartbreak as a laboring factory child, and he does not merely consent to it in financial desperation, as Dickens's kindly and helpless father did, but decrees it in bitter ill-will.

Under Murdstone's domination the gentle and seraphic mother sinks into her early grave and is replaced in her home by his carping sister, who dislikes boys and to whom Murdstone has always been more truly wedded than he was to his timid and shrinking wife. This stony-hearted pair, coldly murdering love with their hard doctrine of "firmness," are not drawn from John and Elizabeth Dickens, of course; they are symbols of the cruel face that life had come to wear for the child torn from his paradise and condemned to humiliating slavery in a world where parental love seemed catastrophically to have turned into indifference and neglect.

Hard upon this exile reappear Dickens's actual parents, disguised as Mr. and Mrs. Micawber. When David begins work washing bottles and pasting on labels, they are introduced merely as the struggling couple within whose house a place is found for him to sleep. In his misery and degradation during that lonely life they stand *in loco parentis* to the orphaned boy, but once more, even in fiction, Dickens cannot nerve himself to the open admission that his own parents were like this. They must be portrayed as a pair of strangers whom chance has brought into intimacy with him. Mr. Micawber, with his plump figure, imposing shirt collar, and tasseled walking stick, represents the pompous, financially slipshod, irresponsible side of John Dickens's character. Poor careworn Mrs. Micawber, always nursing her twins, pawning the spoons, making blurred, ineffectual plans to establish a girls' school, elastically recovering from fainting fits to eat lamb chops and drink warm ale, is drawn from Elizabeth Dickens as she was in Bayham Street and Gower Street. But there is no trace of the angel-mother, and no such thing as the father-god, hardly even the father-friend, little more than the jovial pot-companion.

Micawber has all of John Dickens's grandiloquence of utterance. "Under the impression," he tells David at their first meeting, "that your peregrinations in this metropolis have not as yet been extensive, and that you might have some difficulty in penetrating the arcana of the Modern Babylon in the direction of the City Road—in short, that you might lose yourself—I shall be happy to call this evening, and install you in the knowledge of the nearest way." [6] Speaking of his father-in-law, Micawber says: "Take him for all in all, we ne'er shall—in short, make the acquaintance, probably, of anybody else possessing, at his time of life, the same legs for gaiters, and able to read the same description of print, without spectacles." [7]

Forster illustrates the parallel with quotations from the elder Dickens: "I must express my tendency to believe that his longevity is (to say the least of it) extremely problematical"; "The Supreme Being must be an entirely different individual from what I have every reason to believe Him to be, if He would care in the least for the society of your relations." [8] Writing from Genoa of the departure of an English physician in 1844, Dickens genially parodied his father's style: "We are very sorry to lose the benefit of his advice—or, as my father would say, to be deprived, to a certain extent, of the concomitant advantages, whatever they may be, resulting from his skill, such as it is, and his professional attendance, in so far as it may be so considered." [9]

There is only a fond teasing in these details of the Micawber portrayal, but behind them are huddled many of the darker shadows of Dickens's unhappy childhood. The Micawber house in Windsor Terrace is really Gower Street, with angry creditors forcing themselves into the passage demanding payment and John Dickens oscillating between despair and rebound. With the dirty-faced bootmaker bawling abuse, "Mr. Micawber would be transported with grief and mortification, even to the length (as I was once made aware by a scream from his wife) of making motions at himself with a razor; but within half an hour afterwards, he would polish up his shoes with extraordinary pains, and go out, humming a tune with an air of greater gentility than ever." [10] Mrs. Micawber is no less mercurial: "On one occasion, when an execution had just been put in . . . I saw her lying (of course with the twins) under the grate in a swoon, with her hair all torn about her face; but I never knew her more cheerful than she was, that very same night, over a veal-cutlet before the kitchen fire, telling me stories about her papa and mama, and the company they used to keep." [11]

Mr. Micawber's incarceration in the King's Bench prison is John Dickens's imprisonment in the Marshalsea, and David pawning books and spoons in the City Road is Dickens disposing of the "library" and the family's poor scraps of silver. All the facts of the jail sojourn that Dickens wrote out for Forster are in the story: the tears, the selling of the furniture and camping out in the denuded parlors, the removal from the house, with the rest of the family going to the prison and the boy to a garret "commanding a pleasant prospect of a timber-yard." [12] The humiliations that these experiences were in actuality, however, are all softened by the alteration of David's relationship to the Micawbers.

Dickens takes pains, furthermore, not to be unfair to the virtues of his parents even while painting their weaknesses. Micawber is always in debt and in difficulties, but he is neither lazy nor incompetent. Traddles pays tribute to his industry: "I must do Mr. Micawber the justice to say," he remarks, "that although he would appear not to have worked to any good account for himself, he is a most untiring man when he works for other people. I never saw such a fellow." The "distracted and impetuous manner," Traddles goes on, in which he dives "among papers and books; to say nothing of the immense number of letters he has written . . . is quite extraordinary." [13] Even the portrayal of Dickens's mother is tinged with affectionate forgiveness

My magnificent order at the public house

and understanding: "There was a great deal of good in Mrs. Micawber's heart, which had not been dunned out of it in all those many
years." [14] And, indeed, Dickens goes beyond the facts when he de-
lineates the Micawbers as unwilling to take money from David, al-

though they appeal readily enough to Traddles and everyone else. Few of Dickens's family ever had any delicacy of that kind.

The soul-wrenching agony with which Dickens sank into the loneliness and neglect of washing and labeling bottles in Hungerford Stairs shadows all of David's bewildered and hopeless desolation as he toils for Murdstone and Grinby. Only the sick humiliation with the very smell of blacking is omitted; David's imaginary employers are in the wine trade, a shade above being makers of shoe-blacking, and David is spared that nauseated visceral loathing that made Dickens even as a man cross the Strand to avoid the odor of Robert Warren's blacking establishment. But otherwise David's slavery in that rat-infested, tumble-down tenement is steeped in all the anguish of Dickens's solitary ordeal, day after day, and in all his sense of being rejected by his natural protectors, and cast into a bottomless abyss of pain. The misery that pervades David's small odyssey of despair reveals with heartrending intensity how a child can suffer. In the light of that story, who can fail to understand Dickens's confession that his old way home through the Borough made him weep even after his eldest child could speak?

It clarifies the reasons, too, for that long sequence of rejected children, fatherless or motherless, neglected or abandoned, who move through almost all Dickens's stories. Oliver Twist is an orphan with no home but the starvation workhouse, at the mercy of Bumble and the ferocious Mrs. Corney, and later of the Sowerberrys, Sikes, and Fagin. Kit Nubbles has no father, only his hard-working washwoman mother; Nell, neither father nor mother, but a crazed grandfather of whom she must take care, as if he, not she, were the child. Barnaby Rudge has been abandoned by his murderer father; Nicholas Nickleby has no father and a brainless, gabbling mother; Martin Chuzzlewit no parents; Florence Dombey, no mother and a father whose earlier indifference changes to hatred. Even in *Pickwick Papers* only old Wardle has a mother and only the Wardle girls and Mr. Winkle have a father, and none of the parental roles are very important as such.

Most of the other characters in these novels are either parentless or provided only with very unsatisfactory parents: Smike and the other victims of Squeers at Dotheboys Hall; Noah Claypole and Fagin's gang of young pickpockets; Jo Willet with his fat, slow-witted father;

Edward Chester and Hugh of the Maypole, both sons of the polished and self-centered Sir John Chester; Jonas Chuzzlewit, the Pecksniff girls, Mary Graham, Tom and Ruth Pinch. The Toodles children in *Dombey and Son* and the Cratchits in *A Christmas Carol* are almost the only ones that have a really cheerful home life and a pair of devoted parents. And the novels that follow *David Copperfield* continue the theme of orphaned, unfortunate, or neglected childhood, with Esther Summerson, the Jellyby children, and poor Jo in *Bleak House*, Sissy Jupe and the Gradgrind children in *Hard Times*, Maggy, Clennam, and the heroine of *Little Dorrit*, Pip and Magwitch in *Great Expectations*, John Harmon, Jenny Wren, and little Johnny in *Our Mutual Friend*.

This dearth of happy homes and good parents is startling in a writer whose warm celebration of family life and fireside has created a glow in which readers overlook how relatively seldom he portrays what he praises. The dark pit of the blacking warehouse had made the bright and vanished safety of loving parents and protective hearth infinitely precious to Dickens by revealing it as dreadfully fragile. As he was to write his friend Thompson in 1844, the greater part of the parents who came under his observation seemed to him selfish in their behavior to their children.[15] Even after he was freed from the bondage of the warehouse and sent back to school again, the security of the happy time in Chatham was gone forever. That home which he had known and lost became for his heart a radiant center in his vision of the good life. And its loss, of which he reveals the very essence in the weeping child washing the bottles in his tears, molded his entire response to all the unhappy and misused of the world.

David's flight from the warehouse is the dream-flight that Dickens must often have visioned in his childhood grief, and it is significant that, although he disguises his goal as Dover, the first haven for which he makes like a homing arrow is Rochester and the grass-grown batteries of Chatham. And it may well be that David's grotesque and frightening experience with the crazy old slops seller exclaiming "Goroo!" [16] (suggested by "old Charley," a drunken madman of Chatham memory) [17] symbolizes a childhood fear that even Chatham, like the rest of his world, would have turned inhospitable, strange, and terrifying. But then at last comes the blessed peace and safety of curling up in the protective custody of Miss Betsey Trotwood, who is as plainly as may be the fairy godmother of the nursery tales, hiding a soft heart beneath a harsh exterior. Miss Betsey, his father's aunt, is the longed-for return of the angel-mother, even though it must be no more in the form of girlish beauty but with the worn face and gaunt frame of middle age. And with a single wave, as it were, of her wand, she sends the hateful Murdstones reeling backward, and the warehouse, that dark place of tears, disappears forever.

And so David falls under the joint guardianship of Miss Betsey and her middle-aged and woolly-witted protégé, Mr. Dick, who become the final and benign parent surrogates of the story. It is Mr. Dick, indeed, who speaks the words that decide Miss Betsey to keep the boy: "Have him measured for a suit of clothes directly" [18]—just as John Dickens had made the decision that sent Dickens back to school. In the exquisite relief of it, Dickens can even make Mr. Dick into another laughing burlesque of parental ineptitude, the grown-up child who gabbles forever and writes long memorials that never accomplish anything (both his monosyllabic nickname "Mr. Dick" and his actual surname "Mr. Babley" are suggestive), but whose goodness shines transparently through his incapacity to deal with the world. Remarking that he was "vexed" with "that father of mine," Dickens had exclaimed to Mitton in 1842, "How long he is, growing up"; [19] and just as Micawber indubitably paints one aspect of John Dickens's character, so Mr. Dick gently and fantastically exaggerates him into a figure of absurd and yet noble-hearted foolishness.

In all these intermingled strands of fact and fantasy, the shining memory of early childhood, the nightmare reality of boyhood, the unrealized dreams of what might have been, the softenings of some humiliations Dickens still felt too sick at heart to portray as they were, and the lurid enhancement of griefs that had swelled too bitterly into misery to be remembered with literal accuracy, the sad distortions and the playful exaggerations too, these pages of *David Copperfield* have one deep and undeniable significance. Often fictional as to the mere event, they are undeviatingly true to the emotional reality. They pierce to the very heart of how Dickens felt about those buried days upon which, since the hour when they had come to an end, he and his parents had been as if they were struck dumb. Their very elements of invention are truer than the fact, because they symbolize that emotional reality. In them Dickens made a profound and tremendous effort to come to grips with himself, to evaluate the influences that had made him what he was, to understand himself and the meaning of his own experience. That is what gives its greatness to the entire earlier third of the book.

It fills with only a slightly lesser significance the middle part, where the theme is modified into the struggles of youth. Here the minor events are variations upon Dickens's employments as shorthand writer and Parliamentary reporter leading into the opening out of his career as an author. Most significantly, though, the major ones flower out of his infatuation with Maria Beadnell and shine with all the emotion of that time of ecstasy and anguish. David's love for Dora Spenlow is Dickens's love for Maria, both as it was to him then and as it has come to seem to him across the intervening years. Relived with all its unbearable beauty and shining wretchedness, it is also seen with some of the sad irony of maturity fusing pity with bitterness, pain with tender laughter, even resentment with long-remembered devotion and a hurt never entirely healed.

Foolish, pretty Dora, with her childish ways and her childish mind, shaking her curls and behaving like a divinely babyish imbecile, is at once the little beauty who filled Dickens's youthful heart with longing and delight and the vision of her that has come to his soberer judgment. But, unlike Maria, she is merely silly, not cruel and flirtatious, and her little heart holds for David all the affection it can. On David's sudden descent into poverty again Mr. Spenlow indignantly forbids their courtship, but then obligingly dies (as the beefy Mr. Beadnell had shown no signs of doing) and David's labors, unlike Dickens's, are at last rewarded by carrying home his child-bride. The desperate desire that had never been realized in the world of fact is consummated in the world of dream.

Few writers have more successfully re-created the shimmering enchantment of youthful love than Dickens does in these scenes. David so lost in infatuation with Dora that dining at her father's table he does not know if he eats anything, or what he eats; David feeling that to drink a cup of punch would somehow be a profanation of the holiness of his sentiments; David lost in luminous dreams of the delight of being allowed to call her Dora, or of having reason to believe that when she is among other people she still thinks of him; David filled with adoration even for her little dog Jip and with revential awe of her father because he is her father—all are vibrant with the blurred radiance of dawning love.

Or David riding horseback behind Dora's carriage, unaware of the dust because he is lost in a mist of love and beauty. Or David strolling under the trees with Dora's shy arm in his, "and Heaven knows," Dickens has him exclaim, "folly as it all was, it would have been a happy fate to have been struck immortal with those foolish feelings, and have strayed among the trees forever!" [20] Or their first great quarrel, when Dora "used the terrible expression that 'our love had begun in folly, and ended in madness!' which dreadful words occasioned me to tear my hair, and cry that all was over!" [21] "What an unsubstantial, happy, foolish time!" Dickens writes in tender valedictory. "Of all the times of mine that Time has in his grip, there is none that in one retrospect I can smile at half so much, or think of half so tenderly." [22]

But movingly as he conveys it, Dickens does not lose himself in the illusion. As he looks back upon that boyish love, he knows now that it could have led to no happy marriage. "Blind, blind, blind!" says David's Aunt Betsey,[23] and both when she says it and later when he hears a blind beggar crying the same words in the street he feels "a vague unhappy loss or want of something" [24] overshadow him. "Are you happy now, you foolish boy?" asks Dora when they are married, "and are you sure you don't repent?" [25]

Without ceasing to be the artless, childish creature that Dickens's memory painted Maria Beadnell as having been, Dora acquires after her marriage more and more of a coloring derived from Kate. David is obliged to take upon himself the management of the household, the purchases from butcher and grocer and baker, the keeping of the accounts. He learns that Dora is no mental companion for him, and tries to "form her mind" by reading to her or gravely giving her useful information. But the only effect on Dora is "to depress her spirits, and make her always nervous" with apprehension. Finding that "I had effected nothing," David says, "it began to occur to me that Dora's mind was already formed." [26] And gradually "the old unhappy feeling" his aunt had evoked by her exclamation pervades David's life "like a strain of sorrowful music faintly heard in the night." [27]

He knows at last what is its cause: "it would have been better for me if my wife could have helped me more, and shared the many thoughts in which I had no partner; and that this might have been; I knew." [28] Instead, he is obliged to keep his work and his anxieties locked in his own heart. "There can be no disparity in marriage," he repeats to himself forlornly, "like unsuitability of mind and purpose." [29] And later still another phrase recurs and echoes in his memory: "The first mistaken impulse of an undisciplined heart." [30] It is Dickens's ultimate judgment of his youthful infatuation, gently but firmly seen, for all its beauty, as a boyhood folly. But it goes deeper and further into his life than those days of joy and sorrow. It not merely assays the strong unlikelihood that he and Maria Beadnell could ever have been happy in marriage, it hints all the unspoken feelings that lurked below the surface of his relationship to Kate. And, in the book, with deep pathos, but unwaveringly, Dickens shapes the story toward the death of the brainless pretty creature who is both his own youthful sweet-heart and a wife.

Is there a trace of resentful wish fulfillment hidden in this, is it merely a rendering in art of the knowledge that the dream could never have been, or does it express an unhappy judgment of the marriage he did contract? Probably a mingling of all three, and if the last it contains, too, in David's avowal of his own weaknesses and failures a confession that Dickens recognized some of his own. The whole truth about his own temperament, his willful temper, his impatience and impetuosity, it does not reveal: despite David's efforts to "form" Dora's mind, he is more tender with her feeble ineptitude than Dickens was likely to have been. Dickens did not realize what a strain his furious energies, his wild alternations of exhilaration and gloom, and his tyrannical insistence on precision all put upon his wife and family. But a great deal of self-understanding he did attain, and it was enormously valuable to him to have confronted himself thus honestly. The achievement brought him a kind of peace for which he had long been struggling vainly. Facing the truth as he knew and felt it, he resolved, for the time at least, some of the conflicts that struggled within him.

These facts endowed his story for Dickens with meanings unusually deep and personal. "Of all my books," he confessed in the year before he died, "I like this the best. It will easily be believed that I am a fond parent to every child of my fancy, and that no one can ever love that family as dearly as I love them. But, like many fond parents, I have in my heart of hearts a favourite child. And his name is DAVID COPPERFIELD." [31]

* * * * *

His feeling for this loved child of his imagination springs from its triumphant total achievement. In it he had poured all his comprehension of himself from childhood to maturity, unified and given the form which was its meaning. If Dickens draws within the frame of his self-portrayal no picture of David's practice as a novelist, that is because Dickens, in his enormous fluency and fruitfulness, felt within himself no problems peculiar to the fact of being a writer. He had the difficulties every writer knows, of making himself work against inclination, of clarifying in imagination what he wanted to do, and of rendering in words the sharp realization of what he had conceived. But although he struggled—and sometimes gigantically—with these problems, they did not involve him in the critical agonies of Flaubert or the conscious meticulosities of Henry James. He felt, strictly as a writer, no troubled areas that he needed to explore as he did those of personal emotion.

There is a different reason for the way in which, to some readers, David Copperfield himself seems to fade out of the picture as his story moves toward the time of his life when he is supposed to be writing it. David does not really disappear, but it is true that he is conveyed through altered means. He is not so much looking inward upon himself or backward upon an image of the child he was, as looking out upon those around him. Therefore, as the book nears its close, it is Uriah Heep, Micawber, Steerforth, Daniel Peggotty, and Betsey Trotwood that we are more conscious of seeing than we are of David, because we are looking at them through his eyes. And, as Professor E. K. Brown points out, "he is much more than a mere medium. It is to him that almost everything happens, and since he is a person of a sensitive nature the happenings set up vibrations in him, and affect us as accompanied by those vibrations." [32] But there is already a separation between him and the child who visited the Peggottys in their boat at Yarmouth, or the youth who squeezed his feet into tight shoes for Dora, that enables him to portray those earlier avatars of himself from without as well as from within. Both the earlier and the later portrayal, however, are bathed in the light of emotional veracity.

This suffusion of feeling with a translucent truth to experience is what gives the story its singular magic. Its intensity is especially note-worthy in the scenes of childhood because writers have not often found its essence easy to recapture. But even the most successful por-trayals of childhood do not surpass *David Copperfield*. In the sur-realist fantasy of *Alice in Wonderland* Lewis Carroll reflects the unin-telligible strangeness of the child's world, but not its griefs and ter-rors. In the brilliant first chapter of *A Portrait of the Artist as a Young Man* Joyce paints the bewilderment and unhappiness of childhood, but not its delights and affections. His bleak emotional tone and rapidly telescoped transitions from infancy through boyhood to adolescence are altogether colder than the glow and bloom of Dickens, and have more of the adult's sense of time than of the timelessness of childhood. *Tom Sawyer* and *Huckleberry Finn*, superb though they are, do not have the scope nor even quite the depth of *David Copper-field*. No other boy has known exactly the same circumstances as David Copperfield, and yet all childhood is there.

Out of the blurred cloud of infancy there first emerge the pretty mother and the bumpy servant Peggotty, with "cheeks and arms so hard and red" that the child wonders "the birds didn't peck her in preference to apples." [33] Next comes an uncertain image of tottering unsteadily across the floor between their stooped figures. Then there is the house, with its two parlors and the long passage to the kitchen, past a threatening dark storeroom full of mingled smells of soap, pickles, candles, and coffee; and the back yard where tall fowl stalk about "in a menacing and ferocious manner" and terrifying geese stretch out their long necks.[34] In the garden, "a very preserve of butter-flies," the mother gathers clusters of fruit and the child bolts "furtive gooseberries." [35] During lamplit evenings, Peggotty sews and David props his sleepy eyelids open to keep on looking at her wonderful workbox with its pink-domed picture of St. Paul's Cathedral on the lid. How naturally and yet subtly out of this domestic serenity comes David's innocent question, "Peggotty, were you ever married?" and her mysterious crossness, followed by the remorseful hug so tight that the buttons burst off the back of her gown and fly across the room.[36] The scene leads immediately to the introduction of the tall dark-haired man with the shallow black eyes, whom the child intuitively dis-likes to see touching his mother's hand.

Mr. Murdstone is seen entirely through David's fear, as an incarnation of cold ferocity and formidable power. When "bewitching little Mrs. Copperfield" is once his bride, her son becomes for him simply a rebellious small animal to be whipped and tamed. "God help me, I might have been improved for my whole life," David says, "I might have been made another creature perhaps, for life, by a kind word at that season. A word of encouragement and explanation, of pity for my childish ignorance, of welcome home, of reassurance to me that it *was* home, might have made me dutiful to him in my heart henceforth, instead of in my hypocritical outside, and might have made me respect instead of hate him." [37]

But the Murdstone firmness, "the grand quality on which both Mr. and Miss Murdstone took their stand," had no place for being gentle with a child. And David understood clearly enough that, whatever they might call it, "it was another name for tyranny; and for a certain gloomy, arrogant, devil's humour, that was in them both. The creed, as I should state it now, was this. Mr. Murdstone was firm; nobody else in his world was to be firm at all, for everybody was to be bent to his firmness. Miss Murdstone was an exception. She might be firm, but only by relationship, and in an inferior and tributary degree. My mother was another exception. She might be firm, and must be; but only in bearing their firmness, and firmly believing there was no other firmness on earth." [38]

"The gloomy taint that was in the Murdstone blood, darkened the Murdstone religion, which was austere and wrathful." [39] Little Mr. Chillip, the doctor who delivered David, quotes his wife on the dark roots of Mr. Murdstone's faith. " 'Mrs. Chillip,' " he reports, " 'quite electrified me by pointing out that Mr. Murdstone sets up an image of himself, and calls it the Divine Nature. . . . And do you know I must say, sir,' he continued, mildly laying his head on one side, 'that I *don't* find authority for Mr. and Miss Murdstone in the New Testament?' " [40]

Nevertheless, and it is one of the great artistic triumphs of the book, even to Mr. Murdstone David achieves the justice of seeing that he is not entirely a monster, but a man whose self-righteous cruelty has not quite frozen all warm emotion. This saves the Murdstone portrayal from melodrama and endows it with human complexity. Mr. Murdstone has not married David's mother merely for her small estate: "He seemed to be very fond of my mother," David admits, and, with another burst of psychological honesty, "—I am afraid I liked him none the better for that—and she was very fond of him." [41] And when the timid, affectionate creature whom he has tormented into her grave is gone, there is no doubt of his sorrow. "Mr. Murdstone took no heed of me, when I went into the parlour, where he was, but sat by the fireside, weeping silently, and pondering in his elbow-chair." He "took a book sometimes, but never read it that I saw. He would open it and look at it as if he were reading, but would remain for a whole hour without turning the leaf, and then put it down and walk to and fro in the room." [42]

There is another penetrating touch in Dickens's portrayal of David's behavior when he receives word at school that his mother is dead. Even in his sincere grief he feels that his affliction confers a kind of dignity upon him. Walking in the playground while the other boys are in school, and seeing them glancing at him out of the windows, "I felt distinguished," he says, "and looked more melancholy, and walked slower. When school was over, and they came and spoke to me, I felt it rather good in myself not to be proud to any of them, and to take exactly the same notice of them all, as before." [43]

Even the bleak and meager schooling at Mr. Creakle's is now ended; the boy sinks into the hopeless loneliness of his toil at the warehouse. His flight to Dover and the frightening reappearance of the Murdstones in Miss Betsey's parlor bring into focus one of the major themes of *David Copperfield*, which is to recur later with still more power: the struggle in the world between simple goodness and cruel cunning. Until now we have seen the Murdstones only through the eyes of a helpless child. They have banished him from his home, condemned him to the slavery of washing bottles in a warehouse, in essence killed his mother, seized her money. "But their physical strength, their awful visages, their hypocritical assumptions of respectability, are no match for the goodness and directness of one brave frail old woman, whose only support is the lunatic innocence of Mr. Dick." [44] Miss Betsey minces no words in describing Mr. Murdstone's treatment of his wife:

"Do you think I don't know what a woeful day it was for the soft little creature when *you* first came in her way—smirking and making great eyes at her, I'll be bound, as if you couldn't say boh! to a goose! ... And when you had made sure of the little fool—God forgive me that I should call her so, and she gone where *you* won't go in a hurry—because you had not done wrong enough to her and hers, you must begin to train her, must you? begin to break her, like a poor caged bird, and wear her deluded life away, in teaching her to sing *your* notes? . . . Mr. Murdstone, you were a tyrant to the simple baby, and you broke her heart. She was a loving baby—I know that; I knew it years before *you* ever saw her—and through the best part of her weakness you gave her the wounds she died of." [45]

And with an inspired touch of insight, Miss Betsey puts her finger on the underlying reason for Mr. Murdstone's dislike of David, "the poor child you sometimes tormented her through afterwards, which is a disagreeable remembrance, and makes the sight of him odious now." The stroke pierces home: Mr. Murdstone "had stood by the door, all this while, observant of her, with a smile upon his face, though his black eyebrows were heavily contracted. I remarked now," David writes, "that, though the smile was on his face still, his colour had gone in a moment, and he seemed to breathe as if he had been running." [46]

Her final bolt is one not of denunciation but of sheer ridicule, suddenly dropped upon Miss Murdstone: "Good day to you, too, ma'am. Let me see you ride a donkey over *my* green again, and as sure as you have a head upon your shoulders, I'll knock your bonnet off, and tread upon it!" [47] It is a splendid victory. In an instant these two dark ogres of childhood have been deflated to life size, and their power shown to have been only the weakness of their victims. Anyone good and courageous enough to defy them can defeat them.

Miss Betsey determines to send David to school again. There follows the serener interlude of his Canterbury days, with his boyish infatuation for Miss Shepherd, upon whom he bestows Brazil nuts and kisses behind a cloakroom door, his fight with the young butcher, who appears "like the apparition of an armed head in Macbeth," his adolescent devotion to the eldest Miss Larkins, who plays the harp, wears blue flowers in her hair, and marries an elderly hop-grower. And while David rises to be head boy at Dr. Strong's, the Doctor delights the awed and happy Mr. Dick by reading aloud scraps of his Dictionary as they walk together in the courtyard, "Mr. Dick listening, enchained by interest, with his poor wits calmly wandering God knows where, upon the wings of hard words . . ." [48] At the close of David's schooling, we find him apprenticed to Spenlow and Jorkins to become a proctor in Doctors' Commons.

The few satiric elements in *David Copperfield* are almost all centered in this part of the book. The Commons, says Mr. Spenlow enthusiastically, "was the most conveniently organized place in the world. It was the complete idea of snugness. It lay in a nut-shell. For example: You brought a divorce case, or a restitution case, into the Consistory. Very good. You tried it in the Consistory. You made a quiet little round game of it, among a family group, and you played it out at leisure. Suppose you were not satisfied with the Consistory, what did you do then? Why, you went into the Arches. What was the Arches? The same court, in the same room, with the same bar, and the same practitioners, but another judge, for there the Consistory judge could plead any court-day as an advocate. Well, you played your round game again. Still you were not satisfied. Very good. What did you do then? Why, you went to the Delegates. Who were the Delegates? Why, the Ecclesiastical Delegates were the advocates without any business, who had looked on at the round game when it was playing in both courts, and had seen the cards shuffled, and cut, and played, and had talked to all the players about it, and now came fresh, as judges, to settle the matter to the satisfaction of everybody!" [49]

It is while David is at Doctors' Commons that he is a dinner guest of the Waterbrooks at the appalling genteel party where the diners are all as iced as the wine and where everyone talks about "the Aristocracy—and Blood." "We might have been a party of Ogres," David observes, "the conversation assumed such a sanguine complexion." "Other things are all very well in their way," says Mr. Waterbrook, "but give me Blood!" A lady in black velvet, with a great black velvet hat, who looks as if she might have been Hamlet's aunt, agrees with him: "There are some low minds," she observes loftily, "(not many, I am happy to believe, but there are *some*) that would prefer to do what *I* should call bow down before idols. Positively Idols! Before services, intellect, and so on. But these are intangible points. Blood is not so. We see Blood in a nose, and we know it. We meet with it in a chin, and we say, 'There it is! That's Blood!'" [50]

Meanwhile, the strands of the story are weaving together the lives of Peggotty's family and the life of David's boyhood friend Steerforth. From Hampstead, where he meets Steerforth's mother and her companion Rosa Dartle, David goes down to Yarmouth for a visit to Peggotty's brother Daniel and his adopted children, Ham and Little Em'ly. Innocently David introduces Steerforth to his fisherman friends. How should he foresee that his admired companion will seduce the little beauty for whom he himself had felt a baby infatuation in childhood?

Steerforth we see, as is natural, only through David's hero-worshiping eyes, and therefore glimpse only by degrees the self-centered and Byronic corruption that lurks in the core of his brilliance. But even in their school days it is revealed in his demands that the adoring David, despite his sleepiness, remain awake to entertain him with hours of storytelling every night after they have gone to bed. And it is still more brutally declared in his indifferent response to Rosa Dartle's question whether the lower classes are mere "animals and clods" without feeling: "Their delicacy is not to be shocked, or hurt very easily. They are wonderfully virtuous, I daresay. Some people contend for that, at the least; and I am sure I don't want to contradict them. But they have not very fine natures, and they may be thankful that, like their coarse rough skins, they are not easily wounded." [51]

Rosa Dartle's retort is an ironic comment on this inhumanity: "Really!" she exclaims. "Well, I don't know, now, when I have been better pleased than to hear that. It's so consoling! It's such a delight to know that, when they suffer, they don't feel! Sometimes I have been quite uneasy for that sort of people; but now I shall just dismiss the idea of them altogether. Live and learn. I had my doubts, I confess, but now they're cleared up. I didn't know, and now I do know, and that shows the advantage of asking—don't it?" [52]

Steerforth's charm, in fact, is merely a refinement of egoism. "If any one had told me, then," David exclaims, "that all this was a brilliant game, played for the excitement of the moment, for the employment of high spirits, in the thoughtless love of superiority, in a mere careless course of winning what was worthless to him, and next minute thrown away: I say, if any one had told me such a lie that night, I wonder in what manner of receiving it my indignation would have found a vent!" [53] But Steerforth himself bitterly knows his own nature. "It would be better to be this poor Peggotty," he says moodily, "or his lout of a nephew, than to be myself, twenty times richer and twenty times wiser, and be the torment to myself that I have been . . ." "I wish with all my soul that I had been better guided! I wish with all my soul I could guide myself better!" "David, I wish to God I had had a judicious father in these last twenty years!" [54]

Save for momentary outbursts, such as this, however, Steerforth is never revealed from within. If this is mainly because the narrative is restricted to what is known to David, it may be partly, too, because for Dickens, with his impassioned purposefulness and conviction of the meaningfulness of effort, the cynicism and disillusion of a Byron was not inwardly conceivable. He could believe in the existence of disillusion, and he could be bitterly disappointed and indignant at the cruelties of the world, but he could not enter into that despairing mood that sees all striving as futility and all its objects as dead-sea fruit. He was able, nevertheless, to imagine Steerforth's feelings of compunction and self-contempt, and there is an exquisite pathos in Steerforth's last farewell to David with its foreshadowings of the betrayal that will estrange them forever:

"Daisy," Steerforth says, "—for though that's not the name your Godfathers and Godmothers gave you, it's the name I like best to call you by—and I wish, I wish, I wish, you could give it to me! . . . Daisy, if anything should ever separate us, you must think of me at my best, old boy. Come! Let us make that bargain. Think of me at my best, if circumstances should ever part us!" And later, in the dull dawn, David sees him sleeping, "lying easily, with his head upon his arm, as I had often seen him lie at school," and bursts into a sorrowing valedictory: "Never more, Oh God forgive you, Steerforth! to touch that passive hand in love and friendship. Never, never more!" [55]

The rest of Little Em'ly's story is less well handled, although Ham's heartbroken grief and Mr. Peggotty's devotion are moving. But the reader sometimes feels that Em'ly's self-abasement and remorse are intensified to a sentimental luxuriance, and that there is too much of the assumption that she is irretrievably stained forever, and that her life thereafter can be nothing but one long and hopeless penance. There is something wearisome, too, about the fallen Martha Endell dragging herself around, "making the same low, dreary, wretched moaning in her shawl," [56] and always wandering around the nocturnal streets of London and making her way down to the muddy banks of the river.

While all these events are moving toward the denouement, the major theme of the battle between craft and innocence—which is also exemplified in the contrast between Steerforth and the simple Yarmouth family of fishermen and boatbuilders—is working up to its greatest climax in the unmasking of Uriah Heep. The subtle knave who has gradually entangled Mr. Wickfield, Miss Betsey's man of business, in his web and who intends to make Mr. Wickfield's daughter Agnes "his Agnes," is the Murdstone threat grown ten times more cunning and grinningly unscrupulous. His hypocritical assumption of " 'umbleness," his damp bony hands, his fawning hatred of those he has deceived, his calculated dependence upon their very loyalties and affections, his ingenuity in spinning his web, make him despicable and dangerous to a degree far transcending the Murdstones, who could tyrannize only over weak women and helpless children. Uriah Heep can worm his way into the confidence of an experienced man of affairs, gradually get the upper hand of his weaknesses, and reduce him to subservience.

With his symbolic twistings and contortions of the body, Uriah is at once comic, revolting, and frightening. In one of those echoes from the fairy tales which constantly recur in Dickens, seeing Uriah with Agnes Wickfield reminds David "of an ugly and rebellious genie watching a good spirit." [57] Just as Rosa Dartle recalls the evil princess, and Miss Betsey, again, the fairy godmother whom the bad spirit cannot terrify: "If you're an eel, sir," she exclaims as Uriah jerks himself about, "conduct yourself like one. If you're a man, control your limbs, sir! Good God!" she goes on indignantly, "I am not going to be serpentined and corkscrewed out of my senses!" [58]

But Dickens understands and explains the forces that have made Uriah what he is. "Father and me," Uriah tells David, "was brought up at a foundation school for boys; and mother, she was likewise brought up at a public, sort of charitable, establishment. They taught us all a deal of umbleness—not much else that I know of, from morning to night. We was to be umble to this person, and umble to that; and to pull off our caps here, and to make bows there; and always to know our place, and abase ourselves before our betters. And we had such a deal of betters! Father got the monitor-medal for being umble. So did I. . . . 'Be umble, Uriah,' says Father to me, 'and you'll get on. It was what was always being dinned into you and me at school; it's what goes down best. Be umble,' says father, 'and you'll do!' And really it ain't done bad!" [59]

"It was the first time," David comments, "it had ever occurred to me, that this detestable cant of false humility might have originated out of the Heep family. I had seen the harvest, but had never thought of the seed." With this speech, however, "I fully comprehended now, for the first time, what a base, unrelenting, and revengeful spirit, must have been engendered by this early, and this long, suppression." [60]

But this skillful and vindictive schemer is also brought to defeat. Micawber, still looking for something to turn up, has become Uriah's clerk; he ferrets out his employer's secrets and brings them to the knowledge of David's friend Traddles. And just as Miss Betsey and Mr. Dick routed the Murdstones, so the ingenuous and generous Tommy Traddles and the improvident Micawber unravel the complex plottings of Heep. "What is the matter, gentlemen?" Mr. Micawber asks in his indignation. "What is *not* the matter? Villainy is the matter; baseness is the matter; deception, fraud, conspiracy are the matter; and the name of the whole atrocious mass is—HEEP! . . . I'll put my hand in no man's hand," he continues, puffing, gasping, and sobbing, "until I have—blown to fragments—the—a—detestable—serpent—HEEP!" [61]

The scene in which Uriah is confronted by Mr. Micawber, flourishing the ruler he has drawn from his breast, and reading from his foolscap document, represents the culmination of that struggle of forces that has pervaded the book. Upon Uriah's darting at the document, "Mr. Micawber, with a perfect miracle of dexterity or luck, caught his advancing knuckles with the ruler, and disabled his right hand. It dropped at the wrist, as if it were broken. The blow sounded as if it had fallen on wood."

"Approach me again, you—you—you HEEP of infamy," Mr. Micawber gasps, "and if your head is human, I'll break it. Come on, come on!" [62]

It is the end. Uriah has some half-dozen more writhes and twists left in him, but essentially he is caught by the heels. Once more the good and the brave have triumphed, although not without difficulty and pain, over treachery and cruelty, just as the devotion of Daniel Peggotty has ultimately found and brought peace to Little Em'ly. If this seem a simple philosophy, it might be asked whether the belief that evil always carries off the victory is so much more worldly-wise. Dickens can hardly be accused of closing his eyes to the existence of suffering and injustice, but he believed that courage and integrity, supported by labor and intelligence, could overcome the obstacles in their path. He believed that a persevering energy and determination were the strong points in his own character and the roots of his success. He believed that that was the significance of his life story. "My meaning simply is," he has David Copperfield say, "that whatever I have tried to do in life, I have tried with all my heart to do well . . ." [63]

This emphasis, fusing with the autobiographic content of *David Copperfield*, shapes all the ramblings and twistings of its plot into a structure beautifully appropriate to its purposes. An autobiography or an autobiographic novel must have the flexibility that admits all that crowding world of accident and contingency which characterizes the multiplicity of life it seeks to mirror. The art that excludes everything but the rigidly logical and necessary, the art of a Racine or Flaubert, would not be appropriate here. It would be too orderly, too severely patterned, to convey all the richness and variety of episode needed to suggest the events of half a lifetime. Dickens has superbly adjusted all the details of his crowded canvas so that they reinforce its reality without falling in chaos. His dominant themes are always there, but they never crush his life story into the sort of intellectual geometry that Henry Adams makes of his autobiography. Dickens has ordered his materials so that for all their skillful appearance of artlessness they give meaning to his interpretation of his experience. Into *David Copperfield* he has not merely precipitated the painful experiences of his childhood and youth; he has so surrounded them with life itself as to make them part of a larger world.

CHAPTER SEVEN

Household Words

Long before *David Copperfield* had run its course, Dickens had transformed his "dim design" of a periodical into a reality. A weekly miscellany—his old enthusiasm for the *Bee* or *Spectator* type of publication coming out again—it was to be written by various hands and sold for twopence a copy. Innumerable subjects seethed in his mind: a history of piracy, a history of knight-errantry "and the wild old notion of the Sangreal," a history of remarkable characters, a history of savages, showing the ways "in which civilized men, under circumstances of difficulty, soonest become like savages," essays, reviews, fiction, letters, theatrical criticism, "as amusing as possible, but all distinctly and boldly going to what . . . ought to be the spirit of the people and the time." [1]

Binding these together, Dickens imagined "a certain SHADOW, which may go into any place, by sunlight, moonlight, starlight, firelight, candlelight . . . and be supposed to be cognizant of everything . . ." The Shadow would issue "warnings from time to time, that he is going to fall on such and such a subject; or to expose such and such a piece of humbug . . . I want him to loom as a fanciful thing all over London; and to get up a general notion of 'What will the Shadow say about this, I wonder? What will the Shadow say about this? Is the Shadow here?' and so forth. . . . Now do you make anything of this? which I let off as if I were a bladder full of it, and you had punctured me." [2]

But Forster robustly pooh-poohed this insubstantial Shadow, and Dickens gave it up in the end. With the New Year of 1850 he began bombarding Forster with a fusillade of other titles: *The Robin, Mankind, Charles Dickens: A Weekly journal designed for the instruction*

and entertainment of all classes of readers: Conducted by Himself,
The Household Voice, The Household Guest, The Household Face,
The Comrade, The Microscope, The Highway of Life, The Lever, The
Rolling Years, The Holly Tree, and finally *Household Words.*
This was chosen as the name, with a motto adapted from Shake-
speare: "Familiar in their mouths as Household Words." [3]

For subeditor Forster suggested William Henry Wills, who had
been Dickens's secretary on the *Daily News* and continued with that
paper after Dickens resigned.[4] Still so thin that his friends said he
could tuck himself away in a flute case,[5] Wills was nevertheless a steel
spring of indefatigable industry. Though not of a lively imagination
—he was, Dickens said, "decidedly of the Nutmeg-Grater, or Fancy-
Bread-Rasper School" [6]—his faithfulness and sharp efficiency made
him an excellent man to handle the business part of the publication.
Dickens offered and Wills accepted a salary of £8 a week and one-
eighth of all profits so long as he retained his post.[7]

Dickens's own salary as what he preferred to call "Conductor" he
set at £500 a year.[8] Remembering, no doubt, his contentions with
Bentley as well as the frictions between himself and the proprietors
of the *Daily News,* he designated himself as half owner. Bradbury and
Evans had a quarter share and Forster the remaining eighth, for which
he was to contribute occasional literary articles. These arrangements
amounted to giving Dickens a clear three-quarters control.

The rest of the editorial staff was not numerous. Richard Henry
Horne, poet and a colorful descriptive journalist, was taken on at five
guineas a week. George Hogarth also seems to have had editorial
duties, as did John Dickens.[9] Public announcement of the magazine
was made, and Dickens wrote personally to literary friends and acquaintances suggesting that they become contributors.[10] Throughout
these first few months of getting *Household Words* started, Dickens
was also writing *David Copperfield.*

At 16 Wellington Street, just north of the Gaiety Theatre on the
Strand, he took a small building for offices. Its three stories and garret
were of brick neatly edged with stone quoins. A small door opened
on the slanting sidewalk, to the left of a round bay window two stories
high, and above, on the third floor, a single window opened on a bal-
ustraded balcony. Here Dickens arrived at eight on the mornings he
spent in the office, and strode up and down the floor thinking and dic-

tating, combing his hair over and over again while he paced, a trick he had when he worked.[11]

He knew exactly the kind of magazine he wanted to create. It was to be entertaining, and at the same time the instrument of serious social purpose. It should portray the "social wonders, good and evil," in "the stirring world around us." It should tell the thousand and one marvelous tales of knowledge, science, and invention, and render vividly both their color and their meaning. Giving no encouragement to those who glorified the good old times, emphasizing the present as "this summer-dawn of time," it should range over past and present, and over every nation, with an eye sharp for what was wrong and a heart warm for what was right. It should fight for tolerance and the progress of human welfare, and give no quarter to chicanery and oppression.[12]

Many of these aims were identical with those of radical reform, but in one way *Household Words* was to be very different. Animated by "No mere utilitarian spirit, no iron binding of the mind to grim realities," it should "cherish that light of Fancy which is inherent in the human breast" and insist that no class was to be "excluded from the sympathies and graces of imagination." Woe betide that day, said Dickens's Preliminary Word in the first number, when the workers were taught that their lot was to be only a moody, brutal slavery at the "whirling wheel of toil"! Not harsh efficiency, not the clanking of an economic machine, were the goal of society, but the loving union of multitudes of human lives in generous feeling and noble purpose. "The adventurer in the old fairy story, climbing the steep mountain," the announcement concluded, "was surrounded by a roar of voices, crying to him, from the stones in the way, to turn back. All the voices *we* hear, cry Go on! . . . We echo back the cry, and go on cheerily!" [13]

Dickens did go on. He arranged with his brother-in-law Henry Austin, now Secretary of the Sanitary Commission, to provide the facts for a series of articles on sanitary reform—water supply, lack of light and air in the slums, refuse disposal—on which he intended to hammer away in the magazine.[14] To Charles Knight, who had written him on the injustice of the high duty on paper which made publishing costs excessive, he replied that he agreed, but thought the window duty pressing down on the great mass of the people a far greater evil. "They cannot read without light. They cannot have an average chance of life and health without it." [15] Their wrongs came first. To other possible contributors he wrote that he most needed short stories imbued by "such a general purpose" of calling attention to things wrong in the world.

One of these writers was Elizabeth Cleghorn Gaskell, whose *Mary Barton* had given a sympathetic picture of the sufferings of Manchester factory workers, suggested by the Chartist petition, riots, and general strike of 1842, and by the bitter distresses of the following years. There was "no living English writer," Dickens told her, whose aid he more desired: "I should set a value on your help which your modesty can hardly imagine . . ." Would she write "a short tale, or any number of tales," for his pages? [16] He was gratified to receive from her a gloomy but impressive story entitled *Lizzie Leigh*, centering around a seduced servant girl and her illegitimate child. He suggested a few changes in narrative detail, which Mrs. Gaskell accepted, and the tale appeared as a serial in the first three numbers.

Not all those friends Dickens asked became contributors. For he was adhering to the custom, still widespread among magazines at that time, of signing no authors' names to any of the contents, and there were writers who rebelled against this procedure. "But the periodical is anonymous throughout," protested Dickens to Douglas Jerrold. "Yes," replied Jerrold, reading aloud the words that appeared at the top of every page, " 'Conducted by Charles Dickens.' I see it is— *mon*onymous throughout." [17]

And, indeed, some of the younger writers felt that there was an unintentional injustice in this system: everything good in the magazine was credited to Dickens, so that years of successful work might still leave a man unknown to the public. But Dickens himself, "the kindliest, the justest, and the most generous of mankind," said one of them, had "no remotest notion that he was putting a bushel over the lights of his staff . . ." [18]

* * * * *

The first number of *Household Words* was dated March 30, 1850. It contained twenty-four double-column pages of reading matter, roughly something over twenty thousand words. After the Preliminary Word and *Lizzie Leigh* came an article, "Valentine's Day at the Post-Office," a brief dramatic parable in verse, entitled "Abraham and the

Fire-Worshipper" and emphasizing religious tolerance, another article, "The Amusements of the People," on the theaters popular among the working class, a biographical "Episode in the Life of Mademoiselle Clairon," a famous eighteenth-century French actress, a short poem, and an article supporting Mrs. Caroline Chisholm's society for helping poor people emigrate to Australia, illustrated by a group of emigrants' letters.

Of these, only "The Amusements of the People" was entirely by Dickens, although he had a hand in the post-office article, which was by Wills, and probably wrote the introduction to the emigrants' letters, which had been supplied by Mrs. Chisholm. The anecdote of Mlle. Clairon was by Hogarth.[19] They all, however, illustrate both Dickens's point of view and his insistence on color and imagination in handling even the most baldly factual material. No matter how brilliant, wise, or true something was, unless it were readable it might as well be left unsaid. ("Let John Hollingshead do it," Dickens would say to Wills in later years: "he's the most ignorant man on the staff, but he'll cram up the facts, and won't give us an encyclopaedical article." [20]) Everything must sparkle with vitality.

"Valentine's Day at the Post-Office," for example, is an informational article dealing with the bulk of mail passing through London's central office. But all the statistical data are presented in a rapid narrative full of descriptive vigor. Glance at the account of the mailing of newspapers. These had to be posted by six o'clock; we begin at quarter to the hour: "It was then just drizzling newspapers. . . . By degrees it began to rain hard; by fast degrees the storm came on harder and harder, until it blew, rained, hailed, snowed, newspapers. A fountain of newspapers played in at the window. Water-spouts of newspapers broke from enormous sacks, and engulphed the men inside. . . .

"Suddenly it struck six. Shut Sesame! Perfectly still weather. Nobody there. Not a trace of the late storm—Not a soul, too late!

"But what a chaos within! Men up to their knees in newspapers on great platforms; men gardening among newspapers with rakes; men digging among newspapers as if a new description of rock had been blasted into those fragments; men going up and down a gigantic trap . . . taking with them nothing but newspapers!" [21]

Dickens's own article, "The Amusements of the People," describes going with one "Joe Whelks, of the New Cut, Lambeth," to the Victoria Theatre, where prices ranged from one shilling down to three-pence.[22] The gallery was jammed to the roof; the pit crowded with young mechanics and their wives, so many of them accompanied by "the baby" that one looked down on a sea of quiet baby faces fast asleep.[23] In the play, a fantastic melodrama called *May Morning, or The Mystery of 1715 and the Murder!,* the actors ranted through a plot of the wildest improbability. "I ster-ruck him down, and fel-ed in er-orror!" exclaims a repentant assassin, and continues, "I have liveder as a beggar—a roader-sider vaigerant, but no ker-rime since then has stained these hands!" Learning of another murderous scheme, "What! more bel-ood!" he cries, and falls flat.[24]

Dickens has (and so does the reader) a good deal of fun with these absurdities, but his point is that "Joe Whelks" must have entertainment, and that, although such plays might easily be improved, even they are better than if he were to have no training for his imagination and his sympathies at all. People "formed *entirely* in their hours of leisure by Polytechnic Institutes would be an uncomfortable community."[25] A young man whose boyhood had been passed exclusively among cranks and cogwheels would not be likely to respond with much feeling to an appeal in behalf of sufferings he had never experienced. But happily, there is "a range of imagination in most of us, which no amount of steam-engines will satisfy . . ." Joe Whelks "is not much of a reader, has no great store of books, no very commodious room to read in, no very decided inclination to read, and no power at all of presenting vividly to his mind's eye what he reads about." But in the theater he follows a story with rapt attention, and its portrayals of good and evil strike home to him. That is why, Dickens insists, the popular theater is of tremendous importance.[26]

From the start *Household Words* hit the mark it was aimed at; one hundred thousand copies of the first number are reported to have been sold.[27] Nevertheless, elated though he was, Dickens did not feel quite satisfied as he looked over the plan of the second number. It needed some touch of deeper and gentler emotion than anything in it thus far. Impelled by this feeling, he wrote "A Child's Dream of a Star," with its memories of Chatham and St. Mary's Church and himself and Fanny when they were small.[28] "And here's a man for you!" he jokingly told William Bradbury. ". . . The amazing undersigned feels a little uncomfortable at the want of Household tenderness . . . So he puts away Copperfield at which he has been working like a Steam Engine—writes (he thinks) exactly the kind of thing to supply the deficiency—and sends it off, by this post, to Forster! What an amazing man!" [29]

The second and third numbers maintained the level of the first. Horne's "True Story of a Coal-Fire" described the formation of coal from prehistoric forests, its extraction from the mines, and the hideous working conditions of the men, women, and children who worked them. "Heathen and Christian Burial" contrasted the crowded and unsanitary graveyards of London with the burial customs of other times and nations.[30] In "The Troubled Water Question" Wills used the facts provided by Henry Austin to attack the excessive charges and the dirty water of the monopolies and the consequent lack of a decent water supply for the poor.[30a] An article on the lucifer match pointed out its cheapness and efficiency in comparison with the old-fashioned tinderbox. "Short Cuts Across the Globe" advocated building canals across Panama and the Isthmus of Suez.[31]

The third number also announced the inauguration of a monthly supplement at the same price as the magazine itself, *The Household Narrative of Current Events*.[32] Although handled by John Dickens, this publication permitted him no Micawberian flights of eloquence. It presented without editorial comment a skillfully condensed summary of all important news, under the main headings of Parliament and Politics, Law and Crime, Accident and Disaster, Social, Sanitary, and Municipal Progress, Obituaries, Colonies and Dependencies, Foreign Events, Commercial Record, Stocks and Shares, and Emigration Figures.[33] A marked innovation, *The Household Narrative* was in essence identical with the modern news magazine, which it anticipated by almost one hundred years.

Dickens maintained a vigorous, a dictatorial control over every detail in both publications. His hand was everywhere, supplying titles, criticizing stories, eliminating fuzzy or pretentious verbiage, rewriting passages and injecting color, tightening structure, sharpening clarity, cutting out dull patches. "I wonder," he wrote Wills, "you think 'A Night with the Detective Police' would do for a title! After all those nights with Burns and the Industrious Fleas, and Heaven knows what else!! I don't think there could be a worse one within the range of the human understanding." [34] Mrs. Gaskell's "The Heart of John Middleton," he commented, was very good, but the girl crippled by a stone hitting her in the back was going to remind readers of other victims of accident in her stories, "the girl who fell down at the Well, and the child who tumbled down stairs. I wish to Heaven her people would keep a little firmer on their legs!" [35] Harriet Martineau's "The Sickness and Health of the People of Bleaburn" was "heavy"; [36] and the end of her story "The Home of Woodruffe the Gardener" was long-winded. "I have cut Woodruffe as scientifically as I can, and I don't think Miss Martineau would exactly know where." [37] Sometimes, having all these tasks to perform in addition to his own writing almost overwhelmed him. "I really can't *promise* to be comic," he replied to a request from Wills for a humorous piece or two. "As to *two* comic articles, or two any sort of articles out of me, that's the intensest extreme of nogoism." [38]

In May we find Dickens writing to Faraday, the famous scientist, and suggesting that articles based on his "lectures on the breakfast-table" and those "addressed last year, to children" would be exceedingly beneficial to the public. "May I ask you whether it would be agreeable to you, and, if so, whether you would favour me with the loan of your notes of those lectures for perusal." [39] Faraday replied graciously, putting the notes at Dickens's disposal. "I really cannot tell you," Dickens responded, "how very sensible I am of your great kindness or what an honour I feel it to be to have interested you in my books.

"I think I may be able to do something with the candle: but I would not touch it, or have it touched, unless it can be relighted with something of the beautiful simplicity and clearness of which I see the traces in your notes." [40]

Household Words for August 3rd carried an article called "The Chemistry of a Candle," in which a young boy who has attended one of the lectures outlines to his family all that he has learned on the subject.[41] Later in the year, "The Laboratory in the Chest" and "The Mysteries of a Tea-Kettle" are probably derived, at least in part, from the same source.[42] Throughout the whole long course of the publication, in fact, there is a constant stream of articles on science and invention, "The Planet-Watchers of Greenwich," "A Shilling's Worth of Science," "Greenwich Weather-Wisdom," "The Fire-Annihilator" (a new chemical fire-extinguisher), "Ballooning," "India

Rubber," "The Stereoscope," "The Power Loom," "Decimal Measures," "Some Account of Chloroform," "Electric Light," and many others.[43]

* * * * *

With the able lieutenancy of Wills, *Household Words* was soon running so efficiently that Dickens felt free in June to run over to Paris with Maclise for ten days' vacation. In spite of a frightful hot spell, they went to the theater with Régnier, dined with Sir Joseph Olliffe, physician to the British Embassy, called on Lord Normanby at the Embassy, and visited broken-down old John Poole (to whom Dickens was still regularly doling out money raised in the benefit performances) in his fifth-floor hovel in the Rue Neuve Luxembourg.[44] "Poole is staggering around like a bad automaton," Dickens reported to Wills, "and the English people are perpetually squeezing themselves into courtyards, doorways, blind alleys, closed edifices, and other places where they have no sort of business. The French people, as usual, are making as much noise as possible about everything . . ." And, probably thinking of the repressions by which Louis Napoleon was transforming himself into a dictator, Dickens added: "They made a mighty hullabaloo at the Theatre last night, when Brutus (the play was Lucretia) declaimed about Liberty." [45]

Even in the appalling heat, however, Dickens sent Wills directions about *Household Words* and toiled through an article for one of the next month's numbers. "I am writing at this moment with nothing on but a shirt and pair of white trousers, and have been sitting four hours at this paper, but am as faint with the heat as if I had been at some tremendous gymnastics. And yet we had a thunderstorm last night!" [46]

On his return to England, Dickens was shocked by the fatal accident in which Sir Robert Peel was thrown by his horse. Since Peel's display of courage and statesmanship in the abolition of the Corn Laws in 1846, Dickens's respect for him had been steadily rising. "I am in a very despondent state of mind," he wrote Mrs. Watson, "over Peel's death. He was a man of merit who could ill be spared from the Great Dust Heap down at Westminster. When I think of the joy of the D'Israelis, Richmonds, and other impostors and Humbugs, I think of flying to Australia and taking to the Bush." [47]

Throughout the effort and excitement of finishing *David Copper-*

field, he continued to deal with constant demands from *Household Words.* An article attacking the dirt and cruelty of the Smithfield cattle market had aroused scandalized comment; Dickens planned a return to the attack.[48] He corrected proofs, wrote some half-dozen further pieces used during the next few months, read contributions. "I think the Bank Note *very good indeed.* D? the Hippopotamus. D? Swinging the Ship." [49]

Besides keeping a sharp watch on the contributors, Dickens sometimes had to deal with friction in the office. Wills felt that Horne was not pulling his weight. He pointed out that he himself had too many duties to make up for Horne's negligence, and estimated that in consequence every article Horne wrote cost the publication some £8 out of a weekly budget for contributions averaging £16.[50] Dickens replied that he thought highly of Horne's abilities, had always found him willing to work, and had no intention of changing his engagement. He would, however, pass on Wills's criticisms.[51] Horne professed himself willing to help in any desired way, and remained in his post.[52] In the following year, when Wills returned to the charge, Horne offered to resign. In 1852 he went to Australia,[53] from whence he continued as a contributor at intervals.

From the middle of August to the end of October Dickens's children were with Georgina at Fort House, Broadstairs, a brick dwelling on the cliff above the bay. Kate, however, who was again in what Dickens called "an anti-Malthusian state," [54] remained in Devonshire Terrace until some weeks after the child was born, and Dickens himself constantly shuttled back and forth between the two places. Signing himself "Wilkins Micawber," he wrote Forster on August 15th, "Mrs. Micawber is still, I regret to say, in statu quo." [55] The next day, however, a baby girl was born, whom they named Dora Annie.[56] As soon as it was clear that Kate was making a good recovery, Dickens left her in charge of her mother and went down to see the children and work on his book. "I have still Dora to kill—I mean the Copperfield's Dora—" [57]

From the sea he wrote Kate news of the children and some of the guests at Fort House, although he saw her each time he went up to London.[58] "The Spectre in great glory." (This was three-year-old Sydney, whom Dickens had nicknamed the Ocean Spectre, because of a strange, faraway look in his eyes, as if he saw some phantom out at sea.) "A fresh wind blowing, and nearly blowing him off his legs in the garden—His hair all over his face—his hat nowhere in particular—and he lugging a seat about—equal in weight, I should think, to six legs of mutton." [59] "Forster was in a tip top state of amiability, but I think I never heard him *half so loud* (!) He really, after the heat of the walk, so disordered me that by no process I could possibly try, could I get to sleep afterwards." [60]

On September 6th Dickens brought Kate down to Broadstairs.[61] From there he continued to supervise *Household Words* with an eagle eye. He approved an article on the "Steam Plough," by Horne, emphasizing the increase that such devices of machine farming would achieve in the land brought under cultivation.[62] Another dealt with the scientific measurement of the height attained by Atlantic waves in a storm.[63] An entire series, "The Doom of English Wills," written by Dickens in collaboration with Wills, castigated the dirty, dilapidated, and disorderly way in which ecclesiastical records were kept, moldering away in damp and crowded depositories, almost deliberately inaccessible to the public, while their guardians drew salaries as high as £7,000 for letting them decay.[64]

At Broadstairs there were almost daily swims and jollity with a constant succession of guests. During one time, when Horne and Wills and their wives had rooms in Fort House, Frank Stone and Augustus Egg overflowed into a supplementary cottage, and Dickens invited Thomas Beard to join them.[65] "Your continued absence from the Stairs," he wrote, "occasions great surprise and consternation. Come, and all will be forgiven. September is a fine month. October also. Why do you try the feelings of your friends by prolonged absence?" [66]

Frederick Dickens was still trying to extort financial aid from his brother. He had at last married Anna Weller [67] and was tangled deep in debt. Perhaps, if Dickens wouldn't lend him money, he would lend his name. "It gives me extraordinary pain to refuse you anything," Dickens replied, "but I cannot make up my mind to be security for the performance of so extensive a contract. I am uneasy in the lightest thought of bequeathing such an obligation to those of these nine children who may outlive me, if I bequeath anything. . . . I cannot undertake it." [68] Subsequently, however, he may have weakened: "My dear Fred," we find him writing, "What is the nature of the Security that I should be required to give . . . ." [69]

With the end of October and the completion of *David Copperfield*, the pressure of Dickens's labors slackened. But he had forestalled any danger of gloomy letdown from having too little to do by arranging another whirl of amateur theatricals, first with Bulwer Lytton at his estate of Knebworth, and second with the Watsons at Rockingham Castle.[70] And of course the endless round of editorial work kept on. "This proof of Morley's . . . will require to be very carefully looked to. I had better go over it myself." (This was "Mr. Bendigo Buster on Our National Defenses Against Education," an ironical parody of the arguments of those who opposed state support of education out of fear that it would lead to "centralization." The name of the imaginary speaker is modeled on "The Great Bendigo," a well-known prize-fighter of the day.) "I can't make out," Dickens continued, "whether he means Mr. Buster to be actually a prize-fighter, or . . . a gentleman with prize-fighting tastes. I have adopted the latter hypothesis, as involving less inconsistency and incongruity." [71]

* * * * *

From this time on until the close of his life Dickens's activities as an editor were unceasing. His vigilance never slackened. He read, rejected, accepted, rewrote. Though none of the articles were signed, the signature of his style was so obvious that readers often imagined the entire magazine to be written by Dickens. (Sometimes, in fact, they were not far from the truth—John Hollingshead says that in 1854 Dickens read nine hundred unsolicited contributions and used eleven after entirely rewriting them.[72]) No matter where he was—in Broadstairs, Paris, Boulogne, Italy, America—packets of manuscripts and proofs constantly traveled back and forth between him and the offices at Wellington Street, accompanied by letters to Wills containing reams of advice. "Keep Household Words imaginative," he reiterated again and again.[73] "I have been looking over the back Numbers. Wherever they fail, it is in wanting elegance of fancy. They lapse too much into a dreary, arithmetical, Cocker-cum-Walkingame dustyness that is powerfully depressing." [74] "Brighten it, brighten it, brighten it!" [75]

He tossed off new ideas for pieces, discovered new writers. The young George Meredith had poems in *Household Words*. Wilkie Collins rode to fame there. A group known as "Dickens's young men" made their start in literature or journalism through his encouragement: George Augustus Sala, Edmund Yates, James Payn, Percy Fitzgerald. Other contributors included Wilkie Collins's gifted brother (who became Dickens's son-in-law) Charles Allston Collins, Georgiana Craik (Mrs. Mulock), William Hepworth Dixon, James Hannay, William and Mary Howitt, Charles Knight, Elizabeth Lynn (later Mrs. Lynn Linton), Sheridan Le Fanu, Charles Mackay, Coventry Patmore, Adelaide Anne Procter, William Moy Thomas, and Chauncey Hare Townshend. Dickens was among the first to recognize the genius of George Eliot, although he tried in vain to persuade her to write a serial for him. Among the authors of already established reputations who appeared in his pages were Charles Lever, Bulwer Lytton, Charles Reade, and Thomas Adolphus Trollope.[76]

The range of subject matter in the pages of *Household Words* is fascinating and extraordinary. The informational articles alone exhibit the widest variety. Here is an almost random selection: a description of San Francisco during the Gold Rush, the savings to litigants effected by the Small Claims Courts, the work of John Hullah (Dickens's old friend) in providing free classes in choral singing to the poor, the operation of a Paris newspaper, the banking rooms, treasure vaults, and banknote engraving at the Bank of England, the hunting of seals and whales, the use of ice for preserving food and making cool drinks and desserts, the industrial exploitation of the great dust-heaps formed from the refuse of London, the possibility of crossing the English Channel either by a tunnel or by an enormous bridge arching between a series of artificial islands! [77]

Brief biographical articles, taken almost equally at random, include Sydney Smith, Angelica Kauffmann the artist, Peter the Great, Fanny Burney, the piano manufacturer Pierre Érard, the two poisoners Mme. Ursinus and the Marquise de Brinvilliers, Abelard and Héloise, William Cobbett, Handel, Napoleon, Robert Burns, Dr. Johnson, Philip Sidney and Fulke Greville, Lesage, the author of *Gil Blas*, and the philosopher Pierre Ramus. There were literary articles, among others, on Pepys's *Diary*, Margaret Fuller, *Beowulf*, Hazlitt's works, the poems of Caedmon, Leigh Hunt's stories in verse, *Hamlet*, the *Golden Ass* of Apuleius, Robert Herrick, Ebenezer Elliott, the "Corn-Law Rhymer," Edmund Waller, Carlyle's *Frederick the Great*, the plays of Lope de Vega, the Celtic bard Oisin, and a warmly appreciative

review of Turgenev's beautiful *Sportsman's Sketches* in its first English translation. Throughout, there is a fusion of freshness and accuracy, neither an archeological dustiness nor a narrow concentration
on the merely contemporary.[78]

The most characteristic feature of *Household Words*, however, is
its treatment of current problems. Hardly a week goes by in which it is
not attacking some abuse. It consistently opposes racial, national, religious, and class prejudices. It crusades against illiteracy, and in favor
of government aid for public education and free elementary and industrial schools for the poor. It crusades for proper sewage disposal, cheap
and unlimited water supply, and the regulation of industries vital to
health. It demands the replacement of slums by decent housing for
the poor, pleads for the establishment of playgrounds for children, and
advocates systematic municipal planning. It supports thoughtful
prison reform but protests against coddling criminals. Devote half
the sums spent on jails, it argues, to improving the surroundings and
training the capacities of the innocent, and you won't have to exert
so much effort in a largely unsuccessful attempt to reform the guilty.
It insists that industrialists must not be allowed to mutilate and kill
their laborers in order to save the cost of preventing accidents. It scandalously affirms that workingmen have the right to organize into
unions, and calls upon the working class to use its power to turn "the
Indifferents and Incapables" out of Downing Street and Westminster
and force the government to remedy the ills from which poor men
suffer.[79]

Illustration of more than a few of these themes would run to too
great length, but from the beginning to the close of its career *Household Words* never ceased repeating them. It was especially emphatic
on the importance of education. "The Schoolmaster at Home and
Abroad" points out that in "the whole of northern Europe" one child
"to every 2¼ of the population" received "the rudiments of knowledge; while in England there is only one such pupil to every *fourteen*
inhabitants." [80] "The Devil's Acre" lauds the work of the Ragged
Schools and their more advanced industrial counterparts in the slum
districts of London, especially in reforming young criminals and teaching them a trade.[81] "Infant Gardens" praises the work of Froebel and
those of his disciples who started the first English kindergartens.[82]
"New Life and Old Learning" satirically notes that the only conces-

sion to the changing times Oxford has made in its curriculum is to permit the study of modern history—up to the year 1790 but not beyond.[83] "Minerva by Gaslight" hails the achievements of the Working Men's College in Great Ormond Street, and the recent inauguration of evening session classes by King's College in the University of London.[84]

Articles on sanitary reform and slum clearance are no less numerous. Statistical analyses demonstrate that the most crowded slums have the highest mortality rates. "Health by Act of Parliament," arguing for London's inclusion within the Public Health Act, quotes figures to prove that the monetary loss in the metropolis caused during the year 1848 by typhus alone was £440,000. "This cold-blooded way of putting the really appalling state of the case," it adds, "is, alas! the only successful mode of appealing to . . . John Bull . . . His heart is only reached by his pocket, except when put in a state of alarm. Cry, 'Cholera!' or any other frightful conjuration, and he bestirs himself." [85] Cholera, however, is only the most spectacular of many preventable diseases caused by polluted sewers, bad or insufficient water, and crowded, dirty houses. "A Home Question," "Commission and Omission," [86] and countless other articles gird repeatedly at the incompetence and negligence of the public bodies supposed to deal with these matters.

Until these "epoch-making articles appeared in *Household Words*," says W. W. Crotch, "housing reform had been scarcely heard of." [87] But Dickens missed no chance to reinforce them by constant blasts of all kinds. The state of public health in London, he said in a speech before the Metropolitan Sanitary Association in 1850, was "the tragedy of *Hamlet* with nothing in it but the gravedigger." Opposition to improvement came from two main classes: landlords, clamorous to protect their pockets, and weak-minded gentlemen who talked of self-government and thought what happened in the next parish none of their business. But such a slum as Jacob's Island could be made decent at a weekly cost of less than two glasses of gin for each inhabitant. As for self-government, let them talk of that when any court or street could keep its diseases within its own bounds.[88]

A few nights later Sir Peter Laurie, the London alderman Dickens had satirized in *The Chimes*, told a public meeting that Jacob's Island "ONLY existed" in the pages of *Oliver Twist*. Dickens fell

upon him savagely in the preface to a new edition of that book. By
Sir Peter's logic, he said, "When Fielding described Newgate," it
"ceased to exist"; "when Smollett took Roderick Random to Bath,
that city instantly sank into the earth"; and "an ancient place called
Windsor was entirely destroyed in the reign of Queen Elizabeth by
two Merry Wives of that town, acting under the direction of a person
of the name of Shakespeare." But on reflection was it not equally
clear, since Sir Peter Laurie had once been described in a book too,
"that there CAN be no such man!" [89]

The following year Dickens addressed the Metropolitan Sanitary
Association again. That the horrors of filth and disease knew no boundaries was as certain, he said, as "that the air from Gin Lane will be
carried by an easterly wind into Mayfair, or that the furious pestilence
raging in St. Giles no mortal list of lady patronesses can keep out of
Almack's." [90] This was why neither education nor religion could do
anything useful for the poor until the way was prepared by cleanliness
and decency. "Give them a glimpse of heaven through a little of its
light and air; give them water; help them to be clean . . ." And let
people cease to be intimidated from clearing up these evils by the use
of terrifying words like "centralization." [91]

It would be hard to exaggerate the power of Dickens's aid to the
pioneers in sanitation and housing. "Lord Shaftesbury, and the Association for Improving the Dwellings of the Poor," Crotch summarizes,
"were, like the first Housing Acts, the outward and visible signs of his
energies," and the housing developments fostered by these and by
other public-spirited foundations erected "not only homes for the
people, but monuments to their champion . . ." [92]

Fierce even beyond these attacks on slums and the neglect of public
health, however, was the campaign *Household Words* carried on
against factory accidents. Since 1844 there had been a law that dangerous machines must be fenced in, but it had been very largely
evaded or ignored. "Ground in the Mill" detailed dozens of hideous
deaths and mutilations: boys caught in a piece of belting and smashed
a hundred and twenty times a minute against the ceiling, men wedged
in a shaft getting battered to pulp, their lungs broken, their heads
scalped, their skulls smashed. There were two thousand of these victims killed or mutilated by machinery in a half-year, [93] "Fencing with
Humanity" reported, and told of the formation of a Manufacturers'

Association to defy the law and pay the fines of its members if they were convicted. Ten pounds was the penalty in one such case: "When the mill-owner sets that price on his workman's brains," the article said grimly, "who can wonder if the workman sets a price still lower on his master's heart!" [94] The accidents amounted to fewer than 6/10 per cent, argued the factory owners, and the deaths to only 42 a year. "Death's Ciphering-Book" suggested that if percentages had anything to do with the moral issues, one might as well forgo punishing burglary and murder, of which the percentages were far smaller in a population of twenty-one million.[95]

The viewpoint dominating all these articles, and hundreds of others on scores of additional subjects, represented an uncompromising humanitarian radicalism in almost every field they touched upon, social, political, and economic. Week after week Dickens or his henchmen hammered away, wielding every conceivable weapon: reasoned argument, cajolery, facts and figures, humor, insinuation, irony, parable and allegory, sarcasm, repetition, angry diatribe. In total the contents of *Household Words* are a striking testimony to the enlightenment of Dickens's policy on most of the problems of nineteenth-century society and the breadth of his interests. But more than that, they are a proof of his editorial skill as well. For unlike the liberal-radical magazines of our own day, *Household Words* was not limited to a small specialized group of intellectuals but had a huge and steadily growing audience ranging in both directions from the middle and upper middle classes.

It was probably this extraordinary achievement that led Lord Northcliffe to declare Dickens the greatest magazine editor either of his own or any other age.[96] Although unmatched, however, the achievement is not mysterious: its secret lies in the pattern of broad appeal to which almost every number of *Household Words* conforms—a pattern that explains how Dickens could persuade his readers to swallow so much radicalism along with their entertainment. For although *Household Words* fought on every issue its conductor had at heart, and never pulled its punches, it did not limit itself to crusading. Among the six to nine items filling its twenty-four pages, there were never more than two or three devoted to reform causes; usually there was only one. The tone might be indignant, but never embittered.

Thus, in the very issue in which one article points out that the workhouse diet is worse than that of the criminal jail, another article gives a dream-vision of all the cruelties that darkened the "good old times." All the rest of the contents was entertainment, colorful information, humor, or sentiment. Great pains were taken to be vivid, great pains were taken to be clear. But, at the same time, the tone of *Household Words* was never patronizing. "Don't think," Dickens warned, "that it is necessary to write *down* to any part of our audience."

At last, with *Household Words*, Dickens had found the instrument toward which he had been groping, years back, in the opening, unsuccessful numbers of *Master Humphrey's Clock*. And in the intervening time, he had learned how to work with and at the same time control a group of collaborators as he had not been able to do on the *Daily News*. Both in its business and its editorial structure *Household Words* ideally met Dickens's long-felt need for a periodical in which he could say to his readers, profitably and without interference from anyone else, everything about all the subjects in the world that he was bursting to say.

CHAPTER EIGHT

Splendid Barnstorming

THE play, Dickens wrote Bulwer Lytton in July of 1850, "stirs my blood like a trumpet." [1] Lytton had invited the dramatic amateurs to be his guests at Knebworth—the Hertfordshire estate he had inherited from his mother—and play *Every Man in His Humour* before an audience of his county neighbors. But the combined labors of *Household Words* and *David Copperfield* compelled Dickens to defer the glorious idea until fall. Meanwhile, he promised, he would take counsel with Forster, and then "report myself to you touching Bobadil." Before the summer was over, their plans were being made.

Dickens and Bulwer Lytton had known each other, and been friendly though not intimate, for well over a decade. Edward Bulwer —he had not then taken the additional surname of Lytton—was in Parliament when Dickens was in the Gallery. Handsomely aquiline, auburn-curled, beringed and ornate of dress, he had been, together with D'Orsay and Disraeli, one of the glittering dandies emulated by the youthful Boz. Nine years Dickens's senior, and, until the triumph of *Pickwick*, the most popular novelist of the day, he might easily have been resentful, but he greeted his rival only with the heartiest praise. He was far less intimate with Dickens, however, than with Macready, who had successfully appeared in his *Richelieu* and *The Laly of Lyons*. "Without our friend," Bulwer told Dickens in grave modesty, the latter play "might have been a hideous failure." [2] And Dickens knew that he was not only generous in words. The number of unfortunate literary men he had helped more than justified Macready's tribute to him as the most warm-hearted and high-minded of men. [3]

Nevertheless, even in mid-career, Bulwer continued to be pursued by literary animosity. His birth, his hauteur, his dress, the high circles in which he moved, all aroused bitter sneers. The violent termination of his brief marriage and the half-insane slanders of his estranged wife Rosina were seized upon with snarling joy. And when, on his mother's death, he added her maiden name of Lytton to his own surname, malice could not contain its chortles at the grandiosity of calling one-self Sir Edward George Earle Lytton Bulwer Lytton. But he re-mained proudly silent, went on writing copiously and successfully, and collected stained glass and medieval armor. Now, at the age of forty-seven, his tastes were still exotic and luxurious. He smoked a chibouk and wore oriental dressing gowns no less rich than the splendors of his youth. Moving through the long library of Knebworth, with his premature slight stoop, grizzled reddish hair, and beaked nose above flaming whiskers, he looked, in his somber magnificence, strangely like a refined and elegant Fagin.

Out of Bulwer Lytton's proposal of a "Dramatic Festival" at Knebworth were to grow further plans that would bring him and Dickens into closer association and deepen their mutual esteem. At the moment, however, all Dickens thought of was the excitement of acting again. He suggested the end of October for the play and hoped the neighborhood of Knebworth could produce enough aspirants for dramatic laurels to fill the vacancies in their cast. "Do you know Mary Boyle, the Hon. Mary, daughter of the old Admiral?" he asked. She was one of the very best actresses he had ever seen. "I have acted with her in a country house in Northamptonshire, and am going to do so again, next November." If they could get her to play Mrs. Kitely, his "little sister-in-law"—Georgina—"would 'go on' for the second lady," and they could do without professional actresses.[4]

Dickens was exhilarated to learn that Miss Boyle could join them, and booked her also to play Lisette in *Animal Magnetism*, one of the farces given in 1848, at which he had seen people laugh until they "hung over the front of the boxes like ripe fruit." [5] This might also, Dickens thought, be included among their Rockingham theatricals later in the year. *My Grandmother*, suggested and rather pertina-ciously defended by Miss Boyle's brother, Captain Cavendish Boyle, Dickens insisted would never "go." Its jokes were hoary-headed when Old Parr was a baby and the dialogue gave one the feeling of "being rubbed down with a gigantic Baker's-rasp." Instead, Dickens proposed a piece called *Louison,* of which he admitted having only the vaguest memories, but which he was sure would be a success. "It may have been some anecdote of the French Revolution—I don't know—I think a pistol was fired in it—perhaps it was only a bell rung—I can't say. . . . I have a wild dream that in this mysterious piece (one scene, one act) somebody was hid somewhere on account of something." [6]

Early in October all these plans were deferred, the Knebworth performances until November 18th, 19th, and 20th, and the Rockingham theatricals until after Twelfth Night in the new year.[7] This simply gave more time for rehearsals, however, and furbishing up the costtumes. More serious was the loss of Miss Boyle, who was prevented from joining them by a death in her family, but to take her place Dickens got little Anne Romer, who had played the role of Mary in *Used Up.*[8] Rehearsals were held once more in Miss Kelly's theater in Soho.[9]

Almost at the outset, Kate, who had the part of Tib (a character who made four brief appearances and spoke a total of thirty lines), managed to fall through a trap door on the stage. Her ankle was so severely sprained that Mrs. Lemon took her place.[10] With the course of years, in fact, the clumsiness Dickens had noted in America and humorously exaggerated in Tilly Slowboy seemed to be growing more marked. Richard Horne, who had been at Broadstairs with the Dickenses during the summer and often dined with them at Devonshire Terrace, observed that bracelets would even slide off her arms and fall with a splash into her soup, while Dickens threw himself back in his chair laughing uproariously, his eyes streaming with mirth.[11] Kate's lack of physical control strongly suggests nervous disturbance and Dickens's laughter sounds like the hilarity with which we hide a secret irritation from ourselves. But in behavior Dickens was all solicitude, and when it was clear that Kate would still be unable to walk on the 18th he arranged that she be taken to Knebworth in a brougham so that she could at least make one of the audience.

The last rehearsal in town took place on the 14th of November.[12] "Ah, sir," said the master carpenter at Miss Kelly's, to whom Dickens explained some ideas he had about adapting *Used Up* to a small stage, "it's a universal observation in the profession, sir, that it was a great loss to the public when you took to writing books!"— "which," remarked Dickens, "I thought complimentary to Copper-

field." [13] The rehearsal was no sooner over than Dickens took the train
to Stevenage, the Knebworth railway connection. All week-end he
spent seeing to the final details of installing the theater, testing the
brilliance of the oil lamps ("without smell") which they had to use in
the absence of gas, and drilling his cast through the very dress rehearsal on Saturday night.[14]

The theater itself was a portable unit complete, some twenty feet
high, erected at one end of the double-storied great hall, leaving the
rest of its stone-floored expanse back to the entrance under the minstrel gallery for the seats of the guests.[15] Through one of the enormous
windows, hoisted over the window seat, had also been brought a huge
hybrid instrument called a "choremusicon," clad in "an immense
crimson silk waistcoat" and guaranteed to be "better than three musicians." [16]

For three nights the carriages of Bulwer Lytton's county friends
("Dukes, Duchesses, and the like," [17] Dickens said mischievously)
rolled into the great rectangular court with its gargoyle-surmounted
walls, and the guests trooped among his suits of armor, under his
stained-glass windows and the medieval tapestries hung on the dark-
paneled walls, and responded enthusiastically to the dramatic entertainment. "Everything," Dickens wrote Mrs. Watson, "has gone off in
a whirl of triumph, and fired the whole length and breadth of the
county of Hertfordshire . . ." Georgina, he added, had "covered herself with glory" as Mistress Bridget.[18]

Only one semicomic rift marred the amenity of the occasion. In
order to allow the curtain to go up at seven-thirty, dinner was at six,
and on the first night, after the performance, the host provided only
cake, biscuits, and wine for refreshments. For a group of actors raven-
ous from their exertions this was insufficient, and most of the cast
went to bed gnawed by hunger. Next morning they held a council.
Forster, blunt as usual, said they should ask for more to eat. Delmé
Radcliffe, one of the county men in the cast, was for bribing the cook.
Mark Lemon proposed getting supplies in the village and sneaking up
to a surreptitious supper in Jerrold's room at the top of the tower.
This schoolboyish suggestion carried the day, Fred Dickens and
Augustus Egg were sent for food, and that evening there was "a stifled
stampede" of actors smuggling glasses and mugs upstairs under their
costumes. Unhappily, Bulwer Lytton was told and felt solemnly an-

noyed until Dickens joked him out of it. On the next night, however, he served a sumptuous supper.[19]

Contact with Dickens and these three performances crystallized in Bulwer Lytton's mind a set of ideas that had long been amorphous there. He had pitied and sent anonymous help to more than one talented writer like poor Laman Blanchard, who had cut his throat in 1844 when the struggle to support a family by journalism proved too hard. And Dickens and his amateurs had collected large sums for the benefit of such literary veterans as Leigh Hunt, Sheridan Knowles, and John Poole. The first two of these were now receiving government pensions, but although such provisions did exist for the aid of writers and artists, they were inadequate, often political or capricious in origin, and even, on occasion, rather humiliating to their beneficiaries. There were able writers who had met with misfortunes, promising young writers who had not yet made their way, scholarly writers whose work could not expect a popular audience. Artists, too, experienced the same difficulties. What was needed for all these was something more dignified than the charity of private donations or government pension list and more flexible than a college lectureship, with its prescribed duties and academic qualifications.[20]

Could they not build, Bulwer Lytton suggested, an endowment which might combine these purposes with the bestowing of an honorable distinction? He himself would write a comedy all the earnings of which he would present to the endowment; Dickens's company would act this play throughout England for its benefit. With the eloquent fame of such a brilliant beginning, they might then make public appeal for additional contributions to the fund. For, said Bulwer Lytton, "This is a great power that has grown up about you, out of a winter-night's amusement, and do let us try to use it for the lasting service of our order." [21]

So the Guild of Literature and Art was born. As it matured in their minds it grew more ambitious. Bulwer Lytton would present the Guild with the use of a plot of land on his estate, where a group of neat cottages would be built, and in them would dwell rent-free a little fellowship of artists and men of letters chosen in accordance with the Guild's purposes. Over them would preside a Warden, with a house and £200 a year. Resident Members would receive £170 a year and nonresident Members £200 a year. These were to be men of established names.

Finally, there would be a number of Associates, young men of promise, with one-year grants of £100.[22] "I do devoutly believe," exclaimed Dickens, "that this plan carried, will entirely change the status of the literary man in England, and make a revolution in his position, which no Government, no power on earth but his own, could ever effect." [23]

*   *   *   *   *

His enthusiasm for the project was fired by efforts in which he was even then engaged to obtain further help for John Poole. The proceeds from his benefit had at last been exhausted, but Poole was so completely shattered in intellect that writing "the most ordinary sentence in a letter" had become "a work of infinite labor to him." "In the sunny time of the day, he puts a melancholy little hat on one side of his head, and, with a little stick under his arm, goes hitching himself about the Boulevards; but for any power he has of earning a livelihood he might as well be dead." [24]

Through Lord John Russell, Dickens obtained for him a small sum from the Queen's Bounty, but what he really needed, Dickens explained to Russell, was a pension. The last time Dickens had visited him was a cold dark day, with Dickens sitting by a tiny wood fire and Poole quivering nervously in bed, while a series of violent bumping noises sounded from the ceiling. Trembling beneath the bedclothes, Poole explained that a vaudeville troupe who did "the poses plastiques" were rehearsing in the attic overhead. "They—they begin—with Ajax defying the lightning—at daybreak. They—they—defy the lightning all day. I—I know I shall die, die here. They are my murderers." [25] Fortunately, the troupe soon had to flee their debts, but "I do not think," Dickens wrote Russell, "he would hold a small pension very long." On Christmas Eve, he received a reply announcing that Poole had been granted £100 a year, dating "from the end of June last." [26]

Happy in what he had accomplished for Poole, Dickens turned his attention now to the approaching theatricals in Northamptonshire. The portable theater used at Knebworth was too lofty for any of the ancient low-ceiled rooms of Rockingham Castle. He consequently suggested to Mrs. Watson that she rent scenery from Nathan, the "costume-maker" who dressed his company.[27] Presently Dickens found he had to explain to Mrs. Watson that a backdrop with a practicable door couldn't be put right against the wall of the room unless there was a room door in the same place: otherwise "the door of the room might as well be in Africa." [28] Finally, a special set was assembled under his direction, and adapted to the purpose.[29] After looking this over at Nathan's and finding it new-painted and elegant, Dickens decided he had better make a one-day trip to Northamptonshire to superintend its installation.[30]

There were also botherations about the cast. Was Captain Boyle playing or wasn't he? [31] And how about Mrs. Watson's brother, Captain Quin? [32] Mr. Watson himself would do wonderfully as the lawyer in *Used Up* (which they had decided to do instead of *Louison*), but Dickens had set his heart on giving *him* the pleasure of seeing the play.[33] If the Watsons' friend Mr. Stafford O'Brien was unable to take part, would they like him to get Mr. Lemon? [34] Finally, what *was* this confusion of a Mr. Stafford, a Mr. Stopford, and a Mr. Stafford O'Brien: were there two or three of them, and would Mrs. Watson clear up the muddle of their too similar names? [35]

Even when all these tangles were straightened out there was one last-minute oscillation. Dickens had suggested that Charley, who would be home from Eton, play the part of a little page—called a "tiger"—in *Used Up*, and on Mrs. Watson's agreement had him measured for his costume.[36] Then arrived word that Captain Quin might take the role.[37] On top of this came still another letter: let Charley take it. "As your letter is *decided*," Dickens replied, "the scaffolding shall be re-erected round Charley's boots (it has been taken down, and the workmen retired to their respective homes in various parts of England and Wales) and his dressing proceeded with. I have been very much pleased with him in the matter, as he never made the least demonstration of disappointment or mortification, and was perfectly contented to give in. (*Here I break off to go to Boxall.*) (*Here I return much exhausted.*)" [38]

These two parentheses refer to sittings for his portrait then being painted by Sir William Boxall. "As Boxall (with his head very much on one side and his spectacles on) danced backward from the canvas incessantly with great nimbleness, and returned, and made little digs at it with his pencil, with a horrible grin on his countenance, I augur," Dickens reported, "that he pleased himself this morning." [39] But the portrait seemed to Dickens himself to get worse and worse as the sittings went on, and finally he discontinued them. Sometimes, he said, the picture "was like Ben Caunt"—a very ugly prize-fighter—then like Greenacre—a murderer. "At last, by Jove, I found *I was growing like it!*—I thought it time to retire, and that picture will never be finished if it depends upon any more sittings from me." [40]

On the 7th of January, Dickens arrived at Rockingham, and after frenzies of preparation and rehearsal their program came off on the 15th: *A Day After the Wedding, Used Up,* and *Animal Magnetism.*[41] His burlesque love affair with Mary Boyle had reached the point where he was writing her, as he had Mrs. Colden years before, incoherent notes of misery and devotion. One of these, dated from "Loft over Stable," laments that "the call of honor stands between me and my rest—baulks my inclination—beckons me from happiness . . . (do you understand, my angel?)" Even with every apparent blessing, including "a domestic hearth," many things may be lacking for a man's happiness, "and he may be confoundedly miserable—As I am—Ever Affectionately my darling." [42] At Rockingham began the custom, whenever they were together, of Dickens's bestowing a chaste goodnight kiss on Mary's brow. Henceforth, using both her own name and the names of their roles in *Used Up,* she was his "dearest Mary" or "darling Meery" and he was her "Joe."

Kate assumed in the same play the small part of Lady Maria Clutterbuck—by this time, of course, her ankle was entirely healed—but we do not hear that she "covered herself with glory." Even Georgina, though she played again in *Animal Magnetism,* was quite forgotten. No other woman compared with Mary Boyle, enchanting in lemon muslin as Lisette and demure in pink as Mary.[43] Following the three plays, country dances lasted until far into the morning. Next day, after the hundred-and-twenty-mile railway journey to London, Dickens dined with the Russells, where Lady John Russell talked about Mrs. Watson with an affection that relieved his despondency at the visit being over.[44] "I am still feeble, and liable to sudden outbursts of causeless rage and demoniacal gloom, but I shall be better presently." [45]

Unlike his father, young Charley ended his holiday in great spirits. It was a wet night and a servant took him to the train for Eton. "Master Charles went off very gay, sir," he reported. "He found some young gen'lmen as was his friends in the train, sir." "Come," said Dickens, "I am glad of that. How many were there? Two or three?" "Oh dear, sir, there was a matter of forty, sir! All with their heads out o' the coach windows, sir, a-hallowing 'Dickens!' all over the station!" [46]

Meanwhile Bulwer Lytton had sent Dickens the first three acts of his comedy—a costume piece set in the reign of George II. It was *"most admirable,"* Dickens told him, "and *certain to go nobly."* He could already, in imagination, see his companions in the roles they would play. He himself would love to take the part of Sir Gilbert (probably Sir Geoffrey Thornside in the final version of the play). "Assumption has charms for me—I hardly know for how many wild reasons—so delightful, that I feel a loss of, oh! I can't say what exquisite foolery, when I lose a chance of being someone in voice, etc., not at all like myself." But he knew that in the central role of Lord Wilmot nobody else could hold the play together like himself. I think I could touch the gallant, generous, careless pretence, with the real man at the bottom of it, so as to take the audience with him from the first scene." Therefore he would forgo the other part, throw up his cap for Wilmot, and "devote myself to him, heart and head!" [47]

Dickens in fact almost completely surrendered himself to this project for close to a year. He did not even begin thinking about a new novel until August, when the London engagements of the play were concluded.[48] He did not begin writing it until the end of November.[49] There was always, of course, the unceasing round of supervising *Household Words*, week by week, on which he never relaxed. But that, for his superhuman energy, was almost routine. Discovering a new writer of ability like George Augustus Sala was all in the day's work.[50] The writing of his own contributions he wedged into any odd hour or two. His *Child's History of England*, beginning to appear irregularly in the magazine from January 25th on, was a compilation derived from Keightley's *History*, which he dictated to Georgina in spare moments.[51] But all his most earnest efforts, for almost a full year, and much time for another nine months beyond that, were dominated by working for the Guild of Literature and Art.

Bulwer's play, it was agreed, they would try to get off to a great start, by inviting the Queen and Prince Albert to the first performance. This should be, Dickens suggested, about three weeks before the opening on May 1st of the Great Exhibition in Hyde Park, so that it might be "the town talk before the country people and foreigners come." He proposed constructing a special stage that could be erected at first in the Hanover Square Rooms, and then taken down and put up wherever they might play in the provinces; the set he had had made for Rockingham had been "a sort of model" of what he had in mind and a test of its "working powers." [52]

Macready was to read the completed play to the assembled company at Forster's on February 19th.[53] In the course of the month, shivering in furs, Dickens let Joseph Paxton show him and W. P. Frith through the vast and icy exhibition hall, not yet completely enclosed in glass; [54] and then he made his escape to Paris, where it was frosty but fine, for a five-day holiday with Leech and Spencer Lyttleton, a man who was "a capital companion," [55] "the jolliest of the jolly," and "up to anything." [56] Returning to London, he saw Macready's last stage appearance, in Macbeth at Drury Lane, and arranged the farewell dinner at the London Tavern.[57]

Bent and feeble, the famous Charles Kemble, who had acted with Mrs. Siddons, his still more famous sister, came to the dinner to do Macready honor, and was greeted with a deafening applause and waving of glasses, napkins, and decanters. Macready spoke haltingly, too deeply moved to notice when he said his heart was fuller than his glass that he held an empty glass.[58] Dickens spoke well, but what he felt most profoundly he wrote in a letter: "I have told you sometimes, my much-loved friend, how, when I was a mere boy, I was one of your faithful and devoted adherents in the pit . . . No light portion of my life arose before me when the quiet vision to which I am beholden, in I don't know how great a degree, or for how much—who does?—faded so nobly from my bodily eyes last night." [59]

After further deliberations with Bulwer Lytton about their play, Dickens determined on a bold stroke. He asked the Duke of Devonshire—whom he knew but slightly beyond his reputation as a patron of artists and man of letters—for permission to give its first performance, before Her Majesty and the Court, in Devonshire House, His Grace's palatial residence on Piccadilly.[60] Within two hours the Duke replied: "My services, my house, and my subscription will be at your orders. And I beg you to let me see you before long, not merely to converse upon this subject, but because I have long had the greatest wish to improve our acquaintance, which has, as yet, been only one of crowded rooms." [61] "This," Dickens commented, "is quite princely, I think, and will push us along as brilliantly as heart could desire." [62]

Dickens was soon in those turmoils of preparation that he loved. Bulwer's comedy, now entitled *Not So Bad as We Seem* ("but a great deal worse than we ought to be," quipped Douglas Jerrold [63]), had been read before its prospective cast. Dickens had offered Wills a small part as a valet to Lord Wilmot, but Wills felt that it might conflict with his duties on *Household Words*,[64] and Dickens therefore suggested to Augustus Egg that a young writer named Wilkie Collins might take it. "He would have an opportunity of dressing your humble servant—frothing some chocolate with an absolute milling-machine that must be revived for the purpose— . . . and dispatching other similar 'business' dear to actors." [65] Shortly after Collins's acceptance, rehearsals were under way at Covent Garden, beginning on March 18th, and continuing every Monday and Tuesday thereafter.[66]

Frank Stone, Dickens complained, was "a Millstone—I shall have to go over that part with him (out of rehearsal) at least fifty times— around my neck." [67] Horne was "the very worst actor that the world ever saw, and . . . must not on any account, be entrusted with more words than he has already." Forster was "going a little wrong" and Lemon was making his part "too farcical." [68] But gradually everyone did better. Told that he was "too loud and violent," Forster "subdued himself with the most admirable pains, and improved the part a thousand per cent." Stone surprised Dickens by playing "inexpressibly better than I should have supposed possible in him"; he wound up by making his character of the Duke of Middlesex "the best man in the play." "They are all most heartily anxious and earnest, and, upon the least hitch, will do the same thing twenty times over." [69]

In addition to drilling his company five hours a night two nights a week, Dickens was in a "maze of bewilderment . . . with carpenters, painters, tailors, machinists, and others." [70] His "ingenious theatre" was under construction. David Roberts and other well-known painters, including Stanfield, Grieve, Telbin, Pitt, and Absolon, had been asked to donate scenery: the Mall, a distressed poet's garret, a sinister alley called Deadman's Lane, an open space near the Thames.[71] These, and the furniture, were "rapidly advancing towards completion, and will be beautiful. The dresses are a perfect blaze of colour, and there is not a pocket-flap or a scrap of lace that has not been made according to Egg's drawings to the quarter of an inch. Every wig has been made from an old print or picture. From the Duke's snuff-box to Will's Coffee-house, you will find everything in perfect truth and keeping." [72]

The Queen had replied to Dickens's invitation by appointing the evening of April 30th for the performance, but events in his own family compelled Dickens to postpone it.[73] Early in February the baby daughter, Dora Annie, had been so gravely ill with congestion of the brain that they had hastily had her baptized at once.[74] Then, a month later, Kate became seriously unwell, with "a tendency of blood to the head," "giddiness and dimness of sight," and "an alarming confusion and nervousness." [75] Southwood Smith advised placing her under medical care at Great Malvern and subjecting her to "a rigorous discipline of exercise, air, and cold water." [76]

As Dickens reflected on it now, it seemed to him that he could detect signs of this trouble in Kate as far as three or four years back.[77] He wrote Dr. James Wilson, to whom it was recommended that he entrust her, that her case was "a nervous one," and that when they met in person he would "state what Dr. Southwood Smith has particularly requested me to mention to you as rendering great caution necessary." Instead of living in Dr. Wilson's house, for reasons "founded on my knowledge of her" she would stay in some cheerful cottage in the neighborhood.[78] Dr. Wilson replied by urging that she stay in his house after all.[79] But Dickens refused emphatically; he was sure, he said, that she could not possibly form a favorable impression of Malvern if she were in any house but her own.[80] This belief he based on "what I have lately observed when we have been staying in the country houses even of intimate friends." [81] The words clearly refer to their recent visits to Knebworth and Rockingham, and unmistakably hint as much of psychological disturbance as they do of physical illness.

Oscillating between London and Malvern, Dickens was then shocked to receive word that his father was mortally ill.[82] His old urinary complaint, mentioned a quarter of a century ago in applying for retirement from the Navy Pay Office, he had ignored and neglected ever since. His family knew nothing of his condition until inflammation of the bladder brought on mortification and delirium. Dickens was hastily summoned to his bedside in Keppel Street.[83] A surgeon "was called in, who instantly performed (without chloroform) the most terrible operation known in surgery, as the only chance of saving him. He bore it with astonishing fortitude, and I saw him directly afterwards—his room, a slaughter house of blood." [84]

The next day, in the midst of a dreary and incessant rain, Dickens wrote Kate again. "My father slept well last night, and is as well this morning . . . as anyone in such a state, so cut and slashed, can be." [85] But in spite of being "wonderfully cheerful and strong-hearted," John Dickens grew weaker and weaker. On March 31st, "My poor father died this morning," Dickens wrote Forster, "at five and twenty minutes to six. . . . He began to sink at about noon yesterday, and never rallied afterwards." Dickens arrived at Keppel Street shortly after eleven that night, but by then his father did not know him or anyone. "I remained there until he died—O so quietly." [86] As he looked on his father's dead face, what were the grandiloquence, the improvident borrowings, the extravagance, the irresponsibility, the disappearances to escape the bailiff? He could remember only the hard work, the irrepressible gusto and love of living, the old companionship of walks to Gad's Hill, the loving pride in a small boy's singing, the tenderness that throughout many a night had nursed a sick child.[86a]

Barely a fortnight later fell another blow. On the 14th of April Dickens came from Malvern to London to preside at the dinner of the General Theatrical Fund. He spent part of the afternoon in Devonshire Terrace playing with little Dora Annie, who had recovered from her illness and was in happy spirits. Shortly before Dickens rose to speak, Forster was summoned out of the room. It was a message that the child had suddenly died in convulsions. Returning to the banquet room, Forster painfully decided to let Dickens give his speech before telling him what had happened.[87] In an agony, he heard Dickens saying how often the actor was obliged to come from "scenes of sickness, of suffering, ay, even of death itself," to play his part.[88] At the end of the speech, Forster and Lemon broke the news. Dickens hurried home, arranged with Forster to bring Kate back from Malvern, and spent the rest of the night beside his child's body with Lemon. "I have not forgotten (and never shall forget)," he said, "who sat up with me one night when a little place in my home was left empty." [89]

In Kate's already upset state, it was necessary to deal with her very thoughtfully. Dickens provided Forster with a letter that did not tell the whole truth, but prepared for her hearing it when she arrived

home: "Now observe. You must read this letter, very slowly and carefully," it began. "If you have hurried on thus far without quite understanding (apprehending some bad news), I rely on your turning back,
and reading again.

"Little Dora, without being in the least pain, is suddenly stricken
ill. She awoke out of a sleep, and was seen, in one moment, to be
very ill. Mind! I will not deceive you. I think her *very* ill.

"There is nothing in her appearance but perfect rest. You would
suppose her quietly asleep. . . . I do not—why should I say I do, to
you my dear!—I do not think her recovery at all likely."

She would not like to be away, the letter continued, and he would
not keep her away. Forster would bring her home. But he begged her
to be composed and remember their other children. Finally, "if—*if*—
when you come, I should even have to say to you 'our little baby is
dead,' you are to do your duty to the rest, and to shew yourself worthy
of the great trust you hold in them." [90]

The shock of this bereavement compelled Dickens to postpone rehearsals and take a few days' rest. A week's rehearsals had already been
lost at the time his father died, when he had been unable to sleep,
taken long night walks through the slums, and distracted the slow
hours of one sleepless night observing the routine of the Bow Street
Station House.[91] Consequently he was obliged to ask the Queen to
set a later date for the performance of the play, and Her Majesty deferred it to May 16th.[92]

Kate was so overwhelmed with grief that she wanted only to get
away as soon as possible. Dickens rented Fort House in Broadstairs
from the middle of May and decided to sublet Devonshire Terrace
until September,[93] when his twelve-year lease would expire. He had for
some time been feeling that they needed a larger house, and had even
made an offer on one place. Now he tried to distract Kate by taking
her out under various pretenses, including that of inspecting others
they might consider.[94] Gradually they resigned themselves to the loss
of the child, "our poor little pet," Dickens called her.[95] After a time
he was able to write, "I am quite happy again, but I have undergone
a great deal." [96]

*   *   *   *   *

When rehearsals began again, they took place in Devonshire House,
where the Duke had set aside the picture gallery for the audience and

the adjacent library for the stage.⁹⁷ The paintings in the gallery were covered with planks masked behind crimson velvet draperies, and the portable theater was installed without any nails in either walls or floor by the lateral pressure of padded beams against upright stanchions. Behind the theater, the remainder of the library was screened off as a "green room" for the players.⁹⁸

Entering through the high gates on Piccadilly, the actors were shown upstairs by liveried footmen with epaulettes of silver bullion. At the first rehearsal, one of them noticed a gentleman in rusty black puttering about under a heavy roller of scenery being hoisted in the air. "Now, sir!" he exclaimed sharply, "do for Heaven's sake keep out of the way! Do you want to get your back broke?" The gentleman bowed, gave a deprecating smile, and retired. The actor was not a little startled, however, after the rehearsal, when a "profuse and elegant cold collation, with the choicest wines" was being served, to discover that his brusque words had been addressed to the Duke.⁹⁹

The fact that the Queen was coming added to their difficulties. In one scene Horne was supposed, as "Colonel Flint of the Guards," to be smoking a clay pipe with his back to the glowing fireplace of Will's Coffee House. "The Queen can't bear tobacco," Dickens warned. "No tobacco," replied Horne, "dried herbs—got them in Covent Garden." Then the pipe must be foul, Dickens suggested; Horne said it was perfectly new. Nevertheless, another pipe was obtained. This time Paxton smelled tobacco, in spite of being shown that Horne was smoking a mixture of thyme and rose leaves. So Horne obtained some whorls of fine cotton on twirls of invisible wire to imitate wreaths of smoke curling from the pipe. But it was still no use: "Her Majesty would *think* she smelled tobacco, and that would be just as bad." ¹⁰⁰

Dickens was now tyrannically rehearsing his company all day long three days a week.¹⁰¹ He went over and over the weak places, resolved to make them strong ones. "My legs," he said, "swell so, with standing on the stage for hours together, that my stockings won't come off. I get so covered with sawdust among the carpenters, that my Infants don't know me. I am so astonishingly familiar with everybody else's part, that I forget my own. I roar to the Troupe in general, to that extent that the excellent Duke (who is deaf) thinks in the remoteness of his own little library that the wind is blowing hard." ¹⁰²

Finally everything was ready. There were even two decorative tickets of admission, designed by Joseph Jenkins, of the Water Colour Society, and the painter E. M. Ward, which were to be used for alternate nights.[103] Dickens had doubtfully asked the Duke if three guineas a ticket would be too much, and on that nobleman's advice had then calmly agreed to demand five.[104] One final precaution he was obliged to take to see that all went smoothly. Rosina Bulwer Lytton sent a violent letter to the Duke threatening to make her way in disguised as an orange-girl and create a disturbance.[105] To Dickens she wrote a hysterical outburst, denouncing the Queen as "sensual, selfish, and pig-headed," the actors as "a disreputable set of charlatans," and her estranged husband, "Sir Liar Coward Lytton," as "a ruffian and a scoundrel." [106] It was just possible, Dickens considered, that she might have laid her hands on a ticket for someone else or obtained one under a false name. He therefore placed on guard in the hall a detective in plain clothes, who was prepared "very respectfully" [107] to "shew our fair correspondent the wrong way to the Theatre, and not say a word until he had her out of hearing . . . ." [108] There is no record, however, of Rosina's having tried to force an entrance.

The dress rehearsal, attended only by friends of the actors and the Duke, took place on May 14th. The Queen's Night followed on the 16th.[109] A large audience crowded the entire picture gallery. After an overture composed for the occasion, played by the Duke's private band, the lights were lowered, the scented oil footlights grew bright, and the curtain rose on Lord Wilmot's lodgings. There were spectators and even fellow actors who did not think Dickens ideally successful in portraying a witty eighteenth-century man of mode—Horne found him more like a sunburnt captain of an East Indiaman and his gestures more quarter-deck than elegant—but there can be no doubt that the play triumphed with its audience. At the end the Queen led the hearty applause. There followed a luxurious supper at which Victoria sat in a chair surmounted by a Gothic arch elaborately decorated with roses, magnolias, jasmine, and honeysuckle, festooned with orchids, and surmounted by night-flowering cereus, all strewn with opals in simulation of dewdrops.[110]

The Duke, "all smiles," was so delighted with the success of the evening that he begged them to play once more in his residence before beginning at the Hanover Square Rooms.[111] There was consequently an additional performance at Devonshire House on May 27th. No farce had been acted the first night: *Not So Bad as We Seem* was long, it did not begin until nine, and "the Queen gets very restless towards 12 o'clock." [112] Dickens had intended, however, to write a farce for the later performances. He had even produced a first scene that he thought "very rapid and droll," but then bogged down.[113] In its place he collaborated with Lemon on a hilarious absurdity they called *Mr. Nightingale's Diary*. The second-night audience now screamed with laughter at this piece, and were flabbergasted near the end to discover that Dickens in rapid succession had disguised himself to play no fewer than six parts: a lawyer, a Sam Wellerish waiter, a maniacally enthusiastic walker, a hypochondriac, a gabbling Sairey Gamplike old woman, and a deaf sexton.[114] The Duke rounded off the evening with a magnificent ball and supper for the actors, at which Douglas Jerrold was thrown into such a state of romantic admiration by some of the society beauties present that he moved about with gleaming eyes, "uttering glowing and racy ejaculations." [115]

Dickens experienced his usual sense of letdown when these initial performances were over, even though he knew they would soon be resuming again in the Hanover Square Rooms. From Fort House at Broadstairs, where he had joined Kate and the children, he wrote the Duke that he was in a favorite house of his, "with the green corn growing all about it, and the larks singing invisible all day long." Nevertheless, despite the garden full of flowers and the freshness of the sea, there was "the melancholy of having turned a leaf in my life. It was so sad," he explained, "to see the curtain dropped . . . that something of the shadow of the great curtain which falls on everything seemed . . . to be upon my spirits." [116]

But the Duke must certainly come to the first Hanover Square performance, postponed from June 3rd to the 18th in order to make sure all the tickets were sold.[117] "I really believe the actors will go all wrong and want all heart, if they don't see you in your box." [118] Here, too, the production was tumultuously applauded, and a fortnight later, on July 2nd, the curtain rose and fell repeatedly in a whirlwind of enthusiasm.[119] But Forster and Jerrold were beginning to blow cold on going into the provinces: "Jerrold because he is constitutionally inconsistent and unsettled," Dickens said, "—Forster, because he thinks he is not appreciated in Hardman." Both had lately been "wet-blanketing the proceedings," and pains must be taken at the third and "final" London performance on July 21st "to keep the stragglers" in line.[120] With Bulwer Lytton's persuasion and more of Dickens's bludgeoning, they *were* kept in line, and on August 4th there was a "positively the last" London performance.

The endless editorial activities were, of course, continuing as ever. The author of a paper on the treatment of lunatics must be told that it was too didactic and too long. If he would allow Dickens to rewrite and shorten it, well and good; if not, it must be rejected.[121] An unknown young man named George Augustus Sala had written "a very remarkable piece of description" entitled "The Key of the Street," "quite good enough for a first article—but we will not put it first for fear we should spoil him in the beginning." [122] Dickens himself wrote an article called "Whole Hogs" on the uncompromising fanatics who insisted on all-or-nothing positions, to whom a teaspoonful of wine in a glass of water was a violation of Temperance, a single sentry before the Queen's palace a denial of Peace, and a bone in a pot of vegetables a fall from the Garden of Eden.[123]

The provincial performances of *Not So Bad as We Seem* began late in the fall. Forster was "disabled by illness and occupation" from acting,[124] but somehow managed to go to Bath as a spectator on November 11th and thence to Clifton for the Bristol performances on the 12th and 14th.[125] Jerrold, still somewhat reluctantly a member of the company, was "in extraordinary force. I don't think I ever saw him so humorous." Although the great room at Bath was full, it was "a horribly dull audience"; but the response from the fourteen hundred people who crammed the still greater room at Bristol was "prodigious." [126]

During the following year *Not So Bad as We Seem* went luxuriously barnstorming through the provinces.[127] They had already cleared over £3,000, Dickens told his company, and should keep on till they had £5,000. In February they filled the Free Trade Hall in Manchester and twice played to three thousand in the Philharmonic Hall at Liverpool. People laughed so hard at *Mr. Nightingale's Diary* that half of it was inaudible. Jerrold, to be sure, had deserted them after the walls of both towns were plastered with bills listing him in his part, but young Wilkie Collins took it over and came up to scratch nobly.[128] Forster, who was with them at Manchester, was "absolutely stunned" by the "fury of delight" with which their audiences rose after the performance. "I sincerely believe," Dickens wrote excitedly, "that we have the ball at our feet, and may throw it up to the very Heaven of Heavens." And, again, "Believe me we may carry a perfect fiery cross through the North of England . . . I have been so happy in all this that I could have cried . . ." [129]

He left Liverpool almost "blinded by excitement, gas, and waving hats and handkerchiefs." [130] In May came the Music Hall at Shrewsbury on the 10th, and the Birmingham Town Hall on the 12th and 13th. Almost always on these trips Dickens took the two largest rooms and almost all the beds of the principal hotel; sometimes he took the entire hotel.[131] In addition to the thirty or so members of the acting company and the orchestra conductor, there was "a perfect army of carpenters, gasmen, tailors, barbers, property-men, dressers, and servants" [132] who all told might easily exhaust the accommodations of a provincial hotel. In Manchester, Dickens reluctantly declined Mrs. Gaskell's invitation to stay with her and her husband. "I can't imagine what the company would think, if the Manager were away. As to their ever producing themselves in due costume at the proper time, under such circumstances—or as to any of the many unseen workmen doing what they ought to do—*that*, I am quite clear about." [133] The whole company lunched together, dined lightly before the performance, and then had supper together afterwards, inviting the mayor of the town, the chief civic magnates, and any of their friends as guests. After supper they relaxed their spirits in noisy hilarity, sometimes playing leap-frog all around the supper table, with Lemon making so enormous a "high back" as few could surmount.[134]

In August, the tour was whirling to a close. On the 23rd they were at Nottingham. On the 25th, at Derby, the Duke of Devonshire happily turned up at a rehearsal.[135] At Newcastle, on the 27th, they squeezed six hundred people at twelve and sixpence "into a space reasonably capable of holding three hundred." On the 28th the deafening cheers from an audience of twelve hundred in the just-erected Lyceum at Sunderland filled Dickens with trepidation. There were rumors that the structure was unsafe, and at every round of applause he imagined he "saw the gallery out of the perpendicular, and fancied the lights in the ceiling were not straight." On the 30th, they played at Sheffield.[136]

In September the tour ended, with return performances in Man-

chester on the 1st and Liverpool on the 3rd.*137* *Used Up* was also on
the bill for the former of these nights. "O, think of that!" he wrote
Mary Boyle. "With another Mary!!! How can I ever say, '*Dear* Joe, if
you like!' The voice may fully frame the falsehood, but the heart—
the heart, Mr. Wurzel—will have no part in it." [138] Bulwer Lytton
spoke brilliantly about the Guild at a public dinner in Manchester,
and in Liverpool Dickens gave an appreciative supper to the stage-
hands and other helpers of the cast.[139]

The later course of the Guild of Literature and Art cannot be followed in detail. Dickens gave it faithful service throughout the rest
of his life; the records of the Guild show some thirty-five council meetings and general meetings, some of them very protracted, which he
attended, and such minutes, of course, do not show how much additional time he gave to its business.*140* All the funds accumulated for its
endowment were invested in government securities in the names of
Dickens and Wills, who were its Chairman and Secretary.

On June 2nd, 1854, Bulwer Lytton succeeded in getting through
Parliament a charter incorporating the Guild. Unfortunately, the
charter prohibited granting any pensions under it until seven years
from that date. Dickens recommended that the capital and interest
be allowed to accumulate over that time, and offered meanwhile rent-
free accommodations in the *Household Words* offices. When the excitement of the theatricals was once over, however, general interest
in the Guild fell off. There was never the widespread support which
Dickens had confidently expected, and donations from the public
were but meager. At the end of the seven years during which its funds
were frozen, the crowds that had laughed and cheered the performances of *Not So Bad as We Seem* had entirely forgotten the Guild.

Nor did the artists and writers for whose benefit it had been inaugurated take to it very kindly. In spite of its laudable aims and its
brave words about financial independence, the plan seemed to them
to have an unpleasant coloring of patronage; it suggested a slur of
pauperism that both writers and artists resented. Some of these objections are suggested in a letter Macaulay wrote Bulwer Lytton the
day after the Devonshire House performance:

"Suppose ten or twelve charming cottages built on the land which
you so munificently propose to bestow. Suppose funds to be provided
for paying your Warden and ten or twelve fellows. . . . Whom will

you choose. Form a list of the thirty best writers now living in the United Kingdom. Then strike off from this list first all who require no assistance, and secondly all who do indeed require assistance, but receive from the State pensions as large as you propose to give." Hardly more than four or five, Macaulay believed, would remain. He therefore felt that they would be driven, even with the very best intentions and using the best possible judgment, to fill up the Guild with second-rate writers.[141]

Macaulay's forecast proved justified by the event. Annual pensions went to a few mediocrities; the widows of a few journalists and illustrators received donations. And yet the problem to which Dickens and Bulwer Lytton generously addressed themselves was a real one never entirely solved. As we look on it today, the Guild seems a far-sighted anticipation of those modern endowments—for artists, writers, musicians, scientists, philosophers—that enable creative workers to concentrate without other preoccupations on a chosen project.

We are still far short, however, of dealing soundly with great abilities. The learned foundations and the universities are not wealthy enough to endow more than a few of many valuable works of scholarship that cannot command an audience numerous enough to pay their way. And those who would aid the artist, the seminal thinker, have the even harder task of distinguishing talent from mere oddity or charlatanism. Enigmatic young inspiration derided, mature attainment still without reward, are sad twin phenomena of the entire history of the arts, as Dickens and Bulwer Lytton well understood despite their own success having been almost instantaneous. Their vision of the Guild was a noble effort that with better fortune might have given priceless aid to learning and genius.

The Darkening Scene

1851–1858

PART EIGHT

The Darkening Scene

1851–1858

CHAPTER ONE

Fog Over England

WITH the mid-century mark Dickens reached almost exactly the halfway point in his literary career. He was just in his fortieth year. Though his novels followed one another less swiftly than in his amazing first five years, if there be thrown in the balance his editorial work on *Household Words*, the large amount of writing he did for it, his enormous correspondence, and his acting and play producing, he revealed little if any slackening of energy. And artistically he was at the height of his powers. Firmer in structure, deeper in intellectual grasp, sharper in social criticism, even imaginatively richer, his work assumed new dimensions of profound significance.

The two great novels immediately preceding this period laid the foundations for its tremendous achievement. In *Dombey and Son* he had for the first time portrayed society as a single interlinked system poisoned by the heartlessness of a money ethic. In *David Copperfield* he had made a mighty effort at self-understanding, facing up to the painful elements in his past that had shaped him for good and ill, and striving to clarify his image of his own character and fortune in life. He had taken measure of himself and of the world.

In the books that followed he was to attempt nothing less than an anatomy of modern society. *Bleak House* articulates its institutions, from government and law to philanthropy and religion—on every level, from Sir Leicester Dedlock's Lincolnshire estates to the rotting tenements of Tom-all-Alone's—as a corrupt and entangled web of vested interests and power. *Hard Times* unmasks the cold-hearted rationalizations of political economy and the industrial greed that uses economic "laws" to justify its callous exploitation of the laboring classes. *Little Dorrit* paints this entire system as a vast jail imprisoning every member of society, from the glittering admirers of Mr. Merdle to the rack-rented dwellers in Bleeding Heart Yard.

The grimmer and more comprehensive vision Dickens brought to his enlarged purpose fills these novels with somber hues. His sense of the ludicrous, of course, never ceases to be lively, but it does not play with the sparkling profusion that once made it a fountain of ir-repressible hilarity. Boythorn and the young man named Guppy, de-lightful as they are, and even the voluble Flora Finching and Mr. F's Aunt, are only effervescent flashes in comparison with Dick Swiveller, Mrs. Gamp, and Captain Cuttle. The satiric characters—Mr. Vholes, the Smallweeds, Mr. Bounderby, the Merdles and Tite-Barnacles—are bitten in now with burning acid. But if the old high spirits gleam less frequently, there is in these books a new intensity and integration, rich, dark, sulphurous, that weights every observation and cuts like a knife.

Dickens began no new novel, however, until the end of November, 1851,[1] after the first provincial performances of *Not So Bad as We Seem* at Bath and Bristol. From the early spring on, almost all the attention he could spare from Guild affairs and *Household Words* had been centered upon finding a larger house.[2] One property at High-gate he lost through insisting that the owners convey to him at their expense the freehold of an adjacent bit of land to which their title was dubious.[3] He then offered £2,700 for Balmoral House, overlooking the Regent's Park. Luckily for him, this was also refused: a few years later a barge of gunpowder passing through the Regent's Canal exploded and wrecked the building.[4] Keeping up his search while the family was at Broadstairs and Devonshire Terrace sublet, he installed iron bedsteads in his Wellington Street offices for use when he had to be in town during the summer.[5]

On July 1, 1851, Dickens took Charley and three of his Eton chums on a boating excursion down the Thames from Windsor.[6] The day began very rainy, and when he arrived at Slough he found the boys wearing long faces with fear that the picnic would be called off. "When they saw us, the faces shut up as if they were upon strong springs, and their waistcoats developed themselves in the usual places." As the hampers from Fortnum and Mason were unloaded the boys danced with excitement; as one proved to be filled with bottles "they all stood wildly on one leg." At the boathouse a waterman shrilly greeted as "Mahogany," "Hog," and "Hogany" stowed the delicacies "in a galley with a striped awning," and under a clear sky now, "all rowing hard," they went down the river.[7]

They lunched in a field, Dickens suffering agonies lest the boys get drunk on the light champagne he had provided: "I feel, even now, old with the anxiety of that tremendous hour. They were very good, however. The speech of one became thick, and his eyes too like lobsters' to be comfortable, but only temporarily. He recovered, and I suppose outlived the salad he took." They had tea and rashers of bacon at a public house, coming home through a prodigious thunderstorm, the boys singing a song with a chorus that ended:

> *"I don't care a fig what the people may think,*
> *But what WILL the governor say!*

"which was shouted," Dickens added, "with a deferential jollity towards myself, as a governor who had that day done a creditable action, and proved himself worthy of all confidence." [8]

Coming up to London from Broadstairs not long after this picnic, Dickens learned that Frank Stone was moving next door to the house he had formerly occupied.[9] These two dwellings, Tavistock House and Russell House, made with the adjoining Bedford House a group of three buildings facing Tavistock Square, having an iron-railed front garden and a tree-shaded carriage sweep common to them all.[10] Like its neighbors, Tavistock House had a basement mostly below ground from which it rose three full stories to a mansard-roofed attic with servants' rooms. On the ground floor two windows in the coursed stone façade looked out on the trees and shrubs of the drive. To the left there was a shallow entrance porch with Doric columns. The walls above were brick, with three high rectangular windows on the first floor, and three round-arched ones beneath a plain cornice.[11] A lane on the right connected the front and rear gardens and gave light and air on that side. Wider than Devonshire Terrace, and a full story higher, Tavistock House would have ample room for Dickens's entire brood of children.

This property could be "bought," as British legal phraseology has it, for a term of forty-five years, the purchaser being responsible during that period for paying the taxes and making his own repairs. "It is decidedly cheap," Dickens wrote Henry Austin, "—most commodious—

and might be made very handsome." But it was "in the dirtiest of all possible conditions"; so, before committing himself, Dickens asked Austin to obtain an expert opinion "as to the likelihood of the roof tumbling into the kitchen, or the walls becoming a sort of brick and mortar minced veal." [12] These fears being dissolved, Dickens authorized Stone to offer £1,450 in his behalf. "I am convinced it is the prudent thing for me to do, and that I am very unlikely to find the same comforts for the rising generation elsewhere, for the same money. . . . I don't make any apologies for thrusting this honour upon you, knowing what a thorough-going old pump you are." [13]

* * * *

While the legal details were being settled, Dickens began pondering, with all his usual unhappy symptoms, the subject of his new book: "Violent restlessness, and vague ideas of going I don't know where, I don't know why . . ." [14] "I very nearly packed up a portmanteau and went away, the day before yesterday, into the mountains of Switzerland, alone! Still the victim of an intolerable restlessness, I shouldn't be at all surprised if I wrote you one of these mornings from under Mont Blanc. I sit down between whiles to think of a new story, and, as it begins to grow, such a torment of a desire to be anywhere but where I am . . . takes hold of me, that it is like being *driven away*." [15]

Some of the titles and subtitles he mulled over reveal how the theme was shaping itself in his mind: *Tom-all-Alone's: The Ruined House; Bleak House Academy; The East Wind; Tom-all-Alone's: The Solitary House where the Grass Grew; Tom-all-Alone's: The Solitary House that was always Shut up and never Lighted; Tom-all-Alone's: The Solitary House where the Wind howled; Tom-all-Alone's: The Ruined House that Got into Chancery and never got out; Bleak House and the East Wind: How they both got into Chancery and never got out; Bleak House.*[16] The name "Tom-all-Alone's" floated up of course, out of his childhood memories of the lonely house in the waste places outside of Chatham, wrecked by the mines the army had exploded within its walls. But in it fused the image of the desolate London slum with its falling houses and the idea of a social system rotten with the forces of its own decay and ultimate self-annihilation.

Writing the book, however, soon had to be set aside until the move to Tavistock House was made. Dickens drew a plan for the garden and instructed the gardener to transplant as many of the shrubs as possible from Devonshire Terrace. "I put them all there, and don't want to leave them there."[17] Inside, he altered the house radically. The entrance hall was to be carried right through the ground floor to the private garden in the rear. What had been Stone's painting room on the first floor was to become the drawing room, and the drawing room transformed into a schoolroom. Plans for a conservatory were made and abandoned. A door must be cut between the drawing room and the study.[18] Perhaps a pillar should be constructed in the kitchen to make sure the floor above it was safe. "Let us dance in peace, whatever we do, and only go into the kitchen by the staircase." [19]

The equipment and fittings of the house had to be thoroughly modernized. Speaking as the taker of a shower bath every morning, Dickens wrote, he insisted that the water closet be partitioned off from the bath, not allowed to "demonstrate itself obtrusively." "I believe it would affect my bowels. It might relax, it might confine, but I mistrust its having some influence on the happy mediocrity it is my ambition to preserve." [20] Then there was a new range to be installed in the kitchen, brass ventilators in the dining room,[21] bookshelves and built-in mirrors in drawing room and study,[22] and bells in all the bedrooms and connecting the best bedroom, dining room, and drawing room with the nursery.[23] "Curtains and carpets, on a scale of awful splendor and magnitude, are already in preparation . . ." [24]

The delays and confusions usual to such alterations drove Dickens almost to frenzy. To Austin, who was superintending them, he wrote in large capitals:

"NO WORKMEN ON THE PREMISES

". . . I have torn all my hair off, and constantly beat my unoffending family. Wild notions have occurred to me of sending in my own Plumber to do the Drains. . . . Then Stone presents himself, with a most exasperatingly mysterious visage, and says that a Rat has appeared in the kitchen, and it's his opinion (Stone's, not the Rat's) that the drains want 'compoing'; for the use of which explicit language I could fell him without remorse." Followed still more lamentations and directions, ending madly:

"P.S.—NO WORKMEN ON THE PREMISES!

"Ha! ha! ha! (I am laughing demoniacally.)" [25]

When the workmen did arrive, the chaos they created was so awful that Dickens escaped to Broadstairs. But he could not resist fretting and imagining how things were going on in his absence. "I am perpetually wandering (in fancy) up and down the house and tumbling over the workmen. When I feel that they are gone to dinner I become low. When I look forward to their total abstinence on Sunday, I am wretched. The gravy at dinner has a taste of glue in it. I smell paint in the sea. Phantom lime attends me all the day long. I dream that I am a carpenter and can't partition off the hall." [26]

Then he would become distracted, dash back to town, look at the house, and fall into discouragement. "They are continually going up ladders, and never appear to come down again. They roll barrels of lime into the garden, and tap them by the dozen, like a sort of dusty beer. They peck at walls with iron instruments (for no reason that I can discover), and the walls fall down. . . . They stand on scaffolds, whistling, in the most sacred chambers. There is no privacy anywhere. Yesterday week, I saw a hairy Irishman cultivating mortar with spade-husbandry in the room I am to write in!" [27]

From these preoccupations he was sometimes diverted and amused by his Broadstairs guests: "Here has Horne been (with a guitar) bathing at 'Dumblegap,' the flesh-colored Horror of maiden ladies. Here has Forster been and gone, after patronizing with suavity the whole population of Broadstairs, and impressing Tom Collins with the fact that he (F) did the Ocean a favor when he bathed. Here likewise has Mrs. Horne been, full of beauty, also Wills, with a frosty nose and a dribbling pretence of shower-bath." Then back would come the vision of "workmen, scooping, grooving, chiseling, sawing, planing, dabbing, putting, clinking, hammering" while, he exclaimed, "I am wild to begin a new book, and can't until I am settled—" [28]

But slowly progress was made. When Dickens and Catherine returned from Broadstairs on October 20th, order was beginning to establish itself.[29] "The painters still mislaid their brushes every five minutes," he wrote several days later, "and chiefly whistled in the intervals . . . but still there was an improvement, and it is confirmed today. White lime is to be seen in the kitchens—faint streaks of civilization dawn in the water-closet—the Bath-room is gradually resolving itself into a fact . . ." On the other hand, "The drawing-room encourages no hope whatever. Nor the study. Staircase painted. Irish labourers howling in the school-room, but I don't know why: I see nothing. . . . Inimitable hovering gloomily through the premises all day, with an idea that a little more work is done when he flits, bat-like, through the rooms, than when there is no one looking on." [30] Catherine was "all over paint, and seems to think that it is somehow being immensely useful to get into that condition." And making all these trials more distressing, he had caught, he announced, "a tre-mendous cold, which has shut up my right eye—made a mere steel button of my left—communicated the lively expression of a codfish to my mouth—muffled my voice—rasped the inside of my chest with a rough file—and reduced my mental condition (as you may perceive) to one of mere drivel and imbecility." [31]

By the fourth week in November, however, the delays were over and the move into Tavistock House was completed. With a recur-rence of high spirits, Dickens addressed Mrs. Gaskell as "Schehera-zade," whose narrative powers were "good for at least a thousand nights and one," and jocularly described the kitchen as "an apartment painted in the arabesque manner, with perfumes burning night and day on tripods of silver" and "crimson hangings of silk damask con-cealing the saucepans." [32] But he was genuinely delighted with the outcome. Every detail about the house was exactly as he—and he only —had determined that it should be.[33] Even the dummy book-backs on the imitation shelves of the door between his study and the draw-ing room were so impressively successful as to make it seem part of an unbroken wall of books.[34]

Dickens had derived considerable amusement from inventing titles for these imaginary volumes. Some are purely facetious: *Five Minutes in China*, 3 vols., *Forty Winks at the Pyramids*, 2 vols., *Drowsy's Recollections of Nothing*, and *Heaviside's Conversations with No-body*. Others are puns: *A Carpenter's Bench of Bishops*, *The Gun-powder Magazine, Steele. By the Author of "Ion," Teazer's Commen-taries*. But there is a more satiric bite to *The Quarrelly Review, Kant's Eminent Humbugs, King Henry the Eighth's Evidences of Christi-anity*, and *Hansard's Guide to Refreshing Sleep* in "as many volumes as possible." Later Dickens added still more which run the same gamut: *Lady Godiva on the Horse, Cockatoo on Perch, Socrates on*

Wedlock (in which Dickens on Wedlock is inferable), *Strutt's Walk*, *Noah's Arkitecture, Shelley's Oysters, Cat's Lives* (in 9 vols.), *Drouet's Farming* and *Malthus's Nursery Songs* ("baby farms" and the political economists again!), *History of a Short Chancery Suit*, 21 vols., and *The Wisdom of Our Ancestors*, of which the successive volumes were labeled: "I. Ignorance. II. Superstition. III. The Block. IV. The Stake. V. The Rack. VI. Dirt. VII. Disease." Alongside this bulky work was *The Virtues of Our Ancestors*, a single volume so narrow that the title had to be printed sideways. All told, Dickens devised over seventy such titles.[35]

*   *   *   *   *

Sealed away in his study from the rest of the house, he was now ready to begin *Bleak House*. Opposite the two windows a console mirror framed in the mahogany bookcases reflected the trees and sky.[36] His writing table looking out into the garden was neatly decked with all its knickknacks—the duelling green-bronze frogs, the man with squirming puppies overflowing all his pockets, the ivory paper knife, and the rest—and equipped with its supply of writing paper, blue ink, and quill pens. Soon his imagination was swirling with the raw mist of Chancery Lane and the dense fog of Jarndyce and Jarndyce. On the 7th of December he had only a "last short chapter to do, to complete No. 1." [37]

At the turn of the year Catherine Dickens became the author of a volume which Bradbury and Evans published as the work of "Lady Maria Clutterbuck" and which was entitled *What Shall We Have for Dinner? satisfactorily answered by numerous Bills of Fare for from two to eighteen persons*.[38] Its contents were compiled from the dinners served at Devonshire Terrace. The book was favorably received, although one reviewer declared that "no man could possibly survive the consumption of such frequent toasted cheese." This certainly represented Dickens's own taste, however; his son Charley remarked in later years, "I wonder . . . how many dinners were begun with a glass of Chichester milk-punch; how many were finished with a dish of toasted cheese . . ." [39]

The turn of the year also saw published in *Household Words* the first of Mrs. Gaskell's charming village sketches later collected under the title of *Cranford*, which appeared irregularly for the next year and a half.[40] Mrs. Gaskell was irritated when in his own periodical Dickens modestly substituted Hood's *Poems* for her laudatory reference to *Pickwick Papers*, but allowed herself to be mollified by his explanation.[41] His praise of her own work, though, she suspiciously dismissed as "soft sawder." [42]

The first Christmas season in the new house was marked by a burst of festivities. The Dickens children, coached by their father, put on a Twelfth-Night performance of Albert Smith's burletta *Guy Fawkes* in the big schoolroom, transformed into a theater for the occasion. And it must have been from around this time that Thackeray's daughter Annie remembered a "shining" party that seemed to "go round and round" in an enchanted way. She and her younger sister Minnie, almost the same ages as the two Dickens girls, were lost in a blur of music, streams of children, Miss Hogarth finding dancing partners for them, a vision of Mamey and Katey with white satin slippers and flowing white sashes, more dancing, radiant confusion.

In the supper room Dickens, with his arm around a curly-headed very little girl named Miss Hullah, coaxed her to sing, which she did, trembling and blushing, in a small sweet voice. Then came more dancing and more people arriving, and crowds of little boys shouting and waving arms and legs. And finally, in the hall hung with Christmas greens, as Thackeray arrived to take his daughters home and stood with his white head towering above the throng, young Charley marshaled the boys on the broad staircase to give three cheers. "That is for you!" Dickens laughingly told Thackeray, who settled his spectacles, surprised and pleased, and nodded gravely at the boys.[43]

Mamey and Katey were now growing up rapidly. Mamey, almost fourteen, was still quiet and docile; Katey, just turned twelve, had the fiery disposition that had given her the nickname Lucifer Box, and revealed enough talent for art so that Dickens enrolled her this year for drawing lessons at Bedford College.[44] The two girls shared a room at the top of the house, which they were allowed to decorate as they pleased, but Dickens insisted that they keep it with military precision. Every morning he inspected their bureau drawers, and left "pincushion notes" to reprimand any untidiness or praise something new and pretty as "quite slap-up." [45] The boys, too, each had pegs for their hats on the hall rack, and woe betide the one who failed to use his! Once, Alfred Tennyson Dickens remembered, "I was busily engaged in brushing my coat in the dining room instead of outside," when his father came in, "and I never by any chance committed that particular offence afterwards." [46] Dickens demanded neatness—"if the wind blew his locks in the garden he would fly for his hair-brush" [47]—and he demanded punctuality; but he was "wonderfully good and even-tempered," Alfred said, and even when there had been a flurry of excitement the next moment would be "like the sun after a shower." [48]

The first number of *Bleak House* came out in March, 1852, and was at once a much greater success than *David Copperfield* had been. "Blazing away merrily," it soon sold thirty-five thousand copies every publishing day,[49] and there is no estimate of how many in back sales or spread out through the month. In spite of its intricate but closely articulated structure, Dickens wrote more easily, or at least with fewer groans of misery and despair, than for years past. Through *David Copperfield*, for all the evasions and omissions in its public self-revelation, he had achieved some inner catharsis, some coming to terms with himself, that left him more at peace. He was also able to blow off steam in the whirlwind theatrical trips and footlight excitements that punctuated most of the year. And possibly he was stimulated by a varied and amusing social life and by living in new places—when he was not touring with *Not So Bad as We Seem*—in Dover from the middle of July through September and Boulogne for a few weeks in October.

Now and then, to be sure, there is still one of the familiar outbursts: "Wild ideas . . . of going to Paris—Rouen—Switzerland—somewhere —and writing the remaining two-thirds of the next No. aloft in some queer inn room. I have been hanging over it, and have got restless. Want a change I think. Stupid." [50] The plaint anticipates by no more than a week Kate's giving birth, on March 13, 1852, to another child, "a brilliant boy of unheard-of dimensions," [51] who was named Edward Bulwer Lytton Dickens. But although Dickens reported himself happy that both mother and son were in a "blooming condition," he added, "I am not quite clear that I particularly wanted the latter . . ." [52] And to another correspondent he wrote: "What strange kings those were in the Fairy times, who, with three thousand wives and four thousand seven hundred and fifty concubines found it necessary to offer up prayers in all the Temples for a prince as beautiful as the day! I have some idea, with only one wife and nothing particular in any other direction, of interceding with the Bishop of London to have a little service in Saint Paul's beseeching that I may be considered to have done enough towards my country's population." [53]

Recovering speedily enough, however, from this mood, Dickens was soon struggling cheerfully with the proofs of the second number of *Bleak House*. In the dilettante parasite Skimpole, in this number, he had imitated Leigh Hunt's playful vivacity of manner and the willful gaiety of his paradoxes. (Just as in the following number, the gentle but leonine Boythorn was, he wrote confidentially, "a most exact portrait of Walter Savage Landor." [54]) But Skimpole was clearly revealed as, beneath his charm, a selfish cheat; and Forster objected that readers who recognized his mannerisms might attribute his moral qualities to Hunt as well. Though Hunt was neither mean nor idle, but a hard-working and warm-hearted man, there was in fact some color of reason for attributing to him a trace of Skimpole's financial irresponsibility. It is only fair to note, however, that some of the unpaid debts charged against Hunt were secretly contracted in his name by his brandy-drinking wife, upon whose faults his lips were loyally sealed.[54a]

Dickens did not know these facts, but he was fond of Hunt and did not wish to give him pain. He therefore took the opinions of other friends, toned down the portrayal, introduced traits which were not those of Leigh Hunt, and changed Skimpole's first name from Leonard to Harold.[55] Browne, too, in the illustrations, "helped to make him singularly unlike the great original." [56] The whimsically paraded superiority to financial obligation still remained the same, though, and the unmistakable description of Skimpole looking more like "a damaged young man, than a well-preserved elderly one." [57]

During the months that followed Dickens did a dozen different things with all his customary energy. He advised Miss Coutts on a slum-clearance and cheap housing project which she was now considering. Small separate houses, he told her, were both more expensive to build and less satisfactory than multiple dwellings. The jerry-builders had already laid waste the countryside and shut out the air for miles around London with "absurd and expensive walnut shells" that forced their inhabitants to travel miles to their work and cut them off from any glimpse of green fields. Blocks of flats could have spacious public gardens, soundly constructed walls, good foundations, gas, water, drainage, and a variety of other advantages that would be prohibitively costly in one-family houses. In the course of elaborating these ideas, Dickens outlined an entire plan of schools, savings banks, and public libraries to be established with each group of buildings.[58] From these discussions, in which Dickens was a guiding mind throughout, developed the razing of a slum area in Bethnal Green and the Columbia Square model flats which Miss Coutts built there.

Through Dickens's eyes, around this time, we get another glimpse of Samuel Rogers. Now eighty-nine, lamed by an accident, the old creature lived in his armchair, had it "lifted in and out of his carriage, wheeled to his table, carried upstairs with him in it, . . . and put to bed with him I suppose. In all other respects he is the same as ever. Vivacious enough and vicious enough,—tells the same stories, in the same words, to the same people, twenty times in a day, and has his little dinner parties of four, where he goes mad with rage if anybody talks to anyone but himself." [59]

In May the Guild company swooped down upon Shrewsbury and Birmingham, where Dickens kept everything "under the Managerial eye," played Lord Wilmot and Gabblewig, which together were "something longer," he said, "than the whole play of Hamlet—am dressed fourteen times in the course of the night—and go to bed a little tired." [60] Early in June Dickens arranged a farewell dinner at the Albion which some of the members of the company gave to Richard Henry Horne, who was soon leaving for Australia as Commissioner for Crown Lands.[61]

During this same month a young American girl, a Miss Clarke, was a visitor at Tavistock House, and later recorded her impressions. They talked of *Uncle Tom's Cabin*, published just that spring, which Dickens told her he thought a story of much power, "but scarcely a work of art." "Uncle Tom," she reported, "evidently struck him as an impossible piece of ebony perfection . . . and other African characters in the book as too highly seasoned with the virtues . . ." "Mrs. Stowe," Dickens said, "hardly gives the Anglo-Saxon fair play. I liked what I saw of the colored people in the States. I found them singularly polite and amiable, and in some instances decidedly clever; but then," he added, with a comical arching of his eyebrows, "I have no prejudice against white people." In the course of the evening Miss Clarke expressed her pleasure at seeing that his servants did not wear livery;

Dickens replied, "I do not consider that I own enough of any man to hang a badge upon." [62]

July found Dickens in Dover, praising the sea and the country walks to Mary Boyle, but remarking that the place was "too bandy (I mean musical, no reference to its legs) and infinitely too genteel." Once again her Joe was archly tender: "Watson seemed, when I saw him last, to be holding on as by a sheet-anchor to theatricals at Christmas. Then—O rapture!—but be still, my fluttering heart." Insensibly led on from this to voice an undercurrent of deeper emotion, he added, "This is one of what I call my wandering days, before I fall to work. I seem to be always looking at such times for something I have not found in life, but may possibly come to a few thousands of years hence, in some other part of some other system. God knows." [63]

Suddenly his feelings were given more tangible cause by the death of Watson. Only three weeks before they had dined together merrily in London, full of projects for the future. "I loved him as my heart," Dickens wrote, "and cannot think of him without tears." [64] "When I think of that bright house, and his fine simple honest heart, both so open to me, the blank and loss are like a dream." [65] Hard upon this came the news that D'Orsay was dead. "Poor d'Orsay! It is a tremendous consideration that friends should fall around us in such awful numbers as we attain middle life. What a field of battle it is!" [66] And within less than another two months Catherine Macready was also no more.

Visiting Macready in his retirement at Sherborne the year before, Dickens had been the last friend outside her family circle to see Mrs. Macready, even then sinking in her final illness. "The last flush of pleasure that passed over her face was caused by the sight of him; and as he took her hand to say farewell, she, sinking back exhausted in her chair, said feebly and faintly, 'Charles Dickens, I had almost embraced you—what a friend you have been!' He stooped and kissed her forehead . . ." [67] Now she too was dead. "Ah me! ah me!" Dickens wrote mournfully. "This tremendous sickle certainly does cut deep into the surrounding corn, when one's own small blade has ripened." [68]

In November occurred another death less personal in its meaning, that of the Duke of Wellington. Dickens obtained leave for Charley to come from Eton to see the funeral procession of the great old man,[69] and Alfred recalled being awakened at three in the morning with Frank and Sydney (and probably Walter) to be taken to the office of *Household Words*, from which they saw the guns and the colors, the troops and the dignitaries, and the Duke's famous charger, Copenhagen, as the dead march moved along Fleet Street to St. Paul's.[70] Catherine and Georgina, Mamey and Katey, numbers of friends, and some of the contributors to the magazine also witnessed the procession.

"The military part of the show," Dickens said, "was very fine." But "for forms of ugliness, horrible combinations of color, hideous motion, and general failure, there never was such a work achieved as the Car." [71] In addition, he violently detested the "barbarous show" and "ghastly folly" encouraged by such mortuary pomp. Undertakers, he thought, were a crew of funereal harpies and mercenary wretches who took advantage of grief to enforce an expensive display. In an article for *Household Words* called "Trading in Death" Dickens attacked these perversions of sorrow and especially the ghouls who coined money out of the old hero's death by renting windows and balconies along the route of the procession and selling mementos, autograph letters, and locks of hair.[72].

Dickens continued writing *Bleak House* steadily throughout the year. Its circulation was by this time "half as large again as Copperfield." [73] Once, in December, an assemblage of dogs took it into their heads to gather in Tavistock Square every morning and bark for hours without stopping, "positively rendering it impossible for me to work," Dickens complained, "and so making what is really ridiculous quite serious for me." [74] But these were dispersed finally by a few charges of small shot, and from then on the work continued with no variation except for a trip to Birmingham in January, when the Society of Artists gave Dickens a silver-gilt salver and a diamond ring.

On this occasion Dickens again voiced his disbelief in "the coxcombical idea of writing down to the popular intelligence" and his belief in the people. "From the shame of the purchased dedication, from the scurrilous and dirty work of Grub Street, from the dependent seat on sufferance at my Lord Duke's table today, and from the sponging-house or Marshalsea tomorrow . . . the people have set literature free." Many workingmen were now better versed in Shakespeare and Milton than many fine gentlemen in the days of dear books, and it was the general public that read Macaulay's *History*, Layard's *Re-*

searches, and Tennyson's *Poems*, and applauded the discoveries of Herschel and Faraday.[75]

After this excursion the writing of *Bleak House* progressed uneventfully through the spring of 1853. In March, Dickens spent a fortnight's holiday at Brighton, and May saw the arrival in England of Cornelius Felton, the beaming Pickwickian Greek professor from Harvard of whom Dickens had become so fond when he was in America. "He was one of the jolliest and simplest of men," Dickens said, "and not at all starry, *or* stripey." [76] During the course of the next month, in the time he had free from his work, Dickens piloted Felton around London, showing him the Guild Hall and the Monument and Greenwich Hospital, and introduced him to all his friends, from Forster and Clarkson Stanfield to old Rogers, sitting with a black skullcap on his head and looking out of his drawing-room window on the Green Park.[77]

*　　*　　*　　*　　*

Despite his steel-coil vitality, by the approach of summer Dickens felt tired and overworked. "The spring does not seem to fly back again directly," he noted, "as it always did when I put my own work aside, and had nothing else to do." [78] He had written more than four-fifths of *Bleak House*'s 380,000 words, and during the past two and a half years had dictated over 125,000 words of the *Child's History of England* to Georgina. What with these, he said, "and Household Words . . . and Miss Coutt's Home, and the invitations to feasts and festivals, I really feel as if my head would split like a fired shell if I remained here." [79] In fact, he had a severe recurrence of the kidney trouble that had afflicted him at irregular intervals since childhood, and spent six painful days in bed.[80]

Against everyone's advice but Dr. Elliotson's, he insisted, however, before he was completely recovered, on setting out for Boulogne, which had pleased him so much the previous October that he had determined to go there for the summer.[81] After a few days at Folkestone during which he still felt aches and pains when he sat up to write,[82] he crossed the Channel with his family on June 12th and settled in the Château des Moulineaux, which had once been occupied by an acquaintance he had made in Switzerland.[83]

Located on a wooded hillside in the midst of a great terraced garden, the villa had all of Boulogne piled and jumbled before it. On

one side it was only a single story; on the other, two. It was approached
by an avenue of hollyhocks and surrounded by thousands of roses and
other flowers, with "five great summerhouses, and (I think) fifteen
fountains—not one of which (according to the invariable French custom) ever plays," [84] but all stocked with "gasping gold fish." [85] Inside,
the house had countless little bedrooms and drawing rooms, a billiard-
room, a dining room looking into a conservatory through a picture
window over the fireplace, a glitter of mirrors everywhere, and a profusion of clocks keeping "correct Australian time—which I think,"
Dickens explained, "is about ten or twelve hours different from
French or English calculation." [86]

The landlord, M. Beaucourt, a portly jolly fellow, was enormously
proud of what he always called "the property," and so obliging about
instantly supplying whatever one asked that Dickens became embarrassed to make any further requests. "The things he has done in the
way of unreasonable bedsteads and washing-stands, I blush to think
of." All M. Beaucourt wanted was that his little estate be admired.
"You like the property?" he asked. "M. Beaucourt," Dickens replied,
"I am enchanted with it; I am more than satisfied with everything."
"And I, sir," said M. Beaucourt, laying his cap upon his breast and
kissing his hand, "I equally!" [87]

There was a detailed plan of the property in the hall, looking "about
the size of Ireland," whereon every single feature was identified by
name. "There are fifty-one such references, including the Cottage of
Tom Thumb, the Bridge of Austerlitz, the Bridge of Jena, the Hermi-
tage, the Bower of the Old Guard, the Labyrinth (I have no idea
which is which); and there is guidance to every room in the house,
as if it were a place on that stupendous scale that without such a clue
you must infallibly lose your way, and perhaps perish of starvation
between bedroom and bedroom." [88]

As the names of some of these architectural features suggest, M.
Beaucourt was a staunch admirer of Napoleon. "Medallions of him,
portraits of him, busts of him, pictures of him, are thickly sprinkled
all over the property. During the first month of our occupation, it was
our affliction constantly to be knocking down Napoleon: if we
touched a shelf in a dark corner, he toppled over with a crash; and
every door we opened shook him to the soul." [89]

In these Napoleonic surroundings, Dickens was soon able to report himself "brown, well, robust, vigorous, open to fight any man in England of my weight, and growing a moustache. Any person of undoubted pluck, in want of a customer, may hear of me at the bar of Bleak House, where my money is down." [90] Here, early in July, came the children, "all manner of toad-like colors" from a stormy Channel passage.[91] Here came Frank Stone to a house Dickens found him in the Saint-Omer road, and the Leeches, and Wilkie Collins. Here, in August, came Forster, not at all understanding the customs officers when they asked, "Est-ce que Monsieur ait quelque chose à déclarer?" In consequence of which, said Dickens, he replied, "after a moment's reflection with the sweetness of some choice wind instrument 'Bon jour!' and was immediately seized." [92] And here Dickens continued to keep an iron hand on *Household Words*, bombarding Wills with countless letters in which he was ruthlessly bidden to exclude, rewrite, and rearrange.

"Justice to Bears" wouldn't do as a title. "We have already had Justice to the Hyaena." Change it to "Brother Bruin." A "forlorn attempt at humour" in another article must be "ferociously decapitated." As for a garbled sentence like "And the onus of the idea task strangles every newly born smile that struggles for existence"—"strike it out with a pen of iron." "Gore House," by Leigh Hunt, was very poor. The passage in it about the Graces must be deleted: "It is Skimpole, you know—the whole passage." Of still another piece: "Look to the slang talk of it, and don't let 'Ya' stand for 'You.' " [93]

Amid a burst of stormy weather at the end of August, Dickens wrote the last pages of *Bleak House*. It had retained its immense circulation from the first, "beating dear old Copperfield," he said, "by a round ten thousand or more. I have never had so many readers." [94] The end of his long effort left him in a state of drowsy lassitude. "I should be lying in the sunshine by the hour together if there were such a thing. In its absence I prowl about in the wind and rain. Last night was the most tremendous I ever heard for a storm of both." [95]

There is a poetic fitness about this nocturnal violence that marked the close of *Bleak House*, for it is a dark and tempestuous book. The fog choking its opening scene, the rain swirling over the Ghost's Walk at Chesney Wold amid the dripping funeral urns on the balustrade, the black and verminous ruins of Tom-all-Alone's crashing at intervals with a cloud of dust, the besmeared archway and iron-barred gate that lead to the rat-infested graveyard, insinuate their oppressive gloom even amid the genial sunlit scenes. A turbulent and furious hostility to vested evils storms savagely through its pages.

Its numerous readers responded to this sharpened intensity with extremes of agreement and dissent. Only a few days after the very first number appeared, one of them sent Dickens a pamphlet about a Chancery case the essence of which he embodied in the story of Gridley, the embittered man from Shropshire.[96] The smashing attack of Jarndyce and Jarndyce was so effective that the Vice-Chancellor felt it necessary to defend the Court—at a Mansion House dinner, where his eye rested on Dickens among the guests—by arguing that any slight leisureliness in its legal pace was the fault of a stingy public, which had until recently resisted increasing the number of judges to seven, and that now its business would be carried on very much more rapidly.[97] "This seemed to me," Dickens commented in his Preface, "too profound a joke to be inserted in the body of this book, or I should have restored it to Conversation Kenge or Mr. Vholes, with one or other of whom I think it must have originated." [98]

Many other readers were disturbed and bewildered by Dickens's bitter ironies on the missionary zeal that worried about savages abroad and felt no concern for its own homeless waifs. A clergyman wrote in a personal letter, "Do the supporters of Christian missions to the heathen really deserve the attack that is conveyed in the sentence about Jo seated in his anguish on the doorstep of the Society for the Propagation of the Gospel in Foreign Parts?" [99] Lord Chief Justice Denman, who had been friendly with Dickens, wrote a series of articles in the Standard, first deriding his onslaught against the legal system as "belated and now unnecessary," and then angrily replying to the portrayal of Mrs. Jellyby and her enthusiasm for the natives of Borrioboola-Gha: "We do not say," Lord Denman noted, "that he actually defends slavery or the slave trade, but he takes pains to discourage by ridicule the effort now awaking to put them down." [100]

Lord Denman's violence was partly the result of declining health—he died in the following year—of which his son sent Dickens an apologetic explanation. "I know I deserve his former and wiser judgment," Dickens replied gently, "and I cancel the rest for ever." [101] To his clerical critic he responded in more detail. "There was a long time," he said, "during which the benevolent societies were spending immense sums on missions abroad, when there was no such thing as a Ragged School in England," or any attempt to deal with the "horrible domestic depths in which such schools" were found. He repeated his conviction that the best way of Christianizing the world was making good Christians at home and allowing their influence to spread abroad, not allowing "neglected and untaught childhood" to wander on the streets. "If you think the balance between the home mission and the foreign mission justly held in the present time—I do not." [102]

Sometimes even those as critical of society as he was himself overlooked his larger intention by magnifying or misreading some minor point. John Stuart Mill, the heir of Benthamite radicalism, might well have sympathized with Dickens's smashing indictment of the law and of political institutions as instruments for keeping power in the hands of those who had it. But Mill saw nothing except the satire on Mrs. Jellyby and Mrs. Pardiggle, which he interpreted as an impudent sneer at the rights of women—done "in the very vulgarest way," he wrote his wife with angry redundancy, "just the style in which vulgar men used to ridicule 'learned ladies' as neglecting their children and household." [103]

Mill's understanding, of course, was misted by his noble enthusiasm for the equality of the sexes, for Dickens had nothing but admiration for the efforts of women like Mrs. Gaskell and Harriet Martineau, who were deeply concerned in activities of public welfare. That was very different, however, from admiring women who assumed family responsibilities and then ignored them or made benevolence a device for bullying the poor. But when even so clear a mind as Mill's could fail to realize the entire scope of *Bleak House* in an excited misreading of a part, it is not remarkable that many readers should have been blind to its tremendous pattern and the immensely broadened outlook with which Dickens had come to look upon society.

CHAPTER TWO

The Anatomy of Society

CRITICISM: *Bleak House*

THE key institution of *Bleak House* is the Court of Chancery, its key image the fog choking the opening scenes in its dense brown obscurity and pervading the atmosphere of the entire story with an oppressive heaviness. But both law and fog are fundamentally symbols of all the ponderous and murky forces that suffocate the creative energies of mankind. They prefigure in darkness visible the entanglements of vested interests and institutions and archaic traditions protecting greed, fettering generous action, obstructing men's movements, and beclouding their vision. Surviving out of the miasmal swamps and ferocities of the past, these evils, like prehistoric monsters, unwieldly, voracious, and dreadfully destructive to human welfare, move stumbling and wallowing through layer upon layer of precedent as if through quagmires of encrusted mud. *Bleak House* is thus an indictment not merely of the law but of the whole dark muddle of organized society. It regards legal injustice not as accidental but as organically related to the very structure of that society.

Though the fog-enshrouded Court is only a symbol for this more sweeping arraignment, it is nevertheless the central symbol of the book. "The raw afternoon is rawest," the opening chapter tells us, "the dense fog is densest, and the muddy streets are muddiest, near that leaden-headed old obstruction, appropriate ornament for the threshold of a leaden-headed old corporation: Temple Bar. And hard by Temple Bar, in Lincoln's Inn Hall, in the very heart of the fog, sits the Lord High Chancellor in his High Court of Chancery." Here, surrounded by innumerable barristers mistily engaged upon an endless case, "tripping one another up on slippery precedents, groping knee-deep in technicalities," running their heads against walls of words, in a courtroom like a well where "you might look in vain for Truth at the bottom," all dim with wasting candles and wasting lives, the Chancellor gazes up from his dais "into a lantern that has no light in it, and . . . the attendant wigs are all stuck in a fog-bank!" [1]

"This," Dickens continues, "is the Court of Chancery; which has its decaying houses and its blighted lands in every shire; which has its worn-out lunatic in every madhouse, and its dead in every churchyard; which has its ruined suitor, with his slipshod heels and threadbare dress, borrowing and begging through the round of every man's acquaintance; which gives to monied might, the means abundantly of wearying out the right; which so exhausts finances, patience, courage, hope; so overthrows the brain and breaks the heart; that there is not an honourable man among its practitioners who would not give—who does not often give—the warning: 'Suffer any wrong that can be done you, rather than come here!' " [2]

From this point the story sweeps relentlessly on, showing how the glacial processes of the court wreck the lives of countless victims. The protracted struggle destroys Gridley, the angry man from Shropshire, "who can by no means be made to understand that the Chancellor is legally ignorant of his existence, having made it desolate for half a century." [3] Prolonged waiting overthrows the sanity of poor little Miss Flite, the tiny spinster dwelling with her birds in her starved tenement, and saying, "I was a ward myself. I was not mad at that time. I had youth and hope. I believe, beauty. It matters very little now. Neither of the three served, or saved me . . . I have discovered," she goes on, "that the sixth seal mentioned in the Revelations is the Great Seal"; she expects a judgment "on the Day of Judgment." How heart-rending is this crazed and helpless small creature, curtsying and smiling, and repeating, "Youth. And hope. And beauty. And Chancery." [4] She and Gridley bathe the long perspective of waste in flames of molten indignation and pathos.

The great lawsuit of the book is the classic case of Jarndyce and Jarndyce, "a monument," as the lawyer Conversation Kenge remarks, "of Chancery practice." In it, "every difficulty, every contingency, every masterly fiction, every form of procedure known in that court, is represented over and over again," and in it the court costs have already amounted to between sixty and seventy thousand pounds. "It is a cause," he adds with unconscious irony, "that could not exist, out of this free and great country." [5] And in it, in one way or another, almost every character of the story is involved.

There are the parties to the case, John Jarndyce, his wards Ada Clare and Richard Carstone, Esther Summerson through her aunt Miss Barbary, Sir Leicester Dedlock through his wife Honoria Dedlock. There are those who have only some vague connection with it, like Miss Flite and Gridley. There are the lawyers, Kenge and Carboy, Sir Leicester's solicitor Mr. Tulkinghorn, and Richard Carstone's representative Mr. Vholes. There are the lawyers' clerks and law writers, Mr. Guppy, his friend Tony Jobling, and "Nemo," the mysterious lodger above Krook's legal junkshop. There are the bailiff Neckett and his children. There is Snagsby, the law stationer. There are the rapacious Smallweeds, moneylenders, and through them Trooper George, who is in their clutches and who possesses letters that Tulkinghorn wants to secure as evidence. There is the illiterate and half-mad Krook, who calls himself "the Lord Chancellor," with his crazy collection of tattered lawbooks, ink bottles, old bones, skinned cats, rags, crackled parchment, and dog's-eared law papers. There is the police detective, Inspector Bucket. There is the foul and decaying slum tenement, Tom-all-Alone's, which is going to ruin while the case remains unsettled, in the noisome corners of which sleeps the waif and crossing-sweeper Jo. All these and many more are caught up in the convolutions of Jarndyce and Jarndyce.

What Dickens has done here, in fact, has been to create the novel of the social group, used as an instrument of social criticism. Though to a certain extent, in *Vanity Fair*, Thackeray had anticipated him, Thackeray used his story more in the spirit of *Everyman* or *Pilgrim's Progress*, as a moral commentary upon human nature, hardly more than suggesting that people's lives were shaped and twisted by social institutions. But Dickens had from the beginning of his career been deeply concerned with institutions, although at first he was able to do no more than sandwich his attacks on them between episodes of melodrama and comedy or relate them to his story only by implication. With *Dombey and Son* he had attempted a more integral suffusion of social criticism and narrative, but for all its successes *Dombey* achieves neither the scope nor the depth of *Bleak House*. Modern writers who have followed Dickens in employing the novel to criticize society and its institutions—like Wells and Galsworthy, and even

Shaw, in *An Unsocial Socialist*—have striven for no such close-knit cohesion of dramatic plot; Aldous Huxley, in *Point Counter Point*, drops out the plot almost entirely, and leaves many of his characters either quite unconnected with each other or associated only by the most fortuitous of links.

From one point of view this is a gain in "realism," but from another it is an artistic loss. For if there is a danger of Dickens's intricate structures seeming contrived and overmelodramatic, with their missing documents and hidden sins rising up out of the past, there is also a strength in tightness and intensity of development. This advantage Dickens potently exploits by creating a sense of taut inevitability that deepens immeasurably the emotional impact. The movement of *Bleak House* becomes a centripetal one like a whirlpool, at first slow and almost imperceptible, but fatefully drawing in successive groups of characters, circling faster and faster, and ultimately sucking them into the dark funnel whence none will escape uninjured and where many will be crushed and destroyed. In pure emotional power *Bleak House* ranks among Dickens's greatest books.

This is not to say that it has no weaknesses. Among them is the almost purposeless malignance with which Mr. Tulkinghorn pursues Lady Dedlock, a deep animosity that patiently unearths her secret and strives only to reduce her pride to subservience. But he has no practical goal, and it is not merely her proud indifference that challenges him; Sir Leicester is no less proud, and Mr. Tulkinghorn has no desire to humiliate him. When this sinister and implacable old man has gathered all the threads in his hands, knows about Lady Dedlock's soldier lover and her bastard child, he himself is uncertain what to do with his knowledge—whether or not to tell Sir Leicester, how to tell him, what the consequences may be. He knows merely that he could not rest until he had dragged up all the facts out of the past and forced this haughty woman to cringe before him.

If Mr. Tulkinghorn has no clearly defined motives, Lady Dedlock's motives and her situation fall too much into the domain of melodrama, although Dickens has tried to give them deeper significance. Like Edith Dombey, she is one of those defiant spirits who have got into a false position and who therefore despise themselves and revenge their own self-contempt by treating the world with arrogant scorn. Ambitious for aristocratic rank, she had not married Captain Hawdon and had been deceived into believing that their baby daughter had died at birth. Later, as Sir Leicester's wife and a leader of fashionable society, she has found her triumph dead-sea fruit. Having denied the forces of love and life, she can find no sound basis for rebellion. Mingled with the false guilt imposed by a conventional code of ethics is the real guilt of her submission to its standards, her hidden cowardice, her failure to be faithful to her lover and child. The fictitious conception of honor dictated by the morality of society has involved her in a tragic emotional dilemma, of which her very name, Honoria Dedlock, is symbolic.

Esther Summerson, the daughter of whose survival she has been kept in ignorance, is completely successful neither as a character nor as an instrument of the story's literary technique. Suggested probably, like Agnes Wickfield in *David Copperfield*, by what Dickens saw as Georgina Hogarth's sacrificial dedication to the welfare of others and her immersion in household duties, Esther is almost cloyingly unselfish, noble, and devoted, and rather tiresome in her domestic efficiency. The reader wearies of her jingling her keys as the little housekeeper of Mr. Jarndyce's home, and of her being called Dame Durden, Dame Trot, and Little Old Woman, and other nicknames, of everyone's affectionately confiding in her and seeking her advice, and of her so invariably resigning her own desires, repressing her griefs, and telling herself that she is very fortunate.

The fact that she sometimes exasperates us, however, reveals that she has genuinely been endowed with life, even if we do not share the estimate of her that we are intended to accept. But technically she exemplifies another defect in the handling of the narrative. All the scenes in which she appears are represented as seen through her eyes and are told in the first person as her story. This fact involves her in the difficulty of constantly reporting the tributes others pay to her virtues, which none of her own modest disclaimers can make sound quite ingenuous. In addition, although Dickens begins by trying to portray the things she tells through her eyes and to tell them in her words, he often loses sight of that objective and has her say things much more natural to him than to her. Her first visit to Krook's junkshop, when she sees the rags as looking like counsellors' gowns torn up and the bones as those of legal clients picked clean,[6] is brilliant satire, but it is not the observation of a young girl who has had no experience of the law. And only a little later there is the same mordancy in her description of the domineering Mrs. Pardiggle and the hordes of clamoring philanthropists as distinguished by a "rapacious benevolence." [7] Throughout many other passages one has to concede and overlook the fact that Dickens himself wrests from Esther Summerson the pen he placed in her hands.

Few of the other main characters are so richly or deeply realized as those in either *Dombey and Son* or *David Copperfield*. Ada Clare, one of the wards in Chancery under Mr. Jarndyce's protection, is a reversion to the colorlessness of Madeline Bray and Mary Graham. Richard Carstone, the other ward, is a spirited sketch—but only a sketch—of psychological and moral deterioration. (It was a theme Dickens had conceived in his original plans for Walter Gay, before deciding to have him marry Florence Dombey, but only much later, in the hero of *Great Expectations*, was he to be entirely successful in painting a gradually changing character.) Mr. Jarndyce probably makes amends to the nobler aspects of Dickens's father for the good-humoredly derisive caricature of Micawber: even the name John Jarndyce is a softened echo of John Dickens. Like Mr. Pickwick, a lovable old fool who rescues all the victims of oppression (just as John Dickens had brought his son out of the despair of the blacking warehouse), John Jarndyce is a noble-hearted eccentric who protects every sufferer from misfortune and saves those who will let themselves be saved. Unlike Mr. Pickwick, however, he is gently purged of all trace of absurdity. But though his harmless oddities help to humanize his goodness, he does not escape a certain sentimentality of delineation.

Surrounding these central characters crowd a host of others who stand for all the forces or classes of society—philanthropy, art, manners, religion, trade, industry, the poor, the aristocracy, law, government, politics. And, aside from those altogether broken or brutalized by misery, like the crossing-sweeper Jo and the colony of brickmakers near St. Albans, almost all these figures are revealed as corrupted by a predatory and selfish pursuit of their own interests. Those who come off best are the small tradesman and the industrialist—Mr. Snagsby the law stationer and Mr. Rouncewell the ironmaster. But even Mr. Snagsby is portrayed as afraid of and subservient to Mr. Tulkinghorn and unable to prevent his wife from exploiting the poor workhouse slavey Guster, who comes cheap because she is subject to fits; he can express his gentle heart only by silent donations of half-crown pieces to those who have touched his sympathies. And Mr. Rouncewell is one of those craftsman entrepreneurs who have made their way by invention and hard work; he has contributed to the welfare of society and is not a financial spider preying on its prosperity like Mr. Bounderby, the banker industrialist of *Hard Times*. In *Bleak House* the nearest analogues to Mr. Bounderby are the Smallweeds, that horrible family of little goblin usurers.

What a gallery are all the rest! There is Mrs. Jellyby, dreaming moonily of helping the African natives on the banks of Borioboola-Gha while she ignores the horrors of the London slums and neglects her own family. (In her unconcern for her children, Mrs. Jellyby was suggested by Mrs. Caroline Chisholm, whose Australian emigration schemes Dickens had aided.[8]) There is Mrs. Pardiggle, who browbeats the poor and bullies her children to enhance her own sense of power. There is Harold Skimpole, with his iridescent chatter about art and music and his whimsical paradoxes disguising his parasitic idleness. There is Mr. Turveydrop, that bloated parody of the Prince Regent, in his stays and rouge and padding, using his elegant deportment to batten on his devoted son and deluded daughter-in-law. There are the oily Chadband and the bitter Mrs. Chadband, he with his flatulent pseudo-religious magniloquence and she with her gloomy iron-bound harshness satirizing the emptiness and the cruelty of the evangelical creeds.

All these people exemplify the decay of the lofty principles and noble ideas that they profess, into irrelevance, flippancy, indifference, selfishness, and hatred. Chadband's sermonizing is nothing but the deliquescence of religion into a self-righteous substitution of words for deeds of love. "What is peace?" he demanded fatuously. "Is it war? No. Is it strife? No. Is it lovely, and gentle, and beautiful, and pleasant, and serene, and joyful? O yes! Therefore, my friends, I wish for peace, upon you and yours." [9] But all Chadband thinks of doing for the crossing-sweeper Jo is to tell him that he is "in a state of darkness," "a state of sinfulness," "a state of bondage," from which if he chose to profit by this discourse he might emerge into the joyfulness of becoming "a soaring human boy!" [10] And Mrs. Chadband, once the servant of Esther Summerson's aunt, Miss Barbary, echoes the relentlessness of that woman, who would tell a small child that it would have been better if she had never been born: "Your mother, Esther, is your disgrace, and you were hers." [11] What is Miss Barbary's vengeful rigor but the decay of religion into ferocity and wrath?

In such a society, where religion degenerates into perversions of its inspiration, culture into the cheating and cadging of Skimpole, and courtesy into the cold-hearted parental cannibalism of Turveydrop, mere self-preservation also sinks at its lowest into the hideous rapacity of Grandfather Smallweed. "The father of this pleasant grandfather . . . was a horny-skinned, two-legged, money-getting species of spider, who spun webs to catch unwary flies, and retired into holes until they were entrapped. The name of this old pagan's god was Compound Interest. He lived for it, married it, died of it. Meeting with a heavy loss in an honest little enterprise in which all the loss was intended to have been on the other side, he broke something—something necessary to his existence; therefore it couldn't have been his heart—and made an end of his career." [12]

*   *   *   *   *

Cumulatively, these characters make *Bleak House* both an anatomy of society and a fable in which its major influences and institutions are portrayed by means of sharply individualized figures. They are instruments through which the meaning of the story is enlarged and extended to one of the broadest social significance. But everywhere its statements are conveyed not in abstractions but embodied in character and action organically related to the analysis. Archibald MacLeish is wrong in saying that a poem should not mean but be: like any work of literature, it may legitimately both mean and be. Into the very existence of *Bleak House* Dickens has precipitated the understanding of nineteenth-century society that he has achieved.

His method is at the same time realistic and figurative. Mrs. Jellyby, never seeing anything nearer than Africa, Mrs. Pardiggle, forcing her children to contribute their allowances to the Tockahoopo Indians, are themselves; but they are also the types of a philanthropy that will do nothing to diminish the profitable exploitation of England's poor. Mrs. Pardiggle will hand out patronizing little booklets to debased brickmakers who are unable to read; she will not work to obtain them a living wage or decent homes with sanitary facilities. Neither she nor

Mrs. Jellyby will do a thing to abolish a pestilent slum like Tom-all-Alone's or to help an orphan vagrant like Jo.

"He is not one of Mrs. Pardiggle's Tockahoopo Indians," Dickens says bitterly; "he is not one of Mrs. Jellyby's lambs, being wholly unconnected with Borrioboola-Gha; he is not softened by distance and unfamiliarity; he is not a genuine foreign-grown savage; he is the ordinary home-made article. Dirty, ugly, disagreeable to all the senses, in body a common creature of the common streets, only in soul a heathen. Homely filth begrimes him, homely parasites devour him, homely sores are in him, homely rags are on him: native ignorance, the growth of English soil and climate, sinks his immortal nature lower than the beasts that perish. Stand forth, Jo, in uncompromising colours! From the sole of thy foot to the crown of thy head, there is nothing interesting about thee." [13]

Even more marked, however, in *Bleak House* is the use of poetic imagery and symbolism to underline and parallel the meaning of its patterns. The fog of the opening chapter is both literal and allegorical. It is the sooty London fog, but it covers all England, and it is the fog of obstructive procedures and outmoded institutions and selfish interests and obscured thinking as well. Miss Flite's caged birds symbolize the victims of Chancery, and the very names she has given them in her insanity are significant: "Hope, Joy, Youth, Peace, Rest, Life, Dust, Ashes, Waste, Want, Ruin, Despair, Madness, Death, Cunning, Folly, Words, Wigs, Rags, Sheepskin, Plunder, Precedent, Jargon, Gammon, and Spinach." "That's the whole collection," adds Krook, the sham Lord Chancellor, "all cooped up together, by my noble and learned brother." [14] Later, Miss Flite adds two more birds to the collection, calling them "the Wards in Jarndyce." [15] And always outside the cage lurks the cat Lady Jane, waiting, like the lawyers, to seize and tear any that might get free. Lady Jane is sometimes seen as a tiger and sometimes as the wolf that cannot be kept from prowling at the door. Mr. Vholes, skinning his tight black gloves off his hands as if he were flaying a victim, is constantly described, as are the other lawyers, in metaphors drawn from beasts of prey. And there is a further imagery of spiders spinning their traps, entangling flies within strand upon strand of sticky and imprisoning filaments, hanging their meshes everywhere in gray and dusty clotted webs.

The most elaborately worked out of these symbols is the parallel between Krook and the Lord Chancellor. "You see I have so many things here," Krook explains, "of so many kinds, and all, as the neighbours think (but *they* know nothing), wasting away and going to rack and ruin, that that's why they have given me and my place a christening. And I have so many old parchmentses and papers in my stock. And I have a liking for rust and must and cobwebs. And all's fish that comes to my net. And I can't abear to part with anything I once lay hold of (or so my neighbours think, but what do *they* know?) or to alter anything, or to have any sweeping, nor scouring, nor cleaning, nor repairing going on about me. That's the way I've got the ill name of Chancery. *I* don't mind. I go to see my noble and learned brother pretty well every day when he sits in the Inn. He don't notice me, but I notice him. There's no great odds betwixt us. We both grub on in a muddle." [16]

And to sharpen the point still more, as Lady Jane, at his bidding, rips a bundle of rags with tigerish claws, he adds, "I deal in cat-skins among other general matters, and hers was offered me. It's a very fine skin, as you may see, but I didn't have it stripped off! *That* warn't like Chancery practice though, says you!" [17]

Nor are these sharp and bitter strictures unjustified by the actualities. The Day case, nowhere near settled at the time Dickens wrote, dated from 1834, had always involved seventeen lawyers and sometimes thirty or forty, and had already incurred costs of £70,000.[18] The case of Gridley, the man from Shropshire, was based upon an actual case that had been called to Dickens's attention.[19] Jarndyce and Jarndyce was suggested by the notorious Jennings case, involving the disputed property of an old miser of Acton who had died intestate in 1798, leaving almost £1,500,000. When one of the claimants died *in* 1915 the case was still unsettled and the costs amounted to £250,000.[20]

Such facts give cogency to Dickens's conclusions: "The one great principle of the English law is, to make business for itself. There is no other principle distinctly, certainly, and consistently maintained through all its narrow turnings. Viewed by this light it becomes a coherent scheme, and not the monstrous maze the laity are apt to think it. Let them but once perceive that its grand principle is to make business for itself at their expense, and surely they will cease to grumble."

"But not perceiving this quite plainly," the laity *do* grumble, and then the "respectability of Mr. Vholes is brought into powerful play against them. 'Repeal this statute, my good sir?' says Mr. Kenge to a smarting client, 'repeal it, my dear sir? Never, with my consent. Alter this law, sir, and what will be the effect of your rash proceeding on a class of practitioners very worthily represented, allow me to say to you, by the opposite attorney in the case, Mr. Vholes? Sir, that class of practitioners would be swept from the face of the earth. Now you cannot afford—I will say, the social system cannot afford—to lose an order of men like Mr. Vholes. Diligent, persevering, steady, acute in business. My dear sir, I understand your present feelings against the existing state of things, which I grant to be a little hard in your case; but I can never raise my voice for the demolition of a class of men like Mr. Vholes.' " [21]

The respectability of Mr. Vholes "has even been cited with crushing effect before Parliamentary committees" and been no less reiterated in private conversations affirming "that these changes are death to people like Vholes: a man of undoubted respectability, with a father in the Vale of Taunton, and three daughters at home. Take a few steps more in this direction, say they, and what is to become of Vholes's father? Is he to perish? And of Vholes's daughters? Are they to be shirtmakers, or governesses? As though, Mr. Vholes and his relations being minor cannibal chiefs, and it being proposed to abolish cannibalism, indignant champions were to put the case thus: Make man-eating unlawful, and you starve the Vholeses!" [22]

But the law is only the archetype of those vested interests that plunder society under the guise of being society, that strangle the general welfare, that grow fat on the miseries of the poor. It is one of the instruments that give "monied might the means abundantly of wearying out the right," [23] the visible symbol behind which lurk the forces of greed and privilege spinning their labyrinthine webs of corruption. Spread out over the fair English landscape are Chesney Wold, with its noble dignity, its green garden terraces and stately drawing rooms, Bleak House, with its orderly comfort and generous master, Rouncewell's, with its productive and self-respecting industry. But Rouncewell's is no more than part of the whole—a part, too, that will reveal its own dark evils under the deeper analysis of *Hard Times*. Bleak House, at its best and for all its warm intentions, is itself helplessly enmeshed and can make only frustrated gestures to reach out a helping hand. And Chesney Wold has its corollary and consequence in

Tom-all-Alone's

Tom-all-Alone's and the wretched hovels of the brickmakers: its dignity is built on their degradation.

Chesney Wold and Tom-all-Alone's are thus also symbols in the symbolic structure. For Dickens does not mean that Sir Leicester Dedlock, or even the aristocracy as a class, is personally responsible for social evil, any more than are the Lord Chancellor or Carboy and Kenge or Inspector Bucket. Individually they may all be amiable enough, but they are instruments of a system in which the stately mansion and the rotting slum represent the opposite extremes. Inspector Bucket, officially the bloodhound of the law, is personally a bluff and kindhearted fellow, Conversation Kenge merely a florid rhetorician, the Lord Chancellor a harmless old gentleman. And to Sir Leicester, who epitomizes the system, Dickens is chivalrously magnanimous.

Sir Leicester is a good feudal landlord, a kind and generous master to his servants, loyal to his family, devoted to his wife. "He is a gentleman of strict conscience, disdainful of all littleness and meanness, and ready, on the shortest notice, to die any death you may please to mention rather than give occasion for the least impeachment of his integrity. He is an honourable, obstinate, truthful, high-spirited, intensely prejudiced, perfectly unreasonable man." [24] Beneath his high demeanor and occasional absurdity there is a core of true nobility. When he learns the story of Lady Dedlock's past, and falls moaning to the floor, paralyzed and unable to speak, his devotion to his wife and his distress at her flight are greater than the horror of the revelation, and his faltering hand traces upon a slate the words, "Full forgiveness. Find——" [25]

But, for all his private virtues, he has no hesitation about trying to bully or buy a victory in Parliamentary elections, although he bitterly resents the corrupt opposition to his own purposes that makes this expensive course necessary. The "hundreds of thousands of pounds" required to bring about the triumph of his own party he blames on the "implacable description" of the opposition and the "bad spirit" of the people. His dependent spinster cousin, the fair Volumnia, with her rouge, her still girlish ways, and her little scream, is innocently unable to imagine the need for this enormous outlay; Sir Leicester freezes her with his displeasure: "It is disgraceful to the electors. But as you, though inadvertently, and without intending so unreasonable a question, asked me 'what for?' let me reply to you. For necessary expenses." [26]

The "implacable" opposition is, of course, merely a rival faction contending for the spoils of office, and no matter which party wins, the country is still dominated by wealth and privilege manipulating all the puppetry of political juntas. This is true even when the candidates of Mr. Rouncewell the ironmaster capture a few seats, and will continue to be true when they fill the House, despite Sir Leicester's gasping conviction that "the floodgates of society are burst open, and the waters have—a—obliterated the landmarks of the framework of the cohesion by which things are held together!" [27] All that the rising power of the industrialists really means is that they too will force their way into the coalition of exploitation formed by their predecessors, the landed aristocracy, the lawyers and politicians, the merchants, and the bankers.

The political aspects of this situation Dickens conveys with a wonderful burlesque brilliance. "His description of our party system, with its Coodle, Doodle, Foodle, etc.," writes Bernard Shaw, "has never been surpassed for accuracy and for penetration of superficial pretence." But Shaw's feeling that Dickens "had not dug down to the bedrock of the imposture" is derived from a failure to notice that Dickens portrayed Tom-all-Alone's and the brickmakers as much more than a mere indictment of "individual delinquencies, local plague-spots, negligent authorities." [28] In reality Dickens links all these phenomena with each other, the political bargains and combinations no less so than the slow-moving chicaneries of law.

Lord Boodle points out to Sir Leicester that the formation of a new Ministry lies "between Lord Coodle and Sir Thomas Doodle—supposing it to be impossible for the Duke of Foodle to act with Goodle, which may be assumed to be the case in consequence of the breach arising out of that affair with Hoodle. Then, giving the Home Department and the Leadership of the House of Commons to Joodle, the Exchequer to Koodle, the Colonies to Loodle, and the Foreign Office to Moodle, what are you to do with Noodle? You can't offer him the Presidency of the Council; that is reserved for Poodle. You can't put him in the Woods and Forests; that is hardly good enough for Quoodle. What follows? That the country is shipwrecked, lost, and gone to pieces . . . because you can't provide for Noodle!

"On the other hand, the Right Honourable William Buffy, M.P., contends across the table with some one else, that the shipwreck of the country—about which there is no doubt; it is only the manner of it that is in question—is attributable to Cuffy. If you had done with Cuffy what you ought to have done when he first came into Parliament, and had prevented him from going over to Duffy, you would have got him into alliance with Fuffy, you would have had with you the weight attaching as a smart debater to Guffy, and you would have brought to bear upon the elections the wealth of Huffy, you would have got in for three counties Juffy, Kuffy, and Luffy, and you would have strengthened your administration by the official knowledge and business habits of Muffy. All this, instead of being as you now are, dependent upon the mere caprice of Puffy!" [29]

Beyond their witty parody of the language of political manipulation, these two paragraphs ingeniously exploit the mere ludicrous rhyming sounds of their alphabetical succession of names and the derogatory implications of many of those names. Boodle is not an auspicious name for a politician, nor do Noodle and Poodle convey the most promising insinuations. Doodle and Noodle were names of two of the characters in one of the versions of Fielding's burlesque *Tom Thumb*. And from the time immediately before his reporting days Dickens may well have remembered that the notoriously incompetent Lord Dudley, Secretary of State for Foreign Affairs under the Duke of Wellington in 1828, was widely known as Lord Doodle,[30] and that "doodle" meant to trifle or to make droning noises. Guffy, Huffy, Muffy, and Puffy may also be made to yield derisive associations, and possibly even Buffy, Cuffy, and Luffy.

With biting satire Dickens paints the ensuing political corruption. "England has been in a dreadful state for some weeks. Lord Coodle would go out, Sir Thomas Doodle wouldn't come in, and there being nobody in Great Britain (to speak of) except Coodle and Doodle, there has been no Government. . . . At last Sir Thomas Doodle has not only condescended to come in, but has done it handsomely, bringing in with him all his nephews, all his male cousins, and all his brothers-in-law. So there is hope for the old ship yet." In the process, he "has found that he must throw himself upon the country—chiefly in the form of sovereigns and beer," "in an auriferous and malty shower" while "mysterious men with no names" rush backward and forward across the country on secret errands. Meanwhile Britannia is "occu-pied in pocketing Doodle in the form of sovereigns and swallowing Doodle in the form of beer, and in swearing herself black in the face that she does neither." [31]

All this structure of venality rises upon a foundation of exploitation, destitution, and misery. We are shown the wretched hovels of the brickmakers at St. Alban's, "with pigsties close to the broken win-dows," old tubs "put to catch the droppings of rainwater from a roof, or . . . banked up with mud into a little pond like a large dirt-pie." [32] Within their damp and musty rooms we see their dwellers, "a woman with a black eye nursing a poor little gasping baby by the fire; a man all stained with clay and mud, and looking very dissipated, lying at full length on the ground, smoking a pipe; a powerful young man, fas-tening a collar on a dog; and a bold girl, doing some kind of washing in very dirty water." [33] As Professor Cazamian points out, contempo-rary official reports all more than justify the hideous picture. [34]

Into this scene Mrs. Pardiggle pushes her way, hectoring its inhabit-ants in her loud, authoritative voice and ignoring the growling resent-ment of the man on the floor. "I wants a end of these liberties took with my place. I wants an end of being drawed like a badger. . . . Is my daughter a-washin? Yes, she *is* a-washin. Look at the water. Smell it! That's wot we drinks. How do you like it, and what do you think of gin, instead! Ain't my place dirty? Yes, it is dirty—it's nat'rally dirty, and it's nat'rally onwholesome; and we've had five dirty and onwhole-some children, as is all dead infants, and so much the better for them, and for us besides. Have I read the little book wot you left? No, I ain't read the little book wot you left. There ain't nobody here as knows how to read it; and if there wos, it wouldn't be suitable to me. It's a book fit for a babby, and I'm not a babby. If you was to leave me a doll, I shouldn't nuss it. How have I been conducting of myself? Why, I've been drunk for three days, and I'd a been drunk four, if I'd a had the money. Don't I never mean for to go to church? No, I don't never mean for to go to church. I shouldn't be expected there, if I did; the beadle's too gen-teel for me. And how did my wife get that black eye? Why, I giv' it her; and if she says I didn't, she's a Lie!" [35]

Worse still is the urban slum of Tom-all-Alone's, a black, dilapi-dated street of crazy houses tumbling down and reeking with foul stains and loathsome smells, dripping with dirty rain, and sheltering within its ruined walls a human vermin that crawls and coils itself to sleep in maggot numbers on the rotting boards of its floors among fetid rags. "Twice, lately, there has been a crash and a cloud of dust, like the springing of a mine, in Tom-all-Alone's; and each time a house has fallen. These accidents have made a paragraph in the newspapers, and have filled a bed or two in the nearest hospital. The gaps remain, and there are not unpopular lodgings among the rubbish." [36] There dwells Jo, with his body exuding a stench so horrible that Lady Dedlock cannot bear to have him come close to her; and thence comes Jo, munching his bit of dirty bread, and admiring the structure that houses the Society for the Propagation of the Gospel in Foreign Parts. "He has no idea, poor wretch, of the spiritual destitution of a coral reef in the Pacific, or what it costs to look up the precious souls among the cocoa-nuts and bread-fruit." [37] And when Jo lies dead of neglect, malnutrition, and disease, the narrative swells into an organ-toned and accusing dirge: "Dead, your Majesty. Dead, my lords and gentlemen. Dead, Right Reverends and Wrong Reverends of every order. Dead, men and women, born with Heavenly compassion in your hearts. And dying thus around us every day." [38]

Counterpointed with the death of Jo is that of Richard Carstone, for high-spirited and generous youth, with every advantage, is no less prey to the infection of an acquisitive society than helpless ignorance and misery. All Richard's buoyancy and courage, his gentleness and frankness, his quick and brilliant abilities, are not enough to save him. Gradually he becomes entangled in the fatal hope of getting something for nothing, stakes everything on the favorable outcome of the Chancery suit, neglects his capacities, fosters his careless shortcomings, dissipates the little money he has, feverishly drifts into suspicion and distrust of his honorable guardian, argues that Mr. Jarndyce's appearance of disinterestedness may be a blind to further his own advantage in the case. How, Richard asks, can he settle down to anything? "If you were living in an unfinished house, liable to have the roof put on or taken off—to be from top to bottom pulled down or built up—tomorrow, next day, next week, next month, next year,—you would find it hard to rest or settle." [39] By early manhood his expression is already so worn by weariness and anxiety that his look is "like ungrown despair." [40] Not until it is too late, and he is dying, does he speak of "beginning the world," and confess his mistakes and blindnesses to his wife. Esther Summerson reports his words:

"'I have done you many wrongs, my own. I have fallen like a poor stray shadow on your way, I have married you to poverty and trouble, I have scattered your means to the winds. You will forgive me all this, Ada, before I begin the world?'

"A smile irradiated his face, as she bent to kiss him. He slowly laid his face down upon her bosom, drew his arms closer round her neck, and with one parting sob began the world. Not this world, O not this! The world that sets this right.

"When all was still, at a late hour, poor crazed Miss Flite came weeping to me, and told me she had given her birds their liberty." [41]

Richard Carstone and poor Jo, Miss Flite driven insane, Gridley dying broken on the floor of George's shooting gallery and George in the toils of the moneylenders, Mr. Tulkinghorn shot through the heart in his Lincoln's Inn Fields chambers beneath the pointing finger of allegory, Sir Leicester humbled, heartbroken, and paralyzed, Lady Dedlock dead, disgraced, and mud-stained outside the slimy walls of the pauper graveyard where her lover lies buried—all are swept on to frustration or defeat in the titanic intensity of this dark storm of story. Everywhere the honest, the generous, the helpless, the simple, and the loving are thwarted and crippled. John Jarndyce, the violently good master of Bleak House, can rescue only a distressingly small number of those he sets out to save. In a life of poverty and struggle imposed by a society where nature itself is deformed and tainted, poor Caddy Jellyby and her husband Prince Turveydrop can give birth only to an enfeebled deaf-and-dumb child. For *Bleak House* (like Shaw's *Heartbreak House*, of which it is a somber forerunner) is in its very core symbolic: *Bleak House* is modern England, it is the world of an acquisitive society, a monetary culture, and its heavy gloom is implied by the very adjective that is a part of its title.

* * * * *

But the mood of *Bleak House* is not one of resignation or despairing sorrow; it is that of indignation and grim fire-eyed defiance. Dickens is no longer, as Shaw points out, merely the liberal reformer who takes it for granted that "the existing social order" is "the permanent and natural order of human society, needing reforms now and then and here and there, but essentially good and sane and right and respectable and proper and everlasting." He has become instead a revolutionist, to whom "it is transitory, mistaken, dishonest, unhappy, pathological: a social disease to be cured, not endured." [42] It is this that troubles numbers of readers in Dickens's later books, which are his greatest ones, and makes those readers prefer the earlier stories. It is now the very root-assumptions of that social order that Dickens is attacking and insisting must be destroyed.

One of the forms taken by the discomfort of such readers is the repeated criticism that Dickens could not portray a gentleman. At the time of Sir Mulberry Hawk and Lord Frederick Verisopht this might have been true; by the time of Sir Leicester Dedlock it was so no longer. It should be observed that Thackeray, who was never accused of a failure to understand gentlemen, paints them far more savagely than Dickens does; he makes Sir Pitt Crawley mean, dirty, illiterate, and brutal, and almost the entire aristocracy profligate, sycophantic, ill-bred. But Thackeray took the stability of society for granted, whereas Dickens was by now demanding a radical reconstruction of society. So Thackeray may be smiled upon as a genteel satirist who merely exposed the flaws of the polite world, and Dickens must be thrown out of court as one who had no understanding of the upper classes. "It would be nearer the mark," Shaw says dryly, "to say that Dickens knew all that really mattered in the world about Sir Leicester Dedlock," and that Thackeray "knew nothing that really mattered about him. . . . Thackeray could see Chesney Wold; but Dickens could see through it." [43]

He could see through Lombard Street and Threadneedle Street and the City, too; and, as he was soon to prove, he could see through Birmingham, Manchester, Leeds, and Preston. He sees the world about him as a conflict between the forces of love and life and those of acquisition, retention, and greed, with pride and cruelty everywhere inflicting the most frightful mutilations upon helplessness. But not without having recoil back upon themselves the inevitable consequences of the system that embodies their working, nor without evils being engendered that spread almost at random everywhere. Sir Leicester cannot protect the woman he loves and honors; the Lord Chancellor himself cannot speed the slow movement of Chancery or prevent it from grinding its victims, of whatever class they may be. Esther Summnerson's face cannot be saved from having its beauty ruined as long as there are waifs like Jo and plague spots like Tom-all-Alone's.

In this society of shocking extremes the highest and the lowest are inextricably linked to each other. Dickens had shown this before, in *Barnaby Rudge* with Sir John Chester and Hugh, in *Dombey and Son* with Edith Dombey and Alice Marwood, but in *Bleak House* it becomes central to the very structure and meaning of the plot. Tom-all-Alone's, Dickens shows us, has his revenge. "Even the winds are his messengers, and they serve him in these hours of darkness. There is not a drop of Tom's corrupted blood but propagates infection and contagion somewhere. It shall pollute, this very night, the choice stream (in which chemists on analysis would find the genuine nobility) of a Norman house, and his Grace shall not be able to say Nay to the infamous alliance. There is not an atom of Tom's slime, not a cubic inch of any pestilential gas in which he lives, not one obscenity or degradation about him, not an ignorance, not a wickedness, not a brutality of his committing, but shall work its retribution, through every order of society, up to the proudest of the proud, and to the highest of the high. Verily, what with tainting, plundering, and spoiling, Tom has his revenge." [44]

And just as Tom-all-Alone's sends out its noxious vapors poisoning society, its waifs bearing pollution and infection, its criminals returning evil for the evil that has formed them; just as Tom-all-Alone's slowly and piecemeal crumbles into ruins from the rottenness of its old beams and reeking plaster, now one and now another house crashing down into dust and rubbish: so the internal rottenness of the social structure that not merely tolerates but perpetuates Tom-all-Alone's must inevitably destroy itself in the end, die of its own self-engendered diseases, annihilate itself by its own corruption. Such is the symbol of Krook's death by Spontaneous Combustion:

"Here is a small burnt patch of flooring; here is the tinder from a little bundle of burnt paper, but not so light as usual, seeming to be steeped in something; and here is—is it the cinder of a small charred and broken log of wood sprinkled with white ashes, or is it coal? O Horror, he IS here! and this from which we run away, striking out the light and overturning one another in the street, is all that represents him.

"Help, help, help! come into this house for Heaven's sake!

"Plenty will come in, but none can help. The Lord Chancellor of that Court, true to his title in his last act, has died the death of all Lord Chancellors in all Courts, and of all authorities in all places under all names soever, where false pretences are made, and where injustice is done. Call the death by any name Your Highness will, attribute it to whom you will, or say it might have been prevented how you will, it is the same death eternally—inborn, inbred, engendered in the corrupt humours of the vicious body itself, and that only—Spontaneous Combustion, and none other of all the deaths that can be died." [45]

It is Dickens speaking with the voice of prophecy. For the sham Lord Chancellor and his shop clearly symbolize not only the real Court of Chancery and all the corruptions of all law, but "all authorities in all places under all names soever"—all the injustices of an unjust society. And they are no longer subjects for local cure or even amputation. Nothing will do short of the complete annihilation that they will ultimately provide by blowing up of their own corruption.

CHAPTER THREE

"The Heaviest Blow in My Power"

BLEAK HOUSE represents a tremendous effort and a tremendous creative achievement. Dickens had so organized its very structure as to image his sense of society as one monolithic whole dominated by the powers of privilege and wealth. The thick-coiled fog of the law, the clotted web of tradition, the plausible orthodoxies of manners, art, philanthropy, religion, parliamentary government, were only defenses and disguises for the predatory forces they concealed. He was to return to the attack again in his next book, *Hard Times*, when he would unmask the arid, hollow, heartless scheme of values behind these forms and institutions, the dusty, destructive ethics that stunted love, imagination, life itself.

But the struggle to forge the gigantic attainment of *Bleak House* into its huge unity had momentarily exhausted Dickens's powers. He must have rest before he undertook another work of fiction. And so, after his heavy spell of labor, he made ready now in the autumn of 1853 to set out on a two-month holiday in Switzerland and Italy that he had been planning from the proceding January to take with Augustus Egg and Wilkie Collins.

Since Egg had induced Collins to play the valet in *Not So Bad as We Seem*, a genial association had developed between Dickens and the younger writer. Twenty-six years of age when his first novel, *Antonia*, was published, he was twelve years Dickens's junior. Slight in build, with dainty feet and hands so small that he wore women's gloves, but with an enormous brow bulging above his spectacles, Collins looked both smug and prim. But his crimson ties and blue-striped shirts insinuated another vein in his character, colorful, Bohemian, running into a taste for rowdy fun. He loved rich food, champagne, and music halls; he was often involved in intricate tangles with several women at once; he was amusing, cynical, good-humored, unrestrained to the point of vulgarity. As godfather to the first baby of the painter E. M. Ward he celebrated so heartily that, trying in vain to focus on the infant lying in the clergyman's arms, he exclaimed, "The baby sheems moving in a very odd way, and is making funny faces. Why, 'pon my soul, the baby's drunk, the baby's drunk!"

Collins gave only bachelor parties and was regarded askance by nice-minded women. He was lazy, skeptical, slovenly, unpunctual; but he was also gentle, warm-hearted, and unpretentious—he was not at all irritated at being told that his books were "read in every back-kitchen." He hated pugnacity, competition, and cruelty, and was interested only in enjoying himself. All these qualities help to explain the appeal he had for Dickens, who was coming to feel more and more skeptical of society and its conventions himself, and more and more rebellious against them. He craved color and variety in his life, of which he found too little in his staid older friends as they grew steadily more respectable and sober—certainly not in Forster, who every day grew more starchified and buttoned up. Collins stood for fun and freedom. With him it was easy for Dickens to be "Albion's Sparkler," as he loved to call himself, seething with champagne gaiety. Gradually, in the course of the last year, whenever Dickens wanted to spend a night out he had taken to summoning Collins to "forage pleasantly for a dinner in the City" or "revel in the glories of the eccentric British Drayma" at one of the cheap theaters. Or, holding out the enticement of a bowl of gin punch, he would playfully announce "the National Sparkler" prepared to give his guest "a bellyful if he means anything but Bounce."

In preparation now for the holiday tour, Dickens "cleared the way through Household Words," so that Wills could handle it in his absence. He dictated the remainder of the Child's History of England to Georgy,[1] unceremoniously dropping it at the Revolution of 1688 and rounding it off with a hasty list of the reigns from the time of William and Mary to the marriage of Victoria and Albert. Kate, Georgy, and the children were to be sent home from Boulogne, except for Alfred and Frank, who were being left there at a private school.[2]

Back in London, the Guild of Literature and Art gave a gorgeous

dinner for Dickens at the London Tavern, "four immense red scaffolds covered with gold plates—turtle cooked in six ways—astonishing
wines—venison—pine[apple]s—all manner of luxuries." The evening "would have been perfect" but that Forster, who realized and
jealously resented Dickens's new friendship with Collins, made "a
very uncomfortable and restless Chairman." [3] Another hurried trip to
Boulogne, and then, on the 10th of October, Dickens was off for
Paris, where he, Egg, and Collins were invited to a great dinner given
by Miss Coutts,[4] and then started for Strasbourg and Switzerland.[5]

In Lausanne they were guests of Chauncey Hare Townshend, and
Dickens met his old friend Cerjat, now thin and very gray, and Haldimand, as loud-laughing and disputatious as ever.[6] At the Blind Institute the blind, deaf, and dumb protégé he used to supply with cigars
had entirely forgotten him and only "muttered strange eager sounds
like 'Town' and 'Down' and 'Mown,' " which Townsend ludicrously
tried to wrest into an effort to speak *his* name. "As he evidently had
no more idea of Townshend than of any lamp-post in London, it was
so inexpressibly absurd that I laughed disgracefully, and could not be
stopped." [7] In Geneva they stayed at the Écu, and at Chamonix
ascended the Mer de Glace.[8] Then they crossed the Simplon and Dickens was delighting in hearing "the delicate Italian once again." [9] and
sending greetings home to Catherine and Georgy and all the children,
including the baby, now called by the nickname of Plornishghenter.

In imitation of Dickens's mustache and beard, which were now
"formidable," [10] the sad-faced Egg and the wispy Collins were letting
their own grow, achieving results, Dickens said, "more straggling,
wandering, wiry, stubbly, formless, more given to wandering into
strange places and sprouting up noses and dribbling under chins, than
anything . . . since the Flood." Suffering from the sight of "these terrific objects," Dickens seized his razor and shaved off his beard as an
example; but utterly without effect, "they merely observing with complacency that 'it looks much better so.' " [11] Egg sometimes wanted accommodations that could hardly be obtained even in a large city,[12]
Collins spat and snorted in the morning more than Dickens thought
necessary,[13] and both men were a little stingy with servants. As for
Dickens, he dragged them across glaciers, hauled them up mountains,
raced them along roads, dragooned them into punctuality, and forced
them through a fury of sighteeing with a relentless energy that must

have worn them down. Nevertheless they all enjoyed each other's company and got on very well together.

At Genoa, Dickens found the Palazzo Peschiere converted into a girls' school.[14] He wrote Kate a gossipy account of their friends and acquaintances there, including the Thompsons, who lived at Nervi, some fourteen miles toward Porto Fino. Thompson, with a pointed beard, "in a disorderly old billiard room wth all manner of messes in it," was teaching the multiplication table to his daughters, two pale untidy little girls with no stockings and oddly cropped hair. Christiana, daubed with oil paint and greatly flushed, "said she had invented this head gear as a picturesque thing—adding that perhaps it was and perhaps it wasn't." Dickens got the impression that, what with music and oil painting, "household affairs went a little to the wall." [15] The ethereal creature who had made his heart leap was clearly no longer an angel in his eyes.

The steamer from Genoa to Naples was scandalously overcrowded with passengers who had been sold first-class tickets far in excess of the accommodations, so that ladies were obliged to sleep on deck among heaps of carpetbags, hatboxes, and life buoys. In the midst of this came a tropical downpour that drenched everyone, and the rest of the night was passed in a jumble on the stairs. During the second day Dickens "facetiously" led the captain "such a life" that he found a place for Egg and Collins in the storeroom, "where they slept on little dressers, with the pickles, spices, tea, fruits, and a very large double Glo'ster cheese." [16] Dickens slept in the steward's cabin on a pallet "four feet and a half by one and a quarter," with the engine "under the pillow," an "extremely nervous" wall, "and the whole in a profuse perspiration of warm oil." [17]

At Naples the travelers visited a public bath to rid themselves of the odors of groceries and oil. Dickens was soaped by an old attendant who frothed him all over, rubbed him down, and scrubbed him with a brush, and who "was as much disappointed (apparently) as surprised, not to find me dirty . . . ejaculating under his breath 'O Heaven how clean this Englishman is!' He also remarked that the Englishman was as fair as a beautiful woman—but there, he added, the resemblance ended." [18]

Naples was full of people whom Dickens knew: Sir James Emerson Tennent and Lady Tennent, who had been on the steamer from

Genoa; the British Chargé d'Affaires, who had been one of the guests at the Rockingham theatricals; [19] Austen Henry Layard, the excavator of Nineveh and as uncompromising a radical as Dickens himself, "with whom we ascended Vesuvius in the sunlight and came down in the moonlight, talking merrily." [20] And at near-by Capri, Dickens learned, a son of Mrs. Norton, "Young Brinsley Norton, two and twenty years old," had married "a bare-footed girl off the Beach, with whom he had previously fulfilled all matrimonial conditions except the ceremony." The bride had "no idea of a hair brush and is said to be extremely dirty—which her young husband particularly admires, observing that it is 'not conventional.' " [21]

Politically, Dickens soon realized, Italy was in an even more gloomy state of reaction than before the revolutions of 1848. In every street of Milan "the noble palace of some exile" was a barrack with dirty soldiers "lolling out of the magnificent windows." In Naples, under "King Bomba" there were a hundred thousand troops. Dickens asked a Neapolitan Marchese what had happened to a cultivated man he had known there. "In exile," was the reply. "What would you have? He was a remarkable man—full of knowledge, full of spirit, full of generosity. Where should he be but in exile!" [22]

On arriving in Rome, Dickens was disappointed not to find an expected letter from Kate, and wrote to Georgina his "doubts respecting the plainness of its direction." [23] Sending a special inquiry to the post office next day, he did discover a letter, but so illegibly addressed, he wrote Kate, that no "Frenchman or Italian could ever make out the first necessary condition—that my name begins with a D—." [24] From Forster he received two indignant letters reporting that Wills was running *Household Words* without asking any advice from him.[25]

The Roman antiquities were smaller than Dickens's imagination in nine years had made them, but the Pantheon he thought "even nobler than of yore" and was fascinated to find the wires of the electric telegraph going "like a sunbeam through the cruel old heart of the Coliseum." Malaria from the Pontine Marshes was gradually "encroaching on the Eternal City as if it were commissioned to swallow it up"; "from the Coliseum through the Street of Tombs to the ruins of the old Appian Way" there was nothing "but ruined houses from which the people have fled, and where it is Death to sleep." [26]

Arriving early for a performance of *Moses in Egypt* at the opera, the three travelers found a party of Americans behind them in the almost empty theater. "I expect we ain't no call to set so nigh to one another neither," said one of them, "—will you scatter, Kernel, will you scatter sir?" So, said Dickens, they "scattered" all over the pit—"for no earthly reason apparently but to get rid of one another." When the audience began coming in, they were forced to resume their right places—all except one. About an hour later, though, "when Moses was invoking the darkness," a disturbance broke out. "What is it neow, sir?" said one American to another; "—some person seems to be getting along against streeem." "Waal sir," replied the other, "I dunno. But I xpect 'tis the Kernel sir, a holdin on." "So it was," said Dickens. "The Kernel was ignominiously escorted back to his right place, not in the least disconcerted, and in perfectly good spirits and temper." [27]

Collins and Egg also continued to give Dickens much amusement. "To hear Collins learnedly holding forth to Egg (who has as little of that gammon as an artist *can* have) about reds, and greens, and things 'coming well' with other things, and lines being wrong, and lines being right, is far beyond the bounds of all caricature." Dickens ostentatiously refrained from participating in these arty conversations, "always appearing to fall into a profound reverie" while they went on. Collins was also very learned on music, "and sometimes almost drives me into frenzy by humming and whistling whole overtures—with not one movement correctly remembered from the beginning to the end. I was obliged to ask him, the day before yesterday, to leave off whistling the overture to William Tell. 'For by Heaven,' said I, 'there's something the matter with your ear—I think it must be the cotton—which plays the Devil with the commonest tune.' " [28]

"He occasionally expounds a code of morals," Dickens told Catherine, "taken from modern French novels, which I instantly and with becoming gravity smash. But the best of it is, that he tells us about the enormous quantities of Monte Pulciano and what not, that he used to drink when he was last there, and what distinguished people said to him in the way of taking his opinion, and what advice he gave them and so forth—being then exactly thirteen years of age. On this head, Egg is always very good, and makes me laugh heartily. All these absurdities are innocent enough. I tell them in default of having anything else to tell. We are all the best of friends, and have never had the least difference." [29]

* * * * *

Before going on to Florence, Dickens sent Wills a little story for the Christmas number of *Household Words*, called "The Schoolboy's Story," and at Venice he succeeded in doing another entitled "Nobody's Story." [30] Under a cold but bright blue winter sky, the fantastic city enchanted Dickens as it had on his first visit. By day the water was a blazing ultramarine, by night a gleaming black, and under the exquisite starlight "the front of the cathedral, overlaid with golden mosaics and beautiful colours, is like a thousand rainbows even in the night." More than ever, though, Dickens felt "that one of the great uses of travelling is to encourage a man to think for himself," and have the boldness to ignore the genteel subserviencies about works of art. "Egg's honest amazement and consternation when he saw some of the most trumpeted things was what the Americans call a 'caution.' " Dickens refused to fall into conventional raptures over what did not move him, or to follow the guidebook in patronizing Tintoretto, whose *Assembly of the Blest* he thought "the most wonderful . . . picture ever painted." It was through the extension of such slavish orthodoxies that the world got "three-fourths of its frauds and miseries." [31]

When he had been at Genoa, Dickens had joyfully visited the De la Rues.[32] Mme. De la Rue was still haunted by her phantoms, but otherwise well and in brave spirits. She and her husband both referred warmly and generously to Kate, and Mme. De la Rue sent her love. But beyond mentioning the fact that he had seen them,[33] Dickens said nothing about them when he was writing to Kate until he was in Turin on his way home. Then he reminded her of the time she had constrained him "to make that painful declaration of your state of mind to the De la Rue's," and asked her if what had "looked large in that little place" had not since then "shrunk to its reasonable and natural proportions." His effort to cure Mme. De la Rue, he reminded her, was simply an illustration of the intense pursuit of any idea that took complete possession of him, and was one of the qualities that made him different from other men. "Whatever made you unhappy in the Genoa time had no other root, beginning, middle, or end, than whatever has made you proud and honored in your married life . . ." [34]

"Now I am perfectly clear," he told her, "that your position beside these people is not a good one, is not an amiable one, not a generous one—is not worthy of you at all." Kate had the power to set this right by sending Mme. De la Rue "a note to say that you have heard . . . of her sufferings and her cheerfulness—that you couldn't receive her messages of remembrance without a desire to respond to them—and that if you should ever be thrown together again . . . you hope it will be for a friendly association without any sort of shadow upon it." He would never ask her if she had followed his suggestion, he ended, and it would be "utterly valueless" for her to do so "through a grain of any other influence than that of your own heart." [35] But evidently Catherine now felt persuaded that she had suffered from a mistaken jealousy in those miserable Italian days, and did as he suggested. The following spring Dickens was even asking De la Rue if his wife had received Kate's "letter about the Italian dishes"—an inquiry of which it is impossible to say whether it refers to recipes or pottery. [36]

Dickens had arranged that at Paris he was to be met by his son Charley, who had been spending the past year in Germany. [37] The boy had decided that he did not want to enter any of the learned professions, and on his father's advice had given up an inclination for the army and was planning to become a businessman. [38] He had consequently withdrawn from Eton the preceding Christmas and gone to Leipzig to study German as a serviceable tool for a mercantile career. [39] He was now almost sixteen, and Dickens found "his arms and legs so grown out of his coat and trousers" as to necessitate smuggling him "under cover of night, to a ready-made establishment . . . where they put him into balloon-waisted pantaloons, and increased my confusion." [40]

At Dover, on Sunday, December 11th, the authorities of the railroad, hearing that Dickens was crossing from Calais, "detained train for London for distinguished author's arrival, rather to the exasperation of British public. D. A. arrived at home between ten and eleven that night, thank God, and found all well and happy." [41] Almost at once he plunged into rehearsing a Twelfth-Night play with the children and preparing three readings he had agreed to give for the benefit of the newly established Birmingham and Midland Institute. [42] Kate and Georgy went along to Birmingham to hear him.

These were Dickens's first public readings from his books. The

Birmingham Town Hall was an enormous place, "but I had considered all that carefully," he said, "and I believe made the most distant person hear as well as if I had been reading in my own room." The first night's reading of A *Christmas Carol* on December 27th was attended by two thousand people, who listened spellbound for three full hours, and repeatedly burst into tumultuous applause. After an almost equally successful reading of *The Cricket on the Hearth*, on the 29th, he gave a second reading of the *Carol* on the 30th, at reduced prices, before an assemblage of twenty-five hundred working people, for whom Dickens had requested that most of the vast auditorium be reserved. These, he thought, were the best audience of the three. "They lost nothing, misinterpreted nothing, followed everything closely, laughed and cried . . . and animated me to that extent that I felt as if we were all bodily going up into the clouds together." [43]

Between £400 and £500 was added to the endowment of the Institute, its grateful founders gave Dickens and Kate a silver flower basket and another piece of plate,[44] and the performance made such a furore that Dickens was deluged with invitations to read elsewhere.[45] All these last, however, he refused or evaded, and returned to helping the children get up their Twelfth-Night performance of Fielding's *Tom Thumb* in the schoolroom. (This was now the third year of such high jinks: the year before they had done Robert Brough's extravaganza *William Tell*.[46]) Little Betty and Lally Lemon trotted over to rehearsals from Gordon Place with their father, and Dickens "improvised costumes," one of the childish performers remembered, "painted and corked our innocent cheeks, and suggested all the most effective business of the scenes." [47]

On the night of the performance, Dickens, who played the Ghost of Gaffer Thumb, billed himself under the pseudonym of "the Modern Garrick," and Mark Lemon, who played the Giantess Glumdalca, as "the Infant Phenomenon." The little girls were gravely irresistible as Huncamunca and Dollalolla. A small boy named Alfred Ainger, who performed Lord Grizzle, sang the ballad of "Villikins and His Dinah" so drolly that Thackeray, who was among the guests, rolled off his chair in helpless convulsions of laughter. But the hit of the evening was the small helmeted hero, Tom Thumb, acted with solemn conviction by four-year-old Henry Fielding Dickens.[48]

Caught up in this seasonal turmoil, Dickens had not yet seen two

American friends, Mrs. David Colden and her brother Dr. Wilkes, whom he remembered happily from his New York days, although he had learned of their presence in London on the Sunday night of his own arrival. His first impulse had been to dash around to the Burlington Hotel at once.[49] " 'Good God!' said I, 'I must go and see them directly.' 'You can't,' said Catherine and Georgina both together, 'for they are going to Brighton tomorrow for a few days.' " [50] Then came the Birmingham expedition, and then the children's play. When Dickens did call on January 8th, Mrs. Colden, hurt, received him rather frostily. He went home and immediately wrote her a note of explanation.

"Life is not long enough," he pleaded, "for any little misunderstanding among friends who are really friends at heart . . ." He had come as soon as he had cleared away the demands upon his time, and could say, "where shall I go with you, what companionship can we project together, how will you use me in this great place that I know something about. . . . Now do dismiss all but that," he concluded, "and let us be as cordial as when I left you a dozen years ago. If there be any blame, I take it all; if there be any slight, you shall have it all. Let it be past in any case." Mrs. Colden melted, and agreed that he was not, as he put it at the end of his letter, "a neglectful—And callous—Ruffian—but your old friend—Quite unchanged." [51]

* * * * *

No sooner were the New Year's festivities over than Bradbury and Evans called a business conference to consider plans for the future. The six months' profits of *Household Words* on the preceding September 30th had been only around £528, about half what they had been for the corresponding periods in the preceding two years, and the circulation was still shrinking. After having steadily bettered its initial success, it was now slipping badly.[52] Something drastic would have to be done.

The last installment of *The Child's History of England* had been published in December, and Bradbury and Evans urged that Dickens spring to the rescue by writing a new serial in weekly numbers especially for the pages of the magazine. It had always been understood that he would occasionally contribute a long story, though at the moment he had intended no effort of the kind for a full year.[53] But

Bradbury and Evans pressed; Forster and Wills concurred; and Dickens agreed. There was "such a fixed idea," he announced, "on the part of my printers and co-partners . . . that a story by me, continued from week to week, would make some unheard of effect . . . that I am going to write one." [54]

Even so, he might have sought other means to swell *Household Word's* circulation had not the idea for the novel he was to write "laid hold of me," as he put it, "by the throat in a very violent manner." [55] Within him, the conception of the forces shaping society foreshadowed by *Dombey and Son* and darkly, volcanically dominant throughout the entire design of *Bleak House,* was still fermenting and seething with creative fury. Deeper still, indeed, the roots of the new story went back even further, into the beginnings of his development: they were twisted in the flaring gloom of the Black Country and his first horrified vision, sixteen years ago, of mines like underground dungeons and mills filled with clamor and cruelty. He had sworn then "to strike the heaviest blow in my power" for their victims. [56]

In *Nicholas Nickleby* he had hardly been ready to carry out that oath, but, in one sense, all that he had written since had done so. His warm, loving, humorous portrayal of the poor, his sympathy and wrath at their mistreatment, strengthened the emotions behind every effort for their welfare. Dickens would not stand for any patronizing talk of the laboring class being stupid or lazy or of their not minding dirt and squalor. He utterly rejected the dogma that their earnings must be determined by an iron law of wage, and insisted on their right to a decent livelihood. He demanded that the Government recognize and fulfill a duty to them and their children. As a writer, as an editor, as a public figure, he hammered repeatedly at these issues.

But the cruel and ugly world of mechanized industry had loomed through his stories only in a few nightmare glimpses—from the train windows of Mr. Dombey's journey to Leamington or in *The Old Curiosity Shop* as a blur of angry workers silhouetted against the glare of furnaces. Scrooge is not a millowner nor an ironmaster, though he voices their relentless economic creed. And the working people Dickens had so colorfully painted were not the miners, the mill hands, or the pottery workers, but the humble folk already crowded in great cities and coastal towns before the factory wheels began turning. Mr. Kenwigs, Mrs. Nubbles, Bob Cratchit, Toby Veck, Mr. Peggotty and

Ham Peggotty are their representatives: the small craftsman, the washerwoman, the poor clerk, the ticket porter, the fisherman and boatbuilder, and, beside them, the apprentices, milliners' assistants, seamstresses, domestic servants, brickmakers, and waifs like Jo the crossing-sweeper. Will Fern, an out-of-work farm laborer; Mick Walker and Mealy Potatoes, sealing Murdstone and Grimby's bottles by hand; Mr. Toodle, fireman and locomotive engineer: there are no factory machine-minders among them.

Meanwhile, through all the first half of the nineteenth century, the power of the industrial system had been growing until it dominated society. Chimneys smutted the sky and killed grass and trees, chemical waste fouled the streams, bleak miles of sordid tenements spread like a cancerous blight over the countryside. Row upon row of flimsy houses, three-quarters of them with no privies, crammed thousands of human beings into damp rooms and cellars. Heaps of ordure and garbage outside drained into ditches which often provided the only water people had to drink.[57] The owners of the factories fought by every evasion against obedience to the Ten Hours Bill, cynically defied sanitary regulations in unventilated workrooms whose air was thick with fluff from the looms, and recklessly ignored the law requiring that dangerous machinery be fenced in. The philosophy of the industrialists savagely denied that they had any duty to their employees except to pay them the wage established by the law of supply and demand, and insisted that the prosperity of the country depended upon high profits and cheap labor. The industrial system established a tyranny all the deadlier because it professed to be based upon scientific laws inherent in the very structure of society.

This fusion of brutal act and harsh theory was the core of what Dickens had always fought. But he now understood it far more deeply and clearly. He had been right in seeing Sir Leicester Dedlock as the symbol of landed power and inherited wealth; right in seeing Mr. Dombey as the symbol of mercantile power making itself an accomplice in social miseries that it even deepened; right in seeing Coodle and Doodle as the tools of both. He was right, too, in seeing that, in comparison with Sir Leicester, Mr. Rouncewell the ironmaster was a progressive force—as Mr. Dombey's father, or perhaps his grandfather, had been. Mr. Rouncewell had created a new power, however crude; added to the world's wealth, however greedy he had been with it. In Parliament he was already disputing the control of England with Sir Leicester and Mr. Dombey. He had torn the chains from his own limbs. What Dickens was now about to demonstrate was that he had proceeded to rivet them even more firmly on the limbs of the poor. [58]

But more horrible to Dickens even than the hard reality was the fact that the factory owners confronted it with a clear conscience. Their philosophic principles, so far as they had any, were identical with their practice. Many of them acted simply in straightforward greed, though they were glad enough to use the abstract defenses the economists devised for them. And the abstractions represented their true feelings: nothing was real except the statistics of profit and loss; anything else was mere sentimentality, intangible fancy. The degree to which Dickens insisted on this hard materialism as the essential feature of the industrial system is indicated in the bitter list of titles he drew up for the story that became Hard Times: "According to Cocker. Prove it. Stubborn Things. Mr. Gradgrind's Facts. The Grindstone. Hard Times. Two and Two are Four. Something Tangible. Our Hardheaded Friend. Rust and Dust. Simple Arithmetic. A Matter of Calculation. A Mere Question of Figures. The Gradgrind Philosophy." [59]

With his usual thoroughness Dickens prepared the ground for his story. He had already determined on its opening scene in Mr. Gradgrind's school, which he documented by studying the Educational Board's questions for the examination of teachers.[60] Though he had so recently passed through the blast furnaces and belching chimneys of Wolverhampton on his way to Birmingham, and looked down from the high railway arches upon the pit mouths and the flaming kilns in the blackened landscape, he decided on a trip to Preston, to observe the stubborn and long-drawn-out strike among the workers in its cotton mills.

At the end of January, 1854, he made the journey. Opposite him in the railway carriage a bitingly emphatic gentleman whom Dickens mentally called Mr. Snapper told him sharply that the men on strike "wanted to be ground," "to bring 'em to their senses." If that was all they wanted, replied Dickens, they must be very unreasonable, for surely they had had a little grinding already. Mr. Snapper glared, asked if he was a friend to the strike, a friend to the lockout, denied that he might be a friend to both masters and hands: there was nothing, he said firmly, "in the relations of Capital and Labor, *but* Political Economy." Dickens suggested that there might be understanding and consideration; Mr. Snapper laughed at him. Did Dickens, he demanded aggressively, think the hands had a right to combine? Surely, said Dickens, as perfect a right to combine as the combined Preston masters.[61]

Preston he found a nasty place, but entirely quiet and orderly despite the fact that the strikers were not too well fed and had been out of employment for twenty-three weeks. The chimneys were cold and smokeless, and small groups at street corners read placards about the strike, but mostly, he was told, the people sat at home and moped. Dickens was staying at the Bull Hotel, before which, some time ago, a crowd had assembled, demanding an interview with the masters, whom they supposed to be meeting inside. He remembered seeing an account of it in an Italian paper, "in which it was stated that 'the populace then environed the Palazzo Bull, until the Padrona of the Palazzo heroically appeared to them at one of the upper windows and addressed them!' One can hardly conceive anything less likely to be represented to an Italian mind, by this description," he remarked, "than the old, grubby, smoky, mean, intensely formal red brick house with a narrow gateway and a dingy yard, to which it applies." [62]

*   *   *   *

In London he was soon wrestling with the trouble of writing in weekly installments which he had not known since the days of *Master Humphrey's Clock.* The task was made still more arduous by the brevity necessary in *Household Words.* "The difficulty of the space," he complained, "is CRUSHING. Nobody can have an idea of it who has not had an experience of patient fiction-writing with some elbow-room always, and open places in perspective. In this form, with any kind of regard to the current number, there is absolutely no such thing." [63]

While Dickens was still engaged on the opening chapters, he was grieved to learn of the death of his old friend Talfourd. He recalled how kind Talfourd had been to him when he was an obscure beginner at his profession, his generosity and greatness of heart.[64] And he remembered a moonlit night at Broadstairs when Talfourd had told of his earnest pleasure at being made a judge and the two of them had playfully disputed at what age he should retire and what he would do at three-score and ten. "So amiable a man," Dickens wrote, "so gentle, so sweet-tempered, of such a noble simplicity, so perfectly unspoiled by his labours and their rewards, is very rare indeed upon this earth." [65]

Hard Times began appearing in *Household Words* on April 1st. The story doubled the circulation in the course of the first ten weeks,[66] and the final profits make it clear that before the end the sales must have multiplied by four or five.[67] But there were readers who were worried by the radical sound of the story. Dickens robustly insisted that its purpose was not to foment discord, but to foster understanding between employers and employed. "The English people," he said, "are . . . the hardest-worked people on whom the sun shines. . . . They are born at the oar, and they live and die at it. Good God, what would we have of them!" [68] And "I often say to Mr. Gradgrind that there is reason and good intention in much that he does—but that he overdoes it. Perhaps by dint of his going his way and my going mine, we shall meet at last at some halfway house where there are flowers on the carpets, and a little standing-room for Queen Mab's chariot among the Steam Engines." [69]

During April, Dickens was obliged to spend much time attending to *Household Words*: Wills was in ill health and taking the water cure at Malvern. The office looked desolate in his absence, Dickens wrote him, "but O Heavens how tidy!" And Kate and Georgina were disappointed not to hear that Wills was drinking twenty-two tumblers of water every day.[70] Dickens himself claimed to have been reading "a soul-stirring Drama called the Larboard Fin," an imaginary work of which he pretended that Wills was the author, "which *looks* to me like an undiscovered play by Shakespeare, surreptitiously modernized." [71]

Meanwhile Dickens had arranged to begin publishing a serial novel by Mrs. Gaskell in September when *Hard Times* should have run its course. Her story was also to have its setting in a mill town and a theme of industrial conflict. She was worried that there might turn out to be too much sameness in their choice of incidents; Dickens wrote her to relieve her fears. "The monstrous claims at domination made by a certain class of manufacturers, and the extent to which the way is made easy for working men to slide down into discontent under such hands, are within my scheme"; but she might feel at ease on the point raised, he was not going to have a strike in his tale.[72]

Tired, sometimes "dreary" with his work, Dickens sought distraction whenever it allowed him a little freedom. How about going for the evening, he asked Mark Lemon, to that public house on the Thames where they had the performing dogs: "it will do us good after such a blue-devilous afternoon as this has been." [73] He summoned Wilkie Collins for a jaunt to Tunbridge Wells, for a stroll on Hampstead Heath.[74] He took Mrs. Colden's brother, Dr. Wilkes, on the rounds of what he called "the low and vicious haunts of London." He welcomed Felton back from a tour of the Continent and a visit to Scotland, somewhat baffled to understand why Felton should consider Rome "a failure" and Edinburgh so immeasurably " 'the drollest' place he had ever seen" that he was unable to speak of it without bursting into fits of laughter.[75]

One more visitor this spring was a young man named Edmund Yates, the son of Frederick Yates, the actor, who thought Dickens might receive him kindly for his father's sake. Giving his card at the door of Tavistock House, he was shown into the large drawing room. Soon Georgina Hogarth, who by now almost ran the house, was explaining to him that Dickens was too busy on his book to see him at the moment, but would be glad to receive him next Sunday afternoon at two.

"God! how like your father!" was Dickens's greeting when Yates was shown into his study. But Yates, who had formed his image of Dickens from the poetic Maclise portrait of 1839, was surprised by his thinning hair, mustache, and "door-knocker" beard, and by his hearty, almost aggressive manner. Sitting with one leg under him and a hand in a pocket, Dickens talked enthusiastically of old days at the Adelphi Theatre and how he had admired Yates's mother. He told Yates he was off to Boulogne for the summer at the end of the coming week, but hoped to see him in the fall.[76]

Dickens crossed the Channel to Boulogne on June 18th or 19th.[77] He had rented the Villa du Camp de Droite, another of M. Beaucourt's houses, a larger cottage with more spacious rooms, located at the top of the hill.[78] "Range of view and air, most free and delightful; hill-side garden, delicious; field, stupendous; speculations in haycocks already effected by the undersigned, with the view to the keeping of a 'Home' at Rounders." [79] A mile away a French military camp was being constructed—the Crimean War had begun at the end of March. With magic speed there were whole streets of mud huts, tents like immense sheets hung out to dry, and soldiers making the roads and bridges red with their trousers.[80]

Promptly on his arrival, Dickens "moved every article of furniture in the house," besides effecting "a variety of ingenious devices in the Robinson Crusoe way . . . which must be *studied*, to be appreciated." [81] Three days later came the children, "in every stage and aspect of sea-sickness," a nurse, also prostrate, Mamey's and Katey's governess, and twenty-seven pieces of luggage.[82] With them too came Lally and Betty Lemon, "whose parents had discreetly packed two dozen pairs of bran new stockings in their luggage. Duty on said stockings, 8 francs." [83]

What with making these changes and getting the family and their guests settled in, he wrote only seventy-two words of *Hard Times* during the first five days.[84] But before the middle of July he had made such progress that he was hoping to finish the book and take the last chapters of it to London on the 19th. "Bobbing up, corkwise from a sea of Hard Times," he wrote to suggest that Collins join him in five days "of amiable dissipation and unbounded license in the metropolis," and then return with him to Boulogne. "If you will come and breakfast with me about midnight—anywhere—any day, and go to bed no more until we fly to these pastoral retreats, I shall be glad to have so vicious an associate." [85]

He was "stunned with work," [86] he informed Wills. And to Forster he wrote, "I am three parts mad, and the fourth delirious, with perpetual rushing at Hard Times. I have done what I hope is a good thing with Stephen, taking his story as a whole . . . I have been looking forward through so many weeks and sides of paper to this Stephen business that now—as usual—it being over, I feel as if nothing in the world, in the way of intense and violent rushing hither and thither, could quite restore my balance." [87] Of Carlyle he asked permission to dedicate the book to him. "I know it contains nothing in which you do not think with me, for no man knows your books better than I." [88]

He wrote the last lines of *Hard Times* in a wild burst of energy two days earlier than he had expected to,[89] and felt appallingly "used up." [90] He might well feel exhausted, for all its hundred thousand

words had been written in little over five months. But he took the boat
next day, July 18th, and arrived at ten that night in a London intensely
close, suffocating, and oppressive.[91] After a busy day at the office, he
met Collins at the Garrick for a convivial evening. The next night,
with Miss Coutts, he heard Grisi in *Lucrezia Borgia,* and the night
after that saw the Spanish dancers at the Haymarket and sat up with
Buckstone, the manager, drinking gin slings till daylight. "I have been
in a blaze of dissipation altogether, and have succeeded (I think) in
knocking the remembrance of my work out." [92]

CHAPTER FOUR

Critique of Materialism

CRITICISM: *Hard Times*

Hard Times brings to a culmination an orderly development of social analysis that extends in Dickens's work from *Dombey and Son* through *Bleak House*. That development has its roots, indeed, far earlier, and is to be found, although fragmentarily, in the social attitudes underlying *Oliver Twist* and the prison scenes of *Pickwick Papers*. With *Dombey and Son*, however, Dickens achieved his first clear picture of the workings of a monetary society; and even while he was still writing that story he underlined his hostility to Mr. Dombey's world through Scrooge and the fantasy of *A Christmas Carol*. Although *David Copperfield* is mainly an exploration of personal emotion, the social comment is an organic part of its pattern. It lurks in the legal morasses of Doctors' Commons and runs through the conscienceless exploitation of child labor in the bottling warehouse; its emphasis on money is as clear in the ostentatious display of Mr. Spenlow as in the mean rapacity of Uriah Heep; its spiritual essence is painted in Steerforth's cynical middle-class indifference to the humanity of the poor and the callousness of his seduction of Little Em'ly.

Bleak House carries on that analysis to a detailed examination of the rotten workings of the social system in almost every major institution and activity of society. Except for one: the operations of that colossus of mechanized industry that had swollen its dominion until it had almost all of modern society subjected to its power. That power Dickens saw as an inhuman, life-denying tyranny. *Bleak House* reveals the monstrous tentacles of acquisitive power in general, crushing human fulfillment in its foggy coils. *Hard Times* deals with industrial power, but is not so much a picture of its ramifications as a presentation of its underlying principles. It is an analysis and a condemnation of the ethos of industrialism.

These facts partly explain why *Hard Times* has been unpopular with many readers and has been disliked by most critics. People could laugh unrestrainedly at Dick Swiveller and Pecksniff and Micawber, who can only amuse, not hurt us, but no such irresponsible mirth is possible with Bounderby and Gradgrind, who have the world appallingly under their control. In Dickens's earlier novels it had been easy to think of him as a warm-hearted, unphilosophic humanitarian indignant at individual cruelties. Even in *Bleak House* the reader might not realize the total meaning of the indictment, and could comfort himself by imagining that Dickens was merely prejudiced against some groups in society—lawyers, moneylenders, members of the aristocracy, politicians. But there is a desperate endeavor among commentators to ignore or belittle the dark masterpieces of Dickens's maturity because they will not let us close our eyes on the clamorous problems that threaten us with disaster. The harsh truth of Mr. Merdle and the Circumlocution Office in *Little Dorrit* is dismissed as "twaddle," and *Our Mutual Friend*'s astringent satire on Podsnap and the Veneerings as mere clowning in a dusty desert of a book. Except for a few critics such as F. R. Leavis, who do not care for Dickens's earlier work, only radicals and revolutionaries like Ruskin and Bernard Shaw have praised *Hard Times*.

For in *Hard Times* there is no mistaking Dickens's violent hostility to industrial capitalism and its entire scheme of life. Here he is proclaiming a doctrine not of individual but of social sin, unveiling what he now sees as the real state of modern society. "This," Shaw says, "is Karl Marx, Carlyle, Ruskin, Morris, Carpenter, rising up against civilization itself as a disease, and declaring that it is not our disorder but our order that is horrible; that it is not our criminals but our magnates that are robbing and murdering us; and that it is not merely Tom-all-Alone's that must be demolished and abolished, pulled down, rooted up, and made for ever impossible so that nothing shall remain of it but History's record of its infancy, but our entire social system." "Here you will find," Shaw continues, "no more villains and heroes, but only oppressors and victims, oppressing and suffering in spite of themselves, driven by a huge machinery which grinds to pieces the people it should nourish and ennoble, and having for its directors the basest and most foolish of us instead of the noblest and most farsighted." And thus, he summarizes, the indignation with which Dickens began "has spread and deepened into a passionate revolt against the whole industrial order of the modern world." [1]

The change that reaches its climax in *Hard Times*, however, is not only in revolutionary thought, it is in method as well. And this disturbs still another group of Dickens's readers, grown used to a profusion of comic episode and a tremendous crowded canvas thronged with characters almost as numerous as life itself, all painted in vivid contrasting scenes of light and dark with a brilliant external realism. This is the method of *Dombey* and of *Bleak House*, those complicated and elaborate literary structures like some enormous medieval building whose bays and wings and niches are filled with subordinate figures and with bright genre groups of all kinds clustering in a hundred patterns ranging from grotesque fancy to portraits from nature.

Had Dickens been following this method in *Hard Times*, he would have had scenes among the clerks in Bounderby's bank like those in Mr. Dombey's countinghouse and scenes among the hands in Bounderby's factories like those of pasting on the labels in Murdstone and Grinby's warehouse. He would have had scenes of a cotton spinner getting tangled in the threads of his loom as comic as the marchioness smiting herself on the chin with her corkscrew, and extended scenes of clamorous industrial activity as vivid as the brief glimpses of glaring furnace mouths in Little Nell's nocturnal wanderings through the Black Country. He would have had scenes of the home lives of the factory laborers as warm as those of the Toodle family, and as grim as those of the brickmakers in *Bleak House*. All this would have been no less easy for Dickens's creative vitality, perhaps even easier, than the technique he did follow. Dictated partly, no doubt, by the need of compressing his story into a short novel of brief weekly installments, that technique was even more determined by Dickens's resolution to make it a formidable and concentrated blow against the iniquity of a heartless materialism.

In consequence, *Hard Times* is a morality drama, stark, formalized, allegorical, dominated by the mood of piercing through to the underlying *meaning* of the industrial scene rather than describing it in minute detail. Therefore Coketown, which might be Hanley, Preston, Birmingham, or Leeds, or, for that matter, Fall River or Pittsburgh, is drawn once for all in a few powerful strokes: "It was a town of red brick, or of brick that would have been red if the smoke and ashes had allowed it; but as matters stood it was a town of unnatural red and black like the painted face of a savage. It was a town of machinery and tall chimneys, out of which interminable serpents of smoke trailed themselves for ever and ever, and never got uncoiled. It had a black canal in it, and a river that ran purple with ill-smelling dye, and vast piles of buildings full of windows where there was a rattling and a trembling all day long, and where the piston of the steam-engine worked monotonously up and down like the head of an elephant in a state of melancholy madness. It contained several large streets all very like one another, and many small streets still more like one another, inhabited by people equally like one another, who all went in and out at the same hours, with the same sound upon the same pavements, to do the same work, and to whom every day was the same as yesterday and tomorrow, and every year the counterpart of the last and the next." [2]

"The streets were hot and dusty on the summer day, and the sun was so bright that it even shone through the heavy vapour drooping over Coketown, and could not be looked at steadily. Stokers emerged from low underground doorways into factory yards, and sat on steps, and posts, and palings, wiping their swarthy visages, and contemplating coals. The whole town seemed to be frying in oil. There was a stifling smell of hot oil everywhere. The steam-engines shone with it, the dresses of the Hands were soiled with it, the mills throughout their many stories oozed and trickled with it. The atmosphere of those Fairy palaces was like the breath of the simoom: and their inhabitants, wasting with the heat, toiled languidly in the desert. But no temperature made the melancholy mad elephants more mad or more sane. Their wearisome heads went up and down at the same rate, in hot weather and cold, wet weather and dry, fair weather and foul. The measured motion of their shadows on the walls, was the substitute Coketown had to show for the shadows of rustling woods; while, for the summer hum of insects, it could offer, all the year round, from the dawn of Monday to the night of Saturday, the whir of shafts and wheels." [3]

"Seen from a distance, in such weather, Coketown lay shrouded in a haze of its own, which appeared impervious to the sun's rays. You could only know the town was there, because you knew there could have been no such sulky blotch upon the prospect without a town. A blur of soot and smoke, now confusedly tending this way, now that way, now aspiring to the vault of Heaven, now murkily creeping along the earth, as the wind rose and fell, or changed its quarter: a dense formless jumble, with sheets of cross light in it, that showed nothing but masses of darkness:—Coketown in the distance was suggestive of itself, though not a brick of it could be seen." [3a]

Every packed detail of this entire setting is surcharged with significant emotional and intellectual comment, and every character among the small unified group, symbolic and stylized, who act out their drama in the gritty industrial world, serves to deepen and intensify the meaning. Josiah Bounderby, banker and manufacturer, is its blatant greed and callous inhumanity in action. Thomas Gradgrind retired wholesale hardware dealer, man of facts and figures, is the embodiment of utilitarian economic theory and its endeavor to dry up life into statistical averages. Young Thomas Gradgrind, devoted first and only to his own advantage, is the mean product of the paternal theories—"that not unprecedented triumph of calculation which is usually at work on number one." [4] The daughter Louisa is their predestined tragic victim going to her doom, in her face "a light with nothing to rest upon, a fire with nothing to burn." [5] The consummate achievement of Mr. Gradgrind's system is represented by Bitzer, one of the pupils graduated from the day school founded by Gradgrind: for Bitzer everything is a matter of bargain and sale, accessible to no appeal except that of self-interest.

In contrast to these, Sissy Jupe, the strolling juggler's child, spending her childhod among the acrobats and equestrians of Sleary's Horse-riding, symbolizes everything in human nature that transcends the soul-crushing hideousness and mere instrumentalism of Coketown: she is vitality, generosity, uncalculating goodness. It is significant that she has been born and nourished among a people whose activities are not dominated by pure utility, but have at least some association with those of art, self-fulfilling, self-justified, and containing their ends within themselves. The contrast between her "dark-eyed and dark-haired" [6] warmth, glowing with an inward sun-filled luster, and Bitzer's cold eyes and colorless hair and etiolated pallor, renders in pure sensation, as F. R. Leavis points out, the opposition between "the life that is lived freely and richly from the deep instinctive and emotional springs" and "the thin-blooded, quasi-mechanical product of Gradgrindery." [7]

Nor does Dickens concern himself in *Hard Times* with any of the small tricks of verisimilitude in speech. The characters express themselves in a stylized idiom that is as far removed from everyday diction as it is true to the inward essence of their natures. Louisa speaks in a solemn poetry filled from the beginning with vibrant forewarnings of her destiny, and Sissy, the stroller's child, confronts Harthouse, the smart, sarcastic worldling, with the stern justice of an angelic messenger. Bounderby's housekeeper, Mrs. Sparsit, with her Roman nose and Coriolanian eyebrows, has a grotesque and mournful dignity of utterance fitting to a world of mad melodrama. And in the wild exuberance of his humor, Dickens allows Mr. Bounderby to talk with the extravagant absurdity of a figure in an insane harlequinade. When Mrs. Sparsit, rendered inarticulate by an inflamed throat and pathetic with sneezes, is trying in vain to tell Mr. Gradgrind that Louisa has deserted Bounderby for Harthouse, the aggrieved husband seizes and shakes her. "If you can't get it out, ma'am," he exclaims, "leave *me* to get it out. This is not a time for a lady, however highly connected, to be totally inaudible, and seemingly swallowing marbles." [8]

In all Dickens's previous novels there had been scenes in which the characters burst into a theatrical diction of an ornate dignity or talked a gabble fantastically ridiculous. Nicholas and Ralph Nickleby assail each other in words of purple rhetoric and Edith Dombey addresses both her husband and Mr. Carker in the accents of a tragedy queen, but the successes Dickens achieves in such passages are won in the teeth of their language. And with Mrs. Nickleby, Sampson Brass, Pecksniff, Sairey Gamp, Captain Cuttle, Mr. Toots, and Jack Bunsby he had risen to heights of triumphant nonsense. "But now," as Shaw remarks, "it is no longer a question of passages;"—or even of an occasional character—"here he begins at last to exercise quite recklessly his power of presenting a character to you in the most fantastic and outrageous terms, putting into its mouth from one end of the book to the other hardly a word which could conceivably be uttered by any sane human being, and yet leaving you with an unmistakable and exactly truthful portrait of a character that you recognize at once as not only real but typical." [9]

In the same way, the overtones of symbolism and allegory had always moved through Dickens's earlier novels, in solution, as it were, and only at times rendered in definite statement. They are implicit in the social myth of Little Nell's mad grandfather and his mania for the "shining yellow boys" seen against the stock-market-gambling fever of the 1840's. They glimmer in the Christmas pantomime transformation-scenes that end *Martin Chuzzlewit*, with old Martin as the beneficent Prospero bringing the pageant to a close. They are symmetrically balanced in the ice and frozen cupids of Mr. Dombey's dinner table and the warmth of the Little Midshipman where Florence and Captain Cuttle are the wandering princess and the good monster of a fairy tale. They emerge again in the image of Uriah Heep as an ugly and rebellious genie and Betsey Trotwood as the fairy godmother. They underlie that entire symbolic bestiary of wolves, tigers, cats, captive birds, flies, and spiders that moves among the fog and falling tenements and self-consuming rottenness of *Bleak House*. But in these novels, except for the last, the symbolism always lurked below the surface or played over it in a fanciful and exuberant embroidery of metaphor. Even in *Bleak House* symbolism had never taken charge, nor determined and limited every detail in the structure.

* * * * *

Hard Times opens, significantly, in a schoolroom. Here the children are to be indoctrinated in the tenets of practicality, encouraged to think of nothing except in terms of use, crammed full of information like so many "little vessels . . . ready to have imperial gallons of facts poured into them until they were full to the brim." [10] "Now, what I want," Mr. Gradgrind tells the schoolmaster, "is, Facts. Teach these boys and girls nothing but Facts. Facts alone are wanted in life. Plant nothing else and root out everything else. You can only form the minds of reasoning animals upon Facts: nothing else will ever be of service to them. This is the principle on which I bring up my own children, and this is the principle on which I bring up these children. Stick to Facts, sir!" [11]

In the Gradgrind world there are to be no imagination, no fancy, no emotion, only fact and the utilitarian calculus. When Sissy Jupe—

"Girl number twenty," [12] Mr. Gradgrind calls her, obliterating human identity itself in the blank anonymity of a number—defends her taste for a flowery-patterned carpet by saying, "I am very fond of flowers . . . and I would fancy——" the government inspector of schools pounces upon her triumphantly: "Ay, ay, ay! But you mustn't fancy. That's it! You are never to fancy"; and "You are not, Cecilia Jupe," Mr. Gradgrind repeats sepulchrally, "to do anything of that kind." "Fact, fact, fact!" says the government official. "Fact, fact, fact!" echoes Thomas Gradgrind.[13]

For Sissy's loving humanity, though, this bleak factuality is quite impossible. " 'Here are the stutterings,' " she misquotes her school-teacher—"Statistics," corrects Louisa—of a town of a million inhabitants of whom only twenty-five starved to death in the course of a year. What does she think of that proportion? "I thought it must be just as hard on those who were starved whether the others were a million, or a million million." [14] So "low down" is Sissy in "the elements of Political Economy" after eight weeks of study, that she has to be "set right by a prattler three feet high, for returning to the question, 'What is the first principle of this science?' the absurd answer, 'To do unto others as I would that they should do unto me.' " [15]

Mr. Gradgrind's stand at school is the stand he takes among his own children at home. "No little Gradgrind had ever seen a face in the moon; it was up in the moon before it could speak distinctly. No little Gradgrind had ever learnt the silly jingle, Twinkle, twinkle, little star; how I wonder what you are! No little Gradgrind had ever known wonder on the subject, each little Gradgrind having at five years old dissected the Great Bear like a Professor Owen, and driven Charles's Wain like a locomotive engine-driver. No little Gradgrind had ever associated a cow in a field with that famous cow with the crumpled horn . . . or with that yet more famous cow who swallowed Tom Thumb: it had never heard of these celebrities, and had only been introduced to a cow as a graminivorous ruminating quadruped with several stomachs." [16]

But the facts in which Gradgrindery is interested are only the cut-and-dried facts of intellectual definition, not the facts of living and breathing reality. It wants to learn nothing about the behavior of horses and how they are trained, which Sissy Jupe knows from Sleary's Horse-riding: "You musn't tell us about the ring, here." [17]

Instead, it trots out Bitzer's "definition of a horse": "Quadruped. Graminivorous. Forty teeth, namely twenty-four grinders, four eye-teeth, and twelve incisive. . . . Hoofs hard, but requiring to be shod with iron. Age known by marks in mouth."—"Now girl number twenty," says Mr. Gradgrind, "you know what a horse is." [18]

The factual education approved by Mr. Gradgrind is identical in spirit with that which was inflicted upon John Stuart Mill and which left him in his young manhood despairingly convinced that his emotional and imaginative nature had been starved to death. Mr. M'Choakumchild, the schoolmaster, has been "turned out," with "some one hundred and forty other schoolmasters . . . in the same factory, on the same principles, like so many pianoforte legs. . . . Orthography, etymology, syntax, and prosody, biography, astronomy, geography, and general cosmography, the sciences of compound proportion, algebra, land-surveying and levelling, vocal music, and drawing from models, were all at the ends of his ten chilled fingers. He had worked his stony way into Her Majesty's most Honourable Privy Council's Schedule B, and had taken the bloom off the higher branches of mathematics and physical science, French, German, Latin, and Greek. He knew all about all the Water Sheds of all the world (whatever they are), and all the histories of all the peoples, and all the names of all the rivers and mountains, and all the productions, manners, and customs of all the countries, and all their boundaries and bearings on the two and thirty points of the compass. . . .

"He went to work in this preparatory lesson, not unlike Morgiana in the Forty Thieves: looking into all the vessels ranged before him, one after another, to see what they contained. Say, good M'Choakumchild. When from thy boiling store, thou shalt fill each jar brim full by-and-by, dost thou think thou wilt always kill outright the robber Fancy lurking within—or sometimes only maim him and destroy him!" [19]

The principles that dominate Mr. Gradgrind's school are the principles that dominate Coketown and its industry. His hard-facts philosophy is only the aggressive formulation of the inhumane spirit of Victorian materialism. In Gradgrind, though repellent, it is honest and disinterested. In Bounderby, its embodiment in the business world, with his bragging self-interest, it is nothing but greed for power and material success, Victorian "rugged individualism" in its vulgarest and ugliest form. And Bounderby is nothing but the practice of that business ethos, for which "the relations between master and man were all fact, and everything was fact between the lying-in hospital and the cemetery, and what you couldn't state in figures, or show to be purchaseable in the cheapest market and saleable in the dearest, was not, and never should be, world without end, Amen." [20]

The wonderful wit and insight with which Dickens withers laissez-faire capitalism is not to be lost sight of "because he chooses to speak," as Ruskin says, "in a circle of stage fire." [21] Carlyle never voiced a more burning denunciation of the dismal science of classical economic theory or the heartlessness of "cash-nexus" as the only link between man and man. The hundred years that have passed since *Hard Times* was written have done hardly more to date the cant with which businessmen defend industrial exploitation than they have to brighten the drab and brutal thing. Laboring men who protested wanted "to be set up in a coach and six and to be fed on turtle soup and venison, with a gold spoon"; [22] the laboring class "were a bad lot altogether, gentlemen," "restless," "never knew what they wanted," "lived upon the best, and bought fresh butter; and insisted upon Mocha coffee, and rejected all but prime parts of meat, and yet were eternally dissatisfied and unmanageable." [23] As for the Labor unions: "the united masters" should not "allow of any such class combinations." [24]

One more cluster of these sardonic clichés recalls the capitalists of our own day who were going to dispose of their businesses and go to Canada if Franklin Delano Roosevelt were re-elected. The Coketown industrialists, Dickens observes dryly, were always crying that they were ruined: "They were ruined, when they were required to send labouring children to school; they were ruined when inspectors were appointed to look into their works; they were ruined, when such inspectors considered it doubtful whether they were justified in chopping people up with their machinery; they were utterly undone when it was hinted that perhaps they need not always make quite so much smoke. . . . Whenever a Coketowner felt he was ill-used—that is to say, whenever he was not left entirely alone, and it was proposed to hold him accountable for the consequences of any of his acts—he was sure to come out with the awful menace that he would 'sooner pitch his property into the Atlantic.' This had terrified the Home Secretary within an inch of his life, on several occasions.

"However, the Coketowners were so patriotic after all, that they never had pitched their property into the Atlantic yet, but, on the contrary, had been kind enough to take mighty good care of it." [25]

The only weaknesses in Dickens's handling of the industrial scene are his caricature of the union organizer Slackbridge and his portrayal of that noble but dismal representative of the laboring classes, Stephen Blackpool. Slackbridge, with his windy and whining rhetoric ("Oh my friends and fellow-countrymen, the slaves of an iron-handed and a grinding despotism! Oh my friends and fellow-sufferers, and fellow-workmen, and fellow-men!" [26]) is a figment of imagination. "He was not so honest," Dickens says, as the workers he addressed, "he was not so manly, he was not so good-humoured; he substituted cunning for their simplicity, and passion for their safe solid sense. An ill-made, high-shouldered man, with lowering brows, and his features crushed into an habitually sour expression, he contrasted most unfavourably, even in his mongrel dress, with the great body of his hearers in their plain working clothes." [27]

Such a description is a piece of sheer ignorance, not because union leaders cannot be windbags and humbugs as other politicians can, but because labor organizers are not like Slackbridge and do not talk like him, and did not do so in Dickens's day any more than in ours. Dickens knew human nature too well not to know that fundamentally laboring men were like all men, and he knew domestic servants and artisans working for small tradesmen, but of the class manners and behavior of industrial laborers he had made no more than a superficial observation in some half-dozen trips through the Midlands. He had attended only one union meeting in his life, during the Preston strike in January, 1854. "It is much as if a tramp," Shaw comments with witty but not untruthful exaggeration, "were to write a description of millionaires smoking large cigars in church, with their wives in low-necked dresses and diamonds." [28]

There is a possibility, to be sure, that the brief chapter in which Slackbridge appears was designed to reassure a middle-class audience that might otherwise grow restive and worried over the radical sound of the book. Dickens's own personal support of the labor movement, however, is unequivocally clear. He had already stated in *Household Words* his belief that laborers had the same right to organize that their employers had,[29] and shortly after the conclusion of *Hard Times* he was to appeal to working men to force reforms from the Government.[30] *Hard Times* itself burns with indignant sympathy for the injustice under which the workers suffered and is violent in its repudiation of Bounderby's career and Gradgrind's philosophy.

Hardly less typical of the laboring class than Slackbridge is the independent workman Stephen Blackpool, who is ostracized by his fellow workers for not joining the union and blacklisted by Mr. Bounderby for having the courage to defend their cause. Stephen's isolated stand cuts him off from the support of his own class and the patronage of the factory owners. For all this, it is in Stephen's mouth that Dickens puts a dark summation of the life of the industrial workers: "Look round town—so rich as 'tis—and see the numbers o' people as has been broughten into bein heer, for to weave, an to card, an to piece out a livin', aw the same one way, somehows, twixt their cradles and their graves. Look how we live, and wheer we live, an in what numbers, an by what chances, and wi' what sameness; and look how the mill is awlus a goin, and how they never works us no nigher to ony dis'ant object—'ceptin awlus Death." [31]

And to Stephen, too, Dickens gives a denunciation of laissez faire and the hostile division it creates in society: "Let thousands upon thousands alone, aw leading the like lives and aw faw'en into the like muddle, and they will be as one, and yo will be as anoother, wi' a black unpassable world betwixt yo, just as long or short a time as sitch-like misery can last. . . . Most o' aw, rating 'em as so much Power, and reg'latin 'em as if they was figures in a soom, or machines: wi' out loves and likens, wi'out memories and inclinations, wi'out souls to weary and souls to hope—when aw goes quiet, draggin' on wi' 'em as if they'd nowt o' th' kind, and when aw goes onquiet, reproachin 'em for their want o' sitch human feelins in their dealins wi' you—this will never do't, sir, till God's work is onmade." [32]

When Stephen's crushed body is brought up from Old Hell Shaft, into which he had stumbled, his dying words are as if the crushed people themselves were speaking from the pit into which the modern world had fallen: "I ha' fell into the pit . . . as have cost wi'in the knowledge o' old fok now livin, hundreds and hundreds o' men's lives —fathers, sons, brothers, dear to thousands an thousands, an keeping 'em fro' want and hunger. I ha' fell into a pit that ha' been wi' th' Fire-damp crueller than battle. I ha' read on't in the public petition, as onny one may read, fro' the men that works in the pits, in which they ha' pray'n and pray'n the lawmakers for Christ's sake not to let their work be murder to 'em, but to spare 'em for th' wives and children that they loves as well as gentlefok loves theirs. When it were in work, it killed wi'out need; when 'tis let alone, it kills wi'out need. See how we die an no need, one way an another—in a muddle—every day!" [33]

And, in the end, as if from the depths of Old Hell Shaft, Dickens sounds once more a prophetic warning to the "Utilitarian economists, skeletons of schoolmasters, Commissioners of Fact, genteel and used-up infidels, gabblers of many little dog's eared creeds," lest "in the day of [their] triumph, when romance is utterly driven out" of the souls of the poor, "and they and a bare existence stand face to face, Reality will take a wolfish turn, and make an end of you." [34]

* * * * *

Within this larger sweep of *Hard Times* and its social-economic criticism there is a no less significant spiritual core. That core involves a demonstration of the way in which the Gradgrind philosophy denudes and devastates the life of Mr. Gradgrind himself. Not a bad man, "an affectionate father, after his manner," [35] "Mr. Gradgrind, though hard enough, was by no means so rough a man as Mr. Bounderby. His character was not unkind, all things considered; it might have been very kind indeed if only he had made some mistake in the arithmetic that balanced it years ago." [36] Instead, he has gone astray in the aridities of a crude mechanistic theory of human nature, and spends his time in the "parliamentary cinder-heap in London" proving "that the Good Samaritan was a Bad Economist." [37]

His kindness in taking Sissy Jupe under his care enables Dickens to bring in a contrasting picture of the circus folk in Sleary's Horseriding. They symbolize art, and their position in the eyes of Mr. Gradgrind and Mr. Bounderby implies the position of art in Victorian England, just as Gradgrind and Bounderby themselves symbolize the orthodox respectability of that society. For them, art is reduced to the status of mere entertainment, and the artist is a useless Bohemian of dubious respectability, whose work they frown on as frivolous and wasteful, utterly valueless for the utilitarian calculus. Nevertheless, that work ministers to vital human needs and, debased and degraded though it is in social estimate, represents one of the few clear links Coketown has with the life of disinterested achievement and the enrichment of experience.

"There were two or three handsome young women among them . . . and their eight or nine little children, who did the fairy business when required. The father of one of the families was in the habit of balancing the father of another of the families on the top of a great pole; the father of a third family often made a pyramid of both those fathers . . . ; all the fathers could dance upon rolling casks, stand upon bottles, catch knives and balls, twirl hand-basins, ride upon anything, jump over everything, and stick at nothing. All the mothers could (and did) dance upon the slack wire and the tight rope, and perform rapid acts on bare-backed steeds; none of them were at all particular in respect of showing their legs; and one of them, alone in a Greek chariot, drove six-in-hand into every town they came to." [38]

The circus people are also vessels of those simple virtues of sympathy and helpfulness to others for which Mr. Gradgrind's philosophy had no use and Mr. Bounderby's hardened heart no room. When Bounderby harshly tells Sissy that her father has deserted her, "They cared so little for plain Fact, these people," Dickens writes, "and were in that advanced state of degeneracy . . . that instead of being impressed by the speaker's strong common sense, they took it in extraordinary dudgeon. The men muttered 'Shame!' and the women 'Brute!' "—a reaction leading Sleary to give the visitors a hasty warning that they were in danger of being pitched out of the window.[39]

There is no sentimentality in this portrayal of the circus strollers. Dickens admits that "they were not very tidy in their private dress" and grants that they were sometimes rather disorderly in their private lives. He knows the dirt and squalor of their surroundings. He sees Sleary exactly as he is, with his flabby body, game eye, wheezing voice, and brandy-soaked state of never being quite sober and never quite drunk. But he knows that the qualities they exemplify are just as real as those in Mr. Gradgrind, and that they are quite as likely to be found in jugglers and acrobats as in bankers and businessmen.

So the two worlds confront each other, the world of generous feeling and the world of rationalized greed. It is through his heartless philosophy that Mr. Gradgrind is to be struck down, and through his inconsistent deed of kindness that he and his family are ultimately to be saved. Through his blindness to imagination, his failure to understand the life of the emotions, the mechanical crudity of his philosophy, his son becomes a selfish sneak and thief, and Louisa, his favorite child, suffers a dark emptiness in her heart. The love that her father always ignores, the devotion to which he denies any reality, she directs with all her starved and thwarted intensity upon her scapegrace brother. For his sake she accepts the proposal her father brings from Bounderby and prostitutes herself in marriage to a man she does not love.

The scene in which she receives that proposal is a triumph of dramatic subtlety. Her dispassionate chill is disconcerting even to the father who has consistently urged treating every situation in terms of fact. With intervals of silence between them punctuated by the hollow ticking of a "deadly statistical clock," [40] she subjects her father to a cold questionnaire: "Father, do you think I love Mr. Bounderby?" "Father, do you ask me to love Mr. Bounderby?" "Father, does Mr. Bounderby ask me to love him?" [41]

The embarrassed man tries to escape into the realms of abstract definition; the reply, he says, depends "on the sense in which we use the expression." Mr. Bounderby does not do either Louisa or himself "the injustice of pretending to anything fanciful, fantastic, or (I am using synonymous terms) sentimental." [42] Let them reduce the question to one of Fact: "Does Mr. Bounderby ask me to marry him? Yes, he does. The sole remaining question then is: Shall I marry him?"[43]

Throughout the conversation Louisa has been regarding her father fixedly. "As he now leaned back in his chair, and bent his deep-set eyes upon her," Dickens writes, "he might have seen one wavering moment in her, when she was impelled to throw herself upon his breast, and give him the pent-up confidences of her heart. But, to see it, he must have overleaped at a bound the artificial barriers he had for so many years been erecting, between himself and all those subtle essences of humanity which will elude the utmost cunning of algebra . . . The barriers were too many and too high for such a leap. With his unbending, utilitarian, matter-of-fact face, he hardened her again; and the moment shot away into the plumbless depths of the past, to mingle with all the lost opportunities that are drowned there.

"Removing her eyes from him, she sat so long looking silently to-

wards the town, that he said, at length: 'Are you consulting the chimneys of the Coketown works, Louisa?'

" 'There seems to be nothing there but languid and monotonous
smoke. Yet when the night comes, Fire bursts out, father!' she answered, turning quickly.

" 'Of course I know that, Louisa. I do not see the application of the
remark.' To do him justice, he did not, at all." [44]

How beautifully this conversation, in reducing each question to
one of "Fact," empties it of all meaning! No philosophic analysis
could puncture the calculus of fact with more deadly effectiveness.
And with what power it conveys the emotional tensions beneath the
dialogue, Louisa's yearning for sympathy and understanding and the
obtuse, well-meaning father missing it all, even the allusion to those
unquenchable fires of human passion, so often hidden, that burst out
in the dark night of despair. An uncomfortable sense of something
not quite right, however, Mr. Gradgrind does have, and he questions
his daughter whether she has any other attachment.

"Why, father," she replies with fathomless irony, "what a strange
question to ask me! The baby-preference that even I have heard of as
common among children, has never had its innocent resting-place in
my breast. You have been so careful of me, that I have never had a
child's dream. You have dealt so wisely with me, father, from my
cradle to this hour, that I have never had a child's belief or a child's
fear." [45] "What do I know, father, of tastes and fancies; of aspirations
and affections; of all that part of my nature in which such light things
might have been nourished? What escape have I had from problems
that could be demonstrated and realities that could be grasped?" [46]

As Louisa speaks these words, she unconsciously closes her hand,
"as if upon a solid object," and slowly opens it, "as though she were
releasing dust or ash." Mr. Gradgrind is "quite moved by his success,
and by this testimony to it." [47]

When Louisa's disastrous marriage to the braggart Bounderby ends
in flight back to her father, all his past blindness recoils upon his head.
"How could you give me life," she reproaches him, "and take from
me all the inappreciable things that raise it from the state of conscious
death? Where are the graces of my soul? Where are the sentiments
of my heart? What have you done, O father, what have you done,"
and she strikes herself with both hands upon her breast, "with the

garden that should have bloomed once, in this great wilderness here!" [48]

"I never knew you were unhappy, my child."

"Father, I always knew it. In this strife . . . my dismal resource has been to think that life would soon go by, and that nothing in it could be worth the pain and trouble of a contest. . . . I do not know that I am sorry, I do not know that I am ashamed, I do not know that I am degraded in my own esteem. All that I know is, your philosophy and your teaching will not save me. Now, father, you have brought me to this. Save me by some other means!" [49]

And as he clasps her to prevent her falling, and then lays her down upon the floor, he sees "the pride of his heart and the triumph of his system, lying, an insensible heap, at his feet." [50]

The next day he entreats Louisa to believe that he had meant to do right. "He said it earnestly, and to do him justice he had. In gauging fathomless deeps with his mean little excise-rod, and in staggering over the universe with his rusty stiff-legged compasses, he had meant to do great things. Within the limits of his short tether, he had tumbled about, annihilating the flowers of existence with greater singleness of purpose than many of the blatant personages whose company he kept." [51]

But in the crisis of his life, Mr. Gradgrind, unlike Sir Austin Feverel, is able to choose love and his child, not the pride of his system. And she finds her comfort and he finds his redemption through the uncalculated and inconsistent deviation from the system that had led to his taking into his household the strolling juggler's child. Sissy Jupe's affection has been twining through that utilitarian home the ministrations of a loving heart, and on her gentle strength both the father and the daughter in the end come to repose. Through Sissy, too, and Sleary's non-utilitarian gratitude for Mr. Gradgrind's kindness to her, comes the resolution of the remaining part of the story, the escape of young Tom, that other "triumph" of Mr. Gradgrind's system, from going to jail for robbing Bounderby's bank.

This conclusion to the demonstration is trenchant satire. Sulky to the last, disguised as a comic servant with black face and a grotesquely ludicrous livery, the whelp grumblingly defends himself in his father's own jargon: "So many people are employed in situations of trust; so many people, out of so many, will be dishonest. I have heard you talk, a hundred times, of its being a law. How can I help laws? You have comforted others with such things, father. Comfort yourself!" [52]

Swift upon this confrontation arrives Bitzer, the real success of the system, determined to drag Tom back to Coketown and clinch his own succession to Tom's job in the bank. To the anguished father's pleas, Bitzer's replies, with mordant irony, throw in his face every one of his old arguments. Has he a heart? Mr. Gradgrind asks. "Smiling at the oddity of the question," Bitzer retorts with brisk factuality that the circulation couldn't be carried on without one.[53] "If this is solely a question of self-interest with you," Mr. Gradgrind begins. But Bitzer interrupts. "I am sure you know that the whole social system is a question of self-interest." [54] Nor can he be bribed; his advancement at the bank is worth more than any sum Mr. Gradgrind can offer. Mr. Gradgrind tries to appeal to Bitzer's gratitude for his schooling. "My schooling was paid for," says Bitzer; "it was a bargain; and when I came away, the bargain ended." [55]

"It was a fundamental principle of the Gradgrind philosophy," Dickens notes, "that everything was to be paid for. Nobody was ever on any account to give anybody anything, or render anybody any help without purchase. Gratitude was to be abolished, and the virtues springing from it were not to be. Every inch of the existence of mankind, from birth to death, was to be a bargain across the counter. And if we didn't get to Heaven that way, it was not a politico-economical place, and we had no business there." [56]

Bitzer is prevented from giving the alarm and young Tom is smuggled out of the country by a fantastic plot involving the services of the circus's dancing horse and educated dog. Mr. Sleary, no economist to the last, refuses any financial reward, although a collar for the dog and a set of bells for the horse, he agrees, he will be glad to take. "Brandy and water I alwayth take." [57] And privately, to Mr. Gradgrind, over his glass of grog, he makes a final revelation and pronouncement. Sissy's father is dead: his performing dog, who would never have deserted him, had returned to the circus months ago, worn out and almost blind, and there died.

It seems to suggest, Mr. Sleary observes musingly, that there is a love in the world, not all self-interest after all, but something very different; and that love has a way of its own of calculating or not calculating, to which it may be hard to give a name.[58]

And, as for the circus artists and Mr. Gradgrind's former disapproval of them, Mr. Sleary says in his preposterous lisp: "Thquire, thake handth, firtht and latht! Don't be croth with uth poor vagabondth. People mutht be amuthed. They can't be alwayth a learning, nor yet they can't be alwayth a working, they ain't made for it. You *mutht* have uth, Thquire. Do the withe thing and the kind thing too, and make the betht of uth; not the wortht!" [59]

Seen in all its implications against the background of the story, these final scenes hold in solution Dickens's entire indictment of nineteenth-century industrial society and the essence of his defense of art. Against the monstrous cruelty of mine and mill and pit and factory and countinghouse, against the bleak utilitarian philosophy with which they were allied, what power could there be except the flowering of the humane imagination and the ennoblement of the heart?

CHAPTER FIVE

"Fire Bursts Out"

THE unquiet and feverish state of mind toward which Dickens found himself tending when he finished *Hard Times* was more than the aftermath of an intense effort. True, the strain of writing the novel in less than six months had been terrific. But more significant than that was the mingling of his half-acknowledged feelings about his private life with his deepened realization of how many things were fundamentally wrong with England and the world.

For nine years now he had been shouldering enormous burdens of work and adding to them innumerable other distractions. He had founded a newspaper, taken on the editorship of a weekly magazine, devoted days to advising Miss Coutts and actively furthering her projects, dashed about—to Edinburgh, Manchester, Birmingham, Lausanne, Paris, Boulogne, all over Italy—lived in a dozen different places, been restless everywhere, repeatedly organized the most elaborate theatrical benefits, and invariably subsided into cries of misery when each series of dramatic performances was over. He wore out his friends by reiterated demands that they accompany him on twenty-mile walks, and was always proposing some diversion that involved going somewhere and doing something rather than remaining peacefully at home. How long he had been trying to avoid the inward admission of what caused his own disquiet was a secret hidden within him. But it was coming perilously close to the surface at last.

The sharpness of his personal unrest was intensified by the feelings with which he looked upon the world. His own disappointments were not merely for him among the unlucky accidents in a structure that on the whole worked reasonably well. The areas of individual happiness had come to seem no more than islands in an ocean of social misery. It was not that he believed the cosmos radically evil; he was too inveterate a fighter for yielding to despair. No one was further than Dickens from the Byronic mood of futility or the erratic cynicism he had tried to portray in Steerforth. Nor did he believe that human nature was intrinsically bad. But he did feel that the entire machinery of society was built upon principles of greed and class interests that systematically frustrated the general welfare.

He saw well enough that this machinery was not operated for the most part with any deliberate and malignant design of producing human suffering. Ralph Nickleby, Squeers, and Quilp were aberrations, but they shaded into Sir John Chester and the Chuzzlewits, and thence into the cold indifference of Mr. Dombey and Sir Leicester Dedlock's lofty assurance that he and his class were England. That neither the merchant nor the baronet was personally dishonest signified as little as that Mr. Vholes and Mr. Tulkinghorn were not a pair of scoundrels like Dodson and Fogg. The impersonal workings of the social system were as brutal as if those at its controls were an aggregation of villains. And just as Mr. Dombey corrected the optimistic distortion of the Cheerybles, Mr. Rouncewell was replaced by Gradgrind and Bounderby, the one bullying and blustering, the other blind to the imagination and the heart. Land, birth, trade, and industry were all treading the same broad road to destruction down which civilization had disastrously blundered.

No wonder, Dickens thought, that the mechanisms of society could not even serve their masters efficiently, but were always breaking down—symbolic of their final collapse. Privilege could not function without corruption, and corruption undermined itself and the structure of which it was a rotten support. Snobbery, jobbery, red tape, and incompetence defeated the Dedlock interests themselves in the cumbrous, cranky tangle. Sunlight was blotted out in the clinging fog, lungs choked by the black soot. But in the darkness every now and then walls collapsed in a prophetic crash of rubble, and from the monotonous smoke fire burst out.

How Dickens felt about both his personal unrest and the dangerous state of society emerges unmistakably in *Hard Times* through the portrayal of the workman Stephen Blackpool. Bound in marital ties that he can no longer bear, he asks Mr. Bounderby what he can do, only to be told that for him there is no way out, he must simply submit to his fate.[1] And when he makes a reasoned plea for his fellow workers, not as an enemy to the masters, but as a human being drawing attention to the struggling lives of the hands, and pleading for an effort of kindness and understanding to bridge the black unpassable world between the two, he is angrily denounced as an ill-conditioned troublemaker. But it will not solve the problem, he says, to make the one side unnaturally and forever wrong. "The strong hand will never do't." [2] "Look how this ha' growen an' growen, Sir, bigger an' bigger, broader an' broader, harder an' harder, fro year to year, fro generation to generation. Who can look on 't, Sir, and fairly tell a man 'tis not a muddle?" [3]

And as Dickens looked about him, he felt the muddle growing ever worse and more desperate. The outbreak of the Crimean War in March, 1854, had of course been made the excuse for dropping all attempts at social planning. The Reform Bill that Lord John Russell had introduced in February he had been forced to withdraw in April. And with it, Dickens realized, education, slum clearance, sanitation, hours and wages, factory conditions, every necessary social amelioration would go by the board, and "the old cannon-smoke and blood-mists" would "obscure the wrongs and sufferings of the people at home." [4] "I fear I clearly see," he burst out angrily, "that for years to come domestic reforms are shaken to the root; every miserable red-tapist flourishes war over the head of every protester against his humbug ..." [5] "When I consider the Patriotic Fund on the one hand, and on the other the poverty and wretchedness engendered by cholera, of which in London alone, an infinitely larger number of English people than are likely to be slain in the whole Russian war have miserably and needlessly died—I feel as if the world had been pushed back five hundred years." [6]

Though his judgment remained bitterly unwavering, his temperament was as mercurial as ever. The emotional effects of *Hard Times* he threw off in that "blaze of dissipation" with Collins for which he had gone to London. But the book had taken a great deal out of him. He was so immeasurably fatigued that on his Boulogne hillside he spent hours in a haystack with a book, falling asleep, and turning a deep coffee color in the August sun.[7] Through the bright, breezy days he recovered his resiliency. "Every window blows every door open, and all the lighter articles of dress and furniture fly to all points of the compass. A favorite shirt of mine went to Paris (as I judge from the course it took) this morning." [8] He still felt lazy, and told Wills not to send him proofs of *Household Words* to correct on week-ends. "I am not going over to the Sabbatarians, but like the haystack (particularly) on a Sunday morning." [9]

Mrs. Gaskell's story was giving trouble. Dickens had praised the artistry of a first large section of it that she had sent him, and even suggested its title, *North and South*, but as a serial it was slow-moving, the installments were too long, and not enough happened in each part.[10] To include more each week, he said, would ruin *Household Words*. "Therefore it must at all hazards be kept down." [11] But the printers at Whitefriars made a mess of things by giving a fantastically erroneous estimate of how much printed matter the manuscript amounted to.[12] In addition, Mrs. Gaskell began to be difficult about editorial changes, stipulating that the story was not to be "touched 'even by Mr. Dickens.' That immortal creature," Dickens added jocosely, "had gone over the proofs with great pains—had of course taken out the stiflings—hand-plungings, lungeings, and other convulsions—and had also taken out her weakenings and damagings of her own effects. 'Very well,' said the Gifted Man, 'she shall have her own way. But after it's published show her this proof, and ask her to consider whether her story would have been the better or the worse for it.' " [13] Long before the end, the magazine lost some of the additional readers *Hard Times* had gained for it. "I am sorry to hear of the Sale dropping," Dickens said, "but I am not surprised. Mrs. Gaskell's story, so divided, is wearisome in the last degree." [14]

Early in September, Prince Albert came to Boulogne to be entertained by the Emperor with a great review of the troops. "The town looks like one immense flag," [15] Dickens wrote; and he hoisted the British Jack and the French colors over his haystack, "to the glory of England and the joy of Beaucourt." [16] As the royal yacht approached, the cliff tops were lined with soldiers, the Prince appeared on deck in a brilliant uniform, and was greeted with "such an infernal blazing and banging as never was heard." [17] On the day of the review Dickens went for his usual country walk, only to find himself, covered with dust, face to face with Albert and Napoleon, jogging along the Calais road, followed by a staff of horsemen and red-coated royal grooms. Dickens removed his hat, but without stopping, and the Emperor and the Prince raised their cocked hats. The Emperor, Dickens observed, was "broader across the chest than in the old time when we used to see him so often at Gore-house, and stoops more in the shoulders." [18] That evening Dickens added to the festival illuminations of the town by lighting up all eighteen front windows of the villa with one hundred and twenty wax candles,[19] at sight of which his landlord, M. Beaucourt, was so delighted that he "*danced and screamed* on the grass before the door." [20]

The middle of the month brought a sudden alarm: an hour and a half after midnight of Sunday, the 17th, Dickens's daughter Mary was taken desperately ill with the cholera.[21] Her nausea and diarrhea were so acute and she seemed to be sinking so fast that there was not time to wait for a physician. The danger was great in a house full of children. Dickens had often thought of what would have to be done under such circumstances, and now set himself to applying the remedies recommended, although even this was made very difficult "by the frightful sickness." With the morning he was relieved to see that she seemed better. She fell into a slumber at breakfast time and slept twenty-four hours.[22] The next day it was clear that she had "turned the awful corner." [23]

The other children all remained well. Little Harry, next to the youngest, was now between five and six years old, and was called sometimes The Jolly Postboy and sometimes The Comic Countryman. The youngest, now two "and perpetually running about on two mottled legs," [24] had triumphed over Dickens's failure to feel delight at his birth and was a favorite with his father. Dickens always loved children and could not resist babies. When he had been in Italy the previous fall, his letters had been full of "The Plornishghenter," whom he declared "evidently the greatest, noblest, finest, cleverest, brightest, and most brilliant of boys," "an irresistibly attracting, captivating May-Roon-Ti-Goon-Ter." [25] This September he was declaring "The Plornish Maroon is in a brilliant state; beating all former babies into what they call in America (I don't know why) sky-blue fits." [26] And to Collins only a few days later Dickens wrote, "The Plornish-Maroon desires his duty. He had a fall yesterday, through overbalancing himself in kicking his nurse." [27]

The villa had entertained the usual lively succession of visitors. Collins had been there until shortly before Mary's illness,[28] writing in a pavilion in the garden. Wills had passed a fortnight there, planning the Christmas number of *Household Words* with Dickens, and going back to London with Collins.[29] Then came Beard, through a spell of delicious cool weather during which they lit fires, and then Mitton, and Evans, and Egg.[30] Thackeray had been down the Paris road in June, inhabiting a melancholy old château, "with one milk jug as the entire crockery of the establishment," but had tired of it and gone to Spa. Now he came back, and ascended the hill to smoke a farewell cigar with Dickens before going to Scotland.[31]

On the 1st of October, Dickens saw the military review at which Napoleon III was handed the erroneous telegraphic dispath announcing the fall of Sebastopol.[32] (The siege did not in fact come to an end until the following September.) The Emperor and Empress were on horseback, Eugénie a slight, pretty figure gracefully sitting a gray horse. "When the Emperor gave her the dispatch to read, she flushed and fired up in a very pleasant way, and kissed it with as natural an impulse as one could desire to see." [33] Dickens was disturbed to notice that the cheering of the troops at the news was faint and cold, for little as he wished the war to stand in the way of alleviating misery at home, he was convinced "that the future peace of the world" rendered it imperative "that Russia MUST BE stopped." [34]

*   *   *   *   *

But the war thus far had stopped, not Russia, but domestic reform, and Dickens turned back to England with a resumption of all his old feelings, all the desperation that had overwhelmed him at the beginning of the summer. "I have had dreadful thoughts of getting away somewhere altogether by myself." He considered going to the Pyrenees, starting a new book "in all sorts of inaccessible places," "living in some astonishing convent" "above the snow-line in Switzerland." "*Restlessness*, you will say," he told Forster. "Whatever it is, it is always driving me, and I cannot help it." He had rested nine or ten weeks, and could bear idleness no more—"though I had the strangest nervous miseries before I stopped. If I couldn't walk fast and far, I should just explode and perish." [35]

The cholera had taken its toll in London; throughout England and Wales it had killed twenty thousand during the summer.[36] Angrily Dickens wrote for the October 7, 1854, number of *Household Words* a paper of sharper tone than he had taken yet. He told his readers that unless they earnestly set about improving their towns and amending the dwellings of the poor, they were guilty of wholesale murder. He warned working people not to be taken in by "high political authorities" and "sharking mountebanks" interested only in "contesting for places, power, and patronage, loaves and fishes." He enjoined them to insist that they and their children had a "right to every means of life and health that Providence has provided for all." Neither religion nor education would make any headway until the "government discharged its first obligation, and secured to the people Homes, instead of polluted dens." [37]

Any working man of common intelligence, he continued, knew "that one session of parliament" could attain this object if it really wanted to. But neither Government nor Parliament by itself would originate the least step; had not Lord Seymour only the year before cut jokes about sanitation which the House received with laughter while the pestilence was raging? He charged the workers to make their voices heard, to call on the middle class to join with them, to unite and use the power of their numbers. They could see to it that the men who defied their needs were thrown out of office, and by Christmas there could be "a government in Downing Street and a House of Commons within hail of it, possessing not the faintest family resemblance to the Indifferents and Incapables last heard of in that slumberous neighbourhood." [38]

So fiery an appeal made directly to the workers had a frightening sound to many readers. Most of the working class had no vote. Was the suggestion that they use their numbers to demand their will an invitation to violence? Or, hardly less horrifying, did it mean that Dickens approved of labor unions? (He did; he thought their employers left them no other alternative, although, as Hard Times made clear, he believed their leaders were often corrupt demagogues.) The article worried even Miss Coutts, who wrote Dickens that she was "in a maze" about it.[39]

He was sorry, he replied. His meaning was simply that the people would never save themselves or their children from disease and death "until they have cheap water in unlimited quantity, wholesome air, constraint upon little landlords like our Westminster friends to keep their property decent . . . efficient drainage, and such alterations in

building acts" as would preserve open spaces and create new ones.
But they would not receive the least attention from "a worthless
Government which is afraid of every little interest and trembles be-
for the vote of every dust contractor." Therefore these things must
be made election questions, and the working people must "unite to
express their determination to have them, or to keep out of Parliament
by every means in their power, every man who turns his back on these
first necessities." Unless such a change were made, he told Miss Coutts
sternly, the next return of the cholera might bring "such a shake in
this country as never was seen on Earth since Samson pulled the Temple down upon his head." [40]

He poured out the same feelings in letters to other friends. Writing
Mrs. Watson, he mingled "burning desires to cut the Emperor of Russia's throat" with an even fierier indignation at the wrongs of the
people at home.[41] He urged Macready to read in the next number
of *Household Words* an article that ranked these problems of health
and homes above the vote and the other reforms that had been
emphasized in the People's Charter of 1838 and 1848. "It is not written by me, but is generally of my suggesting . . ." [42] Let the people
demand and by the strength of their union obtain the more substantial reforms in the very conditions under which they lived, said the
article, and the political reforms would not fail to come too.[43]

From this theme he turned to making arrangements with Macready
for the reading of the *Christmas Carol* that he would be giving on
December 20th at Sherborne, his old friend's Dorsetshire retreat, and
expressed the pleasure with which he looked forward to their meeting.[44] Although Macready was only sixty-one, he considered himself
an old man: Dickens jestingly called him "old Parr" in allusion to the
seventeenth-century centenarian who was supposed to have reached
the age of one hundred and fifty-two. "I think of opening the next
long book I write with a man of juvenile figure and strong face, who
is always persuading himself that he is infirm. . . . I would make him
an impetuous passionate sort of fellow, devilish grim upon occasion,
and of an iron purpose." In a final paragraph Dickens added that
Forster was "getting a little too fat" and was "troubled by the great
responsibility of directing the whole War. He doesn't seem to be quite
clear that he has got the ships in the exact order he intended, on the
sea point of attack at Sebastopol." [45]

Dickens read the *Carol* at two other gatherings that December, one at Reading on the 19th, in memory of Talfourd, the other in aid of the Bradford Mechanics' Institute on the 28th.[46] There was "a little fireside party" of thirty-seven hundred people so crowding the Town Hall that the authorities there had arranged two rows of seats behind Dickens on the platform. "These (on which the committee immensely prided themselves), I instantly overthrew; to the great terror and amazement of the bystanders, who enquired in a dismal manner 'Where was the Mayor to go then?' I said the Mayor might go—anywhere—but must not come near me." [47]

The children's Twelfth-Night play for 1855 Dickens adapted from Planché's *Fortunio and His Seven Gifted Servants*.[48] The stage was re-erected in the nursery, now billed as "the Theatre Royal, Tavistock House," with "Mr. Vincent Crummles" as "sole lessee and Manager." [49] Large-lettered announcements heralded the "Re-engagement of that irresistible comedian, Mr. Ainger," "Reappearance of Mr. H." (Henry Fielding Dickens) "who created so powerful an impression last year!" "Return of Mr. Charles Dickens Junior from his German engagements!" "Engagement of Miss Kate, who declined the munificent offers of the Management last season!" "First appearance on any stage of Mr. Plornishmaroontigoonter (who has been kept out of bed at a vast expense)." [50]

Among the adult actors, a Mr. Wilkini Collini played the small part of Gobbler, one of the seven gifted servants, and was "dreadfully greedy" in devouring property loaves.[51] Mark Lemon, under the name of Mr. Mudperiod, made a mountainous Dragon for Fortunio to subdue, and that small hero, the six-year-old Harry, watched with sly relish as the sherry with which he had adulterated the monster's drink demoralized his foe into a helpless imbecility.[52] Dickens himself had two roles. As Mr. Measly Servile he was "the Expectant Cousin of the Nobility in General," in which part he "constantly pervaded the stage" with "a fixed and propitiatory smile on his face." [53] As Mr. Passé he was the testy old Baron, and interpolated a song presumed to be sung by the Russian Czar: [54]

> "A despot I am of the regular kind;
> I'm in a fierce mood and I'm out of my mind
> And man was created to swallow the pill
> Of my wrong-headed, Bull-headed absolute will." [55]

But none of these diversions could keep out of Dickens's mind for long his disgust with the way England's affairs were managed. The men who saw "figures and averages, and nothing else," "representatives of the wickedest and most enormous vice of this time," were the ones who were doing all the harm: "the addled heads who would take the average of cold in Crimea during twelve months as a reason for clothing a soldier in nankeens on a night when he would be frozen to death in fur, and comfort a labourer in travelling twelve miles a day to and from his work, by telling him that the average distance of one inhabited place from another in the whole area of England, is not more than four miles. Bah!" [56]

Reports were pouring home from the Crimea by this time of the shameful disorganization of supplies, the horrible bungling in the medical arrangements, and the frightful mortality in the military hospital at Scutari. In the House of Commons after Christmas, Roebuck told in a faltering voice how out of an army of fifty-four thousand men forty thousand had died in the course of a few months, of wounds, of fever, of frostbite, of dysentery and cholera. Of the remainder, nine thousand were unfit for duty. Men lay crowded in filth amid an intolerable stench in verminous hospitals without enough beds, with only canvas sheets, with no towels, soap, brooms, mops, trays, or plates, with scanty medical supplies, inadequate kitchens, preposterous laundries. Roebuck demanded a committee to inquire into the conduct of the war, and in the face of an overwhelming vote of censure the Aberdeen ministry resigned.

But for the new Government that was formed under the premiership of Lord Palmerston, Dickens had no more respect than he had felt for its predecessor. He wrote for *Household Words* a satiric parody of *The Arabian Nights,* which he called "The Thousand and One Humbugs," [57] describing how "Abbadeen (or the Addled) . . . had for his misdeeds been strangled with a garter" and succeeded by "Parmarstoon (or Twirling Weathercock)," "the glib Vizier." Abetted by his daughter, Hansardadade, and a mute named Mistaspeeka, this cunning charlatan then proceeded also to gull the Sultan, "Taxedtaurus (or Fleeced Bull)," with longwinded stories in which night after night was wasted.[58]

So Dickens expressed his distrust of any mere shuffling around of Coodle and Doodle to effect a change for the better. And once again his personal distress sounds in the midst of his political disillusion. He might go to Bordeaux or emigrate "to the mountain-ground between France and Spain. Am altogether in a dishevelled state of mind— motes of new books in the dirty air, miseries of older growth threatening to close upon me. Why is it, that as with poor David, a sense always comes crushing upon me now, when I fall into low spirits, as of one happiness I have missed in life, and one friend and companion I have never made?" [59]

*   *   *   *   *

On his birthday he dined at Gravesend with a group of friends and afterward walked the road to Rochester between walls of snow six feet high.[60] At the top of the hill he had so often trudged with his father, just opposite Gad's Hill Place, he observed for sale a little house that had been hardly less "a dream of my childhood" than the old rosy brick dwelling across the way. With the remembrance of that old happy time an impulse swept over him to buy it.[61] The negotiations later fell through, but the rush of images from those innocent days when he had fancied it would be the height of felicity to be "a learned and distinguished man" made the shadows of the present even darker.

Already, just to get away somewhere, he had desperately determined on a trip to Paris, and persuaded Collins to accompany him. On the way he would stop off at Boulogne to see Alfred and Frank, still at school there, but then he and Collins would have a week of indulgence, dining out every night, and throwing themselves "en garçon on the festive diableries de Paris." [62] On Saturday, February 10, 1855, all his arrangements were made for leaving the following morning. He sat in his study reading by the fire. A handful of letters was brought in and laid on his table. He looked them over carelessly but, recognizing the handwriting of no personal friend, let them lie there and went back to his book.[63]

But as he sat there he found his mind curiously disturbed, and wandering away through so many years to such early times of his life, that he was perplexed to account for it. There was nothing in what he had been reading, or immediately thinking about, to awaken such a train of thought. At last it came into his head that it must have been something in the look of one of those letters. So he turned them

over again—and suddenly recognized the handwriting of one of them.
A riot of heartbreaking memory welled up in him as he remembered
the hand of Maria Beadnell! a tumult of pain and ecstasy reborn out
of those dead days and alive again in a moment! "Three or four and
twenty years vanished like a dream," he wrote her, "and I opened
it with the touch of my young friend David Copperfield when he was
in love." [64]

It was indeed Maria, writing so pleasantly and affectionately of the
past that it all rose magically before him, filled with the fragrance of
a "Spring in which I was either much more wise or much more foolish than I am now," but when certainly "the qualities that have done
me most good since, were growing in my boyish heart." He remembered everything—the odd little court behind the Mansion House
that came out on the corner of Lombard Street, poor Anne buried now
in the near-by church, the time he met Maria and her sisters going
with their mother "to order mysterious dresses—which afterwards
turned out to be wedding garments," Maria bewitching in green
merino, the anguish he had felt when "the Angel of my soul" was
sent to Paris "to finish her education!" [65]

She was married now, he learned from her letter, to a merchant
named Henry Louis Winter, and had two little girls. "In the unsettled state of my thoughts," he replied, "the existence of these dear
children appeared such a prodigious phenomenon, that I was inclined
to suspect myself of being out of my mind, until it occurred to me that
perhaps I had nine children of my own! Then the three or four and
twenty years began to arrange themselves in a long procession between me and the changeless Past . . ." Marianne Leigh, he wrote, he
had seen at Broadstairs once, years ago, and had heard since that
she was married. "My mother has a strong objection to being considered in the least old, and usually appears here on Christmas Day
in a juvenile cap which takes an immense time in the putting on." [66]

He was going to Paris the next day, he told her, but when he returned Catherine would call to arrange a day for having her and her
husband to a quiet private dinner. Meanwhile he would be at the
Hôtel Meurice; if he could discharge any commission for her or bring
home anything for her little girls she had only to write him there.
He ended in an emotion in which he avowed that there was something a little sorrowful. "The associations my memory has with you

made your letter more—I want a word—invest it with a more immediate address to me than such a letter could have from anybody
else." [67]

In Paris he could think of nothing but Maria, although his letters
home spoke only of the weather, Collins, their thickly carpeted apartment, Régnier, the theaters and boulevards, and his terror that he
might run into the staggering form of Poole.[68] But he could not resist
talking about Maria to Lady Olliffe. Was it "really true," she asked,
"that I used to love Maria Beadnell so very, very, very much? I told
her there was no woman in the world, and there were very few men,
who could ever imagine how much." [69]

So he wrote Maria, for she took advantage of his suggestion that he
might get something for her children by requesting two brooches.[70]
In addition Dickens obtained for the older of the little girls a velvet
collar with a clasp of blue stones, and another with similar ornaments
for Maria.[71] It gave him a pleasurable heartache to remember the
little blue gloves he had matched for her when he was nineteen, and
to remember the blue ribbon he had tied around the bundle of letters he had returned to her.[72]

He wondered if she had seen in *David Copperfield* "a faithful reflection of the passion I had for you," and "in little bits of 'Dora'
touches of your old self sometimes and a grace here and there that
may be revived in your little girls, years hence, for the bewilderment
of some other young lover—though he will never be as terribly in
earnest as I and David Copperfield were. People used to say to me
how pretty all that was, and how fanciful it was, and how elevated it
was above the little foolish loves of very young men and women. But
they little thought what reason I had to know it was true and nothing
more nor less." [73]

All the romance, energy, passion, hope, and determination of his
nature, he told her, were inseparable from her. He had begun his
fight out of poverty and obscurity with one perpetual idea of her. He
had never heard anybody addressed by her name without a start. "The
sound of it has always filled me with a kind of pity and respect for
the deep truth that I had, in my silly hobbledehoyhood, to bestow
upon one creature who represented the whole world to me. I have
never been so good a man since, as I was when you made me wretchedly happy. I shall never be half so good a fellow any more." [74]

The nature of the letter from Maria to which this was a reply can only be inferred from what Dickens wrote. Three sentences near the close suggest in part what she must have said: "These are things that I have locked up in my own breast and that I never thought to bring out any more. But when I find myself writing to you again 'all to yourself,' how can I forebear to let as much light upon them as will shew you that they are still there! If the most innocent, the most ardent, and the most disinterested days of my life had you for their Sun—as indeed they had . . . how can I receive a confidence from you, and return it, and make a feint of blotting all this out!" [75]

Perhaps, he suggested at the very end, she would write him another letter—"all to myself," he quoted her—while he was still in Paris.[76] It arrived after he had left, but followed him immediately to London. "Ah! Though it is so late to read in the old hand what I never read before, I have read it with great emotion, and with the old tenderness softened to a more sorrowful remembrance than I could easily tell you. How it all happened as it did, we shall never know this side of Time; but if you had ever told me then what you tell me now, I know myself well enough to be thoroughly assured that the simple truth and energy which were in my love would have overcome everything." [77]

This can have no other meaning than that Maria said she had loved him in those former days and that they had been separated by misunderstandings. And, on Dickens's part, that he accepted and believed her explanations. But now, she told him, she was "toothless, fat, old and ugly"—"which I don't believe," he answered. She was always the same in his remembrance. He had never seen a girl play a harp without being reminded of her and seeing her father's drawing room. He had never seen in a strange face her tendency to draw her eyebrows together without being "carried away at the rate of a thousand miles a second" and thinking "Maria Beadnell!" Within the last twelve months he had gone over the streets he used to walk when they were falling apart from each other asking himself "whether any reputation the world can bestow is repayment to a man for the loss of such a vision of his youth as mine. You ask me to treasure what you tell me, in my heart of hearts. O see what I have cherished there, through all this time and all these changes!" [78]

Maria must have suggested that they meet each other alone before the family dinner that Kate was supposed to arrange, for Dickens wrote her, "I am a dangerous man to be seen with, for so many people know me. At St. Paul's the Dean and the whole chapter know me. In Paternoster Row of all places, the very tiles and chimney pots know me." He wondered whether he should discourage her desire or suggest an alternative plan, for at the moment things still seemed improbable that might "be very natural and probable a fortnight hence." Still, he too would feel more at ease if they met first before others were by. Would she not like, he suggested, to call at Tavistock House on Sunday, "asking first for Catherine and then for me? It is almost a positive certainty that there will be none here but I, between 3 and 4. . . . If you think you would not like to come here, make no change. I will come there."

"Remember," he ended passionately, "I accept all with my whole soul, and reciprocate all." [79]

Who knows what rapturous, impossible dreams were swirling deliriously through his mind? what rainbow-hued visions ambiguously natural a fortnight hence? Maria's warning that she was no longer the ravishing beauty she had been he utterly dismissed. He could not imagine her in any way changed from the radiant image he had preserved in memory. Eagerly he believed that they had been separated only by misunderstandings now swept away like a mist. The days that had had her for their sun were almost as if they had never ceased to be. The tremulous notes of a harp long unheard were sounding once more in his ears with an ecstatic music. What would happen after they had met—what enchantment melting away the dissonances of his life?

As for Maria, her hopes and intentions are as inscrutable as her true feelings had been in earlier days. Perhaps she began only with a wish to boast herself the present friend as well as the former sweetheart of so distinguished a writer. Perhaps she looked forward to a sentimental flirtation spiced by recollections of their old romance. She may even have envisioned the possibility of their renewed acquaintance kindling more dangerous emotions. Possibly she had no clear purposes at all when she first wrote, and found herself caught up by the intensity of his response in a blurred, breathless excitement. But she was neither shocked nor frightened: she made him an avowal that she asked him "to treasure in his heart of hearts," she proposed a rendezvous at which neither her husband nor his wife should be present. And what could she have told him that elicited that last earnest outcry: "Remember, I accept all with my whole soul, and reciprocate all"?

Dickens himself was in a feverish beatific haze of blinding emotion. The past, with all its lyric passion, had come back to life. In his letters to Maria he cast all reserve to the winds. Only on the surface was he careful to maintain the proprieties by arranging to have Catherine call on Maria and invite her and her husband to dinner. And in Paris, Lady Olliffe may well have suspected that his love for Maria Beadnell was not all a memory of days gone by. But it is highly uncertain whether he had any aims beyond the tense anticipations of the immediate moment and whether his thoughts extended into an envisioned future.

From this exalted state their first meeting brought him down to earth with an appalling jolt. Whether Maria came to Tavistock House or Dickens met her elsewhere, on Sunday, February 25th, they did see each other alone.[80] Dickens must have known that at forty-four Maria could hardly be the same ethereal vision he remembered. Nevertheless, for all her warning, it was a surprise to find her so undeniably fat. But it was not the physical change that was shattering. The gay little laugh, so infectious in the young creature she had been, had turned into a silly giggle. The delightful little voice, running on in such enchanting nonsense, had become a muddleheaded and disjointed volubility. The prettily pettish flirtatious little ways, the arch glances and tones of voice that suggested a secret understanding, were merely ridiculous affectations in a middle-aged woman.[81] What had happened to the fascinations that had captivated him? Or, still worse, was it possible that Maria had always been this absurd and brainless chatterer, that her angelic charm had been only the radiant hallucination of youth?

Even more terrifying, this stout monster, "tossing her head with a caricature of her girlish manner," [82] throwing him the most distressing imitations of the old glances, behaved as if this private meeting involved them in some intimate agreement. He felt the most horrible fear that she was expecting him to propose an instantaneous elopement. But "this grotesque revival" of what had "once been prettily natural to her" was now like an attempt to resuscitate an old play "when the stage was dusty, when the scenery was faded, when the youthful actors were dead, when the orchestra was empty, when the lights were out." [83]

All these things he wrote, months later, in *Little Dorrit*, where Flora is avowedly suggested by Maria's reappearance in his life. By that time he had regained his emotional equilibrium about the episode, and was able to see it in a light half rueful, half comic: "Flora, whom he had left a lily, had become a peony; but that was not much. Flora, who had seemed enchanting in all she said and thought, was diffuse and silly. That was much. Flora, who had been spoiled and artless long ago, was determined to be spoiled and artless now. That was a fatal blow." [84]

At the moment, though, the shock was frightful. The shining dream disappeared like a mirage in a desert. And yet, even in the midst of his disturbance, he could see in the foolish creature traces of something warm-hearted that gave her a touch of pathos. And beneath her discursive babble too, he realized, she had in a swift rush of intuition perceived that he was disappointed.[85] "The inconsistent and profoundly unreasonable way in which she instantly went on, nevertheless, to interweave their long-abandoned boy and girl relations with their present interview" made him feel a mingling of dizziness and terror.[86] But it distressed him, both for the sake of what had been and in sympathy for her now, to give her pain. Gently he endeavored to conceal his feelings, and somehow the meeting ended.

But he could not keep his agitation and distress to himself. Desperate, he confided in Forster, who was incredulous, and thought he must be exaggerating his emotions. "I don't quite apprehend what you mean," Dickens replied, "by my over-rating the strength of the feeling of twenty-five years ago." It had excluded every other idea from his head for four years, "at a time of life when four years are equal to four times four"; it had so steeled his ambition and so filled him with suffering "that to see the mere cause of it all, now, loosens my hold upon myself. Without for a moment sincerely believing that it would have been better if we had never got separated, I cannot see the occasion of so much emotion as I should see anyone else. No one can imagine in the most distant degree what pain the recollection gave me in *Copperfield*. And, just as I can never open that book as I open any other book, I cannot see the face (even at four-and-forty), or hear the voice, without going wandering away over the ashes of all that youth and hope in the wildest manner." [87]

The family dinner that he had all unknowingly planned, however, was still to be endured. It took place on March 7th.[88] Mr. Winter was a prosy and colorless merchant. Maria was only a silly, kindly, fat woman, not markedly different from his middle-aged, rather red-faced wife. Despite a cold, Maria tittered and chattered at his side, and Dickens caught her cold. "I think," he wrote her, with an effort at playfulness, "I heard somebody sneezing at my desk half the day yesterday, who sounded like the incomparable author." For in spite of her suspicion of his feelings, Maria had not given up, and wrote again, insinuating her hopes of reassurance. Dickens tried not to sound cruel. "You make me smile," he replied, "when you picture to yourself how weak I might be, and what poor thoughts I might have, and in what unworthy lights it might be my spoiled nature to show myself." [89]

Her proposal that she call on Sunday with her little girl, however, he answered evasively. He thought the family were pretty sure to be at home, but he could not speak positively for himself. He had promised to participate in "some public literary business," and Sunday might be the day chosen for the meeting.[90] When the day came he was not there, and did not return until she was gone.[91] He tried to soften the effect of his absence by sending a few weeks later tickets for a box at the Adelphi and saying that if his work for *Household Words* allowed he would turn up there in the course of the evening.[92] Once again, though, when the evening came he was not there.

Maria tried to see him the next day, and the day after that, but both times he went out. She wrote him a reproachful letter, accusing him of trying to avoid her and asking what was amiss. Surely he could see her for half an hour? Nothing was amiss, he replied; she simply did not understand "the restlessness or waywardness of an author's mind. . . . 'It is only half an hour'—'it is only an afternoon'—'it is only an evening'—people say to me over and over again—but they don't know that it is impossible to command one's self sometimes to any stipulated and set disposal of five minutes—or that the mere consciousness of an engagement will sometimes worry a whole day. These are the penalties paid for writing books. Whoever is devoted to an Art must be content to deliver himself wholly up to it, and to find his recompense in it. I am grieved if you suspect me of not wanting to see you, but I can't help it; I must go my way, whether or no." [93]

As for the present, "A restlessness is upon me now—as at most times —of wandering about in my own wild way, to think. I could no more resist this on Sunday or yesterday, than a man can dispense with food, or a horse can help himself from being driven." "I am going off, I don't know where or how far, to ponder about I don't know what." He might go to France, or to the seacoast to walk the shore for four months, or to Switzerland. Last week he had vowed he would go to Spain. "Two days afterwards Layard and I agreed to go to Constantinople when Parliament rises. Tomorrow I shall probably discuss with somebody else, the idea of going to Greenland or the North Pole. The end of all this, most likely will be that I shall shut myself up in some out of the way place I have never yet thought of, and go desperately to work there.

"Once upon a time I didn't do such things, you say. No, but I have done them through a good many years now, and they have become myself and my life." [94]

With these words he went his way for a second time. But this time it was Maria Beadnell who was dismissed. Rather obtusely, in June, she was still offering to visit him on some Sunday. Dickens replied that he expected to be out of town for Sundays to come.[95] Maria called at Tavistock House now and then; once Dickens accompanied Kate on an afternoon call at Maria's home in Artillery Place, where he observed her little dog Daphne stuffed in the hall and confirmed a disillusioned impression that Maria liked brandy in her tea. Later Dickens wrote her a sympathetic note when her baby died, but she was irrevocably removed from his life.

Nevertheless, the whole experience had shaken him almost unbelievably. Though he tried to think his tension was merely the usual consequence of trying to get started on a new book, and tried to maintain a tone of joking high spirits with most of his friends, he was keyed up as never before. He felt, he wrote Leigh Hunt, "as infirm of purpose as Macbeth, as errant as Mad Tom, and as ragged as Timon." [96] He rejected all engagements, "to have my time to myself, get tired of myself and yet can't come out of myself to be pleasant to anybody else, and go on turning upon the same wheel round and round and over and over again until it may begin to roll me to my end." [97] "I am in a state of restlessness," he told Miss Coutts, "impossible to be described—impossible to be imagined—wearing and tearing to be experienced." And to Collins he wrote, "I feel as if nothing would do me the least good but setting up a Balloon. It might be inflated in the garden in front—but I am afraid of its scarcely clearing those little houses." [98]

His emotional strain was in fact heading inexorably toward a crisis. He felt the desperate state of the nation's affairs more bitterly than ever. Frost had lasted until late in the spring, many of the poor were out of work, and there had been bread riots in the East End, with dock laborers raising the black flag and looting bakers' shops.[99] "A country which is discovered to be in this tremendous condition," he wrote Forster, "as to its war affairs; with an enormous black cloud of poverty in every town which is spreading and deepening every hour, and not one man in two thousand knowing anything about, or even believing in, its existence; with a non-working aristocracy, and a silent parliament, and everybody for himself and nobody for the rest; this is the prospect . . . O what a fine aspect of political economy it is, that the noble professors of science . . . should have tried to make Adulteration a question of Supply and Demand! We shall never get to the Millennium, sir, by the rounds of that ladder . . ." [100]

As his indignation at these evils fermented with his personal agitation they produced an inward disturbance that exploded with more than ordinary violence. He joined fiercely with Austen Layard in a flaming public attack on the incompetence and indifference of the Government. But even the molten vitriol he poured into this denunciation was insufficient to release his pent-up feelings. Without even any pretense of a purpose other than pure distraction he simultaneously plunged into all the excitement of producing another play, alternately bullying his cast and blasting the administration. And while he was doing both together, he began wrestling with the conception of his next novel, a story in which existence itself, for rich and for poor, for the imprisoned and the free, is seen as no more than confinement in a variety of jails.

CHAPTER SIX

"Nobody's Fault"

WITH this sense of frustration on every hand, Dickens felt more than ever the need for furious action. His friend Layard had returned from the Crimea—where from the maintop of the *Agamemnon* he had seen the Battle of the Alma—determined to fight the inefficiency of the administration with every weapon. The conduct of the war was just another disgraceful proof of the incompetence and indifference to human suffering that produced a thousand evils at home. But it was what might be expected, Layard said, from a government so conscienceless as to "go on vacation for eight weeks without ever summoning a cabinet meeting." Now, as radical member for Aylesbury, he intended to press without ceasing for administrative reform. Dickens promised staunch co-operation.

He would enlist Mark Lemon's support as editor of *Punch*, Dickens told Layard, and their friend Shirley Brooks would use the *Weekly Chronicle* and the *Illustrated London News* to bring the issues home to their large bodies of readers. Dickens had begged Jerrold, too, "not to be diverted from the straight path of help" to Layard, "the most useful man in England." He would also speak to Forster, little as that seemed needed. And, "If you ever see any new loophole, cranny, needle's-eye, through which I can present your case in Household Words, I most earnestly entreat you . . . to count upon my being Damascus Steel to the core." [1]

Layard was obstructed in Parliament, of course, with every procedural dodge, and before the public with every device of misrepresentation. When he finally got his motion before the House it was defeated by a vote of 359 to 46. He countered the rejection of his demands with a direct appeal to a discontented public. Miss Coutts, troubled, told Dickens she feared Layard was setting class against class. He differed with her altogether, Dickens retorted: Layard found them "already set in opposition." The upper class had taken the initiative years ago, "and it is *they* who have put *their* class in opposition to the country—not the country which puts itself in opposition to *them*." [2]

"Take my knowledge of the state of things in this distracted land," Dickens lectured her, "for what it may be worth a dozen years hence. The people will not bear for any length of time what they bear now. I see it clearly written in every truthful indication that I am capable of discerning anywhere. And I want to interpose something between them and their wrath." [3]

The sullen discontent in the country, he was convinced, was "the worse for smouldering, instead of blazing openly"; it was "like the general mind of France before the breaking out of the first Revolution." Any of a thousand accidents—"a bad harvest—the last strain too much of aristocratic insolence or incapacity—a defeat abroad—a mere chance at home"—could precipitate "such a devil of a conflagration as never has been beheld since." [4]

Dickens attended a meeting at which it was decided to organize an Administrative Reform Association, and subscribed £20 as a member. He agreed to take the chair at a public meeting to be held at Drury Lane in June. [5] At the annual dinner of the General Theatrical Fund he contrasted the efficiency of dramatic enterprises with governmental blundering in the Crimea. Unlike the War Department, he said, when the Haymarket Theatre staged a battle scene, necessary supplies were not "found packed under 500 tons of iron," nor did it prove impossible "to fire a shot because they had all been left somewhere where they were not wanted." Rounds of applause greeted this sardonic hit. [6]

At the same time Dickens was publishing in *Household Words*, as he had promised, a series of attacks upon the administration. His "Thousand and One Humbugs" article he followed up with another called "Scarli Tapa and the Forty Thieves," in which the robbers' cave, "with the enchanted letters O.F.F.I.C.E.," is entered by pronouncing the words "Debrett's Peerage. Open Sesame!" and in which Scarli Tapa, instead of slaying the thieves, forms an alliance with their Captain. [7] The following week Dickens satirized Palmerston, the Premier, as the talkative barber, Praymiah, "a frisky speaker, an easy shaver, a touch-and-go joker, a giver of the go-by to all complainers," who never did the work he was hired to do, but instead constantly "danced the dance of Mistapit, and sang the song of Mistafoks, and joked the joke of Jomillah." [8]

Hardly a week went by that Dickens was not hammering away in all manner of forms at the same points. Parliament, "with its feeble jokes, logic-chopping, straw-splitting, tape-tying, tape-untying to tie again; double-shuffling, word-eating," was plainly "the house of Parler and Mentir," the place of wordiness and lies.[9] What of a system where there were "Chancery suits sixty years old, and admirals and generals on active service, eighty"? Why was it that even when a reform was promised it always turned out to consist of dismissing a few clerks at £90 a year and retaining all their incompetent superiors? [10] Was it not obvious "that any half-dozen shopkeepers taken at random from the London Directory and shot into Downing Street out of sacks" could do a better job than these Red-Tapers and Sealing-Wax-Chafers? [11]

Meanwhile Dickens was pushing ahead with the plans for his play. Collins had written "a regular old-style melodrama" called *The Lighthouse* which Dickens intended to put on in the children's theater. The stage would be large, so that there would only be room for twenty-five spectators, but it could be given on a number of successive nights. He asked Clarkson Stanfield to paint the one scene, the interior of the lighthouse.[12] "O, what a pity it is not the outside of the Light'us, with the sea a-rowling agin it! Never mind, we'll get an effect out of the inside, and there's a storm and shipwreck 'off'; and the great ambition of my life will be achieved at last, in the wearing of a pair of very coarse petticoat trousers. So hooroar for the salt sea, Mate, and bowse up!" [13]

Stanfield entered into the scheme "with the greatest delight" [14] and was soon in the schoolroom "all day long with his coat off," "bent on desperate effects" and "up to his eyes in distemper." [15] In addition to the interior he painted an act drop showing the Eddystone Light in a raging storm. Dickens, Collins, Egg, and Lemon acted with Mamey and Georgy in the melodrama, and to these were added Katey and Frank Stone in *Mr. Nightingdale's Diary*. Dickens dominated rehearsals with his usual determination to obtain perfection. Charley, who operated the "wind-machine" that produced storm effects, said later, "I could always tell by the very look of my father's shoulders . . . as he sat on the stage with his back to me that he was ready for the smallest mistake." [16]

Four successive audiences crowded the tiny schoolroom theater on the nights of June 15th, 16th, 18th, and 19th. [17] Dickens played the role of Aaron Gurnock, the old lighthouse keeper, with a wild picturesqueness that reminded Carlyle of Poussin's famous painting of the Bacchanalian dance. [18] All the guests cried plentifully during the melodrama and cheered the farce. Among them, with her son, was Mrs. Frederick Yates, who had played Dolly Varden and Sikes's Nancy in the old days at the Adelphi. She had wept so profusely that she still had "a large, red circle round each eye," and exclaimed, "O Mr. Dickens what a pity it is you can do anything else!" "Longman the bookseller was seen to cry dreadfully—and I don't know that anything could be said beyond that!" [19]

The production created such a furore that Dickens was asked to present the play again for the benefit of the Bournemouth Sanatorium for Consumptives on July 10th. [20] Campden House, Kensington, which had a private theater with orchestra, boxes, stage, and footlights, was offered by its owner, Colonel Waugh, to accommodate a larger audience. [21] For this performance a number of "Swell Amateurs" assumed parts in *Animal Magnetism*, which replaced *Mr. Nightingale* on the bill. "If you could have seen me yesterday," Dickens exclaimed, "with a wretched Idiot (of large property) who was yawyawing through the part of a French Viscount"! But he swiftly imbued these amateurs too with "a wholesome dread of the Inimitable," [22] and the charitable performance came off well.

Never for a moment, though, did Collins's melodrama push from Dickens's mind the larger drama on the national stage. He was unable to be present when Layard addressed a meeting at Drury Lane on June 20th, but he was entirely in accord with what Layard said. The evidence of government blue books, Layard charged, revealed "records of inefficiency, records of indifference to suffering, records of ignorance, records of obstinacy," that were a shame to the nation. The Civil Service was grossly overstaffed with men busy making work for each other. Lord Palmerston, personally, he denounced for an attitude of levity toward the sufferings of the people.

Stung by the attack, Lord Palmerston retorted with a sneer about "the private theatricals at Drury Lane." And Dickens, fired with indignation, determined that such a creature "as this Lord Palmerston" must have it rung "into his soul (or what stands for it) that the time for Dandy insolence is gone for ever." [23] At a second Drury Lane gathering on the 27th, he built the first part of his speech around Palmerston's contemptuous epithet. "I have some slight acquaintance with theatricals, private and public," he said ominously, "and I will accept that figure of the noble lord. I will not say that if I wanted to form a company of her Majesty's servants, I think I should know where to put my hand on 'the comic old gentleman'; nor, that if I wanted to get up a pantomime, I fancy I should know what establishment to go to for the tricks and changes . . ." But he *would* tell the reason for these "private theatricals": "The public theatricals which the noble lord is so condescending as to manage are so intolerably bad, the machinery is so cumbrous, the parts so ill-distributed, the company so full of 'walking gentlemen,' the managers have such large families, and are so bent upon putting those families into what is theatrically called 'first business'—not because of their aptitude for it, but because they *are* their families, that we find ourselves obliged to organize an opposition. We have seen the *Comedy of Errors* played so dismally like a tragedy that we really cannot bear it. We are therefore making bold to get up the *School of Reform*, and we hope, before the play is out, to improve that noble lord by our performance very considerably. If he object that we have no right to improve him without his license, we venture to claim that right in virtue of his orchestra, consisting of a very powerful piper, whom we always pay." [24]

England could not "find on the face of the earth," Dickens continued, "an enemy one-twentieth part so potent to effect the misery and ruin of her noble defenders" as she had been herself. In the gloomy silence with which the people stood aloof from the machinery of government and legislation it was "as if they left it to its last remaining function of destroying itself, when it had achieved the destruction of so much that was dear to them." [25] In a state of affairs so menacing, the only wholesome turn things could take was for the people to speak out, to unite, and to achieve a great change in administration.

Three objections, Dickens noted, had been made to the present

Association. First, that it proposed to influence the House of Commons. But the House *was* influenced by interests not at all favorable to the welfare of the people, and needed to be watched and jogged and hustled and pinched into doing its duty. Second, that the Association set class against class. This was mere parrot prattle. Suppose a gentleman to have a crew of incompetent servants, who gave his children stones instead of bread, serpents instead of fish, who consulted "exploded cookery books in the South" when they were ordered to serve "dinner in the North," who wasted and brought everything to ruin. And then, when he says, "I must have servants who will do their duty," his steward cries in pious horror, "Good God, master, you are setting class against class!" The third objection was that the reformers should mind their own business. To which the answer was that this was their business. If the ruling forces of the country persisted in an "obstinate adherence to rubbish," that rotten debris—like the worm-eaten old splints that caught fire and destroyed the Palace of Westminster—would one day break into flames and consume them in its burning. "Let the hon. gentleman find a day for himself," Lord Palmerston had said scornfully when Mr. Layard first asked for a day to present his motion. "Name you the day, First Lord," Dickens warned; "make a day, work for a day beyond your little time . . . and History may then—not otherwise—find a day for you . . ." [26]

* * * * *

The mood that burned in this address was not absent from the new novel he had already started to write. He had experienced more than ordinary difficulty in making a beginning—taking notes, tearing them up, pacing his room all day, staring at a blank first page, prowling about London at night, going out of town, coming back next day, breaking engagements, distraught far beyond anything that getting under way had ever involved before.[27] All of the excitement and subsequent disillusion of seeing Maria again, of course, had a part in his feverish state—as did the labors of producing *The Lighthouse* and the blows he was striking for administrative reform in the pages of *Household Words*. But these last activities served at least in some degree to relieve his feelings. The real source of his difficulty and his tension was the problem of shaping a story that should symbolize the condition of England.

As he had first conceived the book, its central character was to have been a man who brought about all the mischief in it, and then, at every fresh calamity, said "Well, it's a mercy, however, nobody was to blame you know!" [28] But this notion did not emphasize clearly enough his desire to portray a vast impersonal system of inefficiency, venality, and wrong, baffling all endeavor to fasten responsibility anywhere. He therefore dropped this element in his original scheme; no pattern would do that permitted his readers to imagine that isolated individual mischiefs were more than small parts of a corrupt social whole. Not until after he had written the first four numbers, however, and the book was on the verge of publication, did he substitute the name *Little Dorrit* for the bitterly ironic title *Nobody's Fault*.

The great structure that he finally evolved integrated his criticism into a whole of remarkable intellectual and artistic power. All the things he wanted to emphasize were there, connected with each other in dozens of ways. There was the rack-renting of the poor for the profit of their exploiters in the benevolent Casby extorting every last farthing from the inhabitants of Bleeding Heart Yard. There was the obstructionism of a bureaucracy that entangled justice and encumbered progress in the convoluted procedures of the Circumlocution Office. There was the sinister alliance between political leadership and the unscrupulous interests that wielded financial power in the negotiations between Lord Decimus Tite Barnacle and the slinking financial manipulator Merdle. And both literally and symbolically Casby is linked with the Tite Barnacles and the Tite Barnacles with the Circumlocution Office, Merdle, and the entire political, financial, and social structure of the country.

Even after these major points were settled, however, the writing was a struggle. Finally, around the 21st of May, Dickens got into the first chapter, "sitting down to an immensity, getting up after doing nothing," stepping "on particular bits of all the flowers in the carpet— tearing my hair (which I can't afford to do) . . ." [29] But throughout the end of that month he made little headway, filling his manuscript with interlineations and erasures. During June and the earlier part of July he was still wrestling with the first number.[30]

He was exasperated beyond bearing by the fact that Layard's reform endeavors were being completely smothered in Parliament. Dining at Lord John Russell's, Dickens "gave them a little bit of truth . . .

that was like bringing a Sebastapol battery among the polite company," and Meyerbeer, the composer, said admiringly afterward, "Ah, mon ami illustre! que c'est noble de vous entendre parler d'haute voix morale, à la table d'un ministre!" [31] It was grimly clear, though, that the forces of Circumlocution were doing their usual job of rendering all progress impossible by throwing out a tangle of red tape and a labyrinth of official forms.

From the middle of July, Dickens rented 3 Albion Villas, Folkestone, a pleasant little house overlooking the sea and breezy with the scent of thyme from the downs. [32] Here he hoped to write enough of his book to have a comfortable backlog before it began publication in December. At first he found himself utterly unable to concentrate; all the boys were home from school and their feet constantly stamped up and down the wooden stairs, with fourteen-year-old Walter the loudest of all. "Why a boy of that age should seem to have on at all times, 150 pairs of double soled boots, and to be always jumping a bottom stair with the whole 150, I don't know." [33] But at the end of the month Walter went back to his school at Wimbledon, and the house became a little quieter or Dickens grew a little more used to the clatter. And at the end of August, Frank and Alfred returned to their school at Boulogne, taking with them their eight-year-old brother Sydney, and leaving little Harry and Plorn the only small boys remaining with the family. [34]

Dickens stuck to his writing, and went into "the great oven," as he now called London, only when *Household Words* business forced him to. [35] By the middle of August, consequently, he had finished the first number and started the second. [36] His superfluous vitality he expended "in swarming up the face of a gigantic and precipitous cliff in a lonely spot overhanging the wild sea-beach." Here, he wrote Beard, he might generally be seen "from the British Channel, suspended in mid-air with his trousers very much torn, at fifty minutes past 3 P.M." [37] With the completion of the second number he felt steeped in his story, rising and falling by turns into enthusiasm and depression. [38] "There is an enormous outlay in the Father of the Marshalsea chapter, in the way of getting a great lot of matter into a small space." [39] As always, he was coming to live in his tale and feel as if it pervaded all the world around him, "heaving in the sea, flying with the clouds, blowing in the wind." [40] The end of September saw the virtual completion of "No. 3, in which I have relieved my soul," Dickens told Collins, "with a scarifier"—the satiric tenth chapter on "How Not to Do It," "Containing the Whole Science of Government." [41]

Meanwhile, other matters also demanded his attention. Charley, now eighteen, and back from Leipzig since Christmas—presumably with a sufficient stock of German—had to be found a place in business. Dickens had consulted with Miss Coutts, who held out hopes of a post with a firm trading in Turkey, and he had friends in Birmingham who were willing to recommend the young man to a position there. But the Birmingham opening offered only scanty opportunities to learn anything about foreign trade, and the one Miss Coutts mentioned was still uncertain.[42] On the advice of one of the partners in Baring Brothers, Charley had been put in a London brokers' office.[43] After he had been there six months, the same gentleman told Dickens there was an opening in Baring's.[44] He added "that the brokers gave Charley 'so high a character for ability and zeal' that it would be unfair to receive him as a volunteer, and he must begin at a fifty-pound salary, to which I graciously consented."[45] "I expect the Brokers," Dickens commented, "to have been a device and trial altogether—to get a telescopic view of a youth with a double suspicion on him arising out of his being an author's son and an Eton boy." On September 24th Charley assumed his new duties.[46]

Dickens was now on the verge of leaving for Paris, where he planned to spend the fall and winter, but he had a number of engagements to keep first. On October 4th he read the *Christmas Carol* for the benefit of an educational institution at Folkestone. The price of the stalls was five shillings, but he had insisted that there must also be seats at threepence for working men.[47] And on October 11th he presided over a farewell dinner for Thackeray, who was sailing for America to give a series of lectures on *The Four Georges*. Dickens had argued with Thackeray over what he felt the distorted and sentimental praise he had given the Charterhouse Charity in a recent article in the *Examiner* [48]—three years earlier *Household Words* had made an attack on the abuses in the administration of that charity—but Dickens did not allow this difference of opinion to spoil the friendliness of the occasion. Two days later Thackeray sailed from Liverpool and Dickens crossed the Channel to Boulogne.[49]

Georgina had by this time almost completely superseded Catherine

in the control of all domestic matters, and had gone ahead to Paris
to take an apartment for the family. Here Dickens joined her, leaving
Catherine at Boulogne with the children.[50] Paris was crowded and
insanely expensive. Georgy found a little house in the Rue de Balzac
whose tenant was supposed to be leaving, but suddenly he refused to
move out.[51] The owner, M. Arsène Houssaye, director of the Théâtre
Française, offered another house in the Rue de Lord Byron, which
proved to be too small.[52] Finally an entresol and first floor were found
at 49 Avenue de Champs Élysées, near the Barrière de l'Étoile and
the Jardin d'Hiver, with six small sunlit rooms looking out on the busy
street and lots of others tucked away inside. "They are not over and
above well furnished," Dickens wrote Catherine, "but by changing
furniture from rooms we don't care for, to rooms we *do* care for, we
shall be able to make them comfortable and presentable." [53]

The first night there, however, proved the place to be dreadfully
dirty. Georgy was unable to sleep for the smell of her room. Next morning Dickens routed out the porter, the porter's wife, her sister, various
other helpers, and the old lady and little man with a François Premier
beard who were owners of the apartment, and demanded that it be
cleaned. They were astounded: "It's not the custom," they urged. But
gradually they wavered, offered "new carpets (accepted), embraces
(not accepted)," and at last responded "like French Bricks." Dickens
stalked coatless and dirty-faced through the rooms in a fury of "stage-
managerial energies" until by nightfall they were purified to spot-
lessness.[54]

Soon afterward, Catherine arrived with Mamey and Katey and the
two little boys. Through the six windows facing on the wide avenue
the children could watch the constant parading of the regiments
marching out to drill in the country and straggling back picturesquely
in the afternoon. Sometimes "great storms of drums played, and then
the most delicious and skilful bands, Trovatore music, Barber of
Seville music," with "all bloused Paris" following "in a sort of hilarious dance." [55] Again would come striding the Zouaves, sunburnt, with
red petticoat trousers and wild beards and mustaches, preceded by
their regimental mascot, a little black dog marching "with a profound
conviction that he was decorated." [56]

Through the celebrated artist Ary Scheffer, Dickens met Daniele
Manin, the exiled President of the ill-fated Republic of St. Mark, and

from this "best and noblest" of the leaders of 1848 Mamey and Katey began taking lessons in Italian.[57] They also saw a good deal of Thackeray's daughters, who were living just across the avenue with their grandmother while their father was in America. Almost young ladies now, they could all admire the luxurious costumes of fashionable Paris driving past in open carriages, the billowing frothy crinolines and the glowing russets and oranges of the shawls.[58]

Dickens was now well known in France through numerous translations. *Pickwick* had appeared there in 1838, *Nickleby* in 1840, *Oliver* in 1841, and *The Old Curiosity Shop* in 1842. Then, after a pause, there had been a rush of further translation, the Christmas stories in 1847, *Dombey* in 1848, and *Copperfield* in 1851.[59] On his arrival in Paris, he found that daily installments of *Chuzzlewit* were being published in the *Moniteur*, and it was impossible for him to give his name in a shop without being greeted enthusiastically. "Ah! The famous writer! Monsieur bears a very distinguished name. But! I am honored and interested to see Monsieur Dick-in." A man who delivered some vases Dickens had bought was ecstatic about Mrs. Todgers. "That Madame Tojair . . . Ah! How droll, and exactly like a lady I know at Calais!" [60] And in addition to these personal tributes, the *Revue des Deux Mondes* carried in February, 1856, a critical article by Hippolyte Taine, "Charles Dickens, son talent et ses oeuvres," proclaiming his European importance and emphasizing his significance as a social critic. To round out the circle of his recognition in France, in the course of the winter the publishing house of Hachette arranged with Dickens to bring out a uniform edition of all his novels in a carefully supervised translation.[61]

He now mingled constantly with the most distinguished artists and men of letters in Paris. At the diner table of Eugène Scribe he met Auber, whose *Manon Lescaut* was having its première at the Opéra Comique, and a little later he heard Marie Cabel in its title role. "She sings a laughing song in it," he told Forster, "which is received with madness, and which is the only real laughing song that was ever written." On another evening he dined with Amédée Pichot, director of the *Revue Britannique* and translator of *David Copperfield*. Here he renewed his acquaintance with Lamartine, who was exactly as Dickens had remembered him, speaking "with a sort of calm passion . . . very taking indeed." They talked of the genius of Richardson and Defoe, and Lamartine complimented "ce cher Boz" on his command of French, "whereat your correspondent blushed modestly" and at once "choked himself with the bone of a fowl (which is still in his throat)." [62]

The Scribes were among the guests at dinner, but had to leave early, and Dickens was fascinated by Mme. Scribe's youthfulness and beauty. Her eldest son, he said, "must be thirty, and she has the figure of five-and-twenty, and is strikingly handsome. So graceful too, that her manner of rising, curtseying, laughing, and going out after him, was pleasanter than the pleasantest thing I have ever seen done on the stage." [63] And Mme. Régnier and Pauline Viardot, the operatic mezzo-soprano—how did these women retain their grace and charm! It was an observation, though, that he could not make about George Sand, whom he met at Mme. Viardot's. The famous novelist was a "chubby, matronly, swarthy, black-eyed" woman, "whom you might suppose to be the Queen's monthly nurse," with "nothing of the blue-stocking about her, except a little final way of settling all your opinions with hers." [64]

Nothing in Paris startled Dickens more than the glittering opulence of the Second Empire and the mania for speculation among all classes of society. Even the writers had made fortunes on the Bourse. Scribe had a delightful apartment in town, a château in the country, and a "sumptuous carriage and magnificent span of horses." [65] Eugène Sue lived surrounded by pictures, statues, and antiquities, in an ornate apartment with hothouses bursting with flowers and fountains playing on gold and silver fish.[66] But most magnificent of all was the press magnate and political economist Émile de Girardin, who in addition to owning the great political organ, *La Presse,* ran a whole string of weekly magazines, and had built up stupendous wealth in financial manipulations.

Writing with some slight hyperbole, perhaps, Dickens described a dinner at Girardin's.[67] There were "three gorgeous drawing rooms with ten thousand wax candles in golden sconces," a table piled with mounds of truffles, iced champagne in ground-glass jugs, "Oriental flowers in vases of golden cobweb," "Cigarettes from the Hareem of the Sultan," cool drinks flavored with lemons just arrived from Algeria and oranges from Lisbon, "a far larger plum pudding than ever was seen in England at Christmas time, served with a celestial sauce in color like the orange blossom" and described in a gold-framed menu as "Hommage à l'illustre écrivain d'Angeleterre." "That illustrious man staggered out at the last drawing-room door," only to be told by his host, "The dinner we have had, mon cher, is nothing—doesn't count—was quite en famille—we must dine (really dine) soon. Au plaisir! Au revoir! Au diner!" [68]

On a later occasion, after a banquet terminating with every guest's being served "a flower pot out of a ballet . . . piled to the brim with the ruddiest fresh strawberries," Girardin asked Dickens if he would like a cigar. "On my replying yes, he opened, with a key attached to his watch-chain, a species of mahogany cave, which appeared to me to extend under the Champs Élysées, and in which were piled about four hundred thousand inestimable cigars, in bundles or bales of about a thousand each." [69] Among the other diners was a little man "who was blacking shoes 8 years ago, and is now enormously rich—the richest man in Paris—having ascended with rapidity up the usual ladder of the Bourse. By merely observing that perhaps he might come down again, I clouded so many faces as to render it very clear to me that *everybody present* was at the same game for some stake or other!" [70]

The madness of luxury and gambling on the market, in fact, was a fever throughout the city. "If you were to see the steps of the Bourse at about 4 in the afternoon, and the crowd of blouses and patches among the speculators there assembled, all howling and haggard . . . you would stand aghast at the consideration of what must be going on. Concierges and people like that perpetually blow their brains out, or fly into the Seine, 'à cause des pertes sur la Bourse.' On the other hand, thoroughbred horses without end, and red velvet carriages with white kid harness on jet black horses, go by here all day long; and the pedestrians who turn to look at them, laugh, and say, 'C'est la Bourse!' Such crashes must be staved off every week as have not been seen since Law's time!" [71] and the collapse of his notorious speculative scheme, the Mississippi Bubble.

*   *   *   *   *

These scenes incontestably deepened the hues in which Dickens later painted the splendor of the Merdle banquets and the widespread ruin following the crash of the Merdle fortune. But meanwhile the distractions of Paris were making it hard for him even to find time to work on *Little Dorrit*. Before he had been there a week Ary Scheffer had expressed a desire to do his portrait.[72] "He is a most noble fellow," Dickens said, "and I have the greatest pleasure in his society"; but as Dickens sat to him daily throughout most of November he was driven almost wild at being kept away from his desk. His state of mind was not improved by his being unable to find in the picture any faintest resemblance to himself.[73] Ultimately, as the sittings were prolonged into the following year, he was privately calling it "the nightmare portrait." [74] and chafing desperately at his bondage.

Nevertheless, he drove away doggedly at *Little Dorrit*, and managed to get the first three numbers finished by the time the opening number was published in December. As it developed, it rendered ever more darkly his vision of the modern world that it portrayed. "You see what miserable humbugs we are," he said to one correspondent. "And because we have got involved in meshes of aristocratic red tape to our unspeakable confusion, loss, and sorrow, the gentlemen who have been so kind as to ruin us are going to give us a day of humiliation and fasting the day after tomorrow. I am sick and sour to think of such things at this age of the world." The theme of the book, in fact, went "round and round" this idea, with the Dorrits in the Marshalsea, the workers in Bleeding Heart Yard, Mr. Merdle skulking through the heavy magnificence of his mansion, and the world of wealth and fashion rotating in its own prison routine, all like "a bird in his cage." [75]

Despite its somber atmosphere, however, the story from the beginning commanded a greater audience than Dickens had ever had before, and retained that lead throughout its entire career. The day after the first number went on sale, "Little Dorrit has beaten even Bleak House out of the field," Dickens wrote. "It is a most tremendous start, and I am overjoyed at it." [76] Soon Bradbury and Evans were proposing that they greatly increase the £200 they paid him each month, in order to diminish the half-yearly balance, and Dickens made no objection. "It will be as useful to me in six large portions and a moderate lump, as in six small portions and a great lump." [77]

He had been in London for a week at the beginning of November,[78] and in the middle of December he made another brief trip to England, where he had promised to read the *Christmas Carol* for the benefit of Mechanics' Institutes at Peterborough and Sheffield. He found *Little Dorrit* "still going amazingly," and "an enormous sale" of the

Christmas number of *Household Words*, for which he had written three of the short stories.[79] Before the Peterborough reading on the 18th, Dickens spent an evening at Rockingham Castle with Mrs. Watson and saw his dear Mary again, dashed back to London, and then went to Sheffield for the 22nd. Throughout the entire time the weather was polar. Walking to the Birmingham Railway, through "a black East wind that seemed to freeze the hair off one's head," he met people "actually sobbing and crying with the cold." [80]

On the 24th Dickens returned to Paris, and resumed work on *Little Dorrit* with such energy that he finished the fourth number on the very last day of the year. The effort left him feeling depressed and overworked.[81] He was therefore more than usually irritated when the articles on factory accidents which he had been running in *Household Words* were attacked by Harriet Martineau, who had often appeared in its pages.[82] In a violent and one-sided pamphlet published by the National Association of Manufacturers, and based on information supplied by its representatives, she accused *Household Words* of "unscrupulous statements, insolence, arrogance, and cant." [83]

Dickens had Henry Morley, the author of most of the factory articles, write a reply, which appeared on January 18th under the title of "Our Wicked Misstatements." Impeccably polite, the rejoinder smashed Miss Martineau's every argument. It proved that her statistics on factory accidents were grossly underestimated and based upon sophistical definitions of terms. It showed that the Association of Manufacturers was in purpose and in fact an organization to support its members in defying the law. It courteously rebuked the lady's own controversial manners in calling those who wished to see the law enforced "passionate advocates of meddling legislation" and dismissing their viewpoint as "philo-operative cant." Miss Martineau tried to claim that the wise and witty Sydney Smith would have taken her position; where he would really have stood was shown by a paper in which he described the fatalities among the climbing boys as "burning little chimney-sweepers." "What is a toasted child," he asked with grim irony, "compared to the agonies of the mistress of the house with a deranged dinner?" [84]

Dickens himself carefully went over every word of this reply, preserving its politeness but sharpening its bite. The brilliant quotation from Sydney Smith sounds like one of his additions. "I do suppose,"

Dickens commented, "that there never was such a wrong-headed woman born—such a vain one—or such a Humbug." [85]

With the revised proofs of this article Dickens sent back another piece by Morley which he insisted on having drastically rewritten. He would not have *Household Words* say of the strike in Manchester that the men were *"of course* entirely and painfully in the wrong," and he would not be represented as believing that strikes were never justified. He deplored the waste, the angry passions, and the occasional destruction and violence caused by strikes, but what other recourse had those unhappy workers who could not obtain a peaceful hearing? "Nor can I possibly adopt the representation that these men are wrong because, by throwing themselves out of work, they throw other people, possibly without their consent." Such a principle would have meant no resistance to Charles I; "no raising by Hampden of a troop of Horse, to the detriment of Buckinghamshire Agriculture; no self-sacrifice in the political world. And O Good God when Morley treats of the suffering of wife and children," does he suppose the men themselves don't "feel it in the depths of their hearts" and believe devoutly and faithfully "that for those very children when they shall have children, they are bearing all these miseries now!" [86]

The allusion to the Civil War was probably suggested by Macaulay's *History of England*, through which Dickens was struggling against all inclination. He was found by George Augustus Sala, whom he had invited to breakfast, poring over its pages with his head between his hands, in the attitude of a man indomitably determined to accomplish an ungrateful task. What a bitter mockery was all that complacent Whig optimism about progress in the face of England's social problems! [87]

Dickens put aside the volume and listened to Sala, who had written begging to see him. Sala was leading a raffish, Bohemian life in Paris, and was always hard up, but he felt embarrassed to ask for the advance that he wanted. At last he stammered an appeal for £5, and Dickens gave it, in spite of detecting in him "a strong flavour of the wine shop and the billiard table." [88]

The fifth number of *Little Dorrit* was now being started,[89] in the midst of dark drizzly weather that turned the streets into oceans of mud. All the paving stones were torn up in preparation for macadamizing the streets, but Dickens plowed through the deep holes every afternoon, determined to walk all around the walls of Paris. One day he would turn to the right outside the Barrière and re-enter the city beyond the site of the Bastille, the next day to the left, and return smeared to the very eyebrows with mud.[90] Georgina often went with him, and became literally invisible under the liquid coating. "A turned-up nose may be seen in the midst of splashes, but nothing more." [91]

In early February Dickens had to make another trip to London on business. He attended a meeting of the Theatrical Fund, checked up on the running of the Home at Shepherd's Bush, looked into how Charley was getting on at Baring Brothers'—learning that his son had done so well that he had been given a bonus of £10 and an increase in salary of £10 a year.[92] He also brought to a culmination certain efforts he had been making to aid W. H. Wills.

In the previous June, Wills had been offered the editorship of the *Civil Service Gazette,* and asked Dickens if there was any objection to his assuming its duties concurrently with his work as subeditor of *Household Words.* Dickens objected strongly to Wills taking any other editorial post whatever, and Wills dropped the idea.[93] But, aware that his subordinate needed to supplement his income, when Dickens learned from Miss Coutts in November that she desired a confidential secretary to administer her charitable work, he promptly recommended Wills. The duties would not interfere with his work on *Household Words,* "the connexion," he told Wills, "would be valuable and pleasant to you . . . and the post is fit for any gentleman in association with such a lady." [94] Miss Coutts, always deliberate, took two months in finally making up her mind, but now, in conference with Dickens, decided to offer Wills the position at £200 a year.[95] This offer Wills gladly accepted.

At the same time Forster, who had been feeling that he was not sufficiently consulted about *Household Words* and had come to resent Wills, determined to sever his connection with the magazine. For the last two years he had professed himself too busy to contribute to its pages, but it had been agreed that he should retain his one-eighth share on condition of paying his co-proprietors £1,000 by February, 1856.[96] But the "Lincolnian Mammoth" was "in bad spirits," [97] Dickens said; perhaps, too, he was annoyed that Dickens was excitedly looking forward to having Wilkie Collins visit him in Paris, but did not press *him* to come. He failed to make the payment, and Dickens immediately bestowed half of the relinquished share on Wills for so long as he should remain subeditor of the magazine.[98]

Forster's step did not mean, of course, that he was terminating his friendship with Dickens, although certainly they were less close than they had been before Wills became Dickens's trusted lieutenant on *Household Words* and Collins took Forster's place as a boon companion. Forster was changed, like everything else in Dickens's life; he had grown burly, broad-faced, authoritative, with a pugnacious jaw, stern features, a booming voice; his rhinoceros laugh seldom rang out now, and dinners at his table were solemn affairs. He had succeeded Fonblanque as editor of the *Examiner* and made himself a literary dictator demanding a deference little short of that once accorded to Dr. Johnson. On one occasion, after a quarrel with Browning, he gave a reconciliation banquet. When dinner was over, Carlyle lit up his pipe and two young men thereupon ventured to light cigars, only to receive a majestic rebuke: "I never allow smoking in this room, save on this privileged occasion when my old friend Carlyle honours me. But I do not extend that to you Robert Lytton, or to you Percy Fitzgerald. You have taken the matter into your own hands, without asking leave or license; as that is so, and the thing is done, there is no more to be said." [99] And although Forster took no such tone with Dickens, and their fondness for each other was deeply rooted, the old spontaneous intimacy was gone.

When Dickens went to London on another flying trip in March, Forster electrified him by a further announcement. After having reached the age of forty-four and coming to be regarded by everyone who knew him as a confirmed bachelor, Forster had engaged himself to marry the wealthy widow of Henry Colburn the publisher. "Tell Catherine," Dickens wrote Georgy, "that I have the most prodigious, overwhelming, crushing, astounding, blinding, deafening, pulverizing, scarifying secret of which Forster is the hero, imaginable by the united efforts of the whole British population. It is a thing of that kind, that after I knew it (from himself) this morning, I lay down flat, as if an Engine and Tender had fallen upon me." [100]

* * * * *

Shortly after Dickens returned to Paris came the formal ending of the Crimean War. It was received with general apathy and Dickens himself felt that it made little difference to any of the social objects he had hoped for.[101] Layard's strivings had been thwarted; the same forces that had used the war to block progress would go on finding new excuses and erecting new obstacles or merely imposing the ponderous inertia of the Circumlocution Office to wear down the reformers. Although he was never to cease pouring out criticism, Dickens had by now almost entirely lost faith that anything would come of it.

More and more, in fact, he found himself deeply and bitterly skeptical of the whole system of respectable attitudes and conventional beliefs that cemented all of society into a monolithic structure stubbornly resistant to significant change. He derided the pompous self-assurance of the aristocracy and hated the cold-hearted selfishness of the men of wealth. He despised the subservient snobbery of the middle class, which was "nothing but a poor fringe on the mantle of the upper." He was contemptuous of the corruption and inefficiency of the Government and bitter over the brutal workings of an economic system that condemned the masses of the people to ignorance, suffering, and squalor. But there the monstrous *thing* lay in the road of progress, in one enormous mass, higher and more invulnerable than any Chinese Wall.

"As to the suffrage, I have lost hope even in the ballot." Representative institutions were a failure in England because the people were denied the education that was a prerequisite for supporting them. "What with bringing up the soul and body of the land to be a good child, or to go to the beer-shop, to go a-poaching, and go to the devil; . . . what with flunkyism, toadyism," [102] red tape, greed, and apathy, Dickens felt almost hopeless. England was in the hands of Sir Leicester Dedlock, Boodle and Coodle, Mr. Dombey, the Tite Barnacles; worse still, of Mr. Gradgrind, Mr. Bounderby, and Mr. Merdle; and worst of all, England abased itself beneath their feet.

The very values of the imagination and the heart that sustained a healthy culture were deeply undermined. This was why even art and literature were feeble in comparison with what they might be. "Don't think it a part of my despondency about public affairs . . . when I say that mere form and conventionalities usurp, in English art, as in English government and social relations, the place of living force and truth." The Belgians and the French both did better. Among them, at the international art exposition in Paris that winter, there were "no end of bad pictures," to be sure, "but, Lord! the goodness also—the fearlessness, of them; the bold drawing; the dashing conception; the passion and action in them!" Even in the work of his own friends, however, fond as he was of them, Leslie, Frith, Ward, Egg, dear old Stanny, there was something lacking. "It is of no use disguising the fact that what we know is wanting in the men is wanting in their works . . . There is a horrid respectability about most of the best of them—a little, finite, systematic routine in them, strangely expressive to me of the state of England herself." 103

The same limitations explained the shortcomings of English literature. Mrs. Grundy had her grip on everything, smothering courage and truth. What a dishonest state was represented by some smooth gentleman complaining that the hero of an English novel was always "uninteresting—too good—not natural, &c," in comparison with the heroes of Balzac and Sand! "But O my smooth friend, what a shining impostor you must think yourself and what an ass you must think me," when both know "that this same unnatural young gentleman . . . whom you meet in those other books and in mine *must be* presented to you in that unnatural aspect by reason of your morality, and is not to have, I will not say any of the indecencies you like, but not even any of the experiences, trials, perplexities, and confusions inseparable from the making or unmaking of all men!" 104

These feelings, the never-ending toil of his book, and his deep inward unrest, all generated a desperate craving for excitement. Prowling wretchedly about the rooms on the Champs Élysées, "tearing my hair, sitting down to write, writing nothing, writing something and tearing it up, going out, coming in," he said, he was "a Monster to my family, a dread Phenomenon to myself." 105 Sometimes as he planned another scathing chapter on officialdom, he had a grim pleasure "that the Circumlocution Office sees the light" and wondered "what effect it will have." Then, his head stinging "with the visions of the book," he would feel the need to plunge "out into some of the strange places I glide into of nights in these latitudes." 106 One night it was the *fête* of the company of the Folies Nouvelles, "which I should think," he told Collins, "could hardly fail to attract all the Lorettes in Paris." 107 Another night it would be a cheap public ball, with "pretty faces, but all of two classes—wicked and coldly calculating, or haggard and wretched in their worn beauty." 108

Back at his writing table again, he allowed his imagination to revel in the portrayal of Flora Finching. With a rather cruel but not entirely unkind comedy, he was modeling her upon the changed Maria Winter who had shattered the gleaming image of Maria Beadnell. "It came into my head one day," he wrote the Duke of Devonshire, "that we have all had our Floras (mine is living, and extremely fat), and that it was a half serious half ridiculous truth which had never been told." [109] "There are some things in Flora in number seven that seem to me to be extraordinarily droll, with something serious at the bottom of them after all. Ah, well! was there *not* something very serious in it once?" [110] And from this, perhaps, he would dash off with Collins, who was now in Paris and dining at the Dickens table every day, on some "Haroun Alraschid expedition," [111] one of a bachelor "perspective of theatrical and other-lounging evenings." [112]

But early in April, Collins went back to London. A few days later Macready, who had been in Paris for a short visit, also took his departure. Dickens felt dull and lonely in the evenings when they were both gone.[113] He took Kate, Georgy, and the two girls to a French version of *As You Like It* at the Comédie Française, but found it a performance that might have been got up "by the Patients in the Asylum for Idiots. Dreariness is no word for it, vacancy is no word for it, gammon is no word for it, there *is* no word for it. Nobody has anything to do but sit upon as many grey stones as he can. When Jacques had sat upon seventy-seven stones and forty-two roots of trees (which was at the end of the second act) we came away." [114]

Although Dickens had been glad to see Macready, the sight of his old friend had also depressed him. During his retirement the actor had aged more than during all his laborious years upon the stage. "It fills me with pity to think of him away in that lonely Sherborne place. I have always felt of myself that I must, please God, die in harness, but I have never felt it more strongly than in looking at, and thinking of, him. However strange it is to be never at rest, and never satisfied, and ever trying after something that is never reached, and to be always laden with plot and plan and care and worry, how clear it is that it must be, and that one is driven by an irresistible might until the journey is worked out!" [115]

At the end of April his time in Paris drew to a close. He had arranged in January to take M. Beaucourt's breezy hilltop house in Bou-

logne again for the summer,[116] but until then, although his family
would stay on in Paris, he had to be in London. The Hogarths, however, were in Tavistock House, as they had been on a number of other
occasions when Dickens went abroad, and were not leaving till the
3rd of May. And in the course of time, except for Georgina, Dickens
had come to feel an almost unbearable impatience with his wife's
family. They came and remained in his house for long periods. They
cheerfully allowed him to pay their bills for them. Mrs. Hogarth had
been ill in November, but in January Dickens learned that the apothe-
cary's charges for attendance and medicine were still unpaid. He told
the man to charge them to his account, "and say nothing at all about
the matter to her, or her family," but seemingly the Hogarths calmly
accepted all such favors.[117]

During previous visits, they had been so negligent of the housekeeping and had vacated the place in such a dirty condition that Dickens
had felt obliged to remonstrate with them.[118] And even then he returned to find "the dust on the first floor," as he complained to Catherine, "an inch thick," and had to spend hours wallowing in dirt
as the study and drawing room were washed and swept, the windows
opened, and the carpets aired.[119] Maddened, he stood in his dismantled study "with the carpet in the corner like an immense roly-poly
pudding, and all the chairs upside down as if they had turned over
like birds and died with their legs in the air," [120] while the servant
put away a disorder of books and papers and tried to get the dreary
house neat and comfortable again.[121]

In addition to these exasperations, he had come to dislike their very
presence, even their communications. "I never in my days," he told
Georgina, "beheld anything like your mother's letter, for the desperation of its imbecility." [122] And when the Hogarths had been staying
at Tavistock House in March, 1855, "I am dead sick of the Scottish
tongue," he observed to Collins, "in all its moods and tenses." [123]

Now, as the time came for returning, Dickens felt that even for a
few days he could not "bear the contemplation of their imbecility any
more. (I think my constitution is already undermined by the sight
of Hogarth at breakfast.)" He therefore determined to stay at the
Ship Hotel, in Dover, from Tuesday until the following Saturday,
when they would be gone.[124]

But the Hogarths, of course, were only one gray and dusty strand in all the gray fabric that had come to make up the pattern of his life. The English people were "on the down-hill road to being conquered," were "content to bear it," and *would* "NOT be saved." [125] And again and again, "as with poor David," when he fell into low spirits, he found himself lamenting "one happiness I have missed in life, and one friend and companion I never made." [126] All he had left was work. That, to be sure, was something. "It is much better to go on and fret, than to stop and fret. As to repose—for some men there's no such thing in this life. The foregoing has the appearance of a small sermon; but it is so often in my head in these days that it cannot help coming out. The old days—the old days! Shall I ever, I wonder, get the frame of mind back as it used to be then? Something of it perhaps—but never quite as it used to be. I find that the skeleton in my domestic closet is becoming a pretty big one." [127]

CHAPTER SEVEN

"Old Hell Shaft"

IN HIS distraught state of mind, Dickens longed to be able to drown his unhappiness in the turmoil of producing another play. At his suggestion, Collins started writing a melodrama based on the ill-fated arctic expedition of Sir John Franklin, all of whose members had died of starvation and exposure. Early in April, Collins had mapped out so much of the play that Dickens asked Mrs. Wills if she would undertake the part of a Scotch nurse with an eerie and foreboding gift of second sight.[1] But he had already arranged to stay at Boulogne until September, and therefore no more could be done before autumn. Meanwhile, he would have to bear his low spirits as best he could.

In Dover his landlady at the Ship Hotel pursued him with excited anticipations of the imminent arrival of some Baron Brunow until he snapped, "I don't care a damn about the Baron . . . if he were sunk coming over, it would not make the least difference to me." In London, after four dusty hours clearing the mess the Hogarths had left in the dining room and schoolroom, he went to see Miss Coutts and argued hotly with her companion, Mrs. Brown, when she talked "nonsense about the French people and their immorality." In England, Dickens said, people hypocritically pretended that social evils and vices did not exist; in France people were honest about them. "Don't say that!" she cried. "Don't say that! It gives me such pain to hear you say anything I can't agree with!" But he must, Dickens replied, "when, according to our national vanity and prejudice, you disparage an unquestionably great nation." In the end, Mrs. Brown burst into a shower of tears, but Dickens was stonily unyielding.[2]

The next afternoon Stanfield dropped in at Tavistock House, and on hearing about the play became immensely excited. He upset the schoolroom Dickens had straightened out by dragging chairs to represent the proscenium and planning the scenery with walking sticks. "One of the least things he did was getting on the top of the Long table and hanging over the bar in the middle window where that top sash opens, as if he had got a hinge in the middle of his body." [3]

Stanfield also gave Dickens an account of the effect being engaged to marry Forster had had on Mrs. Colburn. "By God Sir the depreciation that has taken place in that woman is fearful! She has no blood Sir in her body—no color—no voice—is all scrunched and squeezed together—and seems to me in deep affliction—while Forster Sir is rampant and raging, and presenting a contrast beneath which you sink into the dust. She *may* come round again—*may* get fat—*may* get cheerful—*may* get a voice to articulate with, but by the blessed Star of Morning Sir she is now a sight to behold!" [4]

Surrounded by his old friends, Stanfield, Maclise, Forster, Macready —who turned out to be in town for a few days—Dickens found himself feeling a little more cheerful. He gave a party at the *Household Words* office, "pigeon pie, collared red partridge, ham, roast fowls, and lobster salad," with "quantities of punch," from which he did not get back to Tavistock House until half past two in the morning.[5] He saw Collins, and spent an evening at Cremorne Gardens with Lemon.[6] By permission of Dean Milman, he took three companions to the top of St. Paul's to see the blazing illuminations with which London on May 29th celebrated the end of the Crimean War.[7]

On June 9th he settled down at the Villa des Moulineaux to work again on *Little Dorrit.* The army camp, dismantled now, looked bleak and miserable with the grass all trodden away and drifted sand choking the ledges of doors and windows. All France was firmly convinced that the British Army had done nothing in Crimea except "get rescued by the French," and at home "the Barnacles and the Circumlocution Office" had things entirely their own way. Dickens did not feel any less disheartened by finding the pier at Boulogne crowded with young British "trippers," male and female, whose vulgarity and insolence made him ashamed for his country.[8]

Stranded in M. Beaucourt's other villa were Dickens's old friend Cattermole and his family. The artist was hard up, and the gentle Beaucourt confessed reluctantly that "Monsieur Cattermole 'promises always,' " but did not pay. There was a nurse who refused to leave

and refused to work because her wages were in arrears; one of the little
boys did the cooking: "They have broken nearly all the glass and
china," said Beaucourt; ". . . I am desolated for them all." "And for
yourself, Beaucourt, you good fellow," asked Dickens. "Don't you say
anything about yourself?" "Ah, Monsieur Dickens, pardon me, it's
not worth the trouble; it's nothing, don't let us speak of it!" With
which, Dickens reported, he "went backing up the avenue with such
a generous, simple, amiable face that I half expected to see him back
himself straight into the Evening Star (which was at the end of it)
without going through the ceremony of dying first." [9]

The gardens had been "a burst of roses" when Dickens arrived,[10]
and Beaucourt had arranged the planting so that the summer's guests
found a constant succession of bloom.[11] Stanfield came for a week
in the middle of July [12] and Mary Boyle a little later. (Addressing
her as "Beloved Mary," Dickens exclaimed "O breezes waft . . . my
Mary to my arms," and signed himself "Ever to distraction Joseph." [13]) Wills came at the end of the month,[14] and when Collins
made his appearance in the middle of August [15] the house was smothered in roses and geraniums, and there was honeysuckle everywhere,
and "sweet peas nearly seven feet high." [16]

The only excitement of the summer was provided by two tigerish,
marauding cats from a near-by mill, who constantly invaded the house
through the open windows to get at the family's canary. They hid
themselves behind draperies, hanging "like bats, and tumbling out
in the dead of night with frightful caterwaulings." One of the servants
borrowed Beaucourt's gun to shoot them, and tumbled "over with the
recoil, exactly like a clown." The children kept watch "on their stomachs" in the garden to give the alarm with horrible whistles. "I am
afraid to go out," Dickens wrote, "lest I should be shot." [17] Tradesmen
cried out as they came up the avenue, "It's me—baker—don't shoot!"
For over a week the household was in a state of siege.[18]

The stay in Boulogne was cut short at the end of August by an outbreak of cholera.[19] Dickens sent the children home at once with Catherine while he and Georgy packed up. The 8th of September saw him
back in Tavistock House.[20] Collins, now a member of the *Household
Words* staff at five guineas a week,[21] was at the same time driving
ahead on the second act of his arctic melodrama, and Dickens gave
him a stream of eager suggestions.[22] On October 2nd, Collins arrived

at Tavistock House in a breathless state of excitement, with the first two acts finished.[23] Already entitled *The Frozen Deep*, the events of the last act were sufficiently mapped out so that Dickens felt able to set about its production.[24] On the 20th, the third act was completed and the play was read aloud to the assembled company.[25] In its ultimate form, Dickens had suggested so many of the situations and written or revised so many of the lines that it was almost as much his work as it was Collins's.[26]

The play opens in Devon, where Clara Burnham, the heroine, is haunted by fears for the life of her betrothed, Frank Aldersley, who has long been away with a polar expedition. With the same expedition is her rejected lover, Richard Wardour, who does not know the identity of his successful rival, but who has sworn to kill him if they ever meet. As Clara agonizes lest some accident reveal them to each other, Nurse Esther has bloody visions in the crimson sunset: "I see the lamb in the grasp of the Lion—your bonnie bird alone with the hawk—I see you and all around you crying, Bluid! The stain is on you —Oh, my bairn, my bairn—the stain o' that bluid is on *you*!"[27]

The second act is in the arctic regions, where chance selects Aldersley and Wardour to seek relief for the stranded expedition. As they start, Wardour discovers that Aldersley is his rival. In the third act Clara has come to Newfoundland, hoping for news of her lover. Into a desolate cavern on the coast staggers an exhausted man who has escaped from an ice floe. Clara recognizes him as Wardour; there is a hysterical accusation that he has murdered Aldersley. He rushes out and returns with Aldersley in his arms. "Often," he gasps, "in supporting Aldersley through snow-drifts and on ice-floes, have I been tempted to leave him sleeping." Weakened by hunger, exposure, and the struggle of bringing his rival to safety, he now dies, with Clara's kiss upon his lips and her tears raining down upon his face.

Georgy, Charley, and the two girls all had parts in the play; Collins and Dickens were to do Aldersley and Wardour, and began growing beards to look their roles. In the schoolroom Stanfield was constantly measuring boards with a chalked piece of string and an umbrella.[28] He was painting the scenery for the second and third acts, William Telbin that for the first act, and nothing could induce either man to explain his plans in the presence of the other.[29] There was "a painter's shop in the school-room," Dickens wrote; "a gasfitter's shop all over the basement; a dressmaker's shop at the top of the house; a tailor's shop in my dressing-room." [30] The house was a chaos of "size always boiling over on all the lower fires, Stanfield perpetually elevated on planks and splashing himself from head to foot, Telbin requiring impossibilities of swart gasmen, and a legion of prowling nondescripts forever shirking in and out." [31] The noise reminded Dickens "of Chatham dockyard" or "the building of Noah's ark." [32]

As early as October 16th Dickens began rehearsing the first two acts, putting Charley and the girls "through fearful drill under their rugged parent." [33] From then on, rehearsals took place every Monday and Friday evening till January. [34] Diners were constantly in the house; four stage carpenters practically boarded there. [35] Dickens ordered such huge quantities of meat that the butcher called to ask if there was no mistake. [36] His own part Dickens got up in a twenty-mile walk through Finchley, Neasdon, and Willesden, shouting it aloud "to the great terror" of the surrounding country. [37] Throughout all this, he was steadily working on his novel: "Calm amidst the wreck," he wrote Macready, "your aged friend glides away on the Dorrit stream, forgetting the uproar for a stretch of hours, refreshing himself with a ten or twelve miles' walk, pitches headforemost into foaming rehearsals, placidly emerges for editorial purposes, smokes over buckets of distemper with Mr. Stanfield aforesaid . . ." [38]

The Frozen Deep had its first night on January 6, 1857, Charley's twentieth birthday, and there were three repeat performances, on the 8th, 12th, and 14th. [39] Close to a hundred people crowded the little schoolroom theater each evening, although the ladies' crinolines made it a tight squeeze. [40] A small orchestra rendered an overture and incidental music composed for the play by Francesco Berger, a young musician Charley had met at Leipzig, who presided at the piano. [41] Then, from behind the darkened scene, the voice of Forster intoned the Prologue written by Dickens, comparing the hidden deeps of the heart with the unplumbed depths of the north, and suggesting

> *"that the secrets of the vast Profound*
> *Within us, an exploring hand may sound,*
> *Testing the region of the ice-bound soul,*
> *Seeking the passage at its northern pole,*
> *Soft'ning the horrors of its wintry sleep,*
> *Melting the surface of that 'Frozen Deep.'"* [42]

Dickens had devised novel lighting effects, simulating the changing hours of the day, from bright sunshine through crimson sunset to the gray of twilight and the misty blue of night.[43] But the emotional power of the play was derived from the intensity he gave to the character of Wardour, into which he poured all his own concealed desperation. "Hard work, Crayford," Wardour exclaims, "that's the true elixir of life! Hard work that stretches the muscles and sets the blood aglowing, that tires the body and rests the mind." When during the last act Dickens rushed in anguish from the stage, he tossed the other men aside like a charging bull and often left them black and blue from the struggle. His death scene was so heart-rending that his fellow actors themselves were in tears and members of the audience sobbed audibly.[44]

After an intermission the spectators were restored to cheerfulness by Buckstone's farce of *Uncle John*, in which they found Dickens as side-splittingly comic as he had been pathetic. The opening-night performance was followed by a supper with champagne and oysters. The next day Dickens wrote Wills excitedly that he was "Calm—perfectly happy with the success—about to make more Gin Punch. Draught of that article enormous;" and added, "Macready has just been here, perfectly raging because Forster took him away, and positively shouldered him out of the Green Room Supper, on which he had set his heart." [45]

When the curtain descended on the last performance, workmen began "battering and smashing down" the theater. Soon it was "a mere chaos of scaffolding, ladders, beams, canvases, paint-pots, artificial snow, gas-pipes, and ghastliness." [46] Dickens felt "shipwrecked" and depressed. "The theatre has disappeared," he wrote Macready gloomily, "the house is restored to its usual conditions of order, the family are tranquil and domestic, dove-eyed peace is enthroned in this study, fire-eyed Radicalism in its master's breast." [47] For, as ever in Dickens, among the shadows of his personal dejection always mingled his deep and implacable condemnation of the way public affairs were conducted in England.

He thought "the political signs of the times," he told Lord Carlisle, the Viceroy of Ireland, "to be just about as bad as the spirit of the people will admit of their being." [48] As for the House of Commons, it seemed to him "to be getting worse every day." The dire influence of privilege had so tainted and perverted all the potentialities of rep-

resentative government as to make it "a miserable failure among us."
The people were far more honest and efficient than the members of
Parliament. "See what you are all about down at Westminster at this
moment with the wretchedest party squabble," Dickens wrote Paxton,
"and consider that poor Workingmen's meeting about emigration,
within a few yards of you all, the other night!" [49]

In consequence of this "political despondency" [50] and the hollow
left by the cessation of the theatricals, Dickens felt a more violent
craving than ever for distraction. Collins must take a trip with him—
to Brighton, somewhere; he needed a change, was heavy with the
galley-slave labor of tugging at his oar.[51] When Collins agreed he was
overjoyed. "I immediately arose (like the desponding Princes in the
Arabian Nights, when the old woman—Procuress evidently, and probably of French extraction—comes to whisper about the Princesses they
love) and washed my face and went out; and my face has been shining ever since." [52] He and Collins were much at the theaters, and in
the green rooms among the actresses, whom they called "little peri-
winkles." [53] "Any mad proposal you please," he told Collins, would
"find a wildly insane response." And "If you can think of any tremendous way of passing the night, in the meantime, do. I don't care
what it is. I give (for that night only) restraint to the Winds!" [54]
And, still again, "if the mind can devise anything sufficiently in the
style of Sybarite Rome in the days of its culminating voluptuousness,
I am your man." [55]

*   *   *   *   *

After these frenzied outbursts, Dickens resigned himself to a quiet
summer in the country. For at long last, and in a frame of mind that
almost destroyed the flavor of the triumph, he had achieved the ambition of his childhood. A year and a half ago Gad's Hill Place, the
old rose-brick dwelling on the hill two miles outside of Rochester, had
come upon the market and he had bought it. Walking past with
Wills, in the summer of 1855, Dickens had called his eye to the ancient cedars in front and told him that early dream. The very next
morning Wills had come to him in great excitement. "It is written,"
he exclaimed, "that you were to have that house at Gad's Hill." [56]

The previous night at dinner, Wills explained, he had sat beside
Mrs. Lynn Linton, one of the contributors to *Household Words*, and
their conversation had turned on the neighborhood. "You know it?"

he asked. "I have been there today." "I know it very well," she replied. "I was a child in the house they call Gad's Hill Place. My father was the rector, and lived there many years. He has just died, has left it to me, and I want to sell it." "So," Wills said to Dickens, "you must buy it. Now or never!" [57]

In August of 1855 Dickens had had Austin look at it to estimate how much it would cost to put the house in repair and raise the old slate roof six feet to provide extra rooms in the attic. At first he had not thought of living there, but of renting it by the month, and using it at other times for himself or as a change for Charley from Saturday to Monday.[58] He had begun by offering £1,500, but his eagerness to own it grew.[59] In the end, he gave £1,700,[60] and then another £90 for the shrubbery across the road which Mrs. Linton valued separately. Concluding the purchase on March 14, 1856, Dickens noted that the day fell in with his belief that all the important events of his life took place on Fridays: he was born on a Friday, had been married on a Friday. "After drawing the cheque, I turned round to give it to Wills (£1790), and said: 'Now isn't it an extraordinary thing—look at the day—Friday! I have been nearly drawing it half-a-dozen times, when the lawyers have not been ready, and here it comes round upon a Friday, as a matter of course.' " [61]

Once the place was his own, he felt as proud of "the property" as if he were M. Beaucourt. "It is old fashioned, plain, and comfortable," he said. "On the summit of Gad's Hill, with a noble prospect at the side and behind, looking down into the Valley of the Medway. Lord Darnley's Park at Cobham (a beautiful place with a noble walk through a wood) is close by . . . It is only an hour and a quarter from London by the Railway. To Crown all, the sign of the Sir John Falstaff is over the way, and I used to look at it as a wonderful Mansion (which God knows it is not), when I was a very odd little child with the first faint shadows of all my books in my head—I suppose." [62]

During the negotiations, the house had been occupied by the Reverend Joseph Hindle, the rector of the parish, and Dickens agreed to let him stay on till the following March.[63] In the course of the year he decided to occupy it as a permanent residence when Mr. Hindle moved out. By February, 1857, he was deep in conferences with Austin about the papering and painting and hiring a builder to overhaul the drainage and raise the roof. His servant John he was constantly sending into furniture stores to buy articles as if for himself (to prevent the shopkeepers from running up the prices) and letting him "bring them away ignobly, in vans, cabs, barrows, trucks, and costermonger's trays. If you should meet such a thing as a Mahogany dining table or two marble washing-stands, in a donkey cart anywhere, or in a cat's-meat cart . . . you may be sure the property is mine." [64]

In April, Dickens received word from Hans Christian Andersen that he was coming to England again, and immediately invited him to stay at Gad's Hill when he should arrive in June.[65] For almost two weeks Dickens was then at Waite's Hotel in Gravesend, from which he went over to Gad's Hill every day to hurry along the workmen "lingering in the yard," who were only to "be squeezed out by bodily pressure." [66] And on May 17th there was a housewarming, with a "small and noble army" of guests who ate "cold meat for the first time 'on the premises.' " [67] With the 1st of June, the family was installed at Gad's Hill for the summer, except for certain missing articles of "luggage wandering over the face of the earth." [68]

Going up to London by train on June 9th, Dickens was shocked to hear a gentleman looking over his newspaper say to another, "Douglas Jerrold is dead." [69] Only nine days before he and Jerrold had dined at Greenwich with William Howard Russell, the war correspondent, and a group of other friends. Jerrold had then been looking unwell, but explained that he had been upset by the smell of a newly painted window in his study. He had soon regained his natural color and gone stamping about, pushing back his hair, laughing in his heartiest manner at some joke Dickens made. At the end of the meal he had felt completely recovered and gone home elated that he had "quite got over that paint!" [70]

Dickens knew that Jerrold's family would not be left well off. Old affection, generous sympathy, and, no doubt, the burning need for distraction that now gave him no peace, all made a single idea leap impetuously into his mind. They must raise a fund; there must be a benefit, a series of performances—T. P. Cooke in revivals of Jerrold's *Black-Eyed Susan* and *Rent Day*, Thackeray giving a lecture, Dickens himself giving a day reading, a night reading, Russell giving a lecture, and, of course, a subscription revival of *The Frozen Deep*, all done in a dignified manner, not "beggingly," but anounced as "In memory of the late Mr. Douglas Jerrold." [71]

A committee was speedily formed, rooms were taken for the series in the Gallery of Illustration on Regent Street, the Queen was asked to give her name in support.[72] Her Majesty was intensely eager to see *The Frozen Deep*, but felt that assent would involve either perpetual compliance in other requests or perpetually giving offense. She therefore suggested that Dickens select a room in Buckingham Palace and let her see the play there. Dickens objected that he "did not feel easy as to the social position" of his daughters "at a Court under those circumstances," and begged that some other way of her seeing the play be devised. He then proposed that the Queen come to the Gallery of Illustration to a private performance for her own invited guests a week before the subscription night. This, within a few hours, her Majesty resolved to do.[73]

Soon hammers were resounding in the Gallery of Illustration as Dickens superintended the workmen reassembling the Tavistock House stage. At all hours he was tearing through rehearsals, working his company to the highest notch of perfection.[74] In charge of the sale of tickets and other business details he placed Arthur Smith, a brother of Albert Smith, the showman and entertainer.[75] But Dickens himself kept a sharp eye on every detail, and was even to be found in the box office on occasion, selling tickets himself. On the two nights before the command performance he drilled his actors until long past midnight.[76]

Meanwhile, Hans Christian Andersen had been welcomed to Gad's Hill, and oscillated happily between there and London. Simple, almost childish, weeping bitterly over a "nasty criticism" of one of his stories and a moment later laughing as he cut a circle of dancing elves or fairies out of a folded square of paper,[77] the author of "The Ugly Duckling" was ecstatic over his host and hostess and their home. Dickens was the greatest author in the world, Kate was charming with her "china blue eyes" and "womanly repose," the children delightful to play with in the near-by field of clover. "The sons and I are often lying there," he wrote, "there is a fragrance of clover, the elder tree is in blossom and the wild roses have an odor of apples . . ."[78] From the top of the hill at sunset the river turned into a ribbon of gold with the ships in black silhouette, while blue smoke curled from the cottages amid a far-off peal of bells.

When Dickens was busy with rehearsals, Catherine took Andersen about London. He heard Handel's *Messiah* with her among an audience of twelve thousand in the Crystal Palace, its vast walls of glass seeming to him like Aladdin's Palace and the music reducing him to tears. With her he saw Ristori in the role of Lady Macbeth. He met all the fashionable world at Miss Coutts's mansion in Stratton Street, and was scared by her "proud servants" but gratefully responsive to Miss Coutts, who could speak German to him and who understandingly heaped his bed high with pillows, as he liked it.[79]

Although Dickens gave Andersen no sign, he did not take so kindly to his guest. They were "suffering a good deal from Andersen," he wrote.[80] "His unintelligible vocabulary was marvellous. In French or Italian, he was Peter the Wild Boy; in English, the Deaf and Dumb Asylum. My eldest boy swears that the ear of man cannot recognize his German; and his translatress declares to Bentley that he can't speak Danish!" In London "he got into wild entanglements of cabs and Sherry, and never seemed to get out of them again until" he was back at Gad's Hill cutting "paper into all sorts of patterns" and gathering "the strangest little nosegays in the woods." [81]

"One day he came home to Tavistock House, apparently suffering from corns that had ripened in two hours. It turned out that a cab driver had brought him back from the City, by way of the unfinished new thoroughfare through Clerkenwell. Satisfied that the cabman was bent on robbery and murder, he had put his watch and money into his boots—together with a Bradshaw, a pocket-book, a pair of scissors, a penknife, a book or two, a few letters of introduction, and some other miscellaneous property." [82]

Andersen was taken to the private performance of *The Frozen Deep*, admired the hothouse flowers provided by the Duke of Somerset, and was thrilled to behold the Queen, Prince Albert, and the King of the Belgians. Although her party numbered no more than fifty, and Dickens had invited only another twenty-five, the audience "cried and laughed and applauded and made as much demonstration," Georgina said, as so small a group could.[83] When the curtain fell on the melodrama it was past midnight, but her Majesty forgot her preference for early hours in her desire to see the farce as well, and gave the word that the evening should go on.[84]

During the interval between the two there took place a curious episode that illustrates Dickens's almost bristling sense of his own dignity. "My gracious sovereign," Dickens explained to Forster, "was so pleased that she sent round begging me to go and see her and accept her thanks. I replied that I was in my Farce dress, and must beg to be excused. Whereupon she sent again, saying that the dress 'could not be so ridiculous as that,' and repeating the request. I sent my duty in reply, but again hoped her Majesty would have the kindness to excuse my presenting myself in a costume and appearance that were not my own. I was mighty glad to think, when I woke this morning, that I had carried the point." [85]

But this private performance was only the beginning of the furore surrounding the Jerrold benefits. The audience for the first public performance on July 8th was positively hysterical. And when Dickens read the *Carol* at St. Martin's Hall he reported to Macready, "The two thousand and odd people were like one, and their enthusiasm was something awful." Further performances of *The Frozen Deep* took place on the 18th and 25th, and another reading of the *Carol* on the 24th.[86] And on July 12th the members of the cast—the "Snow Boys," as Dickens called them—were the guests of Frederic Ouvry, his solicitor, at Ouvry's home in Walham Green, where they spent a glorious afternoon quaffing "great goblets of champagne." [87] And they had played only twice in London when there came a demand that they play in Manchester as well.

In the midst of the London performances, Andersen, who had come for two weeks and remained five, finally took his departure.[88] He had been deeply touched by Dickens's warm desire to help the Jerrold family, although somewhat puzzled by rumors that Jerrold's son protested that they had not been left in "straitened circumstances" and resented "the hat being carried round." [89] At Gad's Hill, Andersen had played with the children, making daisy chains, and once, unobserved, slipping a wreath of daisies over the crown of Collins's wideawake hat, which the latter wore past the Falstaff Inn wondering why the hop pickers laughed at his appearance.[90] Andersen had been entirely unsuspicious of any strain in the relations of his host and hostess, and innocently unaware that he had outstayed his welcome. Dickens kindly drove him to the train at Maidstone, and the gaunt, angular Dane wept as he "travelled alone in the steam serpent to Folkestone." [91] But long before he said good-by Mamey and Katey regarded him as "a bony bore," and when he was gone Dickens stuck a card on his dressing-table mirror, reading "Hans Christian Andersen slept in this room for five weeks which seemed to the family ages." [92]

Five days later, Dickens said another farewell that did move him deeply. His second son Walter was now sixteen years of age, a healthy, vigorous youngster who had done well at school and even won an occasional prize.[93] Although an amiable boy who was a favorite with the whole family,[94] he was not without flashes of temper: at the age of twelve he had ended a dispute with the younger children's nurse by flinging a chair at her.[95] Miss Coutts was going to use her influence to have him nominated for a cadetship, and Dickens had put him to study with a Mr. Trimmer at Putney, who prepared boys for Addiscombe and India.[96] But at Addiscombe it seemed unlikely that Walter could attain high distinction in his studies, "least of all in mathematics and fortification," Dickens said, "without which he couldn't get into the Engineers." [97] He was steady and good, his father thought, and would always do his duty, but was undeniably "a little slow." [98]

Dickens consequently wavered about having Walter put up for the nomination. Alfred seemed to him to have a more remarkable "combination of self-reliance, steadiness, and adventurous spirit," and Frank to come next.[99] But Alfred was only twelve, Frank fourteen, and Walter was approaching the age requirement, which was sixteen. Ultimately, therefore, Walter received the nomination,[100] although Dickens still did not consider him either as forceful or as manly as Macready's son Ned, who had gone out to India at the same age.[101]

In April of 1857 Walter had passed his final examinations and returned home "radiant and gleaming." [102] He was to sail from Southampton on July 20th, as a cadet in the East India Company's 26th Native Infantry. (Later he was transferred to the 42nd Highlanders.[103]) The intervening weeks he spent happily learning to swim, ride, fence, and shoot, and studying Hindustani.[104] The last few days before his departure he spent with his brothers, who were just back from their school in Boulogne.[105]

Dickens bought his outfit, paid his passage, and gave him a generous letter of credit on Calcutta. It was a mournful thing to realize how Time had "flapped his wings over your head" and that another baby had grown to be a young man. When Walter went on board the *Indus*, waving back cheerfully at his father and his brother Charley, Dickens felt the leave-taking like having "great teeth drawn with a wrench." Walter was "in good spirits, as little cast down as, at 16, one could reasonably hope to be with the world of India before one." Dickens came away, though, wondering whether "the best definition of man" might not be that he was "a parting and farewell-taking animal." [106]

During the four weeks between the London performances for the Jerrold Fund and those in Manchester, Dickens was mostly at Gad's Hill, where he struggled with the problems presented by an empty well and clogged drains. The garden had barely begun to look pretty when the drainpipes forced digging up part of it and building two new cesspools.[107] The well ran dry in June,[108] and in August they were "still boring for water at the rate of two pounds per day for wages. The men seem to like it very much, and to be perfectly comfortable." [109] At last, in the middle of the month, they struck a spring and water rushed in ten feet deep.[110] Even then, a pump was needed to get it into the house. "Here are six men perpetually going up and down the well (I know that somebody will be killed) . . . The process is much more like putting Oxford Street endwise, and laying gas along it, than anything else. By the time it is finished, the cost of this water will be something absolutely frightful." [111] The dug-up garden, the black mud, the drying bath, the delay, and the expense, Dickens lamented, were "changing the undersigned honey-pot into a Mad Bull." [112]

* * * * *

Meanwhile, he had read the *Christmas Carol* for the Jerrold Fund at Manchester on July 31st and arranged to give *The Frozen Deep* there on August 21st and 22nd. The play was to be given in the Free Trade Hall, an immense auditorium in which only an experienced actress could make her action seen and her voice heard. He would therefore have to find substitutes for Mamey and Katey and most of the other feminine members of the cast. "I am already trying," he wrote Collins, "to get the best who *have been* on the stage." [113] He wrote Mrs. Henry Compton, but she was unable to fill in.[114] He asked Alfred Wigan, the manager of the Olympic Theatre, for suggestions. Wigan recommended the well-known actress Mrs. Ternan and her two daughters, Maria Ternan and Ellen Lawless Ternan.

Mrs. Ternan had been praised as superior to both Fanny Kelly and Fanny Kemble, and Dickens had probably seen her as the Countess of Rousillon in *All's Well That Ends Well* at Sadler's Wells in 1852 or as Paulina in *The Winter's Tale* at the Princess's Theatre in 1855. Maria had been on the stage since she was a little child, another sister, Frances Eleanor, had acted at least as early as 1855, and Ellen, the youngest, had appeared as Hippomenes in Talfourd's *Atalanta* only the preceding April.[115] All three of the girls were pretty and talented.

Dickens assigned Mrs. Ternan to the part of Nurse Esther, originally played by Mrs. Wills, gave Maria, the most experienced of the sisters, that of Clara Burnham, the heroine, and placed Ellen in the minor one of Lucy Crayford. After "three days' drill of the professional ladies," [116] the entire company set out for Manchester. Gone was Dickens's gloom of the spring and the letdown following the last of the London performances. During a delay of the train, they whiled away the time making up conundrums and passing them through the windows of neighboring compartments on the ends of canes and umbrellas. And when they had all become desperately hungry, came a riddle from Dickens's compartment: "Why is the Manager's stomach like a butler's pantry?"—"Because there's a sinkin' there." [117] Throughout the entire railway journey he was the "sparkler" once more.

At the performance Dickens surpassed himself. Although Maria Ternan had seen the play in London and rehearsed it with him, she feared she would not be able to control her emotion on the stage. During their morning rehearsal in Manchester, Dickens told her, "Why, my dear, how cold your hand is, and what a tremble you are in. This won't do at night." "Oh, Mr. Dickens," she said, "I am so afraid I can't bear it, that I hope you'll be very gentle with me this morning. I cried so much when I saw it, that I have a dread of it, and I don't know what to do." [118]

"She had to take my head up as I was dying," Dickens explained, "and to put it in her lap, and give me her face to hold between my two hands. All of which I showed her elaborately (as Mary had done it before) that morning. When we came to that point at night, her tears fell down my face, down my beard (excuse my mentioning that hateful appendage), down my ragged dress—poured all over me like rain, so that it was as much as I could do to speak for them. I whispered to her, 'My dear child, it will be over in two minutes. Pray, compose yourself.'—'It's no comfort to me that it will be soon over,' she answered. 'Oh it is so sad, it is so dreadfully sad. Oh, don't die! Give me time, give me a little time. Don't take leave of me in this terrible way—pray, pray, pray!!' Whereupon Lemon, the softest-hearted of men, began to cry too, and then they all went at it together. . . . And if you had seen the poor little thing, when the Curtain fell, put in a chair behind it—with her mother and sister taking care of her—and your humble servant drying her eyes and administering Sherry (in Rags so horrible that they would scarcely hold together), and the people in front all blowing their noses, and our own people behind standing about in corners and getting themselves right again, you would have remembered it for a long, long time." [119]

The second night, before an audience of three thousand, Dickens repeated his triumph. "This was, I think," said Wilkie Collins, "the finest of all the representations of *The Frozen Deep*. . . . The trite phrase is the true phrase to describe that magnificent piece of acting. He literally electrified the audience." [120]

The entire enterprise had fully realized Dickens's aspiration of netting £2,000 for the Jerrold family. The sum was ultimately invested, under direction of the Court of Chancery, and the interest paid over, first to Jerrold's widow, and later to his daughter. On the first anniversary of Jerrold's death, Dickens received "a very good and tender letter from his eldest son, expressing his regret that he had ever been so ill-advised as to be less grateful to certain of his father's friends than he might have been. In reply to which, I stretched out my willing hand to him over his father's grave, and made an end of that incongruity at least, I hope forever." [121]

But as soon as the last excitements of those performances were over, Dickens fell back into a deeper wretchedness than ever before. "Low spirits, low pulse, low voice, intense reaction," he lamented. "If I were not like Mr. Micawber, 'falling back for a spring' on Monday, I think I should slink into a corner and cry." [122] In "grim despair and restlessness" he implored Collins to come with him "anywhere—take any tour—see anything . . . Have you any idea tending to any place in the world? Will you rattle your head and see if there is any pebble in it which we could wander away and play at marbles with? . . . I want to escape from myself. For when I *do* start up and stare myself seedily in the face, as happens to be my case at present, my blankness is inconceivable—indescribable—my misery, amazing." [123]

In this state of hopelessness Dickens set off with Collins for the fells of Cumberland. They went by rail to Carlisle, and thence to Wigton, a place "with the wonderful peculiarity that it had no population, no business, no streets to speak of," only an aggregation of linen drapers' shops.[124] From there they went on to Allonby, and Dickens dragged Collins up Carrick Fell, where they got lost on the mountain in a fog and Collins sprained his ankle leaping down a watercourse. Dickens had to carry him the rest of the way, "Wardour to the life!" [125] For the next three days Collins lay in their sitting room with "liniment and a horrible dabbling of lotion incessantly in progress" while Dickens feverishly roamed the country, climbing hills and exploring all the near-by villages.[126]

What the indolent and sybaritic Collins thought of Dickens's frenzied energy is suggested by a dialogue in *The Lazy Tour of Two Idle Apprentices,* a record of their adventures on which the two collaborated for *Household Words.* He doesn't know how to play, says Collins; he makes work of everything. "Where another fellow would fall into a footbath of action or emotion, you fall into a mine. Where any other fellow would be a painted butterfly, you are a fiery dragon. Where another man would stake a sixpence, you would make for Heaven; and if you were to dive into the depths of the earth, nothing short of the other place would content you."

"A man who can do nothing by halves," he concludes, "appears to me to be a fearful man." [127]

But Dickens was totally unable to be any other kind of man. As soon as Collins could hobble around with two thick canes, "like an admiral in a farce," Dickens hurried him back to Carlisle, and from there to Lancaster, where they slept in a quaint old house the state bedroom of which contained two enormous red four-posters, each as large as Charley's bedroom at Gad's Hill. The landlord served them an elaborate dinner—of salmon trout, sirloin steak, partridges, seven dishes of sweets, and five of dessert, including a bowl of peaches and an enormous bridecake—at the thought of all which items on their bill Collins turned pale.[128]

Although Dickens hated gambling and betting on horses, in his agitated need of forgetting his own problems somehow, he even visited "the St. Leger and its saturnalia" when he and Collins reached Doncaster. In sheer desperation at the track he "bought the card; fa-

cetiously wrote down three names for winners of the three chief races"
—never in his life having heard of any of them—"and, if you can believe it without your hair standing on end, those three races were won,
one after another, by those three horses!!!" But he loathed the place
and the crowds he saw there. The men at the race course, the betting
stand, and the betting rooms all seemed to him to look like Palmer,
the notorious poisoner. After the cup race, "a groaning phantom" lay
in the doorway of his bedroom and howled all night. The landlord
apologized in the morning that "it was a gentleman who had lost
£1,500 or £2,000; and he had drunk a deal afterwards; and then they
put him to bed, and then he—took the 'orrors, and got up, and yelled
till morning." If a boy with any good in him, Dickens declared, but
with a dawning tendency to betting, were brought to Doncaster, it
would cure him for life.[129]

Dickens came back from his trip feeling as horribly unsettled as
when he had started out. Collins might be the ideal companion for
an unrestrained holiday, but he was too young and cynical to give
comfort or counsel. Neither age nor experience could enable him to
understand the hopeless despair from which Dickens was suffering.
For with the final performance of *The Frozen Deep*, the efforts to
control his life to an outer decorum that Dickens had long been making at last gave way. He realized that he could not go on forever fleeing
his marital unhappiness in violent theatrical dashings from London
to the provinces. This last time only the Jerrold benefits had saved
him from breakdown, and now he felt the dreadful return of all the
desperation they had only deferred. His married life was unbearable,
but there seemed nothing he could do except bear it.

In this crisis of his distress, before going off with Collins Dickens
had turned for understanding to the faithful Forster, staid, heavy,
pompous, but always willing to devote his whole heart in sympathy
and help to those he loved. To Forster, Dickens now frankly confessed
at last what his old friend had long known without speech between
them. "Poor Catherine and I are not made for each other, and there
is no help for it. It is not only that she makes me uneasy and unhappy,
but that I make her so too—and much more so. She is exactly what
you know, in the way of being amiable and complying; but we are
strangely ill-assorted for the bond there is between us. God knows she
would have been a thousand times happier if she had married another

kind of man, and that her avoidance of this destiny would have been at least equally good for us both. I am often cut to the heart by thinking what a pity it is, for her own sake, that I ever fell in her way . . ." [130]

If he were sick, Dickens went on, he knew that she would be sorry for him. "But exactly the same incompatibility would arise, the moment I was well again; and nothing on earth could make her understand me, or suit us to each other. Her temperament will not go with mine. . . . What is now befalling me I have seen steadily coming, ever since the days you remember when Mary was born; and I know too well that you cannot, and no one can, help me. Why I have even written I hardly know; but it is a miserable sort of comfort that you should be clearly aware how matters stand. The mere mention of the fact, without any complaint or blame of any sort, is a relief to my present state of spirits—and I can get this only from you, because I can speak of it to no one else." [131]

In the face of this appeal Forster put aside whatever jealousy he may have felt of Dickens's other companions, and responded with a generous flow of comfort and advice. But with his sturdy common sense he underlined Dickens's confession that the shortcomings were not all on Catherine's side. Dickens's own temperament, he reminded him, was impatient, over-intense. The disharmonies Dickens mentioned were to be found in many other marriages. "To the most part of what you say," Dickens replied, "—Amen. You are not so tolerant as perhaps you might be of the wayward and unsettled feeling which is part (I suppose) of the tenure on which one holds an imaginative life, and which I have, as you ought to know well, often only kept down by riding over it like a dragoon—but let that go by. . . . I agree with you as to the very possible incidents, even not less bearable than mine, that might and must often occur to the married condition when it is entered into very young." [132]

Nor did he disguise from himself, he went on, "what might be urged on the other side. I claim no immunity from blame. There is plenty of fault on my side, I daresay, in the way of a thousand uncertainties, caprices, and difficulties of disposition; but only one thing will alter that, and that is, the end which alters everything." He was deeply grateful for the wonderful exercise he had "of life and its highest sensations," and had said and felt for years that these personal qualities were "the drawback to such a career," and were "not to be complained of. . . . But the years have not made it easier to bear for either of us; and, for her sake as well as mine, the wish will force itself upon me that something might be done. I know too well it is impossible." [133]

He knew, too, that in going off with Collins he had merely run away from his problem, not solved it, and his unappeasable heartache gave him no rest. He could not, as Forster urged, resign himself to the state of affairs in his home. It gave him no consolation to reflect that there were others besides himself who led lives of enchained desperation. His misery pressed upon him so relentlessly that he could not concentrate his imagination upon the design of another novel or command the discipline to work on it. Only some fury of distraction could blunt the sharpness of his despair. Forster remonstrated with him in vain.

"Too late to say, put the curb on, and don't rush at hills," Dickens responded wearily, "—the wrong man to say it to. I have now no relief but in action. I am incapable of rest. I am quite confident I should rust, break, and die, if I spared myself. Much better to die, doing. What I am in that way, nature made me first, and my way of life has of late, alas! confirmed." [134]

CHAPTER EIGHT

The Prison of Society

CRITICISM: *Little Dorrit*

"LITTLE DORRIT," says Bernard Shaw, "is a more seditious book than *Das Kapital*. All over Europe men and women are in prison for pamphlets and speeches which are to *Little Dorrit* as red pepper to dynamite." But the prisons threatening the rebels and the revolutionaries are only grimmer manifestations of the even more deadening constraints on men's very minds that Dickens now saw organized society imposing. Its fundamental structure made society a vast jail, the new novel proclaimed, in which the people and their governors were captives and wardens dwelling within the same confining walls.

"Fortunately for social evolution," Shaw continues, "Governments never know where to strike. Barnacle and Stiltstalking were far too conceited to recognize their own portraits. Parliament, wearing its leaders out in a few years by the ceaseless drudgery of finding out how not to do it, and smothering it in talk, left members and ministers no time to read the Coodle-Doodle discussions in Sir Leicester Dedlock's drawingroom. . . . Mr. Sparkler was not offended; he stuck to his sinecure and never read anything. . . .

"The mass of Dickens readers, finding his politicians too funny to be credible, continued to idolize Coodle and Doodle as great statesmen, and made no distinction between John Stuart Mill in the India Office and Mr. Sparkler. In fact the picture was not only too funny to be credible; it was too truthful to be funny. But the fun was no fun to Dickens: the truth was too bitter. When you laugh at Jack Bunsby . . . you have no doubt that Dickens is laughing with you like a street boy, despite Bunsby's tragic end. But whilst you laugh at Sparkler or

[883]

young Barnacle, Dickens is in deadly earnest: he means that both of them must go into the dustbin if England is to survive." [1]

This is the significance of William Dorrit, the Marshalsea debtor-prisoner. Indelibly marked by the more than twenty years to which the Circumlocution Office has condemned him behind those walls, it is forever impossible for him, even when he is released, to lose those psychological scars. Hardly less deep are the wounds inflicted on his children, growing up while their father is in jail, and hardly less deadly the paralysis of Mrs. Clennam, and the helplessness of the impoverished artisans of Bleeding Heart Yard.

This sense of imprisoned helplessness that Dickens felt enveloping all England fills *Little Dorrit* everywhere. Its pervading image is the prison. The narrow, sordid old Marshalsea dominates the entire book; jailyard walls loom mistily about the golden opulence of the Merdle banquets in Cavendish Square, and their spiked shadows stretch into the painted salons of Venice and pierce the heart of gorgeous palazzos in Rome. The prison bars darken every scene, from Mrs. Clennam's smoke-blackened house in the City and the rookeries of Bleeding Heart Yard to Park Lane and Grosvenor Square, from the stone cells of the jail at Marseilles to the corridors of Hampton Court Palace. Everyone—the poor debtor, the hard-working London artisan, the bored cosmopolitan traveler fluctuating over the Continent—is immured within the impalpable barriers of a system no less confining than if it were constructed of blocks of masonry and bars of iron.

In part, this emphasis is simply another manifestation of Dickens's lifelong preoccupation with prisons. From the early "Visit to Newgate" in *Sketches by Boz*, through Mr. Pickwick's detention in the Fleet, the frightful description of Fagin in the condemned cell, and Mr. Micawber's incarceration in the King's Bench, to the unwritten ending of *The Mystery of Edwin Drood*, in which the murderer was to gasp out his confession in another prison cell, the somber theme runs like a dark thread through all Dickens's work. And everywhere, in London, in the cities of the United States, and on the Continent, he had been an assiduous visitor of every kind of prison. Something almost compulsive in this hovering return to the Marshalsea once more reveals how deep had been the wound of his childhood humiliation and grief. It shows that he still felt a need to explore the meaning of that painful area in his own past on a deeper level than he had been able to plumb in *David Copperfield*. And it bears witness to how profoundly the prison had sunk into his consciousness as a symbol of misery and defeat.

All these emotions of disastrous, unbearable, but helpless desperation Dickens had come to feel again as he struggled with his unhappy, hopeless marriage. Life had given him friends, prosperity, freedom, laughter, fame—every gift but one: that "one happiness I have missed in life," that "one friend and companion" he had never known, without which his home itself had become a prison. Divorce was as impossible for him as it was for Stephen Blackpool; neither he nor Catherine had given the other legal cause. The welfare of the children held them together. He shrank from the scandal of a separation. His fatherly affections, his responsibilities, his reputation, his respectability, even the pity he was still able to feel for Catherine in the midst of his intolerable wretchedness, all held him as impotent a prisoner as Mr. Dorrit was rendered by his debts, his incompetence, and his gentility.

And, more, Dickens's own plight seemed to him emblematic of all society, caught in the toils of a system through which people could not break. From the hideous lazar houses where England's defenders had suffered and died in the Crimea to the gloomy labyrinths of the War Office and the Civil Service and all the government departments of Whitehall and Westminster, obstructing every endeavor at improvement, what was society but one huge house of bondage? What were the red tape of administration and the entangling forms of Parliamentary procedure but gyves binding men's limbs? What were the mills and mines of the Black Country and the dank homes of the workers but jail cells filled with the clanking of machinery and the odor of hot oil, hemmed in by bars of smoke and the overshadowing pall of dark fog between them and the sunlit sky? Finally, what else were those fettering constraints upon men's very thoughts that made them servile to their oppressors and that left those oppressors themselves close-locked within the imprisoning conventions that ruled them? In *Barnaby Rudge* he had imagined with mingled emotions of horror and exultation a violent uprising battering down the gates and firing the walls of Newgate, but how desperate was the hope of smashing that vaster dungeon that enclosed all the modern world!

*   *   *   *   *

Such is the atmosphere that permeates *Little Dorrit* from its very opening in the criminal jail at Marseilles, with its heavy masonry and grated barriers cemented in the stone. Here are little Cavaletto, mistakenly suspected of smuggling, and Rigaud, alias Lagnier, alias Blandois, unprovably but all too justifiably accused of a cowardly murder. Presently both are to be released into the larger prison of the world, the harmless little fellow uncorrupted, cheerfully chirping his way through life, the pretentious villain unregenerate, still seeking his corrupt advantage in spying and blackmail. Both are constrained by impersonal forces greater than themselves, far more powerful for ill than Rigaud. Mean and ugly as he is in his swaggering viciousness, it is not Rigaud but the respectable members of society who are responsible for its most baneful and widespread evils.

It may be no accident, however, that Rigaud, with his embittered belief that the world owes him a luxurious living, his false good manners, and his pose of being a fine gentleman, is revealed as parasitic on the business of Mrs. Clennam, through whose dubious past transactions he comes to sit swaggering in a place of power in her house. Both the descriptions of him in the text and the illustrations suggest that he was conceived as a caricature of Napoleon III, "whose régime," as Edmund Wilson points out, "Dickens loathed—in which case the tie-up between Blandois and the Clennams may figure a close relationship between the shady financial interests disguised by the flashy façade of the Second Empire and the respectable business interests of British merchants, so inhuman behind their mask of morality. Blandois is crushed in the end by the collapse of the Clennams' house, as people were already predicting that Napoleon would be by that of his own." [2]

The funereal Clennam house, tottering against the slanting beams that prop its outer walls and with faint internal creakings and siftings of dust from the crumbling joists of its floors, is a spiritual jail. Here dwells Mrs. Clennam, moving in a wheel chair, "like Fate in a go-cart," [3] between her bed and "a black bier-like sofa" with "a great angular bolster" [4] resembling an executioner's block, the prisoner of her wrathful Calvinist theology and a dark inward sense of guilt. She embodies at once the harsh Puritan conscience and the relentless business morality of a monetary society. But Mrs. Clennam is both prisoner and jailer; she has made their home a place of confinement to her husband and his son.

"I am the only child," say Clennam, "of parents who weighed, measured, and priced everything; for whom what could not be weighed, measured, and priced had no existence. Strict people as the phrase is, professors of a stern religion, their very religion was a gloomy sacrifice of tastes and sympathies that were never their own, offered up as a part of a bargain for the security of their possessions. Austere faces, inexorable discipline, penance in this world and terror in the next—nothing graceful or gentle anywhere, and the void in my cowed heart everywhere—this was my childhood, if I may so misuse the word as to apply it to such a beginning of life." [5]

Returning to England as a man in the neighborhood of forty, after years devoted to the family business in the Orient, the son finds nothing different in that grim house except the paralysis that now confines the widowed Mrs. Clennam to her tomblike chamber. Fiercely the severe old woman still reads from her Bible, "praying that her enemies (she made them by her tone and manner expressly hers) might be put to the edge of the sword, consumed by fire, smitten by plagues and leprosy, that their bones might be ground to dust, that they might be utterly exterminated. As she read on, years seemed to fall away from her son like the imaginings of a dream, and all the old dark horrors of his usual preparation for the sleep of an innocent child to overtake him." [6]

West and a little north of the City is Bleeding Heart Yard, whose inhabitants—artisans, laborers, and small shopkeepers—are no less the prisoners of poverty than Mrs. Clennam is the prisoner of her creed. Their landlord, the patriarchal Christopher Casby, late Town-agent of Lord Decimus Tite Barnacle, parades his benevolent white locks and mild blue eyes almost daily through the Yard for their reverential admiration. They believe in the goodness of this rack-renting humbug and imagine that the grinding demands that harry them are all the unrelenting harshness of Mr. Pancks, his grimy and snorting little rent-collector; but it is Casby who keeps Pancks forever at it.

"What were they up to? and What did they mean by it? sounded all over the Yard. Mr. Pancks wouldn't hear of excuses, wouldn't hear of complaints, wouldn't hear of repairs, wouldn't hear of anything but unconditional money down. Perspiring and puffing and darting about in eccentric directions, and becoming hotter and dingier every moment, he lashed the Yard into a most agitated and turbid state." [7] And in the evening Casby remarks, "A very bad day's work, Pancks, very bad day's work. It seems to me, sir, and I must insist on making the observation forcibly in justice to myself, that you ought to have got much more money, much more money." [8]

At the uppermost end of the economic scale is Mr. Merdle, the great finance capitalist, master magician of a thousand combinations. "Mr. Merdle was immensely rich; a man of prodigious enterprise; a Midas without the ears, who turned all he touched to gold. He was in everything good, from banking to building. He was in Parliament, of course. He was in the City, necessarily. He was Chairman of this, Trustee of that, President of the other. The weightiest of men had said to projectors, 'Now, what name have you got? Have you got Merdle?' And, the reply being in the negative, had said, 'Then I won't look at you.' " [9]

But Mr. Merdle too is a prisoner. Forever worried by the manipulations needed to keep his slippery enterprises pyramiding higher and higher, he slinks miserably through the magnificence by which he is surrounded. His unfeeling wife is only an expanse of cold white bosom for the display of jewels, he is afraid of his portentous butler, at his luxurious dinner table he dyspeptically consumes a scant eighteen-pennyworth of food. Inarticulate, uneasy, with a broad overhanging head and dull red cheeks, forever taking his wrists into custody within his own coat sleeves, he oozes muddily and sluggishly about his gold and crimson drawing room, carrying solitary confinement with him into the most glittering of scenes. His very name suspiciously resembles the French word *merde*, with its besmeared and odorous associations.

This "uncouth object of so much adulation," this "roc's egg of great ladies' assemblies," [10] was inspired by the financial career of John Sadleir, M.P., banker, company promoter, and forger, who on the collapse of his schemes in 1856 slit his throat on Hampstead Heath, although some features of Merdle's story are derived from that of George Hudson, the "railway king," who fled to France in the panic of 1847-8. "If I might make so bold as to defend that extravagant conception, Mr. Merdle," Dickens wrote in the preface to the first edition, "I would hint that it originated after the Railroad-share epoch, in the times of a certain Irish bank," and that the Merdle crash recalled in its unsavory details the facts at that moment being revealed by "the public examination of late Directors in a Royal British Bank." [11] The time in which *Little Dorrit* is laid, of course, makes the Merdle failure coincide with the great disasters of 1825, in which Sir Walter Scott was one of those ruined.

Mr. Merdle is in fact simply a nineteenth-century Samuel Insull or Ivar Kreuger, or even, on a more grandiose level, a Charles Ponzi. Like Pierpont Morgan or Jay Gould, however, he has grown so powerful that he can bring pressure to bear upon the Government itself, and so opulent that he can dazzle the loftiest circles of the aristocracy and buy his way into their midst by playing upon their greed. The frigid leader of society whom he has purchased as his wife, her dear friend Mrs. Gowan, and the latter's son Henry Gowan all serve from different angles to mirror his hollow triumph. "I had the general idea of the Society business," Dickens told Forster, "before the Sadleir affair, but I shaped Mr. Merdle himself out of that precious rascality. Society, the Circumlocution Office, and Mr. Gowan are of course three parts of one idea and design. Mr. Merdle's complaint, which you will find in the end to be fraud and forgery, came into my mind as the last drop in the silver cream-jug on Hampstead Heath." [12]

Round about Mr. Merdle, chorusing adulation, gyrate all the magnates of the realm. Court and City, Commons and Lords, Horse Guards, Admiralty, Treasury, Bench, all are avid to bathe in the fountain of fabulous riches. Dining in the great man's house, Bishops come "undesignedly sliding in the direction of the sideboard" [13] to suggest a contribution to "our Combined Additional Endowed Dignitaries Committee," [14] and over him hang luminaries of the Bar with a "little insinuating Jury droop" and "persuasive double eye-glass." [15] At Mr. Merdle's feasts the overwhelming Lord Decimus Tite Barnacle himself is called into treaty to bestow a sinecure in the Circumlocution Office upon Edmund Sparkler, Mr. Merdle's vacuous stepson. Down to dinner on his arm Mr. Merdle takes a Countess secluded in the core of an immense gown "like a richly brocaded Jack in the Green." [16] And, from afar, impoverished connections of the ruling class, like Mrs. Gowan and Lord Lancaster Stiltstalking, pensioners on the Crown tucked away in inconvenient little apartments at Hampton Court

Palace, look with envy and bitterness on the flow of privilege in which they feel that they are excluded from their just share.

All these are as closely confined within the constricting barriers of the social system as the struggling artisans of Bleeding Heart Yard or the indigent debtors of the Marshalsea. Indeed, the noble parasites of Hampton Court even resemble the poor slum dwellers and insolvents in their cramped living quarters and makeshift arrangements; "screens not half high enough," which "warded off obscure corners where footboys slept at night with their heads among knives and forks"; "many objects of various forms, feigning to have no connection with their guilty secret, a bed; disguised traps in walls, which were clearly coal-cellars"; doors behind which callers "pretended not to smell cooking three feet off"; and partitions of thin canvas with "a page and a young female at high words on the other side." [17]

Even those affluent members of high society who can winter on the Continent and dwell in Italian palaces are as narrowly immured within their own psychological prison walls as any debtor in a jail. To Little Dorrit's wondering gaze they "greatly resembled a superior sort of Marshalsea. Numbers of people seemed to come abroad, pretty much as people had come into the prison; through debt, idleness, relationship, curiosity, and general unfitness for getting on at home. They were brought into these foreign towns in the custody of couriers and local followers, just as the debtors had been brought into prison. They prowled about the churches and picture-galleries, much in the old, dreary, prison-yard manner. They were usually going away again tomorrow or next week, and rarely knew their own minds, and seldom did what they said they would do, or went where they said they would go: in all this again, very like the prison-debtors. They paid high for poor accommodation, and disparaged a place while they pretended to like it: which was exactly the Marshalsea custom. A certain set of words and phrases, as much belonging to the tourists as the College and the Snuggery belonged to the jail, was always in their mouths. They had precisely the same incapacity for settling down to anything as the prisoners used to have; they rather deteriorated one another, as the prisoners used to do; and they wore untidy dresses, and fell into a slouching way of life; still, always like the people in the Marshalsea." [18]

Conversely, the social pretenses and the snobbery of Little Dorrit's father, William Dorrit, the Marshalsea prisoner of twenty-five years, are only a pathetic echo of the pretenses and the snobbery of the aristocracy—just as the vices of his son Tip, the billiard marker and race-track tout, are the same vices as those of the aristocracy. Mr. Dorrit's disguised cadging for handouts which he calls "Testimonials" is no different from the unabashed pursuit of privilege by that "noble Refrigerator," [19] Lord Lancaster Stiltstalking, and Mr. Dorrit's indignation at being refused no different from Henry Gowan's resentment at the fact that his relatives the Barnacles do not place him in a sinecure. Mr. Dorrit's horror at his daughter's giving her arm to old Nandy, a workhouse pauper in a "livery," is of a piece with Mrs. Gowan's snobbish contempt for the middle-class Meagles family— "the Miggles people," [20] she calls them—whose gentle and lovely daughter her son wants to marry. Henry Gowan's idleness and dissipated extravagance are only a polished and more corrupt version of poor Tip's incompetent uselessness.

In all these people, the prisoners of rank and of lower-class hardship alike, Dickens reveals the same emotional forces at work and the same restricting states of mind. Old Nandy's daughter, Mrs. Plornish, excites a resentful envy in Bleeding Heart Yard by parading her acquaintance with the genteel Dorrit family and magnifying enormously the amount of Mr. Dorrit's insolvency. Mr. Meagles, for all his knowledge of how the Barnacle family battens on the body politic, cannot contain his pride at having as a guest a younger representative of that family. "As a mere flask of the golden water in the tale became a full fountain when it was poured out, so Mr. Meagles seemed to feel that this small spice of Barnacle imparted to his table the flavour of the whole family-tree. In its presence, his frank, fine, genuine qualities paled; he was not so easy, he was not so natural, he was striving after something that did not belong to him, he was not himself. What a strange peculiarity on the part of Mr. Meagles, and where should we find such another case!" [21]

Complementary to these weaknesses in Mr. Meagles are the smooth depreciations with which Henry Gowan disposes of all superiorities. Everyone he knows he finds more or less an ass or a knave, but still the most lovable, dearest, and best that ever lived. "I claim," Dickens summarizes his attitude, "to be always book-keeping, with a peculiar nicety, in every man's case, and posting up a careful little account of

Good and Evil with him. I do this so conscientiously, that I am happy to tell you I find the most worthless of men to be the dearest old fellow too; and am in a condition to make the gratifying report that there is much less difference than you are inclined to suppose between an honest man and a scoundrel." The effect of which is, as Dickens points out, "that while he seemed to be scrupulously finding good in most men, he did in reality lower it where it was, and set it up where it was not." [22]

Gowan's lack of moral integrity and earnestness is reflected in his attitude to his profession. To punish his family for their failure to provide for him, he has set up as an artist, knowing they will feel humiliated at his following that Bohemian course. But he displays the same cynical carelessness about his art as about everything else. "Clennam, I don't like to dispel your generous visions, and I would give any money (if I had any) to live in such a rose-coloured mist. But what I do in my trade, I do to sell. What all we fellows do, we do to sell. If we didn't want to sell it for the most we can get for it, we shouldn't do it. Being work, it has to be done, but it's easily done. All the rest is hocus-pocus." [23]

As Hesketh Pearson points out, Gowan is not a portrait of Thackeray, but he is a rendering of the attitude in Thackeray toward both life and the art the two men practiced which Dickens found distasteful. "Thackeray's habit of blowing hot and cold," Pearson notes, "his way of interspersing cynical comments on life with enthusiastic appreciations," [24] are both there: "Most men are disappointed in life, somehow or other, and influenced by their disappointment," Gowan says. "But it's a dear good world, and I love it! . . . It's the best of old worlds! And my calling! The best of old callings, isn't it?" [25] Thackeray was clever enough to perceive the echo of his own way of speaking, and that may have been why, with "a strange, half-humorous, half-serious look," he told a companion, "Between ourselves, Little D— is d—d stupid." [26]

The bonds constraining everyone in Little Dorrit lie in certain ways much more heavily upon Gowan with his destructive cynicism, Mrs. Merdle in her loveless luxury, and the Barnacles with their pursuit of power, than they do upon the poor. In Bleeding Heart Yard there is more generosity and helpfulness than there is in Society. The debtors in the Marshalsea are neither hard nor cold. "People are not bad because they come there," says Little Dorrit. "I have known numbers of good, persevering, honest people, come there through misfortune. They are almost all kind-hearted to one another." [27]

The ultimate imprisonment thus is no more one of oppressive institutions than it is of mental states conditioned by those institutions. This is strikingly brought out in the portrayal of Miss Wade and in her autobiographic narrative, the chapter near the close of the book entitled "The History of a Self-Tormentor." An orphaned and illegitimate child, her own resentments and her consciousness of the attitude of society to her birth have built up in her an inability to believe that she can ever be loved, a determination to twist every expression of kindness or consideration into insulting patronage. Her jail is purely a state of mind, but from it she can never emerge.

*   *   *   *   *

For the great structure of society, however, all the forces of petrifaction that interpose barriers against every generous and fruitful and creative impulse are symbolized in *Little Dorrit* by the Circumlocution Office. It is no such limited thing as any single government department; it has a deadening hand on everything, diplomacy, the licensing of inventions and the regulation of business and industry, every branch of government. It is no mere aristocratic bureaucracy, though it is also that, nor even all bureaucracies, though it is all bureaucracies too, but a hardening of the arteries that penetrates all institutions. It is the imprisonment of habit, custom, convention, established forms swollen to more importance than the uses for which they were invented, and confined by inertia, profit, selfishness, and privilege. It is rigidity grown supreme.

"No public business of any kind could possibly be done at any time, without the acquiescence of the Circumlocution Office. Its finger was in the largest public pie, and in the smallest public tart. It was equally impossible to do the plainest right and to undo the plainest wrong, without the express authority of the Cirmumlocution Office. If another Gunpowder Plot had been discovered half an hour before the lighting of the match, nobody would have been justified in saving the parliament until there had been half a score of boards, half a bushel of minutes, several sacks of official memoranda, and a family-vault full of ungrammatical correspondence on the part of the Circumlocution

Office. . . . Whatever was required to be done, the Circumlocution
Office was beforehand with all the public departments in the art of
perceiving—HOW NOT TO DO IT. . . .

"It is true that How not to do it was the great study and object of
all public departments and professional politicians all round the Circumlocution Office. It is true that every new premier and every new
government, coming in because they had upheld a certain thing as
necessary to be done, were no sooner come in than they applied their
utmost faculties to discovering How not to do it. . . . It is true that
the debates of both Houses of Parliament the whole session through,
uniformly tended to the protracted deliberation, How not to do it.
It is true that the royal speech, at the close of such session, virtually
said, My lords and gentlemen, you have through several laborious
months been considering with great loyalty and patriotism, How not
to do it, and you have found out; and with the blessing of Providence
upon the harvest (natural, not political), I now dismiss you. All this
is true, but the Circumlocution Office went beyond it.

"Because the Circumlocution Office went on mechanically, every
day, keeping this wonderful, all-sufficient wheel of statesmanship,
How not to do it, in motion. Because the Circumlocution Office was
down upon any ill-advised public servant who was going to do it, or
who appeared to be by any surprising accident in remote danger of
doing it, with a minute, and a memorandum, and a letter of instructions, that extinguished him. . . .

"Numbers of people were lost in the Circumlocution Office. Unfortunates with wrongs, or with projects for the general welfare (and
they had better have had wrongs at first, than have taken that bitter
English recipe for certainly getting them), who in slow lapse of time
and agony had passed safely through other public departments; who,
according to rule, had been bullied in this, over-reached by that, and
evaded by the other; got referred at last to the Circumlocution Office,
and never reappeared in the light of day. Boards sat upon them, secre-
taries minuted upon them, commissioners gabbled about them, clerks
registered, entered, checked, and ticked them off, and they melted
away. In short, all the business of the country went through the Circumlocution Office, except the business that never came out; and *its*
name was Legion.

"Sometimes, angry spirits attacked the Circumlocution Office.

Sometimes, parliamentary questions were asked about it, and even parliamentary motions made or threatened about it, by demagogues so low and ignorant as to hold that the real recipe of government was, How to do it. Then would the noble lord, or right honourable gentleman, in whose department it was to defend the Circumlocution Office, put an orange in his pocket, and make a regular field-day of the occasion. . . . Then would he keep one eye upon a coach or crammer from the Circumlocution Office sitting below the bar, and smash the honourable gentleman with the Circumlocution Office account of this matter. And although one of two things always happened; namely, either that the Circumlocution Office had nothing to say and said it, or that it had something to say of which the noble lord, or right honourable gentleman, blundered one half and forgot the other; the Circumlocution Office was always voted immaculate, by an accommodating majority." [28]

The smarting indignation with which Dickens had seen the defeat of Austen Layard and the Administrative Reform Association inflames these brilliant and angry paragraphs. Nor was his picture of public abuses basically exaggerated. Lord Melbourne as Prime Minister had been in the habit of wearily asking reformers, "Can't you let it alone?" The famous *Black Book* of 1832 estimated that sinecures in the law courts amounted to more than £62,000 a year. It listed one clergyman who had eleven livings, others holding seven or eight, and pointed out that of eleven thousand livings in the kingdom only five thousand were resident.[29] The Registrar and Deputy Registrar of York in 1850 received £20,000 a year for work that was done entirely by their clerks, while the wills that had to be filed with them rotted away and were eaten by rats in a filthy old mildewed shed in the Cathedral Close, old records were often sold as wastepaper, and the public were charged half a crown for being told that the documents they desired to consult were lost or unavailable.[30] A minister offering a highly paid post in the Civil Service to a friend told him that he could do in two hours all the work he would be called upon to perform in two months, adding, "It will not interfere with your shooting." A Government Report in 1855 said that lucrative posts were bestowed even on the mentally and physically incapacitated. Evidence before a Parliamentary Committee in 1873 listed fifty-five persons appointed between 1836 and 1854, some of whom were incompetent through age, others "perfectly unqualified," and one of whom "was almost anidiot," who "could not read or write." [31]

It is easy to see, therefore, where Dickens found his description of Henry Gowan's father, who, "originally attached to a legation abroad, had been pensioned off as a Commissioner of nothing in particular somewhere or other, and had died at his post with his drawn salary in his hand, nobly defending it to the last extremity." [32] Behind this system were the massed Barnacles and Stiltstalkings, its camp followers packed in Parliament, "waiting their orders to make houses or not to make houses; and they did all their hearing, and ohing, and cheering, and barking, under directions from the head of the family; and they put their dummy motions on the paper in the way of other men's motions; and they stalled disagreeable subjects off until late in the night and late in the session, and then with virtuous patriotism cried out that it was too late; and they went down into the country, whenever they were sent, and swore that Lord Decimus had revived trade from a swoon, and commerce from a fit, and had doubled the harvest of corn, quadrupled the harvest of hay, and prevented no end of gold from flying out of the Bank. . . . And there was not a list, in all the Circumlocution Office, of places that might fall vacant anywhere within half a century, from a Lord of the Treasury to a Chinese consul, and up again to a governor-general of India, but, as applicants for such places, the names of some or of every one of these hungry and adhesive Barnacles were down." [33]

The effects of this spoils-system organization of politics and patronage Dickens had attacked many times in *Household Words*. One of these attacks, "A Poor Man's Tale of a Patent," anticipates the experiences of Clenman's partner, Daniel Doyce, in trying to make a useful invention available to the country. The "poor man" who is its narrator tells how he spends weeks petitioning the Queen, being made to bring a declaration before a Master in Chancery, taking petition and declaration to be signed by the Home Secretary, having them shunted to the Attorney-General, then back to the Home Office, back to the Queen, back to the Home Secretary to sign again, then to the Patent Office, on to the Signet Office and the Privy Seal and the Engrossing Clerk, circling back for resignature to several of the others once more, then to the Lord Chancellor, the Lord Keeper of the Privy

Seal, the Clerk of the Hanaper, the Deputy Chaff-Wax, paying fees to them all.[34]

In the end, this official run-around takes weeks to undergo, involves passing through thirty-five stages, and costs its victim £96 7s. 8d. "I should like to see the Deputy Chaff-Wax," he says bitterly. "Is it a man, or what is it?" And, although he is careful to say that he is not a Chartist, he concludes by deciding that he agrees with a friend, William Butcher, who *is* a Chartist. "In William Butcher's delivering 'that the whole gang of Hanapers and Chaff-waxes must be done away with, and that England has been chaffed and waxed sufficient,' I agree." [35]

Doyce is subjected to a more protracted frustration, handled with burning burlesque. Dickens tells "How, after interminable attendance and correspondence, after infinite impertinences, ignorances, and insults, my lords made a Minute, number three thousand four hundred and seventy-two, allowing the culprit to make certain trials of his invention at his own expense. How the trials were made in the presence of a board of six, of whom two ancient members were too blind to see it, two other ancient members were too deaf to hear it, one other ancient member was too lame to get near it, and the final ancient member was too pig-headed to look at it. How there were more years; more impertinences, ignorances, and insults. How my lords then made a Minute, number five thousand one hundred and three, whereby they resigned the business to the Circumlocution Office. How the Circumlocution Office, in course of time, took up the business as if it were a bran new thing of yesterday, which had never been heard of before; muddled the business, addled the business, tossed the business in a wet blanket. How there was a reference of the business to three Barnacles and a Stiltstalking, who knew nothing about it; into whose heads nothing could be hammered about it; who got bored about it, and reported physical impossibilities about it. How the Circumlocution Office, in a Minute number eight thousand seven hundred and forty, 'saw no reason to reverse the decision at which my lords had arrived.' How the Circumlocution Office, being reminded that my lords had arrived at no decision, shelved the business. How there had been a final interview with the head of the Circumlocution Office that very morning, and how the Brazen Head had spoken, and had been, upon the whole, and under all the circumstances, and looking at it from the various points of view, of opinion that one of two courses was to be pursued in respect of the business: that was to say, either to let it alone for evermore, or to begin it all over again." [36]

Although some of the worst anomalies in patent procedure had been abolished by the Patent Law Amendment Act of 1852, enough still remained.[37] And all the larger outlines of the attack on the Circumlocution Office were, as Humphry House says, "substantially fair." [38] The implications for society as a whole amounted to an endorsement of the entire Chartist criticism and an acceptance of its aims. "As they went along," Dickens says after Doyce has received a decisive repulse, "certainly one of the party, and probably more than one, thought that Bleeding Heart Yard was no inappropriate destination for a man who had been in correspondence with my lords and the Barnacles—and perhaps had a misgiving also that Britannia herself might come to look for lodgings in Bleeding Heart Yard, some ugly day or other, if she over-did the Circumlocution Office." [39]

*   *   *   *   *

The most tragic prisoner, in *Little Dorrit*, of this involved, chaotic system of inefficiency and injustice which is "nobody's fault," is William Dorrit, who has been confined in the Marshalsea since long years before the opening of the story. A gentleman with money invested in some enterprise of which he knew nothing except his financial connection with it, when it fails he is helplessly unable to explain the spiriting away of some of its assets. The principal creditor is the Circumlocution Office, apparently by virtue of fines for a failure to perform government contracts, and the innocent Mr. Dorrit stands out as the only victim who can be imprisoned in lieu of payment. Nothing can be made of his case, nobody understands it, and in the course of years he sinks into a confinement made hopeless by the fact that the Circumlocution Office itself comes eventually to forget what the claim against Mr. Dorrit is. At last the very circumstance that he is still a prisoner falls into oblivion.

Various external details in the portrayal of William Dorrit—his insistence on being taken as a gentleman, his pompous speech, his ornately ringed fingers, and, in the days when he is first in the Marshalsea, the way his nervous hands wander to his trembling lips—are indubitably derived from John Dickens and his son's memories of the prison experience. But, aside from these mannerisms, Mr. Dorrit is not, as many commentators have suggested, a deeper attempt to understand John Dickens and how he had come to be the kind of man he was. Mr. Dorrit had not been brought to the prison by improvidence, and John Dickens's improvidence was the cause, not the consequence, of his prison experiences. He was not a helpless baby, like Mr. Dorrit, but a hard-working and competent professional man, without a particle of Mr. Dorrit's horrified gentility at the idea that he should be suspected of doing anything for a living. His borrowings and his other weaknesses of character were not the mutilation of twenty-five years' imprisonment; he had spent little more than three months in the Marshalsea.

Mr. Dorrit's helplessness, his humiliation, his snobbery, and his shame are instead an amazingly brilliant feat of independent character creation. If they have any personal roots at all, however, those roots lie in Dickens himself. It was Dickens who was the terrified and uncomprehending child at the time his father was imprisoned, Dickens whose heart was torn with despair at his own incarceration in the agony of the blacking warehouse, Dickens to whose misery those months seemed to prolong themselves into tear-stained years, Dickens who felt the need of burying those days as deep in oblivion as Mr. Dorrit tries to do upon his release. Of course Mr. Dorrit is not Dickens's portrait of himself, but in Mr. Dorrit's concealments, Dickens is facing the elements in himself that had sealed his lips upon the Marshalsea and the blacking warehouse.

In the entire range of his work Dickens never drew a character with more delicate subtlety and psychological penetration. Innumerable touches of wonderful sensitivity reveal Mr. Dorrit sinking to greater and greater depths of spurious pride and moral self-abasement, pretending not to know that his favorite daughter, Amy, "Little Dorrit," works as a seamstress to provide him with small comforts and luxuries, affecting unawareness of his brother's playing the clarionet in a cheap theater and his daughter Fanny's dancing there as a chorus girl, superbly accepting the homage of his fellow prisoners as the "Father of the Marshalsea," unashamedly hinting for donations, and all the time maintaining his shabby pretense of genteel superiority.

There is an incomparable scene growing out of the fact that Young John Chivery, the son of a turnkey, falls in love with Little Dorrit and is gently refused. Fearful lest the father will retaliate for his son's rejection, Mr. Dorrit invents a story about a previous episode of the same kind, designed to suggest that Little Dorrit might tolerate her humble lover and "lead him on." But in doing so he grows more and more embarrassed until his voice dies away, only to burst out presently, "O despise me, despise me! Look away from me, don't listen to me, stop me, blush for me, cry for me—Even you, Amy! Do it, do it! I do it to myself! I am hardened now, I have sunk too low to care long even for that." [40] He weeps tears of self-pity and she soothes and rests him against her heart.

When his tears are dried and he has been persuaded to resume his dinner, for the first time he thinks of his daughter. "My love, you have had a life of hardship here. No companions, no recreations, many cares I am afraid. . . . I have not been able to do much for you; but all I have been able to do, I have done." "Yes, my dear father," she rejoins, "I know, I know." "I am in the twenty-third year of my life here. It is all I could do for my children—I have done it. Amy, my love, you are by far the best loved of the three; I have had you principally in my mind—whatever I have done for your sake, my dear child, I have done freely and without murmuring." [41]

"Only the wisdom that holds the clue to all hearts and all mysteries," Dickens comments, "can surely know to what extent a man, especially a man brought down as this man had been, can impose upon himself. Enough, for the present place, that he lay down with wet eyelashes, serene, in a manner majestic, after bestowing his life of degradation as a sort of portion on the devoted child on whom its miseries had fallen so heavily, and whose love alone had saved him to be even what he was." [42]

As for Little Dorrit herself, half ashamed of her father, half admiring him and proud of him, she is all devotion to him. She hopes only that people will understand and not judge him. "Not," she says defensively, "Not that he has anything to be ashamed of for himself, or that I have anything to be ashamed of for him. He only requires to be understood. I only ask for him that his life may be fairly remembered. All that he said was quite true. It all happened just as he related it. He is very much respected. Everybody who comes in, is glad to know him. He is more courted than anyone else. He is far more thought of than the Marshal is." [43]

Little Dorrit's Marshalsea Room

When the day comes on which it is learned that Mr. Dorrit is the heir to a great fortune and that he can leave the prison, all her joy is for him. He has told her how different he used to be, in the days when he was young, in the days before she was born. "I shall see him," she exclaims, "as I never saw him yet. I shall see my dear love, with the dark cloud cleared away. I shall see him, as my poor mother saw him long ago." [44]

But with a sad irony Little Dorrit learns that no sudden gleam of magnificent fortune can melt away the prison shadows of a quarter of a century. Resplendently garbed, with a retinue of retainers and couriers, rolling in magnificent carriages over the Great St. Bernard, gorgeous in Venice, glittering in Rome, Mr. Dorrit is forever afraid that someone will know about his former incarceration. He suspects scorn in his servants, falls into rages at imagined sneers in their tones of voice, is in terror lest, listening at keyholes, they might catch some whispered reference to his past. The daughter from whom he once took everything now angers him if she tries to perform the slightest personal service: someone might guess that she had formerly done menial tasks. And in this bondage to the denial of his own past Little Dorrit recognizes the well-known shadow of the Marshalsea wall. "It took a new shape, but it was the old sad shadow." [45] She would never see her father as he used to be.

At last, at a great banquet in Rome, Mr. Dorrit comes face to face, for the final time, with that terror and that past. His mind gives way and he believes himself back in the prison again. Confusedly seeing the faces around him, he presents his daughter to them: "Born here," he says, shedding tears. "Bred here. Ladies and gentlemen, my daughter. Child of an unfortunate father, but—ha—always a gentleman. Poor, no doubt, but—hum—proud. Always proud. It has become a—hum—custom for my—ha—personal admirers—personal admirers solely—to be pleased to express their desire to acknowledge my semi-official position here, by offering—ha—little tributes which usually take the form of—ha—Testimonials—pecuniary Testimonials. . . . I beg to have it understood that I do not consider myself compromised. Ha. Not compromised. Ha. Not a beggar." [46]

Little Dorrit is not ashamed of his revelation, nor ashamed of him. "She was pale and frightened; but she had no other care than to soothe him and get him away, for his own dear sake. She was between him and the wondering faces, turned round upon his breast with her own face raised to his." [47] Ten days later he passes away. "Quietly, quietly, the reflected marks of the prison bars and of the zig-zag iron on the wall-top faded away. Quietly, quietly, the face subsided into a far younger likeness of her own than she had ever seen under the grey hair, and sank to rest." [48]

In the end, with all the golden shower of sudden wealth melted away in the Merdle ruin, with even Clennam's modest patrimony lost in the same crash, Little Dorrit and Clennam are joined in marriage at the altar of St. George's Church, in the shadow of the Marshalsea, and go down its steps "into a modest life of usefulness and happiness."

For in spite of Dickens's disillusion with the world that the Scrooges, Dombeys, Dedlocks, Bounderbys, Gradgrinds, Merdles, and Barnacles have forged, he has not surrendered. He had faith that the decency and good will of common humanity might with hard work still overcome the obstacles that confusion placed in its path. Without closing his eyes on evil and unhappiness he believed that goodness could win a modest victory. Of Clennam, Dickens remarks that "this saved him from the whimpering weakness and cruel selfishness of holding that because such a happiness or such a virtue had not come into his little path, or worked well for him, therefore it was not in the great scheme, but was reducible, when found in appearance, to the basest elements." [49] That reservation expresses Dickens's own basic creed, bursting irrepressibly through all his social disillusion and discouragement. With the very evolution in which his analysis of society grew ever more penetrating and deepened his anger almost to despair, his unbreakable belligerence roused him again and again to voice his passionate hopes in the power of mankind to solve its problems.

Little Dorrit is not in its entirety as gray a book as it is in its major themes. There is a great deal of delightful comedy in Young John Chivery, in Mrs. Plornish's belief that she is speaking Italian to Cavaletto when she says, "Me ope you leg better soon," in Flora Finching and the implacable animosity of Mr. F's Aunt, in Mr. Pancks and Mr. Sparkler, even in Mr. Dorrit himself. In general, however, like *Bleak House* and *Hard Times*, *Little Dorrit* is more deeply shadowed with an awareness of the deep-rooted troubles of society than the buoyant novels of Dickens's youth.

With gigantic force and social insight it carries Dickens, in its revolutionary unmasking of finance capitalism, to the maturest height of genius that he had yet attained. But even so, his growth was not yet ended. In *Great Expectations* he was to pursue still more deeply the self-analysis of *David Copperfield*, and in *Our Mutual Friend* to make an ultimate survey of that dust-heap of modern civilization from which mankind must strive to be reborn.

CHAPTER NINE

Breaking Point

DURING the months following the completion of *Little Dorrit,*
Dickens's misery in his marriage was swelling into the anguish
of an endless nightmare. Only the excitement of putting on *The
Frozen Deep* had enabled him to endure the previous winter. With
the spring, he fell into the depths of depression, seeking in vain to dull
the ache by haunting theatrical greenrooms with Collins, passing
nights in "Haroun Al Raschid" wanderings and "Sybarite" distractions. In the Jerrold benefits he "tore himself to pieces" [1] rendering
Wardour's agony and despair, yet felt a kind of agitated relief in projecting and symbolizing an emotion not unlike his own. But as soon
as the last night was over, his frustration was clawing at him more
fiercely than ever. He returned from the "lazy tour" with Collins as
desperate as before.

"I am incapable of rest," he lamented. "Much better to die, doing." [2]
Useless to think of sitting down to a new novel; his unhappiness tore
through him with the violence of a powerful electric current agitating
his very body. There could be no relief but in constant action. "What
do you think," he wrote Forster from Gad's Hill, "of my paying for
this place, by reviving that old idea of some Readings from my books.
I am very strongly tempted. Think of it." [3]

The notion had first come to him, not altogether seriously, years
before at Lausanne. But as he had done the *Christmas Carol* for charity, and felt the laughter and tears of his audience course through him,
more and more he had asked why not? Forster, of course, obdurately
opposed. It was a public exhibition for private gain unworthy of a
man of letters and a gentleman. It was true that other writers, including Thackeray, had given lectures for their own profit, but this was

like descending to the vulgarity of the stage. The fact that Forster himself had acted for charitable causes he considered beside the point. So was the fact that their good friend Macready and many other actors were men of the highest characters. For a literary artist to become a sort of professional showman was still a lowering of dignity.[4]

But Dickens did not at all agree. He saw no loss of dignity in reading from his own books. And if charitable causes might legitimately profit from it, why should not he? Above all, it would keep him busy, provide an outlet for his nervous tension, bring him and his public into a close contact from which he derived both stimulation and support, and take him away from a domestic association that he found intolerable.

"I believe," he at last brought himself to the point of telling Miss Coutts, "that no two people were ever created, with such an impossibility of interest, sympathy, confidence, sentiment, tender union of any kind between them, as there is between my wife and me. It is an immense misfortune to her—it is an immense misfortune to me—but Nature has put an insurmountable barrier between us, which never in this world can be thrown down.

"You know me too well to suppose that I have the faintest thought of influencing you on either side. I merely mention a fact which may induce you to pity us both, when I tell you that she is the only person I have ever known with whom I could not get on somehow or other, and in communicating with whom I could not find some way to come to some kind of interest. You know that I have many impulsive faults which often belong to my impulsive way of life and exercise of fancy; but I am very patient and considerate at heart, and would have beaten out a path to a better journey's end than we have come to, if I could." [5]

The truth was worse than that he had ceased to love Kate. In scores of ways she rasped him beyond bearing. Even in Italy, four years earlier, when he had felt during his absence a momentary recurrence of tenderness for her, he had been unable to restrain his impatience at her inability merely to address an envelope legibly. Daily contact with her clumsiness, lassitude, and inefficiency set his teeth on edge. For Dickens, who knew exactly where every article should be in every room in his house, who inspected his children's bedrooms like a drill sergeant every morning, who had a precise place on his desk for every ornament, whose every movement and gesture were made with precision, poor Catherine's mishaps were as irritating as if they were deliberate. In earlier years he had tried to make a joke of these accidents, roaring with laughter when her bracelets fell off her arm with a splash into the soup. But burlesquing her as Tilly Slowboy and exaggerating her bruised elbows and ankles did not ultimately drain off his exasperation. A mounting residue remained undischarged.

Related to these shortcomings were her practical incapacities. When they had moved to Tavistock House, Dickens had settled almost every detail of its reconstruction and furnishing himself. Kate's part, he remarked only half jestingly, was limited to wandering about getting herself "all over paint" and seeming to think that "somehow immensely useful." It was common report in London that Dickens did most of the family shopping, "making bargains at butchers and bakers," and taking on himself such housewives' duties.[6] As for the internal running of the establishment, it was in the hands of Georgina, who also took charge when they moved to Paris, Boulogne, or any of their English summer residences.

Even the children had been more directly under the supervision of their Aunt Georgy than of their mother. Since 1842 Georgina had devoted herself to their care, teaching each in succession to read and write. To be sure, there was a nurse, and later a governess, and one by one the little boys had gone to school, but in a family of nine growing children there had still been enough to do. Catherine's role seemed limited to bringing them into the world.

Nor, Dickens insisted, was there an emotional tie between her and the children. Though she wept at being separated from them when she went to America, "she has never attached one of them to herself, never played with them in infancy, never attracted their confidence, as they have grown older, never presented herself before them in the aspect of a mother. I have seen them fall off from her in a natural— not unnatural—progress of estrangement, and at this moment I believe that Mary and Katey (whose dispositions are of the gentlest and most affectionate conceivable) harden into stone figures of girls when they can be got to go near her, and have their hearts shut up in her presence as if they were closed by some horrid spring. . . . It is her misery to live in some fatal atmosphere which slays every one to whom she should be dearest."[7]

What was true of the girls, Dickens emphasized, was true of the others as well. "She does not—and she never did—care for the children," he told Miss Coutts; "and the children do not—and they never did—care for her. The little play that is acted in your Drawing-room is not the truth, and the less the children play it, the better for themselves, because they know it is not the truth. (If I stood before you at this moment and told you what difficulty we have to get Frank, for instance, to go near his mother, or keep near his mother, you would stand amazed.)" [8]

There may possibly, of course, be another side to these observations. Dickens was of a masterful and domineering temperament; it is conceivable that he seized the control even of all domestic details from Kate's unresisting hand. Georgina, too, has sometimes been seen as a sly and insidious maneuverer, gradually drawing into her own grasp the reins of authority that rightfully belonged to Kate. Neither suggestion, however, is entirely plausible. Dickens was not incapable of delegating power. Although on *Household Words* he retained a firm grasp on policy, he left all routine details to Wills. His egoism was not of a kind that needed to assert itself over every roast of meat or scuttle of coal. And when Georgina joined the household she was a girl of fifteen and Kate a young matron of twenty-seven already six years married. Kate was like Jane Austen's Lady Bertram, reclining indolently day after day upon a sofa. Though Georgina was certainly far the cleverer of the two, and though later she indubitably enjoyed playing hostess, there is no evidence for depicting her as a scheming intriguer and Kate as her helpless victim or for believing that Kate resented or did anything but welcome the ministrations of her more efficient sister.

It is true that in fifteen years Kate had given birth to ten children and suffered a number of miscarriages. But physically her health was good; she survived her more vigorous husband by nine years, dying of cancer at the age of sixty-four. Her illness after the birth of Dora Annie was a nervous one; Dickens's letters to her doctor at the time speak of her having behaved oddly when visiting the homes of friends. And many Victorian wives had quite as many children as Kate and continued to be lively companions to their husbands. Probably Dickens would have required, as Hesketh Pearson says, "a forty-wife power partner," [9] but even so Kate suffered from "an indescribable lassitude," [10] of which Dickens felt that he observed traces in their son Charley.

She had never been a success as the wife of a celebrity, even less so as the wife of one with Dickens's galvanic vitality. She had none of the talents of a hostess; as a guest she was a colorless nullity. Dickens had to remind her of their obligations to the Macreadys when Mrs. Macready's sister was their guest in Genoa. Although Rogers wrote her playful little notes, he did not invite her to his celebrated breakfast table, nor did she enter the great salons where her husband was received. Miss Coutts was undeviatingly kind to her, but always spoke of her in terms of gentle sarcasm: the "Poor dear Mrs. Dickens" with which Miss Coutts invariably alluded to her was pronounced in a tone of illimitable disparagement.[11]

So little impression did Kate make on Dickens's large circle of friends and acquaintances that during many periods she almost seems to disappear from his life. Aside from the usual courtesies, letters to Dickens seldom mention her. The few surviving letters in her own hand are almost without exception utterly flat. Now and then there is a glimpse of her, giggling and girlish in their early married life, fresh-colored and elaborately dressed at a ball in America, in tears at an angry scene between Dickens and Forster, stout and red-faced in middle life. Journeying across the United States, she stumbled and fell in and out of stagecoaches and river steamers; only the help of an unusually competent maid got her through all the ordeals of travel. In Italy, and later in France, there were the services of a cook, nurse, maids, and other servants, all falling more and more under the directions of Georgina.

Undoubtedly Kate had come to realize her husband's impatience, and nervous apprehension intensified her awkward blunders. At Montreal she had surprised Dickens by doing very well in the amateur theatricals, but it was a success she never repeated. She no sooner began rehearsing for *Every Man in His Humour*, in 1850, than she tumbled through a trap door and sprained her ankle. Thereafter we hear little more of her participating in any theatricals. Dickens had no tolerance for ineptitude; Charley had observed the very back of his head tensely waiting for someone to make a mistake at rehearsals of *The Lighthouse*. As Dickens contrasted Kate's middle-aged dullness and incapacity with the well-preserved youthful charm of Mme. Scribe or the grace and ease of Mme. Régnier and Mme. Viardot, all the qualities he had imagined he found in her when she was twenty seemed to have disappeared. As he now saw her, she was sluggish, vague-minded, incompetent, stirring out of self-indulgent idleness only to fall into amorphous self-pity. Amiable and devoted in a torpid way, she was otherwise completely negligible and dim.

Except in one respect. Terrified though she might be of her husband's displeasure, Kate could not believe there was no more than an innocent gallantry in his response to other women or restrain her resentment of the fascination he exercised over them. There is no evidence, to be sure, that she objected to his mock flirtation with the middle-aged Mrs. Colden in 1842, or to his playful later flirtation with Mary Boyle. Nor does she seem to have been aware of his brief though more serious eruption of emotion over Christiana Weller. But she had the direst suspicions of his relations with Mme. De la Rue in Genoa; not even the serenity of that lady's husband could convince her there was nothing wrong. What tears, recriminations, hysteria, there had been—even public scenes, for which Dickens had been obliged to invent flimsy excuses that the De la Rues had tactfully pretended to believe. And in the course of the years these frictions had not ceased.

"Between ourselves," Dickens wrote M. De la Rue in October, 1857, ". . . I don't get on better in these later times with a certain poor lady you know of, than I did in the earlier Peschiere days. Much worse. Much worse! Neither do the children, elder or younger. Neither can she get on with herself, or be anything but unhappy. (She has been excruciatingly jealous of, and has obtained positive proof of my being on the most intimate terms with, at least fifteen thousand women of various conditions in life, since we left Genoa. Please to respect me for this vast experience.) What we should do, or what the girls would be, without Georgy, I cannot imagine. She is the active spirit of the house, and the children dote upon her. Enough of this. We put the Skeleton away in the cupboard, and very few people, comparatively, know of its existence." [12]

Over and over again in these later years, Dickens said, Catherine had suggested that they would be happier separated: "it would be better for her to go away and live apart." But the children, he had always insisted, must be "the first consideration," and must bind them "together 'in appearance.'" For the children's sake he and she must bear their misfortune "and fight the fight out to the end." [13] And so things might have gone on, even during these months of agitation and misery, but for one element in the situation. This was Ellen Ternan, the fair-haired, blue-eyed actress who played Lucy Crayford in the Manchester performances of *The Frozen Deep*.

A rather dubious story says that Dickens had first seen Ellen backstage at her theatrical début in *Atalanta* at the Haymarket, weeping bitterly because of the brief chiton she was obliged to wear in her part as the Grecian youth Hippomenes.[14] Supposedly she was deeply distressed by having to display so much leg. But Ellen must have worn the costume already in rehearsals, and, besides, she came of an old family of actors, so that she was not likely to have been upset by a garb far from unusual on the stage. She might, of course, have felt that she would be more interesting to a great author if discovered in a role of outraged modesty and prettily timorous purity.

Even so, Dickens did not think of her when it became necessary to fill the feminine roles in *The Frozen Deep* with professional actresses. He applied in several other quarters first, the suggestion of having Mrs. Ternan and her daughters did not originate with him, and he gave Ellen only a minor part rather than that of Wardour's love, Clara Burnham.

But during the course of rehearsals and the frenzied last performances in the north, the impression she made upon him deepened. While he was buffeting the other characters out of his way and "rending the very heart out of his body" [15] as Richard Wardour, feeling the tears of Maria Ternan showering down upon his face and beard, his heart was weeping its own lamentation over the "one friend and companion" he had never made, the "one happiness he had missed in life." [16]

How his feeling for the fair young actress wrought upon his impetuous nature is suggested by a conversation in *The Lazy Tour of Two Idle Apprentices* between the two characters who represent Collins and Dickens. Collins has been lying in a meadow, singing "Annie Laurie." What an ass and sniveler the poet was, Dickens exclaims bitterly: "do you think I'd lay me doon and dee? No, sir," he proceeds, with a disparaging assumption of the Scottish accent, "I'd get me oop and peetch into somebody. Wouldn't you?"

"I wouldn't have anything to do with her," yawns Collins. "Why should I take the trouble?"

"It's no trouble to fall in love . . . ," says Dickens, shaking his head.

"It's trouble enough to fall out of it, once you're in it," Collins retorts. "So I keep out of it altogether. It would be better for you, if you did the same." [17]

The advice, however, was wasted upon one with Dickens's disposition. He found a despairing relief in describing his feelings to Mrs. Watson as if they were merely the restlessness of the artistic temperament: "I am the modern embodiment of the old Enchanters, whose Familiars tore them to pieces. I weary of rest, and have no satisfaction but in fatigue. Realities and idealities are always comparing themselves before me, and I don't like the Realities except when they are unattainable—*then*, I like them of all things. I wish I had been born in the days of Ogres and Dragon-guarded Castles. I wish an Ogre with seven heads (and no particular evidence of brains in the whole of them) had taken the Princess whom I adore—you have no idea how intensely I love her!—to his stronghold on the top of a high series of mountains, and there tied her up by the hair. Nothing would suit me half so well this day, as climbing after her, sword in hand, and either winning her or being killed.—*There's* a frame of mind for you, in 1857." [18]

On his return from the "lazy tour" it seemed to Dickens that he could not bear allowing his life to go on unaltered. Sharing the same bedchamber with Kate, with all its domestic intimacies, as he had done these many years, but feeling as he now did, was intolerable to him. With a sudden determination he wrote to Anne Cornelius, their old servant, who was in charge at Tavistock House, directing her to transform his dressing room into his bedroom. The washstands were to be taken into the bathroom. The doorway between the dressing room and Kate's room was to be closed by a wooden door and the recess filled with shelves. He would rather not have these changes talked about, he told Anne, but the sooner they were made the better.[19] But for all his desire that it be done quietly, the closing of that door after twenty-one years of married life was, in the tragedy of Dickens, symbolically as significant as Nora's slamming of the door in *A Doll's House*.

It may have come to the attention of the Hogarths, who were again staying at Tavistock House. Toward the middle or end of October, Dickens had to come from Gad's Hill to London on *Household Words* business, and went home to sleep. Some upset took place, it cannot be said what. Perhaps it grew out of his annoyance with the mere presence of the Hogarths; perhaps there was some question about the change in his sleeping arrangements. Whatever it was, he was "very much put out"; and as he lay afterward, unable to rest, he thought, "After all, it would be better to be up and doing something, than lying here." So up he rose, and at two o'clock in the morning dressed, and tramped all the thirty miles to Gad's Hill through the dead of night.[20] He did not return to Tavistock House again until the Hogarths were gone forever.

*   *   *   *   *

Meanwhile, his outward life continued much as usual. He begged aid of Lord Brougham for Lady Blessington's niece, Marguerite Power, who had fallen into poverty, and later in the year he joined with Thackeray and Forster in raising a purse of £200 for her from old friends of her aunt and D'Orsay.[21] In November he spoke at a dinner in behalf of the Warehousemen and Clerks' School at New Cross, contrasting it with the school he had gone to himself, and with such institutions as the Yorkshire and Charitable Grinders' schools he had described in his books.[22]

But Tavistock House, during these months, was an unhappy home. There were no children's theatricals on Twelfth Night. Kate wept in her lonely room, Georgina kept the house going, and Dickens debated trying to begin a new book instead of inaugurating the course of readings that Forster opposed. "If I can discipline my thoughts into the channel of a story," he wrote his friend, "I have made up my mind to get to work on one: always supposing that I find myself, on the trial, able to do well. Nothing whatever will do me the least 'good' in the way of shaking off the one strong possession of change impending over us that every day makes stronger . . . Sometimes, I think I may continue to work; sometimes, I think not." [23]

On February 9th, Dickens spoke at a dinner in behalf of the Hospital for Sick Children. There were spoilt children, he said, allowed to sit up too late at adult dinner tables, dabbling their faces in the dessert, propping their sleepy eyelids open but fractiously refusing to go to bed, carried off at last kicking and protesting. But these were not the kind of spoilt children he meant to speak of. "The spoilt children I must show you are the spoilt children of the poor in this great city . . . for ever and ever irrevocably spoilt out of this breathing life of ours by tens of thousands . . . The two grim nurses, Poverty and Sickness, who bring these children before you, preside over their births, rock their wretched cradles, nail down their little coffins, pile up the earth above their graves." [24]

Some years ago, he went on, he had visited one of the most foul-smelling slums of Edinburgh. There, in a damp-stained room with an empty porridge-pot on the cold hearth, lay an old egg-box, holding a sick child with a "little wasted face, and his little hot, worn hands folded over his breast, and his little bright attentive eyes." He seldom cried, the mother said; he seldom complained; " 'he lay there, seemin' to woonder what it was a' aboot.' " It seemed to Dickens as if the sick child were "saying, in his silence, more pathetically than I have ever heard anything said by any orator in my life, 'Will you please tell me what this means, strange man? and if you can give me any good reason why I should be so soon, so far advanced on my way to Him who said that children were to come into His presence, and were not to be forbidden, but who scarcely meant, I think, that they should come by this hard road by which I am travelling, pray give me the reason for it, for I seek it very earnestly and wonder about it very much' "; and ever since then Dickens had seen his "poor little drooping friend in his egg-box" and "always found him wondering what it meant, and why, in the name of a gracious God, such things should be!" [25]

"Now, ladies and gentlemen, such things need not be, and will not be, if this company, which is a drop of the life-blood of the great compassionate public heart, will only accept the means of rescue and prevention which it is mine to offer." In the hospital in Great Ormond Street which was once a courtly old mansion, state bedrooms had been converted into airy wards where the tiny convalescents had trays of toys, bright Noah's arks with their animals, and rows of tin soldiers, and where pleasant, childish pictures hung upon the walls. "This is the pathetic case which I have to put to you; not only on behalf of the thousands of children who live half developed, racked with preventible pain, shorn of their natural capacity for health and enjoyment. If these innocent creatures cannot move you for themselves, how can I possibly hope to move you in their names." [26]

The appeal brought in, Forster says, "greatly over three thousand pounds,"and in addition Dickens agreed to read the *Christmas Carol* in April for the same cause.[27] This undertaking raised once more in his mind the question why he should not read for his own profit as well. He had tried in vain to concentrate upon a theme for a story. Everything reminded him of his own frustration. Seeing a performance of a new play by his friend Westland Marston, he protested against the way the hero crushed in his hand a letter from the woman he loved. "Hold it to his heart unconsciously and look about for it the while, he might; or he might do anything with it that expressed a habit of tenderness and affection in association with the idea of her; but he would never crush it under any circumstances. He would as soon crush her heart." [28]

Now he asked once more if he might not find relief in the readings after all. "The domestic unhappiness remains so strong upon me that I can't write, and (waking) can't rest, one minute. I have never known a moment's peace or content, since the last night of The Frozen Deep. I do suppose there never was a man so seized and rended by one Spirit. In this condition, though nothing can alter or soften it, I have a turning notion that the mere physical effort and change of the Readings would be good, as another means of bearing it." [29]

Forster continued to protest, although he was gloomily coming to believe that Dickens had already made up his mind. He had not, Dickens told him; but he felt Forster's resistance to be irrational. Forster had raised no objection to his reading for charity; was he not "exhibiting" himself equally when he did that, no matter who got the money? And did not a good part of the public even now suppose him to be paid? Half Scotland believed he was to be paid for the reading he was to give on March 26th in aid of the Edinburgh Philosophical Institute.[30]

Not absolutely sure of himself, however, Dickens referred Forster's objections to Miss Coutts. She was surprised at first, but almost immediately said she saw nothing derogatory in the project. "I think upon the whole that most people would be glad you should have the money, rather than other people." Her companion, Mrs. Brown, without knowing what Miss Coutts had said, expressed the same opinion.[31]

Dickens had feared Miss Coutts would share Forster's view, and was strengthened by her agreement in pressing his own position. By the time he returned from Edinburgh (where he had been presented with a silver wassail bowl [32]) his determination was all but taken.

"I must do *something*," he told Forster, "or I shall wear my heart away." [33] And a few days later, "quite dismiss from your mind any reference whatever to present circumstances at home. Nothing can put *them* right, until we are all dead and buried and risen. It is not, with me, a matter of will, or trial, or sufferance, or good humour, or making the best of it, or making the worst of it, any longer. It is all despairingly over. Have no lingering hope of, or for, me in this association. A dismal failure has to be borne, and there an end." [34]

What Dickens now proposed was therefore a series of four or six Thursday evening readings in London at St. Martin's Hall throughout May and the beginning of June. These would be followed by an autumn tour of "the Eastern Counties, the West, Lancashire, Yorkshire, and Scotland," "extending through August, September, and October," and running to thirty-five or forty all told. Dickens himself would be entirely dissociated from the business management, which would be handled by Arthur Smith, whose efficiency he had proved during the Jerrold benefits. By the following April, Dickens believed, he might gain a very large sum, even without counting Ireland. And there would still remain America, which he thought (if he could resolve to go there) might be worth £10,000.[35]

While these reading plans were being determined, Dickens was also engaged in an attack on the mismanagement of the Royal Literary Fund. As far back as 1855, at an annual dinner of the Fund, he had indicted the extravagance and nepotism with which its affairs were administered.[36] Needy applicants were turned down or given insignificant doles as small as £5 while the widows of prosperous members received grants as large as £100. The commodious headquarters of the Fund in Bloomsbury were for the most part empty and unused. Forty per cent of its income was swallowed up in the expenses of management. Its main activity seemed to be the luxurious annual dinners for noble guests of honor. Did the organization exist, Dickens asked, to relieve men of genius and learning, or to bolster its own pride with costly banquets and toady to men of title? [37]

Together with Forster and Charles Dilke, Dickens had spearheaded a running fight against these abuses. The administrative committee made a few concessions, but continued to oppose any major changes. By 1858, however, under continued agitation, they felt sufficiently hard-pressed to issue a pamphlet answering the charges against them. The proportion of expense to expenditure, they argued, was not higher than it had always been; certain abuses complained about had been already abolished at the time they were attacked; some of the reformers had in the past been members of the committee without dissenting from decisions they now scored.[38] Dickens drafted a reply. The "sharp needle of fact," he pointed out, in the committee's "haystack of words," was that it still cost £532 to distribute relief of only £1,225. No other like institution had such expenses. The claim that these expenditures were devoted to sustaining the income of the organization was nonsense; almost three-quarters of its funds came in automatically from rents, dividends, and subscriptions.[39] The reformers made but small headway, however, and Dickens continued to be at odds with the committee in later years.

During the course of turning out this reply, Dickens had given his reading for the Children's Hospital at St. Martin's Hall on April 15th and inaugurated the series for his own profit on the 29th.[40] Success was immediate and enormous. "They have let five hundred stalls for the Hospital night," Dickens reported; "and as people come in every day for more, and it is out of the question to make more, they cannot be restrained at St. Martin's Hall from taking down names for other Readings." [41] Somehow, on the second night, they crammed in an additional seventy people; [42] the demand for seats was so strong that the series was expanded from six to sixteen readings extending to the 22nd of July.[43] In addition to A Christmas Carol, Dickens read The Chimes, although at first he found it hard to maintain his composure during some of its more affecting parts. "I must harden my heart," he said, "like Lady Macbeth." [44] By the middle of June he had devised two more reading programs that included the death of little Paul Dombey and some Sairey Gamp scenes from Martin Chuzzlewit.

But at home, even as these public triumphs were initiated, the tension between Dickens and Catherine had at last mounted to a crisis. Dickens had purchased a bracelet to give Ellen Ternan, and the jeweler had made the mistake of sending it to Tavistock House, where it fell into Catherine's hands.[45] It was not unusual for Dickens to ex-

change little gifts and mementos with participants in the theatricals;
he had done so with Mary Boyle, and with Mrs. Cowden Clarke and
her sister Miss Novello. And only recently he had given Francesco
Berger a set of three shirt studs in blue enamel with diamonds as a
token of appreciation for his musical contributions to *The Frozen
Deep*.[46] But to Catherine this was different, and she violently resented it.

Grieving over her husband's alienation, it was impossible for her
to believe the bracelet a mark of innocent esteem. In *Uncle John*, the
farce following *The Frozen Deep*, Dickens and Ellen had played the
parts of an elderly gentleman and his ward, a young girl with whom
he falls in love and whom he loads with "wonderful presents—a pearl
necklace, diamond ear-rings." [47] How else could one interpret these
personal attentions to a beautiful girl of eighteen, even though, like
"Uncle John," Dickens was old enough to be her father? Catherine
flared into angry reproaches. Dickens furiously denied any guilt in his
relations with Ellen. In the indignant fervor of his emotion he resented the accusation as a slur on Ellen's purity; swirling in a luminous
mist, his feelings presented themselves to him as a shining and sanc-
tified devotion and Ellen as the far-off princess on the unscalable
mountain. He was in that lyrical and anguished state which could not
bear having itself imaged, even in its own eyes, as the desire to defile
that fair beauty in a libertine embrace. His wife's bitter suspicions
enraged him as hideous and degrading.

All his violent will power hardened itself into battering her to surrender. He would not have Catherine, he would not have his daughters believing Ellen was his mistress. For of course the girls were old
enough now to feel the tension in the household and would be bound
to realize the cause of their mother's agitation. Catherine must do
something to disavow her groundless charge. She could show her confidence in him, he told her, and her belief in Ellen's innocence, by calling on her and her mother. Going past Catherine's door, eighteen-
year-old Katey found it open and heard sobs from within. Entering,
she found her mother seated at the dressing table, weeping and putting on her bonnet. When she asked why, Catherine, with streaming
eyes, choked, "Your father has asked me to go and see Ellen Ternan."
"You shall not go!" exclaimed Katey, stamping her foot. But Cath-

erine Dickens was not strong enough to resist her husband's determination. She went.[48]

Nevertheless, unable to bear her grief, she finally told her story to her father and mother. Mrs. Hogarth and her youngest daughter Helen flatly refused to believe Dickens's denials. They had long realized and resented his dislike of them; their own bitterness was no less sharp for the favors they had accepted at his hands. Mrs. Hogarth, a far stronger character than her husband, dominated the family discussions. She brought matters to an unexpected climax. Catherine must leave Dickens at once, she insisted, and demand a separate maintenance. Catherine, reinforced in her original unhappy suspicions, wept and yielded.

Georgina, however, took Dickens's side. Her devotion to Dickens was as great as his admiration for her; a half dozen years earlier she had refused a proposal of marriage from Augustus Egg, and although Dickens had thought it would have been a good match for her he felt obliged to admit to himself that she was mentally far the artist's superior; "but five out of six men would be," he added, "for she has one of the most remarkable capacities I have ever known. Not to mention her being one of the most amiable and affectionate of girls." [48a] Georgina's declaration of loyalty to Dickens infuriated her family; their position would be much weakened if the sister who had been a constant member of the household for the past sixteen years supported him before the world. But Georgina refused to be moved. When Catherine left Tavistock House, Georgina remained behind.

This unforeseen and unconventional decision snarled the situation into an even worse tangle. If Georgina had left the house but sought shelter elsewhere than with her parents, that might have forestalled criticism of her conduct and still showed that she believed in Dickens's innocence. But where in nineteenth-century England, except with her family, could a thirty-year-old spinster go, and how would she live? Georgina had been trained to do nothing that would earn a livelihood; the Hogarths themselves had allowed her to become a dependent in Dickens's household. How could she abandon the man for whom she felt admiration and devotion, and join his accusers? It is possible that she had been in love with Dickens herself—in later years she betrayed much bitterness against Catherine—but no imputations against her conduct had been made before the separation crisis. Now, however, if there were some who were convinced by her remaining in Tavistock Square that the accusations against Dickens were groundless, there were others who spread rumors even more scandalous.

Meanwhile, however, Dickens had himself temporarily left Tavistock House and taken up quarters in the *Household Words* office, leaving Mrs. Hogarth to do what she could to get Catherine "away to some happier mode of existence if possible. They all know," he told Miss Coutts, "that I will do anything for her Comfort, and spend anything upon her. . . . I think," he added sorrowfully, "she has always felt herself to be at the disadvantage of groping blindly about me, and never touching me, and so has fallen into the most miserable weaknesses and jealousies."

But as he looked on their situation now, it seemed to him that there was no way in which Catherine could be happy with anyone. "I know that the mother herself could not live with her. I am perfectly sure that her younger sister and brother could not live with her. An old servant of ours is the only hope I see, as she took care of her, like a poor child, for sixteen years. But she is married now, and I doubt her being afraid that the companionship would wear her to death." [48b] At last, forlornly, Catherine took her departure.

For some time, though, only a few people knew his wife had left his house. And Dickens made desperate endeavors to bring about some compromise short of a public separation. His marriage was an unhappy failure and could never be anything else, but surely they could maintain appearances. Dickens professed no Bohemian indifference to the judgment of society and feared its censures might gravely impair his earning powers. It was true that his friend Bulwer Lytton had survived the breakdown of his own marriage and retained his position as a novelist. Dickens was known, however, for his celebration of the happy home and the domestic virtues; his literary popularity might well suffer. If readers ceased to buy his books, stayed away from his readings, what would happen to his children? He was devoted to them, and all except the two eldest boys were still entirely dependent upon him. Their father's good name was the very foundation of their present welfare and their future prospects.

Dickens therefore asked Forster to try to work out some arrangement that might avoid these dangers. But Catherine distrusted Forster as a partisan. She had long felt that he shared and abetted her husband's contemptuous attitude toward her. She consequently requested that stout, tender-hearted Mark Lemon be brought in to represent her interests. Various suggestions were proposed. One was that Catherine have her own rooms, apart from Dickens's, but still appear as his hostess on social occasions. Another was that she stay at Gad's Hill when he was at Tavistock House, and vice versa. Both these proposals Catherine declined. Although the thought of altogether breaking up her home distressed her terribly, if Charles felt like that about her it would be better for her to go away or to die. Always inclined to low spirits, she now passed days in weeping. But, strengthened by the Hogarths, she held to a complete separation.[49]

Slowly the details were worked out. On May 14th Lemon wrote Forster in Catherine's behalf, accepting the proposed settlement.[50] Catherine was to live in a house of her own and receive £600 a year. Charley, the eldest son, would go with her and the other children remain with their father, although they might visit her and she them at any time.[51] Charley was deeply disturbed when Dickens asked him to decide if he would live with his mother, although he concluded that it would be his duty. "Don't suppose," he told his father, "that in making my choice, I was actuated by any preference for my mother to you. God knows I love you dearly, and it will be a hard day for me when I have to part from you and the girls." [52] Walter was in India, the next three boys mostly at school, only Harry and Plorn would still be at home with Mamey and Katey and under the care of their Aunt Georgy. Nine and six years old respectively, they were bewildered and confused by the unhappy turmoil of their home, but hardly understood what was going on.

* * * * *

Suddenly all these arrangements were shattered. Dickens learned that Mrs. Hogarth and Helen Hogarth were circulating the story that Ellen Ternan was his mistress. The news turned him into a maniac of indignant fury. He had assured Catherine that he had not been unfaithful to her. For these two members of a family upon whom he had heaped favors to be seeking to destroy his good name, to endanger the welfare of his children, was the blackest depth of falsehood and ingratitude. Fiercely Dickens refused to make any agreement, any settlement whatsoever. They must retract their wicked accusations, formally and in writing, for themselves and for Catherine, or he would do nothing, pay not a penny. Let them try to ruin him. He would defy them.

The Hogarths did not believe him. They refused to put their names to the document he demanded that they sign and he refused to give way an inch. As in the old days of his struggle with Bentley, he was determined that no court in Christendom should make him yield. His home was in a turmoil with the hysteria of his anger. "My father," Katey said later, "was like a madman . . . ." [53] Catherine asked Miss Coutts to serve as an intermediary between them; a sad little note makes it seem likely that she even hoped for a reconciliation.[53a] Miss Coutts tried, but Dickens rejected her endeavors. "I think I know what you want me for," he wrote. "How I value your friendship and how I love and honor you, you know in part, though you never can fully know. But nothing on earth—no, not even you—no consideration, human or Divine, can move me from the resolution I have taken.

"And one other thing I must ask you to forgive me. If you have seen Mrs. Dickens in company with her wicked mother, I can not enter—no, not even with you—upon any question that was discussed in that woman's presence." [54]

It was clear that Dickens could not be moved. "Many many thanks," Catherine wrote Miss Coutts, "for your kindness in doing what I asked. I have now—God help me—only *one* course to pursue. One day though not now I may be able to tell you how hardly I have been beset." [54a]

For almost two weeks the Hogarths held out. Dickens, however, was still more obdurate. Finally Mrs. Hogarth and Helen gave way before his ultimatum and on May 29th signed the retraction he was bent on extorting from them: "It having been stated to us that in reference to the differences which have resulted in the separation of Mr. and Mrs. Charles Dickens, certain statements have been circulated that such differences are occasioned by circumstances deeply affecting the moral character of Mr. Dickens and compromising the reputation and good name of others, we solemnly declare that we now disbelieve such statements. We know that they are not believed by Mrs. Dickens, and we pledge ourselves on all occasions to contradict them, as entirely destitute of foundation." [55]

Meanwhile all clubland and literary London had been humming with rumor. Going into the Garrick Club, Thackeray was told that the separation was caused by a love affair between Dickens and Georgina. "No such thing," said he with his usual clumsiness; "it's with an actress." His intention was only to scotch the more scandalous story, but the remark came back to Dickens, who wrote him furiously denying all charges against Ellen Ternan and against himself. "We shall never be allowed to be friends," Thackeray said sadly, "that's clear." As he thought of poor Catherine, though, his heart swelled with pity. "To think of the poor matron after 22 years of marriage going away out of her house!" [56]

Dickens, however, in his indignation, had no sympathy to spare for Catherine. "As to Mrs. Dickens's 'simplicity' in speaking of me and my doings, O my dear Miss Coutts," he wrote, "do I not know that the weak hand that could never help or serve my name in the least, has struck at it—in conjunction with the wickedest people, whom I have loaded with benefits!" [57] To his seething imagination it seemed that the whole world must be clamoring with the hideous story. Filled with this delusion, he rushed into more feverish action. He would send out a public statement explaining the truth, and this would set the minds of his admirers at rest and silence the tongue of scandal. Forster advised against it, Lemon advised against it, even young Edmund Yates, to whom Dickens chanced to show the statement in proof, earnestly added his voice.[58] But Dickens was set on his own course. The utmost he would concede was that he would consult John Delane, the editor of the London *Times*, and abide by his opinion.[59]

Forster himself advised with Delane for an hour and a half.[60] Unhappily, Delane was for publication. Thereupon Dickens took the maddest step he had yet made in his unhappy and hysterical state. In a brief note to Catherine, "I will not write a word," he said, "as to any *causes* that have made it necessary for me to publish the enclosed in Household Words." He felt, however, that she ought to see it and say that she had no objection to it. "Whoever there may be among the living, whom I will never forgive alive or dead, I earnestly hope that all unkindness is over between you and me." [61] Catherine docilely agreed to the statement's publication, and under the heading PER-

SONAL the statement appeared on the front page of *Household Words* for June 12, 1858.

"Some domestic trouble of mine, of long-standing," Dickens told the public, had "lately been brought to an arrangement" involving "no anger or ill-will," and all the details of which were known to his children. "By some means, arising out of wickedness, or out of folly, or out of inconceivable wild chance, or out of all three, this trouble has been made the occasion of misrepresentations, most grossly false, most monstrous, and most cruel—involving, not only me, but innocent persons dear to my heart . . . I most solemnly declare, then—and this I do both in my own name and in my wife's name—that all the lately whispered rumours touching the trouble at which I have glanced, are abominably false. And that whosoever repeats one of them after this denial, will lie as wilfully and as foully as it is possible for any false witness to lie, before Heaven and earth." [62]

This statement he not only published himself, but sent to the newspapers to be copied. He quarreled furiously with Mark Lemon and with Bradbury and Evans for feeling that it was not appropriate for inclusion in the pages of a comic magazine and for consequently refusing to print it in *Punch*. Newspapers did print it, often with unfavorable comments, and bewildered readers, who knew nothing of Dickens's domestic affairs, asked each other what it was about. His friends were embarrassed, although they loyally rallied to his defense, and wrote him notes of sympathy.[63] Dickens, growing constantly more rigid and unyielding throughout the furore, was determined to face it down.

But there remained a still worse ordeal. In his excitement, Dickens gave Arthur Smith, his manager, a much more explicit letter, to which he attached a copy of the Hogarths' retraction of their accusations. This he empowered Smith to show "to anyone who wishes to do me right, or to anyone who may have been misled into doing me wrong." [64] In an excess of zeal, Smith allowed a newspaperman to see it. Presently it appeared in the New York *Tribune*, from which later in the summer it was copied by English newspapers. "Nothing has, on many occasions, stood between us and a separation," Dickens said in this statement, "but Mrs. Dickens's sister, Georgina Hogarth. From the age of fifteen, she has devoted herself to our home and our children. . . . In the manly consideration toward Mrs. Dickens which I owe to my wife, I will merely remark of her that some peculiarity of her character has thrown all the children on someone else. I do not know—I cannot by any stretch of fancy imagine—what would have become of them but for this aunt, who has grown up with them, to whom they are devoted, and who has sacrificed the best part of her youth and life to them.

"She has remonstrated, reasoned, suffered, and toiled, again and again, to prevent a separation between Mrs. Dickens and me. Mrs. Dickens has often expressed to her her sense of her affectionate care and devotion in her home—never more strongly than within the last twelve months.

"For some years past Mrs. Dickens has been in the habit of representing to me that it would be better for her to go away and live apart; that her always increasing estrangement made a mental disorder under which she sometimes labours—more, that she felt herself unfit for the life she had to lead as my wife and that she would be better away. . . .

"Two wicked persons who should have spoken very differently of me, in consideration of earned respect and gratitude, have (as I am told, and indeed to my personal knowledge) coupled with this separation the name of a young lady for whom I have a great attachment and regard. I will not repeat her name—I honour it too much. Upon my soul and honour, there is not on this earth a more virtuous and spotless creature than this young lady. I know her to be as innocent and pure, and as good as my own dear daughters. Further, I am quite sure that Mrs. Dickens, having received this assurance from me, must now believe it, in the respect I know her to have for me, and in the perfect confidence I know her, in her better moments, to repose in my truthfulness." [65]

The publication of this statement provoked even more severe comment in the press than its predecessor had. *John Bull* noted dryly, "Qui s'excuse, s'accuse," and said Dickens had "committed a grave mistake in telling his readers how little, after all, he thinks of the marriage tie." The Liverpool *Mercury* struck a still sharper note: "This favourite of the public informs some hundreds of thousands of readers that the wife whom he has vowed to love and cherish has utterly failed to discharge the duties of a mother; and he further hints that her mind is disordered. . . . If this is 'manly consideration,' we should like to be favoured with a definition of unmanly selfishness and heart-lessness." [66]

On the assumption, which it was natural for the newspapers to make, that Dickens had authorized the publication of this statement no less than of the one he had sent out to the press himself, the rebuke was well merited; and, indeed, considering the vagueness of the instructions Dickens had given Smith, it is difficult to see how he could have expected that the letter would not sooner or later get into print. But Dickens always referred to it as the "violated letter," and was much upset at its publication.[67] To Catherine, through her solicitor, he sent assurances that he was "exceedingly pained" that this "private and personal communication" had reached the newspapers; he wished her to know "that I am no consenting party to this publication; that it cannot possibly be more offensive to any one than it is to me; and that it has shocked and distressed me very much." [68]

With horrible and needless publicity, Dickens had at last become freed from his wife. Through all the cruel pillorying she suffered she had remained meekly silent. But Dickens too had undergone bitter emotional turmoil and dreadful abrasions of the spirit.

If, deep within him, he had longed to be rid of Catherine, he had considered it hopeless, and had not wanted an open break nor willed any of the circumstances that had been forced upon him with this separation. It had come only through the public separation he had sought to avoid and amid a noise of slander that his very efforts to silence had made even more clamorous. He had not been able to control either the course of events or their outcome.

Nor, though he could not admit it even in his own heart, had his own behavior been altogether stainless. He had seized with ruthless intensity upon the advantage the venom of the Hogarths gave him. He had been far from chivalrous to poor Kate—much less generous than she in her uncomplaining silence had been to him. No sooner had her family assailed his good name than he hastened to proclaim her deficiencies in ways that were bound to be published to all the world. And although he had not precipitated the final breach, secretly he knew he was not without reproach in the events of the months that led up to it, technically innocent though he might be of the Hogarth's accusations.

He felt that he had been hideously wronged at the hands of those from whom he might justly have expected gratitude. Contending with his indignation, however, and suppressed by it, was a dark frustration and an unavowed sense of guilt. During the entire struggle he was half deranged with hysteria and anguish. "Nothing," said Katey, "could surpass the misery and unhappiness of our home." [69] But Catherine was gone now, and Dickens could take his way through life unimpeded by having to drag her in his wake. It remained to be seen how happy he would be.

PART NINE

The Last Assay

1858–1865

CHAPTER ONE

"The Track of a Storm"

O N A Thursday evening in the middle of June, Dickens stepped out onto the brightly lighted platform of St. Martin's Hall. It was his first reading after the publication of his "personal" statement in *Household Words*; London was buzzing with scandal. His friends were worried lest he be greeted by an outburst of indignation. His manager, Arthur Smith, a timidly nervous man, was tremulous with fears of his being hooted from the stage. Dickens kept his own counsel and maintained a demeanor of absolute calm. Walking rather stiffly, right shoulder aggressively forward, flower in buttonhole and gloves in hand, he strode across the stage and confronted the audience.

The applause that roared through the hall, swelling again and again, might have been heard half a mile away at Charing Cross. His devoted admirers had not deserted him; their cheers were a tumultuous testimony of loyalty and support. Dickens showed no emotion. Taking his place at his reading desk, he opened his book and began with as much composure as if he were in his own study.[1] Throughout the remaining six weeks of his London season there were enthusiastic crowds at every reading.

But he was keeping an iron restraint upon himself. Wild rumor linked his name infamously with Georgina's, with Ellen's, with those of various other actresses. The storm raging through his heart left it "jagged and rent and out of shape" under the sense of wrong and strain.[2] In his bitterness he broke off relations with everyone he associated with the Hogarth accusations. Although Mark Lemon withdrew from representing Catherine when these charges became a part of the negotiations, and declined to forward any communications dealing with them, Dickens could not forgive the refusal to insert his statement in *Punch*.[3] Forgetting the faithful heart that had comforted him all night beside his baby daughter's body, he angrily read the decision as the treacherous act of a false friend denying him a means of self-defense.

There is no telling whether it occurred to Dickens that Bradbury and Evans rather than Lemon might have been responsible for the *Punch* veto, but he was vehement in his resentment of them as well. He was so strongly convinced that Evans above all was aligned with his detractors that he forbade his family even to remain in the same company with the publisher. "I have had stern occasion to impress upon my children," he wrote Evans, "that their father's name is their best possession and that it would indeed be trifled with and wasted by him, if either through himself or through them, he held any terms with those who have been false to it, in the only great need and under the only great wrong it has ever known. You know very well, why (with hard distress of mind and bitter disappointment), I have been forced to include you in this class." [4]

With Thackeray too the separation troubles were partly to blame for bringing about an enduring breach. The two men had never really been congenial, and several times their relationship had been strained. The difference that now developed between them brought out all that each most disliked in the other. Its immediate cause, however, lay not in Dickens's marital discords or even in Thackeray's luckless remark about his having a liaison with an actress, but in an article written by Edmund Yates.

For some time the young son of Dickens's old friend Frederick Yates had been supplementing his income as a Post Office employee by literary journalism, and had recently taken a place on the staff of a little weekly called *Town Talk*. Coming into the office one warm June evening to make up the paper, Yates discovered that one of the contributors was ill and had not sent in his copy. Stripping off his coat, Yates mounted a stool and cudgeled his brains for something to fill in the gap. Only the previous week he had written a brief pen-portrait of Dickens and his readings; the best he could think of on the spur of the moment was a gossipy column about Thackeray's manner, appearance, and character. Dashing this off hastily, he rushed it to the printer and forgot all about it.[5]

But Thackeray, always more sensitive than he thought it reasonable

for others to be, no sooner saw this article than he fell into a violent
fury about it. There was, indeed, cause for offense in Yates's hurried
improvisation, although Thackeray, who lampooned his friends and
acquaintances in print, could hardly express resentment without con-
demning his own practice. "No one meeting him," Yates had written,
"could fail to recognize in him a gentleman; his bearing is cold and
uninviting, his style of conversation either openly cynical, or affectedly
good-natured and benevolent; his *bonhomie* is forced, his wit biting,
his pride easily touched . . . No one succeeds better than Mr.
THACKERAY in cutting his coat according to his cloth: here he
flattered the aristocracy, but when he crossed the Atlantic, GEORGE
WASHINGTON became the idol of his worship, the 'Four Georges'
the objects of his bitterest attacks. . . . Our own opinion is that his success is on the wane . . . there is a want of heart in all he writes, which
is not to be balanced by the most brilliant sarcasm and the most perfect knowledge of the workings of the human heart." [6]

Some of these remarks were silly, some of them were false, and all
of them were wounding to Thackeray's pride. The savage portraits
of the Crawley family and the Marquis of Steyne in *Vanity Fair* did
not flatter the aristocracy, and Thackeray's lectures on the four
Georges had been delivered in both England and America. Tenderly
affectionate with his friends, he was often in scrapes through a sense
of humor that, without meaning any more harm than an awkward
puppy, managed to sound rude and cutting. To his already shaky
friend Forster, who was born the day after April Fool's, the same day
of the year as that on which Dickens was married, Thackeray wrote,
"I wish you many happy returns of your birthday, Dickens of his mar-
riage-day, & both of you of the day previous." [7] Beneath these gauch-
eries Thackeray was really a shy sentimentalist who disguised his diffi-
dence as hauteur and his soft-heartedness as cynicism. His pride and
his modesty combined to make him assume the uneasy tone of de-
preciating both "society" and art and behaving as if he thought more
of being a gentleman than of being a genius.

One other aspect of Yates's strictures stabbed a tender nerve in
Thackeray. Despite the humiliating inferiority of his sales to those
of Dickens, he knew that there were many people who regarded him
as a better writer, and he had never ceased to be wonderingly and
humbly grateful for his own success. But he was also conscious of the

fact that he was beginning to repeat himself and feared that his creative vein was running dry.[8] He felt hardly less wounded in these secret doubts by the suggestion that his popularity was on the wane than he did in his self-esteem by the imputations against his integrity. In his anger he wrote Yates a letter of stinging rebuke:

"As I understand your phrases, you impute insincerity to me when I speak good-naturedly in private; assign dishonourable motives to me for sentiments which I have delivered in public, and charge me with advancing statements which I have never delivered at all. . . . We meet at a club, where, before you were born I believe, I and other gentlemen have been in the habit of talking without any idea that our conversation would supply paragraphs for professional vendors of 'Literary Talk;' and I don't remember that out of that Club I have ever exchanged six words with you. Allow me to inform you that the talk which you have heard there is not intended for newspaper remark; and to beg—as I have a right to do—that you will refrain from printing comments on my private conversations; that you will forego discussions, however blundering, upon my private affairs; and that you will henceforth please to consider any question of my personal truth and sincerity as quite out of the province of your criticism." [9]

Infuriated in turn by this castigation, Yates drafted an insolent reply, pointing out how often Thackeray had caricatured their fellow members in the Garrick Club in his writings: Captain Shindy, for example, in the *Book of Snobs*, and Foker, in *Pendennis*, who were recognizable parodies of the phrases, gestures, and appearance of well-known members. In *Punch's Prize Novelists*, moreover, Thackeray had ridiculed Ainsworth, Disraeli, Lever, and Bulwer Lytton in a way holding them up to contempt; his pursuit of Lytton, indeed, "Mistaw Edwad Lyttn Bulwig," had verged upon persecution. This sharp *tu quoque*, Yates thought, would make Thackeray draw in his horns.[10]

Before sending it, however, Yates sought the advice of Dickens, in whose behalf he had just published a warm defense against the storm of slander raised by his domestic upheaval. Dickens was in a state of emotional agitation, he was grateful for Yates's support, he had not forgotten Thackeray's blundering reference to the rumors about himself and Ellen Ternan. Had Dickens been under less strain he might have told Yates to apologize at once. As it was, he said the sketch was indefensible and the reply too violent and flippant, but he agreed that Thackeray's tone made an apology impossible. After some further consultation, Yates sent an answer concluding, "If your letter to me were not both 'slanderous and untrue,' I should readily have discussed its subject with you, and avowed my earnest and frank desire to set right anything I have left wrong. Your letter being what it is, I have nothing to add to my present reply." [11]

Thackeray promptly appealed "to the Committee of the Garrick Club to decide whether the complaints I have against Mr. Yates are not well founded, and whether the practice of publishing such articles . . . will not be fatal to the comfort of the Club, and is not intolerable in a society of gentlemen." [12] The Committee notified Yates that they would consider the complaint at a special meeting. Yates, surprised, replied that he felt they had no jurisdiction: his article did not mention the Club and referred to no conversation that had taken place there. It might be in bad taste and unintentionally incorrect in its details, but the Committee was "not a Committee of taste." [13]

Dickens told the Committee they had nothing to do with a private quarrel between two members, but the Committee did not agree and ordered Yates "to make an ample apology to Mr. Thackeray, or to retire from the Club." [14] Dickens thereupon resigned from the Committee, writing them that "I cannot take upon myself the very difficult and unsatisfactory functions which you understand to attach to your Body, but which I believe that Body has no right to assume." [15] Yates refused to withdraw from the Club and appealed to a General Meeting of its members. Meanwhile, in the ninth number of *The Virginians*, which had just made its appearance, Thackeray alluded to Yates as "young Grubstreet, who corresponds with three penny papers and describes the persons and conversation of gentlemen whom he meets at his 'clubs.' " [16] Not long afterward, he returned to the attack with some sneering remarks about "Tom Garbage," "an esteemed contributor to the *Kennel Miscellany*." [17]

Dickens voiced his feelings about Thackeray's course by summarizing this stage of the controversy: "Committee thereupon call a General Meeting, yet pending. Thackeray *thereupon*, by way of showing what an ill thing it is for writers to attack one another in print, denounces E. Y. (in Virginians) as 'Young Grub Street.' Frightful mess, muddle, complication, and botheration ensue. Which witch's broth is now in full boil." [18] "Like Fox," he told another correspondent, "I should 'boil with indignation' if I had not found a vent. But I have. Upon my soul, when I picture them in that back-yard, conceiving that they shake the earth, I fall into fits of laughter which make my daughters laugh—away at Gad's Hill—until the tears run down their cheeks." [19]

Neither Thackeray nor Yates attended the General Meeting on July 10th. A letter from Yates was read, offering to apologize to the Club, but not to Thackeray. Dickens supported Yates, saying he had been on good terms with Thackeray many years and was sorry to be opposed to him. The Meeting sustained the Committee by a vote of seventy to forty-six, giving Yates a period of grace in which to apologize to Thackeray or be expelled from the Club.[20] On his refusal to yield, his name was erased from the list of members: "Y's conduct," wrote a friend of Thackeray's, "has been very un-Y's." [21] Following Dickens's advice, Yates took Counsel's opinion on the legality of his expulsion and was told that if he were forcibly refused admission to the Club he could bring suit. He consequently made a formal attempt, in the presence of witnesses, to enter its premises, and had himself ejected by the Secretary.[22] These moves in the wrangle had protracted themselves throughout the whole summer and fall, during which time Dickens had been away on his provincial reading tour. On November 24th Dickens appealed to Thackeray for a peaceful settlement.

"Coming home from my country work," he wrote, "I find Mr. Edwin James's opinion taken on this painful question of the Garrick Club and Mr. Edmund Yates. I find it strong on the illegality of the Garrick proceeding." Could there not be a conference, he asked, "between me, as representing Mr. Yates, and an appointed friend of yours, as representing you, with the hope and purpose of some quiet accommodation of this deplorable matter, which will satisfy the feelings of all concerned?" Yates had consulted him from the first, he admitted, and he had told him the article in *Town Talk* could not be defended but confirmed his feelings that the strong language of Thackeray's letter made an apology impossible. He would be glad to mediate between them, Dickens concluded—"and God knows in no hostile spirit towards any one, least of all to you. If it cannot take place, the thing is at least no worse than it was; and you will burn this letter, and I will burn your answer." [23]

But Thackeray bitterly read Dickens's words as a confession that he had been a secert enemy guiding all Yates's moves. "I grieve to gather from your letter that you were Mr. Yates's adviser in the dispute between him and me. His letter was the cause of my appeal to the Garrick Club from insults against which I had no other remedy." Thackeray did not believe that the Club would be frightened by the opinion of any lawyer, and since he had submitted the case to the Club it was out of his hands. "Yours, &c., W. M. Thackeray." [24] Forster had a burst of rage when Dickens showed him this letter. "He be damned with his 'Yours, &c.' " [24a]

Thackeray was annoyed to hear from a youthful acquaintance that even his admirers blamed him for forgetting his dignity over "a few saucy words, and . . . condescending to quarrel with so young and unimportant a person as Mr. Yates." "You may not think, young 'un," he exclaimed, "that I am quarrelling with Mr. Yates. *I am hitting the man behind him.*" [25] But to the Committee of the Garrick Club he addressed a letter quoting Dickens's offer and saying that if they could devise any peaceful means of ending the affair no one would be better pleased than he.[26] The Committee, however, were in no mood for compromise, and after some further legal skirmishing Yates learned that he could pursue the matter only by bringing a Chancery suit that would cost him £200 to £300 if he lost. This risk he could not afford and gloomily gave up any further proceedings.[27]

The affair ended any semblance of cordiality between the two novelists. Thackeray imagined Dickens jealous of him as a dangerous rival. Dickens blamed Thackeray for an undignified stooping to public resentment and for using his prestige to punish so cruelly a younger and weaker man. He was exasperated too by the violation of his confidence in quoting to the Committee any part of a letter that he had suggested should be burned if Thackeray refused his offer of mediation. All visiting ceased between Dickens and Thackeray, although their daughters continued to be friends. Some two years later, in May, 1861, Thackeray was in the stalls at Drury Lane when Dickens entered the next stalls with Wilkie Collins. "Dickens & I shook hands," Thackeray wrote, "and didn't say one single word to each other. And if he read my feelings on my face as such a clever fellow would he knows now that I have found him out." [28] Not until a few weeks before Thackeray's death in 1863 did he and Dickens ever speak to each other again.

* * * * *

The country reading tour from which Dickens had returned in mid-November had been as spectacularly triumphant as his London readings. Everywhere, in England, Ireland, and Scotland, he was greeted with tumultuous applause. Standing calmly behind his desk, glancing keenly over the audience, Dickens always waited until the last latecomer had been seated and quiet settled over the house. He was in no hurry; he waited for absolute hush. Then the amazing performance began. It was more than a reading; it was an extraordinary exhibition of acting that seized upon its auditors with a mesmeric possession. Like Ruth Draper, but without moving from the center of the stage, without a single prop or bit of costume, by changes of voice, by gesture, by vocal and facial expression, Dickens peopled his stage with a throng of characters.

He had countless voices and countless faces. His Scrooge was harsh and grating, his Mrs. Gamp snuffy, husky, and unctuous with the oozing corpulence of a fat old woman, his Paul Dombey the weary alto of a tired child, his Justice Stareleigh a series of sudden snorts and convulsive starts, his Bob Cratchit a frightened gasp in the thinnest and meekest of tones. He could be a stout old gentleman with a yawn in his very voice, a cockney medical student, a country yokel, an overbearing London alderman, the Boots at a rural inn, the plump sister at the Christmas party crying out, "It's your uncle Scro-o-o-o-oge!" His face could flash from the pinched, avaricious countenance of Scrooge to the jolly features of a schoolboy, from the imbecile pomposity of the little Judge to the browbeaten and bewildered Mr. Winkle. Simply by drumming on his desk top he suggested all the dash and gaiety of Mr. Fezziwig's ball, and by a licking of the lips and a humbly placatory bob Trotty Veck's relish of tripe and his respect for Alderman Cute. Spectators noted how monstrous he looked as Squeers, how murderous as Jonas Chuzzlewit, and in their enthusiasm even insisted that in the scene between Fanny Squeers and Nicholas one side of his face looked like Fanny and the other like Nicholas.[29]

When Dickens had first read the *Christmas Carol* for charity, it had taken him three hours. Gradually he had subjected it to increasingly drastic cuts until it could be performed in two hours. Descriptive passages he ruthlessly pruned or entirely omitted, conveying the appearance and manner of his characters by sheer histrionic brilliance. He speeded up the narrative, tightened the dialogue and made it more sharply typical of each speaker. In his reading copy, whole areas of text were blocked out in a wash of red ink and changed wordings written between the lines or bulging out in encircling balloons. In the margins there were stage directions to himself in blue, such as "Snap your fingers," "Rising action," "Scrooge melted," and "Soften very much." [30]

He prepared similar reading versions of *The Chimes*, *The Cricket on the Hearth*, "The Story of Little Dombey," and a group consisting of "Mrs. Gamp," "The Poor Travellers," and "The Boots at the Holly Tree," the last two of which were shorter Christmas stories from *Household Words*. A little later he added the "Trial Scene" from *Pickwick* and "Bob Sawyer's Party." All these he practiced hundreds of times in his study, striving for perfection in the intonation of every word, achieving absolute mastery over every episode. The time came when he knew each reading by heart, keeping the book before him only for safety, allowing himself impromptu variations, "gagging" on sudden inspiration, magnetizing his hearers to follow him at will.

His first provincial reading was at Clifton on August 2nd. In the large room there "the people were perfectly taken off their legs by The Chimes," and "burst into a storm of applause." [31] The following night, at Exeter, "was a prodigious cram"; then, during the same week, came Plymouth, and Clifton again. In spite of the fact that the Plymouth room was at "the top of a windy and muddy hill leading (literally) to nowhere" and looked like the Ark "after the subsidence of the Deluge," all the local notables were there and one hundred and thirty stalls were sold. [32] "The Boots" on the second night "was a shout all through." [33] Arthur Smith was kept as busy with correspondence as a Secretary of State and was forever dragging forms about, with his coat off, like a furniture dealer. [34] On the closing night at Clifton, "a torrent of five hundred shillings bore Arthur away, pounded him against the wall, flowed on to the seats over his body, scratched him, and damaged his best dress suit. All to his unspeakable joy." [35] The week's receipts were nearly £400. [36]

From Worcester the following week, Dickens wrote to Wilkie Col-

lins of the fatigues of this roving life. "But perhaps it is best for me
. . . to wear and toss my storm away—or as much of it as will ever calm
down while the water rolls—in this restless manner." "As to that furtive and Don Giovanni purpose at which you hint, that may be all very
well for *your* violent vigour, or that of the companions with whom
you have travelled continentally, or the Caliph Haroun Alraschid
with whom you have unbent metropolitanly; but anchorites who read
themselves red hot every night are as chaste as Diana (If I suppose *she*
was by the bye, but I find I don't quite believe it when I write her
name.)" [37]

At Liverpool on one of the three nights of the readings there were
twenty-three hundred people in the audience and receipts of two hundred guineas. "Arthur bathed in checks, took headers into tickets,
floated on billows of passes, dived under weirs of shillings, floated
home, faint with gold and silver." [38] From there, Dickens crossed
over to Ireland, where he read at Dublin, Belfast, Cork, and Limerick.
The Irish audiences were highly excited, and of the quickness of their
response to humor Dickens had no question, but he did not feel at
first that they were as sensitive to pathos. "Generally, I am happy to
report," Dickens wrote Georgina, "the Emerald press is in favour of
my appearance, and likes my eyes. But one gentleman comes out with
a letter at Cork, wherein he says that although only forty-six I look
like an old man. *He* is a rum customer, I think." After his first night's
reading in Dublin, Dickens found the Boots of his hotel waiting for
him at the door. " 'Whaa't sart of a hoose, sur?' he asked me. 'Capital.' 'The Lard be praised fur the 'onor o' Dooblin!' " [39]

For his third night's reading there was such a crowd that Dickens
had trouble forcing his way through the lobby and passages. "They
had broken all the glass in the pay-boxes. Our men were flattened
against walls and squeezed against beams. Ladies stood all night with
their chins against my platform. Other ladies sat all night upon my
steps. And the reading went tremendously." [40] Dickens soon revised
his idea that the Irish were not responsive to pathos. "I have never
seen *men* go in to cry so undisguisedly as they did at that reading
yesterday afternoon. They made no attempt whatever to hide it, and
certainly cried more than the women. As to the Boots at night, and
Mrs. Gamp too, it was just one roar with me and them, for they made
me laugh so that sometimes I *could not* compose my face to go on." [41]

Everywhere he was received with a warmth of personal affection almost overwhelming. People stopped him on the street, saying, "Do me the honour to shake hands, Misther Dickens, and God bless you, sir; not ounly for the light you've been to me this night, but for the light you've been in mee house, sir (and God love your face!) this many a year." Every night ladies begged John, his personal servant, for the flower from his coat. One morning, when the petals from his geranium showered on the platform while he was reading "Little Dombey," the women swarmed up on the platform after he was gone, and picked *them* up as keepsakes.[42]

These blossoms for his buttonhole Dickens found himself receiving everywhere he traveled, by order of Mary Boyle. "Dearest Meery," he wrote her, "First let me tell you that all the magicians and spirits in your employ have fulfilled the instructions of their wondrous mistress, to admiration. Flowers have fallen in my path wherever I have trod; and when they rained upon me at Cork I was more amazed than you ever saw me. . . . Touching that other matter on which you write me tenderly and with a delicacy of regard and interest that I deeply feel, I hope I may report that I am calming down again. I have been exquisitely distressed. It is no comfort to me to know that any man who wants to sell anything in print, has but to anatomize my finest nerves, and he is sure to do it—It is no comfort to me to know (as of course those dissectors do), that when I spoke in my own person it was not for myself but for the innocent and good, on whom I had unwittingly brought the foulest lies—Sometimes I *cannot* bear it. I had one of these fits yesterday, and was utterly desolate and lost. But it is gone, thank God, and the sky has brightened before me once more." [43]

During all this time Ellen Ternan was living in London at the family lodgings, 31 Berners Street, Oxford Street, with her sister Maria. Dickens had taken all the Ternans under his protection. The eldest sister, Frances Eleanor, he told Wills, he had sent to Italy with her mother to complete her musical education.[44] There, a number of years later, she became the second wife of Thomas Adolphus Trollope. Dickens also tried to advance the theatrical career of Maria. "She is accomplished and attractive," he wrote Benjamin Webster, "well used to the stage, sings prettily, and is favorably known to London audiences." [45] "I have a great friendship for her and know her to be one of the best and bravest of little spirits and most virtuous of girls," he told Yates, ". . . and believe her to have more aptitude in a minute than all the other people of her standing on the stage in a month." [46]

Returning to London for a week-end in October, Dickens angrily learned that the two sisters, living alone, had been subjected to indecent persecution from a policeman. Wills must go at once to Scotland Yard and demand an investigation of such "Dangerous and unwarrantable conduct" and insist on learning "what the Devil the mystery means." "Maria is a good deal looked after. And my suspicion is, that the Policeman in question has been suborned to find out all about their domesticity by some 'Swell.' If so, there can be no doubt that the man ought to be dismissed." The young ladies were "in all things most irreproachable," Dickens said indignantly; if the facts were published in the *Times*, "there would be a most prodigious public uproar." [47] The outcome of the episode is unknown, but the personal and protective outrage in Dickens's tone is unmistakable.

Meanwhile, his reading tour had moved on through the Midlands and the north of England—York, Scarborough, Hull, Leeds, Halifax, Sheffield, Durham, Sunderland. His reception everywhere continued to be an ovation. Arthur Smith rubbed his legs sore with a black bag bulging with silver. At Harrogate their landlord asked if he could obtain a little change in silver and Smith gave him £40 worth. At the reading there one man "found something so very ludicrous in Toots, that he *could not* compose himself at all, but laughed until he sat wiping his eyes with his handkerchief. And whenever he felt Toots coming again he began to laugh and wipe his eyes afresh, and when he came he gave a kind of cry, as if it were too much for him. It was uncommonly droll, and made me laugh heartily." [48]

At Newcastle-on-Tyne, Dickens was joined by Katey and Mamey, who went on with him into Scotland.[49] Edinburgh the readings took by storm: "The Chimes shook it; Little Dombey blew it up." [50] During the stay there, Dickens took the girls on a walk to see Hawthornden, the old castellated home of William Drummond, the poet and friend of Ben Jonson. It turned out that it was not a visitors' day and the custodians had never heard of Dickens, but after some persuasion the party was admitted. In the end Dickens gave the gatekeeper a tip so lavish that his parting salutation "could not have been more deferential had the author of *Pickwick* been the Lord of the Isles." [51]

The readings in Dundee, Aberdeen, Perth, and Glasgow were also a triumph. At the last of them people thundered and waved their hats in a way "that for the first time in all my public career," he said, "took me completely off my legs, and I saw the whole eighteen hundred of them reel on one side as if a shock from without had shaken the hall." [52] With the middle of October he was starting on the last part of his tour. Bradford, Manchester, Birmingham, Nottingham, Derby, Leamington, Wolverhampton, and Southampton were all crowded into a single month. He wound up in Brighton on November 13th.[53] In less than three and a half months he had given eighty-seven readings. After deducting all expenses he found that he had cleared over a thousand guineas a month.[54]

More than the money, though, was the comfort and reassurance of the loving faces and grateful words with which he was greeted everywhere. The separation from Catherine and the bitterness with which he was still assailed subjected him to almost unbearable anguish. The continuing newspaper castigations of his "violated" letter made him wince with a pain all the more severe because his conscience must have whispered that it was not entirely undeserved. For all these distresses the warmth of his audiences was a balm. "The manner in which the people have everywhere delighted to express that they have a personal affection for me," he wrote Miss Coutts, "and the interest of tender friends in me, is (especially at this time) high and far above all considerations. I consider it a remarkable instance of good fortune that it should have fallen out that I should, in this autumn of all others, have come face to face with so many multitudes." [55]

These feelings must have been deepened if he knew of certain events in Scotland while he was winding up his tour in the south of England. One group of students at Glasgow had nominated Bulwer Lytton for Rector of the University and another group had nominated Lord Shaftesbury. This was a purely honorary post, bestowed by the vote of the student body, and usually given to some distinguished literary or political figure. A third group, during the last five days of the campaign, and without consulting him, nominated Dickens. The election took place amid a violence of derogatory broadsides and abusive doggerel ballads. Dickens, said the opposing students, was "a vulgar Cockney, with the heart and manners of a Snob," "the poor giggling writer of cricket carols and comic songs," "the itinerant showman, the cowardly calumniator, the cuckoo of his own merits!" He was roundly beaten, with Lytton getting 217 votes and Shaftesbury 204 to his 69.[56] Though "the youth of colleges" might, as Dickens wrote, "cheer me away at night," [57] there was as well a strong undercurrent of condemnation of his conduct.

*   *   *   *   *

During the Irish part of Dickens's journeyings, in Belfast, he had been astonished to receive a visit from his brother Frederick.[58] It had been more than a year and a half since Dickens had firmly refused to incur any further financial responsibilities for his undependable brother. "I have already done more for you," Dickens told him, "than most dispassionate persons would consider right or reasonable in itself. But, considered with any fair reference to the great expenses I have sustained for other relatives, it becomes little else than monstrous. The possibility of your having any further expenses from me is absolutely and finally past." [59] Thereupon Fred had managed to obtain money from both Wills and Henry Austin, failed to repay it, and then, unabashed, asked Dickens for a loan of £30. Dickens repeated his refusal of further aid:

"Firstly, because I cannot trust you, and because your bad faith with Wills and Austin makes the word 'lend' an absurdity.

"Secondly, because if this were otherwise it would do you no real good and would not in the least save you against the creditors who have already the power of taking you in execution." [60]

Now, however, at the sight of the wastrel for whom he had tried to do so much, Dickens's heart melted. "I was dreadfully hard with him at first," he wrote Georgina, "but relented." [61] The warmer relationship did not last long. Barely had Dickens ended his tour than he learned from his old friend Thompson, Fred's brother-in-law, that Fred was in deeper trouble. He had never got on with his wife's family, the marriage that the Wellers and Dickens had both opposed had turned out badly, Fred and Anna quarreled furiously, and Fred left her, bitterly refusing to make her any allowance.

At Thompson's request Dickens now saw Fred in London, but was able to make no impression on him. "He left me, declaring that I had made none; and I have not the faintest reason to suppose that he attached a feather's weight to anything I said." [62] In a later interview, however, Fred agreed to come to reasonable terms, whereupon Dick-

ens wrote Thompson suggesting that the family stay the legal proceedings they had begun.[63] Frederick then disappeared, and ignored
repeated letters from Dickens. When he was at last heard from, more
than a month later, in December, he withdrew his previous agreement.
"Judge," Dickens asked Thompson, "what it is possible to do, under
such circumstances." [64]

This was the end, at last, of Dickens's efforts to help Frederick in
any way. No record has been found of the outcome of his wrangle
with his wife and her family, and there are only scattered references
to him in Dickens's later correspondence. Once he turns up at Canterbury, characteristically demanding a free pass to one of Dickens's
readings for an acquaintance; [65] a few years later we find Dickens telling a friend, "I have written to Frederick, and earnestly hope he is
doing well." [66] Then Frederick is heard of no more until his death in
1868.

On Dickens's return to London from his tour, he took up the
threads of his quarrel with Bradbury and Evans. He had not ceased
to feel harshly about them and was determined to break off all relations. For the publication of his books he would go back to Chapman and Hall. Now a large and prosperous organization with offices
in Piccadilly, the firm was not too great to be delighted at the return
of the prize they had lost fifteen years earlier. William Hall was dead
and would no longer irritate Dickens by any troublesome shadowing
of the brow over doing exactly what Dickens had made up his mind
must be done. Edward Chapman was thinking of retirement, and his
cousin Frederic, now a partner, was a bluff, cheery businessman bent
on giving Dickens anything he wanted. The only thing Dickens
wanted was that his publishers should not cross any of his desires, and
that was the way it was henceforth to be.[67]

But Bradbury and Evans must be ousted from having any connection with the production of Household Words as well. They had always
printed the periodical, and Evans claimed that the other proprietors
had no control over its manufacture.[68] Dickens insisted that as the
largest proprietor he could change the printer and publisher at will.[69]
Evans tried in vain to make conciliatory advances; Dickens refused to
see him and ignored them.[70] He gave Forster a power of attorney to
act for him.[71] Forster rode over the unfortunate printers like a majestic
human steam-roller. It would be best for Bradbury and Evans, he told

them, to sell their share of *Household Words* to Dickens. When they refused to do this, Forster threatened that Dickens would destroy the value of the magazine by announcing that he was withdrawing from it and starting another of exactly the same kind. Wills, who was present, admired the forcefulness with which Forster conducted the interview, and Dickens repeated his praise to Forster. But that Lincolnian Mammoth had never forgiven Wills's failure to defer to him in the running of *Household Words*. "I am truly sorry, my dear Dickens," he rejoined crushingly, "that I cannot reciprocate your friend's compliment, for *a damneder ass I have never encountered in the whole course of my life*." [72]

No agreement with Bradbury and Evans proved possible, and Dickens promptly set about putting his threat into effect. He flabbergasted Forster by suggesting for the new magazine a title drawn from Shakespeare's *Henry VI: Household Harmony*. When Forster pointed out what derisive capital could be made out of the recent lack of harmony in his own household, Dickens was curtly irritable: "I could not invent a story of any sort, it is quite plain, incapable of being twisted into some such nonsensical shape." [73] But he knew Forster was right, and threw out a cluster of other ideas: *Once a Week, The Hearth, The Forge, The Crucible, The Anvil of the Time, Charles Dickens's Own, Seasonable Leaves, Evergreen Leaves, Home, Home Music, Change, Time and Tide, Twopence, English Bells, Weekly Bells, The Rocket, Good Humour*.[74]

None of these chimed, however, with his desire to use with his title a quotation from Shakespeare. A few days later he found one in *Othello*, which he slightly altered for his purpose: "I have just hit upon a name that I think really an admirable one—especially with the quotation *before* it, in the place where our present H. W. quotation stands.

"'The story of our lives, from year to year.'—*Shakespeare*.

"ALL THE YEAR ROUND.

"A weekly journal conducted by Charles Dickens." [75]

With his usual energy Dickens made all the business arrangements. "I have taken the new office; have got workmen in; have ordered the paper; settled with the printer; and am getting an immense system of advertising ready." [76] The new editorial headquarters were at 11 Wellington Street, only a few doors from those of *Household Words*. Dickens owned three-quarters of the venture and Wills the remaining quarter. Dickens was editor at a salary of £504 a year, and Wills subeditor and general manager at £420. If Wills retired, his share was to be reduced to one-eighth, and the good will of the name *All the Year Round* was Dickens's exclusive property.[77]

Bradbury and Evans brought suit to restrain Dickens from "injuring their joint property." [78] Dickens received the news with deadly and self-assured calm, Forster with an explosion of partisan rage. "The dear fellow was here yesterday morning," Dickens wrote, "smoking all over his head, and fuming himself like a steamboat ready to start." [79] But it was obvious that Dickens could not be forced to continue editing *Household Words* or prevented from starting another periodical. Nor could Bradbury and Evans, who owned only a one-quarter share in *Household Words*, appoint another editor without Dickens's consent. The Master of the Rolls, before whom the case was argued, therefore decided on March 26, 1859, that the magazine should be sold at auction.[80] Meanwhile, Dickens had confidently advertised that the last number of *Household Words* would be published on May 28th and that the first number of *All the Year Round* would apppear on April 30th. The two magazines thus overlapped each other by five weeks.

When the auction took place on May 16th, Dickens had arranged that Arthur Smith should bid for him, but that Frederic Chapman, as a feint, should bid against him up to a certain point. Smith amused himself by telling stories to Evans and his representative and putting in his bids "as it were accidentally—to the great terror and confusion of all the room." Misled by Chapman's bidding, nobody could make out why Smith was bidding or whom he represented. Dickens acquired the property, including its stock and stereotype plates, for £3,550. Inasmuch as he valued the stock and plates at £1,600 and paid only one-quarter of the purchase price to Bradbury and Evans, he estimated that he had acquired the name and prestige of *Household Words* for less than £500.[81]

In the May 28th number of *All the Year Round* he consequently added to its title the words "with which is incorporated *Household Words*," and published a triumphant valedictory in the final number of the magazine he had killed. Its last page, he wrote, was closed by the hand of the same writer who had penned its first, ten years ago. "He knew perfectly well, knowing his own rights, and his means of attaining them, that it could not be but that this work must stop, if he chose to stop it. He therefore announced, many weeks ago, that it would be discontinued on the day of which this final Number bears date. The Public have read a good deal to the contrary, and will observe that it has not in the least affected the result." [82]

Bradbury and Evans struck back by establishing a rival magazine called *Once a Week*, one of the titles, as it chanced, that Dickens had considered and rejected. They circularized the *Household Words* authors for material, but Dickens bore off with him most of those whose contributions he valued. The result of their efforts, he predicted, would simply be "to heap over them, a vast accumulation of expensive miscellaneous matter." [83] They tried slavishly and blindly to imitate Dickens's editorial policies. "What fools they are!" he exclaimed contemptuously. "As if a mole couldn't see that their only chance was in a careful separation of themselves from the faintest approach or assimilation to All the Year Round!" [84] *Once a Week* is reported to have limped along for a number of years, and to have proved a costly failure. [85] This may have been true during its earlier stages, but could hardly have continued to be so, for it was still being published long after Dickens's death.

All the Year Round, however, from the very first was a phenomenal success. Its only striking innovation was that its first pages were always reserved for a serial story by a well-known writer, who was no longer left anonymous but advertised with the magazine. To start off with a bang, Dickens began with his own new novel, *A Tale of Two Cities*. This was followed in November by Wilkie Collins's *The Woman in White*. For the right to publish an American edition of the magazine one day after it appeared in England, Dickens received £1,000 a year. [86] Its circulation at home rose with hardly a break. By its fifth number it had trebled that of *Household Words*. [87] Within three months Dickens was reporting to Forster, "So well has All the Year Round gone that it was able yesterday to repay me, with five per cent. interest, all the money I advanced for its establishment (paper, print &c. all paid down to the last number), and yet to leave a good £500 balance at the banker's." [88] *Household Words* during its very best years had sold perhaps some forty thousand copies a week. [89]

Within ten years *All the Year Round* reached three hundred thousand.

At the same time that Dickens sold the American rights to the magazine he was considering the possibility of a reading tour in the United States. He went so far as to draft a conditional agreement with an American named Thomas C. Evans to give eighty American readings provided Evans could deposit £10,000 to his account in advance, but then hesitated to sign it.[90] Though Dickens felt attracted by the idea, his emotions made it painful for him to think of leaving England. "Several strong reasons," as he cautiously wrote an American correspondent, "would make the journey difficult to me . . ." [91] "I should be one of the most unhappy of men if I were to go," he confessed to Forster, "and yet I cannot help being much stirred and influenced by the golden prospect held before me." [92] But Evans turned out to be "a kind of *un*accredited agent," desirous of selling the agreement "to any buyer who would pay enough," and proved unable to lay his hands on the money.[93] Ultimately, therefore, the scheme fell through. "Driven into a corner," Dickens wrote, "I thought of signing it, but Ouvry was so strong against it that I struck—refused—and knocked the whole thing on the head . . ." [94]

*   *   *   *   *

The idea for his new novel had come to Dickens more than a year before, in the midst of the turmoil and anguish of his disintegrating marriage. At first he thought of calling it *One of These Days*. Then, "What do you think," he asked Forster, "of *this* name for my story —BURIED ALIVE? Does it seem too grim? Or THE THREAD OF GOLD? Or, THE DOCTOR OF BEAUVAIS?" [95] But at the time, and for months therafter, he was too agitated to compose himself for any protracted work of creation. In February, 1859, when it became necessary for him to make a start if the tale was to begin in the first number of *All the Year Round*, he still had trouble getting under way. "I cannot please myself with the opening of my story, and cannot in the least settle at it or take to it." [96]

To aid him in the writing of the book, with its background of eighteenth-century England and France, Dickens appealed to Carlyle, whose *French Revolution* he deeply admired, to suggest some source materials that he might consult. He was grateful but stag-

gered when Carlyle sardonically chose two cartloads of books at the
London Library and had them all sent to him.[97] The more of them
that Dickens waded through, however, the more he felt with amazed
admiration that Carlyle had torn out the vitals of them all and fused
them into his fuliginous masterpiece, "which was aflame with the very
essence of the conflagration." [98] Thanks to Carlyle, he felt able to
say that his portrayal of "the condition of the French people before
or during the Revolution" was "truly made, on the faith of trust-
worthy witnesses." [99]

By March his difficulties in writing had smoothed themselves
out. "I have got exactly the name for the story that is wanted," he
reported exultantly; "exactly what will fit the opening to a T. A
TALE OF TWO CITIES. Also . . . I have struck out a rather original and bold idea. That is, at the end of each month to publish the
monthly part in the green cover, with two illustrations at the old
shilling. This will give All the Year Round always the interest and
precedence of a fresh weekly portion during the month; and will
give me my old standing with my old public, and the advantage (very
necessary in this story) of having numbers of people who read it in
no smaller portions than a monthly part." [100] With his usual business astuteness he thus simultaneously appealed to a weekly and a
monthly audience.

When Edmund Yates was considering taking legal action against
the Garrick Club, Dickens had accompanied him to a consultation
in the chambers of Edwin James, a pushing and unscrupulous barrister who was later debarred for malpractice. Dickens quietly observed
his florid, hard-faced bluster; in the sixth and seventh numbers of the
Tale of Two Cities he brought in the character of Mr. Stryver, for
whom Sydney Carton serves as legal "jackal." "Stryver is a good
likeness," Yates observed to Dickens. He smiled. "Not bad, I think,"
he agreed. "Especially after only one sitting." [101]

Meanwhile, Dickens himself had begun sitting for his own portrait to W. P. Frith. It had been commissioned by Forster a year or
two before, but when Dickens grew a mustache Forster asked Frith
to put off painting it. "This is a whim," Forster said authoritatively,
"—the fancy will pass. We will wait till the hideous disfigurement
is removed." But, instead, Dickens grew a beard, and, alarmed lest
whiskers be allowed to spread over his entire face, Forster now gave

orders to go ahead.[102] During one of the sittings Edwin Landseer
called. "Let's have him up," Dickens suggested; "he hasn't seen my
beard and moustache yet." Landseer ignored the change. "Well,
Lanny," Dickens said at last, "what about all this? D'you like it?
Think it an improvement?" "Oh, a great improvement," Landseer
replied gravely. "It hides so much more of your face." [103]

When Ary Scheffer was painting Dickens's portrait in Paris, he had
thought he looked like a Dutch skipper; Frith thought his expression
that of a man "who had reached the topmost rung of a very high ladder and was perfectly aware of his position." [104] Of Frith's portrait of
Dickens Landseer commented, "I wish he looked less eager and
busy, and not so much out of himself, or beyond himself. I should
like to catch him asleep and quiet now and then." Dickens himself
said, "It is a little too much (to my thinking) as if my next-door
neighbor were my deadly foe, uninsured, and I had just received ti-
dings of his house being afire . . ." [105]

During the course of the sittings Frith heard Dickens do the *Carol*
and the "Trial Scene" from *Pickwick* at one of a series of eight readings begun on Christmas Eve and spaced out through January and
February.[106] He was disappointed at the timorous, almost shamefast
way Dickens delivered the repartees of Sam Weller and had the
temerity to tell the author so. Dickens listened with a smile, but
made no answer.

A few days later a friend upbraided Frith for having given him
a false impression of the Weller speeches: they came, he said, "like
pistol-shots; there was no 'sneaking' way of talking, as you described
it." Frith reported back to Dickens, who replied with a twinkle in
his eye, "I altered it a little—made it smarter." Frith was dum-
founded, and naïvely expressed his astonishment at Dickens taking
his advice. "On the contrary," Dickens responded, "whenever I am
wrong I am obliged to anyone who will tell me of it; but up to the
present I have never been wrong." [107]

While Dickens was crowding audiences into St. Martin's Hall,
Ellen Ternan, a few blocks away at the Haymarket, was pursuing her
career as an actress. In the middle of December she appeared as
Alice in Bayle Bernard's *The Tide of Time* and later in the spring
had a part in Palgrave Simpson's *The World and the Stage*.[108] There

is no record, however, that she electrified her auditors as Dickens was doing.

With the coming of June, Dickens settled down in Gad's Hill to working on his story. Mamey and Katey were away visiting the Whites,[109] their old friends from whom Dickens had rented Bonchurch in the summer of 1849, and Dickens and Georgina were alone in the house with Plorn, the servants, and the two dogs, Turk, a bloodhound, and Linda, a St. Bernard. While the old bridge at Rochester was being torn down and replaced by a modern structure, the contractor asked Dickens if he would like to have one of the balustrades as a relic. Dickens gratefully accepted, and set it up on a stone foundation in the lawn behind the house, with a sundial for the top.[110] Occasional guests he had met at Higham Station by a brilliant red jaunting car ordered in Belfast.[111]

He was still suffering from the remains of a cold contracted in the late spring, which obstinately lingered on, but he did not allow it to interfere with his toiling away on his weekly installments. "I have been getting on in health very slowly," he wrote Forster in July, "and through irksome botheration enough. But I think I am round the corner. This cause—and the heat—has tended to my doing no more than hold my ground, my old month's advance, with the Tale of Two Cities. The small portions thereof drive me frantic; but I think the tale must have taken a strong hold. The run upon our monthly parts is surprising, and last month we sold 35,000 back numbers." [112]

Dickens had by this time reached Book Three, "The Track of a Storm," in which his pen caught fire portraying those wild tumults of the Revolution that he understood with a deeper sympathy through the bitterness and turmoil, the intolerable sense of wrong, that had agitated his nights and days. The boiling caldron of the Terror was a macrocosm filled with huge and flaming projections of his own raging emotions. As they poured out of him, he achieved a kind of relief.

If he still did not feel happy, he was calmer in mind. Like an aroused people punishing its rulers, or an angry lion attacking its tormentors, he had lashed out and severely mauled his publishers for daring to disobey his mandates. It made no difference that they had been his faithful servants for sixteen years past. He had severed connections with them and established a new periodical even more profitable than the one he had destroyed. Caught up in the excitement of his new story, he had already proved that he had not lost his hold upon his public. In his paid readings he had struck into a novel and enormously remunerative course that at the same time relieved his need of distraction, satisfied his appetite for theatrical excitement, and gratified his love of establishing a close personal contact with an audience. The affection with which he was received everywhere was grateful to his torn feelings; the laughter, the tears, the emotional tension he could induce were a tribute to his power and a sign of the sympathy between him and his hearers.

All these emotions are still to be found in a letter written to Miss Coutts the following spring. "I am not so weak or wicked as to visit any small unhappiness of my own, upon the world in which I live. I know very well, it is just as it was. As to my art, I have as great a delight in it as the most enthusiastic of my readers; and the sense of my trust and responsibility in that wise, is always upon me when I take pen in hand. If I were soured, I should still try to sweeten the lives and fancies of others, but I am not—not at all.

"Neither do I ever complain, or ever touch that subject. What I have written to you respecting it, I have written merely because I wished you to understand me thoroughly.

"Lastly, I do not suppose myself blameless, but in this thing as in all others know, every day more and more, how much I stand in need of the highest of all charity and mercy. All I claim for myself, is, that when I was very young, I made a miserable mistake, and that the wretched consequences which might naturally have been expected from it, have resulted from it." [113]

And yet the storm through which he had passed, the angry battles he had fought, the relentless spirit he had displayed, had not left him unmarked. The look of exultant enmity Dickens had caught in Frith's portrait of him was a true echo of the passions to which he had given rein during these fifteen months of contention and unsettlement that followed his separation from Catherine. Though he humbly confessed himself in need of charity and mercy, he believed that all his sufferings had resulted from the mistake of a marriage contracted in his youth. He had never shown the least sign of deviating from the conviction that his every step during and after the dis-

solution of that marriage had been moderate and just. He even professed to believe that he was altogether gentle and mild. "You surprise me," he wrote Mrs. Watson, "by supposing that there is ever
latent a defiant and roused expression in the undersigned lamb!" [114]

CHAPTER TWO

Surface Serene

A LL the summer of 1859, save for business trips to London, Dickens remained at Gad's Hill. The girls had returned in July from the Isle of Wight,[1] and now and then there were visitors: F. D. Finlay, the editor of the Belfast *Northern Whig*, who had helped Dickens buy his red jaunting car, Wilkie Collins in July, Tom Beard in August, and a young Irish writer named Percy Fitzgerald, who had contributed to *Household Words* and whom Dickens had met in Dublin.[2] Occasionally Dickens went rowing on the Medway, and he had awakened immense enthusiasm in his daughters by planning a boat, "oak outside, white within, touch of blue here and there, pink striped awnings, Dick at the Prow, and Wilkie at the helm." [3] In September he spent a few days at Broadstairs, where he hoped the sea air and sea water would enable him to get rid of his cold. Here he stayed at the Albion with Charles Collins, Wilkie's younger brother, and the two saw a ludicrous entertainment billed as "The Rigid Legs," in which a dirty young lady pretended to mesmerize a boy who tumbled over into the audience.[4]

During the autumn Dickens directed his attention chiefly to three aims: planning for the futures of his sons, finishing *A Tale of Two Cities* before undertaking another brief reading tour in October, and lining up further serial stories for *All the Year Round*, to succeed *The Woman in White* when it finished the following summer.

Upon the prospects of the boys Dickens looked with various degrees of solicitude. Charley, to be sure, seemed to be doing well; he had spent several years with Baring Brothers, where he was highly praised, and since 1858 had been looking forward to establishing an out-of-London connection and ultimately setting up in business.[5]

In the spring of 1860, he went to Hong Kong, "strongly backed up by Barings, to buy tea on his own account . . . before starting in London for himself." [6] Walter, too, in India, had distinguished himself with the 42nd Highlanders during the Mutiny and been made a lieutenant before his eighteenth birthday.[7]

But Frank presented more difficult problems. Afflicted with a painful stammer, he also suffered on occasion from deafness.[8] Dickens had sent him to Germany to learn the language, all agog to be a doctor.[9] But there Frank became convinced that he would never get over his stammering and that consequently all professions were barred to him; the only thing he would like to be was a gentleman-farmer, at the Cape, in Canada, or Australia. "With my passage paid, fifteen pounds, a horse, and a rifle, I could go two or three hundred miles up country, sow grain, buy cattle, and in time be very comfortable." "I perceived," commented Dickens, "that the first consequence of the fifteen pounds would be that he would be robbed of it—of the horse, that it would throw him—and of the rifle, that it would blow his head off . . ." [10] Back in England, Frank again veered toward medicine, but Dickens was not convinced that he had any steadinesss of purpose. He himself thought he might get the boy into the Foreign Office.[11]

Alfred, a dependable and self-reliant boy of fourteen, was studying at Wimbledon to qualify for an army commission in the Artillery or the Engineers.[12] Sydney, now twelve, the "Ocean Spectre" of his baby days, was mad about the sea and wished to enter the Navy, although Dickens was not sure that this desire was uninfluenced by his having spent the last holidays with a young midshipman "in glorious buttons and with a real steel weapon in his belt." [13] Nevertheless, in May Dickens had placed him in a preparatory school at Southsea and later obtained his nomination as a Naval Cadet.[14] The following year, after passing his examination, Sydney went on board his training ship at Chatham.[15] Of diminutive stature, "the Admiral," as Dickens now affectionately called him, was almost obliterated by his equipment. "His sextant (which is about the size and shape of a cocked hat), on being applied to his eye, entirely concealed him. Not the faintest trace of the distinguished officer behind it was perceptible to the human vision." [16]

For the two youngest boys, Harry, aged ten, and Plorn, only seven, it was too early to make plans. Plorn was still so much the baby and pet of the family that his eldest sister did not want him sent to Boulogne, where most of the other boys had started school. Harry was consequently brought back from Boulogne, in order that he might join Plorn in attending the near-by Rochester Grammar School.[17]

Meanwhile Dickens had been applying himself doggedly, but "with tremendous interest and fervor," to completing *A Tale of Two Cities*.[18] "Nothing but the interest of the subject, and the pleasure of striving with the difficulty of the forms of treatment, nothing in the mere way of money, I mean, could also repay the time and trouble of the incessant condensation. But I set myself the little task of making a *picturesque* story, rising in every chapter with characters true to nature, but whom the story itself should express, more than they should express themselves, by dialogue." [19] By mid-October the tale was completed.[20] "Carlyle says 'It's wonderful' " (although he complained of having to read it by "teaspoonfuls") "and Forster turns white with admiring approval." [21]

Then came a crowded two weeks of reading in the Midlands, at Cambridge, Peterborough, Bradford, Nottingham, Oxford, Birmingham, Cheltenham, a new place almost every night.[22] "Cambridge beyond everything," Dickens wrote; Arthur Smith reported that "he turned away twice Peterborough"; the hurry and brevity of the visit to Oxford compelled Dickens to refuse the Vice-Chancellor's invitation to stay at his house.[23] In spite of persistent rain the University came out brilliantly. "Great doings at Oxford," Dickens said. "Prince of Wales and what not." [24] On the concluding night at Cheltenham the profits for that single occasion were £70.[25]

Promptly on his return to London in November, Dickens flung himself into obtaining the next serial for *All the Year Round*. The first person to whom he wrote was George Eliot, whose *Scenes of Clerical Life* he had tremendously admired when she sent him a copy in 1858. Although at that time he had no idea of who the author was, he shrewdly suspected her sex. "I have observed what seem to me to be such womanly touches, in those moving fictions," he wrote her, "that the assurance on the title-page is insufficient to satisfy me, even now. If they originated with no woman, I believe that no man ever before had the art of making himself, mentally, so like a woman, since the world began." [26]

Later, in sending him a copy of *Adam Bede*, George Eliot revealed her identity. He received the information in confidence, he told her, and repeated what "a rare and genuine delight" it had been "to become acquainted in the spirit with so noble a writer." *Adam Bede* intensified his admiration of her genius: "Every high quality that was in the former book, is in that, with a World of Power added thereunto. The conception of Hetty's character is so extraordinarily subtle and true, that I laid the book down fifty times, to shut my eyes and think about it. . . . The whole country life that the story is set in, is so real, so droll and genuine, and yet so select and polished by art, that I cannot praise it enough to you."

This letter Dickens concluded by saying, "if you should ever have the freedom and inclination to be a fellow labourer with me, it would yield me a pleasure that I have never known yet, and can never know otherwise; and no channel that even *you* could command should be so profitable as to yourself." [27] Now, on November 14th, he wrote to her companion, George Lewes, specifically proposing that she write a story for *All the Year Round* to begin publication some eight months hence. Terms should be arranged completely satisfactory to her, she should retain the copyright of the book, and be free on its completion as a serial to bring it out in book form with any publisher she chose.[28] At first George Eliot demurred merely that she felt this arrangement would not give her enough time, and Dickens suggested eagerly that he extend it by having in the meanwhile a shorter story by Mrs. Gaskell.[29] Not until the following February did he learn that "Adam Bede" felt the serial form of publication sacrificed too much "to terseness and closeness of construction" and must disappoint him by refusing to undertake it.[30]

During these negotiations he asked Mrs. Gaskell to write a story to run for twenty-two weeks, about four hundred manuscript pages, for which he offered her two hundred guineas.[31] While this was under discussion he joyfully concluded an arrangement with Charles Lever, the author of *Harry Lorrequer*, to publish a novel by him, either at the conclusion of *The Woman in White* or that of its successor.[32] When neither Mrs. Gaskell nor George Eliot proved able to oblige, Lever's novel, now called *A Day's Ride: A Life's Romance*, was definitely scheduled for the following July. "Hurrah!" Dickens wrote Lever, "I think the name *a very good one*, and we will fall to as soon as you please in the way of making preparations ahead. Do not be afraid to trust the audience with anything that is good. Though a very large one, it is a fine one." [33]

When Dickens received the first installments of Lever's story in June he was delighted, although he thought a little condensation was needed. But it was "full of life, vivacity, originality, and humour": "I think the rising of invention in the drunken young man, extraordinarily humourous; it made me laugh to an extent and with a heartiness that I should like you to have seen and heard. Go on and prosper!" He did not foresee anything ominous in the slight prolixity he had noticed.[34]

Another book Dickens had read with loyal admiration only a few weeks before was Forster's *The Arrest of the Five Members*, a continuation of his extended treatment of the history of the Great Rebellion against Charles I. "I admired it all, went with it all, and was proud of my friend's having written it all. I felt it to be all square and sound and right, and to be of enormous importance in these times. . . . When the Great Remonstrance came out, I was in the thick of my story, and was always busy with it. But I am very glad I didn't read it then, as I shall read it now to much better purpose. All the time I was at work on the Two Cities, I read no books but such as had the air of the time in them." [35]

That spring Dickens had been heartily glad to hear that Macready at the age of sixty-seven was going to remarry and leave his gloomy Sherborne retreat for a handsome new home at Cheltenham, only four or five hours from London. "God bless you, and God bless the object of your choice!" Dickens replied. "Your letter came with the sunshine of the Spring morning . . ." "I do not believe that a heart like yours was made to hold so large a waste-place as there has been in it." And, teasing his old friend's favorite assumption of enfeebled superannuation, he added: "Aha!—what do you say NOW to those noble remarks I was making at Forster's the other day, about the stout Englishmen all over the world who are always young? I feel a grin of intolerable (except to me) self-complacency mantle all over me as I think of my wisdom." [36]

*　　*　　*　　*　　*

But all the news of Dickens's friends was not so cheerful. Leigh Hunt had died the preceding August, and in November Frank Stone, his old companion of the splendid barnstorming days and next-door neighbor at Tavistock House. In *All the Year Round* Dickens published an article regretting that he had imitated Hunt's "gay and ostentatious wilfulness" in the portrayal of Harold Skimpole, and denying again that Skimpole was intended to be like Hunt in any except these whimsical and airy qualities. "He no more thought, God forgive him!" Dickens reiterated editorially, "that the admired original would ever be charged with the imaginary vices of the fictitious creature, than he has himself ever thought of charging the blood of Desdemona and Othello, on the innocent Academy model who sat for Iago's leg in the picture." [37] For Stone, too, Dickens grieved. "On what strange, sad errand do you think I am going now?" he wrote Wills. "To Highgate to choose a Grave for—poor Stone, who died yesterday." [38] Dickens also busied himself trying to obtain commissions as an illustrator for young Marcus Stone, who, like his father, was an artist.[39]

There were troubles and bereavements in Dickens's family as well. His youngest brother, Augustus, the pet child of twenty years ago, had proved even more of a disappointment than Frederick. Augustus's wife had gone blind and he had finally deserted her, running away to America with another woman and leaving Dickens with still one more dependent relative to be provided for.[40] Even under these circumstances Augustus continued to clamor for help. "I have been painfully restrained from communicating with Augustus," Dickens wrote, "by the knowledge (gained from a stern experience), that the least communication with him would be turned to some account, and that some suddenly virtuously indignant person would proclaim that but for me he would never have been drawn into those social relations, or to that advance of money, or to that recommendation, or what not. Augustus had not been in America three months (I think), when he wrote me asking me to correspond with some man or other who had done something for him, and who would write to recommend me to advance him a sum of money. He did write, and what could I do but hold my peace? . . .

"It is a dreadful state of things that he should have fallen into this position, but I declare to you that I do not see how he is to be helped in it. He has always been, in a certain insupportable arrogance and presumption of character, so wrong, that, even when he had some prospects before him, I despaired of his ever being right." He did "not write a word of this reproachfully towards the unfortunate fellow," Dickens concluded, but his judgment on the subject was fixed. "I have no hope of him." [41]

On July 27, 1860, another brother, Alfred Lamert, died of pleurisy.[42] He had always been a hard-working engineer, employed in railway construction, but never managed to do more than earn a living. "He had had no opportunity of providing for his family," Dickens wrote, "died worth nothing, and has left a widow and five children—you may suppose to whom. Day after day I have been scheming and contriving for them, and I am still doing so, and I have schemed myself into broken rest and low spirits. My mother, who was also left to me when my father died (I never had anything left to me but relations), is in the strangest state of mind from senile decay; and the impossibility of getting her to understand what is the matter, combined with her desire to be got up in sables like a female Hamlet, illumines the dreary scene with a ghastly absurdity that is the chief relief I can find in it." [43] Later in the fall Elizabeth Dickens was established with Alfred's widow, Helen, in a house Dickens found for them on Haverstock Hill, a little south of Hampstead heath.[44] Here he visited them one day in November. His mother "was not in bed, but down-stairs. Helen and Letitia were poulticing her poor head, and, the instant she saw me, she plucked up a spirit, and asked me for 'a pound.' " [45]

But these distresses and the ever-pressing and ever-deepening weight of responsibility they imposed upon Dickens do not altogether explain the restless uneasiness that still lay heavily upon his spirits despite all his lively sallies. His freedom from the old domestic unhappiness had not brought him the peace of heart he had dreamed of. Even when he had imaged Ellen Ternan as an unattainable princess prisoned from him by the ogres of law and convention on some inaccessible mountain summit, he had despairingly exclaimed that "never was a man so seized and rended by one Spirit." But there is no evidence that his emotions had found any happy response; only that agonized outcry of horror at policemen prowling around Berners Street and all too probably trying to serve as panders to the indecent desires of some lustful "swell" lurking in the darkness. The distractions of toil at his desk or the feverish and theatrical thrill of moving enthralled audiences to laughter, excitement, and tears were again all he had.

Beneath a surface of serenity Gad's Hill was filled with undercurrents of unhappiness. Mary was officially her father's hostess, and delegated some of the household responsibilities to her Aunt Georgy and Katey. Mary adored her father and sided with him in the separation, but during this last year she had been in love and refused her suitor because Dickens did not approve. Her submission left her low-spirited and dejected.[46] Katey sided with her mother and felt a vague suspicion that Aunt Georgy had played some devious and underhanded role in the separation. ("Auntie," she said in later years, "was not quite straight." [47]) Mary never saw her mother again until after Dickens's death, but Katey defiantly paid her visits to which Dickens had agreed, but which he felt were meant as a reproach to him. Katey was so miserable at home that when Wilkie Collins's brother Charles proposed she accepted him, although she did not love him.[48]

Charles Allston Collins was thirty-one years of age, very tall, with a white face and flaming, floating orange hair. He had been a member of the Pre-Raphaelite Brotherhood with Rossetti, Burne-Jones, and Holman Hunt; his best painting, *May in the Regent's Park*, had been hung on the walls of the Academy in 1852. He also had talents as a writer that Dickens respected sufficiently to publish a series of his "Eyewitness" sketches in *All the Year Round*, and wrote two small descriptive books of delicacy and humor, *A New Sentimental Journey* and *A Cruise on Wheels*.[49] But he was almost twelve years older than Katey, of a strange, nervous temperament, and often in ill health. Dickens sensed, moreover, that he had not won Katey's heart and advised against the match. But fiery Katey was not her mild and malleable sister. She loved yet resented her father, chafed against him, and shared much of his obstinate self-will. She wanted to get away, she refused to listen to his counsel, and Dickens was obliged to yield. The marriage was set for the 17th of July. "Lord, how the time and Life steal on!" Dickens exclaimed. "It was but yesterday that Katey always had a scratched knee, and it was but the day before yesterday when there was no such creature." [50]

Holman Hunt was best man, and among the other guests were Thomas Beard, Wilkie Collins, the Willses, Chauncey Hare Townshend, Edmund Yates, Henry Chorley the music critic, Percy Fitzgerald, the actor Charles Fechter, Marguerite Power, and Mary Boyle.[51] But there was one person not present whose absence remained conspicuously unmentioned. It was Catherine Dickens.

Gad's Hill neighbors crowded the little church, "the people of the village strewed flowers in the churchyard," "and the energetic blacksmith of the village had erected a triumphal arch in the court, and fired guns *all night* beforehand—to our great amazement: we not having the slightest idea what they meant." [52] "One very funny thing was, the entrance into church of the few friends whom I had caused to be brought down straight from town by a special Train. They didn't know whether they were to look melancholy, beaming, or maudlin; and their uncertainty struck me as so uncommonly droll, that I was obliged to hide my reverend parental countenance in my hand on the altar railing." [53]

"Mary and all the boys were very much cut up when the parting moment came, but they soon recovered; Mary in particular commanded herself extremely well." Dickens does not say whether he and Mary were thinking, on her sister's bridal day, of the marriage Mary had surrendered as Katey had not. "Georgy and I acted as universal bottleholders." [54] "There was no misery of any kind, not even speechifying, and the whole was a great success—SO FAR." [55]

But at last, rustling and billowing in her crinoline, Katey was off for Dover, to spend her honeymoon in France. The red-faced infant, the small child Dickens had taken to Holborn every Christmas for toys, the little girl with scratched knees, the fiery-tempered "Tinderbox," the young girl dancing at Tavistock House in satin shoes and flowing white sash, the talented youthful artist, had grown up, changed to a woman, married, and gone. When the house was quiet and empty of all the departed guests, Mary found her father in Katey's bedroom alone. He was on his knees, sobbing, with his head buried in her wedding gown. "But for me," he wept brokenly, "Katie would not have left home." [56]

* * * * *

For some time Dickens had been desirous of selling Tavistock House and living entirely at Gad's Hill. Ever since he had lived abroad he had disliked London, with its filthy and evil-smelling river and the great heavy canopy of smoke forever lowering over its house-tops. And his home there of the past nine years was overshadowed with memories of misery and desperation poisoning even the glow of Christmas festivities and the feverish glitter of Twelfth-Night theatricals. Forster ponderously argued that it would gravely damage his standing if he did not maintain a town house for the girls, but with Katey's marriage Dickens now determined that he would spend a large part of his time at Gad's Hill and merely rent a furnished house in London during the winter season. Most of the furniture of Tavistock House could be moved to the country, and there was enough to furnish a sitting room and two bedrooms at the *All the Year Round* office that could be used whenever any of the family wanted to come into town.[57]

Tavistock House was accordingly put up for sale, and shortly a Jewish banker named J. P. Davis presented himself as a purchaser. Dickens instructed Anne Cornelius to show him the house, with all the fixtures to be sold with it, "all the Looking-glasses, all the Cornices, the Drawing-room satin window-curtains, large ottoman, and two fixed ottomans at the sides of the fire, the Dining-room curtains, all the blinds, and the painted room curtains," as well as "the great Dining Table" which extended to fit the whole room.[58] A bargain was soon struck. "I must say," Dickens told Wills, "that in all things the purchaser has behaved thoroughly well, and that I cannot call to mind any occasion when I have had money-dealings with any one that have been so satisfactory, considerate, and trusting." [59]

Clarkson Stanfield's scenes for *The Frozen Deep*, which Dickens had transformed into wall decorations, were accordingly taken down and rolled for transportation, together with all the other household effects that were to be moved.[60] "When you come down here next month," Dickens wrote Forster from Gad's Hill, "we have an idea that we shall show you rather a neat house. What terrific adventures have been in action; how many overladen vans were knocked up at Gravesend, and had to be dragged out of Chalk Turnpike in the dead of night by the whole equine power of this establishment; shall be revealed at another time." [61]

Dickens had turned the downstairs bedroom at Gad's Hill to the right of the little entrance porch into his study. Here the books from the Tavistock House library and the door with the dummy book-backs were installed. From its bow window he was able to look out across the lawn with its beds of scarlet geraniums to where the steps of a brick tunnel he had built under the Dover Road gave access to his shrubbery on the other side. All morning long in the bright autumn weather as he sat at his writing table he could raise his eyes and see the blue sky between the green of the two great ancient cedars casting their shadows upon the sunlit road and its floating population of tramps and hop pickers.

During this time of breaking up Tavistock House, Dickens seemed torn by a mania for breaking with the past. In the field behind Gad's Hill he burned all the accumulated letters and papers of twenty years. The reason he gave was that he felt "shocked by the misuse of the private letters of public men," [62] and for the rest of his life he destroyed every personal letter he received as soon as he had answered it. So innumerable letters from Ainsworth, Talfourd, Lady Blessington, Lady Holland, Jeffrey, Sydney Smith, Rogers, Maclise, Cruikshank, Captain Marryat, Carlyle, Macready, Tennyson, Browning, Forster, Bulwer Lytton, Wilkie Collins, and many others all went up in the flames, and the boys, Harry and Plorn, as they later remembered, "roasted onions in the ashes of the great." [63] The burning pile "sent up a smoke," Dickens said, "like the Genie when he got out of the casket on the sea-shore; and as it was an exquisite day when I began, and rained very heavily when I finished, I suspect my correspondence of having overcast the face of the Heavens." [64] When the last sheets had been consumed he said, "Would to God every letter I had ever written was on that pile!" [65] But John Bigelow, the American Minister to France, to whom Dickens told the story, indignantly exclaimed that he deserved to have been burned with them.[66]

While Gad's Hill was still unsettled by painters and carpenters Dickens began writing in the best spare room.[67] Since the conclusion of *A Tale of Two Cities*, his only contributions to *All the Year Round* were a series of personal essays, often reminiscent in tone, under the title of *The Uncommercial Traveller*. "Figuratively speaking," the first of these explained, "I travel for the great house of Human-interest Brothers, and have rather a large connection in the fancy goods way. Literally speaking, I am always wandering here and there from my rooms in Covent Garden, London . . . seeing many little things, and some great things, which, because they interest me, I think may interest others." [68] Among these "Dullborough," "Nurses' Stories," "Travelling Abroad," "Birthday Celebrations," and "Chatham Dockyard" all contain fragments of autobiography.

The little pictorial sketch on which he now started, however, developed so surprisingly that he decided to cancel it and reserve the idea for a new book. "You shall judge as soon as I get it printed," he wrote Forster. "But it so opens out before *me* that I can see the whole of a serial revolving on it, in a most singular and comic manner." [69] At first Dickens intended that it should become one of his long stories in twenty monthly numbers. The needs of *All the Year Round* forced him to reconsider this decision.[70]

The Woman in White had been a sensation, but Lever's story, *A Day's Ride,* was not taking with the public, and for the first and only time the circulation of *All the Year Round* began to fall off. After its comic opening, Dickens complained, the story became too discursive and had no vitality in it.[71] Years later, Bernard Shaw was to suggest in addition that its hero, Potts, a self-deceived and mendacious daydreamer, was "a piece of scientific natural history" who so painfully revealed the weaknesses of all his readers as to hit them "full in the conscience" and make "their self-esteem smart." [72] Whether or no this was the cause, the magazine was suffering badly. "We drop," Dickens wrote, "rapidly and continuously, with The Day's Ride." [73]

"I called a council of war at the office on Tuesday. It was perfectly clear that the one thing to be done was, for me to strike in. I have therefore decided to begin a story, the length of the Tale of Two Cities, on the First of December—begin publishing, that is. I must make the most I can out of the book. . . . The name is, GREAT EXPECTATIONS. I think a good name?" [74]

Although it was a sacrifice to turn the story into a weekly serial, Dickens pointed out, it was a sacrifice for his own welfare. He could no longer, as in earlier days, write two novels simultaneously; if he made *Great Expectations* a story of twenty monthly parts he would be unable for almost two years to write a serial for *All the Year Round,* and that magazine was a property far too valuable to be endangered. "On the other hand, by dashing in now, I come in when most wanted; and if Reade and Collins follow me, our course will be shaped out handsomely and hopefully for between two and three years. A thousand pounds are to be paid for early proofs of the story to America." [75]

"The book will be written in the first person throughout, and during these first three weekly numbers you will find the hero to be a boy-child, like David. Then he will be an apprentice. You will not have to complain of the want of humour as in the Tale of Two Cities. I have made the opening, I hope, in its general effect exceedingly droll. I have put a child and a good-natured foolish man in relations that seem to me very funny. Of course I have got in the pivot on which the story will turn too—and which, indeed, as you remember, was the grotesque tragi-comic conception that first encouraged me. To be quite sure I had fallen into no unconscious repetitions, I read David Copperfield again the other day, and was affected by it to a degree you would hardly believe." [76]

The one part of the situation that troubled Dickens was the blow to Lever's self-esteem. He liked and admired Lever, and did not know that Lever privately sneered at the "fast writing and careless composition" of books like *Dombey and Son* and traced Dickens's popularity to his "low verbiage and coarse pictures of unreality." [77] Dickens tried to break the news to Lever gently. "The best thing I can say in the beginning," he wrote, "is, that it is not otherwise disagreeable to *me* than as it imposes this note upon me. It causes me no other uneasiness or regret." Their stories would have to go on side by side, however, for as long as Lever's continued. "Now do, pray, I entreat you," Dickens pleaded, "lay it well to heart that this might have happened with any writer. It was a toss-up with Wilkie Collins, when he began his story, on my leaving off. But he strung it on the needful strong thread of interest, and made a great success. The difficulties and discouragements of such an undertaking are enormous, and the man who surmounts them today may be beaten by them to-morrow." [78]

Lever felt deeply mortified. Dickens applied himself generously to assuage the wound. "I do entreat you most earnestly," he wrote, "to understand that my original opinion of your serial remains quite unchanged—that I believe it to be the best you ever wrote—that I think it full of character and humour—that I have not in my mind the slightest atom of reservation respecting it—that I am proud and glad to have it—that I value it exactly as I valued it when we first corresponded about it. I implore you to understand that, and not to let any feeling interfere to obscure this truth. For *such a purpose*, it does not do what you and I would have it do. . . . Some of the best books ever written would not bear the mode of publication . . . Surely, my dear Lever, not quite to succeed in such a strange knack, or lottery, is a very different thing from having cause to be struck in one's self-respect and just courage."

In his humiliation Lever had spoken of bringing his own story to a speedy conclusion. "As to winding up," Dickens replied, "— you are to consider your own reputation, your own knowledge of the book as a whole, your own desire what it shall be, and your own opinion what it ought to be. In considering all these things you best consider me. Our connexion never can be a 'misfortune' to me, so long as you will think of me in it as if I were your other self . . . Now, do take heart of grace and cheer up." [79] A *Day's Ride* consequently limped along beside *Great Expectations* in the pages of *All the Year Round* from the beginning of December, when the latter began, until almost the end of March, 1861. In spite of Dickens's kindly generosity of feeling toward Lever, the protraction of the story reduced his readers to such desperation that he was obliged seven weeks before it came to an end to begin advertising its approaching conclusion.[80]

Dickens paid Lever £750 for the unsuccessful serial, went to great pains to persuade Chapman and Hall to publish both it and its successor, *Barrington*, and mediated disputes between the author and the publishers. Lever complained that he was not sufficiently advertised; Edward Chapman complained that the firm lost £650 on the latter book; Dickens soothed both back to tranquillity. He continued to publish articles by Lever in *All the Year Round*, paying for them on acceptance. And Lever inscribed *Barrington* to Dickens: "Among the thousands who read and re-read your writings, you have not one who more warmly admires your genius than myself; and to say this in confidence to the world, I dedicate to you this story." [81]

* * * * *

On the 1st of November, Dickens and Wilkie Collins went into North Devon together, to gather material for "A Message from the

Sea," a story they had arranged to write in collaboration for the Christmas number of *All the Year Round*. At "a beastly hotel" in Bideford, "We had stinking fish for dinner, and have been able to drink nothing, though we have ordered wine, beer, and brandy-and-water. There is nothing in the house but two tarts and a pair of snuffers." [82] Back in London, Collins wrestled with the difficulties of his part of the story, "getting up spasmodically all day, and looking, in high-shouldered desperation out at window." [83] Then things came right and he shot ahead. Dickens wrote the final part, which was sent to the printer at the end of the month.[84]

Christmas at Gad's Hill was so cold that the boys were able to skate all the five miles from Chatham to Gravesend on the frozen Medway. "My beard froze as I walked about," Dickens reported, "and I couldn't detach my coat and cravat from it until I was thawed at the fire." [85] The next night, in town, during a pantomime at Covent Garden, all the scenery suddenly fell flat on its face, "and disclosed Chaos by gaslight behind! . . . In the uproar some mooncalf rescued a porter pot six feet high (out of which the clown had been drinking when the accident happened) and stood it on the cushion of the lowest proscenium Box . . . beside a lady and gentleman who were dreadfully ashamed of it. The moment the House knew that nobody was injured, they directed their whole attention to this gigantic porter pot in its genteel position (the lady and gentleman trying to hide behind it), and roared with laughter. When a modest footman came from behind the curtain to clear it, and took it up in his arms like a Brobdingnagian baby, we all laughed more than we had ever laughed in our lives." [86]

Dickens felt in better health at the turn of the year than he had for some time. At the end of the month he took a furnished house at 3 Hanover Terrace, Regent's Park, until midsummer. Charley was now back from China, looking for his business partnership, and Dickens believed that he had solved the problem of what to do with Frank by taking him into the office of *All the Year Round*. "If I am not mistaken," Dickens said hopefully, "he has a natural literary taste and capacity, and may do very well with a chance so congenial to his mind, and being also entered at the Bar." [87]

The move into London made it easier for Dickens to see Ellen Ternan, who was now established with her mother in a house at

No. 2 Houghton Place, Ampthill Square, just off the Hampstead Road, and not far from the Polygon, one of Dickens's boyhood homes. Here he was able to visit her, coming up from Wellington Street, and perhaps trudging home, in the late hours, through Regent's Park. Francesco Berger, the young composer who had written the music for The Frozen Deep, tells of card games there on Sunday evenings and playing the piano part while Dickens and Ellen sang duets together.[88]

In the course of the spring Dickens made such headway with Great Expectations that he felt able to give a series of six readings in London between March 14th and April 18th. They were given in St. James's Hall, Piccadilly, St. Martin's Hall having burned down.[89] "The result of the six was, that, after paying a large staff of men and all other charges, and Arthur Smith's ten per cent. on the receipts, and replacing everything destroyed in the fire at St. Martin's Hall (including all our tickets, country-baggage, cheque-boxes, books, and a quantity of gas-fittings and what not), I got upwards of £500. A very great result. We certainly might have gone on through the season, but I am heartily glad to be concentrated on my story." [90]

Dickens was now well into the last third of Great Expectations. "Two months more will see me through it, I trust. All the iron is in the fire, and I have 'only' to beat it out." [91] For the last week in May he went to Dover to work by himself awhile and try to get rid of an attack of facial neuralgia. "Of course I am dull and penitent here," he wrote Wilkie Collins, "but it is very beautiful. I can work well, and I walked, by the cliffs, to Folkstone and back today . . ." [92] Early in June he was back in London again, and finished the book on the 11th, feeling rather worn out but satisfied with his accomplishment.[93]

As Dickens had originally conceived it, in the end Pip was to lose Estella, to realize that his love for her had always been mad and hopeless, and know that they could never have been happy together. Thus, like his belief that he was Miss Havisham's chosen heir and like the wealth Magwitch really intended for him, the passion of Pip's life was to melt away, and all of his "great expectations" to come to naught. But such an ending distressed Bulwer Lytton, who read it in proofs while Dickens was staying a few days with him at

Knebworth.[94] He urged Dickens to change it for one closing on a happier note. Could not Estella's heart be softened by sorrow and she and Pip brought together after all?

Lytton "was so very anxious" [95] and "supported his views with such good reasons" that Dickens determined to take his advice.[96] It may be, too, that the changed ending reflected a desperate hope that Dickens could not banish from within his own heart. And there could be no doubt that such an ending would be more agreeable to many of his readers than the twilight melancholy he had envisioned. So, "I have resumed the wheel," he wrote Collins, "and taken another turn at it." [97] "I have put in a very pretty piece of writing," he told Forster, "and I have no doubt the story will be more acceptable through the alteration." [98]

With the conclusion of *Great Expectations* Dickens went down to Gad's Hill to relax during the summer and get ready to resume another series of his provincial readings in the autumn. He planned to add a reading made from the Dotheboys Hall scenes of *Nicholas Nickleby*, and another embodying the Peggotty, Steerforth, and Dora parts of *David Copperfield* and including the great storm at Yarmouth in which Steerforth was drowned. After getting these into shape he rehearsed himself in their delivery some two or three hours every morning, and then collapsed into doing nothing in the afternoon—except for taking walks and playing cricket and rounders with the boys, whose "holiday war-whoop" resounded about the grounds.[99]

He was looking forward, he wrote Macready, to reading at Cheltenham in November and seeing his old friend there. Carlyle, he reported with derisive irony, had so "intensified his aversion to Jews" that he represented King John as an enlightened sovereign for drawing their teeth to extract money from them. Ferociously Carlyle imagined Queen Victoria haling Baron de Rothschild into Court, and addressing him: " 'Sir you sow not, neither do you work, nor make any useful thing upon the surface o' God's airth; you merely accumulate; and Sir we do require to have such accumulation out of ye, and by the strong dentist hand and the permission of the Eternal Ruler o' this Universe, we will draw every tooth out of your Mosaic head unless you here and now put down Seventeen Millions of ill gotten

Money, which shall be held sufficient for this day and this day only, for tomorrow we will have other teeth or other millions, See you!' " [100]

The tone of the anecdote suggests that Dickens had at last lost his awe of Carlyle, although the Sage of Chelsea continued to feel much the same mingling of affection and amusement he had always had for Dickens, and raised an outcry each week to read "that Pip nonsense" with roars of laughter.[101]

But indeed the whole pattern of Dickens's life had changed. The great old men whom he had known in his startling youth were almost all gone: Rogers dead, Hunt dead, Jeffrey dead, Sydney Smith dead, Landor far off in Italy, Carlyle growing ever more atrabilious and prophetically intolerant. Many of Dickens's closer associates were gone or scattered, too. Talfourd dead, Frank Stone dead, Stanfield enfeebled and ailing. Maclise isolated in an eccentric valetudinarianism, Cruikshank withdrawn to his fanatical teetotalism, Lemon estranged. Ainsworth, the close companion of the Cerberus Club days, the friend who introduced him to his first publisher, had vanished into obscurity. At a dinner given by Frederic Chapman, Browning said, "A strange, forlorn-looking being stopped me today, and reminded me of old times. He presently resolved himself into—whom do you think?—Harrison Ainsworth." "Good Heavens!" cried Forster. "Is he still alive?" [102] Phiz was soon to disappear, too; when *Great Expectations* appeared in book form, Dickens's old illustrator was dropped and the volume came out with designs by young Marcus Stone. Only three of Dickens's old intimates remained: Macready rusticating down at Cheltenham, Lytton amid the gargoyles and medieval trappings of Knebworth, Forster tightly buttoned up and armored in dogmatic complacency.

The companions who surrounded Dickens now were mostly younger men, many of them literary dependents: Wilkie Collins, Edmund Yates, Percy Fitzgerald, Francesco Berger, the actor Charles Fechter. Although Dickens was only forty-nine, his health was failing under the strain of the labors to which he subjected himself and the maniacal swift-paced walks in which he still indulged, but he touched up his grizzling hair, dressed as gaily as ever, and continued to act like a young man. It was as if he were under a compulsion to fight his body and deny the waning of his physical vigor. In Ampthill Square there was Ellen Ternan, "Nelly," as he now called her, glamorous in all her fair young beauty. But the separation from Catherine, which had forced so much distress and bitterness upon Dickens, had not worked out at all as he had thought. He was still a prey to restlessness and emptiness. Labor and the fever of his readings were only anodynes. His imagination, his demoniacal creative power alone remained, but that was deeper, more vibrant, more penetrating than ever, exploring his world with an insight constantly more profound, ascending in *Great Expectations* to new triumphs even as the beating wings began to falter.

CHAPTER THREE

The Tempest and the Ruined Garden

CRITICISM: *A Tale of Two Cities* and *Great Expectations*

"I HAVE so far verified what is done and suffered in these pages,"
Dickens wrote in the Preface to *A Tale of Two Cities*, "as that
I have certainly done and suffered it all myself." [1]

The statement was true. The idea for the story had come to him
while he was tearing himself apart as Richard Wardour in *The
Frozen Deep*,[2] and Sidney Carton's sacrifice of his life amid the
flames of revolution magnifies into chords of exaltation Wardour's
death struggle among the ice floes of the arctic. Watching Dickens
die every night during the Manchester performances, while Maria
Ternan's tears rained down upon his face, was the fair and unattainable creature whom his imprisoning marriage rendered hopelessly remote, whom it rent and tortured his spirit to give up, but who
seemed as inaccessible as the princess of a dragon-guarded crag or as
the blue sky of freedom to a wretched captive in a jail. During the
months that followed, Dickens had thought of separation from
Catherine as impossible, of his marriage as an iron-barred and stone-
walled misery weighed down with adamantine chains from which
he could never escape. It is not strange that in the fantasy from
which imagination is born he should dream of a prisoner bitterly
immured for years and at last set free, of a love serenely consummated and a despairing love triumphantly rising to a height of noble
surrender. These emotions were his; he had known and suffered them
all.

This is not to declare that Dr. Manette, Charles Darnay, and
Sydney Carton are all projections of Charles Dickens, or that Lucie
Manette is a portrayal of Ellen Ternan. None of these characters

[972]

was conceived as a literal rendition of anyone. Lucie, indeed, is given hardly any individualized traits at all, although her appearance, as Dickens describes it, is like that of Ellen, "a short, slight, pretty figure, a quantity of golden hair, a pair of blue eyes," and it may be that her one unique physical characteristic was drawn from Ellen too: "a forehead with a singular capacity (remembering how young and smooth it was), of lifting and knitting itself into an expression that was not quite one of perplexity, or wonder, or alarm, or merely of a bright fixed attention, though it included all the four expressions." [3] But, so far as psychological characteristics are concerned, Lucie has only those that any lover might attribute to his beloved and only those generalized emotions appropriate to the drama of the story.

Nor is Charles Darnay, the serious, plodding, unimaginative, rather pedestrian teacher of language, in the least like the mercurial, flashing Dickens, with his keen eye for the ludicrous. Although Darnay shares Dickens's initials and has a high sense of responsibility and honor, he is all sobriety and quite incapable of making a joke. Sydney Carton can direct a bitter jibe against himself, but in his feckless, irresponsible, and dissolute waste of his own talents there is as little of Dickens as there is in Darnay. The fact that Lucie and Dr. Manette at the time of his release from the Bastille are of almost the same ages as Ellen and Dickens does not mean that the Doctor's feeling for his daughter is the emotion Dickens feels for the pretty, blue-eyed actress, although the two merge perhaps in his fervent declaration that he knows Ellen to be as "innocent and pure, and as good as my own dear daughters." [4]

What the persons in the book do reflect as a group and in their several relations to the main situations of the story are the various individual aspects of Dickens's emotional dilemmas: his longing for an ideal love that might flower in a domestic warmth of tenderness and understanding, his haunting fear that he might never find it, his anguished sense of the grandeur of renunciation, his personal rebellion against the imprisoning codes of a society that deprived him of his desire rising into impersonal rebellion against all the frustrations and miseries that society inflicted upon mankind.

Like William Dorrit, Dickens has felt himself walled in behind the barriers of social humiliations and shames; like Dr. Manette, he has known the solitary confinement of the man of talent, shut away within his own breast from all the deep companionship of understanding. Deeply, painfully reserved, he had never been able to express, not even to Forster, the one man who knew the facts, the full intensity of his hurt. But his very silence seemed to him the universal fate: "every beating heart," he exclaimed, "is, in some of its imaginings, a secret to the heart nearest it!" [5]

Dr. Manette's imprisonment symbolizes this supreme isolation. *Recalled to Life* Dickens once thought of calling the tale: but though Dr. Manette is recalled to life by love, he emerges from the Bastille frightfully mutilated in spirit and but slowly capable of achieving an unstable reintegration. He has been even more cruelly changed by a more dreadful incarceration than Mr. Dorrit by his confinement in the Marshalsea. If all of modern society, as *Little Dorrit* implied, is a prison, it is more terrible for the man of ability, of inspiration, of genius, like Charles Dickens, who beats against its bars more fiercely and understands it more clearly, though only he, perhaps, can painfully burst through its doors.

In this way Dickens bears locked within his memory the hidden reproach of the debtors' prison and the blacking warehouse, but he shares in his heart the despair of those victims of the workhouse "bastilles," feels the miseries of emaciated toilers condemned to hard labor in factories like jails, has experienced the anguish of wronged and deserted children. Can such evils ever be righted, such sufferings ever be expiated? Can the Bastille Prisoner ever be *recalled to life?*— can the past with all its dreadful weight of guilt and pain ever be blotted out? Will not wrong generate wrong, flaming into all the horrors of the Revolution, engulfing both the innocent and the guilty in a sacrificial cataclysm?

*   *   *   *   *

So it is that Dickens returns in *A Tale of Two Cities* to the theme of revolution, which had fascinated him in *Barnaby Rudge*, but with a new and flaming power born out of his sense of intolerable oppression and his sympathy with sufferings generating an inevitable upheaval. The French Revolution was the decisive convulsion that had changed the eighteenth-century world and, amid howling horrors, shattered the power of the aristocracy in France, shaken it even in the rest of Europe. Unless the landowners, the capitalists, and the

industrialists learned from that example, unless justice and love superseded force and greed, would not revolution recur again and again?

Dickens was aware of the fact that the condition of the peasants
and the poor of the cities was not so desperate on the eve of the
French Revolution as it had been earlier in the century. But taxes were
still inequitable and bore heavily on the masses; the clergy and the
nobles were exempt from the hated *taille*; and the salt-tax, the *gabelle*,
was execrated by the poor. The nobility were even endeavoring to revive feudal dues that had lapsed and claiming the last *sou* of those
that remained. The peasant risings in Dauphiné, Provence, and Bur-
gundy and the outbreak of the Paris mob were caused by suffering and
hunger.[6] The concessions and reforms that had been made were too
little and too late. To reminders of these from Forster and Lytton,
who questioned the historical accuracy of Dickens's picture of pre-
Revolutionary France, he replied:

"I had of course full knowledge of the formal surrender of the
feudal privileges, but these had been bitterly felt quite as near to the
time of the Revolution as the Doctor's narrative, which you will remember dates long before the Terror. With the slang of the new
philosophy on the one side, it was surely not unreasonable or unal-
lowable, on the other, to suppose a nobleman wedded to the old cruel
ideas, and representing the time going out as his nephew represented
the time coming in. If there be anything certain on earth, I take it
that the condition of the French peasant generally at that day was
intolerable. No later enquiries or provings by figures will hold water
against the tremendous testimony of men living at the time. There
is a curious book printed at Amsterdam, written to make out no case
whatever, and tiresome enough in its literal dictionary-like minute-
ness; scattered up and down the pages of which is full authority for
my marquis. This is Mercier's Tableau de Paris. Rousseau is the authority for the peasant's shutting up his house when he had a bit of
meat. The tax-tables are authority for the wretched creature's impov-
erishment." [7]

This vision of the Revolution as the relentless consequence of the
past luridly illumines all the scenes of violence and turmoil in *A Tale
of Two Cities* and reverberates even through its last chapter in the
rumble of the death carts trundling to the guillotine. "Crush humanity out of shape once more, under similar hammers," Dickens ex-

claims, "and it will twist itself into the same tortured forms. Sow the same seed of rapacious license and oppression over again, and it will surely yield the same fruit according to its kind.

"Six tumbrils roll along the streets. Change these back again to what they were, thou powerful enchanter, Time, and they shall be seen to be the carriages of absolute monarchs, the equipages of feudal nobles, the toilettes of flaring Jezebels, the churches that are not my father's house but dens of thieves, the huts of millions of starving peasants!" [8]

With somber brilliance, from almost the opening pages, the dark background is established against which there is to burst forth the volcanic fury culminating in those processions of bloodshed. There are the gutters of Sainte Antoine running red from the shattered wine cask, and the red stains on the bare feet and wooden shoes, the red marks on the old rag wound round the head of the woman nursing her baby, the tigerish smear about the mouths of those who have lapped the wine up from the broken staves, the tall joker who scrawls upon the wall with the dark fluid the word BLOOD.[9] There are the wildly plunging horses, the sickening jolt at the street-corner fountain, and the man in a nightcap huddled in the mud and wet, howling like a wild animal over a motionless dirty bundle.[10] There is the sunset striking over the top of the hill into the traveling carriage and steeping the figure of the Marquis St. Evrémonde in crimson.[11] There are everywhere the signs "of a people that had undergone a terrible grinding and regrinding in the mill . . . that grinds young people old," and of a hunger that leaves in a "filthy street . . . no offal, among its refuse, of anything to eat." [12]

What wonder that among the stone faces of gargoyles at the château of the Marquis, looking as if the Gorgon had surveyed them, there should presently lie upon the pillow of the Marquis another stone face, like "a fine mask, suddenly startled, made angry, and petrified," with a knife driven into the stone figure of which it was a part? [13] What wonder that in time the château itself should grow luminous with a strange internal red glow, that the stone faces should show in the blaze as if they were in torment, molten lead boil in the marble fountain, the extinguisher tops of the towers melt like ice and trickle down into four rugged wells of flame? [14]

With a frightful energy and a hideous power the book traces the

rising tumult of the revolutionary storm. As always in delineations of
mob fury, Dickens's emotions are divided; but though he pities the
victims, his deepest understanding is now unmistakably with a people
driven mad. As a prosperous member of the middle class he may de-
plore the rapine and destruction, as a merciful human being he sickens
with the cruelty of mass murder, but in his heart there is a sympathy
with these frenzied victims of oppression turned wolfish that rises into
a fierce exultation. Dickens can understand the harmless little wood-
sawyer, once a village road-mender, and gentle enough in himself,
gradually brought to gloat in the bath of blood.[15] He can understand
these maddened people, at one moment weeping tears of sympathy
and joy for Dr. Manette and the next howling for more heads.[16] He
can understand the wild emotions of the Carmagnole, a "ghastly apparition of a dance-figure gone raving mad," "keeping a ferocious
time . . . like a gnashing of teeth in unison," with dancers who "advanced, retreated, struck at one another's hands," spun, "clutched,
and tore," and then, "with their heads low down, and their hands high
up, swooped screaming off." [17] He understands the "species of fervour
or intoxication, known . . . to have led some persons to brave the guillotine unnecessarily, and to die by it," and comprehends it as "a wild
infection of the wildly shaken public mind. In seasons of pestilence,"
he adds profoundly, "some of us will have a secret attraction to the
disease—a terrible passing inclination to die of it. And all of us have
like wonders hidden in our breasts, only needing circumstances to
evoke them." [18]

Thus the red phantasmagoria of horror passes like a dreadful and
rushing pageant. From the storming of the Bastille, with its seven
gory heads on pikes,[19] it races to the attack on the Hôtel de Ville, with
men terrible in their bloody-minded anger and women famished and
naked, hair streaming, beating their breasts, urging each other on with
wild cries. Here is made captive the aged Foulon, "who told the famished people that they might eat grass." Screams ring out: "Foulon,
who told my baby it might suck grass, when these breasts were dry
with want! O mother of God, this Foulon! O Heaven, our suffering!
Hear me, my dead baby and my withered father: I swear on my knees,
on these stones, to avenge you on Foulon! Husbands, brothers, and
young men, Give us the blood of Foulon, Give us the head of Foulon,
Give us the heart of Foulon, Give us the body and soul of Foulon,

The Sea Rises

Rend Foulon to pieces, and dig him into the ground, that grass may grow from him!" [20]

Into the street he is dragged to be hanged. "Down, and up, and head foremost . . . now, on his knees; now, on his feet; now, on his back; dragged, and struck at, and stifled by the bunches of grass and straw that were thrust into his face by hundreds of hands; torn, bruised, panting, bleeding, yet always entreating and beseeching for mercy; now full of vehement agony of action . . . now, a log of dead wood drawn through a forest of legs . . . Once, he went aloft, and the rope broke, and they caught him shrieking; twice, he went aloft, and the rope broke, and they caught him shrieking; then, the rope was merciful, and held him, and his head was soon on a pike, with grass in the mouth for all Sainte Antoine to dance at the sight of." [21]

So, like a tempest, like an earthquake, the Terror rises, engulfing new victims, taking toll of those who were judges and jurymen, whirling hosts to the guillotine: "long ranks of the new oppressors, risen on the destruction of the old," as Sydney Carton's prophetic vision sees at the close, "perishing by this retributive instrument, before it shall cease out of its present use." But then, "I see a beautiful city and a brilliant people rising from this abyss, and, in their struggles to be truly free, in their triumphs and defeats, through long years to come, I see the evil of this time and of the previous time of which this is the natural birth, gradually making expiation for itself and wearing out." [22]

* * * * *

A *Tale of Two Cities* has been hailed as the best of Dickens's books and damned as the worst. It is neither, but it is certainly in some ways the least characteristic, and that fact explains the divergent opinions of it. Its greatest admirers have usually been those who did not otherwise care much for Dickens. The run of Dickens enthusiasts do not find in the story the delights they love in his other fictions.

It is true, for example, as his friend Forster complained, that it has little humor. The oddities of Lucie Manette's nurse, Miss Pross, and Jerry Cruncher, with his spiky hair, rust-stained fingers, and habit of knocking his wife's head against the bed to prevent her "flopping," are feeble substitutes for Flora Finching's breathless and disjointed volubility, Mrs. Plornish's command of foreign languages, Mr. F's Aunt, and Mr. Pancks despoiling Mr. Casby's bald poll of its benevolent ring of encircling curls.

The few ventures the story makes into pathos are not among Dickens's greatest triumphs in that realm. The scene in Defarge's attic, for example, where Lucie rocks her father's scared white head upon her breast, is marred by the obtrusive literary artifice of tearful cadence in her words, with their recurrent "weep for it, weep for it"; [23] and there are many readers for whom even the death of Sydney Carton seems drenched in over-indulged sentiment, with the trusting little seamstress preceding him to the scaffold and the heavily mournful nobility of his last words: "It is a far, far better thing that I do, than I have ever done; it is a far, far better rest that I go to than I have ever known." [24]

Nor is there in A Tale of Two Cities that rich profusion of character creation and thronging incident with which Dickens elaborated the vaster canvas of his longer novels. The number of people and events are fewer and their intricately linked plot relationships seem more artificial in this tightly constructed, concentrated, and swiftly moving story than they do when Dickens is working on a larger scale. It is too neat that the wineshop-keeper Defarge should be Dr. Manette's old servant, that Mme. Defarge should be a younger sister of that wronged pair whose deaths the Doctor witnessed, that Darnay, his son-in-law, should turn out to be a scion of the wicked St. Evrémonde family, that the innocent Darnay should be drawn to Paris as to a loadstone rock and Defarge find the papers that make it possible to denounce him to the revolutionary tribunal, that John Barsad, the prison spy and turnkey, should be Miss Pross's brother, and—supreme coincidence of all—that Carton should so closely resemble Darnay as to be able without detection to substitute for him. Even Dickens's consummate technical skill leaves so many coincidences a little unconvincing.

The aim that Dickens set himself of making the story one of action, in which the characters should be expressed by incident rather than by dialogue or by any exploration of their inner consciousness, resulted, in so brief and crowded a tale, in a certain psychological thinness. Charles Darnay is hardly more than a walking gentleman and Lucie Manette than a pretty ingénue. Stryver is only a good sketch of the sort of pushing, red-faced vulgarian who feels entirely at home in a world that defeats Sydney Carton; and Jarvis Lorry, the old banker, is well drawn in a few strokes, with his tender heart hidden by the rigid pretense of being a mere business machine forever "turning an immense pecuniary Mangle." [25] Dr. Manette, though sharply and even penetratingly observed, is but an outline in comparison with so subtly and sensitively developed a character as Mr. Dorrit.

Of all the figures in the book Sydney Carton is the one who comes nearest to being deeply realized and the one with whom Dickens identifies himself most closely. This aspect of the work, Hesketh Pearson says, "was the direct outcome of Dickens's emotional life at a time when he had fallen in love, believed himself to be shamefully used and wrongfully abused by people who owed everything to him, experienced the open criticism and implied disapproval of many friends, and felt the loneliness of being generally misunderstood. As a defense against this seemingly hostile outer world, and to comfort his conscience, he dramatized himself both in fact and in fiction, saw himself as a much-wronged deeply-suffering but heroic soul, and produced a work the wide popularity of which shows how many much-wronged deeply-suffering but heroic souls there must be in the world." [26]

This is witty comment, but it is not entirely just either to Dickens or to the readers who have emotionally identified themselves with Sydney Carton. If Carton is a suffering but heroic soul, he is also one who feels within himself a deep sense of having done wrong, of guilt and remorse, and of the need of atoning for his errors. In such a vision of oneself there is none of the sentimentality and deception of dramatizing oneself as an innocent victim. Carton's renunciation is a deed of purification and redemption that is at once the consummation of a deeper justice amid the excesses of vengeance called revolutionary justice and a triumphant assertion of the saving and creating power of love.

Ultimately, however, the two themes of love and revolution are not successfully fused. Dickens tried to portray the French Revolution as the inevitable fruit of seed that had been sowed over many long generations, as the harvest of the past, the working out of a historical necessity imbued with a certain dreadful and tragic social justice even when the innocent were among its victims. And he tried to make Carton's sacrifice both an expiation and a victory, an unselfish surrender of the will melting into peace. But in the process, instead of merging, the truth of revolution and the truth of sacrifice are made to appear in conflict. The flaming melodrama to which the action mounts as it hastens to its end transforms the stern social retribution of the Revolution into a cruel and ferocious bestiality, makes its agents into a mob of monstrous demons, and suffuses Carton's martyrdom in a haloed radiance of personal grandeur that blurs the social criticism of the story, and, for all its power, half destroys its revolutionary meaning.

* * * * *

With *Great Expectations* Dickens returned to familiar scenes. The village where Joe Gargery had his forge is the tiny village of Cooling, a few miles north of Gad's Hill, and the small lozenge-shaped gravestones in a row beside the two parent stones, which Pip describes as those of his father and mother and little brothers, are to be found in Cooling Churchyard. The gray neighboring marshes across which Magwitch limps, shivering, with his fettered limbs, are those of the surrounding countryside sinking muddily to the winding river. The black prison hulk lying out in the stream "like a wicked Noah's ark" [27] is one of the convict ships Dickens had known in the Chatham of his boyhood. The near-by country town is Rochester, the Blue Boar is the Bull, Uncle Pumblechook's house an ancient half-timbered structure in the High Street, and Satis House, where Miss Havisham lives, is really Restoration House, the Elizabethan mansion south of Rochester Cathedral, across the Vines.

The impulse that sent Dickens back to this world of his childhood, now the landscape of his daily walks, was more, however, than the desire to have an appropriate setting for his story. It rose from some deeper need to explore once again, more profoundly even than he had been able to do in *David Copperfield,* his formative years and the bent they had given him, to weigh the nature of his response to them and discover what it revealed. In the intervening years he had written *Bleak House, Hard Times,* and *Little Dorrit;* there were crucial ways in which he had developed tremendously beyond the man he had been. *Great Expectations* shows no trace of *David Copperfield's* self-pity. It pierces fathoms down in self-understanding. It is relentless in self-judgment.

Though the story is told as an autobiographical narrative, Pip, its hero, is much less literally a portrayal of Dickens than David Copperfield was, and the outward events of his life have no resemblance to those in the career of his creator. But, with an emblematic significance, they are so shaped as to enable Dickens to plumb those youthful humiliations and griefs whose wounds even in maturity he buried from all the world. Of his grandfather, the butler at Crewe, he breathed never a syllable, and his grandmother, the housekeeper, peeps out only as Mrs. Rouncewell, down at Chesney Wold in *Bleak House*. Of the debtors' prison and the blacking warehouse he could not bear to tell his own children. Subtly disguised, but now seen in a new light, these shames recur as central themes in *Great Expectations*.

Of far humbler origin than Dickens, Pip is an orphan child whose fierce-tempered sister is married to a village blacksmith. A bony, black-haired termagant, she bullies both her simple-minded, sweet-tempered husband, Joe, and the small boy whom it is her boast that she is bringing up "by hand." [28] That hand is often heavy in blows and in soaping the youngster's face with rasping impatience and harrowing it with a harsh towel. "I suppose myself to be better acquainted than any living authority," Pip says, "with the ridgy effect of a wedding-ring passing unsympathetically over the human countenance." [29] Joe Gargery is a gentle, brawny, almost wholly illiterate giant of a man who makes a pet of the boy and looks forward to the "larks" they will have when Pip is apprenticed to him at the forge. Impressively powerful and adroit in his smithy, in his Sunday clothes he looks "like a scarecrow in good circumstances." [30]

Even in childhood, when Pip is taken to the home of the wealthy and half-mad Miss Havisham, he is tortured by the disdain of her adopted child Estella for his coarse hands, clumsy boots, and common speech. He thinks Estella very pretty, very insulting, and wishes Joe had not taught him to call the knaves of playing cards Jacks. Grown to youth, Pip toils in the sweat and soot of the *black*smith shop, a place in the social scale even lower than wrapping bottles in a *black*ing warehouse. He and his background are unmistakably proletarian, with none of the genteel pretension of the Navy Pay Office, not even the modest dignity of the upper ranks in domestic service.

Wandering as a small boy in the churchyard through the raw marshland mists of a late afternoon, Pip had been terrified by an escaped convict starting up from among the graves. Seizing the child in his arms and tilting him far back over a tombstone, the convict fiercely demanded that Pip secretly bring him a file and food. "You fail, or you go from my words in any partikler, no matter how small it is, and your heart and your liver shall be tore out, roasted and ate. Now, I ain't alone, as you may think I am. There's a young man hid with me, in comparison with which young man I am a Angel. That young man hears the words I speak. That young man has a secret way pecooliar to himself, of getting at a boy, and at his heart, and at his liver . . . I am a keeping that young man from harming you at the present moment, with great difficulty. I find it very hard to hold that young man off your inside." [31]

Quaking, Pip pilfers his sister's pantry before dawn and gets a file from the forge. But the convict is recaptured and transported to Australia. Later, released there on a ticket-of-leave, he prospers and grows rich. Remembering the small boy who had tried to help him on the marsh, he determines to pay for the child's education and turn him into a "gentleman." The offer is made, through a London lawyer named Jaggers, who is also Miss Havisham's man of business, and who gives Pip strict injunctions not to pry into the identity of the unknown benefactor.

Joe generously and affectionately releases Pip from his apprenticeship. "Pip is that hearty welcome," Joe says, "to go free with his services, to honour and fortun', as no words can tell him. But if you think as Money can make compensation to me for the loss of the little child —what come to the forge—and ever the best of friends!—" His voice breaks down and his hand hides his eyes. "O dear good Joe, whom I was so ready to leave and so unthankful to," the narrative exclaims, ". . . I feel the loving tremble of your hand upon my arm, as solemnly this day as if it had been the rustle of an angel's wing!" [32]

The mysterious source of Pip's prosperity, however, is a former tinker's boy, a man of violence, an uneducated criminal. Worse than having been confined in a debtor's prison, the man who is to stand in the place of a father to him had been behind the bars of a common jail and worn clanking chains in the hold of a convict vessel. The story of *Great Expectations* is the story of how all these facts shape Pip's character.

The change in his fortunes transforms him into a mean snob. Associating Jaggers with Miss Havisham, he imagines that she has fantastically determined to make him her heir and dreams that she destines him to marry the dazzling and tormenting Estella. Forgetting Joe's tender comradeship in times past, he feels ashamed of Joe's ignorance and clumsiness, neglects him, and lets him feel uncomfortable when the good fellow visits him in London. When Biddy, who helps about Joe's house, gently reproaches Pip with his attitude, he tries to believe that she is jealous of his good fortune, and tells her, "It's a—it's a bad side of human nature." ("In this sentiment," the narrative adds, "waiving its application, I have since seen reason to think I was right." [33]) Pip acquires the education and the manners of a gentleman, but becomes idle, extravagant, ungrateful, servile to conventional judgments, mortified by his own origins, in terror of having them thrown in his face, pierced by a thousand fears that others are alluding to them or may discover them.

He is not so stupid as to think that his new associates are really better than those he has left behind; he sees clearly enough that Bentley Drummle, one of the young men studying under his own tutor, is a vulgar and overbearing lout. But he is more afraid of Drummle's sneers than of the opinions of those he respects. "So, throughout life," he says, "our worst weaknesses and meannesses are usually committed for the sake of the people whom we most despise." [34] In consequence Pip is never entirely free from the gnawings of inward guilt. "Dissatisfied with my fortune, of course I could not be; but it is possible that I may have been, without quite knowing it, dissatisfied with myself." [35]

Meanwhile Pip's perverse infatuation with Estella brings him as little happiness as his rise in social rank. Miss Havisham, who was jilted by the man she loved, has brought Estella up with one aim, to avenge that injury upon the entire masculine sex, and has molded her into a heartless tormentor. Even in childhood Pip has suffered from her cruelty. "Why don't you cry again, you little wretch?" she taunts him. "Because I'll never cry for you again," he replies; and then reflects: "Which was, I suppose, as false a declaration as ever was made; for I was inwardly crying for her then, and I know what I know of the pain she cost me afterwards." [36]

He knows that Estella despises him and knows that it would be better for him if he could get her out of his head. "I asked myself the question whether I did not surely know that if Estella were beside me at that moment . . . she would make me miserable? I was obliged to admit that I did know it for a certainty, and I said to myself, 'Pip, what a fool you are!' " [37] "According to my experience, the conventional notion of a lover cannot be always true. The unqualified truth is, that when I loved Estella with the love of a man, I loved her simply because I found her irresistible. Once for all; I knew to my sorrow, often and often, if not always, that I loved her against reason, against promise, against peace, against hope, against happiness, against all discouragement that could be. Once for all; I loved her none the less because I knew it, and it had no more influence in restraining me, than if I had devoutly believed her to be human perfection." [38]

"I have no heart," Estella warns him frankly. "Oh! I have a heart to be stabbed in or shot in, I have no doubt," she admits, "and, of course, if it ceased to beat I should cease to be. But you know what I mean. I have no softness there, no—sympathy—sentiment—non-sense." [39] "When you say you love me," she underlines it, "I know what you mean, as a form of words; but nothing more. You address nothing in my breast, you touch nothing there." [40] Nevertheless, "Love her, love her, love her!" whispers Miss Havisham fiercely. "If she favours you, love her. If she wounds you, love her. If she tears your heart to pieces—and as it gets older and stronger it will tear deeper—love her, love her, love her!" [41] And to his pillow, "I love her, I love her, I love her!" Pip repeats a hundred times. "Ah me! I thought those were high and great emotions. But I never thought there was anything low and small in my keeping away from Joe, because I knew she would be contemptuous of him. It was but a day gone, and Joe had brought the tears into my eyes; they had soon dried, God forgive me! soon dried." [42]

From the elevation in rank that has done him so little real good, Pip is thrown down by the return of his benefactor to England. For the old convict can defy his sentence of exile only at the risk of death and confiscation of his property if he is caught, and yet he cannot resist the desire to see the "gentleman" he has made. In a late nocturnal interview in Pip's chambers in the Temple he reveals his identity. "Yes, Pip, dear boy, I've made a gentleman on you! It's me wot has done it! I swore that time, sure as ever I earned a guinea, that guinea should go to you. I swore arterwards, sure as ever I spec'lated and got rich, you should get rich. I lived rough, that you should live smooth; I worked hard that you should be above work. What odds, dear boy?

Do I tell it fur you to feel an obligation? Not a bit. I tell it, fur you to know as that there hunted dunghill dog wot you kept life in, got his head so high that he could make a gentleman—and, Pip, you're him!" [43]

But all of Pip's class-consciousness recoils in loathing from this Abel Magwitch, this crude, vulgar ruffian, laying claim to be regarded as his second father. It is almost as if he smelt the stench of the prison ship about him, the fetid reek of unwashed bodies. "The abhorrence in which I held the man, the dread I had of him, the repugnance with which I shrank from him, could not have been exceeded if he had been some terrible beast." [44] Though Pip's baseless self-respect had not been troubled by the belief that he was dependent upon Miss Havisham, the heiress to a fortune, to owe everything to a low convict, "guilty of I knew not what crimes," [15] and liable to be hanged at the Old Bailey, is shattering to his pride. But, as Bernard Shaw points out, "If Pip had no objection to be a parasite instead of an honest blacksmith, at least he had a better claim to be a parasite on Magwitch's earnings than, as he supposed, on Miss Havisham's property." This, although Shaw imagined that Dickens did not perceive it and shared Pip's feelings, verges on the main point of the story. But Shaw's understanding of Dickens pierced deeper when at the same time he declared that "nothing could exceed the bitterness of his exposure of Pip's parasitism." [46]

Now, however, a nobler manifestation of feeling dictates Pip's course. For Magwitch is in danger of capture; his presence in England is known and he is being sought. In mere loyalty Pip cannot desert this wretched man who has loaded him "with his gold and silver chains," [47] risked his life for Pip's sake, and placed that life in his hands. He must get Magwitch safely out of the country. Pip plans, with his friend Herbert Pocket, to smuggle Magwitch aboard a steamer for Rotterdam from a rowboat on the river. In the attempt Magwitch is captured, desperately wounded. But in the course of the intervening weeks, Pip's attitude toward him has slowly changed. "For now my repugnance to him had all melted away, and in the hunted wounded shackled creature who held my hand in his, I only saw a man who had meant to be my benefactor, and who had felt affectionately, gratefully, and generously towards me with great constancy. I only saw in him a much better man than I had been to Joe." [48] When

Magwitch urges that Pip leave him, saying, "It's best as a gentleman should not be knowed to belong to me now," Pip refuses. "I will never," he vows, "stir from your side when I am suffered to be near you. Please God, I will be as true to you as you have been to me!" [49]

Magwitch dies in prison, touching Pip's hand to his lips, and not knowing, what Pip knows, that his entire fortune has been forfeited to the Crown. Thus all Pip's "great expectations" melt away into nothing. The only good, as he looks back upon them, that he can see they have done is the partnership that Pip, unknown to Herbert Pocket, had obtained for his friend in a mercantile business trading in the East. It had required the revelation of the source of his expectations and then their loss to bring home to him the full depth of his own snobbery and selfish ingratitude. Pip becomes a clerk in Herbert's firm, works hard, pays his debts, and in the course of years is made a partner. "I must not leave it to be supposed that we were ever a great House, or that we made mints of money. We were not in a grand way of business, but we had a good name, and worked for our profits, and did very well." [50]

*   *   *   *   *

So, with the tacked-on addition of a belated marriage to Estella, end Pip's "great expectations." Surely the entire drift of the story reveals how clearly Dickens had at last "come to see that making his living by sticking labels on blacking bottles and rubbing shoulders with boys who were not gentlemen, was as little shameful as being the genteel apprentice in the office of Mr. Spenlow, or the shorthand writer recording the unending twaddle of the House of Commons and its overflow of electioneering bunk on the hustings of all the Eatans-wills in the country." [50a]

In that curious and brilliant novel, *Evan Harrington*, George Meredith does penance for his own snobbery in concealing the fact that he came of a family of naval outfitting tailors in Portsmouth. Paying fictional tribute to the character of his grandfather, portrayed as "the great Mel," the fox-hunting tailor, the story heaps witty scorn on the Countess de Salazar and the other daughters who love the old man and yet hide their relationship to him. *Great Expectations* is Dickens's penance for his subservience to false values. The blacksmith and "the taint of prison and crime" [51] which have so mortified Pip, and of which he comes to feel a remorseful humiliation at ever having been ashamed, are both more humbling to genteel thought than the blacking warehouse and the debtors' prison. "The reappearance of Mr. Dickens in the character of a blacksmith's boy," as Shaw remarks, "may be regarded as an apology to Mealy Potatoes." [52]

There is a layer of criticism, however, in *Great Expectations* still deeper than this personal triumph over false social values. It pierces to the very core of the leisure-class ideal that lurks in the heart of a pecuniary society. This is symbolized in Pip's dream of becoming a gentleman living in decorative grandeur on money he has done nothing to earn, supported entirely by the labors of others. It was the dream of nineteenth-century society, willing to base its hopes of comfort and ostentation on the toil of the laboring classes. Pip's "great expectations" were the great expectations of Victorian society, visions of a parasitic opulence of future wealth and glory, a materialistic paradise of walnut, plush, gilt mirrors, and heavy dinners. The aim of the fashionable world was an eternal and luxurious ease, the goal of the middle-class businessman to retire to a surburban villa on a fortune.

Although Dickens never expected to be exempt from work himself, and worked hard all his life, earlier in his career he had accepted this ideal. There is no suggestion that Mr. Winkle, Mr. Tupman, or Mr. Snodgrass need ever think of doing anything for a living. Mr. Brownlow and Mr. Grimwig have no occupations. At the close of *Nicholas Nickleby*, Nicholas retires to a country villa and lives upon his share from the profits of the Cheeryble business which others carry on. Little Nell's grandfather sounds the first warning note against the false dream of gaining a luxury one has not earned. Martin Chuzzlewit, after a few abortive efforts to make a living, returns to living on his grandfather. Mr. Dombey leaves to Mr. Carker and a host of subordinates almost all the management of the enterprise from which he derives his wealth. Even the benevolent Mr. Jarndyce seems to be merely a man of property, although Richard Carstone now strikes another warning note against depending upon "expectations" instead of making oneself of use to the world. Stephen Blackpool in *Hard Times*, and Arthur Clennam in *Little Dorrit*, represent the emergence of a new kind of hero in Dickens's novels: the earnest, sober, industrious worker who contributes his share to the efforts of the world.

But Pip has no occupation and no ideal save that of an empty good form. He and the "Finches of the Grove," [53] the club of young men of leisure to which he belongs, do nothing but spend money, play cards, drink toasts, buy elaborate wardrobes, drive horses, and go to the theater. They have no culture, no interest in the arts, in music, in the world of reflective thought. Pip "reads" with his tutor and has books on his shelves, but we never learn what he reads or perceive that it has had any effect on him. He has no philosophy, only a set of conventions. The virtues that ultimately save him are mainly those that he unconsciously absorbed from Joe in his childhood. His return to a life of modest usefulness is a repudiation of the ideal of living by the sweat of someone else's brow. And Dickens's analysis of the frivolity, falseness, emptiness, loss of honor, loss of manhood, and sense of futility that the acceptance of that ideal imposed upon Pip is a measure of the rottenness and corruption he now found in a society dominated by it. The system of that society and its grandiose material dreams, he realizes, involve a cheapening, a distortion, a denial of human values.

From another angle, in the portrayal of the lawyer Jaggers, *Great Expectations* conveys the same judgment. It is impossible not to see in him, T. A. Jackson points out, "Dickens' deepening sense that success in business in the bourgeois world can be won only at the expense of everything nobly generous, elevating, sympathetic, and humane." [54] Mr. Jaggers specializes in representing accused criminals, whose unsavory cases he handles with the most unscrupulous and triumphant skill. But with the departure of every felonious visitor he goes to a closet and cleans his hands with scented soap, as if he were washing off the client. On one occasion, Pip remarks, "he seemed to have been engaged on a case of a darker complexion than usual, for we found him with his head butted into this closet, not only washing his hands, but laving his face and gargling his throat. And even when he had done all that, and had gone all round the jack-towel, he took out his penknife and scraped the case out of his nails before he put his coat on." [55] Though Mr. Jaggers is a highly successful and respected professional man, his own sense of the necessities his life imposes on him is one of degradation and pollution. Could there be a clearer symbolic suggestion that much of the business of such a society is dirty business?

Its consequence is almost to force upon a man of any sensitivity a dual personality, a division and antagonism between the selfish-acquisitive and all that is warmly human. Mr. Jaggers's clerk Wemmick dwells in the kindest domestic affection at Walworth with his deaf and ancient father, "the aged parent," [56] in a little wooden villa with a narrow moat, a plank drawbridge, a miniature cannon which he fires at night, and a small Gothic entrance door. But all this feeling and imagination he keeps for his home; in the office his mouth is a dry slit like a mailbox, he is dead against Pip's desire to serve his friend Herbert, and harps on the dominant necessity of acquiring "portable property." [57] Only at home will he tell Pip, "This is devilish good of of you." [58] "Walworth is one place," he says, "and this office is another." [59]

Both for Wemmick and for Mr. Jaggers, then, their office in Little Britain is a kind of prison in which they lock up their better selves and subdue them to the world of venality. Thus the symbolism of *Great Expectations* develops that of *Little Dorrit* and of *A Tale of Two Cities*. The Marshalsea and Mrs. Clennam in the dark house of greed and Mr. Merdle in the glittering mansion of speculation and the world of "society" are all immured in the same vast outer dungeon of imprisoning ideas. Darnay and Carton are the jailed victims of revenge for past deeds of exploitation and cruelty, and Dr. Manette is driven mad in the Bastille, broken and goaded to a destroying curse by that past injustice. Now, in this last story of the three, Jaggers, Wemmick, Magwitch, Pip, are under like shadows of prison walls; and Miss Havisham, her heart broken by a rapacious adventurer, creates in Estella a living curse, and, surrounded by greedy relatives, wanders self-incarcerated in her dark, decaying house. And intertwined like an iron chain with all of these is Pip's despairing and disillusioned obsession with Estella, the darkest emotional imprisonment of them all.

It is inevitable that we should associate Pip's helpless enslavement to Estella with Dickens's desperate passion for Ellen Lawless Ternan. The very name "Estella" seems a kind of lawless anagram upon some of the syllables and initials of Ellen's name. The tone of Dickens's unhappy letters to Collins and Forster during all the time between the last night of *The Frozen Deep* and the time of the separation discloses an entirely new intensity of personal misery far exceeding the restlessness of years before. His insistence that since that last night he had "never known a moment's peace or content" centers his distress unmistakably not on the "domestic unhappiness" alone but on a person: "never was a man so seized and rended by one Spirit." [60] His allusion in a letter to Mrs. Watson to "the princess I adore—you have no idea how intensely I love her!" [61] points in the same direction, like the desire he there expresses to go "climbing after her, sword in hand," and either win her "or be killed." The words are a kind of desperate playing with his frustration, a half unveiling disguised in ambiguity. And later still there is the black mingling of fear and bitterness and rage in his outburst about the policeman endeavoring to enact the role of a go-between in Berners Street.

With these things must be seen the unprecedently somber hues in which Dickens depicts Pip's feeling for Estella. Never before had he portrayed a man's love for a woman with such emotional depth or revealed its desperation of compulsive suffering. Dolly Varden's capriciousness is a childish coquetry beside Estella's cold obduracy. The unhappiness that breathes in Dickens's youthful letters to Maria Beadnell is the suffering of a boy, whereas Pip's is the stark misery of a man. David Copperfield's heartache for Dora Spenlow is an iridescent dream-grief to this agonized nightmare-reality. Only with Philip Carey's dreadful servitude to the pallid indifference of the sluttish Mildred, in *Of Human Bondage*, or, in Proust's masterpiece, with Swann's craving for Odette, is there anything like Pip's subjection to Estella's queenly and torturing disregard. Pip's love is without tenderness, without illusion; it reveals no desire to confer happiness upon the beloved; it is all self-absorbed need. Where in all his past career as a novelist had Dickens painted such passions and in what abyss of personal agony had he learned them?

In love, too, then, Pip's "great expectations," like Dickens's own, have been disappointed and deceived, and ideally the story should have ended on that loss, as Dickens originally planned. Pip's desire for Estella is as selfish as his desire to be a gentleman, not at all the desire to give, only the desire to receive. It is the culminating symbol and the crowning indictment of a society dedicated to selfish ends. It is a bitter revelation of the emptiness of its values and of the distortions they inflict upon all generous feeling, even upon the need to love and to be loved. Pip is not all selfish; he is capable both of generosity and of love. Indeed, at the end he has learned from his experience, learned to work, learned to love, learned to think for others.

Both as art and as psychology it was poor counsel that Lytton gave in urging that the shaping of a lifetime in Estella be miraculously undone. Save for this, though, *Great Expectations* is the most perfectly constructed and perfectly written of all Dickens's works. It should close with that misty moonlight scene in Miss Havisham's ruined garden, but, as Shaw suggests, with Pip and Estella then bidding each other a chastened farewell and Pip saying, "Since that parting I have been able to think of her without the old unhappiness; but I have never tried to see her again, and I know I never shall." [62]

In spite of its theme of disillusion *Great Expectations* is not in its pervading atmosphere a melancholy book. Not merely does it move to an ending of serene and twilight peace, but there are many scenes of high-spirited enjoyment and of the comic gusto Dickens had always been able to command even in the midst of his deepest despair. There is the child Pip's flight into a series of fantastic whoppers when Uncle Pumblechook is badgering him to tell what happened at his first visit to Miss Havisham's and he invents a picture of Miss Havisham sitting in a black velvet coach having cake and wine on gold plates while they feed veal cutlets from a silver basket to four large dogs, wave flags, and shout hurrahs.[63] There is Mr. Wopsle's famous performance of *Hamlet*, with the Danish nobility represented by "a noble boy in the wash-leather boots of a gigantic ancestor, a venerable Peer with a dirty face, who seemed to have risen from the people late in life, and the Danish chivalry with a comb in its hair and a pair of white silk legs presenting on the whole a feminine appearance," and the church in the graveyard scene resembling a "small ecclesiastical wash-house." [64] There is Trabb's boy imitating Pip's progress down the High Street by pulling up his shirt collar, twining his side hair, sticking an arm akimbo, smirking extravagantly, and drawling, "Don't know yah, don't know yah, 'pon my soul don't know yah!" [65] There is Joe's description of how the robbers looted Pumblechook's shop: "and they drinked his wine, and they partook of his wittles, and they slapped his face, and they pulled his nose, and they tied him up to his bedpust, and they giv' him a dozen, and they stuffed his mouth full of flowering annuals to perwent his crying out." [66]

But these joyous moments do not undermine the predominant seriousness of *Great Expectations* and its theme. As Pip and Estella, with linked hands, leave that misty and forlorn garden of their childhood they are reminiscent of the parents of humanity exiled, but not utterly without hope, from another Garden:

The world was all before them, where to choose
Their place of rest, and Providence their guide.
They hand in hand, with wandering steps and slow,
Through Eden took their solitary way.[67]

CHAPTER FOUR

Intimations of Mortality

GOLD now poured itself out for Dickens in an endless stream. Advance sheets of his novels brought him handsome sums from Harper and Brothers in New York. Whenever he wished he could obtain £1,000 for a short story. The sales of *All the Year Round*, already risen with the publication of *Great Expectations* to several thousands higher than the London *Times*, continued rising when Lytton's *A Strange Story* began coming out.[1] *Great Expectations* went into a fourth edition within a few weeks of its appearance in book form.[2]

But Dickens struggled with personal distresses that weighed upon him ever more heavily. The careers of the boys still presented problems. Frank was proving of little use in the office.[3] Alfred, who had been destined for the Royal Military Academy at Woolwich, was not a good enough student to meet the competition.[4] Plorn, now at Wimbledon with Harry, was shy, lonely, and ill-adjusted.[5] Deaths among old friends and associates gave Dickens the feeling that he was part of a forlorn charge steadily mown down upon the field: "We must close up the ranks," he would say, "and march on." [6] Deaths in his family loaded him with more griefs and responsibilties. His own "miserable anxieties," he lamented, "gathered and gathered"; [7] they were swollen into a dreadful burden that afflicted him with an anguish of unrest. He chafed bitterly at the troubles of society and the state of the world. His health was gradually breaking, but his will refused to recognize any warnings and relentlessly laid upon his body the most wearing exertions.

He had arranged that on the completion of *Great Expectations* in *All the Year Round* on August 3, 1861, it should be immediately followed by Lytton's *A Strange Story*. "I would gladly pay you £1,500," he had written in the preceding December; and he promised that in addition he could obtain Lytton £1,200 "for the right of re-publication in collected form for two years," as well as £300 for the transmission of weekly proofs to America, a total of £3,000.[8] Reading advance sheets of the first third in his bedroom at night, "I COULD NOT lay them aside," he wrote the author, but "got into a very ghostly state indeed. . . . If you were the Magician's servant instead of the Magician, these potent spirits would get the better of you; but you *are* the Magician . . ."[9]

During the middle of June, with Georgy and Mamey, Dickens paid a visit to Lytton at Knebworth,[10] and saw the houses for the Guild of Literature and Art that were now rising near by at Stevenage. Across the road, they also looked in curiously on Mr. James Lucas, the "Hertfordshire Hermit," a man of means who chose to live with matted hair and unwashed body, clad only in a blanket, in the foul kitchen of his decaying mansion. He is impaled satirically, "blanketed and skewered and sooted and greased," as Mr. Mopes in "Tom Tiddler's Ground," the Christmas story of the following winter.[11]

Despite neuralgic pains in his face, Dickens practiced assiduously on the readings for the fall, adding to them "the Bastille prisoner from the Tale of Two Cities" and "Mr. Chops the Dwarf," from the Christmas story of 1858.[12] Arthur Smith, his manager, was seriously ill, but even in his "wakings and wanderings" so desperately unwilling to relinquish his work that Dickens hesitated to replace him. "With a sick man who has been so zealous and faithful, I feel bound to be very tender and patient." "You may imagine how anxious it makes me, and at what a dead stop I stand." Finally he engaged Thomas Headland, an assistant of Smith's, to take over all the heavy part of his duties. "Of course I pay him," Smith said faintly, "and not you."[13]

Shortly before the tour was to begin Dickens received a group of photographs he had had taken of himself. To one of them his family took exception. "A general howl of horror greeted the appearance of No. 18," he told Watkins the photographer, "and a riotous attempt was made to throw it out of window. I calmed the popular fury by promising that it should never again be beheld within these walls. I think I mentioned to you when you showed it to me, that I felt persuaded it would not be liked. It has a grim and wasted aspect, and perhaps might be made useful as a portrait of the Ancient Mariner."[14]

In the first few days of October, Arthur Smith died; "it is as if," said Dickens, "my right arm were gone." [15] Hard upon this Henry Austin died, and Dickens found that his sister Letitia, Austin's widow, would be left in straitened circumstances. In virtue of Austin's useful services as Secretary to the Board of Health it seemed that Letitia might be given a government pension, but it was not until almost three years later, after interminable memorializing and patient letter-writing, that the slow-moving processes of the Circumlocution Office at last approved a grant of £60 a year.[16] Meanwhile, Dickens as trustee took charge of Letitia's affairs. Even here he was pursued with unreasonable demands. "I can only pay Mr. Henry Austin's own lawful debts," he wearily told one creditor. "His father's I have nothing to do with." [17]

November saw the marriage of Charley Dickens to Bessie Evans, the daughter of Frederick Evans. Dickens did not approve the match and feared it would be disastrous. He believed that Charley cared nothing for the girl, but had been "committed by his foolish mother, chiefly because her hatred of the bride used to know no bounds." [18] Dickens's depreciatory judgment of Catherine had not softened in the three and a half years they had been separated. Nor had his antagonism to Frederick Evans diminished. "Of course," he wrote to Beard, Charley's godfather, "I understand your responding to any request on the part of Charley, or of his mother, to attend the dear fellow's marriage. But I must add the expression of my earnest hope that it is not your intention to enter Mr. Evans's house on that occasion." [19] And, just as Catherine had not been present at Katey's wedding, Dickens was absent from Charley's. But a year later, when Bessie had borne her first child, she and Charley and Dickens's baby granddaughter were at Gad's Hill for Christmas. "Think of the unmitigated nonsense," Dickens exclaimed, "of an inimitable grandfather!" [20]

The readings got off to a poor start with *Copperfield* on October 28th at Norwich. Headland had mismanaged things; the audience was sparse and "lumpish," [21] the auditorium was "a great, cold, stone-paved Gothic Hall," with wind howling in the arches, Dickens missed Arthur, and felt that he himself was reading badly.[22] Headland did his best, Dickens said, but "the look of him is very different from the poor lost fellow in his evening dress. Besides which, Headland and the rest of them are always somewhere, and he was always every-where." [23] But the next night went better. The reading was *Nickleby*, which went off with a roar throughout. "The people were really quite ridiculous to see when Squeers read the boys' letters." [24]

Mistakes, however, continued to be made. At Newcastle all the bill-posters announcing the readings were lost and finally turned out to have been sent by Johnson, the printer, to the reading hall, "where they had been lying in some vault or other, and might have lain there until Doomsday." "Johnson's mistake," said Headland. Somehow *Little Dombey* was announced for an evening when Dickens had de-cided on *Copperfield*; "Johnson's mistake," said Headland again.[25] From Edinburgh came frantic complaints that no posters and no tickets had arrived; hundreds upon hundreds of people could be told nothing except that Dickens *was* coming. " 'Johnson's mistake,' says the unlucky Headland. Of course, I know that the man who never made a mistake in poor Arthur's time is not likely to be always making mistakes now." [26]

At one of the Newcastle readings Dickens's authoritative quick-ness prevented a disaster. "Suddenly, when they were all very still over Smike," the gas-batten lighting his figure from above the plat-form came down with a crash, "and it looked as if the room was falling. There were three great galleries crammed to the roof, and a high steep flight of stairs, and a panic must have destroyed numbers of people. A lady in the front row of stalls screamed, and ran out wildly towards me, and for one instant there was a terrible wave in the crowd." [27] "So I addressed her, laughing, and half-asked and half-ordered her to sit down again; and in a minute, it was all over." [28] "It took some few minutes to mend, and I looked on with my hands in my pockets; for I think if I had turned my back for a moment there still might have been a move." [29] His own crew of men "had such a fearful sense of what might have happened (besides the real danger of Fire) that they positively shook the boards I stood on, with their trembling when they came up to put things right. I am proud to re-cord that the gas-man's sentiment, as delivered afterwards, was, 'The more you want of the master, the more you'll find in him.' " [30]

On the first night at Edinburgh, through some further blunder, countless tickets had been sold for which there were no seats. "There was a tearing mad crowd in all the passages and in the street, . . .

forcing a great turbid stream of people into the already crammed hall."
When Dickens appeared, a hundred frantic men mounted upon
ledges and cornices shouted objections. He expressed regret for the
mismanagement, and offered to adjourn to the Music Hall or to cancel
this engagement "and come back later and read to all Edinburgh if
they would." There were cheers and a cry, "Go on Mr. Dickens.
Everybody will be quiet now." But uproarious spirits clamored, "We
won't be quiet. We won't let the reading be heard. We're ill-treated."
Calmly closing his book, Dickens assured them the reading would not
be given until they were all agreed.

When quiet was restored and Dickens was about to begin, a gentleman "with full dressed lady torn to ribbons on his arm" cried out
a suggestion that some of the ladies, at least, might be accommodated
on the platform. "Most certainly," Dickens agreed. "In a minute the
platform was crowded. Everybody who came up, laughed, and said
it was nothing when I told them in a low voice how sorry I was; but
the moment they were there, the sides began to roar, because they
couldn't see." Dickens proposed that those on the platform sit down.
"Instantly they all dropped into recumbent groups, with Respected
Chief standing up in the centre. I don't know what it looked like
most—a battlefield—an impossible tableau—a gigantic picnic. There
was one very pretty girl in full dress lying down on her side all night,
and holding on to one leg of my table. So I read Nickleby and the
Trial. From the beginning to the end they didn't lose one point, and
they ended with a great burst of cheering." [31]

Despite Headland's incompetent management, the readings themselves were a prolonged series of triumphs. If the new reading from
Nickleby was a "wonderful success," the *Copperfield* was "without
precedent in the reading chronicles. Four rounds when I went in—
laughing and crying and thundering all the time—and a great burst
of cheering at last." [32] When Dickens got to Cheltenham in January,
Macready, "with tears running down his face," [33] was rendered utterly
incoherent. "I found him quite unable to speak, and able to do nothing but square his dear old jaw all on one side, and roll his eyes (half
closed), like Jackson's picture of him. And when I said something
light about it, he returned: 'No—er—Dickens! I swear to Heaven that,
as a piece of passion and playfulness—er—indescribably mixed up together, it does—er—No, really, Dickens!—amaze me as profoundly

as it moves me. But as a piece of Art—and you know—er—that I—No, Dickens! By God!—have seen the best Art in a great time—it is incomprehensible to me. How it is got at -er—how it is done—er— how one man can—well! It lays me on my—er—back, and it is of no use talking about it.' With which he put his hand upon my breast, and pulled out his pocket handkerchief," and Dickens felt as if he were playing in his tragic role of Werner.[34]

The sequence of the readings was temporarily interrupted at Liverpool on December 14th by the death of the Prince Consort, but then resumed at the end of the month and brought to its planned conclusion on January 30, 1862.[35] In recognition of the public sympathy with the Queen, Dickens felt that the half-dozen readings scheduled between the middle of December and Christmas should be canceled, all the more because the Queen had "always been very considerate and gracious to me, and I would on no account do anything that might seem unfeeling or disrespectful." [36] The endless national lamentations, however, after a time struck him as exaggerated: "the Jackasses that people are at present making of themselves on that subject!" [37] he exclaimed, and privately confessed himself "shocked by the rampant toadyism" and "blatant speeches" that were "given to the four winds." [38] In the course of later years the legend of the Prince's marmoreal perfections filled him with impatience. Seeing the words "Prince Albert Pudding" on the dinner menu at Gad's Hill, he crossed them out and substituted "Flunkey Pudding," although later still he allowed that dessert to be called "The Great and Good Pudding." [39]

With the end of February Dickens exchanged Gad's Hill for a house at 16 Hyde Park Gate South for a few months, and in March began his London series of readings.[40] He was enthusiastic about Collins's No Name, which was soon to begin in All the Year Round,[41] but he disliked the London residence and complained that "this odious little house seems to have stifled and darkened my invention" so that he could hit upon nothing for a story of his own.[42] He was saddened, too, by the death of the erratic and lovable Angus Fletcher,[43] and by the death of Cornelius Felton. "Poor dear Felton! It is 20 years since I told you of the delight my first knowledge of him gave me," he wrote Forster, "and it is as strongly upon me to this hour. . . . Alas! alas! all ways have the same finger post at the head of them, and at every turning in them." [44]

Dickens was anxious about Georgina, too, who had developed "degeneration of the heart" and who was "very low about herself." "No one can ever know what she has been to us, and how she has supplied an empty place and an ever widening gap, since the girls were mere dolls." [45] He planned, therefore, to take her and Mary to Paris in the autumn, hoping the rest and change would do her good. "Georgina very, very poorly," he wrote Collins. "Excruciating pain in the left breast is the last symptom. It seized her at dinner yesterday, and she seems to me—but I might overstate the case—to grow steadily worse." [46]

With this fear haunting him and "with my own old load (of which you know something)," he confessed to Collins, "I am become so restless that I cannot answer for anything."[47] These "miserable anxieties . . . I must impart one of these days when I come to you or you come to me. I shall fight out of them, I daresay: being not easily beaten—but they have gathered and gathered." [48] The desperate infatuation mirrored in Pip's obsession with Estella was gnawing with ever sharper fangs into his heart. It seems evident that Ellen was unresponsive to his need and cold to his emotion. Though he would speak of it only to Collins and Forster, his mood was one of repressed misery.

*   *   *   *   *

He had by now hit upon an idea for another twenty-number serial and even found a title for it, *Our Mutual Friend*; "but whether, with all this unsettled fluctuating distress in my mind, I could force an original book out of it, is another question." [49] And yet his consciousness of all those dependent upon him made him feel that he ought to do something to spur his earnings. The American Civil War rendered impossible the reading tour in that country which he had considered a few years earlier, but more and more earnest invitations were now coming from Australia. Only that June an Australian in London had offered him £10,000 outright for an eight months' tour,[50] and there were others who considered £12,000 a low estimate for the profits of a six months' absence. "If the notion of these speculators be anything like accurate, I should come back rich." [51]

Dickens consequently considered this Australian venture. He might take Charles Collins with him as his secretary and, while he was there, do a series on "The Uncommercial Traveller Upside Down" for *All the Year Round.*[51a] A little later he proposed this post, in the event of his going, to his old friend Beard: in money, he pointed out, it would represent for Beard "some four or five years of present employment at home" and the "repute attaching to such an experience and trust" might "be helpful afterwards." [52] "How painfully unwilling I am to go," he exclaimed to Forster, "and yet how painfully sensible that perhaps I ought to go—with all the hands upon my skirts that I cannot fail to feel and see there, whenever I look round. It is a struggle of no common sort, as you will suppose, you who know the circumstances of the struggler." [53]

But the more Dickens reflected upon this long separation from all that was dear to him, the more his heart sickened at the exile. "I know perfectly well before-hand how unspeakably wretched I should be." [54] "The domestic life of the Readings is all but intolerable to me when I am away for a few weeks at a time merely, and what it would be—" "If I were to go it would be a penance and a misery, and I dread the thought of it more than I can possibly express." [55] In the end, he found the idea unbearable, and rejected it.

On October 16th Dickens started for Paris and three days later came back to Boulogne to meet Georgina and Mary and take them on to the capital.[56] In the Rue du Faubourg Saint-Honoré Dickens took a pretty apartment, "but house-rent here," he lamented, "is awful to mention." Mary's tiny Pomeranian, Mrs. Bouncer, he announced in the same letter, had to be muzzled, by order of the Paris police, and was "a wonderful spectacle to behold in the streets, restrained like a raging Lion." [57]

Settled as was Dickens's "animosity towards the French Usurper," [58] Napoleon III, he thought the Emperor right in proposing to England and Russia that they join with France in making an earnest "appeal to America to stop the brutal war." [59] Dickens had no sympathy with either side, and was surprised when an American friend told him that the North would win.[60] Slavery he believed had nothing to do with the quarrel, save insofar as the industrial and more powerful North found it convenient to lay down a line beyond which slavery should not be permitted to extend lest the South be able to recover its old political power.

"Any reasonable creature may know, if willing, that the North hates the Negro, and that until it was convenient to make a pretence that sympathy with him was the cause of the war, it hated the abolitionists and derided them up hill and down dale. They will both rant and lie and fight until they come to a compromise; and the slave may be thrown into that compromise or thrown out of it, just as it happens. As to Secession being Rebellion, it is distinctly possible by state papers that Washington considered it no such thing—that Massachusetts, now loudest against it, has itself asserted its right to secede, again and again." [61]

Wilkie Collins was ill, and worried lest he might not be able to keep up to schedule with the installments of *No Name*. Dickens begged him to dismiss that fear from his mind. "Write to me at Paris at any moment, and say you are unequal to your work, and want me: and I will come to London straight and do your work. I am quite confident that, with your notes and a few words of explanation, I could take it up at any time, and do it. Absurdly unnecessary to say that it would be a makeshift! But I could do it, at a pinch, so like you as that no one should find out the difference. Don't make much of this offer in your mind—it is nothing—except to ease it. If you should want help, I am as safe as a Bank. The trouble would be nothing to me, and the triumph of overcoming a difficulty—great." [62] It is not known whether Collins needed to accept Dickens's services.[62a]

During Dickens's stay in Paris he also wrote his last known letter to Maria Winter. In 1858 her husband had failed in business and after a fruitless appeal to George Beadnell, her father, she had turned to Dickens for aid. "I wish to Heaven," he had replied, "it were in my power to help Mr. Winter to any new opening in life. But you can hardly imagine how powerless I am in such a case. . . . Commercial opportunities above all are so removed from me, that I dare not encourage a hope of my power to serve Mr. Winter with my good word, ever coming within a year's journey of my will and wish to do so.

"But I really think that your Father who could do so much in such a case, without drawing at all heavily upon his purse, might be induced to do what—I may say to you, Maria—it is no great stretch of sentiment to call his duty. . . . Forgive my recommending this, if you have so anticipated the recommendation as to have done all that possibly can be done to move him. But what you tell me about George seems so strange, so hard, and so ill balanced, that I cannot avoid the subject." [63]

Now, in November, 1862, George Beadnell died, leaving an estate of £40,000. "Of course I could not be surprised, knowing his great age, by the wearing out of his vitality," Dickens wrote Maria; "but—almost equally of course—it was a shock too, for the old Past comes out of its grave when I think of him, and the Ghosts of a good many years stand about his memory." [64]

The stay in Paris improved Georgina's health, and she and Mary returned to Gad's Hill with Dickens for Christmas with the boys, Katey and her husband, and Charley, his wife, and "his preposterous child." [65] "Somebody's Luggage," the Christmas story of that year, had sold 185,000 copies by December 22nd.[66] "The house is pervaded by boys," Dickens wrote Mary Boyle; "and every boy has (as usual) an unaccountable and awful power of producing himself in every part of the house at every moment, apparently in fourteen pairs of creaking boots. My dear Mary, ever affectionately yours, Joe." [67]

In the middle of January, leaving Georgina and Mary at Gad's Hill, Dickens returned to Paris, where he now took a suite of rooms at the Hôtel du Helder. On the 17th and again, by clamorous demand, on the 29th and 30th, he read for charity at the British Embassy. "The Reading so stuns and oversets the Parisians," he reported to Wills, "that I shall have to do it again. Blazes of Triumph!" [68]

"They are so extraordinarily quick to understand a face and gesture, going together, . . . that people who don't understand English, positively understand the Readings! I suppose that such an audience for a piece of Art is not to be found in the world. . . . I got things out of the old Carol—effects I mean—so entirely new and so very strong, that I quite amazed myself and wondered where I was going next. I really listened to Mr. Peggotty's narrative in Copperfield, with admiration. When Little Emily's letter was read, a low murmur of irrepressible emotion went about like a sort of sea. When Steerforth made a pause in shaking hands with Ham, they all lighted up as if the notion fired an electric chain. When David proposed to Dora, gorgeous beauties all radiant with diamonds, clasped their fans between their two hands, and rolled about in ecstasy. . . . As to the Trial, their perception of the Witnesses, and particularly of Mr. Winkle, was quite extraordinary. And whenever they saw the old Judge coming in, they tapped one another and laughed with that amazing relish that I could hardly help laughing as much myself. All this culminated on the last night, when they positively applauded and called out expressions of delight, out of the room into the cloak room, out of the cloak room into their carriages, and in their carriages away down the Faubourg." [69]

Although Dickens could not resist the infection of their hilarity, his own emotional state was far different. There is no undeniable evidence pointing at this time to the development of his connection with Ellen Ternan, as there is later, but it seems not unlikely that either now or perhaps during the previous period of almost a month in England, Ellen's obduracy had at last given way. If so, her surrender brought him little of that shining ecstasy with which throbbing imagination conceives the world will be transfigured by triumphant love. The fatal confluence established by his old unhappy passion for Maria Beadnell, his ideal vision of Mary Hogarth, the deepening misery of his life with Catherine, and the painful evaporation of a dream with Maria's reappearance, all led almost inevitably to his longing for the solace of a beautiful and youthful tenderness and to his desiring to know, before it was too late, the enchantment that had always eluded him, but it did not lead to his finding happiness or understanding.

Nor, though Collins had been able to draw him in the desperation of his later married years into nocturnal adventures beginning in the greenrooms of London theaters or mingling with the *Lorettes* of Paris, could Dickens ever really share those "furtive Don Giovanni purposes" so easy to the younger man. Dickens was no Don Giovanni, flitting carelessly from Donna Elvira to Zerlina, toying lightly with the triumphs of sexual conquest. All his heart yearned for loyalty, devotion, and ideal love. The domestic serenity and romance he had not found with Catherine, and that his separation from her rendered forever impossible, was the very essence of his need. His was no Bohemian flouting of moral standards, but an irresistible compulsion.

Whether or no this was the period when the relationship between Dickens and Ellen deepened into a liaison—and in the nature of things such matters must usually be conjectural—their intimacy, though as much hidden from the world as possible, was known to numbers of those surrounding him. Though even when Dickens was dead they were guarded in referring to their knowledge, they reinforce the conclusive evidence in Dickens's own hand that emerged later still. ". . . There are circumstances connected with the later years of the illustrious novelist," wrote George Augustus Sala in 1893, "which should not and must not be revealed for fifty years to come at the very least." [70] And Edmund Yates, in 1884, said: "My intimacy with Dickens, his kindness to me, my devotion to him, were such that my lips are sealed and my tongue is paralyzed as regards circumstances which, if I felt less responsibility and delicacy, I might be at liberty to state." Both these statements transparently hint that the secrets they refuse to reveal are of a kind that the world ordinarily regards as gravely compromising.[71]

It was legally impossible for Dickens and Ellen to marry, but from the middle sixties, according to Katey, Ellen often stayed at Gad's Hill, Georgina called her "dearest Ellen," and Dickens provided her with "an establishment of her own at Peckham." [72] In 1865 Ellen was with Dickens when he was returning from a short vacation in Paris, and traveled in the same compartment of the boat train from Folkestone to London.[73] Planning his American reading tour in 1867, he longed desperately to be able to have Ellen join him, and settled with her that, after he had arrived there and decided whether her presence could be arranged without scandal, he would send Wills a cablegram in code for transmisison to her. In his diary, opposite the calendar for November of that year, with emphatic underlinings he entered the memorandum:

> "IN ANY CASE. TEL:
> Tel: all well means
> *You come*
> Tel: safe and well, means
> *You don't come.*" [74]

And in a sheet of instructions to Wills he included two items concerning Ellen:

> "NELLY
> "If she wants any help will come to you, or, if she changes her address will immediately let you know the change. Until then, it will be Villa Trollope, a Ricorboli, Firenze, Italy. . . .
> "On the day after my arrival out, I will send you a short Telegram at the office. Please copy its exact words (as they will have a special meaning for her) and post them to her by the very next post after receipt of Telegram. . . .

"FORSTER

"has an ample power of attorney from me, in case you should want any legal authority to act in my name. He knows Nelly as you do, and will do anything for her if you want anything done." [75]

There is no word of what Dickens's daughter Mary thought of this relation between her father and a young woman born a year later than herself. Katey, however, was less restrained. Although Dickens had assured Miss Coutts that there had never been any closeness of affection between his daughters and their mother, Katey sympathized with her and bitterly resented Ellen. "Do you think he is sorry for me?" Catherine once asked her daughter.[76] "My poor, poor mother!" [77] Katey exclaimed. And coming down to Gad's Hill for a visit once, shortly after Ellen had been there, and hearing that Ellen had taken a hand at cricket, Katey observed tartly, "I am afraid she did not play the game." [78]

But as Katey looked back on the tangled and unhappy story in after years, her judgment of Ellen softened. "She flattered him," Katey said, "—he was ever appreciative of praise—and though she was not a good actress she had brains, which she used to educate herself, to bring her mind more on a level with his own. Who could blame her? He had the world at his feet. She was a young girl of eighteen, elated and proud to be noticed by him." [79] "I do not blame *her*. It is never one person's fault." [80]

About her father, Katey's feelings were ambiguous and confused, a mingling of antagonism and irresistible fascination. Though she fought him, she feared and loved him at the same time, as if he were both the ogre and the Prince Charming of a fairy tale. He stormed her heart with tenderness and overwhelmed it with awe. "What could you expect from such an uncanny genius?" she exclaimed. The life of Dickens that she began writing, she burned: "I told only half the truth about my father, and a half-truth is worse than a lie. . . ." [81] "I knew things about my father's character that no one else ever knew; he was not a good man, but he was not a fast man . . . he was wonderful." [82]

The relationship between her father and Ellen Ternan, Katey declared, was "more tragic and far-reaching in its effect . . . than that of Nelson and Lady Hamilton." [83] It was not happy. There is reason for believing that Dickens had won Ellen against her will, wearing down her resistance by sheer force of desperate determination, and that her conscience never ceased to reproach her. In later years, according to Thomas Wright, she confided the story and her remorse to a clergyman. " 'I had it,' said Canon Benham, 'from her own lips, that she loathed the very thought of the intimacy.' " [84]

There are overtones in Dickens's later novels which suggest that he too was troubled by the feeling that this was a guilty love. Even in 1863, something of his distress is hinted by the emotion with which he heard *Faust*—probably for the first time—at the Paris Opéra on January 31st. He was passionately and personally moved by "that noble and sad story" so "nobly and sadly rendered." [85] Mephistopheles, he observed, was "surrounded by an infernal red atmosphere of his own" and "Marguerite by a pale blue mournful light. The two never blending. After Marguerite has taken the jewels placed in her way in the garden, a weird evening draws on, and the bloom fades from the flowers, and the leaves of the trees droop and lose their fresh green, and mournful shadows overhang her chamber window, which was innocent and gay at first. I couldn't bear it, and gave in completely." [86] And in another letter, to Georgina, he repeats, "I could hardly bear the thing; it affected me so, and sounded in my ears so like a mournful echo of things that lie in my own heart." [87]

What were the mournful things that echoed within his heart to that story and that music? What analogies did he feel to the infernal red atmosphere surrounding Mephistopheles and the innocent brightness of Marguerite's chamber window? What intimate meaning was there for him in the acceptance of those jewels which shows that Marguerite has already yielded to Faust in her heart and that the ultimate surrender will soon take place? What symbolic identification between himself and Faust, who wields magical powers? What foreshadowing of the future in those fading leaves and flowers and in that fading light?

* * * * *

Georgina and Mary were not with Dickens on this return to Paris, and at its conclusion he dropped out of sight for a ten-day trip during which he stayed at Arras and Amiens. Not until the middle of February did he turn up in London.[88] There, however, in March he began another series of readings, this time at the Hanover Square Rooms, which lasted until the end of May. Carlyle came to the "Trial from Pickwick" on Dickens's invitation,[89] grumbling that he did so "to the complete upsetting of my evening habitudes and spiritual composure." [90]

When Dickens came out on the stage, he and Carlyle exchanged a nod and the reading began. "I thought Carlyle would split," said one spectator, "and Dickens was not much better. Carlyle sat on the front bench and he haw-hawed right out over and over till he fairly exhausted himself. Dickens would read and then he would stop in order to give Carlyle a chance to stop. . . . I laughed till my jaws ached, and I caught myself involuntarily stamping. Now and then some fellow would astonish himself and the audience by a loud bawl." [91]

During the intermission Dickens came and took Carlyle backstage with Thomas Woolner the sculptor, and over a glass of brandy and water Carlyle, nodding again, said, "Charley, you carry a whole company under your own hat." [92] Next day he praised the performance to his youngest sister, but with that mingling of depreciation he customarily brought to everything: "Dickens does it capitally, such as *it* is, acts better than any Macready in the world; a whole tragic comic heroic *theatre* visible, performing under one *hat*, and keeping us laughing—in a sorry sort of way some of us thought—the whole night." [93]

When the Princess Alexandra of Denmark came to England to be married to the Prince of Wales, Dickens, Georgina, and Alfred, from the balcony of the *All the Year Round* office, saw the procession pass along the Strand. Afterward, Dickens had a dinner engagement in Westbourne Terrace and sent Alfred out to get a cab. The young fellow scoured all around the Strand, Regent Street, Haymarket, and Leicester Square, but in the gala circumstances found none disengaged. Returning to the neighborhood of the Lyceum in despair, he saw a well-appointed brougham there, and explained his trouble to the coachman. "Well," said the latter, "I do not expect my master will be back for about three-quarters of an hour, and as I would chance a good deal for Charles Dickens, I will drive him over." Dickens told Alfred he had "a good considerable amount of assurance," but he took the brougham.[94]

On the royal marriage night Harry and Plorn were allowed home from Wimbledon "to see the illuminations." Dickens "chartered an enormous Van at a cost of five pounds, and we started in majesty from the office in London, fourteen strong," with a party that included the

Forsters, the Willses, Wilkie and Charles Collins, and others. "We crossed Waterloo Bridge," Dickens wrote Macready, "with the happy design of beginning the Sight at London Bridge, and working our way through the City to Regent Street. In a bye-street in the Borough, over against a dead wall and under a Railway Bridge, we were blocked for four hours! We were obliged to walk home at last, having seen nothing whatever. The wretched Van turned up in the course of the next morning. And the best of it was that at Rochester here they illuminated the fine old castle, and really made a very splendid and picturesque thing (so may neighbours tell me)." Though willing enough to take part in the festivities, however, Dickens added, "We really have been be-princed to the last point of human endurance, haven't we?" [95]

With the close of the summer Dickens's thoughts were turning more and more purposefully to his new serial, *Our Mutual Friend*. Late in September he signed an agreement with Chapman and Hall giving them a half share of the profits in return for a payment of £6,000.[96] He wanted to start publication in the spring, but was determined not to begin with fewer than five numbers done. "I see my opening perfectly, with the one main line on which the story is to turn; and if I don't strike while the iron (meaning myself) is hot, I shall drift off again, and have to go through all this uneasiness once more." [97]

Only a short time earlier there had come to him a communication that curiously influenced the design of his story. Mrs. Eliza Davis, the wife of the gentleman who had bought Tavistock House, wrote him a letter telling him that Jews regarded his portrayal of Fagin in *Oliver Twist* as "a great wrong" to their people. Only once before had this reproach come to his eyes, in 1854, when the *Jewish Chronicle* had asked "why Jews alone should be excluded from the sympathizing heart" of this great author and powerful friend of the oppressed. At that time, responding to an invitation to an anniversary dinner of the Westminster Jewish Free School, he had replied: "I know of no reason the Jews can have for regarding me as 'inimical' to them. On the contrary, I believe I do my part towards the assertion of their civil and religious liberty, and in my *Child's History of England* I have expressed a strong abhorrence of their persecution in old time." [98] Now he felt impelled to defend himself in more detail.

If Jews thought him unjust to them, he replied, they were "a far less sensible, a far less just, and a far less good-tempered people than I have always supposed them to be." Fagin, he pointed out, was the only Jew in the story (he had forgotten the insignificant character of Barney) and "all the rest of the wicked *dramatis personae* are Christians." Fagin had been described as a Jew, he explained, "because it unfortunately was true of the time to which that story refers, that that class of criminal almost invariably was a Jew." (Which was not to say, of course, that all, or even many, Jews were receivers of stolen goods.) And finally, Dickens continued, in calling Fagin a Jew no imputation had been suggested against the Jewish religion; the name had been intended in the same way in which one might call a Frenchman or Spaniard or Chinese by those names. "I have no feeling towards the Jews but a friendly one," Dickens concluded his letter. "I always speak well of them, whether in public or private, and bear my testimony (as I ought to do) to their perfect good faith in such transactions as I have ever had with them . . ." [99]

Nevertheless, although Dickens felt it absurd to regard Fagin as typifying his feelings about Jews, he was troubled at being so seriously misinterpreted. In *Our Mutual Friend* he therefore included a group of Jewish characters, of whom the most important is Mr. Riah, a gentle and upright old Jew caught in the toils of a *Christian* money-lender. Lizzie Hexam, one of the two heroines, takes refuge in affliction among a community of Jews, who treat her with the most generous tenderness. To a clergyman worried about her remaining with them, she defends her Jewish employers: "The gentleman certainly is a Jew," she says, "and the lady, his wife, is a Jewess, and I was brought to their notice by a Jew. But I think there cannot be kinder people in the world." [100]

Near the end of the book there is a passage showing that Dickens had reflected upon Mrs. Davis's reproach and understood how it came to be made, even though it imputed to him an injustice he had never intended. "For it is not in Christian countries with the Jews as with other peoples," Mr. Riah reflects. "Men say, 'This is a bad Greek, but there are good Greeks. This is a bad Turk, but there are good Turks.' Not so with the Jews. Men find the bad among us easily enough —among what peoples are the bad not easily found?—but they take the worst of us as samples of the best; they take the lowest of us as presentations of the highest; and they say 'All Jews are alike.' " [101]

Mrs. Davis saw the meaning of this group of Jewish characters. During the course of the novel's serial publication she wrote Dickens in terms that can be inferred from his reply: "I have received your letter with great pleasure, and hope to be (as I have always been in my heart) the best of friends with the Jewish people." [102] Some years later she gave him a copy of Benisch's Hebrew and English Bible, inscribed: "Presented to Charles Dickens, in grateful and admiring recognition of his having exercised the noblest quality men can possess—that of atoning for an injury as soon as conscious of having inflicted it." [103] These words, Dickens told her, were more gratifying than he could possibly express, "for they assure me that there is nothing but good will left between you and me and a people for whom I have a real regard, and to whom I would not wilfully have given an offense or done an injustice for any worldly consideration." [104]

During this summer of 1863 Dickens continued to be troubled about his sons. At Wimbledon, Plorn felt confused and homesick in the impersonal largeness of the school, and felt that he would do better in a smaller place where there were only some half-dozen or dozen boys.[105] At the new year, on the recommendation of M. De la Rue, Dickens confided him to the Reverend W. C. Sawyer, at Tunbridge Wells. "He is a shy boy of good average abilities, and an amiable disposition," Dickens told his new master. "But he has not yet been quite happy away from home, through having lived—as the youngest of my children—a little too long at home with grown people. He has never been a spoiled child, however, for we are too fond of children here to make them disagreeable." [106]

Frank had adapted himself so poorly to his duties at the *All the Year Round* office that Dickens had sometimes felt tempted to cut off his allowance.[107] Now, at twenty, he expressed a strong desire to enter the Bengal Mounted Police, and Dickens took steps to obtain a nomination for him.[108] Near the end of January he went out to India, where he expected to see his brother Walter.[109] But before he arrived, Dickens received word that Walter had died of hematemesis on the last day of the old year.[110] He had been only twenty-two. "My poor boy was on his way home from an up-country station, on sick leave. He had been very ill, but was not so at the time. He was talking to some brother-officers in the Calcutta hospital about his preparations for home, when he suddenly became excited, had a rush of blood from the mouth, and was dead." [111]

Death, indeed, was striking on every hand. The preceding April, Augustus Egg had died, "good dear little fellow." [112] On September 13th died Dickens's mother, who had long been sunk in hopeless senility. [113] And a week before the death of Walter, Thackeray died of apoplexy on Christmas Eve in his home at Palace Green. There had been a reconciliation between him and Dickens only a few days earlier. [114]

Calling on Katey at her London house, Trackeray had voiced his regret at the disagreement with her father, and she had urged him to "say a few words—" "You know," Thackeray interrupted, "he is more in the wrong than I am." But, "he is more shy of speaking than you are," she returned, "and perhaps he mightn't know you would be nice to him." "In that case," Thackeray said, with a glare of his spectacles, "there will be no reconciliation." Then, after a long pause, "And how do I know he would be nice to me?" Thackeray mused. "Oh," exclaimed Katey joyfully, "I can answer for that. There is no need for me even to tell him what has passed between us, I shall not say a word; try him, dear Mr. Thackeray, only try him, and you will see." [115]

Not long afterward, Thackeray was talking with Sir Theodore Martin in the great pillared hall of the Athenaeum Club. Dickens came out of the morning room on his way to the staircase, passing close to them with no sign of recognition. Suddenly Thackeray broke away, and reached Dickens just as he had his foot on the stair. "It is time this foolish estrangement should cease," he exclaimed, "and that we should be to each other what we used to be. Come; shake hands." Dickens held out his hand, and some friendly words were exchanged. Returning to his companion, Thackeray said, "I love the man, and I could not resist the impulse." [116]

Thackeray reported to Katey with radiant face. "How did it happen?" she asked. "Oh," he said gaily, "your father knew he was wrong and was full of apologies—" "You know you are not telling me the truth, you wicked man. Please let me hear immediately what really did happen." Thackeray's eyes were gentle as he told how he had held out his hand: "your father grasped it very cordially—and—and we are friends again, thank God!" [117]

Dickens heard of Thackeray's death on his way to Gad's Hill on Christmas Eve. Young Marcus Stone was meeting him at the station; as soon as he saw Dickens he knew something had distressed him. "What is it?" Stone asked. In a breaking voice, Dickens said, "Thackeray is dead." "I know you must feel it very deeply, because you and he were not on friendly terms." Dickens put his hand on Stone's arm. "Thank God, my boy, we were!" he exclaimed earnestly; and then told about the meeting at the Athenaeum only the week before.[118]

Five days later Dickens stood beside Thackeray's grave in Kensal Green. There was "a look of bereavement in his face which was indescribable. When all others had turned aside from the grave he still stood there, as if rooted to the spot, watching with almost haggard eyes every spadeful of dust that was thrown upon it. Walking away with some friends, he began to talk, but presently in some sentence his voice quivered a little, and shaking hands all round rapidly, he went off alone." [119]

* * * * *

The Christmas number of *All the Year Round*, a story called "Mrs. Lirriper's Lodgings," had shot far ahead of even the story of the previous year, selling about 220,000 copies.[120] "Mrs. Lirriper is indeed a most brilliant old lady," Dickens wrote Wills. "God bless her!" [121] With that work out of the way, Dickens settled down seriously to *Our Mutual Friend*. Marcus Stone was doing the illustrations, and Dickens bombarded him, in his usual way, with a series of instructions. "Note, that the dustman's face should be droll, and not horrible." [122] "Mrs. Boffin, as I judge of her from the sketch, 'very good indeed.' I want Boffin's oddity, without being at all blinked, to be an oddity of a very honest kind, that people will like." [123] "The doll's dressmaker is immensely better than she was. I think she should now come extremely well. A weird sharpness not without beauty is the thing I want." [124] Marcus Stone called Dickens's attention in St. Giles to the articulator of skeletons who inspired the character of Mr. Venus.[125]

Laboring away thus, in the house at 57 Gloucester Place, Hyde Park Gardens, which he had taken from February to June, Dickens got *Our Mutual Friend* in train for publication. The first number came out at the beginning of May, and sold thirty thousand copies in three days.[126] A fortnight before it appeared, Catherine wrote to Frederic Chapman at Chapman and Hall's, and asked to have a copy of each month's number sent her as it came out.[127]

Near the end of June, Dickens was off on a ten or twelve days' trip in France and Belgium,[128] and then returned to Gad's Hill for the summer and fall. Gradually he had transformed his little freehold, which he had "added to and stuck bits upon in all manner of ways," so that it was "as pleasantly irregular," he boasted, "and as violently opposed to all architectural ideas, as the most hopeful man could possibly desire." [129] The outside, with its rosy brick and little entrance porch and bell turret, he had left almost untouched. But under the gambrel roof on the third floor he had built in two bedrooms facing the garden,[130] and he had enlarged the drawing room, first by building an additional one and then by throwing the two together into one large and handsome room.[131] He had erected new stables and replaced an old coach house by a servants' hall with a schoolroom for the boys in the loft above.[132] In what had been part of the orchard he made a walled croquet ground.[133] He rounded out the property by obtaining an eight-acre meadow at the back of the house, through an exchange of land with the trustees of the Rochester Free School.[134] He was now enormously proud of his small estate and warmly attached to its homely comfort.

But he was not in good health and his writing went slowly. He had already fallen behind one number from the advance with which he had started. When he began work on the next Christmas issue of *All the Year Round*, he would lose another number. "This week I have been very unwell," he wrote Forster at the end of July; "am still out of sorts; and, as I know from two days' slow experience, have a very mountain to climb before I shall see the open country of my work." [135] Hot weather slowed him still further in August, and Wills became ill, so that Dickens had to take over the duties on *All the Year Round* that his subeditor ordinarily performed.[136]

Although Dickens thought little of Wills's imaginative powers, he had a high regard for his business efficiency and devoted loyalty, and had come to feel a cordial friendship for the scrawny, blotch-faced fellow. When he put Wills up for membership in the Garrick Club in the fall of 1864 and his nominee was blackballed, Dickens was consequently infuriated. To mark his feeling he resigned—for the third and last time—and Collins, who had seconded the nomination, resigned with him.[137] The actor Charles Fechter, with whom Dickens was growing more and more intimate, also resigned in sympathy, explaining to the Club that "he would trust himself to no community of men in which such things were done." [138]

Dickens was also disgusted, more impersonally, by matters within the public realm. The contentions among the Christian churches and their common endeavors to oppose the advance of scientific knowledge infuriated him. The excited controversy about Bishop Colenso's commentary on the Pentateuch and the Book of Joshua seemed to him so much obscurantist superstition. Was it not clear that "ever since there was a sun and there was vapour, there *must have* been a rainbow under certain conditions"? "Joshua might command the sun to stand still, under the impression that it moved round the earth; but he could not possibly have inverted the relations of the earth and sun, whatever his impressions were." The "science of geology is quite as much a revelation to man as books of an immense age and of (at the best) doubtful origin." It was stupid of the Church to "shock and lose the more thoughtful and logical of human minds," to "call names," and assume revelation "to be finished and done with." "Nothing is discovered without God's intention and assistance, and I suppose every new knowledge of His works that is conceded to man to be distinctly a revelation by which men are to guide themselves." [139]

Hardly less revolting were "the indecent squabbles of the priests of most denominations" with those of opposing faiths, and the rancor of their differences. "And the idea of the Protestant establishment, in the face of its own history, seeking to trample out discussion and private judgment, is an enormity so cool, that I wonder the Right Reverends, Very Reverends, and all other Reverends, who commit it, can look in one another's faces without laughing . . . How our sublime and so-different Christian religion is to be administered in the future I cannot pretend to say, but that the Church's hand is at its own throat I am fully convinced. Here, more Popery, there, more Methodism—as many forms of consignment to eternal damnation as there are articles, and all in one forever quarrelling body—the Master of the New Testament put out of sight and the rage and fury always turning on the letter of obscure parts of the Old . . . these things cannot last. The Church that is to have its part in the coming time must be a more Christian one, with less arbitrary pretensions and a stronger hold upon the mantle of our Saviour, as He walked and talked upon this earth." [140]

On the heels of this outburst comes another cry of personal lamentation. John Leech had just died. "I have not done my number," Dickens says. "This death of poor Leech . . . has put me out woefully. Yesterday and the day before I could do nothing; seemed for the time to have quite lost the power; and am only by slow degrees getting back into the track today." [141]

*   *   *   *   *

More and more his body gave him trouble. Christmas, 1864, went by, and during a protracted winter at Gad's Hill his left foot swelled with excruciating pains and had to be treated with poppy fomentations. But he would not have it that he had gout. "I got frost-bitten by walking continually in the snow," he insisted to Forster, "and getting wet in the feet daily. My boots hardened and softened, hardened and softened, my left foot swelled, and I still forced the boot on; sat in it to write, half the day; walked in it through the snow, the other half; forced the boot on again next morning; sat and walked again; and being accustomed to all sorts of changes in my feet, took no heed. At length, going out as usual, I fell lame on the walk, and had to limp home dead lame, through the snow, for the last three miles—to the remarkable terror, by-the-bye, of the two big dogs." [142]

At the end of April he was still calling it his "frost-bitten foot," but claimed that he could again walk his ten miles in the morning without inconvenience—although he was then "absurdly obliged to sit shoeless all evening." "I am working like a dragon at my book," he wrote Macready from London, "and am a terror to the household, likewise to all the organs and brass bands in this quarter. Gad's Hill is being gorgeously painted, and we are here until the first of June. I wish I might hope you would be there any time this summer; I really *have* made the place comfortable and pretty by this time." [143]

After his son Alfred had given up his medical ambitions and his desire to be a farmer, Dickens had used the help of friends to get him a position in a City mercantile house, hoping that he might ultimately go out to some firm in Ceylon or China. [144] Alfred had taken hopefully to the idea too, but after two years in London felt that he would like to go to Australia. This also Dickens aided him to do, telling him that he might return home again if Australia did not suit him. On May 29, 1865, Alfred sailed for Melbourne.[145]

At the end of May, Dickens went to Paris for a week's vacation. "Work and worry, without exercise, would soon make an end of me," he wrote Forster. "If I were not going away now, I should break down. No one knows as I know today how near it I have been." [146] It is probable that Ellen Ternan was with him on this brief holiday; it is certain that she returned with him from it. In Paris Dickens picked up rapidly. "Before I went away," he wrote Mary, "I had certainly worked myself into a damaged state. But the moment I got away, I began, thank God, to get well. I hope to profit by this experience, and to make future dashes from my desk before I want them." [147]

June 9th, the day of their return, was clear and beautiful. The sun shone on the water and the Channel was without a ripple. Steamers could enter Folkestone Harbor only at high tide, which that day was a little after two. Dickens and Ellen boarded the "tidal" train, which waited for the boat at its varying times of arrival, and a little later they were spinning along the rails at fifty miles an hour. The only other occupant of their compartment was an old lady who sat opposite.

At eleven minutes past three the train went through Headcorn and entered on a straight stretch of track between there and Staplehurst. The engineer was going full speed. One-third of the way there came a slight dip in the level country to a stream bed crossed by a railway bridge of girders supporting the heavy beams that bore the rails. Suddenly the driver clamped on the brakes, reversed his engine, and whistled for the guards to apply their hand brakes. He had seen a flagman with a red flag and a gap of ripped-up rails.

A crew of repairmen were carrying on a routine replacement of worn timbers, but their foreman had looked at the timetable for the next day and imagined the train would not be along for another two hours. The flagman was supposed to be 1000 yards beyond the gap and to have laid down fog signals, but he had neglected the signals and was only 550 yards from the bridge. When the engineer saw him it was too late. As he reached the bridge the train was still going almost thirty miles an hour.

The engine leaped the 42-foot gap in the rails and ran to the farther bank of the river bed. The guards' van that followed was flung to the other track, dragging the next coach with it. The coach immediately behind was that in which Dickens and Ellen were seated. It remained coupled to the one ahead and jolted partly over the side of the bridge, ten feet above the stream, with its rear end on the field below. The coupling behind broke, and the other coaches ran down the bank, buckling and turning upside down in the marshy ground, where four of them were smashed to matchwood. Only the very rear of the train remained on the rails.[148]

"Suddenly," Dickens said, "we were off the rail, and beating the ground as the car of a half-emptied balloon might do. The old lady cried out, 'My God!' " Ellen screamed. "I caught hold of them both . . . and said: 'We can't help ourselves, but we can be quiet and composed. Pray don't cry out.' The old lady immediately answered: 'Thank you. Rely on me. Upon my soul I will be quiet.' We were then all tilted down together in a corner of the carriage, and stopped." [149]

Dickens saw that at the moment they were in no further danger. He asked his companions to remain motionless lest they disturb the perilous balance of the carriage; he would clamber out the window and obtain means to open the door. Standing on the step, he saw the timbers of the bridge gone and the river ten feet below. "Some people in the other two compartments were madly trying to plunge out of window, and had no idea that there was an open swampy field . . . down below them . . ." Two guards were running wildly up and down. Dickens called authoritatively to one of them and demanded the key that would open the carriage doors. With the aid of a laborer and a few planks, Dickens brought Ellen and the old lady to safety and freed the occupants of the other compartments.[150]

Then he went back for his brandy flask, filled his hat with water, and began trying to help the injured and dying. Remains of shattered carriages were projecting wheels-upward from the water. The screams of the sufferers were appalling. A staggering man covered with blood had "such a frightful cut across the skull," Dickens said, "that I couldn't bear to look at him. I poured some water over his face, gave him some drink, then gave him some brandy, and laid him down in the grass . . ." There was a lady with "blood streaming over her face (which was lead-colour) . . ." [151] One lady who had been crushed to death was laid on the bank just as her husband, screaming "My wife!

my wife!" and running frantically about, came up and found her a mangled corpse. Dickens was everywhere, helping everyone.[152]

When he had done everything he could, he remembered that he had had the manuscript of the next number of Our Mutual Friend with him, and coolly climbed back into the carriage once more to retrieve it.[153] Only when it was all over and he was back at Gad's Hill did he realize how shaken he was. His hand was so unsteady that to most of the inquiries that poured in about his health he responded by dictating his replies. But he nerved himself to write the Station Master at Charing Cross in Ellen's behalf:

"A lady who was in the carriage with me in the terrible accident on Friday, lost, in the struggle of being got out of the carriage, a gold watch-chain with a smaller gold watch-chain attached, a bundle of charms, a gold watch-key, and a gold seal engraved 'Ellen.'

"I promised the lady to make her loss known at headquarters, in case these trinkets should be found. . . . I would have spoken to you instead of writing, but that I am shaken;—not by the beating of the carriage, but by the work afterwards of getting out the dying and the dead." [154]

Throughout the month Dickens was unable to throw off the effects of the accident. His pulse was feeble. "I am curiously weak—weak as if I were recovering from a long illness," he told Forster. And a little later, "I begin to feel it more in my head. I sleep well and eat well; but I write half a dozen notes, and turn faint and sick." "I am getting right, though still low in pulse and very nervous. Driving into Rochester yesterday I felt more shaken than I have since the accident." [155]

In his weakness and shock he did not forget about Ellen. Solicitously he sent her little delicacies by John, his personal servant. "Take Miss Ellen tomorrow morning, a little basket of fresh fruit, a jar of clotted cream from Tuckers, and a chicken, a pair of pigeons, or some nice little bird. Also on Wednesday morning, and on Friday morning, take her some other things of the same sort—making a little variety each day." [156]

At the end of June, "I cannot bear railway travelling yet," Dickens wrote Forster. "A perfect conviction, against the senses, that the carriage is down on one side (and generally that is the left, and not the side on which the carriage in the accident really went over), comes upon me with anything like speed, and is inexpressibly distressing." [157]

Indeed, he never fully recovered. "To this hour," he wrote over three years later, "I have sudden vague rushes of terror, even when riding in a hansom cab, which are perfectly unreasonable but quite insurmountable. I used to think nothing of driving a pair of horses habitually through the most crowded parts of London. I cannot now drive, with comfort to myself, on the country roads here; and I doubt if I could ride at all in the saddle." [158] For a while he could bear railway travel only if he went by slow trains, but long journeys and boredom were worse than the tension of the express. It became his invariable habit, however, to carry a flask of brandy with him.[159] "My reading secretary and companion knows so well when one of these odd momentary seizures comes upon me in a railway carriage, that he instantly produces a dram of brandy, which rallies the blood to the heart and generally prevails." [160] Even so, when the train jolted across switches or over intersections, he often clutched the arms of his chair, his face whitened, and his brow broke out in perspiration.[161] Exactly five years later he died on the aniversary of that sunny June day that had brought him so close to death.

CHAPTER FIVE

The Great Dust-Heap

CRITICISM: *Our Mutual Friend*

A LITTLE more than halfway through *Our Mutual Friend* that honest "waterside character" Rogue Riderhood, run down by a steamer on the Thames and almost drowned, slowly struggles back to life and consciousness. "And yet—like us all, when we swoon—like us all, every day of our lives when we wake—he is instinctively unwilling," Dickens writes, "to be restored to consciousness, and would be left dormant if he could." [1] *Like us all, every day of our lives.* So far has life altered for Dickens since the sunny days when Mr. Pickwick was "begun in all his might and glory" [2] that he now takes it to be beyond all doubt that only reluctantly do men each day return from sleep to waking.

Not so did Mr. Pickwick feel when with the first radiance of dawn he "burst like another sun from his slumbers" and threw wide his window to look out on Goswell Street. Not so did Dickens himself feel in the times when he would leap out of bed in the middle of a winter's night to practice the polka on an icy bedroom floor. But, in his early fifties now, he no longer dwells in that glorious *Pickwick* world nor even among the brightly colored scenes of *David Copperfield.* The east wind that began smothering *Bleak House* in fog has spread a heavy pall over all the landscape, and with Dickens's darkened vision of reality his world has changed. No Sam Weller makes lively quips in the grimmer and dustier atmosphere of *Our Mutual Friend*. In the earlier novels the very villains—Mr. Jingle, Sir Mulberry Hawk, the diabolic Quilp, the writhing Uriah Heep—had a violent vitality, a eupeptic bounce, a delight in evil, that are altogether absent from the sordid little schemes of Alfred Lammle, Esquire, or the sour malignance of Silas Wegg. The gloom and despair of Mr. Toots are more high-spirited than the hopes of the Golden Dustman.

London itself, as it has swollen in size, has become for Dickens what it became for Henry Adams, a barren and stony desert, "cheaper as it quadrupled in wealth; less imperial as its empire widened." [3] Eugene Wrayburn and Mortimer Lightwood, those two weary idlers of *Our Mutual Friend*, reside in the Temple, but for them the fountain that played for little Ruth Pinch never laughs and dimples the waters of its basin. This London is a London of dusty corners and muddy gutters, of dingy houses with dim windows and blank back premises, of narrow and dirty streets where wastepaper and grit are blown by a grating wind, "a hopeless city, with no rent in the leaden canopy of its sky." [4] In the descending fog it is a city of dark yellow and brown deepening into rusty black, "a heap of vapour charged with muffled sounds of wheels and enfolding a muffled catarrh." [5] Always either a gray dusty city or a dark muddy one, steeped in a general gloom like a dismal and enormous jail.

The image of the city as a jail is a recurrence, of course, of the fundamental metaphor of *Little Dorrit*. But with it there reappear in *Our Mutual Friend* almost all those other images with which, ever since *Dombey and Son*, Dickens had reflected his judgment of the social system, now fused and wrought to a more bitter intensity. Mr. Dombey's icy Barmecide feasts are paralleled by the Veneering dinners, where saltcellars shaped like silver camels cross the arid board, and the guests despise their hosts, and the butler, referred to as "the Analytical Chemist," [6] improves upon Mr. Merdle's chief butler by despising them all. The cancerous spread of the city with the sprouting of railroads and the growth of commerce, first noted in *Dombey*, is here seen as a chaos of dilapidated villas, unfinished streets, warehouses, rank fields, black ditches, and brick viaducts, like something built "by a child of particularly incoherent mind." [7] The dense legal fog of *Bleak House*, too, envelops the book, mingled with the pall of smoke that hung over Coketown in *Hard Times*; and within them coil the same monetary greeds and struggles for political power that animated Mr. Bounderby and Sir Leicester Dedlock and exalted Mr. Merdle to an uncouth national idol. The cruel exploitation that in *A Tale of Two Cities* transforms the mob into howling wolves *Our Mutual Friend* reveals in the very process of mutilation: making poor

little R. Wilfer a clerical wage-slave, poisoning his family with financial envy, steeping his wife in a martyred nagging and embittering his
daughter Bella, turning the crippled little dolls' dressmaker, Miss
Jenny Wren, into a creature half sorrowful child and half acid shrew,
bringing out the selfishness in young Charley Hexam that renders him
a nastier Pip, monstrous in his ingratitude.

Though Dickens emphasizes more sharply than ever the class structure of society, he has long ceased to see the power of the aristocracy
as crucial. Domination has passed to the middle class, represented by
Mr. Podsnap, whose self-complacency is not in the least humbled by
the snobbish respect with which he looks on the engraved portraits
of Lord Snigsworth "snorting at a Corinthian column, with an enormous roll of paper at his feet, and a heavy curtain going to tumble
down on his head." [8] Mr. Podsnap is entirely satisfied with his wealth,
his importance, and the world. He has "thriven exceedingly in the
Marine Insurance way," [9] and he knows perfectly well that he and
his fellow company-directors together with the bankers, promoters,
and large-scale contractors really own that world. The values of pecuniary respectability are the only ones he recognizes as having any
genuine currency.

Finance capitalism and the stock exchange are the supreme tri-
bunals of merit. "As is well known to the wise in their generation,
traffic in Shares is the one thing to have to do with in this world. Have
no antecedents, no established character, no cultivation, no ideas, no
manners; have Shares. Have Shares enough to be on Boards of Direction in capital letters, oscillate between London and Paris, and be
great. Where does he come from? Shares. Has he any principles?
Shares. What squeezes him into Parliament? Shares. Perhaps he never
of himself achieved anything, never originated anything, never produced anything! Sufficient answer to all; Shares. O mighty Shares! To
set those blaring images so high, and cause us smaller vermin, as under
the influence of henbane or opium, to cry out night and day, 'Relieve
us of our money, scatter it for us, buy us and sell us, ruin us, only we
beseech ye take rank among the powers of the earth, and fatten
on us!' " [10]

Even more than in *Great Expectations*, this society is a society of
monetary barbarism, devoid of culture, and emptier still of sincerity,
generosity, integrity, and warmth of feeling. The significantly named

Veneerings can bribe their way into acceptance with magnificent dinners and receptions, can even buy a seat in Parliament to represent the independent borough of Pocket-Breaches. "Mr. and Mrs. Veneering were bran-new people in a bran-new house in a bran-new quarter of London. Everything about the Veneerings was spick and span new. All their furniture was new, all their friends were new, all their servants were new, their plate was new, their carriage was new, their harness was new, their horses were new, their pictures were new, they themselves were new, they were as newly married as was lawfully compatible with their having a bran-new baby, and if they had set up a great-grandfather, he would have come home in matting from the Pantechnicon without a scratch upon him, French polished to the crown of his head." [11]

Around their table assemble those powers who constitute the voice of society. There is old Mr. Twemlow, an impoverished little gentleman who ekes out an insufficient allowance from his second cousin, Lord Snigsworth, by dining wherever he is invited. There is Lady Tippins, with her yellow throat and her false hair and her grisly fiction that she is a siren besieged by lovers, rattling off smart tittle-tattle, and so dyed and varnished for her appearances in public that "you might scalp her, and peel her, and scrape her, and make two Lady Tippinses out of her, and yet not penetrate to the genuine article." [12] (Lady Tippins, Dickens notes, is the widow "of the late Sir Thomas Tippins, knighted in mistake for somebody else by His Majesty King George the Third, who, while performing the ceremony, was graciously pleased to observe, 'What, what, what? Who, who, who? Why, why, why?' " How ingeniously this parody of the crazy old King gabbling his gibberish is made the vehicle of the author's mordant insinuation: What is being done here? Who is being knighted, and why? [13])

Present at the Veneerings' table, too, are Miss Sophronia Akershem, mature and well powdered, pretending to be a young lady of property, and Alfred Lammle, Esquire, "with too much nose in his face, too much ginger in his whiskers, too much torso in his waistcoat, too much sparkle in his studs, his eyes, his buttons, his talk, and his teeth," pretending to be a gentleman of property. [14] There, also, are Eugene Wrayburn and Mortimer Lightwood, both present in that sheer indolence which finds it easier to accept an invitation than to write an excuse. There are Buffer, Boots, and Brewer, filling in. "There is the Contractor, who is Providence to five hundred thousand men. There is the Chairman," [15] "in such request at so many Boards, so far apart, that he never travels less by railway than three thousand miles a week." There is the Promoter without "a sixpence eighteen months ago," who "through the brilliancy of his genius in getting those shares issued at eighty-five, and buying them all up with no money and selling them at par for cash, has now three hundred and seventy-five thousand pounds." [16]

Above all, there is Mr. Podsnap, the pompous embodiment of respectable and complacent middle-class riches and its standards. Everything disagreeable or improper Mr. Podsnap puts out of existence by refusing to recognize. " 'I don't want to know about it; I don't choose to discuss it; I don't admit it!' Mr. Podsnap had even acquired a peculiar flourish of his right arm in often clearing the world of its most difficult problems, by sweeping them behind him (and consequently sheer away) with those words and a flushed face." [17] It was part of the Gospel of Podsnappery that he "always knew exactly what Providence meant" and "that what Providence meant was invariably what Mr. Podsnap meant." [18]

"A certain institution in Mr. Podsnap's mind which he called 'the young person' may be considered to have been embodied in Miss Podsnap, his daughter. It was an inconvenient and exacting institution, as requiring everything in the universe to be filed down and fitted to it. The question about everything was, would it bring a blush to the cheek of the young person. And the inconvenience of the young person was, that, according to Mr. Podsnap, she seemed always liable to burst into blushes when there was no need at all. There appeared to be no line of demarcation between the young person's excessive innocence, and another person's guiltiest knowledge." [19]

Thus, Mr. Podsnap is affronted by a fellow guest's referring to the fact that "some half-dozen people had lately died in the streets, of starvation. It was clearly ill-timed, after dinner. It was not adapted to the cheek of the young person. It was not in good taste. 'I don't believe it,' said Mr. Podsnap, putting it behind him." The fellow guest, though a man of meek demeanor, repeats that the facts support his statement, and suggests "that there must be something appallingly wrong somewhere" which they should try to set right.[20]

" 'Ah!' said Mr. Podsnap. 'Easy to say somewhere; not so easy to say where! But I see what you are driving at. I knew it from the first. Centralization. No. Never with my consent. Not English.'

"An approving murmur rose from the heads of tribes; as saying, 'There you have him! Hold him!'

"He was not aware (the meek man submitted of himself) that he was driving at any ization. He had no favourite ization that he knew of. But he certainly was more staggered by these terrible occurrences than by names, of howsoever many syllables. Might he ask, was dying of destitution and neglect necessarily English?" [21]

But Mr. Podsnap, after verbally bullying and buffeting the meek man a few more times, soon feels "that the time has come for flushing and flourishing this meek man down for good." " 'I must decline to pursue this painful discussion. It is not pleasant to my feelings. It is repugnant to my feelings. I have said that I do not admit these things. I have also said that if they do occur (not that I admit it), the fault lies with the sufferers themselves. It is not for *me*'—Mr. Podsnap pointed 'me' forcibly, as adding by implication though it may be all very well for *you*—'it is not for me to impugn the workings of Providence. I know better than that, I trust, and I have mentioned what the intentions of Providence are. Besides,' said Mr. Podsnap, flushing high up among his hair-brushes, with a strong consciousness of personal affront, 'the subject is a very disagreeable one. I will go so far as to say it is an odious one. It is not one to be introduced among our wives and young persons, and I—' He finished with that flourish of his arm which added more expressively than any words, And I remove it from the earth." [22]

"Mr. Podsnap's world was not a very large world, morally; no, nor even geographically: seeing that although his business was sustained upon commerce with other countries, he considered other countries, with that important reservation, a mistake, and of their manners and customs would conclusively observe, 'Not English!' when, PRESTO! with a flourish of the arm, and a flush of the face, they were swept away. Elsewise, the world got up at eight, shaved close at a quarter-past, breakfasted at nine, went to the City at ten, came home at half-past five, and dined at seven. Mr. Podsnap's notions of the Arts in their integrity might have been stated thus. Literature; large print, respectively descriptive of getting up at eight, shaving close at a quarter-past, breakfasting at nine, going to the City at ten, coming home at half-past five, and dining at seven. Painting and Sculpture; models and portraits representing Professors of getting up at eight, shaving close at a quarter-past, breakfasting at nine, going to the City at ten, coming home at half-past five, and dining at seven. Music; a respectable performance (without variations) on stringed and wind instruments, sedately expressive of getting up at eight, shaving close at a quarter-past, breakfasting at nine, going to the City at ten, coming home at half-past five, and dining at seven. Nothing else to be permitted to those same vagrants the Arts, on pain of excommunication. Nothing else To Be—anywhere!" [23]

In Podsnap Dickens exemplifies all the forces he has spent a lifetime fighting. Podsnap is the smug and deliberate complacence, comfortable in its own ease, that refuses to be told of any shortcomings in society. Podsnap is the blind toryism that resists every effort at reform. Podsnap is the Mrs. Grundyism that seeks to smother independent thought in heavy layers of conventional propriety. He is Philistinism secretly mistrustful of the arts and despising the artist as a mountebank. He is British insularity contemptuous of foreigners and everything "Not English." He is the incarnate materialism of a monetary barbarism that masquerades as civilization. Podsnappery is the dominant attitude of respectable society: a vast, vulgar, and meretricious idolatry, with Podsnap as its oracle, Lady Tippins its priestess, and the Veneerings, the Lammles, and the others its aspirants and acolytes.

*   *   *   *   *

The central symbol of their worship is figured in that mountain range of profitable dust-heaps that forms the inheritance of old Noddy Boffin, the Golden Dustman. No sooner is it known that he is the legatee of the miserly dust-contractor Harmon who was his employer than the world is at his feet. The "divine Tippins" may snigger, but she leaves cards. The regal Podsnap may swell, but he leaves cards. Little Twemlow leaves cards. The Veneerings leave cards, "requesting the honour of Mr. and Mrs. Boffin's company at dinner with the utmost Analytical solemnities." [24] "Tradesmen's books hunger, and tradesmen's mouths water, for the gold dust of the Golden Dustman." [25] Bland strangers try to corrupt his servants. Begging letters pour in from scores of rapacious charities, from hundreds of greedy

The Evil Genius of the House of Boffin

individual mendicants. Behold "all manner of crawling, creeping, fluttering, and buzzing creatures, attracted by the gold dust of the Golden Dustman." [26] And out on the mounds of dust, the wily and rapacious Wegg, whom Noddy has installed as caretaker, stumps with his wooden leg over the piles of muck, taking soundings with an iron rod.

Rubbish, in the mid-nineteenth century, was removed by private contractors and piled in huge dumps in North London. These were enormously lucrative to their owners. Jewels, coins, and other valuables were often found in them. Odorous and soggy, infested by rats and flies, these piles of soot, cinders, broken glass, bottles, crockery, worn-out pots and pans, old paper and rags, bones, garbage, human feces, and dead cats, were picked over and sorted for sale to brickmakers, soap boilers, paper manufacturers, road makers, dealers in metal and glass, concrete makers. The soot was used as fertilizer, decayed animal and vegetable matter as manure; even the dead cats were sold for their skins. In 1850 there was an article by R. H. Horne in *Household Words* which noted that a rich dust-contractor had offered his daughter as a wedding present either £20,000 in cash or one of his mounds. She chose the cash and he later sold the mound for £40,000.[27]

The image of wealth as filth, the supreme goal of nineteenth-century society as dust and ordure, gave a deep and savage irony to Dickens's hatred for its governing values. (At the same time he himself was driven on by his worry over the unending needs of all his dependents to a wearing exhaustion of his energies in the profitable toil of his readings. Despite his frequent display of a marked exultation over his earnings, however, the compelling forces behind his course were less those of cupidity than of a nagging demand for excitement and a painful awareness of how many looked to him for support.) Early in his career Dickens had realized that those dusty values were the realities behind all the loud slogans of political battle. It is significant that since his reporting days he had repeatedly described Parliament as a "dust-heap," and that in *Hard Times* he refers to Mr. Gradgrind's "parliamentary duties" in "the national cinder-heap" as "sifting for the odds and ends he wanted" and "throwing dust into the eyes of other people." [28] Like images are implied in the rag-and-bone shop of Krook, the symbolic Lord Chancellor of *Bleak House*, and in the "merde" which lurks within the name of Mr. Merdle.

Ultimately the dust-heaps are magnified into an all-embracing metaphor of mistaken endeavors directed to the piling up of rubbish, mounds marking the dust and ashes of buried aspiration. This aspect of their meaning emerges in a powerful outburst while Boffin's dust-heaps are being carted away for sale: "My lords and gentlemen and honourable boards, when you in the course of your dust-shovelling and cinder-raking have piled up a mountain of pretentious failure, you must off with your honourable coats for the removal of it, and fall to the work with the power of all the queen's horses and all the queen's men, or it will come rushing down and bury us alive.

"Yes, verily, my lords and gentlemen and honourable boards, adapting your Catechism to the occasion, and by God's help so you must. For when we have got things to the pass that with an enormous treasure at disposal to relieve the poor, the best of the poor detest our mercies, hide their heads from us, and shame us by starving to death in the midst of us, it is a pass impossible of prosperity, impossible of continuance. It may not be so written in the Gospel according to Podsnappery; you may not 'find these words' for the text of a sermon, in the Returns of the Board of Trade; but they have been the truth since the foundations of the universe were laid, and they will be the truth until the foundations of the universe are shaken by the Builder. This boastful handiwork of ours, which fails in its terrors for the professional pauper, the sturdy breaker of windows and the rampant tearer of clothes, strikes with a cruel and a wicked stab at the stricken sufferer, and is a horror to the deserving and unfortunate. We must mend it, lords and gentlemen and honourable boards, or in its own evil hour it will mar every one of us." [29]

The criminal jails that failed to diminish crime, the debtors' prisons that crippled men's characters and murdered their pride, the red tape and the chafing wax of a money-and-power-driven social order, the Poor Laws and the Workhouse against which Dickens had fulminated from *Oliver Twist* to *Little Dorrit*, were all part of the same corrupt system. In *Our Mutual Friend* old Betty Higden, who has always earned her way, speaks of the Poorhouse with a shiver of repugnance and a dark vibration of hatred in her voice. " 'Kill me sooner than take me. Throw this pretty child under cart-horses' feet and a loaded waggon, sooner than take him there. Come to us and find us all a-dying, and set a light to us where we lie, and let us all blaze away with the house into a heap of cinders, sooner than move a corpse of us there!'

"A surprising spirit in this lonely old woman," Dickens exclaims, "after so many years of hard working and hard living, my Lords and Gentlemen and Honourable Boards! What is it that we call it in our grandiose speeches? British independence, rather perverted? Is that, or something like it, the ring of cant?" [30]

" 'Do I never read in the newspapers,' " Betty goes on, " 'God help me and the like of me!—how the worn-out people that do come down to that, get driven from post to pillar and pillar to post, a-purpose to tire them out! Do I never read how they are put off, put off, put off— how they are grudged, grudged, grudged the shelter, or the doctor, or the drop of physic, or the bit of bread? Do I never read how they grow heartsick of it, and give it up, after having let themselves drop so low, and how they after all die out for want of help? Then I say, I hope I can die as well as another, and I'll die without that disgrace.'

"Absolutely impossible, my Lords and Gentlemen and Honourable Boards, by any stretch of legislative wisdom to set these perverse people right in their logic? . . . A brilliant success, my Lords and Gentlemen and Honourable Boards, to have brought it to this in the minds of the best of the poor! Under submission, might it be worth thinking of, at any odd time?" [31]

And so old Betty Higden, with her burial money stitched into her decent dress, when she feels weakness and decrepitude creeping upon her, flees the charity of the "great blank barren Union House" as if it were the County Jail, from which "in its dietary, and in its lodgings, and in its tending of the sick" it differs only in being "a much more penal establishment." "It is a remarkable Christian improvement to have made a pursuing Fury of the Good Samaritan . . ." [32]

In the Postscript to *Our Mutual Friend*, lest any reader imagine that he has been indulging in the license of fiction, Dickens calls attention to recent revelations in *The Lancet* of deaths by freezing and slow starvation among the poor who had preferred that to the mercies of Relieving Officers and Union Houses, and states his own deliberate judgment: "I believe there has been in England, since the days of the STUARTS, no law so often infamously administered, no law so often openly violated, no law habitually so ill-supervised. In the majority of the shameful cases of disease and death from destitution, that shock the Public and disgrace the country, the illegality is quite equal to the inhumanity—and known language could say no more of their lawlessness." [33]

Hardly less dreadful, though, are the monstrosities of character that swell among those of superior rank. Privilege deforms almost as surely as destitution destroys. Is Lady Tippins a nobler human being than Betty Higden? Is the wealthy Podsnap a better man, or even a brighter one, than trotting, warm-hearted Mr. Boffin, who had been a dustman all his life until riches befell him? Is Alfred Lammle superior to Rogue Riderhood? Is Gaffer Hexam, beating up and down the river in his dirty boat despoiling the bodies of drowned men, any worse than Fascination Fledgeby, dwelling luxuriously in the Albany, but secretly a usurer dealing in promissory notes and squeezing the last drop out of his living victims?

Among the poor, too, however, the struggle for survival enslaves and distorts. For Fledgeby's unsavory business old Mr. Riah, the humble Jew entangled in his debt, is obliged to serve as a front and assume the onus of his employer's greed. Crippled little Miss Jenny Wren, whose back is bad and whose legs are queer, toils at her trade as a dolls' dressmaker and tries to take care of the alcoholic parent whom she calls her "bad child." [34] But it is not only her body that is misshapen. She has none of the angelic patience Little Nell displays with her gambler grandfather; Jenny Wren, for all her childish pathos and wistful dreams, is a sharp-tongued and suspicious scold, forcing her abject, shaking wretch of a father to turn over to her what money he has not spent and sometimes in her exasperation even knocking his head against the wall. "Oh, you prodigal old son!" [35] "Oh, you disgraceful old chap!" [36] "I wish you had been poked into cells and black holes, and run over by rats and spiders and beetles." [37] Charley Hexam, ambitiously bent on rising to a superior class, selfishly repudiates his sister Lizzie, whose love first persuaded him to seek an education. His schoolmaster, Bradley Headstone, is moody and sullen about his own low origins, with "a naturally slow or inattentive intellect that had toiled hard to get what it had won," [38] a man of mechanical acquirements forever suspicious and uneasy with care. Eugene Wrayburn has all the ease and assurance that Headstone lacks, but he cares no more for his family than Charley Hexam does for his father and sister, and Wrayburn's father has even less feeling for him than Jenny

Wren's father for his hard-working child. There is, in fact, rather more devotion among the poor than among the rich, for Lizzie loves her callous brother and Jenny devotes herself to the drunkard who is the misery of her life. But on every level this society is permeated by selfishness, sharp dealing, struggle, undutiful parents and ungrateful children, labor and generous sacrifices ill repaid, hardness of heart and trampled affection.

On every level, everywhere, Dickens shows the money ethic of an acquisitive society crippling human nature and blighting the flowering of humane values. Bradley Headstone, the self-educated man, he no longer sees as a theme for rejoicing, because Headstone has accepted the standards of the world into which he is striving to rise and has distorted the essence of self-respect by which he might have been animated. "By bettering himself," as Lindsay says, "he has destroyed himself; he has become a frenzied cog in a mechanistic universe of phoney knowledge and money-values. Dickens, in his picture of this frustrated man, makes a decisive rejection of Victorian educational methods, the whole outlook which imagined progress as mechanistic reduplication and which wanted education to further a false concept of man." [39]

* * * * *

Headstone's very name proclaims him to be headed and self-devoted to destruction. But distinguished from him there are two other characters, Bella Wilfer and Eugene Wrayburn, who are each brought to a change of heart. Wrayburn is the gentlemanly idler whom Dickens has despised in the past and held up to scorn as the selfish dilettante Henry Gowan, the rebel and misfit who can find nothing to believe in and nothing worth doing in the world. But Wrayburn's skepticism of received values now makes him an effective instrument for Dickens's criticism of society. How is his merely passive rejection of conventional aims to be transformed into affirmation and positive action? Eugene, half idly in the beginning, becomes interested in Lizzie Hexam, whom he first sees when her father drags out of the river a drowned body identified as a client of Mortimer Lightwood. Without knowing whether his own purpose is disinterested or directed toward seduction, he offers her his aid, has her taught to read, besets her with more and more deeply absorbed attention. Her self-respect and integrity of character ultimately fix his devotion; at last, to the scandal of good society, he marries her. But in the denial of pure snobbery he has at the same time learned affirmation; in asking, accepting, and deserving love he has achieved purpose and self-respect.

Dickens's contempt for the artificial judgments of mere "society" was never voiced more witheringly than in the final chapter of *Our Mutual Friend*, where Lady Tippins canvasses its opinion of Eugene's marriage to "a female waterman." [40] Podsnap heatedly proclaims "that my gorge rises against such a marriage—that it offends and disgusts me—that it makes me sick—and that I desire to know no more about it." [41] The genius at promotion thinks that if the young woman had no money it was madness and moonshine. "A man may do anything lawful, for money. But for no money!—" [42] Only little Mr. Twemlow defends the quixotic absurdity. "If this gentleman's feelings of gratitude, of respect, of admiration, and affection, induced him (as I presume they did) to marry this lady—"

"This lady!" sneers Podsnap.

"Sir," returns Twemlow, "*you* repeat the word; *I* repeat the word. This lady. What else would you call her, if the gentleman were present?"

("This being something in the nature of a poser for Podsnap," Dickens interpolates, "he merely waves it away with a speechless wave.")

"I say," Twemlow resumes, "if such feelings on the part of this gentleman, induced this gentleman to marry this lady, I think he is the greater gentleman for the action, and makes her the greater lady. I beg to say, that when I use the word, gentleman, I use it in the sense in which the degree may be attained by any man." [43]

As an inverted parallel to Eugene, who rises in true dignity when he lifts a poor girl to his side, Bella Wilfer is able to respect herself for the first time only after surrendering her snobbish and mercenary determination to marry for money and descending, as she would once have thought it, into matrimony with the mere secretary whom she believes a poor man. Beautiful and willful, spoiled and petulant, she chafes impatiently at the poverty of the miserable box of a house in Holloway with her snapping sister Lavinia and a mother always lurking "like the Tragic Muse with a face-ache in majestic corners." [44]

and the meek little father whom she pets and teases. "I love money," she proclaims, "and want money—want it dreadfully. I hate to be poor, and we are degradingly poor, offensively poor, miserably poor, beastly poor." [45]

To John Harmon, the son of the dead dust-contractor, she is dishearteningly enchanting, dishearteningly selfish. "So insolent, so trivial, so capricious, so mercenary, so careless, so hard to touch, so hard to turn!" [46] Masquerading under the name of Rokesmith, with the connivance of Mr. and Mrs. Boffin, as their secretary, he resists their earnest desire to give him his father's fortune. "To come into possession of my father's money, and with it sordidly to buy a beautiful creature whom I love—I cannot help it; reason has nothing to do with it; I love her against reason—but who would as soon love me for my own sake, as she would love the beggar at the corner. What a use for the money, and how worthy of its old misuses!" [47]

Mr. Boffin pretends to be spoiled by his supposed fortune, to turn mean and grasping, and to encourage Bella, whom he has adopted as his protégée, in her plans of marrying for money. He has Silas Wegg read him the lives of misers and imitates their conduct. "These good looks of yours (which you have some right to be vain of, my dear, though you are not, you know) are worth money," he tells Bella, "and you shall make money out of 'em." [48] Looking "stealthily towards him under her eyelashes," Bella can see now "a dark cloud of suspicion, covetousness, and conceit, overshadowing the once open face." [49] "Its old simplicity of expression got masked by a certain craftiness that assimilated even his good-humour to itself. His very smile was cunning, as if he had been studying smiles among the portraits of his misers. Saving an occasional burst of impatience, or coarse assertion of his mastery, his old good-humour remained to him, but it had now a sordid alloy of distrust . . ." [50]

His progressive rudeness and overbearingness to his secretary makes Bella more and more ashamed of the disdain and insolence she had herself displayed to that person. Rokesmith's admiration, which she had resented when she first realized it, makes a steadily deeper impression on her. "Oh, it's all very well to call me your dear," she exclaims to Lizzie Hexam with a pettish whimper, "and I am glad to be called so, though I have slight enough claim to be. But I AM such a nasty little thing!" "Such a shallow, cold, worldly, Limited little brute!" [51]

When Mr. Boffin pretends to discharge the secretary with insults for presuming to tell Bella he loves her, she can bear no more. "Oh, Mr. Rokesmith, before you go, if you could but make me poor again! Oh! Make me poor again, Somebody, I beg and pray, or my heart will break if this goes on! Pa, dear, make me poor again and take me home! Don't give me money, Mr. Boffin, I won't have money. Keep it away from me, and only let me speak to good little Pa, and lay my head upon his shoulder, and tell him all my griefs. Nobody else can understand me, nobody else can comfort me, nobody else knows how unworthy I am, and yet can love me like a little child. I am better with Pa than anyone—more innocent, more sorry, more glad!" [52]

And to Mr. Boffin she bursts out: "I hate you!—at least, I can't hate you, but I don't like you! . . . You're a scolding, unjust, abusive, aggravating, bad old creature! I am angry with my ungrateful self for calling you names; but you are, you are; you know you are! . . . I have heard you with shame. With shame for myself, and with shame for you. . . . When I came here, I respected you and honoured you, and I soon loved you. And now I can't bear the sight of you. At least, I don't know that I ought to go so far as that—only you're a—you're a Monster!" [53]

Then, to the secretary again: "There is not an ungenerous word that I have heard addressed to you—heard with scorn and indignation, Mr. Rokesmith—but it has wounded me far more than you, for I have deserved it, and you never have. . . . The only fault you can be truly charged with in having spoken to me as you did . . . is that you laid yourself open to be slighted by a worldly shallow girl whose head was turned, and who was quite unable to rise to the worth of what you offered her. Mr. Rokesmith, that girl has often seen herself in a pitiful and poor light since, but never in as pitiful and poor a light as now, when the mean tone in which she answered you—sordid and vain girl that she was—has been echoed in her ears by Mr. Boffin." [54]

Indignantly but at the same time tearfully she renounces Mr. Boffin and renounces any claim upon his benevolence, running from the room sobbing, but stopping to catch him round the neck and give him a farewell kiss. Presently she marries John Rokesmith. Not until months later does she learn that he is John Harmon, and that the Boffins insist on turning over to him the bulk of his father's fortune. Meanwhile, she happily keeps house on a modest income in a little dwelling on Blackheath. "I want," she tells her husband, "to be something so much worthier than the doll in the doll's house." [55] "In the profusion of Dickens," G. M. Young remarks, "the phrase might pass unnoticed. Twelve years later Ibsen made it the watchword of a revolution." [56]

No one can fail to perceive the resemblance between Bella and Estella in *Great Expectations*, of whose very name Bella is a briefer and less stately echo. Bella is smaller, less majestic, but she is seen with a deeper and more intimate and less dazzled understanding even than Pip's disillusioned knowledge of the fatal and tormenting creature who rung his heart. In her selfishness and charm and greed for money and playful tenderness, she is drawn with a wonderful and compelling clarity that imposes an absolute conviction of her irresistible fascination. Nor does one doubt the sweep of indignant emotion with which she repudiates her own mercenary greed, although one may feel a little less assured of the permanence of that conversion to unselfish devotion. But who could grudge Dickens that flush of eager faith with which he looks forward into her future and believes that henceforth she will always be what she has become in the moment of surrender? If, indeed, Estella and Bella are both drawn in part from Ellen Ternan, who would not hope that the love John Harmon ultimately awakens in his capricious little beauty may have come to Dickens as well? Echoing that unconscious bathos of years ago when the death of Little Nell reverberated with the anguish Dickens felt at the loss of Mary Hogarth—a bathos he was always in danger of falling into when he was most deeply and personally moved—there is now a joyful bathos resounding through the words with which he inaugurates the wedded life of his hero and heroine:

"So, she leaning on her husband's arm, they turned homeward by a rosy path which the gracious sun struck out for them in its setting. And O there are days in this life, worth life and worth death. And O what a bright old song it is, that O 'tis love, 'tis love, that makes the world go round!" [57]

But Dickens had not forgotten those "miserable anxieties" of which Collins knew, and which even late in 1862 had "gathered and gathered" round him.[58] For all the radiant, ecstatic, and rather unreal mist of felicity *Our Mutual Friend* breathes around the future of its lovers, it may be that from Dickens's own life those anxieties had not entirely vanished. Until far into the book John Harmon is possessed with the painful knowledge that Bella is grasping and selfish, and those traits in her are delineated with a vividness and an authoritative force almost entirely new in Dickens's portrayals of young girls. It is no accident that during the period beginning with Estella, when the sacrificial martyr-heroines, the Little Nells and Florence Dombeys, the Esther Summersons and Little Dorrits, disappear from his fictions, their place is filled by young women bearing so unmistakable a stamp of observation and so much less angelic. Pip's love is tortured and without illusion; John Harmon's, through all its earlier manifestations, no less helpless and "against reason."

Let there be no question about it: what a writer has not experienced in his heart he can do no more than coldly image from without. Only what he has proved within emerges from those depths with irresistible power, and when new figures lighted in strong emotion force themselves into his imaginative world they are a projection of that inward reality, no matter how thoroughly the mere surface details may have been changed and disguised. And thus the figure of Bradley Headstone rises up like the armed head in *Macbeth*, still another significant symbol of Dickens's emotional life. Just as in *A Tale of Two Cities* Dickens divided his hopes of happiness and his fears of disappointment between Charles Darnay and Sydney Carton, so in *Our Mutual Friend* he imagines for John Harmon the happiness he himself longs for and portrays in Bradley Headstone all the tortures of jealous fear and unrequited love.

It is noteworthy that, full of lovers as all Dickens's books have been, never before *Great Expectations* has he delineated jealousy save in a humorous light. Sim Tappertit's jealousy of Dolly Varden is merely absurd, Mr. Toots's anguish in the face of Walter Gay has only a comic pathos, Mr. Sparkler's sufferings at the hands of Fanny Dorrit are grotesquely ludicrous. Even David Copperfield's hatred of the young man with red whiskers who monopolizes Dora at a picnic is seen in a mist of tender comedy. But with Pip the desperation aroused by seeing Estella smile on Bentley Drummle is an agony, and Bradley Headstone's devouring and hopeless infatuation for Lizzie Hexam is a burning torment, a bleeding of his heart's blood, untouched in molten fury by anything Dickens has ever done before. No other writer, indeed, in English literature, outside Shakespeare, as Hesketh Pearson observes, portrays the bitterness of rejected love with such poignant horror. There is no evidence, to be sure, that Dickens had reason for jealousy, but even the suspicion of being unloved can fill the breast with unavailing fire.

Of course it would be an error to identify Headstone completely with Dickens. Headstone is a man of plodding abilities, of cramped imaginative horizons, of mediocre judgments and conventional ambitions. He would never see through the outer forms of society and its gilded prizes as Dickens has done. But he is at the same time a man who has elevated himself by laborious effort from humble origins, a man of iron will, of painfully acquired discipline and furious passions. No longer a boy, timorously uncertain of himself, he has so fought his way in the world that it is painfully difficult for him to implore and bitterly humiliating to find all his emotional controls broken down.

"You draw me to you," he tells Lizzie Hexam. "If I were shut up in a strong prison, you would draw me out. I should break through the wall to come to you. If I were lying on a sick bed, you would draw me up—to stagger to your feet and fall there." [59] "You are the ruin of me . . . Yes! you are the ruin—the ruin—the ruin—of me. I have no resources in myself, I have no confidence in myself, I have no government of myself when you are near me or in my thoughts. And you are always in my thoughts now. I have never been quit of you since I first saw you." [60] ("I have never known a moment's peace or content, since the last night of The Frozen Deep. I do suppose that there never was a man so seized and rended by one Spirit." [61]) "Oh, that was a wretched day for me! That was a wretched, miserable day!" [62]

As he speaks, Headstone accompanies his words with a "passionate action of his hands," "which was like flinging his heart's blood down before her in drops upon the pavement-stones"; later he stops and lays "his hand upon a piece of the coping of the burial-ground enclosure, as if he would have dislodged the stone." [63]

"No man knows till the time comes," he continues furiously, "what depths are within him. To some men it never comes; let them rest and be thankful! To me, you brought it; on me, you forced it; and the bottom of this raging sea has been heaved up ever since. . . . I love you. What other men may mean when they use that expression, I cannot tell; what *I* mean is, that I am under the influence of some tremendous attraction which I have resisted in vain, and which over-masters me. You could draw me to fire, you could draw me to water, you could draw me to the gallows, you could draw me to any death, you could draw me to anything I have most avoided, you could draw me to any exposure and disgrace. This, and the confusion of my thoughts, so that I am fit for nothing, is what I mean by your being the ruin of me." [64]

Who could blot out the memory of this scene, with the desperate man wrenching at the stone until the powdered mortar rattles on the pavement, and finally "bringing his clenched hand down upon the stone with a force that laid the knuckles raw and bleeding"! [65]

* * * * *

The mercenary Bella and the tormented Headstone are important to an understanding of Dickens's travail in the years immediately preceding the composition of *Our Mutual Friend*. Like the character of Estella and Pip's passion for Estella, they illumine a realm of emotion that Dickens as novelist had never entered before, and throw some light on the otherwise rather shadowy figure of Ellen Ternan. But it is another of Dickens's triumphs that all this personal and painful material has not merely been fused with the rest of *Our Mutual Friend*; it has been brought into essential relations with its deep-rooted major themes and made a further source of their blazing illumination. Bella's venality is not just one girl's greed, it is the dominant and cherished vice of a pecuniary society; and Headstone's jealous desire to absorb Lizzie Hexam's love and his disastrous endeavor to adapt himself to the dust and ashes of Podsnap's world are stained with the possessiveness and false values of that society.

Every detail is thus woven into a superb union of searching theme and significant symbol that places *Our Mutual Friend* among Dickens's crowning achievements. Intellectually and artistically it is one of the peaks of his stupendous creative power, the synthesis of his developing insight throughout a lifetime. Its view of society and of the world is the goal toward which he began moving early in his career and upon which he marched almost unfaltering through a series of great books to this, which is in certain ways their chief, and one of the supreme works of English fiction.

In it Dickens has utterly renounced the dominant values of conventional and acquisitive respectability, and sharply repudiated the faith he once had in the Cheerybles and the Rouncewells. He sees that the modern world is enslaved to monetary power, that the new financiers and entrepreneurs are but the old aristocracy writ large, and that these pillars of society have no faith and no principles save those of power. The world of Podsnap, Boots, Brewer, and Veneering, the world of promoters, contractors, and company chairmen, with Lady Tippins as its Queen of Love and Beauty, is as corrupt as the world of Sir Leicester Dedlock, less honorable, more callous, and immeasurably cheaper and more vulgar.

The decent values of mankind are found mainly among its misfits and its unsuccessful. They survive rather feebly in little Mr. Twemlow, more firmly in the Reverend Frank Milvey, the poor Christian minister become a social worker. They can be awakened in a Eugene Wrayburn or a Mortimer Lightwood. They may flower in Bella Wilfer, when she has given up her middle-class ambition. But more often they are to be found, though crippled and distorted by bitter pressures, in the poor and in those members of the lower middle class who have sunk into poverty: in the old Jew, Mr. Riah; in Jenny Wren, the dolls' dressmaker; in Betty Higden, who loves the children she minds for a few pennies a day and who has aroused the strongest devotion in Sloppy, the gangling love-child who turns her mangle; in Bella's cherubic Pa, who meekly accepts the teasing of his fellow clerks and the stately nagging of his wife; in Mr. and Mrs. Boffin; in Lizzie Hexam, the unlettered daughter of a Thames water-rat.

But Dickens no longer idealizes the poor either. He sees what poverty has done to Jenny Wren as clearly as he sees what Podsnap is in his prosperity. If the Veneerings represent the glittering corruption of an acquisitive society and Fascination Fledgeby its putrescence, Bradley Headstone, whose very aspirations and ambitions have accepted a false goal, would never have become anything more savory than a schoolroom Bounderby. But whereas Headstone has a certain ugly strength, his weak disciple, Charley Hexam, has merely a whining and nasty selfishness. And lower still we sink to the rats of the waterside, like Rogue Riderhood, "the accumulated scum of hu-

manity . . . washed from higher grounds, like so much moral sewage." [66]
The vermin of the depths are as diseased as the curs and jackals of
power.

Our Mutual Friend is consequently the darkest and bitterest of all
Dickens's novels. If the Golden Dustman after all remains uninfected
by his wealth, his is an individual case. Mr. Boffin's generosity changes
the pattern of society no more than Sophronia Lammle's betrayal of
her husband's plot to trap Georgiana Podsnap into wedlock with the
fortune hunter Fledgeby. John Harmon's marriage to Bella, Eugene
Wrayburn's marriage to Lizzie Hexam, shake the foundations of that
society as little as the Veneerings' bankruptcy and flight to France. At
the end, as at the beginning, Podsnap sits magisterially robed in complacence and the fascinating Tippins screams scandal, coyly berates
her lovers, and gobbles greedily at table.

> *Lo! thy dread Empire, CHAOS! is restored;*
> *Light dies before thy uncreating word;*
> *Thy hand, great Anarch! lets the curtain fall,*
> *And universal Darkness buries All.*[67]

Our Mutual Friend is *The Waste Land* of Dickens's work. Like
that poem, it resorts to the realm of myth, and "for the source of emotional vitality," as Robert Morse points out, "draws upon the deepest
mythology of mankind." [68] "Dickens has gone underground to that
region where the mists of unnameable anxieties and the smoke of in-
fantile terrors prevail. There, at the edge of the sea of sleep, he has
built his London." [69] In the mazes of that dark city dwell the Mino-
taur and the Gorgons, and the Furies are neighbors to Miss Flite's
birds. As in the world of Eliot's poem, this London is a waste land of
stony rubbish and broken images, of dead trees, dry rock, and dust.

> *Unreal City,*
> *Under the brown fog of a winter dawn,*
> *A crowd flowed over London Bridge, so many*
> *I had not thought death had undone so many.*[70]

The Thames of *Our Mutual Friend* is the same river that flows
through the waste land, a river sweating tar and waste, bearing a flot-
sam of debris in its muddy waters. Once a symbol of the renewal of
life, the waters themselves are sullied with the muck of the dust-

heaps infecting their purity in loathsome solution. And along their shore, like Eliot's rats creeping softly through the vegetation and dragging their slimy bellies on the bank, Rogue Riderhood and his fellows are the slinking underworld counterparts of the fatter rats, the Fledgebys and the geniuses at speculation, who are gnawing the foundations of the Rialto.

The mythological image of drowning or near-drowning, symbol at once of death and resurrection, appears and reappears in a dozen variants. The third mate who changes clothing and identities with John Harmon in the waterside tavern actually drowns, as do Bradley Headstone and Rogue Riderhood caught in a death-grip of hate with each other. Earlier in the story Riderhood is nearly drowned, but is brought back to consciousness, only to use his restoration to life for treachery and blackmail. The near-drownings of John Harmon and Eugene Wrayburn are each a prelude to rebirth into a new identity; Eugene's is almost a sort of baptismal immersion that represents the death of his old selfish levity and his spiritual rebirth. The final disposition of the immutably mean-spirited Wegg is the inverse of Eugene's salvation: Sloppy dumps him with a prodigious splash into a scavenger's cart of muck.

Lizzie Hexam hardly needs any conversion, but she too is plunged metaphorically into the waters of suffering, and literally rescues Eugene from the stream in which his bloody and multilated body has been sinking to its death. Last of all, there is the conversion of Bella Wilfer, saved from selfishness by that very stratagem of the Golden Dustman that drowns her in humiliation and shame. Even in the midst of that dark waste of city through which Dickens now images the modern world, redemption is still possible for those who have learned the great lesson that is the burden of the book: Control, Give, Love.

For it is the essence of Dickens's genius that his vision is not simple but complex, and of his spirit that he will admit no irremeable defeat. He has come to see that the pressures of society make most men what they are and that the evils of society are general evils more than they are the work of deliberately vicious men. Though there are men like Sir Mulberry Hawk, Quilp, Sir John Chester, Jonas Chuzzlewit, Fledgeby, and Lammle, who willingly give themselves to brutality and treachery, their spectacular misdeeds produce far less of the suffering of humanity than the respectable virtues of Mr. Dombey and Mr. Gradgrind, or of Bounderby and Podsnap. The Tite Barnacles and the Merdles are not villains; Mr. Dorrit and even Rogue Riderhood are more victims of their environment than they are conscious agents.

But the ever-broadening grasp and deepening penetration that enabled Dickens to see the dominant values of nineteenth-century society as a great dust-heap could not stop at mere negation. Within the framework of necessity, he insists, there is always the possibility of some choice, and the choice a man makes weakens or strengthens his powers of future choice. He believes that the hideous domination of mechanical greed can be broken in society as it can be transcended by the individual—as it is transcended every day by the Betty Higdens and the Lizzie Hexams; as it can be by the Bella Wilfers and Eugene Wrayburns. Dickens is as clear as John Dewey in asserting that, if society in many ways shapes the individual, the individual may also remold society. In the individual, learning control for generous ends, in the love of the human heart, lies the hope that can conquer the dust-heap and bring fruitful bloom back to the waste land.

PART TEN

The Bottom of the Cup

1865–1870

CHAPTER ONE

Pilgrim of Gad's Hill

"THE fifty-eight boxes have come, sir," said Dickens's groom, meeting him one day at Higham Station. "What?" said Dickens. "The fifty-eight boxes have come, sir." "I know nothing of fifty-eight boxes." "Well, sir," returned the man, "they are all piled up outside the gate and we shall soon see, sir." [1]

When they were opened, the astonishing consignment turned out to be packed with all the parts of a small Swiss chalet, in ninety-four pieces made to fit together like the joints of a puzzle.[2] A gift from the actor Charles Fechter, the little building was two stories high, with a narrow outside staircase rising to a fretted balcony on which opened an airy room above. A brick foundation was soon being laid for it across the road deep among the leafy trees of the shrubbery. "The chalet is going on excellently," Dickens reported to Forster, "though the ornamental part is more slowly put together than the substantial. It will really be a very pretty thing; and in the summer (supposing it not to be blown away in the spring), the upper room will make a charming study." [3]

For the donor of the chalet Dickens had conceived an almost extravagant admiration. Strolling one night into a Parisian theater where Fechter was playing the lover in La Dame aux Camélias, Dickens found himself so carried away by the romantic tenderness in which Fechter enveloped the heroine that he felt "they trod in a purer ether and in another sphere quite elevated out of the present. 'By heavens!' I said to myself; 'a man who can do this can do anything.' I never saw two people more purely and intensely elevated by the power of love." [4] The performance took Paris by storm. Meeting the actor and discovering that he spoke English musically and fluently, Dickens pressed him to come to England.

Fechter's passionate Hamlet, played with flaxen hair,[5] startled London by "a remorseless destruction of conventionalities" [6] and a fiery logic of conception; his Iago convincingly deceived his victims instead of giving himself away by sneers and diabolic grins.[7] Dickens thought his performance in the last act of *Ruy Blas* very fine,[8] and in 1863 hailed his production of *The Duke's Motto* as "a brilliant success" enabling Fechter to throw down a "gauntlet in defiance of all comers." [9] In 1864 Dickens aided Fechter as a "play doctor," adapting Bellew's *The King's Butterfly* to more effective stage production.[10] Later he was generous with advice and assistance in putting on *The Master of Ravenswood*, a dramatization of Scott's *The Bride of Lammermoor*,[11] and in staging a revival of Lytton's *Roman Lady*.[12]

Dickens is even supposed to have given Fechter financial aid. During one triumphant but expensive production, Fechter's manager is alleged to have proved to him that instead of being £6,000 ahead, as Fechter had believed, he owed £3,000. Upset and angry, according to the story, the actor told Dickens about it as they walked away from meeting each other in Covent Garden. Dickens made no offer of assistance, but the next morning Fechter's manager said, "The matter was not so pressing as all that, my dear sir." "What do you mean?" "Why, about that £3,000. Charles Dickens came and handed me the cash on your behalf at twelve o'clock last night." [13]

Whether or not anything like this happened, there can be no doubt of the warmth of Dickens's support and friendship.[14] Many of his other protégés thought it an unaccountable infatuation. Marcus Stone insisted that Fechter was no gentleman, and Percy Fitzgerald did not like him. But Dickens "became his helper in disputes, adviser on literary points, referee in matters of management, and . . . no face was more familiar than the French comedian's at Gad's Hill or in the offices of his journal." [15] "I shall be heartily pleased to see you again, my dear Fechter, and to share your triumphs with the real earnestness of a real friend," [16] Dickens wrote; and, again, "Count always on my fidelity and true attachment." [17]

Fechter completed his gift of the chalet "by furnishing it in a very handsome manner" when it was ready for use in August, 1865.[18] Inviting Lytton to Gad's Hill, Dickens suggested his using it to write in.[19] The two had just spent a pleasant day together during the ceremonies of dedicating the Guild of Literature and Art houses at Stevenage. The seven years' delay provided by the Act of Parliament that incorporated the Guild was at last over, and its founders, filled with generous hope, celebrated the occasion with a formal banquet in the dining hall of Lytton's Knebworth estate. They had no anticipation of the slow paralysis to which the Guild would gradually fall prey.

Dickens came up from Gad's Hill for the dedication with Percy Fitzgerald, Mary, and Georgina, reading proofs on the train and stopping off at Wellington Street to pick up Wills and look at the huge orange-and-red posters with which they were advertising a new serial for *All the Year Round*. Thence they drove in great spirits through Seven Dials to the station of the Great Northern, where they met some of Lytton's other guests. Soon they were in the green countryside of Hertfordshire, with Dickens joking and telling stories about Adah Isaacs Menken,[20] who was to be seen at Astley's Circus in *Mazeppa*, bound to a horse, "ascending the fearful precipice not as hitherto done by a dummy." [21]

"Grand old Knebworth," Fitzgerald thought, was like an Elizabethan palace, with its vases, statues, and high green hedges. Dickens took him upstairs to see Lytton, reclining in an oriental dressing gown smoking a chibouk "like an Eastern potentate, with dreamy eyes." Lytton was supposedly too delicate in health to act as host, and John Forster, gloriously majestic, served as his vizier and displayed the three Gothic houses of the Guild partly enclosing their pretty garden-quadrangle. Dickens strode around in high spirits, a flower in his buttonhole and his hat a little on one side. Forster was so grandiose that Fitzgerald half complained to Dickens about his intolerable condescension. Dickens shook with laughter. "Lord bless you, why he *didn't see* ME! . . . He was in the clouds like Malvolio." [22]

Lytton appeared at dinner, hawk-nosed and surprisingly keen of eye again, and the two famous authors indulged in reminiscence about the old days when they had been youthful unknowns beginning their careers. But after dinner the baronial pomp of Lytton's hospitality proved too overpowering for some of the other literary guests, who gradually drifted away to the tavern across the road from the Guild houses. At nine, Dickens's party took the train back to London, where they dropped in at the office again for *pâté de foie gras*, cold game, and wine. Fitzgerald returned to Gad's Hill with the family. Their train reached Gravesend at midnight, and from there Dickens drove them home by moonlight along the white high road.[23]

Although Dickens and Forster maintained their old affection for each other, they were not so often together as in earlier years. There were still bouts of sparring between them, sometimes without gloves, but more and more Dickens found himself amused by Forster's swelling Johnsonian dignity. Sometimes he rolled on a sofa in agonies of enjoyment at some new story grotesquely revealing his friend "impregnably *mailed* in self-complacency." [24] A cabman whom Forster had given a dressing-down ruefully described him as "a harbitrary cove," but Forster was no less overbearing with the great. He had shouldered his way from his post as Secretary to the Lunacy Commission to an even more lucrative appointment as one of the Commissioners. "I never let old Brougham go," he told Fitzgerald. "I came back again and again until I wore him out. I forced 'em to give me this." [25]

Since his wealthy marriage Forster had given up his chambers at Lincoln's Inn, and now lived in ostentatious magnificence in a large mansion at Palace Gate. At his dinner table his guests were astounded, his wife terrified, and only his butler unmoved by his roars of indignation at an incompetent pageboy. "Biscuits," he murmured to the page; then, more loudly, "Biscuits!" and when this went unheeded, with a bellow, "BIScuits!" [26] On the guests, Robert Browning said, he would "wipe his shoes," giving his "rhinoceros laugh," bullying and shouting them down with a rolling "In-*tol*-er-able," "Don't tell me!" "Incredible!" "Monstrous!" [27]

With Dickens's faithful henchman, Wills, he got on as badly as ever. Seldom did Forster turn up in the *All the Year Round* office without the two "growling at each other like angry dogs." On one occasion, "I had at last," Dickens told Fitzgerald, "to say to Wills, 'Please to withdraw.'" Glaring hostility, Wills did withdraw, but muttered, "Never mind, a time will come—all right," while Forster snorted, "That Wills is neither more nor less than a stock-jobber . . ." [28] Then Forster would cool off and ask what was amiss between them. "I said," Dickens reported to Wills, "that I did not know from you that anything was amiss. He rejoined that he had made such and such approaches to you, which you had avoided, and that if there were something wrong between you, it was quite unconsciously on his part." [29]

All Forster's acquaintances recognized his mannerisms embedded in Podsnap—the indignant flush, the sweeping gesture of dismissal—but nobody who knew him doubted his entire inability to see himself there.[30] It is not impossible, however, that they were wrong; just around the time that the chapter on Podsnap appeared in *Our Mutual Friend*, near the end of July, 1864, "Forster fluttered about in the Athenaeum," Dickens wrote Georgina, "as I conversed in the hall with all sorts and conditions of men—and pretended not to see me—but I saw in every hair of his whisker (left hand one) that he saw Nothing Else." [31] Whatever irritation there was, though, did not last long; before the end of August Forster and his wife spent a long week-end at Gad's Hill.[32]

* * * * *

During the summer the house was always filled with guests; sometimes there was even an overflow into the Sir John Falstaff across the road beyond the shrubbery. In Gad's Hill itself, each bedroom had the most comfortable of beds, a sofa, an easy chair, and caned-bottom chairs—which Dickens liked far better than upholstered chairs—and a large writing table with paper, envelopes, and an almost daily change of quill pens. Each room also had a small library of books, a fire in winter, and a shining copper kettle, with cups, saucers, tea caddy, teapot, sugar and milk on a side table.[33]

Life at Gad's Hill reflected a routine of genial if strenuous hospitality on the part of its host. Breakfast was between nine and ten-thirty.[34] Descending the staircase with its Hogarth prints, the visitor saw on the first-floor landing an illuminated plaque: "This House, GAD'S HILL PLACE, stands on the summit of Shakespeare's Gad's Hill, ever memorable for its association with Sir John Falstaff in his noble fancy. *But, my lads, my lads, tomorrow morning, by four o'clock, early at Gad's Hill! there are pilgrims going to Canterbury with rich offerings and traders riding to London with fat purses; I have vizards for you all; you have horses for yourselves.*" [35] Beyond the square entrance hall a wide passage, with Stanfield's paintings decorating the walls between the study and the billiard room, opened on the rear lawn, separated from the meadow by a stone wall and massive iron gates.[36]

In the dining room, bright with mirrors, Dickens gave a morning greeting and recommended some savory dish from the sideboard, perhaps kidneys with an appetizing dressing,[36a] although he was an abstemious eater himself, and seldom took more than a rasher of bacon, an egg, and a cup of tea.[37] After breakfast, Dickens wrote all morning, either in his study or in the chalet, while his guests could please themselves, smoking cigars, reading the papers, strolling in the garden among its clambering honeysuckle, clumped nasturtiums, red geraniums, and mignonette, and perhaps pausing for a chat with Mary, who was looking after her flowers.[38]

Dickens loved mirrors and hung them everywhere. "I have put five mirrors in the chalet where I write," he told an American friend, "and they reflect and refract, in all kinds of ways, the leaves that are quivering at the windows, and the great fields of waving corn, and the sail-dotted river. My room is up among the branches of the trees; and the birds and the butterflies fly in and out, and the green branches shoot in at the open windows, and the lights and shadows of the clouds come and go with the rest of the company. The scent of the flowers, and indeed of everything that is growing for miles and miles, is most delicious." [39]

At one o'clock Dickens emerged for lunch, a substantial meal, though again he himself ate little, usually confining himself to bread and cheese and a glass of ale.[40] The dinner menu was always on the sideboard at lunchtime, and Dickens would discuss the items. "Cock-a-leekie? Good, decidedly good; fried soles with shrimp sauce? Good again; croquettes of chicken? Weak, very weak; decided want of imagination here." [41] For the rest of the day he devoted himself to his guests.

First there might be a trip to the stables to see the horses: Toby, a good sturdy animal,[42] Mary's riding horse Boy,[43] Trotty Veck,[44] and the sober Newman Noggs, a Norwegian pony who drew the basket cart in a jingling harness of musical bells.[45] Romping along came the dogs, Turk the great mastiff, Linda the St. Bernard, tumbling over each other, and, frisking along with them, Mrs. Bouncer, Mary's Pomeranian, for whom Dickens had a special voice and who amused him with her airs because "she looks so preposterously small." [46]

The vagrants who tramped the Dover Road made dogs a desirable protection at Gad's Hill, and one was usually chained on each side of the entrance gate except when they went on walks. In September, 1865, Fitzgerald delighted Dickens with the gift of an Irish bloodhound named Sultan, who turned out to be gentle and obedient with his master but so ferocious with everyone else that he had to be kept muzzled at all times. "He has only swallowed Bouncer once, and temporarily," Dickens wrote Fitzgerald.[47] A little later came Don, a black Newfoundland sent by a friend from America.[48] The rest of the dogs were tractable enough, but Sultan proved fiercely unmanageable. He hated other dogs; he hated policemen; he hated soldiers, and once, with his muzzle tight on, "dashed into the heart of a company in heavy marching order . . . and pulled down an objectionable private." [49] He constantly broke loose and, despite his muzzle, returned home covered with blood. When he attacked a little girl, sister of one of the servants, Dickens decided he would have to be shot.

"You heard," he wrote Fitzgerald, "of his going to execution, evidently supposing the procession to be a party detached in pursuit of something to kill or eat? It was very affecting. And also of his bolting a blue-eyed kitten, and making me acquainted with the circumstance by his agonies of remorse (or indigestion)?" [50] "But observing in the procession an empty wheelbarrow and a double-barrelled gun, he became meditative, and fixed the bearer of the gun with his eyes. A stone deftly thrown across him by the village blacksmith (chief mourner) caused him to look round for an instant, and then he fell dead, shot through the heart. Two posthumous children are at this moment rolling on the lawn; one will evidently inherit his ferocity, and will probably inherit the gun." [51]

Descending through the tunnel and coming into the shrubbery as he showed his guests around the little estate, Dickens would boast of the singing birds who fluttered about there all day, and of his nightingales at night.[52] He gave "a capital imitation of the way a robin-red-breast cocks his head on one side preliminary to a dash forward in the direction of a wriggling victim." He was full of stories about canaries, and liked to show people the small grave of Dick, the favorite canary who had survived by ten years the cat war at Boulogne in 1856.[53]

When everything had been seen, Dickens suggested a walk, but of those who had walked with him before only the bravest dared face the grueling ordeal again.[54] To Chatham and Fort Pitt, over Cooling Marsh, or even, skirting Cobham Wood and Park, to Chalk and Gravesend, Dickens maintained a relentless pace of four miles an hour, swinging his blackthorn stick and talking cheerfully all the while. Only at Chalk would he slacken and gaze meditatively at the cottage where he and Catherine had spent their honeymoon so many years ago,[55] but no one ventured to ask what memories it brought to his mind. Sometimes his perspiring companions gave way to blisters and breathlessness. "I have now in my mind's eye," wrote Edmund Yates, "a portly American gentleman in varnished boots, who started with us full of courage, but whom we left panting by the wayside, and for whom the basket-carriage had to be sent." [56] On their return, tired and dripping, Dickens saluted the energetic survivors: "Well done! Twelve miles in three hours." [57]

No sooner had they returned to Gad's Hill than Dickens plunged into games, usually with those who had pleaded correspondence when he proposed a stroll. He was an expert at rounders, relentless at battle-dore and bagatelle, and loved bowling and quoits.[58] Even when the tall maid in her spotless cap came out to the green turf to announce five-o'clock tea, and the sun warned that they must soon prepare for dinner, Dickens still "played longer and harder than any of the company, scorning the idea of going in to tea at that hour, and beating his ball instead, quite the youngest of the company up to the last moment!" [59]

In the summer he allowed a local working-men's club to hold cricket matches in his meadow, and, encouraged by their appreciation, got up a day of foot races and rustic sports each Christmas season. As he had never yet had a case of drunkenness, he explained, he allowed "the landlord of the Falstaff to have a drinking-booth on the ground. Not to seem to dictate or distrust, I gave all the prizes (about ten pounds in the aggregate) in money. The great mass of the crowd were labouring men of all kinds, soldiers, sailors, and navvies. They did not, between half-past-ten, when we began, and sunset, displace a rope or a stake; and they left every barrier and flag as neat as they found it. There was not a dispute, and there was no drunkenness whatever." From the lawn Dickens made a little speech at the end, "saying that please God we would do it again next year. They cheered most lustily and dispersed. The road between this and Chatham was like a Fair all day; and surely it is a fine thing to get such perfect behaviour out of a reckless seaport town." [60]

After taking a shower bath, which he loved, Dickens would be as fresh at dinner as any of his guests. Though he was not a glittering conversationalist, he sparkled with the pleasure of companionship. He was sometimes so comical that he convulsed the servants and left them quite unable to keep a straight face.[61] His own laughter burst out of him with "a peculiar humorous protest" as if he were exclaiming, "This is *too* ridiculous! This passes all bounds!" It "overwhelmed him like a tide, which carried all hearers away with it." [62] But, better than a brilliant talker, he was a brilliant listener, who stimulated others to their best, filled everyone with the conviction that Dickens delighted in his company, and allowed no man to be a bore. His radiant face and his lustrous eyes shone with life. In those glowing eyes, Fitzgerald said, you could see the first gleam of laughter, "twinkling there" and then spreading downward while "the mobile muscles of the cheek began to quiver," and finally reaching "the expressive mouth" under its grizzled mustache, where it broke into "*crimpled* wrinkles of enjoyment." [63]

Once an old French priest in a railway carriage told Dickens there were no antiquities in England. "None at all?" Dickens said. "You have some ships, however," the priest went on. "Yes; a few." "Are they strong?" "Well," Dickens replied, "your trade is spiritual, father; ask the ghost of Nelson." [64] On another occasion, at the dinner table, to a young writer denouncing the world, "What a lucky thing it is," Dickens insinuated slyly, "you and I don't belong to it?—It reminds me of the two men, who on a *raised* scaffold were awaiting the final delicate attention of the hangman; . . . observing that a bull had got into the crowd of spectators, and was busily employed in tossing one here, and another there . . . one of the criminals said to the other, 'I say, Bill, how *lucky it is* for us that *we are up here.*' " [65]

Following dinner, there would be dancing and games. Dickens was not a very good dancer, his daughter Mary said, but he could do a lively sailor's hornpipe, and was best at Sir Roger de Coverleys and other country dances, though he insisted on jigging even on the sides, clapping his hands, and dancing at the backs of those he thought needed rousing.[66] Card games he did not care for, but he loved charades, "Dumb Crambo," pantomimes, and guessing and memory games. Even years later Marcus Stone was convulsed whenever he tried to imitate Dickens's dumb show of "frog." [67] An American visitor remembered a pantomime of the beheading of Charles I: Dickens with a black handkerchief on his head and a fire shovel as an ax, with Collins brought in as the victim, and the company's desperate attempt, despite Collins's trousers, to identify him as Mary Queen of Scots.[68]

Dickens was always one of the survivors in memory games, where each player added a phrase to a steadily growing total until one after another forgot something and dropped out. Sometimes his fellow players were puzzled by the oddity of his additions, as when with a curious twinkle in his eye and an odd tone of voice he supplied the words, "Warren's Blacking, 30, Strand." [69] He was swift and intuitive in "Twenty Questions," bombarding the other players with such a rapid stream of searching queries that he positively extorted the solution. On one occasion, he failed to guess "The powder in the Gunpowder Plot," although he succeeded in reaching Guy Fawkes; but on the same evening he ferreted out what Fitzgerald had believed impossible, "the left leg of a postilion's boot." [70]

The steaming brandy punch or gin with lemon that Dickens delighted to brew was a ritual, with a devout attention to the proportions and blending of the ingredients, whimsical auguries of the staggering impact the beverage might be expected to have on its imbibers, and a zestful flourish in the serving. But for him the enjoyment lay almost entirely in the associations of clinking cannikins, apples bobbing merrily in the bowl, minstrel glees, and warm conviviality. Instead of drinking tumbler after tumbler, he seldom took more than a glass or two: "Never was there a more abstemious bibber." [71] Later in the evening the men had whiskies and soda in the billiard and smoking room that had been made from the old breakfast parlor. Bending over the green cloth of the billiard table for a shot, with his red but worn cheeks, his thinning grayish hair, the sharp wrinkles around his eyes magnified by the large double-glasses he now wore for reading or playing, he looked unexpectedly middle-aged. At midnight he would retire to sleep, but his guests were under no such obligation, and the first streaks of dawn sometimes found them still playing.[72]

*   *   *   *   *

Although Dickens still took a house in London for the spring, he spent most of the year at Gad's Hill. Now and then, however, he liked to get away by himself. For this purpose he had rooms at the Five Bells Inn, a few miles southeast of London, at the corner of New Cross Road and Hatcham Park Road, and not far from a station of the South Eastern Railway.[73] Less than a mile south was Linden Grove, Nunhead, where from 1867 on, according to Thomas Wright, Ellen Ternan was living at Windsor Lodge, a villa with a large garden that Dickens had taken for her. In the rate-books at Peckham Town Hall between 1867 and 1870 the name of the occupant appears at first as Turnham and later as Tringham. A woman who worked at the Lodge knew Dickens only as Mr. Tringham, although she was aware of the fact that he was a writer. Dickens was known by sight and name, however, to a local hackman who often drove him there. In 1866 Ellen's sister Frances Eleanor had married Thomas Adolphus Trollope; and later neighbors learned that the lady who occupied the villa was related in some way to "Mr. Trollope,—presumably the writer." [74]

Numbers of Dickens's friends knew about Ellen, although he kept her as closely guarded a secret as possible. To Frances Dickinson, an old friend who had acted with him in *The Frozen Deep*, he wrote: "The 'magic circle' consists of but one member. I don't in the least care for Mrs. T. T. [Thomas Trollope] except that her share in the story is (as far as I am concerned) a remembrance impossible to swallow. Therefore, and for the magic sake, I scrupulously try to do her justice, and not to see her—out of my path—with a jaundiced eye.

"I feel your affectionate letter truly and deeply, but it would be inexpressibly painful to N to think that you knew her history. She has no suspicion that your assertion of your friend against the opposite powers ever brought you to the knowledge of it. She would not believe that you could see her with my eyes, or know her with my mind. Such a presentation is impossible. It would distress her for the rest of her life. I thank you none the less, but it is quite out of the question. If she could hear that, she could not have the pride and self reliance which (mingled with the gentlest nature) has borne her, alone, through so much.

". . . Of course you will be very strictly on your guard, if you see Tom Trollope, or his wife, or both,—to make no reference to me which either can piece into anything. She is infinitely sharper than the serpent's Tooth. Mind that." [75]

There are no known facts throwing any light on what Dickens meant by Frances Eleanor Trollope's "share in the story," but the rest of this letter is perfectly clear. Mrs. Dickinson, in defending him against his accusers, had learned the truth and assured him of her sympathy and support, even voiced a desire to meet "N" (Nelly) and be her friend. That plea, out of regard for Ellen's feelings, Dickens felt obliged to reject. And, finally, it is plain that Dickens not only believed the Trollopes to be unaware of Ellen's relationship with him, but desired to keep them so.

Dickens's description in *Our Mutual Friend* of the neighborhood in which Bradley Headstone's school was located, "down in that district tending to the Thames, where Kent and Surrey meet," tallies exactly with what New Cross and Hatcham were like in the sixties. Near by in Lewisham High Street was a private school where a pretty daughter of his Barrow relations was learning French, music, and dancing. Emily Barrow learned that her famous kinsman had rooms at the Five Bells and called on him there with her best friend, Charlotte Elizabeth Lane. Dickens loved pretty faces and girlish chatter, and gave them apples from the pyramid he always had piled on his table, took them to the Bank of England to see "the gold being shovelled up with shovels," and invited them to Gad's Hill. During visits there, the two girls noticed that he was often pensive and silent at the table. Suddenly he would push back his chair, leave in the middle of a meal, and hurry off to his writing. Later the family stole peeps at his manuscript, and came away laughing at what they read. [76]

Throughout all this time, Dickens's health remained a cause for concern. During the winter, changes in weather from mugginess to frost and back brought recurrences of the trouble with his foot, and early in 1866 his pulse was so bad that Frank Beard, his doctor—brother of his old friend Thomas Beard—told him "an examination of the heart was absolutely necessary." "There seems," Dickens reported to Georgina, "to be degeneration of some functions of the heart. It does not contract as it should. . . . I have noticed for some time a decided change in my buoyancy and hopefulness—in other words, in my usual 'tone.' " [77]

Nevertheless, despite his realization that these symptoms resulted from the strain his readings had put upon him, and despite the fact that even after medical treatment he continued "very unwell," Dickens now resolved to undertake another series of thirty readings "in England, Ireland, Scotland, or Paris," as it might be decided. Messrs. Chappell, of New Bond Street, offered him £50 a night in addition to all expenses, and Dickens accepted the offer.[78] He insisted, however, that the shilling seats must be as good as those at higher prices. "I have been the champion and friend of the working man all through my career, and it would be inconsistent, if not unjust, to put any difficulty in the way of his attending my Readings." [79] Chappell's was to handle all business details. "All I have to do is, to take in my book and read, at the appointed place and hour, and come out again." [80]

His opening night at St. James's Hall, London, on April 10, 1866, was devoted to "Doctor Marigold," adapted from his Christmas story of that year, which had sold over 250,000 copies. During the intervening three months Dickens had rehearsed it more than two hundred times. The excitement in the audience was tremendous. The very next day Dickens went on to Liverpool and Manchester.[81] As manager Chappell's had appointed George Dolby, a brother of the well-known singer Mme. Sainton Dolby. Dolby was a tall, bulky, bald-headed man with a stammer and a bluff manner, whom Mark Twain described as "a gladsome gorilla." [82] At the train Dolby met the scrawny Wills, who was to be Dickens's traveling companion, and Dickens himself, in a pea jacket, a Count D'Orsay cloak, and a soft felt hat worn on one side, which gave his lined and bronzed face the look of a "modernized gentlemanly pirate" with eyes in which "lurked the iron will of a demon and the tender pity of an angel." [83]

Wills began by putting Dolby through a severe cross-examination about how he handled his work. Dickens was agitated by the railway journey and, until they reached Bletchley, forty miles from London, wore an expression of anxiety and nervousness. But then the flask of brandy was brought out and they fell into conversation over their cigars.[84] On later journeys, Dolby provided a cold collation of anchovy and hard-boiled egg sandwiches, salmon mayonnaise, pressed beef, cold fowl and tongue, Roquefort cheese, and cherry tart, with wine and gin punch iced in the washstand, and coffee made with a spirit lamp.[85] They played three-handed cribbage, and once Dickens danced a sailor's hornpipe for them to a whistling accompaniment.[86] Another time, when Dickens, glass in hand, was giving them the drinking song from *Der Freischütz*, the suction of air from an express on the opposite track whisked a sealskin cap clear off his head and out of a window.[87]

The provincial tour went with a rush everywhere. There were enormous "lets" in Glasgow and Edinburgh, and even in Aberdeen, where the local agent told Dolby, "I'm no prapared t' state positively what yewr actiel receats 'll be, *for ye see, sir, amangst ma ain freends there are vairy few wha ha' iver haird o' Charles Dickens*." [88] Everywhere the demand for shilling seats was a tidal wave.[89] In Birmingham, Dickens read "Nickleby" instead of the "Trial," which was announced on the program. Discovering his error, he came out on the platform again at ten o'clock "and said that if they liked I would give them the Trial. They *did* like, and I had another half hour of it in that enormous place." [90]

In Portsmouth, where the tour ended near the close of May, Dickens wandered around with Wills and Dolby and found himself in Landport Terrace. "By Jove!" he exclaimed, "here is the place where I was born"; and began trying to identify the house. One must be it, he thought, because "it looked so like his father"; another "because it looked like the birthplace of a man who had deserted it; a third was very like the cradle of a puny, weak youngster . . . and so on through the row." [91] One open square in the town, with red brick houses dotted by white window frames, so resembled the scene for the comic business of a pantomime that Dickens was unable to resist a temptation to imitate the clowning of Grimaldi. Mounting the steps to a brass-plated green door, he gave three raps, and lay down on the top step, when a stout woman suddenly opened the door, and all three men beat a hasty retreat, with Dickens in the rear chased by an imaginary policeman, in the course of which the wind blew off Dickens's hat and the pursuit became a real one.[92]

Despite all these high jinks, Dickens was not well. He found himself unable to sleep at night, and was obliged between halves of his performance to take a dozen oysters and a little champagne as a restorative.[93] He developed a severe pain in his left eyeball that, with the shaking of the trains, made it hard for him to do anything. Early in May he caught a cold that refused to leave him.[94] For weeks, even months, he was troubled by distention and flatulency, with pains in

the pit of the stomach and chest.[95] "Twice last week," he wrote Forster, "I was seized in a most distressing manner—apparently in the
heart; but, I am persuaded, only in the nervous system." [96]

But the demoniac possession that drove him would not let him
rest. The readings closed with three London engagements ending on
June 12th. Their total receipts turned out to be £4,672. Several weeks
before the end, Chappell's tempted him with an offer for fifty more
nights to begin at Christmas. Dickens at first thought of demanding £70 a night, but ultimately offered to give forty-two readings
for £2,500.[98] The Chappells—"speculators," Dickens called them,
"though of the worthiest and most honourable kind" [99]—instantly
accepted this offer.[100] The stimulus and excitement that he had come
to need, the constant nagging sense of family needs that would still
exist even when he was dead, were inexorably driving him to a disastrous course.

"This is a pretty state of things!" he exclaimed to Collins. "—That
I should be in Christmas Labour while you are cruising about the
world, a compound of Hayward and Captain Cook! But I am so
undoubtedly one of the sons of Toil—and fathers of children—that I
expect to be presently presented with a smock frock, a pair of leather
breeches, and a pewter watch, for having brought up the largest family
ever known with the smallest disposition to do anything for themselves." [101]

In July, 1863, fourteen-year-old Harry, aided by his younger brother,
had started a domestic paper, printed by hand, called *The Gad's Hill
Gazette*. The two boys continued to turn it out in the winter and
summer holidays, and in 1865 Wills gave them a small printing press
for the purpose. The paper chronicled arrivals and departures, billiard matches, excursions, and evening amusements, told anecdotes
of the guests, and ran a sprinkling of acrostics and conundrums. Dickens made joking contributions to it and read it with interest, but he
did not feel that its authors had any literary talent.[102]

Harry was hard-working and quick-minded. But over Plorn, so long
his favorite child, Dickens was beginning to feel almost discouraged.
Now fourteen, the boy seemed to have no intellectual talents and
small powers of industry. "His want of application and continuity of
purpose," Dickens felt, were part of an "impracticable torpor . . . in
his natural character," and therefore a misfortune rather than a

fault.[103] "He is most completely self-deceived," Dickens wrote his tutor, "if he supposes that I do not know him better than to trust to his improving himself in anything of his own accord, or to his reading at home." [104] His best course, Dickens decided, would be to look toward becoming a farmer in Australia, to drop Latin, and learn some practical chemistry, carpentry, and smith's work, such as would be of use to him "in a rough wild life" there.[105] But Dickens's belief in the boy died hard. As "he is fond of animals, and of being on horseback, and of moving rapidly through the air, I hope he may take better to the Bush than to Books. His natural abilities may flash up, under such conditions, too." [106]

The lassitude Dickens observed in his youngest son troubled him all the more because he had earlier noted the same failing in Charley, and feared it was a quality that both had inherited from their mother.[107] Charley, after having tried so many other things, was now engaged in a paper-mill business established on capital found by Miss Coutts,[108] but like his brother Walter, who when he died in India had been deep in debt,[109] was finding it difficult to handle money with prudence and understanding.

With all the doubts aroused by most of the other boys, Dickens felt uncertain even about Harry, though he now seemed to be doing well at Wimbledon. Harry had declared he "did not wish to enter the Indian Civil Service"; Dickens replied "that many of us have many duties to discharge in life which we do not wish to undertake, and that we must do the best we can to earn our respective livings and make our way. I also clearly pointed out to him that I bear as heavy a train as can well be attached to any one working man, and that I could by no means afford to send a son to College who went there for any other purpose than to work hard, and to gain distinction." [110]

Dickens finally agreed, however, to ask the Reverend William Brackenbury, the head of the school, if he believed Harry really "worth sending to Cambridge," and really possessed of "the qualities and habits essential to marked success there." If Mr. Brackenbury so advised, "he should study accordingly." If not, "he should decidedly go up for the Indian Civil Service Examination." [111]

Around this time, Catherine, who had some problem concerning her house in Gloucester Crescent, Regent's Park, asked Dickens to come there and advise her. He refused to express any opinion on the matter, and turned her letter over to Georgina for reply. Catherine must "decide the question out of her own daily experience . . . and domestic knowledge"; "I will never go to her house," he declared obdurately, "and . . . it is my fixed purpose (without any abatement of kindness otherwise) to hold as little personal communication with her as I possibly can." [112]

Mary was now in her late twenties, and it began to look as if she would never marry. Dickens had tried without success to interest her in Percy Fitzgerald. "I am grievously disappointed that Mary can by no means be induced to think as highly of him as I do—what a wonderful instance of the general inanity of Kings, that the Kings in the Fairy Tales should have been always wishing for children! If they had but known when they were well off, having none!" [113]

About the world, too, Dickens felt discouraged. The year before there had been the Negro uprising in Jamaica which Governor Eyre had suppressed with a severity that was sharply criticized by such leaders of liberal opinion as Mill, Spencer and Huxley. Judgments on the matter were divided, however, by memories of the bloody Indian mutiny of 1857–8. Ruskin, Tennyson, and Carlyle justified Eyre's stern measures as just and necessary preventatives of further violence. Influenced by Carlyle, Dickens joined Eyre's defenders, but regarded the episode, like the Mutiny, as chiefly significant for showing how the Government had been unaware of the most appalling dangers.

Everywhere he looked he saw equal reason for disillusion. The railroads were a muddle, with "no general public supervision, enormous waste of money, no fixable responsibility, no accountability," and the railway interests thwarting all attempt at regulation.[114] In France there was dangerous unrest; the Army was discontented with the Emperor, and "his secret police" were "making discoveries that render him desperately uneasy." [115] In England "the more intelligent part of the great masses were deeply dissatisfied with the state of representation," while the middle and upper classes continued to oppose any reform in the franchise with "the old insolent resource of assailing" the poor as ignorant and politically indifferent. "I have such a very small opinion of what the great genteel have done for us," Dickens wearily commented, "that I am very philosophical indeed concerning what the great vulgar may do, having a decided opinion that they can't do worse." [116]

* * * * *

In January Dickens turned to the profitable anodyne of his readings again. His old servant John was no longer with him, having been found out in a long series of pilferings from the cashbox of *All the Year Round* and discharged. But Dickens could not bear to cast him off altogether after some twenty years, and tried to find him a place in which he would not have the opportunity or temptation to steal. "What I am to do with or for the miserable man God knows." [117] It was even more distressing that John seemed to feel very little "the enormity of his offense, except as it inconveniences himself. Wills telling him today that he might be able to get him made a waiter at the Reform Club, he replied 'Oh I couldn't do that Sir.'" [118] At last, according to Marcus Stone, Dickens set him up in some small business, saying, "Poor fellow, he has lost his character, and will not be able to get another situation." [119] "It has so shocked me," Dickens wrote, "that I have had to walk more than usual before I could walk myself into composure again." [120]

His new man, Scott, proved splendidly satisfactory. "As a dresser he is perfect. In a quarter of an hour after I go into the retiring room, where all my clothes are airing and everything is set out neatly in its own allotted space, I am ready; and he then goes softly out, and sits outside the door. . . . He has his needles and thread, buttons, and so forth, always at hand; and in travelling he is very systematic with the luggage. What with Dolby, and what with this skilful valet, everything is made as easy to me as it possibly *can* be." [121]

Indeed, Chappell's arrangements were in every way unexceptionable. "Not the faintest trace of the tradesman spirit ever peeps out," Dickens said; and Dolby was "an agreeable companion, an excellent manager, and a good fellow." [122] But Dickens found the strain of traveling and reading harder than ever. He was unable to sleep at night, and after his first Liverpool reading was taken so faint that he had to lie on a sofa at St. George's Hall for half an hour.[123] At Chester his hotel was freezing cold; [124] at Wolverhampton it rained bitterly and after the reading he felt heavily beaten. During the forty-minute ride to Birmingham it was all he could do to hold out the journey.[125]

"If I should be a little more used-up tomorrow than I am today," he told Forster, "I should be constrained in spite of myself, to take to the sofa and stick there." [126] At his hotel in Liverpool he felt so faint and sick that he had to leave the dinner table, and he suffered almost all the time from "a curious feeling of soreness all round the body." [127] To Georgina he wrote that he believed it an effect of the railway shaking. "There is no doubt of the fact that, after the Staplehurst experience, it tells more and more, instead of (as one might have expected) less and less." [128]

At Birmingham, Dickens displayed his usual coolness in emergency. The reflector above his head, projecting out over the stalls, was suspended from its supports by strong copper wire. Under one of these supports a new gasman accidentally placed a burning gas-jet, so that the wire began to get red hot. If it burned through, the heavy reflector would crash into the stalls, perhaps set them on fire. Standing in agony at the edge of the violet-colored screen Dickens used as a background, Dolby pointed to the danger, whispering, "How long shall you be?" Without pausing in his reading, Dickens unconcernedly showed Dolby two fingers, but his manager could not tell whether "The Chief" meant two minutes or two seconds. With almost inconceivable ingenuity, Dickens altered much of the reading and brought it to the speedier termination. He had seen the danger from the middle of the reading, he told Dolby, and calculated how long the wire would last.[129]

During the three days they spent at Newcastle, Dickens went for a two hours' sea-walk at Tynemouth, where there "was a high North wind blowing, and a magnificent sea running. Large vessels were being towed in and out over the stormy bar, with prodigious waves breaking on it . . ." [130] "Suddenly there came a golden horizon, and a most glorious rainbow burst out, arching one large ship, as if she were sailing direct for heaven. I was so enchanted by the scene, that I became oblivious of a few thousand tons of water coming in in an enormous roller, and was knocked down and beaten by its spray when it broke, and so completely wetted through and through, that the very pockets in my pocketbook were full of sea." [131]

Back at Gad's Hill for a brief rest, Dickens received word from Wilkie Collins of old companions in Paris. "Glad to hear of our friend Regnier," he replied; and with a burst of his old fun: "As Car-

lyle would put it: 'A deft and shifty little man, brisk and sudden, of
a most ingenious carpentering faculty, and not without constructive
qualities of a higher than the Beaver sort. Withal an actor, though
of a somewhat hard tone. Think pleasantly of him, O ye children of
men!' " [132]

Then, in spite of the Fenian troubles in Ireland, Dickens was off
to Dublin and Belfast for readings in those cities. Friends in Tipperary
wrote him that they were living fortified in a district in a state of
"acute rebellion." [133] Kingstown was full of armed policemen and
detectives.[134] Menservants in Dublin were reported to be all Fenians.
It was feared that in an uprising they might set fire to all the houses.
In appearance, however, Dublin was perfectly calm. "The streets are
gay all day . . . and singularly quiet and deserted at night. But the
whole place is secretly girt in with a military force." [135]

Within a few weeks more the tour was over. In a day's interval
between two expeditions Dickens visited Clarkson Stanfield.[136] It
was clear that his old friend was dying, and beside that deathbed, on
Stanfield's plea, Dickens was reconciled with Mark Lemon.[137] Before
the very last reading Dickens came again, and still again the following
day, but when he saw upon the door the symbol of what had taken
place he did not have the courage to ring. "No one of your father's
friends can ever have loved him more dearly than I always did," he
wrote Stanfield's son, "or can have better known the worth of his
noble character." [138]

In May the readings were ended. At night Dickens found himself
so tired he could hardly undress for bed.[139] But already he was thinking of another and even more toilsome engagement. Every mail
brought him proposals that he read in America. A committee of private gentlemen in Boston wished for the credit of bringing him across
the Atlantic, desired no profit, and were ready to deposit a guarantee
of £10,000 in advance at Coutts's bank. "Every American speculator
who comes to London repairs straight to Dolby, with similar proposals." [140]

"I am in a tempest-tossed condition, and can hardly believe that I
stand at bay at last on the American question. The difficulty of determining amid the variety of statements made to me is enormous,
and you have no idea how heavily the anxiety of it sits upon my
soul." [141] "Poor dear Stanfield! I cannot think even of him, and of our

great loss, for this spectre of doubt and indecision that sits at the board with me and stands at the bedside." [142] But in the depths of his being the fateful attraction was being felt, the fateful decision being made.

"In the Eastern story," he had written in *Great Expectations*, "the heavy slab that was to fall on the bed of state in the flush of conquest was slowly wrought out of the quarry, the tunnel for the rope to hold it in its place was slowly carried through the leagues of rock and fitted in the roof, the rope was rove to it and slowly taken through the miles of hollow to the great iron ring. All being made ready with much labour, and the hour come, the sultan was aroused in the dead of the night, and the sharpened axe that was to sever the rope from the great iron ring was put in his hand, and he struck with it, and the rope parted and rushed away, and the ceiling fell." [143] ". . . I began to feel myself drawn towards America," Dickens now told Georgina and Mary, "as Darnay in the Tale of Two Cities was attracted to the Loadstone Rock, Paris . . ." [144]

CHAPTER TWO

To the Loadstone Rock

Bᴜᴛ despite the golden lure of America, Dickens wavered. How could he bear the parting from his friends, from Georgina and the children, from Ellen? "I should be wretched beyond expression there," he cried to Forster. "My small powers of description cannot describe the state of mind in which I should drag on from day to day." [1] Ellen had been ill throughout the latter part of April and re-currently to almost the end of May, and had needed the attentions of a doctor, but was better with the return of summer. In his distress at so long a separation, Dickens thought of having her join him in America. [2]

Wills and Forster, who so often disagreed, joined in trying earnestly to dissuade him from making the journey at all. [3] Both feared that his health would break down under the sharpened strain of foreign travel and heavier labor, and Forster had never ceased to feel that the read-ings were unworthy of a man of genius. [4] Dickens dined with Forster and tried in vain to shake his objections. Wills's arguments Dickens vigorously answered in a letter. It was true that twenty-five years ago he had been younger, but he had been worn out from writing *Master Humphrey's Clock* and had just undergone a painful surgical opera-tion. The continual speechmaking to which he had been subjected was quite as wearing as reading, and he was then, he insisted, less pa-tient and more irritable than now. And even in England he would never rest; he had that within which would be "rusting and corrod-ing" him unless he were active. Furthermore, he felt assured that he had wonderful powers of refreshing and strengthening himself in short periods of repose, that would obliterate "a quantity of wear and tear." [5]

Battering down all resistance, Dickens decided to send Dolby over to investigate the lay of the land.[6] On August 3rd [7] Dolby sailed on the *Java*, taking with him the manuscripts of two brief stories, "George Silverman's Explanation" and "A Holiday Romance," for each of which Dickens was to receive £1,000.[8] Both had been commissioned that spring, the first by the Hon. Benjamin Wood, a New York State senator and newspaper publisher, and the second by Ticknor and Fields for appearance in *Our Young Folks*, a children's magazine they published.[9]

"George Silverman" has a strange and suggestive psychological theme. The narrator of the story, rescued from a slum childhood and brought up as a clergyman, seems to himself always to be acting with the most nobly disinterested of motives, but is constantly striking others as selfish and disingenuous. Opinion among those who know him, however, is divided, some thinking him proud, others a sneak, still others generous and unselfish. There are those who feel he has a beautiful face and those who find it frightening, almost cruel. Believing himself cruelly misjudged, Silverman at the same time has a lurking suspicion of his own guilt. What sort of man is he, really? These ambiguities, in fact, represent the very point of the story, and one feels as if it were haunted by Dickens's troubled consciousness of ambiguities within himself. But he could not grapple successfully with the theme; it wavers half-heartedly between apologia and accusation, an unresolved conflict. There can be no doubt, however, that for Dickens the narrator's state of mind had a deep inner significance. "I feel," he exclaimed, "as if I had read something (by somebody else) which I should never get out of my head!!" [10]

The other manuscript was a group of four light and whimsical stories supposedly written by children. "I hope the Americans will see the joke of Holiday Romance," he said. "The writing seems to me so like children's, that dull folks (on *any* side of *any* water) might perhaps rate it accordingly! . . . It made me laugh to that extent that my people here thought I was out of my wits, until I gave it to them to read, when they did likewise." [11]

In Boston, Dolby hastened to turn over "A Holiday Romance" to Ticknor and Fields.[12] Everyone there was sure the readings would be a success, and Dolby tentatively chose for the purpose the Tremont Temple, a somewhat old-fashioned building holding around two thousand people.[13] In New York, Horace Greeley, the editor of the *Tribune,* and William Cullen Bryant, the editor of the *Post,* concurred in saying that Dickens's triumph would "eclipse that of Jenny Lind." [14] James Gordon Bennett, of the *Herald,* insisted that Dickens must "first apologize" for *American Notes* and *Martin Chuzzlewit,* but believed that "in good hands" he might then charge ten dollars a ticket.[15]

The next morning, by way of helping out, Bennett published the offensive *Notes* in a " '*special,*' *free of cost*" supplement to the paper. Unlike the public of 1842, however, the current generation proved untroubled by the book, and Ticknor and Fields subsequently sold large numbers in a twenty-five-cent reprint.[16] "Even in England," said the New York *Times,* "Dickens is less known than here, and of the millions here who treasure every word he has written, there are tens of thousands who would make a large sacrifice to see and hear the man who has made happy so many homes. Whatever sensitiveness there once was to sneering criticism, the lapse of a quarter of a century, and the profound significance of a great war, have modified or removed." [17]

From Senator Wood there had been no reply to repeated messages that he could claim the manuscript of "George Silverman." Suddenly, at the very moment Dolby was leaving New York, Wood appeared and flung "a bag—*supposed* to contain a thousand sovereigns—on the table." But Dolby had been warned that, like Joey Bagstock, the senator was "de-vil-ish sly." He told Wood he no longer had time to count the money, but that he would leave the manuscript with Ticknor and Fields, who were empowered to conclude the business. No more was heard from Wood, and in 1868 the story was published in the *Atlantic Monthly.*[18]

While Dolby was in America, Dickens worked at *No Thoroughfare,* the story for the ensuing Christmas on which he was collaborating with Collins, and helped Collins in making a dramatic version for Fechter.[19] "Welcome back, old boy!" he telegraphed on Dolby's return. "Do not trouble about me, but go home to Ross first and see your wife and family, and come to me at Gad's at your convenience." [20] Dolby's report, when they met at Gad's Hill, enthusiastically supported an American tour, with plans of all the halls in which Dickens would speak, calculations of expenses, and estimates of the profits at various prices of admission.[21] For presentation to Wills and Forster,

Dickens boiled it down to a statement which he entitled "The Case in a Nutshell." The statement concluded that on a series of eighty readings, even allowing seven dollars to the pound for the loss on converting American paper money into gold, the clear profit would be £15,500.[22]

Far from being persuasive to Forster, this argument was like a red rag to a bull. "He had made up *his* mind, and there was an end of the matter." Since the Staplehurst accident, he told Dolby, Dickens had been in a bad state of health: a sea voyage was the worst thing in the world for him. If he went, there would be a recurrence of riots like the Forrest-Macready riots. There was no money in America; if there were, Dickens wouldn't get any of it; if he did, it would be stolen from his hotel; and if he put it in a bank, the bank would fail on purpose. There "was no reason why the interview should be prolonged," he said testily; he had "fully made up *his* mind that Dickens should *never go to America again.*" "I shall write to Dickens by tonight's post," he concluded, "and tell him how fully I am opposed to the idea, and that he must give it up." [23]

For Forster's worry about Dickens's physical condition there was reason enough. Ever since he had seen Dolby off at Liverpool six weeks before, Dickens had again been having trouble with his left foot. "I cannot get a boot on," he wrote Georgina; and to Forster, "I am laid up with another attack . . . and was on the sofa all last night in tortures. I cannot bear to have the fomentations taken off for a moment." Nevertheless, "I make out so many reasons against supposing it to be gouty, that I really do not think it is." He even managed to hypnotize the surgeon who looked at it into diagnosing it as erysipelas supervening upon the irritation of "an enlargement in the nature of a bunion." [24] All through August the foot continued inflamed, and in the middle of September he was still lame and unable to wear a shoe.[25]

Exaggerated rumors of his ill-health spread through all the newspapers. Dickens felt obliged to send their editors letters of denial. He suggested to one that "critical state of health" was a misprint for "cricketing." [26] He asked another to certify him "as combining my usual sedentary powers with the active training of a prize-fighter." [27] He wrote an American friend that Wilkie Collins and Charles Reade, who were staying at Gad's Hill, made a joke of taking his pulse at meals and inveigling "innocent messengers to come over to the summer-house where I write . . . to ask, with their compliments, how I find myself *now*." [28]

"This is to certify," he facetiously told his friend Finlay, of the *Northern Whig*, "that the undersigned innocent victim of a periodical paragraph disease which usually breaks out once in every seven years (proceeding from England by the Overland route to India, and per Cunard line to America where it strikes the base of the Rocky Mountains and rebounding to Europe, perishes on the Steppes of Russia), is NOT in *a critical state of health*, and has NOT consulted *eminent surgeons*, and never was better in his life, and is NOT recommended to proceed to the United States for *cessation from literary labour*, and has not had so much as a headache for twenty years." [29]

On September 30th a cablegram was sent to Ticknor and Fields in Boston: "Yes. Go ahead." [30] Dickens was to leave England early in November. Almost immediately the American press broke out with the old controversies and accusations. Dickens indignantly countered them. For twenty years, he said, his only allusion to the republication of his books in America had been "the good-humoured remark, 'that if there had been international copyright between England and the States, I should have been a man of very large fortune, instead of a man of moderate savings, always supporting a very expensive public position.' " He denied that he had ever expressed himself "with soreness," or talked about "those fellows" who published his books, or said they sent him "conscience money." Every American who had ever spoken to him could testify that he had frankly said, "You could have no better introduction to me than your country." [31]

On November 2nd, Dickens was given a farewell dinner at the Freemason's Hall.[32] Almost all the notables of the literary, dramatic, and artistic world were among an assembly numbering close to four hundred and fifty. Charley was seated with these, but Mary and Georgina were among the hundred feminine guests in the ladies' gallery.[33] Another balcony glittered with the brasses of the Grenadier Guards band.[34] Just two days before, Dickens's sailor son, Sydney, had managed to come up from Portsmouth, where his ship was in harbor, and Dickens begged Charles Kent, the Secretary of the banquet, somehow to squeeze him in at this last moment. "Der—er—oo not cur—ur—urse me, I implore." [35] Sydney had just been made a lieutenant, "with the consequent golden garniture on his sleeve. Which I, God forgive me,"

Dickens said, "stared at, without the least idea that it meant promotion." [36]

White statuary gleamed among the green of exotic plants in lobbies, corridors, and reception rooms. British and American flags decked the dining hall, bright against walls whose twenty arched panels were decorated with golden laurels on a deep red ground, each panel bearing the title of one of Dickens's works in gold letters and a wreath surrounding the initials "C.D." Behind the chairman's seat *Pickwick Papers* had the place of honor.[37] The chairman was Lord Lytton, created a baron in 1866, now sixty-four years old, gaunt, bent, black-clad, and hawk-eyed.

Wild enthusiasm greeted the arrival of the two most famous living novelists as Dickens entered on Lytton's arm. In his buttonhole Dickens wore a camellia encircled with violets.[38] Following in procession were Lord Chief Justice Cockburn, the Lord Mayor of London, Lord Houghton, Sir Charles Russell, and an assemblage of Royal Academicians. To some of the younger guests Lytton seemed a figure strange, powerful, and phantasmal. He spoke with a long drawl ending in a jerk, emphasizing his words with the queer gesture of stretching out his hand with fingers tightly clasped and then drawing it in under his arm, but he spoke with stately fervor.[39] They were there, he said, to do honor to the conquests of art. "Happy is the man who makes clear his title-deeds to the royalty of genius while he yet lives to enjoy the gratitude of those whom he has subjected to his sway. Though it is by conquest that he achieves his throne, he at least is a conqueror whom the conquered bless. . . . . Seldom, I say, has that kind of royalty been quietly conceded to any man of genius until his tomb becomes his throne, and yet there is not one of us now present who thinks it strange that it is granted without a murmur to the guest whom we receive tonight." [40]

A score of times Lytton was interrupted by cheers, but when Dickens rose shouts stormed upon him. Men leaped on chairs, tossed up napkins, waved glasses and decanters above their heads. The ladies' gallery was a flag of waving fans and handkerchiefs. Color and pallor followed each other in Dickens's face, and "those wonderful eyes," said one guest, "flamed around like a searchlight"; tears streamed down his cheeks and as he tried to speak his voice faltered. Even when he found speech, although his words were eloquent, there were those who "felt that the real eloquence of the evening had reached its climax in the silent tears of Dickens." [41]

It was late before the company broke up. Outside, in the street, however, there was still waiting a great crowd of people who wished to pay their tribute of farewell. Among them, as Dickens appeared, was one aged woman who bowed her face upon his hand while he stood motionless and pale.[42]

In the next few days last good-bys were said, including farewells to Charley's children. Dickens disliked the name of "Grandfather," and both little Mekitty, as his granddaughter Mary Angela was called, and her tinier brother Charles were jestingly taught to know him as " 'Wenerables,' which they sincerely believe to be my name," Dickens said, "and a kind of title that I have received from a grateful country." [43] A farewell note came from Catherine. Dickens replied, "I am glad to receive your letter, and to accept and reciprocate your good wishes. Severely hard work lies before me; but that is not a new thing in my life, and I am content to go my way and do it." [44]

Ellen was going to Italy to stay for a while with her sister Frances Eleanor and her brother-in-law Thomas Adolphus Trollope. But Dickens could not bear to surrender his hope that she might be able presently to come to him in America. Carefully he arranged with Wills to forward the code telegram that would tell her what to do. Would he find that he could write "all well" and have her speeding to him across the Atlantic, or would he be obliged to send the words "safe and well" that meant she was to remain in Europe? Meanwhile, Wills was always to have her address, to help her in any unforeseen difficulty, and to invoke Forster's aid for her in case of need. These instructions make it likely, though not beyond all doubt, that Wills also served as Dickens's almoner in taking care during these months of Ellen's financial needs.[45]

*   *   *   *   *

Dolby had already sailed for America again, and Dickens had been given "the Second Officer's cabin on deck" in the *Cuba*, leaving Liverpool on November 9th. With a window and a door he could leave open, it gave him plenty of fresh air—always a chief requirement with him—although it was "of such vast proportions that it is almost large enough to sneeze in." [46] They ran into a head wind halfway across, and rolled and pitched, but Dickens felt wonderfully well except for his foot, which continued rather painful.[47] On the 19th he arrived in Boston.[48]

That staid city was in a state of frenzy resembling the *Pickwick* mania at the inauguration of Dickens's career. "No sooner was the news flashed along the cable, that he was coming," reported the New York *Tribune* facetiously, "than everything was immediately put in apple-pie order. The streets were all swept from one end of the city to the other for the second time in twenty-four hours. The State House and the Old South Church were painted, offhand, a delicate rose pink." There were "Little Nell Cigars," "Mr. Squeers Fine Cut," the "Mantalini Plug," and the genuine "Pickwick Snuff." Pictures of Dickens were everywhere, and there was a "Dickens Collar," ornamented with two rosebuds and a likeness of the author on the tips.[49]

On the customs steamer *Hamblin*, Dolby set out at midday on the 19th, in a choppy and freezing sea, to meet the *Cuba*. He and his companions, Howard Ticknor and James Fields, and their junior partner James Osgood, were joined by a large staff of newspaper reporters. All afternoon passed without the liner being sighted, and it was not until after dark that the vessel appeared. Ignoring a perfect shower of rockets, it tore straight on, portholes alight, as if it were going to run Boston down, with the *Hamblin* puffing after, making the harbor hideous with the shrieks of its whistle. Within fifty yards of the wharf, however, the *Cuba* ran on a mudbank, and while it was snorting, blowing off steam, and backing to get off, Dolby heard his Chief calling his name. A plank was soon lowered to the *Hamblin*, everyone was shaking hands, and at last they were off to the Parker House, where Dolby had taken a third-floor corner suite on the School Street side.[50]

After the excitement of greetings, Dickens felt fatigued and depressed. At supper the waiters left the door of his sitting room ajar, and from the corridor eyes peered in at him through the crack. "These people," he said irritably, "have not in the least changed during the last five and twenty years—they are doing now exactly what they were doing then." [51] But he felt cheered by what Dolby told him of the sale of tickets for the first four readings. The night before the sale, a line had begun forming, and by eight the next morning it was almost half a mile long. The sale lasted over eleven hours, when every ticket was disposed of and $14,000 had been taken in. The box-office price was two dollars, but speculators were already getting as much as twenty-six dollars for a ticket.[52]

To give his Chief time to rest from the voyage Dolby had not scheduled the first reading until a fortnight hence, December 2nd, and Dickens chafed at the delay. Meanwhile, however, there were old friendships to be renewed. The following afternoon Longfellow called, looking benign and handsome with his white hair and long white beard, and later brought Holmes, Agassiz, and Emerson to see him.[53] Longfellow found Dickens as "elastic and quick" as ever, "with the same sweetness and flavor as of old, and only greater ripeness." [54] Within the next two days Dr. Samuel Gridley Howe and Richard Henry Dana, Jr., also wrote and called.[55]

On the 21st, Dickens dined at the Fields home on Charles Street. One of the enraptured young men who had cheered Dickens in 1842, Fields was now a brown-bearded man of almost fifty. In 1859 he had visited Gad's Hill and become one of Dickens's friends. He and his wife, who looked like a pensive Burne-Jones portrait, made an adoring cult of Dickens, proudly displaying the Francis Alexander portrait of him on their drawing-room wall. Besides Longfellow, Agassiz, Emerson, and Holmes, the other guests included Judge Hoar and Charles Eliot Norton.[56] Dickens was gay and entertaining and often had them in tempests of laughter, although Mrs. Fields fancied Holmes "bored him a little by talking at him." At one of his own public lectures, Holmes said, his landlady's face "was the only one which relaxed its grimness"; "probably," Dickens rejoined, "because she saw money enough in the house to pay your expenses." [57]

Dickens's fears that he would be troubled by intrusive strangers proved unfounded. "The Bostonians having been duly informed that I wish to be quiet, really leave me as much so as I should be in Manchester or Liverpool." [58] He walked his seven to ten miles a day without being stopped or followed, but if he paused to look in a shop window a score of passers-by stopped too, and reporters were always in his hotel. But although there was certainly more tact and consideration than there had been twenty-five years ago, it was clear that Ellen could not be with him. The cablegram that Wills received on November 22nd therefore resignedly opened with the words "Safe and well," but went on more cheerfully, "expect good letter full of hope." [59]

On Thanksgiving Day Dickens dined at Longfellow's home.[60] That

morning Fields took him calling on the youthful Mrs. Thomas Bailey
Aldrich in her little "workbox" of a house on Pinckney Street, with
its white muslin curtains looped back by bows of pink and blue ribbon; and Dickens was shown the six-year-old daughter of her housekeeper, demure with braids and a long mouse-colored gown. Acting
as a maid, the little creature dropped a curtsy and offered him wine
and a biscuit on a silver tray. Dickens gave her a deep courtly bow as
he drank a health to them all. When the child left the room, he put
his head back against the cushion of his chair and laughed and
laughed.[61]

From Pinckney Street Dickens went on to Cambridge. Longfellow
now owned the house in which he had roomed twenty-five years ago,
and they dined in the square, white-wainscoted dining room. In the
bookshelves Dickens saw his own works and said with a wink that delighted Longfellow's children, "Ah-h-h! I see you read the best authors." [62] "I suppose you don't remember Longfellow," he wrote
Charley, "though he remembers you in a black velvet frock very well."
But through all the enjoyment of the day Dickens could not blot from
his imagination the dreadful picture of Longfellow's beautiful wife
who had burned to death in that home six years before. "She was in
a blaze in an instant, rushed into his arms with a wild cry, and never
spoke afterwards." [63]

Among Dickens's callers before his readings were due to begin was
his old secretary Putnam. "Grey, and with several front teeth out, but
I would have known him anywhere." [64] "It was quite affecting to see
his delight in meeting his old master again. And when I told him that
Anne was married, and that I had (unacknowledged) grandchildren,
he laughed and cried together." [65] He rose "into the seventh heaven"
when Dickens gave him tickets to a reading, for himself and his wife
and daughter.[66]

Anticipation was now at fever heat. All Cambridge was booked in
a phalanx for the first night,[67] and five hundred undergraduates unable to get tickets begged Longfellow to intercede in their behalf.
Dickens was in despair about what could be done for them.[68] In the
packed audience to hear the *Christmas Carol* that night was Longfellow, "looking like the very spirit of Christmas," Holmes, "crisp and
fine, like a tight little grape-skin full of wit instead of wine," Lowell,
"with his poet's heart smiling sadly through his poet's eyes," even the

elder Dana, a man of eighty, "with long grey hair falling round a face bright with shrewd intelligence." [69] The end of the *Carol* was greeted with cheers and calls.

After the intermission, Dickens read the "Trial." Although one disappointed "down Easter" declared that Dickens knew "no more about Sam Weller 'n a cow does of pleatin' a shirt," most of the ecstatic audience disagreed.[70] Throughout and at the close there were screams of delight. "The old Judge," said Longfellow, "was equal to Dogberry." "In what raptures our dear Felton would be were he now alive." [71] John Greenleaf Whittier was even more emphatic. "Those marvellous characters of his come forth, one by one, real personages, as if their original creator had breathed new life into them. . . . But it is idle to talk about it: you must beg, borrow, or steal a ticket & hear him. Another such star-shower is not to be expected in one's lifetime." [72] All Boston went "absolutely mad" with the sensation.[73]

In his dressing room before the reading, Dickens felt a "glow of pleasure and amazement" to find his usual buttonhole from Mary Boyle. "Ten thousand loving thanks," he wrote her.[74] The Boston *Post* reported that he returned a bouquet to a lady who had sent it on his opening night, thanking her, but saying "that a lady of London supplied him with flowers for his button-hole, not only in England but America." "Oh, Charles," caroled the paper, "at your age and with that bald head and that grey goatee!" [75]

Such journalistic familiarities Dickens attributed to "the public's love of smartness," but he was pleased to observe that in his personal meetings with reporters they treated him with perfect courtesy.[76] Indeed, all America, he came to feel in the course of his stay, was greatly changed "for the better, socially. Politically, no. England governed by the Marylebone vestry and the penny papers, and England as she would be after years of such governing; is what I make of *that*." Newspapers, to be sure, still expressed "the popular amazement at 'Mr. Dickens's extraordinary composure.' They seem to take it ill that I don't stagger on the platform overpowered by the spectacle before me, and the national greatness." [77] "My eyes are blue, red, grey, white, green, brown, black, hazel, violet, and rainbow-coloured. I am like 'a well-to-do American gentleman' and the Emperor of the French, with an occasional touch of the Emperor of China, and a deterioration from the attributes of our famous townsman, Rufus W. B. D. Dodge

Grumsher Pickville. I say all sorts of things that I never said, go to all sorts of places that I never saw or heard of, and have done all manner of things (in some previous state of existence I suppose) that have quite escaped my memory." [78]

The expense of hotel living was enormous—ten pounds a day for the three rooms he and Dolby had together—but the accommodations were excellent.[79] The Parker House had "all manner of white marble public passages and public rooms," there were hot and cold baths, and the dinners provided by Sanizan, its famous chef, were unsurpassed.[80] The only trouble was that the place was so overheated by a great furnace that Dickens felt faint and sick, and had to leave all his windows wide open. "The air is like that of a pre-Adamite ironing-day in full blast." [81]

*　　*　　*　　*　　*

From an opening week in Boston that brought in clear profits of over $9,000 Dickens moved on to New York.[82] It was the first of a series of back-and-forth journeys between the two cities, with a week in one and then a week in the other, that continued until early in January. In New York the state of the public mind was no less delirious than in Boston. On the day he arrived in America, out of the nineteen hundred volumes of his novels in the Mercantile Library, only two remained on its shelves.[83] The night before tickets went on sale, lines of people with blankets and mattresses began forming in front of Steinway Hall, shivering in the bitter cold, singing, dancing breakdowns, making night hideous with fighting; [84] by morning there were at least five thousand, while waiters flew between the line and neighboring restaurants, serving al-fresco breakfasts in the frosty air.[85]

Dolby tried to prevent tickets falling into the hands of speculators, but his efforts gave universal dissatisfaction. If he decreed that no more than six tickets a performance would be sold to any one purchaser, the speculators put fifty dummy buyers at the head of a line; if, noticing that most of these wore caps, he suddenly announced that he would sell only to those wearing hats, all manner of battered hats miraculously appeared. In vain men offered twenty dollars merely for anybody's place. Special precautions had to be taken against bogus tickets.[86] People would not refrain from paying speculators three times the established price, and then reviled Dolby bitterly.[87] The New York *World* exploded, "Surely it is time that the pudding-headed

Dolby retired into the native gloom from which he has emerged"; [88] in consequence of which, Dickens explained, "We always call him P. H. Dolby now." [89] But whether the speculators profited or not, Dolby always came back from the ticket sales and "put such an untidy heap of paper money on the table that it looks like a family wash." [90]

In New York Dickens stayed at the Westminster Hotel, in Irving Place, which he said was "quieter than Mivart's in Brook Street," "quite as comfortable," and its "French cuisine immensely better." [91] He drove out in a carriage and pair, "furred up to the moustache," covered by "an immense white, red, and yellow striped rug," [92] and admired all the new Central Park from a jingling red sleigh "tearing up 14 miles of snow an hour." [93] At Niblo's he saw *The Black Crook*, a preposterous musical comedy that had been running sixteen months. "The people who act in it have not the slightest idea what it is about, and never had"; but Dickens fancied that he had "discovered Black Crook to be a malignant hunchback leagued with the Powers of Darkness to separate two lovers; and that the Powers of Lightness coming (in no skirts whatever) to the rescue, he is defeated." [94]

The New York readings went even more wildly than those in Boston. "Mr. Digguns," said the German janitor at Steinway Hall, showing him out into a hard frost, "you are gread, meinherr. There is no ent to you." Then, reopening the door and sticking his head out, "Bedder and bedder," he added; "Wot negst!" [95] Edwin Coggeshall remembered that his entire family came over from Brooklyn by ferry in a blinding snowstorm. On such a night, some astonished friends said, they wouldn't have come from Brooklyn to hear the Apostle Paul. "No, neither would we," was the reply, "but we came to hear Dickens." [96] At the end of the first week there, Dickens sent £3,000 to England.[97]

On Saturday, December 21st, he went back to Boston, where he found that Mrs. Fields had decorated his hotel rooms with flowers and red-berried holly, while another admirer had imported a branch of English mistletoe. In the Fields home there was a dinner with a blazing plum pudding,[98] and on Christmas Eve, suffering from a dismal cold, Dickens gave another reading of the *Carol*.[99] Christmas Day, doleful with his "American catarrh," he made the return journey to New York.[100]

The railway traveling he found even more distressing than in Eng-

land. The cars were bumped and banged on and off the East River
ferries; they were overheated by a great stove, with the closed windows
making the atmosphere detestable.[101] Sometimes, Dickens found that
the only way he could bear it was to go out on the platform by the
brake, where "it snows and blows, and the train bumps, and the steam
flies at me, until I am driven in again." [102] The baggagemen and
porters handled the luggage with indescribable recklessness. Once
Dickens found Scott, his valet, leaning his head against the side of a
carriage, weeping bitterly over Dickens's smashed writing desk.[103]
" 'The owdacious treatment of the luggage,' " he said, " 'was more
outrageous than a man could bear.' I told him not to make a fool of
himself; but they do knock it about cruelly. I think every trunk we
have is already broken." [104]

His heavy cold brought back that "low action of the heart" from
which he had suffered the preceding spring. After the Christmas night's
reading, he "was laid upon a bed, in a very faint and shady state";
next day he did not get up till afternoon.[105] That night he felt
unfit to read, but forced himself to do so, and the following morning
had to send for a doctor.[106] The physician, Dr. Fordyce Barker,
wanted to "stop the readings altogether for some few days," but Dickens insisted that he must go on.[107] Despite his New York landlord's
prescription of a "Rocky Mountain Sneezer," compounded of brandy,
rum, bitters, lemon, sugar, and snow, the "true American catarrh" refused to budge.[108]

Back in Boston, he still went on, though often he could not sleep
till morning.[109] Longfellow's twelve-year-old daughter "Allegra" later
recalled her joy in those nightly readings: "Sam Weller and Mr. Pickwick, Nicholas Nickleby and the old gentleman and the vegetable
marrows over the garden wall. How he did make Aunt Betsy Trotwood
snap out, 'Janet, donkeys'—and David Copperfield yearn over the
handsome sleeping Steerforth. How the audience loved best of all the
Christmas Carol and how they laughed as Dickens fairly smacked his
lips as there came the 'smell like an eating house and a pastry cook's
next door to each other, with a laundress's next door to that,' as Mrs.
Cratchit bore in the Christmas pudding and how they nearly wept
as Tiny Tim cried 'God bless us every one!' " [110]

In the Harvard Medical School, Dr. Oliver Wendell Holmes
showed Dickens over the rooms in which Professor Webster had mur-

dered his colleague Dr. Parkman and worked so gruesomely to get rid of the body.[111] "They were horribly grim, private, cold, and quiet; the identical furnace smelling fearfully (some anatomical broth in it I suppose) as if the body were still there; jars of pieces of sour mortality standing about, like the forty robbers in Ali Baba after being scalded to death; and bodies near us ready to be carried in to next morning's lecture." [112] At Fields's over the dinner table that night, Longfellow told him a dreadful story of a party Webster gave less than a year before the murder. "As they sat at their wine, Webster suddenly ordered the lights to be turned out, and a bowl of some burning mineral to be placed on the table, that the guests might see how ghostly it made them look. As each man stared at all the rest in the weird light, all were horrified to see Webster *with a rope round his neck*, holding it up, over the bowl, with his head jerked on one side, and his tongue lolled out representing a man being hanged!" [113]

Before heading south for Philadelphia, Baltimore, and Washington. Dickens had another week of readings in New York. This time he also read in Brooklyn, where the only available place turned out to be the Plymouth Church, of which the pastor was Harriet Beecher Stowe's brother, the Reverend Henry Ward Beecher.[114] The usual riotous scenes attended the sale of tickets, with "the noble army of speculators" building bonfires and fighting in the streets and greeting Dolby with roars of "Hallo! Dolby! So Charley has let you have the carriage, has he, Dolby? How is he, Dolby? Don't drop the tickets, Dolby! Look alive, Dolby!" [115] The receipts were so enormous that the manager was "always going about with an immense bundle that looks like a sofa-cushion, but is in reality paper-money, and it had risen to the proportions of a sofa on the morning he left for Philadelphia." [116]

Dickens's cold, however, still would not "stir an inch. It distresses me greatly at times, though it is always good enough to leave me for the needful two hours. I have tried allopathy, homeopathy, cold things, warm things, sweet things, bitter things, stimulants, narcotics, all with the same result. Nothing will touch it." [117] He was hardly able to eat. "I rarely take any breakfast but an egg and a cup of tea, not even toast or bread-and-butter. My dinner at three, and a little quail or some such light thing when I come home at night, is my daily fare. At the Hall I have established the custom of taking an egg beaten up in sherry before going in, and another between the parts. I think that pulls me up; at all events, I have since had no return of faintness." [118]

He had determined by now that he would confine the readings to the East, in spite of anguished outcries from St. Louis, Cincinnati, and Chicago. "Good heavens, sir!" exclaimed George W. Childs, the publisher of the Philadelphia *Public Ledger*, "if you don't read in Chicago the people will go into fits!" "Well," Dickens replied, "I would rather they went into fits than I did." [119] Chicago in fact led a violent assault upon Dickens, with bitter imputations against his reasons for avoiding that city. His brother Augustus, who had deserted his wife in 1858, had died there in 1866, leaving a "widow" and three children.[120] Dickens refused to explain that he had long supported the only legitimate Mrs. Augustus Dickens or that since his brother's death he had been sending £50 a year to Chicago.[121] The newspapers painted lugubrious pictures of his "brother's wife and her helpless children." [122] "Of course my lips are sealed. Osgood and Dolby have really been lashed into madness, and but for my strict charge would have blown the whole thing to pieces regardless of every other consideration. I have imposed silence on them, and they really writhe under it." [123]

Amid these accusations of penurious cruelty, Dickens was telling his daughter Mary to take care of their old servant Anne Cornelius, whose husband had fallen ill and who was very poor. Mary should learn, he told her, whether Anne's sick husband had what he needed, whether she was "pinched in the articles of necessary clothing, bedding, or the like." "The question in the case of so old and faithful a servant, is not one of so much or so little money on my side, but how *most efficiently* to ease her mind and help *her*." [124] And on February 3rd the Boston *Transcript* recorded that Dickens had "sent $1,000 to Mrs. Clemm, Poe's mother-in-law," who had been in needy circumstances since Poe's death.[125] In the course of his various times in Boston, Dickens also arranged with Dr. Samuel Gridley Howe to print 250 copies of *The Old Curiosity Shop* in Braille, to be distributed as a gift to the asylums for the blind, and later sent Dr. Howe $1,700 for that purpose.[126]

Baltimore, Dickens felt, was haunted by "the ghost of slavery" and still wore "a look of sullen remembrance." It was here that "the ladies used to spit when they passed a Northern soldier. . . . The ladies are remarkably handsome, with an Eastern look upon them, dress with a strong sense of colour, and made a brilliant audience." [127] For the first reading in Washington, President Andrew Johnson, the chief members of the Cabinet, the Supreme Court, ambassadors, naval and military officers in full uniform, leading government officials and political figures came almost in a body.[128] The President had a whole row for every reading of the week. During one of the *Carol* evenings there was a dog who kept turning up in different parts of the house looking at Dickens intently. "He was a very comic dog, and it was well for me that I was reading a very comic part of the book. But when he bounced out in the center aisle again . . . and tried the effect of a bark . . . I was seized with such a paroxysm of laughter, that it communicated itself to the audience, and we roared at one another loud and long." [129]

On February 5th the President invited Dickens to call at the White House. He found the Executive quiet and composed in spite of the political storms that were gathering about him (he was impeached on February 24th). "A man not to be turned or trifled with," Dickens thought. "A man . . . who must be killed to be got out of the way." [130] Dickens also dined with his old friend Charles Sumner, and met Secretary of War Stanton, whose dismissal by the President was to set the nation on fire.[131]

Stanton told him a strange anecdote about Abraham Lincoln. Attending a Cabinet meeting one day, Stanton found the President sitting with grave dignity instead of "lolling about" in "ungainly attitudes" and telling "questionable stories," as he usually did. He had had, Lincoln told them, a dream. "And I have now had the same dream three times. Once, on the night preceding the Battle of Bull Run. Once, on the night preceding" another battle unfavorable to the North. His chin sank upon his breast. "Might one ask the nature of this dream, sir?" said the Attorney-General. "Well, I am on a great broad rolling river—and I am in a boat—and I drift—and I drift!—but this is not business—" he suddenly raised his head and looked round the table, "—let us proceed to business, gentlemen." That night he was shot.[132]

On Dickens's birthday in Washington flowers from countless people came pouring into his room in garlands, bouquets, and green baskets, together with other gifts and "letters radiant with good wishes." [133] But his cold was so bad that when Sumner came in at five and found him voiceless and covered with mustard poultice, he said, "Surely, Mr. Dolby, it is impossible that he can read tonight." "Sir, I have told the dear Chief so four times today, and I have been very anxious." But by some mysterious act of will Dickens always managed to overcome his affliction so that "after five minutes of the little table" he was not even hoarse. "The frequent experience of this return of force when it is wanted saves me a vast amount of anxiety," he wrote; "but I am not at times without the nervous dread that I may some day sink altogether." [134]

*　　*　　*　　*　　*

Immediately after his birthday, Dickens turned north again on the second half of his tour. He gave farewell readings in Baltimore and Philadelphia, and then made a week's swing through the New England towns of New Haven, Hartford, Worcester, and Providence. Going on ahead, Dolby discovered that his own advance ticket-agent, a man named Kelly, was responsible for a good deal of the dissatisfaction about sales. [135] Kelly had been speculating in tickets and taking bribes from speculators. [136] In New Haven there was an indignation meeting presided over by the Mayor. Dolby brought consternation to the meeting by promptly canceling the reading and refunding the price of the tickets; but after a scene in which, as Dickens said, he and the Mayor alternately embraced and exchanged mortal defiances, agreed that he would try to work in another evening there later. [137]

Kelly was peremptorily dismissed, and was about to be sent back to England. After a few days, however, Dickens relented and allowed him to remain, although in disgrace and "within very reduced limits." [138] Employees about Steinway Hall swore to give him a beating when he returned to New York. [139] "It is curious," Dickens wrote, "that I conceived a great dislike towards this man, aboard the Cuba coming out. He was ill all the voyage, and I only saw him two or three times, staggering about the lower deck; but I underwent a change of feeling towards him, as if I had taken it in at the pores of the skin." [140]

On February 24th Dickens was back in Boston for another fortnight's readings there. The impeachment of the President, however, cut so drastically the audiences for all entertainments that for the first time there were empty seats. Dickens decided to cancel the second week, which had not yet been announced, and see if his cold would yield to rest.[141] Dolby and Osgood, who were always doing ridiculous things to keep Dickens in spirits, had decided at the beginning of the month to hold a walking match on the 29th. "Beginning this design in joke, they have become tremendously in earnest, and Dolby has actually sent home (much to his opponent's terror) for a pair of seamless socks to walk in." [142]

In Baltimore, Dickens had given them "a breather" of five miles in the snow, half the distance uphill, at a pace of four and a half miles an hour, from which the two returned "smoking like factories." [143] In Washington, coming back from some farewell calls and seeing Dickens looking out of the window, they "put on a tremendous spurt," as if they had been training, and, "rushing up the staircase, and bursting into the sitting-room, . . . sat on the floor, gasping for breath." [144] "They have the absurdest ideas," Dickens wrote, "of what are tests of walking power, and continually get up in the maddest manner and see *how high they can kick* the wall! . . . To see them doing this—Dolby, a big man, and Osgood, a very little one, is ridiculous beyond description." [145]

Dickens drew up burlesque articles of agreement for this "Great International Walking Match," in which Dolby was given the sporting nickname of the "Man of Ross" and Osgood was the "Boston Bantam." The umpires were Fields, "Massachusetts Jemmy," and Dickens, "whose surprising performances (without the least variation) on that truly national instrument, the American catarrh, have won for him the well-merited title of the Gad's Hill Gasper." [146] Going at a tremendous pace, Dickens and Fields laid out the course: six and a half miles along the Mill Dam Road to Newton Centre and then back. It was covered with snow and sheets and blocks of ice.[147]

Despite his cold, Dickens turned up for the race. There was a biting wind and furious snow. "It was so cold, too, that our hair, beards, eyelashes, eyebrows, were frozen hard, and hung with icicles." [148] Just before the turning point Dickens put on a great spurt to establish himself there ahead of the contestants. "He afterwards declared that he received a mental knock-downer . . . to find bright Chanticleer close in upon him, and Rossius steaming up like a locomotive." After the turning the Bantam forged ahead and "pegged away with his little drum-sticks as if he saw his wives and a peck of barley waiting for him at the family perch." [149] "We are not quite decided whether Mrs. Fields did not desert our colours, by coming on the ground in a carriage, and having *bread soaked in brandy* put into the winning man's mouth as he steamed along. She pleaded that she would have done as much for Dolby, if *he* had been ahead, so we are inclined to forgive her." [150]

Afterward, in honor of the contestants, Dickens gave an elaborate dinner for eighteen in the Crystal Room at the Parker House.[151] Among the guests were Fields, James Russell Lowell, Holmes, Charles Eliot Norton, Ticknor, Aldrich, and their wives, "and an obscure poet named Longfellow (if discoverable), and Miss Longfellow." [152] Around ten o'clock, when the other guests had gone, Dickens went upstairs to his room with Dolby and Osgood, in joking high spirits. Water had been drawn for his bath and he entertained his companions by giving an imitation of Grimaldi on the rolling edge of the tub. In the midst of the complicated feat, he lost his balance and, with a tidal wave of a splash, fell in, evening dress, boutonnière, gold chains, brilliantined earlocks, and all.[153]

At a bachelor dinner a few nights later Dickens was in his wildest form. John Bigelow, the ex-Minister Plenipotentiary to France, was one of the guests, and they enacted a burlesque of an English election scene, with Bigelow as Fields's candidate and Dolby as Dickens's. Dickens made a campaign speech pretending that Dolby's superiority to his rival lay in his lack of hair. "We roared and writhed," said Fields, "in agonies of laughter, and the candidates themselves were literally choking and crying . . ." When Fields tried to speak for his man, Dickens interrupted all his attempts to be heard "with imitative jeers of a boisterous election mob," in a variety of voices, including "a pretended husky old man bawling out at intervals, 'Three cheers for the bald 'un!' 'Down with the hairy aristocracy!' 'Up with the little shiny chap on top!' " [154]

With the exposure and exertion of the walking match, the true American had taken "a fresh start, as if it were quite a novelty," and was "on the whole rather worse than ever." [155] Dickens terrified Dolby "out of his wits, by setting in for a paroxysm of sneezing." [156] Under these circumstances, Dickens began a ten days' circuit of one-night stands in western and upstate New York, Syracuse, Rochester, Buffalo, ending with two nights in Albany. At Syracuse he began to have trouble walking, although this time it was something that he called an eruption on his right leg. The hotel there fascinated him with a printed menu which listed "chicken de pullet," "Turpin Soup," "Rolard mutton," and "Paettie de Shay." [157] The last of these, the Irish waiter said with a broad grin, was "the Frinch name the steward giv' to oyster pattie." [158] "You wash down these choice dishes with copious draughts of 'Mooseux,' 'Abasinth,' 'Curraco,' 'Maraschine,' 'Annise,' 'Margeaux' . . . We had an old Buffalo for supper, and an old Pig for breakfast, and we are going to have I don't know what for dinner at 6." [159]

In spite of these jokes, Dickens was constantly tired and depressed and homesick. He was saddened to hear of the death of his old friend Chauncey Townshend.[160] Between Rochester and Albany floods stranded them overnight at Utica after their train had crept on for miles and miles through water. Next day they continued slowly through "drowned farms, barns adrift like Noah's arks, deserted villages," with a hundred booted men pushing blocks of ice out of the way with long poles.[161] On the way they released "a great train of cattle and sheep that had been in the water I don't know how long, and that had begun in their imprisonment to eat each other. I never could have realized the strong and dismal expressions of which the faces of sheep are capable, had I not seen the haggard countenances of this unfortunate flock . . ." [162] Dickens arrived at his hotel in Albany "pretty well knocked up" at half-past ten that night.[163]

On March 20th he entered the last stage of his journeyings. There were still to be ten days of moving through Springfield, Worcester, New Haven, Hartford, and New Bedford, up to Portland, Maine. Then there would remain only the farewell series of readings in Boston and New York. But he reached Portland sick and exhausted. "With the return of snow, nine days ago, the 'true American' (which had lulled) came back as bad as ever. I have coughed from two or three in the morning until five or six, and have been absolutely sleepless. I have had no appetite besides, and no taste. Last night I took some laudanum, and it is the only thing that has done me good." [164] To Forster he admitted, "I am nearly used up. Climate, distance, catarrh, travelling, and hard work have begun (I may say so, now they are nearly over) to tell heavily upon me." If he had engaged to go on into May, he thought he must have broken down.[165]

But the killing odyssey was nearly over. On the train back to Boston, Dickens felt more cheerful and talked briskly with Osgood. From the rear of the car, near the water cooler and the trainboy with his popcorn balls and molasses candy, he was watched by an adoring little girl later known as Kate Douglas Wiggin. When Osgood got up to go to the smoking car, she speeded up the aisle and planted herself timorously "in the seat of honor." [166]

"God bless my soul," Dickens exclaimed, "where did you come from?" "I came from Hollis, Maine," she stammered, "and I'm going to Charlestown to visit my uncle. My mother and her cousin went to your reading last night, but, of course, three couldn't go from the same family, so I stayed at home. . . . There was a lady there who had never heard of Betsey Trotwood, and had only read two of your books." "Well, upon my word! you do not mean to say that *you* have read them!" "Of course I have," she replied; "every one of them but the two that we are going to buy in Boston, and some of them six times." [167]

Under pressing she admitted that she skipped "some of the very dull parts once in a while," and Dickens laughed heartily. Taking out a notebook and pencil, he examined her elaborately on the books in which the dull parts predominated. "He chuckled so constantly during this operation that I could hardly help believing myself extraordinarily agreeable, so I continued dealing these infant blows, under the delusion that I was flinging him bouquets. It was not long before one of my hands was in his, and his arm around my waist . . ." [168]

"Did you want to go to my reading very much?" asked Dickens. This was a question that stirred the depths of her disappointment and sorrow. Her lips trembled as she faltered, "*Yes; more than tongue can tell.*" Only when she was sure the tears in her eyes were not going to fall did she look up, and then she saw that there were tears in his eyes too. "Do you cry when you read out loud?" she asked. "We all do in our family. And we never read about Tiny Tim, or about Steerforth when his body is washed up on the beach, on Saturday nights, or our eyes are too swollen to go to Sunday School." "Yes, I cry when I read about Steerforth," Dickens answered quietly.[169]

They were now fast approaching Boston, and passengers were collecting their wraps and bundles. Several times Osgood had come back, but had been waved away by Dickens. "You are not travelling alone?"

he now asked. "Oh, no, I had a mother, but I forgot all about her."
"You are a passed-mistress of the art of flattery!" Dickens said.[170]

*   *   *   *   *

The return was not too soon. Dickens was not sure his lungs had
not been done a lasting injury.[171] On Forster's birthday—and his own
marriage day—he coughed constantly and was sunk in gloom. He
petulantly refused to see two of Osgood's friends from New Bedford:
"No, I'll be damned if I will!" "I think, too," adds Mrs. Fields, "only
$1,300 in the house was bad for his spirits!" [172] But although Long-
fellow and all his Cambridge friends urged him to give in, he astonished them and even himself by his rendering of the last Boston
readings.[173]

He could hardly eat now, and had established a fixed system: "At
seven in the morning, in bed, a tumbler of cream and two table-
spoonsful of rum. At twelve, a sherry cobbler and a biscuit. At three
(dinner time), a pint of champagne. At five minutes to eight, an egg
beaten up with a glass of sherry. Between the parts, the strongest
beef tea that can be made, drunk hot. At a quarter past ten, soup, and
anything to drink that I can fancy. I don't eat more than half a pound
of solid food in the whole twenty-four hours, if so much." [174]

The final New York readings were all that remained. Only the
daily attention of Dr. Fordyce Barker and the devoted care of Dolby
brought Dickens through the ordeal.[175] "Dolby is as tender as a
woman," he wrote, "and as watchful as a doctor. He never leaves me
during the readings now, but sits at the side of the platform and
keeps his eye upon me all the time." [176] But Dickens's condition was
frightful. In the excitement and exertion of the readings, the blood
rushed into his hands until they became almost black, and his face
turned red and white and red again without his knowing it. After one
of the last three, Mrs. Fields, who had come on to New York with
her husband to be with their friend to the end, found him prostrated,
"his head thrown back without support on the couch, the blood suf-
fusing his throat and temples again where he had been very white a
few minutes before." [177]

There was still a great press banquet at Delmonico's on April 18th
which Dickens had promised to attend. Two hundred and four tickets
were sold at fifteen dollars a plate. The eight large tables were a mass

of confections and flowers.[178] But at five o'clock Dickens felt so un-well that it was not certain he could leave the Westminster Hotel. Messengers ran back and forth between there and Delmonico's with inquiries and bulletins about his condition. Dickens was determined to make the effort, and by the application of lotions and a careful bandaging of his foot and leg Dr. Barker enabled him to get out. He was an hour late when he limped into the restaurant leaning heavily on the arm of Horace Greeley.[179]

The staggering affair progressed through course after course in which the diners had choices of at least three dozen elaborate dishes, includ-ing such items as "Crême d'asperges à la Dumas," "Timbales à la Dickens," "Filets de boeuf à la Lucullus," "Coutelettes à la Feni-more Cooper," "aspic de foie gras historiés," and "Soupirs à la Mantalini." The confectionery triumphs of the pastry cooks in-cluded a "temple de la Littérature; trophées à l'auteur; Stars and Stripes; pavilion internationale; armes Britanniques; la loi du Destin; monument de Washington; and colonne triomphale." "Sairey Gamp and Betsy Prig, and Poor Joe and Captain Cuttle blossomed out of charlotte russe, and Tiny Tim was discovered in pâté de foie gras." [180]

Unaware of how severe was the pain from which Dickens was suffer-ing, Greeley was "One vast, substantial smile." [181] In response to his welcoming speech, with its concluding health, Dickens rose. He was henceforth charged with a duty, he said, "on every suitable occasion . . . to express my high and grateful sense of my second reception in America, and to bear my honest testimony to the national generosity and magnanimity. Also, to declare how astounded I have been by the amazing changes I have seen around me on every side—changes moral, changes physical, changes in the amount of land subdued and peopled, changes in the rise of vast new cities, changes in the growth of older cities almost out of recognition, changes in the graces and amenities of life, changes in the press, without whose advancement no advancement can be made anywhere. Nor am I, believe me, so arrogant as to suppose that in twenty-five years there have been no changes in me, and that I had nothing to learn and no extreme im-pressions to correct when I was here first." [182]

Though he had no intention of writing any other book on America, he wished "to record that wherever I have been, in the smallest places equally with the largest, I have been received with unsurpassable politeness, delicacy, sweet temper, hospitality, consideration, and with unsurpassable respect for the privacy daily enforced upon me by the nature of my avocation here, and the state of my health. This testimony, so long as I live, and so long as my descendants have any legal right in my books, I shall cause to be republished as an appendix to those two books of mine in which I have referred to America. And this I will do and cause to be done, not in mere love and thankfulness, but because I regard it as an act of plain justice and honour." [183]

His feelings he believed representative of those of the majority of the English people. Essentially the two peoples were one, with a common heritage of great achievement. "And if I know anything of my countrymen . . . the English heart is stirred by the fluttering of those Stars and Stripes, as it is stirred by no other flag that flies excepts its own." [184] In conclusion, "I do believe that from the great majority of honest minds on both sides, there cannot be absent the conviction that it would be better for this globe to be riven by an earthquake, fired by a comet, overrun by an iceberg, and abandoned to the Arctic fox and bear, than that it should present the spectacle of these two great nations, each of which has, in its own way and hour, striven so hard and so successfully for freedom, ever again being arrayed the one against the other." [185]

So severe was Dickens's agony by the end of this speech that he was forced to beg to be excused. Hobbling painfully on Greeley's arm, he could not conceal his sufferings. The mechanism of the body, indeed, was disastrously weakened, but the steel-coiled will that dominated it would not surrender. Two nights later, on April 20th, he forced himself to the final reading and bade his American listeners farewell forever. "My future life lies over the sea." [186] But though in some miraculous way the vessel had not been dashed to pieces against the Loadstone Rock and sunk, all its fabric was twisted and broken with the dreadful strain. Could it attempt another such voyage and not go down? Yet it was precisely such a course that Dickens even now was charting.

CHAPTER THREE

Last Rally

THE night before Dickens was to sail, Fields told him he felt like erecting a statue to him for heroism in doing his duty. "No, don't," Dickens gasped, laughing at the same time; "take down one of the old ones instead!" [1] The next day, April 22nd, dawned with a bright blue sky.[2] His bandaged foot swathed in black silk,[3] Dickens limped among so many heaped boxes filled with parting gifts of vintage wines, choice cigars, pictures, books, and photographs that his rooms looked like a combined luggage depot and flower market. Outside, in Irving Place, a carriage waited to take him to a private tug that would put him on board the *Russia*, where it lay moored off Staten Island, instead of exposing him to the enormous crowd waiting at the Cunard pier.[3a]

In the street before the Westminster Hotel, too, a huge crowd was assembled. As he came out, there was a ringing cheer and flowers showered from the windows all around him. A swift drive brought him and Dolby to the foot of Spring Street, where they were joined by Fields and the other friends who were seeing them on board.[4] Here the tug, the *Only Son*, awaited them. When Dickens saw the sparkling water, he exclaimed joyously, "That's *home!*" [5] After a pleasant half-hour sail down the North River and the Bay, they were alongside the *Russia*. The Cunard Company provided a magnificent lunch; Dickens's stateroom—the Chief Steward's, on deck—bloomed with floral tributes. After lunch the passenger tender arrived with the bulk of the voyagers and a group of others coming to say good-by: Du Chaillu, the African explorer, George W. Childs, the Philadelphia publisher, bearing a splendid basket of flowers from his wife, and

Anthony Trollope, who had arrived that very day on the *Scotia* and hastened out to exchange greetings with Dickens.[6]

The tug screamed a note of warning. Fields lingered behind the others returning to shore. Dickens's lame foot came down from the rail and the two men were locked in an embrace. Then Fields scrambled down the side. A cheer went up for Dolby; Dickens patted him on the shoulder, saying, "Good boy." Another cheer for Dickens. The tug was now steaming away, Fields standing at the rail. "Goodbye, Boz." Dickens put his soft hat on his cane and waved it. "Goodbye," he called; "God bless you every one." [7] Even then, a police boat, private tugs, and steam launches followed the *Russia* some distance down the Bay, firing salutes from miniature cannon.[8]

Financially, the American tour had been successful beyond all expectations. The total receipts had been $228,000, and the expenses not quite $39,000, including hotels, traveling, rent of halls, and a 5 per cent commission to Ticknor and Fields on the receipts in Boston. The preliminary expenses in England had been £614, Dolby's commission close to £3,000. The three years that had elapsed since the close of the Civil War had not yet restored American currency to its normal exchange value; if Dickens had invested in American securities and waited for the dollar to go back to par, his profits would have been nearly £38,000. Even paying a discount of almost 40 per cent for conversion to gold, "my profit," Dickens wrote Forster, "was within a hundred or so of £20,000." [9]

But it had been bought at a shattering cost of pain and exhausted endurance. Perhaps if he had given up all further public readings his extraordinary vitality might even now have restored his strength. Since early manhood, though, he had always forced his body to do exactly what he determined; at fifty-six he was not going to change. He would neither give up the prospect of placing his entire large family forever beyond the fear of want, nor strangle those emotional needs the readings relieved with a drugged excitement. He could not bear to give them up—not yet. On his way out to America, he had already begun negotiations with Chappell's for another series, to start in the fall of 1868. Before the first week of Boston readings closed he had settled the terms.[10]

They were glittering but ominous. He was to read one hundred times and receive £8,000. On the American tour an original schedule of around eighty had been reduced by a few cancellations to seventy-six; and under their strain Dickens had been brought to the verge of prostration. In spite of that warning experience, he refused now to alter his plans. The only concession he made was to announce that this would be his farewell tour. For one more series—one hundred more times—he would be "cooked before those lights" and exult in that intoxication, "and then read No More." [11] On the dangers of his determination he closed his eyes.

In part he was deceived by the almost unbelievable resilience with which a little rest reanimated his vigor. Four days out at sea the "true American" turned faithless at last, and for the first time he was able to cram his right foot into a shoe.[12] His spirits and his appetite returned: he "made a Gad's Hill breakfast" and watched Dolby eating his way through "A large dish of porridge into which he casts slices of butter and a quantity of sugar. Two cups of tea. A steak, Irish stew, Chutnee and marmalade." [13] But when a deputation of passengers asked Dickens if he would give *them* a reading, he replied "that sooner than do it" he "would assault the captain, and be put in irons." [14] He arrived in England bronzed and well-looking. "My doctor was quite broken down in spirits when he saw me . . . 'Good Lord!' he said, recoiling, 'seven years younger!' " [15]

At Gad's Hill, Mary and Georgina had got wind of a plan among the villagers to meet Dickens at Higham Station, take his horse out of the shafts of the carriage, and draw him home in triumph. To prevent this, Dickens had himself met by the basket phaeton at Gravesend. Even so, the houses along the road were all decorated with flags and the local farmers turned out in their market chaises, calling "Welcome home, sir!" The two Newfoundland dogs, Don and his son Bumble, who had come to the station, trotted along, lifting their heads to have their ears pulled. The servants at Gad's Hill had so draped the house with flags "that every brick of it was covered. They had asked Mamie's permission to 'ring the alarm-bell' (!) when master drove up, but Mamie, having some slight idea that that compliment might awaken master's sense of the ludicrous, had recommended bell-abstinence." [16]

When Dickens drove into the stable yard, "Linda (the St. Bernard)," he said, "was greatly excited; weeping profusely, and throwing herself on her back that she might caress my foot with her great forepaws. Mamie's little dog, too, Mrs. Bouncer, barked in the greatest agitation on being called down and asked by Mamie, 'Who is this?' and tore round and round me like the dog" in *Faust*. On Sunday, the village choir at the little church made amends for not having been allowed to ring the bell on Dickens's return. "After some unusually brief pious reflections in the crowns of their hats at the end of the sermon, the ringers bolted out, and rang like mad until I got home." [17]

Dolby, at his home in Ross, found his small daughter less excited by the birth of a baby brother than by the arrival of a Shetland pony that Dickens had caused to be sent as a present while the two men were in America. "The little girl winds up her prayers every night," Dickens reported to Mrs. Fields, "with a special commendation to Heaven of me and the pony—as if I must mount him to get there! I dine with Dolby (I was going to write 'him,' but found it would look as if I were going to dine with the pony) at Greenwich this very day, and if your ears do not burn from six to nine this evening, then the Atlantic is a non-conductor." [18]

Return to England brought Dickens no period of rest but a resumption of labor. During his absence Wills had had a serious accident on the hunting field, which led to concussion of the brain. Doctors ordered complete rest; he was forbidden even to write a letter.[19] Even when he had partly recovered he was unable to do the slightest work. "Ah, you cannot divine what it is," he told Fitzgerald, "to hear *doors slamming in your head* all day!" [20] His retirement from the subeditorship of *All the Year Round* forced Dickens to take over all the financial supervision of the magazine, which had always been in Wills's hands, and learn it from A to Z.[21]

His friend Townshend's will had appointed Dickens his literary executor, with the request that he publish "without alteration as much of my notes and reflections as may make known my opinions on religious matters." [22] When the notes were sent from Townshend's home in Lausanne they proved so bulky, repetitious, and chaotic that publishing them "without alteration" was impossible.[23] Dickens murmured that the volume would fall stillborn from the press, and he privately gave it the title *Religious Hiccoughs*, but he faithfully arranged, collated, and selected, and saw the volume published the following year.[24]

No Thoroughfare, the Christmas story on which Dickens and Collins had collaborated, had proved highly successful in their dramatized version at the Lyceum with Fechter. Within a fortnight Dickens saw it twice and was full of suggestions for its improvement.[25] He thought it dragged; a drugging and attempted robbery in the bedroom of a Swiss inn should be done with the sound of a waterfall in the background—it would enhance enormously "the mystery and gloom of the scene." [26] No sooner were these changes made than Dickens took a flying trip to Paris to give a few pointers to the French production before it opened there. Entitled *L'Abime*, and presented at the Vaudeville, the play promised to be a success in Paris as well.[27]

In June, Longfellow, his brother-in-law Tom Appleton, and his three daughters came to England. As soon as Dickens heard of their presence in London he hurried to the Langham Hotel, where they were staying, and invited them to spend the "Fourth of July" weekend at Gad's Hill. On the morning of the 4th, a Saturday, Longfellow was to see the Queen at Windsor, and Monday evening he had to be back in London, but into the brief visit Dickens crowded a breathless hospitality.[28] "I showed them all the neighbouring country that could be shown in so short a time," he wrote Fields, "and they finished off with a tour of inspection of the kitchens, pantry, wine-cellar, pickles, sauces, servants' sitting-room, general household stores, and even the Cellar Book of this illustrious establishment. Forster and Kent . . . came down for a day, and I hope we all had a really 'good time.' I turned out a couple of postilions in the old red jacket of the old red royal Dover road for our ride; and it was like a holiday ride of fifty years ago. Of course we went to look at the old houses in Rochester, and the old cathedral, and the old castle . . ." [29]

Dickens's neighbors, Lord and Lady Darnley, had given him keys to all the gates of Cobham Park; and Alice, Longfellow's eldest daughter, was delighted by the drive over its undulating turf, with the splendid great trees looking as if they were standing up to their knees in ferns and little rabbits dashing in and out. The Gad's Hill meals she found wonderful, "with more cold dishes on the sideboard than we ever dreamed of. In the evening the great tray on wheels was brought into the drawing room, full of bottles and glasses. Punch, hot or cold, lemons, hot water, and every drinkable imaginable." [30]

In the midst of these convivialities, however, Dickens's parental responsibilities were weighing upon him as heavily as ever. Among his sons, only Harry gave him no trouble. Harry had risen to be Head Censor at Wimbledon, was highly praised by Mr. Brackenbury, and was accordingly preparing for Cambridge.[31] But Charley's paper business had gone bankrupt, and although the fault seemed to be more his partner's than his own, Charley was personally in debt for a thousand pounds.[32] "It is clear to me," Dickens wrote him, "that any coming in on my part now, would be very harmful indeed, and would lead the holders of your acceptances for liabilities incurred by the Company, into the preposterous belief that I could and would make some kind of a bargain with them." As for his partner, "I am absolutely certain that so long as you have anything whatever to do with Mr. Lloyd things will go wrong with you. You cannot be very near to such pitch, without getting soiled." [33] At the age of thirty-one Charley still had no settled profession or income. In the end, Dickens took him on *All the Year Round* to assume some of Wills's routine duties. "I must turn his education to the best account I can until we can hit upon some other start in life, and he can certainly take the bag and report on its contents, and carry on the correspondence." [34]

Plorn, who was now almost seventeen, was being sent out to join his brother Alfred in Australia.[35] The expenses of buying his outfit and of getting Harry ready for Cambridge Dickens found staggering. "I can't get my hat on in consequence of the extent to which my hair stands on end at the costs and charges of these boys. Why was I ever a father! Why was my father ever a father!" [36] ". . . On the whole, I am inclined to depart from the text of my dear friend Mrs. Gamp, and say: 'Which blest is the man as has NOT his kiver full of sich?' " [37]

On September 26th Plorn was to sail on the *Sussex*. His father gave him a check for £200.[38] "I need not tell you," Dickens wrote in a farewell letter, "that I love you dearly, and am very, very sorry in my heart to part with you. But this life is half made up of partings, and these pains must be born. . . . Never take a mean advantage of anyone in any transaction, and never be hard upon people who are in your power. . . . I put a New Testament among your books, for the very same reasons, and with the very same hopes that made me write an easy account of it for you, when you were a little child . . . As your brothers have gone away, one by one, I have written to each such words as I am now writing to you. . . . I hope you will always be able to say in after life, that you had a kind father." [39]

Both father and son were greatly distressed at parting. "Just before the train started," Dickens wrote Mary, "he cried a good deal, but not painfully. (Tell dear Georgy that I bought him his cigars.) These are hard, hard things, but they might have to be done without means or influence, and then they would be far harder." [40] As the boy went off, Dickens looked after him sadly. "He seemed to me to become once more my youngest and favourite child . . . and I did not think I could have been so shaken." [41]

In October, Harry went to Cambridge, where Dickens was gratified to hear that he had won a scholarship of £50 a year.[42] So well did Harry work that by the end of his first three terms he won the best mathematical scholarship at Trinity. Excitedly he broke the news to his father, who met him at Higham. "Capital! capital!" exclaimed Dickens, but no more. Deeply self-restrained in whatever moved him deeply, after all his disappointments with the other boys he could not trust himself to speak. Harry felt bitterly hurt. The two started to walk home in silence. Suddenly, half up the road to Gad's Hill, his father turned to him with tears in his eyes, and clasped his hand in a grip of painful intensity. "God bless you, my boy," he said brokenly, "God bless you!" [43]

* * * * *

Even before the farewell readings began there were renewed signs that Dickens's strength was impaired. Although he could call upon a deceptive vivacity, Forster never saw him during that summer without feeling a loss in his elasticity of bearing, even an occasional dimming in the brightness of his eyes. Once, as they walked from Dickens's office to dine with each other in Forster's house at Palace Gate, Dickens alarmed his old friend by confessing that he could read only the right-hand halves of the signs over the shop doors. But this Dickens insisted on attributing to the medicine he was taking.[44]

Barely had the readings got under way than painful symptoms appeared. He got through his opening night at St. James's Hall on October 6th without penalty, but wrote Mary and Georgina three days later, after reading at Manchester, admitting that he was hoarse and croaking all next day.[45] He confessed to Frank Beard that he felt such nausea after his nightly exertions that the next morning he could not even bear the taste of the tincture of myrrh he used for cleaning his teeth. This also he blamed on the prescription, arguing that something in it went against his stomach.[46] "I have not been well," he wrote Forster on October 25th, "and have been heavily tired. However, I have little to complain of—nothing, nothing; though, like Mariana, I am aweary." [47] With the end of the month he was worse. "I cannot get right internally," he told Georgina, "and have begun to be as sleepless as sick." [48]

He had just learned, too, of the death of his brother Frederick. "In reference to the estrangement between him and me," he wrote, "I am glad to remember that it never involved on my side, the slightest feeling of anger. He lost opportunities that I had put in his way, poor dear fellow, but there were unhappy circumstances in his life which demanded great allowances." [49] "It was a wasted life," he wrote Forster, "but God forbid that one should be hard upon it, or upon anything in this world that is not deliberately and coldly wrong." [50]

During November there were no provincial readings, and those Dickens gave in London he did not find so great a strain. But he had decided that his listeners needed a new sensation. From *Oliver Twist* he carved a powerful new reading culminating in the murder of Nancy and Sikes's haunted flight and death, and then felt afraid to use it. "I have no doubt I could perfectly petrify an audience . . . ," he explained. "But whether the impression would not be so horrible as to keep them away another time, is what I cannot satisfy myself upon." [51]

He had indeed made something appalling. One warm afternoon Charley was working in the library with the windows open when he heard a sound of violent wrangling from outside. At first he dismissed it as some tramp beating his wife, but as the noise swelled into an alternation of brutal yells and dreadful screams Charley leaped to his feet, convinced that he must interfere. He dashed out of the door. There, at the other end of the meadow, was his father—murdering an imaginary Nancy with ferocious gestures. After dinner Charley mentioned what he had seen and Dickens acted it for him again. What did he think about it? [52]

"The finest thing I have ever heard," Charley replied, "but don't do it." But he knew his father could not bear any suggestion that his health was failing, and therefore steadily refused to give any explanation of his verdict. Forster also opposed, but would give no reason except that "such a subject was out of the province of reading." [53] Dolby had believed in America that his Chief's illness was mainly due to fatigue and the true American, but now recognized his declining health. He also tried dissuasion, and, when Dickens persisted, proposed that he ask the Chappells for their opinion. They suggested that he canvass the judgments of a private audience of invited friends at St. James's Hall. This was agreed, and Saturday evening, November 14th, determined as the date.[54]

Around a hundred people heard this reading. Beside his usual violet screen, Dickens had two flanking screens of the same hue, and curtains beyond them, narrowing the stage to the space surrounding his own figure. "My dear Dickens," a prominent physician told him just before the performance, "you may rely upon it that if only one woman cries out when you murder the girl, there will be a contagion of hysteria all over this place." Into the reading Dickens threw all his genius as an actor, bringing to life the comic, oily, crafty Fagin, the cowardly and stupid Noah Claypole, the brutal Sikes, and Nancy's terrifying shrieks. The entire audience stared with blanched and horror-stricken faces. It was "a most amazing and terrific thing," the Reverend William Harness wrote Dickens, "but I am bound to tell you that I had an almost irresistible impulse upon me to *scream*, and that, if anyone had cried out, I am certain I should have followed." [55]

Directly Dickens had done, the screens were whisked aside by his crew, revealing a long banquet table and a staff of waiters "ready to open oysters and set champagne-corks flying." Soon the wine restored the color to people's cheeks. When they came up on the stage, "and the gay dresses of the ladies were lighted by those powerful lights of mine, the scene was exquisitely pretty . . . the whole looking like a great bed of flowers and diamonds." Actresses like Mme. Celeste and Mrs. Keeley were enthusiastic, and Dickens was triumphantly excited. Should he do it or not? Dickens asked. " 'Why, of course do it,' " Mrs. Keeley replied. " 'Having got at such an effect as that, it must be done. But,' rolling her large black eyes very slowly, and speaking very distinctly, 'the public have been looking for a sensation these last fifty years or so, and by Heaven they have got it!' With which words, and a long breath and a long stare, she became speechless." [56]

Dickens turned to his son. "Well, Charley, and what do you think of it now?" "It is finer even than I expected," was the reply, "but I still say, don't do it." As Dickens looked at him, puzzled, Edmund

Yates came up. "What do you think of this, Edmund?" Dickens asked. "Here is Charley saying it is the finest thing he has ever heard, but persists in telling me, without giving any reason, not to do it." Yates gave a quick look at Charley, and said gravely, to Dickens's intense amazement, "I agree with Charley, Sir." [57]

But of course Dickens ignored the verdict he did not want to hear. The ominous warnings had been repeated over and over again. That inability to read the street signs on his left side was a plain foreshadowing of paralysis, and his sleeplessness, nausea, and lameness were little less threatening. The attempt to blame them on walking in the snow or on his medicine was either disingenuous or willful self-deception. The danger was clear to all those who knew him intimately. Nevertheless, he chose to close his eyes on what they saw. No matter what the consequences, he would go on doing the thing he loved. In deciding to add the murder of Nancy to his repertory, he was sentencing himself to death.

Perhaps Dickens would have felt shocked had he been accused of a deliberate effort at suicide. Since 1866 he had been reckless in expending his waning energies. But he had ceased to care what happened. All his fame had not brought him the things he most deeply wanted. The long frustration of his marriage had ended in a failure that left him ruthless and embittered toward Catherine. Even when the strained anguish of the separation had receded into the past, he still refused to see her or have any but the most impersonal communication with her, and his only reference to her in the will he was to make was frigidly unforgiving. There is no direct evidence of what part Ellen played in his unhappiness, but there can be no doubt that in some way she, too, failed his need. Did he suspect her, like Bella Wilfer, of being calculating and mercenary, and, unlike Bella, of having remained so? Was his tenderness for her, too, shot through with a disillusioned bitterness that only a wraith like the memory of Mary Hogarth need not fear?

Even his children whom he loved were one after another worrying and disappointing him. And when he looked from his home to the affairs of the world, the gleaming hopes of his earlier career were largely unrealized. Though he had seen the domination of the country pass from a landed aristocracy to the commercial and industrial middle class, inefficiency, cruelty, corruption, and the gangrene of privilege were still entrenched. As he gazed into the future it seemed to him that he could discern no prospects but the decline of England and international conflicts. Only in the people did he still have faith.

But every perspective left him weary of his own struggle. Though he could still relish the comic and still whip himself up at intervals to his old gusty enjoyment of life, more and more these efforts broke down and the darkness and emptiness came crowding back. What was there then but the fearful stimulus of the readings, and returning to them as Jasper in the *Mystery of Edwin Drood* returns to the dangerous excitement of his drugged visions?

*   *   *   *   *

In December the provincial grind began again. Since his return from America the Staplehurst accident seemed to distress Dickens more and more; it was now a constant horror on his journeys. Going to Edinburgh on the "Flying Scotchman," he calculated that traveling such a distance involved "more than thirty thousand shocks to the nerves." [58] With Mrs. Fields he had made a joke about the lights to which he was exposed on his platform, saying, "The hour has almost come when I to sulphurous and tormenting gas must render up myself!" [59] but the heat and glare were intense. In the North the weather was diabolical, and again he had wretched nights.[60] After the first public reading of the "Murder," in London on January 5th, he was still utterly prostrated the next morning.[61]

A few days later there were final readings to be given in Dublin and Belfast. Dickens crossed to Ireland, taking Georgina and Mary with him for the excursion. On the return train from Belfast to catch the mail boat at Kingstown, their carriage was directly behind the engine. Suddenly they heard a crash overhead and there was a severe shock that threw them all forward. Through the windows they glimpsed an enormous fragment of iron tearing along the line and knocking down the telegraph poles. The plate glass was bombarded with flying stones, mud, and gravel. Aghast, they all threw themselves to the floor of the carriage. With a grinding and hissing the train jolted to a standstill.[62]

Controlling his agitation, Dickens climbed out and began talking quietly to the engineer. In a moment they were surrounded by a crowd of terrified passengers. The engineer excitedly explained that the metal tire of the great driving-wheel had been fractured and the fragments shot into the air. It was one of these that had struck the roof of Dickens's carriage. Had it been a little larger or hurled with more force, it might have crashed down through the roof into their midst. The experience did not lessen the nervousness Dickens felt during his almost daily journeyings.[63]

He had arranged his schedule to take in Cheltenham especially so that Macready might hear the "Murder." The famous old Macbeth, seventy-five now, and very infirm, sat in the front row, grimly staring. Afterward, he went to Dickens's dressing room leaning on Dolby's arm. He glared speechlessly at Dickens and took a glass of champagne which Dolby forced on him, scowling as if it had been a personal injury.[64] Dickens tried to laugh away his emotion, but Macready would not have it. " 'No, Dickens—er—er—I will NOT,' with sudden emphasis,—'er—have it—er—put aside. In my—er—best times—er—you remember them, my dear boy—er—gone, gone!—no,'—with great emphasis again,—'it comes to this—er—TWO MACBETHS!' with extraordinary energy. After which he stood (with his glass in his hand and his old square jaw of its old fierce form) looking defiantly at Dolby as if Dolby had contradicted him; and then trailed off into a weak pale likeness of himself as if his whole appearance had been some clever optical illusion." [65]

At Clifton the "Murder" brought about "a contagion of fainting. And yet the place was not hot. I should think we had from a dozen to twenty ladies borne out, stiff and rigid, at various times. It became quite ridiculous." [66] In Bath, Dickens felt as if he were haunted by the ghost of Landor going along the silent streets before him. "The place looks to me like a cemetery which the Dead have succeeded in rising and taking. Having built streets of their old gravestones, they wander about scantily trying to 'look alive.' A dead failure." [67]

Two weeks later Dickens's foot went lame again. The famous doctor, Sir Henry Thompson, refused to let him read that night, and forbade his going to Scotland the following day. "Heaven knows what engagements this may involve in April!" Dickens exclaimed. "It throws us all back, and will cost me some five hundred pounds." [68] But in a few days he felt so much better that, resisting the urgent entreaties of his family and his friends, he set out for Edinburgh on the morning of February 20th. Two days later he collapsed once more and had to consult another doctor.[69] This one prescribed a special kind of boot which gave Dickens relief, but fell in with the theory that the trouble originated in walking in the snow. With the boot Dickens's foot felt better, though at the end of an evening's ordeal both feet were tired and ached in bed.[70]

Dickens professed to feel gratified that the last readings were being disposed of one by one and to be looking forward to their conclusion. With an ominous quotation he anticipated the end: " 'Like lights in a theatre, they are being snuffed out fast,' as Carlyle says of the guillotined in his Revolution. I suppose I shall be glad when they are all snuffed out. Anyhow, I think so *now*." [71]

But he enjoyed the readings. Above all he enjoyed shocking his audiences with the murder and liked to joke about his "murderous instincts." [72] "I have a vague sensation," he said, "of being 'wanted' as I walk about the streets." [73] "There was a fixed expression of horror of me, all over the theatre, which could not have been surpassed if I had been going to be hanged. . . . It is quite a new sensation to be execrated with that unanimity; and I hope it will remain so!" [74] He consequently put the "Murder" on his program again and again. He had by this time given up drinking champagne during the readings, and took only some weak iced brandy and water; "but what he wanted," as Hesketh Pearson says, "was a little strong cold common sense." [75]

After the last Edinburgh reading he reached his dressing room with difficulty and was obliged to lie on the sofa some time before he could utter a word. When they had eaten supper, he handed Dolby the list of readings for the remainder of the tour. "Look carefully through the towns you have given me," Dolby said, "and see if you note anything peculiar about them." "No. What is it?" "Well, out of four Readings a week you have put down three Murders." "What of that?" Dickens asked. "Simply this," Dolby replied; "the success of this farewell tour is assured in every way, so far as human probability is concerned. It therefore does not make a bit of difference which of the works you read . . ." [76]

Dolby went on to say that Dickens should refrain from tearing himself to pieces three nights out of every four and suffering the unheard-of tortures he endured afterward. He should reserve the "Murder" for the larger towns—"Have you finished?" Dickens angrily interrupted. "I have said all I feel on the matter." Dickens bounded up from his chair and threw his knife and fork so violently on his plate that it was smashed to pieces. "Dolby!" he shouted, "your infernal caution will be your ruin one of these days." It was the only time Dolby had ever heard him address an angry word to anyone. "Perhaps so, sir," Dolby replied. "In this case, though, I hope you will do me the justice to say it is exercised in your interest." [77]

Turning aside, he left the table to put the tour list in his writing case. Then he saw that his Chief was crying. "Forgive me, Dolby!" he exclaimed between sobs, going toward him and embracing him affectionately. "I really didn't mean it; and I know you are right. We will talk the matter over calmly in the morning." [78]

But the few concessions he made were too little and too late. He struggled on through deepening exhaustion. In March he learned of the death of Sir James Emerson Tennent, who had stood at Grey's side in the struggle for the Reform Bill of 1832 and supported Peel in the abolition of the Corn Laws. During the Italian visit of 1853 Dickens had spent delightful days with Tennent, and on the completion of Our Mutual Friend had dedicated it to him. The news that this old friend was dead shook him with grief; and by cutting out his intermissions at a York reading he barely managed to make the London train and attend the funeral.[79] To Forster he appeared dazed and worn.[80]

Less than a month later Macready's daughter Katie died. Distressed for his old friend, Dickens responded hotly to the unconscious egoism with which Forster appropriated all the pain of her loss to himself. "God forgive me," Dickens exclaimed to Georgina, "but I cannot get over the mania for proprietorship which is rampant at Palace House." And indignantly he quoted Forster: " 'You may imagine the shock and blow it was to ME'—and all that. Me! Me! Me! as if there were no poor old broken friend in the case. I cannot forget when she gave offence to the dignity enthroned in Montague Square, and one day at dinner when I threw in a word or two for her," Forster's reply was: " 'A very offensive and improper young person and I wish to hear no more about her.' I hate myself for harping on such strings, and yet I should hate myself much more as a monstrous humbug if I didn't." [81]

On April 10th, at St. George's Hall in Liverpool, "the Mayor, Corporation, and citizens," six hundred and fifty strong, gave a dinner in Dickens's honor which he found as exhausting as the reading.[82] He had effusions of blood from his bowels now,[83] and his foot was again so bad that Scott, his valet, carried a supply of flannel and of poppy-heads to make fomentations at a moment's notice.[84] All his giddiness had returned, he was uncertain of his footing, and felt "extremely indisposed to raise" his hands to his head.[85] "My weakness and deadness," he told Georgina, "are all *on the left side*, and if I don't look at anything I try to touch with my hand, I don't know where it is." [86]

Yet he still persisted in trying to believe these symptoms the results of his medicine, and wrote to Francis Beard suggesting that diagnosis. But from Dickens's "exact description," Beard at once recognized what they really meant. "The medicine cannot possibly have caused them," he replied firmly.[87] Hastening the two hundred miles to Dickens's side, he examined him, and insisted that the readings must stop at once.[88] If he took the platform that night, Beard said, "I will not guarantee but that he goes through life dragging a foot after him." Great tears rolled down Dickens's cheeks, and he threw himself on Dolby's neck. "My poor boy!" he sobbed, "I am so sorry for all the trouble I am giving you!" Then, turning to Beard, he pleaded, "Let me try it tonight. It will save so much trouble." Beard refused to take the responsibility. "If you insist on reading tonight I shall have only to stand by and watch the results." "But how will Dolby get through?" "Never mind me," Dolby struck in, "I'll get through somehow; if you and Beard will only leave town at once." [89]

Beard took his patient back to London that very night, and the following day, April 23rd, arranged a consultation with the distinguished physician, Sir Thomas Watson. The latter confirmed Beard's judgment. Dickens's giddiness, the feeling of insecurity about his left leg, the strangeness in his left hand and arm, his inability to lay his hand on a spot unless he looked at it carefully, the unreadiness to raise his hands, and especially his left hand, toward his head, all pointed unmistakably in the same direction. "The state thus described," Watson wrote, "showed plainly that C. D. had been on the brink of an attack of paralysis of his left side, and possibly of apoplexy." [90]

Dickens had managed with his relentless determination to force himself through seventy-four of the hundred planned readings—two

less than the number which in America had brought him so near collapse. Even now he would not refer to his breakdown as having any
other cause than "over-fatigue." As soon as he felt himself recovered,
which was within a few weeks, he began urging Sir Thomas Watson
to authorize his resuming the reading platform. Sir Thomas emphasized the need of caution and warned against overoptimism. "Pre-
ventive measures are always invidious," he said dryly, "for when most
successful the need for them is the least apparent." [91]

Nevertheless Dickens finally got his way. It was understood that the
resumed readings were to number no more than twelve, that they were
to involve no railway travel, and, finally, that they would have to be
deferred at least eight months until early in 1870.[92] Dickens believed
that the joy with which he looked forward to them was only a relief
that the Chappells would more nearly realize the profits they had anticipated. "I do believe," he exclaimed to Forster, "that such people
as the Chappells are very rarely to be found in human affairs. To say
nothing of their noble and munificent manner of sweeping into space
all the charges incurred uselessly, and all the immense inconvenience
and profitless work thrown upon their establishment, comes a note
this morning from the senior partner, to the effect that they feel that
my overwork has been 'indirectly caused by them, and by my great
and kind exertions to make their venture successful to the extreme.'
There is something so delicate and fine in this, that I feel it deeply." [93]

*   *   *   *   *

Sustained by the assurance that he might still slay Nancy a few more
times, Dickens gave himself over to the mere routine of running *All
the Year Round*, living in his rooms above the office. But he knew
in his heart that he had deferred death by a narrower margin than he
would admit, and proceeded early in May to make his will.[93a] His first
bequest was "the sum of £1,000 free of legacy duty to Miss Ellen Lawless Ternan, late of Houghton Place, Ampthill Square," a strange
legacy which he could hardly have believed would fail to arouse scandalized comment after he was dead. It was almost as if he desired to
defy convention from his grave. And in view of his passionate concern
for Ellen's reputation at the time of his separation from Catherine, it
reveals an odd blindness, carelessness, or indifference—surely one of
the three—to the certainty that her name would be coupled with his

when the contents of the will became known. As a provision for Ellen's welfare it seems insufficient, but there is no indication of whether he made any other and no known explanation of his reason for not having done so without naming her in the will at all.[94]

He bequeathed to Georgina Hogarth £8,000 free of legacy duty, and the interest upon an equal sum to Catherine, after which the principal was to descend to his children. Mary was to receive £1,000 and an annuity of £300 if she remained single, but if she married her income was to be divided equally among all his surviving children, who were to share equally in the rest of his estate. Georgina was also given most of his personal jewelry and his private papers, Charley his library, engravings, and prints, and some articles of jewelry and silver, Forster the gold watch presented to Dickens at Coventry and the manuscripts of his books. To each of his servants he gave nineteen guineas. Forster and Georgina were made his executors.[95]

After these formal provisions there was a glowing eulogy of Georgina: "I solemnly enjoin my children always to remember how much they owe to the said Georgina Hogarth, and never to be wanting in a grateful and natural attachment to her, for they know well that she has been, through all the stages of their growth and progress, their ever useful, self-denying and devoted friend." [96] The only further mention of Catherine was cold: "I desire here simply to record the fact that my wife, since our separation by consent, has been in the receipt from me of an annual income of £600, while all the great charges of a numerous and expensive family have devolved wholly upon myself." He concluded by directing that he be buried privately and unostentatiously, "that those who attend my funeral wear no scarf, cloak, black bow, long hatband, or other such revolting absurdity," and that his name be inscribed on his tomb "in plain English letters" with no "Mr." or "Esquire." [97]

Charley was developing into a useful helper on *All the Year Round*. "He is a very good man of business," Dickens told Macready, "and evinces considerable aptitude in sub-editing work." [98] But two of the other boys worried Dickens even more than ever. For the last year or more Sydney, the sailor son, had been drifting into the same courses of extravagance that Walter had been following before he died. As Dickens recalled the strange faraway look in the enormous eyes of the small child he had called "the Ocean Spectre," and his pride in the brightness and popularity of the little "Admiral," he was bitterly distressed. He gave a sharp reproof and warning, but not long afterward the young man was again squandering money and leading a life that Georgina vaguely described as headed toward "*certain misery* on earth." Severely Dickens forbade him to appear at Gad's Hill when he should return to England.[99]

Plorn, too, was failing to settle down into his life in Australia. He had already given up one post with which he had been provided, though Dickens still hoped that he might take better to colonial life. But, "He will not fail," Dickens prophesied with the foreboding of knowledge, "to report himself unfit for his surroundings, if he should find that he is so." [100] A year later, Plorn was so "persistently ignoring the possibility of his holding any other position in Australia" than the temporary one he filled, that Dickens "inferred from it a homeward tendency. He has always been the most difficult of the boys to deal with, away from home. There is not the least harm in him, and he is far more reflecting and more alive *au fond* than any of his brothers. But he seems to have been born without a groove. It cannot be helped. If he cannot, or will not find one, I must try again, and die trying." [101]

Turning from his troubled concern over Plorn, Dickens expressed in these same letters dark fears for the state of the world. The American press was displaying a blustering violence about the Alabama claims and the Northwest Boundary dispute, and the American Minister, John Lothrop Motley, seemed to Dickens a man "of an arbitrary dogmatic turn" unlikely to mend matters. The danger was that the United States might "at last set the patient British back up" and there "come into existence an exasperating war-party on both sides." In France, Dickens perceived, the regime of Napoleon III was on the verge of collapse. In words strongly prophetic of the Commune of 1871, Dickens wrote: "What Victor Hugo calls 'the drop-curtain, behind which is constructing the great last act of the French Revolution,' has been a little shaken at the bottom lately . . . One seems to see the feet of a rather large chorus getting ready." [102] But of the results of the Reform Bill of 1867, which seemed threatening to so many others, Dickens felt calmly confident; "the greater part of the new voters will in the main be wiser as to their electoral responsibilities and more seriously desirous to discharge them for the common good

than the bumptious singers of 'Rule Britannia,' 'Our dear old Church
of England,' and all the rest of it." [103]

Feeling more cheerful in May, Dickens prepared to welcome Mr.
and Mrs. Fields to England, and show them his heartiest hospitality.[104] With these two Boston friends arrived the Charles Eliot Nor-
tons and James Russell Lowell's daughter Mabel, as well as Dr.
Fordyce Barker and Sol Eytinge, the illustrator of the American
"Diamond Back" edition of Dickens's works. To be with them in
London, Dickens took a suite at the St. James's Hotel, in Piccadilly,
for himself, Georgina, and Mary.[105] On one evening, protected by
the detective police, he took Fields, Eytinge, and Dolby through the
lowest criminal dives of the Ratcliffe Highway, the haunts of sailors,
Lascars, and Chinese, and into one of the opium dens where they saw
the hideous old woman who was to serve as a model for the Princess
Puffer in *The Mystery of Edwin Drood*.[106] On another day he showed
Fields over Windsor and took him to dinner at the Star and Garter in
Richmond.[107]

Of course all the glories of Gad's Hill and Rochester were also displayed for his guests. Once again, too, Dickens revived the red jackets
of the old red royal Dover Road, and they dashed merrily to Canterbury, past the apple and cherry orchards of Kent and the hop vines
dancing on the poles. The ancient cathedral was glorious with glowing stained glass and groined vaulting, and in the streets they tried
to decide just which bulging old house with twinkling windows was
Agnes Wickfield's home, Dickens laughingly saying that several
"would do." They drove back in the twilight, the red coats of the
postilions gleaming under an occasional roadside lamp, fireflies shining in the orchards, returning a little after nine to the welcome lantern
and open gates of Gad's Hill Place. It was Dickens's last pilgrimage
to Canterbury.[108]

With the cessation of his provincial readings, Dickens started revolving in his mind the conception of another novel. "What should
you think," he asked Forster in July, "of the idea of a story beginning
in this way?—Two people, boy and girl, or very young, going apart
from one another, pledged to be married after many years—at the end
of the book. The interest to arise out of the tracing of their separate
ways, and the impossibility of telling what will be done with that impending fate." [109] It was a conception that partly shaped the relation

of Edwin Drood and Rosa Bud in the story. But early in August, "I laid aside the fancy I told you of," Dickens wrote Forster, "and have a very curious and new idea for my new story. Not a communicable idea (or the interest of the book would be gone), but a very strong one, though difficult to work.[110]

An agreement with Frederic Chapman was soon drawn. It provided that Dickens was to receive £7,500 for the profits on the first twenty-five thousand copies, and that all profits beyond that were to be shared equally. There was one clause that had never been in a Dickens contract before. It was included by Dickens's own desire: that if he should die or for any other reason be unable to finish the story in twelve numbers, Forster was to serve as an arbitrator to decide what amount should in fairness be repaid to Chapman.[111]

On a Sunday in October one of the Gad's Hill servants knocked on Fields's chamber door with a note from Dickens: "Mr. Charles Dickens presents his respectful compliments to the Hon. James T. Fields (of Boston, Mass., U.S.) and will be happy to receive a visit from the Hon. J. T. F. in the small library as above, at the Hon. J. T. F.'s leisure." [112] Hastening down, Fields heard from Dickens's own lips the opening chapters of *The Mystery of Edwin Drood,* of which the ink on the last page was scarcely dry. With absorbed attention Fields listened to Jasper's awakening from his opium visions in that Ratcliffe Highway dive that he had himself so recently visited, and recognized in the description of Cloisterham the gray and ancient city of Rochester. But the story of which he listened to the beginning that day was destined to have a more disastrous ending than any conceived by its creator.[113]

CHAPTER FOUR

The Dying and Undying Voice

CRITICISM: *The Mystery of Edwin Drood* and Valedictory

The Mystery of Edwin Drood is Dickens's swan song. In its very heart there is a core of death. All its atmosphere is sunset and autumnal. Though the Cloisterham of the story, with its old Cathedral and moldering crypt, its ruined Monks' Vineyard and crumbling houses, is again the Rochester Dickens loved, it is no longer the spring-drenched Rochester of his *Pickwick* days, but a city where darkness already dims the bright colors and the first frost sprinkles the grass of the Cathedral close. Christmas in Cloisterham is no season of glowing cheer; it is a time when murder lurks to strangle its predestined victim and lock his remains within a hollow tomb. The dying mutter of a voice among the choir, sounding through the murky arches and sepulchral vaults until the sea of music rises high and beats its life out, is echoed by the dying chords of this dirge whose notes are broken off unfinished.

Never before has Dickens's control of scene and tone been more masterly. The black rooks flying around the tower, the black-robed Dean and clergy, the waning day and the waning year, the low sun "fiery and yet cold behind the monastery wall," [1] the fallen red leaves of the Virginia creeper on the pavement, the wintry shudder that goes through the little pools on the cracked flagstones, the giant elms shedding their gust of tears, all are heavy and ominous with mortality. When Mr. Jasper goes for an exploratory midnight ramble through the galleries and tower of the Cathedral, he comes in the yard upon the saws of two journeymen, looking like the tools of "two skeleton journeymen out of the Dance of Death" who might be "grinning in the shadow." [2] As Helena Landless leaves her brother at the little

[1115]

postern stair of Jasper's gatehouse, both notice the sky hung with copperous clouds and feel a strange dead weight in the air. Throughout the entire book there is an elegiac precision of observation that not only harmonizes with its dark and secretive story but is as if Dickens were wandering in a last farewell through these familiar haunts and impressing on his mind all the loveliness that he must leave ere long.

This poetic and mournful tone, no doubt, is what led Longfellow to feel that *Edwin Drood* was "certainly one of the most beautiful of his works, if not the most beautiful of all." [3] And it impelled Chesterton to compare this somber half-told mystery to the performance of a dying magician making a final splendid and staggering appearance before mankind.[4] Shaw, more impatiently, dismissed the book as only "a gesture by a man already three quarters dead." [5] Only a few readers have called attention to its curious psychological overtones, and almost none have observed its brooding social implications. Though more commentators have expended their ingenuity upon it than upon any of Dickens's other books, for the most part they have been fascinated, to the exclusion of almost every other interest, by the puzzle of its plot.

That plot is simple and yet baffling. Its main character is John Jasper, a musician, with a beautiful voice, the lay precentor of the Cathedral. But behind his mask of decorum the respected choirmaster is secretly unhappy and has periodical recourse to gorgeous opium visions in which scimitars flash in the sunlight and oriental processions pass with clashing cymbals while ten thousand dancing girls strew flowers. Deeply devoted to his nephew Edwin Drood, a young engineer only a little his junior, Jasper is at the same time painfully in love with his nephew's fiancée, Rosa Bud, a pupil at Miss Twinkleton's school in Cloisterham. Edwin and Rosa are both orphans, betrothed since their infancy by their parents. Though they are fond of each other, they both, unknown to Jasper, half resent the bond that links them, and wish that they might have chosen freely. Rosa is afraid of Jasper, feeling in him a compelling hypnotic influence that forces her to know his feelings and nevertheless to conceal them from Edwin. The young people are to be married after Christmas and will then go to Egypt, where the family engineering interests are located.

The story unfolds in sinister hints. Jasper confesses to his nephew "that even a poor monotonous chorister and grinder of music" [6] may be restless and dissatisfied and take to carving demons out of his heart as the old monks carved them out of the Cathedral stalls: let that knowledge be a warning to him. "You won't be warned, then?" he demands insistently. "You can't be warned, then?" [7] Jasper learns all the nooks and crannies of the Cathedral; he displays a strange interest in a pile of quicklime in the yard; it is implied that he surreptitiously acquires a key to the crypt and access to one of its tombs. He wears around his throat a long black silk scarf. Starting awake out of slumber, he cries, "What is the matter? Who did it?" [8] Following him from London but failing to find him in Cloisterham, the opium woman comes on his nephew and mysteriously warns him that Ned is "A threatened name. A dangerous name." [9] When the lawyer Hiram Grewgious says of the young people, "God bless them both," Jasper responds, "God save them both!" [10]

Shortly before Christmas there arrive in Cloisterham the twins Neville and Helena Landless. They are from Ceylon, exotic and foreign-looking, passionate in nature, half shy, half defiant, with something, "both of face and form, which might be equally likened to the pause before a crouch or a bound." [11] Helena immediately distrusts Jasper, but with none of Rosa's fear of him; Neville immediately falls in love with Rosa, and resents young Drood's air of lazy and patronizing tolerance of her. Jasper observes the spark of antagonism between the young men and insidiously, with the aid of drugged wine the story insinuates, leads them on to a violent quarrel with each other. Then he tells Neville's tutor, Minor Canon Crisparkle, that he fears for his nephew's safety, describing Neville's manner as "murderous"; perhaps through chance, perhaps through eavesdropping, he echoes expressions the young stranger has himself used, "he would have cut him down on my hearth," "There is something of the tiger in his dark blood." [12]

But both young men express regret for their outburst, and Jasper arranges a reconciliation dinner at his gatehouse for Christmas Eve. Meanwhile, Mr. Grewgious has told Edwin that it was never their parents' intention to bind him and Rosa against their will and affection, and the two have gently agreed to dissolve their engagement, although Jasper is not to be informed until after Christmas. On the night of the dinner each in turn goes up the postern stair, Landless, Drood, Jasper with his black silk scarf. The chapter title darkly quotes

Macbeth: "When shall these Three meet again?" [13] Next morning Edwin Drood has disappeared. His watch and tiepin, but not his body, are found caught in a weir of the river by Mr. Crisparkle, who has been drawn there by some influence he is unable to analyze. Neville Landless is arrested on suspicion. There is blood on his stick, but it might have got there in his struggle with the louts who tried to apprehend him without telling him their reason. He is released for lack of proof that Drood is dead.

Jasper announces to Mr. Crisparkle that he is convinced his dear boy has been murdered and that henceforth he devotes himself to fastening the crime upon the murderer. But when Mr. Grewgious tells him that Edwin and Rosa had determined not to marry each other, Jasper shrieks and falls fainting to the floor. Mr. Grewgious looks down upon his ghastly figure with no sign of concern or sympathy. Shortly afterward a new figure turns up in Cloisterham, calling himself Dick Datchery, "a single buffer living idly on his means." [14] With black eyebrows and a great head of floating white hair, he is strongly implied to be disguised, and he devotes himself to spying upon Jasper. The opium woman again traces Jasper back from one of his orgies in London, and this time finds him in the Cathedral. When Datchery sees her surreptitiously shaking her fist at the Choirmaster from behind a pillar, he goes home to his rooms and adds to a curious score he has been chalking on the inside of a cupboard door a thick line running from top to bottom. He has come, plainly, within sight of the end he was seeking.

Here the story breaks off, near the end of its sixth installment. How was the mystery to have been resolved in the remaining six? Scores of writers have devoted vast subtlety to deducing innumerable solutions from the most detailed study of its text, from the revisions and excisions in the manuscript, from Dickens's fragmentary notes, from a preliminary list of possible titles, even from the pictures on the etched cover-page. All the loaded weight of suggestion in the narrative points to Jasper as his nephew's murderer, but there are those who believe that Drood is not really dead and that he had returned disguised as Datchery to bring the would-be murderer to punishment. Others think him dead, but deny that Jasper is the killer. Still others identify Datchery with Neville Landless, with Helena, with Grewgious, with various other characters.

But, in a sense, the more plausible all these arguments, the less conclusive they are. For if Dickens is in control of his story, almost any detail short of outright misstatement may be intended to mislead and confuse. Further, Dickens made a number of declarations on the subject that can be dismissed only if we assume either that he changed the plan of the story or deliberately misinformed those close to him.

Forster says that Dickens did later tell him the idea that he had at first described as "not communicable" if "the interest of the story" was to be maintained. Jasper *was* the murderer, Forster affirms; the novelty of the story "was to consist in the review of the murderer's career by himself at the close, when its temptations were to be dwelt upon as if, not he the culprit, but some other man, were the tempted. The last chapters were to be written in the condemned cell, to which his wickedness, all elaborately elicited from him as if told of another, had brought him. Discovery by the murderer of the utter needlessness of the murder for its object, was to follow hard upon the commission of the deed; but all discovery of the murderer was to be baffled till towards the close, when, by means of a gold ring which had resisted the corrosive effects of the lime into which he had thrown the body, not only the person murdered was to be identified, but the locality of the crime and the man who committed it. So much was told me before any of the book was written; and it will be recollected that the ring, taken by Drood to be given to his betrothed only if their engagement went on, was brought away with him from their last interview." [15]

Other testimony corroborates Forster. Charley reports that he asked his father, "Of course, Edwin Drood was murdered?" and that Dickens replied, with an expression of surprise, "Of course, what else did you suppose?" [16] Forster's jealous and exacting character, Katey believed, made it unlikely that her father would have changed his plan without confiding in his old friend.[17] Luke Fildes, the illustrator, disconcerted Dickens by querying the significance of Jasper's black neckerchief being so long that it went twice around his neck. Muttering something about being afraid he was "getting on too fast," Dickens suddenly demanded, "Can you keep a secret?" and then confided, "I must have the double necktie! It is necessary, for Jasper strangles Edwin Drood with it." [18] This necktie Dickens later changed to the great black silk scarf Jasper wears around his throat or loops over his arm.

* * * * *

Two things emerge darkly from the shadows of the story: that there is a strange fusion and tension between Cloisterham and the Orient, and that Jasper's mad jealousy of the nephew whom he also loves is only one facet of a much more deeply involved division in his soul. In his dreams at Opium Sal's, horrible deeds and dreadful journeys mingle Eastern visions with the Cathedral town; bending over the tumbled bed where he has been lying beside a Chinese and a Lascar, he listens to their mutterings suspiciously before dismissing them with the word, "Unintelligible!" [19] The Landless twins, from Ceylon, are dark, gypsyish, and rich in coloring, and it is insinuated that they may have oriental blood. There is a hint of secrets having their roots somewhere in the Drood family business and the family background in Egypt. Descriptions of the dust of monastic graves in Cloisterham dissolve into allusions to the explorers of Egyptian tombs, "half-choked with bats and dust," [20] and these in turn into Jasper's explorations of the crypt with its debris and moldering dead. In this mingling of East and West, all the imperialist tentacles of England are tangled in a network with this sleepy and decaying old cathedral town.

Jasper, tormented soul, drug addict, dark enigma, is the central figure in this web. It is significant that he is the single major character of whose thoughts we are told nothing. Only when he starts awake from a nightmare and when the opium woman draws ambiguous revelations from him while he is lying in a drugged daze does he give any unintended glimpse of the fiery furnace of his heart. When he knows what he is saying, almost all his words seem moves in his hidden plans. Not until Edwin has vanished does Jasper ever voice his feelings to Rosa, and even then he is careful to ensure that nobody else can hear. There is the possibility, though, that Jasper is a divided personality, and that in his normal state he does not remember what he does under the influence of opium, or know in what ways his everyday doings are influenced by the hidden self that then emerges. He may thus be entirely sincere in writing that he devotes himself to the destruction of a murderer whom he does not realize to be himself.

All his activities, however, in the days before Edwin Drood disappears, as critical comment has shown, have a strange resemblance to those with which the Thugs, Hindu devotees of Kali, the goddess of destruction, set about performing a ritual murder. Concealing his worship of the goddess, the Thug seems a respectable member of the community. He preys upon travelers—and Edwin is about to go upon a journey. He ingratiates himself with his victim by exaggerated endearments. Stupefying him with drugs, the Thug then, a little after midnight, strangles him with a fold of cloth which must previously have been worn and disposes of the body in a secret burial place. (In the actual Thug practice it was a white silver-weighted scarf, although Jasper wore a black scarf.) Omens must be observed, a condition Jasper fulfills when he ascends the Cathedral tower by night and there hears one of the most favorable signs, the cry of a rook within sight of a river. The victim must have no gold upon him; and Edwin's watch and tiepin have been removed, although evidently not the engagement ring, which Jasper did not know he was carrying.

All these details there can be no doubt Dickens must have known. He was personally acquainted with Captain Meadows Taylor, a British officer the Government had employed in the suppression of the Thugs, who in 1839 had written a book, *Confessions of a Thug*. In Paris, Dickens had met Eugène Sue, whose *The Wandering Jew* has among its characters a Thug strangler. He had published in *All the Year Round*, in 1868, Collins's *The Moonstone*, which deals with a secret murder committed in England by a band of Hindu devotees; and during 1869 there was being published James de Mille's *Cord and Creese*, in which there is an Englishman connected with the Thugs.[21]

It is probable that mesmerism, too, was intended to play a part in *Edwin Drood*. When Minor Canon Crisparkle finds himself at the weir, without knowing why he came there, looking fixedly at the glint that turns out to be Edwin Drood's jewelry, again without knowing what made him glance there, it is implied to have been a magnetic suggestion from Jasper that sent him. Jasper's influence over the frightened Rosa so closely approaches the hypnotic that ultimately she flees from him to her lawyer-guardian in London. When Jasper "strikes a note, or a chord," on the piano, Rosa tells Helena Landless, "he himself is in the sounds, whispering that he pursues me as a lover, and commanding me to keep his secret. I avoid his eyes, but he forces me to see them without looking at them. Even when a glaze comes over them . . . and he seems to wander away into a frightful sort of dream in which he threatens most, he obliges me to know it, and to know that he is sitting close at my side, more terrible to me than ever." [22]

But Jasper does not terrify Helena. When asked if she would not be afraid of him too, under similar circumstances, she responds scornfully, "Not under any circumstances." [23] The "slumbering gleam of fire" in her "intense dark eyes" suggests that she is one of whom Jasper had best beware: "Let whomsoever it most concerned look to it!" [24] Devoted to her brother, on whom Jasper seeks to fasten the crime, touched by Rosa's timid affection, already antagonistic to Jasper, Helena's masterful will may turn the tables and mesmerize the mesmerist, eliciting from him, "as if told of another," all the deeds he has done in his drugged second state. Some such denouement seems foreshadowed by an early passage in the book, suggesting that in a way found "in some states of drunkenness, and in others of animal magnetism, there are two states of consciousness that never clash, but each of which pursues its separate course as though it were continuous instead of broken (thus, if I hide my watch when I am drunk, I must be drunk again before I can remember where) . . ." [25]

There are probably "two states of consciousness" in Jasper; certainly he is at war within himself and a man of dreadful passions. In the garden scene, where he at last speaks his love for Rosa, his voice and vehemence are those of Bradley Headstone: "Rosa, even when my dear boy was affianced to you, I loved you madly; even when I thought his happiness in having you for his wife was certain, I loved you madly; . . . even when he gave me the picture of your lovely face so carelessly traduced by him, which I feigned to hang always in my sight for his sake, but worshipped in torment for years, I loved you madly; in the distasteful work of the day, in the wakeful misery of the night, girded by sordid realities, or wandering through Paradises and Hells of visions into which I rushed, carrying your image in my arms, I loved you madly." [26]

To Rosa this speech is a gross hyprocisy which makes her forget her fear in indignation. "How beautiful you are!" he responds. "You are more beautiful in anger than in repose. I don't ask for your love; give me yourself and your hatred; give me yourself and that pretty rage; give me yourself and that enchanting scorn; it will be enough for me." [27] "There is my past and my present wasted life. There is the desolation of my heart and my soul. There is my peace; there is my despair. Stamp them into the dust; so that you take me, were it even mortally hating me!" [28]

Jasper repeats with frightful intensity the agony of frustrated love Dickens had put into each book he had written since the time of *A Tale of Two Cities* and *Great Expectations*. Rosa Bud and Helena Landless echo in divided and inverted forms the two heroines of *Our Mutual Friend*. Rosa shares with Bella her teasing, coaxing, half-petulant charm, and both have Ellen Ternan's fair-haired prettiness. But Jasper feels for her the same painful infatuation Bradley Headstone did for Lizzie Hexam. And as Lizzie unintentionally drew the schoolmaster to his ruin, Helena Landless is prefigured as the Choirmaster's nemesis—Helena Landless, the very syllables of whose name evoke those of Ellen Lawless. Originally Dickens had intended to call her Olympia Heyridge or Heyfort,[29] but he could not banish from his mind reverberations of Ellen's name. Is Helena more than a name?— is that defiant something in her between a crouch and a bound, is that foreshadowed struggle of wills between her and Jasper, a transmuted version of a struggle Dickens had known?

And what of Jasper, with his strange mesmeric power and his fierce longing for the delicate Rosa Bud, who shrinks from him in terror? Like George Silverman, who believed himself to be a wronged and misunderstood man, Jasper poses the problem of what are the truths in the abysses of a man's heart. He becomes a dark rendering of elements his creator has felt within himself. Seen in one light, Jasper is deeply suspect. In another, perhaps, he is a man misjudged, not guilty after all, or, at the very least, a man for whom there are explanations or extenuations not taken into account. And more profoundly still, there is a possibility that Jasper may be the projection of a dilemma Dickens had partly symbolized in *Hard Times*: the position of the artist and his relation to Victorian society.

In Jasper's dreams, visions of oriental splendor mingle with the rook-haunted towers of gray cathedrals. His outwardly staid life is darkened by a life of inward rebellion, in which he sinks down into the filth of the Ratcliffe Highway and ascends to the skies in the musical aspiration of his art. He has disguised himself as a sober choirmaster, just as Dickens appears on the surface a responsible middle-class citizen, but he burns with the fiercest and most violent passions. In the everyday world he, the artist, is a secret misfit, but is it he or that world which is in the wrong? Since the time of Plato the judgment of the world has again and again branded him as evil, but there is another realm, and another vision, in which he is a good and faithful servant. Is the artist a traitor in society's midst, a subverter of its moral standards, or is he a heroic rebel fighting its corruptions, its moldering values, its charnel decay?

Certainly this vision of a dead world lies heavy and brooding over *Edwin Drood*. Forster thought this last book "quite free from the social criticism which grew more biting as Dickens had grown older," [30] but apparently he did not perceive the criticism implicit in its pictures of a crumbling Cloisterham sinking into the dry rot of the dead past. That past, however, is linked to the present in ways no less sinister than those Dickens had seen extending from the Dedlocks and the Tite Barnacles to the Dombeys and Bounderbys and Gradgrinds and Merdles. Deep below the surface, the old forces of privilege and exploitation, which dominated the business and industrial world, had swollen out in a far-flung entanglement of occidental aggression swallowing up the remotest regions of the globe. It is not only the London docks and slums, the smoke-blackened cities of the north, that are strangled in its coils, but India, Egypt, China, the victims of the opium trade, subject peoples, everywhere, falling prey to a greedy imperialism.

Young Drood mouths the catchwords of that imperialism in their most infuriating form. He is "Going to wake up Egypt a little," he says patronizingly.[31] Like any acquisitive materialist, he is condescending about the life of reflective thought. "Reading?" he asks with a trace of contempt. "No. Doing, working, engineering." [32] He talks with insolent and insular contempt of other races. "Pooh, pooh," he sneers to the dark-skinned Neville Landless. "You may know a black common fellow . . . but you are no judge of white men." [33] His words briefly epitomize the whole vainglorious gospel of backward races and the white man's mission.

Instead, therefore, of abandoning the analysis of society, Dickens has deepened it, for he has sensed the extension of the struggle to take in the entire world. Despite its somnolent air of peace, behind Cloisterham lurk all those inhumanities he has spent his life in fighting, grown more monstrous than ever as they threaten now a dark resentful conflict of East and West. Felt more as subtle undercurrents than as sharply defined issues, they breed poisonously in the squalor of stale streets and miserable courts festering off the East India Docks. As personal antagonisms they well up in Drood's race-proud superiority, in Neville Landless's rancor against him, in Helena's hostility to Jasper, and in Opium Sal's malignant fist shaken behind the Cathedral pillar. And just as in the London of *Our Mutual Friend*, all industrial England, though unseen, is sensed in the shadows beyond the slums of Whitechapel and Millbank—the coal mines, the looms of Manchester, the lead mills, the iron foundries, and the potteries— so, in *Edwin Drood*, the shrunken symbols of authority—Mr. Sapsea the Mayor of Cloisterham, the Dean of the Cathedral, the overbearing philanthropist Honeythunder—reveal the insolvency of the institutions for which they stand.

The Mayor of Cloisterham, who is also its leading estate agent, represents both the outlook of its businessmen and the pompous conceit of officialdom. He exemplifies in the moribund world of this provincial backwater the same values that are at work in Lombard Street, Westminster, and Whitehall. The town's chief magistrate, he is easily blinded by any adroit manipulator, and serves Dickens as the instrument for a last fling at the law. "It is not enough that Justice should be morally certain," the egregious old fool observes sententiously; "she must be immorally certain—legally, that is." "His Honour reminds me," Datchery says respectfully, "of the nature of the law. Immoral. How true!" [34]

The smooth, time-serving timidity of the Dean of the Cathedral is morally lower than Sapsea's imbecility. Disturbed by the mere unproved suspicion against Neville Landless, "The days of taking sanctuary are past," he tells Mr. Crisparkle. "This young man must not take sanctuary among us." He has rejected the merciful teachings of his church for a cautious conformity. The clergy, he says, must not "be partisans. Not partisans. We clergy must keep our hearts warm and our heads cool, and we hold a judicious middle course" and "do nothing emphatically." [35]

Honeythunder, however, with his bellowing and intolerant reformatory zeal, is nothing if not emphatic. Love and good works in him are only catchword pretexts for a truculent violence. "Though it was not literally true, as was facetiously charged against him by public unbelievers," Dickens remarks, "that he called aloud to his fellow-creatures, 'Curse your souls and bodies, come here and be blessed!' still his philanthropy was of that gunpowdery sort that the difference between it and animosity was hard to determine." [36] All dissent from his dogmas he tries to bluster down by abuse and distorted misrepresentation. As Sapsea embodies a valedictory jibe at administrative authority, Honeythunder is Dickens's final thrust at Sir Andrew Agnew and the rabid would-be legislators of public virtue. With the Dean, they form a striking secular trinity: the regnant jackass enthroned between the spiritual trimmer and the bigot of reform.

There is no hope for society in the forces represented by these three. But, as always, Dickens's trust is not in the official or self-appointed powers of church and state; it is in the health of human nature itself. And even here in Cloisterham, despite its atmosphere of mortality and the deadly passions seething below its sleepy surface, that vitality is latent. It dwells in the honesty and courage of Mr. Crisparkle, in the awkward rectitude of Mr. Grewgious, in the mysterious operations of Datchery; in Rosa's impulsive warmth of feeling, Neville Landless's quick responsiveness, and Helena's fiery devotion. All these breathe the promise of final victory. Like the gardens of Cloisterham, growing from the graves of abbots and abbesses, this world of graves will again bring forth life. Brought to a burning focus of concealed struggle through the forms of this murder allegory, Dickens portrayed for the last time the fundamental antagonisms and the fundamental problems of his world. And here for the last time he reaffirmed his fundamental creed: his belief in the generous loyalties and affections of the human spirit.

*   *   *   *

Dickens's whole career and achievement, indeed, were singularly consistent. Though he grew and developed, he never lost the living sympathies that lie at the heart of his greatness. Those sympathies were rooted in an almost endless relish for the richness and variety of life and of human nature, a love of experience that exulted in the pure vividness with which things are themselves. Dickens liked and disliked people; he was never merely indifferent. He loved and laughed and derided and despised and hated; he never patronized or sniffed. He could be desperately unhappy; he was never only bored. He had no fastidious shrinkings, no snobberies, no dogmatic rejections.

These are the qualities that give his world such intensity. He was as fascinated by the decaying cabbage-stalks of Covent Garden, or by the fishy smell of Mr. Peggotty's outhouse where crabs and lobsters never left off pinching one another, as he was by the Cratchits' goose in its hissing hot gravy. The grime and foul gutters of Saffron Hill interested him as much as the clowns and spangle-skirted bareback riders of Astley's Circus, the hemp and tangled masts of Limehouse Hole, the shadowy rafters of Westminster Hall, the salt reaches of Cooling Marsh, the dripping urns of Chesney Wold, Boffin's dust-heaps, and the polluted air of the Old Bailey. He was not repelled by a lively scoundrel like Mr. Jingle or revolted by Jo's malodorous body and verminous rags; he felt no scorn for chuckleheaded Mr. Toots or the shabby and bibulous Newman Noggs; even for the merry and black-hearted Fagin in his greasy thieves' kitchen Dickens had a gleam of sympathy.

In his comprehensive delight in all experience Dickens resembles Walt Whitman, but he was innocent of that nebulous transcendental-ism that blurred Whitman's universe into vast misty panoramas and left him, for all his huge democratic vistas, unable to tell a story or paint a single concrete human being. Dickens saw the brilliant indi-vidual quality of each person and experience in its comic or pathetic or dramatic essence, and in so doing he surprisingly realized Walter Pater's aspiration toward "a life of constant and eager observation." [37] Though he burned with a warm and tender, rather than a "hard, gem-like flame," surely Dickens far more than Pater vibrated with the very pulsations "of a variegated, dramatic life." [38] If he fell short of Pater's exquisite sensibility in the rendering of nuance, his grasp was the more muscular because he was vigorously free from the strangulated refine-ment that made Pater a chambered aesthetic nautilus quivering away in his shell from all contact with coarseness and vulgarity. It is the welter of existence that Dickens embraced, not a delicately selected part of it.

But for all the enthusiasm with which he welcomed the multiplicity of experience, Dickens did not fail in a just discrimination of black and white. His very sympathy with life's thronging variety made him stern to whatever impoverished and destroyed. From the hypocritical Stiggins in *Pickwick* to the bullying Honeythunder in *Edwin Drood*, he abominated those who sought to reduce it to a dispirited gray or to subordinate others to their own desire for power. He hated the gloomy and ferocious self-righteousness of the Murdstones. He derided the woolly-mindedness of Mrs. Jellyby, neglecting the poor of London's slums and even her own family while she worried about the natives of Borioboola-Gha, and detested the domineering presumption of Mrs. Pardiggle, pushing her way into the cottages of the poor with useless and arrogant advice. He saw England plundered by Boodle and Coodle, controlled by the landed aristocracy of Sir Leicester Dedlock, the selfish commercialism of Mr. Dombey, the industrial greed of Mr. Bounderby, and the slippery financial machinations of Mr. Merdle; and helplessly obstructed by the Circumlocution Office, while Mr. Gradgrind sifted the ashes of the national dust-heap and formulated the dogmas of political economy. Meanwhile, he beheld with loathing how this dreadful structure of iniquity and suffering spawned a host of lesser parasites, vermin, and beasts of prey, the Fagins, Bumbles, Artful Dodgers, Fangs, Squeerses, Hawks, Tiggs, Slymes, Pecksniffs, Scrooges, Smallweeds, Vholeses, Casbys, Barnacles, Weggs, Lammles, and Fledgebys, all sucking or bludgeoning their own advantage out of their victims.

Not primarily a systematic thinker, but a man of feeling, intuitive and emotional, Dickens had nevertheless a sharp intelligence which pierced through the complexities of the social scene to a comprehension of its shocking realities that was essentially true. His instinctive sympathy with the fruitful and creative enabled him to see how the generous potentialities of human nature were crippled, and he felt his way step by step to a realization of the forces that blighted men's health and happiness. As a young reporter, he watched the landowners resisting to the last ditch the abolition of the rotten boroughs. As a mature man he saw the slum landlords rack-renting their tenants and breeding the cholera by their determination not to spend a penny on sanitary improvement, observed the factory owners mutilating their workers with unfenced machinery, heard them screaming that they would be ruined by a ten-hour day and a living wage. He could put two and two together, and he did. By the time he had reached the middle of his career he understood capitalist industrialism at least as well as most nineteenth-century political economists.

He understood it with unwavering hostility. Every book he produced was not only a celebration of the true wealth of life; it was an attack on the forces of cruelty and selfishness. His heart seized the sword of a sharp and witty logic that slashed contemptuously through innumerable varieties of logical humbug and rationalist special pleading. He had no patience with statistical abstractions and economic theories that ignored the welfare of flesh-and-blood human beings, or with metaphysical systems remote from the hopes and fears of the human heart. Unlike so many of the lovers of humanity who are bitterly unable to love human beings, it was not an abstract humanity constructed in his mind that Dickens loved, but men, women, and children, with all their frailties and absurdities. His hatreds sprang full-armed out of that love.

His weapons were those of caricature and burlesque, of melodrama and unrestrained sentiment. But whether he poured out operatic harmonies of tears or wielded a slapstick whistling through the air and landing with a loud whack, his exaggerations serve mainly to focus a brilliant light of truth upon a squirming absurdity or a vice plausibly disguised as a virtue, to magnify the diseased tissue until its corruption is glaringly obvious. Bernard Shaw, who derived much of his satiric technique from Dickens, explained that his own method was to find the right things to say and then say them with the utmost exaggeration and levity. That is almost precisely the procedure of Dickens. He fought foolishness and evil by exaggerating their excesses. He painted monomania and sophistry in colors of lurid absurdity. He belabored dogmatism and bigotry with fantastic ridicule. Every form of fanatical extremism he attacked with the wildest hyperbole. In a passion of glorious violence he defended the golden mean.

His moderation seems a paradox only because of the gigantic extravagance with which it is presented. Pecksniff is grotesque, but there is nothing immoderate about the judgment on hypocrisy he symbolizes. Bounderby is grotesque, but he might easily be a spokesman for any number of modern organizations of businessmen. Dickens nowhere suggests abolishing business enterprise or individual wealth, but he saw with indignation how incessantly they abused their power. Therefore, though he was well aware of the red tape and inefficiency of government agencies, no fear of "centralization" prevented him from demanding that the Government regulate industry and protect the public from private greed.

The same balance animates his stand at every turn. His delighted descriptions of eating and drinking involve no defense of gorging or drunkenness. Between the fat boy's sluggish and slow-witted gluttony and Scrooge's glum huddle over a solitary bowl of gruel, is not Dickens's position clear? He does not suggest that at Christmas dinner the Cratchits stuffed themselves to torpor or became maudlin on punch. Dickens knew the horrors of alcoholism among the poor but sharply repudiated the intolerant teetotalism of the temperance reformers. The true causes of habitual drunkenness, he insisted, were poverty, misery, and dirt, and they were not cured by forbidding a bottle at the family board. He bitterly opposed the puritanical moralists who grudged the poor any amusements in their laborious lives; he loved to see working people enjoying themselves at the circus and in the theaters. He denounced the gloomy Sabbatarians who fumed piously at Sunday picnics and wanted to close the museums on the one day of leisure the poor had. It is not his views that are bizarre, only his inordinate imagery.

His insistence on weighing everything in terms of human welfare shaped his responses to all the intellectual currents of his time. So strongly did it mold his feelings that commentators as varied as Dean Inge and Bernard Shaw have claimed he was unaware of the cultural upheavals of the nineteenth century and indifferent to all its fierce revivals and revolutionary movements in art, in philosophy, in science, in social theory, and in religion. Shaw quotes Inge's remark that "the number of great subjects in which Dickens took no interest whatever is amazing." [39] But the generalization is far too sweeping. Dickens was himself a revolutionary movement in the art of literature, and had strong and considered judgments on its practice. Except for philosophy, of which he knew little, he was fully alert to the developments of the age, and was at least as well informed as most educated men, not excluding men of letters.

In the realm of music, it is true, his background hardly extended beyond romantic songs, comic ditties, and the old English ballad-operas, which he liked better than he did the Italian opera. He makes no mention of either symphonic or chamber music, and there is no indication that he ever heard of Wagner, but he relished "jolly little Polkas and Quadrilles," [40] and liked Auber's *Masaniello* and *Fra Diavolo*. From the time of his residence in Paris in 1855, and perhaps even from that of his earlier stay in 1846, he enjoyed the opera there, loved *Il Trovatore* and the *Barber of Seville*, and was deeply moved by Gounod's *Faust* and Gluck's *Orpheus*.[41] His daughter Mary testified that he was enchanted by Joachim's playing on the violin, and that he was fond of Mendelssohn's *Lieder* and of Mozart and Chopin.[42]

He had no training in the fine arts, and his responses to Italian art and architecture were not unusually perceptive, but they were vivid and untrammeled. Although at first he derided the Pre-Raphaelites, and wrote an article of sneering mockery about Millais's controversial *Christ in the Carpenter Shop*, he later became an admiring friend of Millais and of Holman Hunt.[43] The Parisian Independent Exhibition of 1855 revealed tremendous further strides in his development; he saw that Ingres, Corot, Manet, Courbet, and Degas left most contemporary English painting in the shade. In comparison with their fearlessness, their bold drawing, their dashing conception, their passion and action, he thought, how timid and conventional seemed his own friends Maclise, Egg, Ward, Frith, and Stanfield.[44]

Of classical literature he knew little and showed hardly the slightest influence. But he knew the entire range of English prose fiction, from Bunyan and Defoe through Swift, Fielding, Richardson, Smollett, Sterne, and Goldsmith, to Cooper, Irving, and Scott. He had a broad knowledge of the drama, from Shakespeare, Jonson, and their fellow Elizabethans, through Congreve, Sheridan, and all the comic playwrights, down to an almost endless number of nineteenth-century comedies and farces. He knew Addison and Steele, Goldsmith's essays, and Aubrey's *Brief Lives*; he loved Pepys's *Diary* and Boswell's *Johnson*. From childhood on he had devoured books of travel and exploration. Wegg's farcical stumblings through the pitfalls of "The Decline and Fall-off the Rooshan Empire," in *Our Mutual Friend*, show that Dickens had a more than superficial if not entirely reverential acquaintance with Gibbon, and among the historians he had also read Macaulay, Carlyle, and Buckle. He deeply admired Cobbett, De Quincey, and Landor; Sydney Smith's *Lectures on Moral Philosophy* was one of his favorite books.[45] He was among the earliest to realize the genius of Browning and Tennyson; he published some of the poems of the young Meredith and praised his *Shaving of Shagpat*; he stimulated the literary career of Mrs. Gaskell; he hailed the very first published fiction of George Eliot as already a work of noble fulfillment. If he did not really care much for the writings of Thackeray and

Anthony Trollope, he always spoke well of them. Almost his last words to one of the companions who saw him sail from America on the *Russia* were a tribute to Matthew Arnold.[46] Among the French writers of his own time, he knew and admired Chateaubriand, Lamartine, Dumas, and Hugo; he was on terms of intimacy with the leading Parisian dramatists. *Household Words* was one of the first English periodicals to praise Turgenev, and Dickens himself had seven volumes of Turgenev's work, in French and English, on the shelves of his library at Gad's Hill.[47]

Dicken's interest in science was reflected less in his writing than in the pages of *Household Words* and *All the Year Round*, both of which were full of articles devoted to the clear and vivid explanation of scientific invention and discovery. Many of these were concerned with the practical applications of science in technology, agriculture, and industry, but an appreciable number dealt with scientific theory. Faraday's lectures on chemistry and physics inspired a series of pieces in *Household Words*. Darwin's *Origin of Species,* which startled so many dovecotes in nineteenth-century thought, was greeted in *All the Year Round* with an article of lucid and respectful exposition calling attention to the far-reaching implications of its theory.[48] The "dreadful hammers" of the geologists clinking away at "every cadence of the Bible phrases," [49] that so distressed Ruskin, had no terrors for Dickens. He read Lyell's *Antiquity of Man,* and calmly ranged himself with Colenso's demonstration that the Pentateuch and the Book of Joshua could not be considered reliable scientific documents.

The full range of any writer's knowledge is seldom mirrored in his books. Some of what fascinates his mind lights no fires beneath those crucibles in which the work of imaginative creation is fused. The poets like Lucretius, Goethe, and Shelley, the novelists like Melville, Dostoevski, and Mann, who are directly inspired by philosophy or science or religion, who strive to incorporate into the cosmos of their work everything that they know, are not the only representatives of literary greatness. Keats shared some of the noble political enthusiasms of his friend Leigh Hunt, but these are seldom the subjects of his poems. The novels of Henry James, save possibly *The Princess Casamassima,* show small concern with the thronging problems of modern industrialism. Whatever concern Shakespeare and a host of other great and lesser literary figures felt for Dean Inge's "great subjects" is indirect and implicit rather than a deliberate and conscious preoccupation.

Seen in this light, Dickens is more conspicuous for the scope of his interests than for their paucity. Though his religious views are imaged only by implication in most of his works, he was sharply concerned with the role of the churches in society. Inclining toward Unitarianism, he had little respect for mystical religious dogma. He hated the Roman Catholic Church, "that curse upon the world," [50] as the tool and coadjutor of oppression throughout Europe. But it was the social and political affiliations of its organization that he fought, not its religious faith. He was so far from being antagonistic to individual Catholics that Clarkson Stanfield and Percy Fitzgerald, both members of that church, were among his closest friends and he had even hoped that his daughter Mary would marry Fitzgerald. The Oxford Movement he despised as an endeavor to revive candles, incense, and all the ornate flimflam of ritualism in England. He applauded the disestablishment of the Irish Church, and believed that ultimately the same course would be forced upon the Church of England.[51] That church, too, he saw as hand in glove with privilege, riddled by nepotism and politics, but crippled by the strength of the dissenting sects. Many of these, however, with their gloomy zeal, their arid creeds, and their antagonism to everything warm and genial in life, he disliked even more than the Established Church. From the ranting pulpit-thumper of *Sunday Under Three Heads* through the gloomy cruelty of the Murdstones and the Old Testament vindictiveness of Mrs. Clennam, he never ceased girding at the bleak self-righteousness and the uncharitable distortion of true benevolence he found in them.

This same spirit animated his feelings about philanthropy and social reform. He could not bear the blind zealots who were more concerned with propagating the Gospel in foreign parts than with helping the victims of poverty and ignorance at home. Vigorously active in philanthropy himself, he consistently satirized those who distorted it into a disguised means of gratifying their own greed for power. His own ideas had been strongly influenced by Benthamism, he had written for the *Examiner*, one of the chief organs of the utilitarians, and he shared many of their aims of radical reform, but he refused to substitute abstract theory for the actual welfare of human beings. No doctrinaire utilitarianism could persuade him to offer up living sacri-

fices on the altar of political economy. Nothing could make him believe that industry would be ruined unless labor was enslaved to an
iron law of wage. He insisted that when men worked long hours in
dangerous or unsanitary surroundings for earnings so small that they
and their families were half starved, something could and must be
done. He insisted that they had a right to light, air, water for drinking
and washing, education, and leisure and enjoyment in their lives.

The obstacle to these goals, he saw, was privilege, and the fact that
government and law were tools of privilege; and he passionately called
on England's ruling classes to set their house in order lest the day
come when violence and disorder sweep them away. He did not believe
that they were all so cruel and selfish as to be utterly callous to human
sufferir 3. He knew that there were landowners and members of the
nobility with warm hearts, merchants capable of a noble generosity,
industrialists earnestly desirous of ameliorating the conditions in
mines and factories. But even these were so caught in the complex web
of the economic system that there was little that they could do as individuals; and the great body of all these groups, he saw, were so blind
and so immersed in retention and acquisition that nothing but shame,
fear, or force would make them yield a fraction of an inch. He therefore called upon the working class to make the weight of its numbers
felt and insist that legislators be elected who would amend the injustices of society.

In that society and its political structure he came finally to have no
faith whatever. Only when the voice of the people was heard might
representative institutions cease to be an utter failure and become instruments of good. But when representative institutions ignored the
people and represented only their exploiters, when wealth dominated
all the proceedings of the legislative body and class prejudice insisted
that the poor must be "kept in their places," elective governments were
only puppets manipulated by the real but hidden rulers, as he had de-
picted them in *Bleak House* and *Little Dorrit*. Under these circumstances, corruption proliferated everywhere, rival forces of privilege
fought each other, each branch and department of the Government
became a hotbed of special interests, each bureau itself became a special interest obstructing outside interference with elaborations of red
tape like the Circumlocution Office.

Two such different critics as Chesterton and Shaw have paid tribute to the social and political insight with which Dickens portrayed modern society. The Circumlocution Office, said Chesterton, is a complete picture of the way England is actually governed at this moment." [52] And Shaw notes: "If Dickens's day as a sentimental romancer is over, his day as a social prophet and social critic is only dawning. Thackeray's England is gone, Trollope's England is gone; and even Thackeray and Trollope mixed with their truth a considerable alloy of what the governing classes liked to imagine they were, and yet never quite succeeded in being. But Dickens's England, the England of Barnacle and Stiltstalking and Hamlet's Aunt, invaded and overwhelmed by Merdle and Veneering and Fledgeby, with Mr. Gradgrind theorizing and Mr. Bounderby bullying in the provinces, is revealing itself in every day's news, as the real England we live in." [53]

All these things Dickens saw as clearly and despised as bitterly as Carlyle, but unlike Carlyle he did not call upon an aristocratic elite or a divine dictator hero to step in, sweep representative institutions aside, and establish a benevolent despotism. Instead, he called upon the people to assert and save themselves. He saw red at the snobberies that, after making education almost a class monopoly, then sneered at the masses as ignorant and brutish. Far from fearing the results of the Reform Bill of 1867, he believed the newly enfranchised masses would take their electoral responsibilities more seriously and discharge them more wisely than most of those who distrusted them. "My faith in the people governing," he said in 1869, "is, on the whole, infinitesimal; my faith in the People governed is, on the whole, illimitable." [54]

Even at the time there were commentators who tried to twist this declaration into something equivocal, as if Dickens's meaning were that he believed not in the people governing themselves but in their being governed by others. Aside from the fact that Dickens was temperamentally incapable of any such tricky word manipulation, he himself, in a speech only a few months later, clearly denied that interpretation. Quoting Buckle's *History of Civilization in England*, he restated his meaning: "They may talk as they will about reforms which Government has introduced and improvements to be expected from legislation, but whoever will take a wider and more commanding view of human affairs, will soon discover that such hopes are chimerical. They will learn that law-givers are nearly always the obstructors of society instead of its helpers, and that in the extremely few cases where their measures have turned out well, their success has been owing to the fact that, contrary to their usual custom, they have implicitly obeyed the spirit of their time, and have been—as they always should be—the mere servants of the people, to whose wishes they are bound to give a public and legal sanction." [55] It was the people, not their governors, whom Dickens trusted, and the people that he wished to see rule.

They represented Dickens's only real hope for the world. He had no panacea to solve all problems. In his own day he worked piecemeal within limited areas for every particular improvement that seemed to him attainable. Though he understood how external circumstance could twist and ruin men's lives, and hoped to make the opportunities for human fulfillment available on the widest scale, he was not an economic determinist and did not believe that people were only the products of environment. Though he saw that government agencies were corrupted by powerful influences, he did not believe that it was an intrinsic defect in the potentiality of government. He never ceased to demand that government continually remake itself into the instrument of human welfare. Unlike those who worry about "creeping socialism," he was no opponent of centralization. But he was not an abstract theorist. He never formulated any blueprints of systematic social reform or any constitution for the ideal political state. Instead of trying to elaborate the entire machinery for the improvement of the world, he sought to portray its human goals. He was "an independent Dickensian, a sort of unphilosophic Radical," [56] who spoke for the hopes of mankind.

Those aims are implicit in the hosts of living people crowding the great panorama of his pages. What writer except Shakespeare has created a larger and more various world or one more rich with the pulsing truth of actuality? If there are novelists whose characters are more subtly realized than those of Dickens, whose creations have a more intricate psychological complexity, there are none whose characters have more vitality or are truer to humanity at its core. His method, to be sure, is neither the enormous and elaborate complexity of Shakespeare and Tolstoy nor the psychological analysis so differently exemplified by Stendhal and Dostoevski. The contrast between Dickens and such writers as these is essentially the same as that painted by Lytton Strachey in a brilliant antithesis of Shakespeare and Molière:

"The English dramatist shows his persons to us in the round; innumerable facets flash out quality after quality; the subtlest and most elusive shades of temperament are indicated; until at last the whole being takes shape before us, endowed with what seems to be the very complexity and mystery of life itself. Entirely different is the great Frenchman's way. Instead of expanding, he deliberately narrows his view; he seizes upon two or three salient qualities in a character and then uses all his art to impress them indelibly upon our minds. His Harpagon is a miser, and he is old—and that is all we know about him: how singularly limited a presentment compared with Shakespeare's bitter, proud, avaricious, vindictive, sensitive, and almost pathetic Jew!" In Tartuffe, Strachey continues, there is the same sharp limitation to essentials. "He displays three qualities, and three only— religious hypocrisy, lasciviousness, and the love of power; and there is not a word that he utters which is not impregnated with one or all of these. Beside the vast elaboration of a Falstaff, he seems, at first sight, hardly more solid than some astounding silhouette; yet—such was the power and intensity of Molière's art—the more we look, the more difficult we shall find it to be certain that Tartuffe is a less tremendous creation even than Falstaff himself." [57]

Such was Dickens's method, too, and in Fagin and Pecksniff, in Uriah Heep and Squeers, it achieves its own astounding triumphs. But with that English exuberance Dickens has in common with Jonson and the comic dramatists of the Restoration, he does not restrict himself to Molière's stripped classical structure. With inordinate gusto, he returns to Micawber again and again, perpetually renewing our joy in recognizing a character that under innumerable variations in circumstance is always richly itself. Like the recurrent themes in a symphony, Dickens's people appear and reappear, David's Dora always pattering her childish-pathetic tinkle of keys, Mr. Bounderby sounding his bombastic brass, Miss Flite or Gridley or Captain Cuttle or Mr. Toots being themselves. But Mr. Dorrit and Pip are there too, reminding us that these figures are not always simple, that they are capable of psychological complexity, that they even change and develop.

To certain readers, however, they seem unreal, vivid perhaps, enormously entertaining, but mere caricatures rather than people. E. M. Forster calls them "flat" characters, and is vaguely worried by the feeling that in consequence they ought to be merely mechanical and Dickens's vision of humanity shallow. Even in the midst of this attack, however, he uneasily recognizes their "wonderful feeling of human depth" and admits Dickens's greatness.[58] It may be argued that no character in literature is ever more than a selection of representative qualities from among the infinite number that constitute the whole of any actual human being, hence that all literary portraits are really a kind of caricature, with omission and exaggeration a part of their very nature, and their appearance of "reality" a victory of their art. Nor does mere accumulation of detail automatically produce greater reality; there are caricatures that in a dozen strokes achieve a truer likeness than the most elaborate portraits. There is no need, however, of resorting to any such mere defense. Santayana hits the very heart of the issue in a direct attack:

"When people say that Dickens exaggerates," he writes, "it seems to me they can have no eyes and no ears. They probably have only *notions* of what things and people are; they accept them conventionally, at their diplomatic value. Their minds run on in the region of discourse, where there are masks only and no faces, ideas and no facts; they have little sense for those living grimaces that play from moment to moment upon the countenance of the world." When Dickens slashes through the convention, the human ego protests. " 'What a bad mirror,' it exclaims; 'it must be concave or convex; for surely I never looked like that. Mere caricature, farce, and horse play. Dickens exaggerates; *I* never was so sentimental as that; *I* never saw anything so dreadful; *I* don't believe there were ever any people like Quilp, or Squeers, or Serjeant Buzfuz.' But the polite world is lying; there *are* such people; we are such people ourselves in our true moments, in our veritable impulses; but we are careful to stifle and hide those moments from ourselves and from the world; to purse and pucker ourselves into the mask of our conventional personality; and so simpering, we profess that it is very coarse and inartistic of Dickens to undo our life's work for us in an instant, and remind us of what we are." [59]

The courage that gave Dickens "a true vision of the world" and the kindness that made it predominantly a comic one, Santayana points

out, also account for his gusto in piling up reiterative detail to mountainous heights that distress shrinking delicacy as overemphatic; "he
mimics things to the full; he dilates and exhausts and repeats; he
wallows. He is too intent on the passing experience to look over his
shoulder, and consider whether we have not already understood, and
had enough. He is not thinking of us; he is obeying the impulse of
the passion, the person, or the story he is enacting. This faculty,
which renders him a consummate comedian, is just what alienated him
from a later generation in which people of taste were aesthetes and virtuous people were higher snobs; they wanted a mincing art, and he
gave them copious improvisation, they wanted analysis and development, and he gave them absolute comedy." 60

Only in his earlier days, however, was his art one of improvisation;
he became a conscientious literary craftsman painstaking to the minut-
est detail of style and structure. He had, to be sure, no such general
theory of the aesthetics of the novel as Flaubert and James agonized
to exemplify in their work. But he took his aims with as much earnestness as they did theirs, and strove to perfect a narrative technique
that should never call attention to the devices whereby the reader was
prepared for each development in the story, but was unobtrusively put
in possession of all that he needed to know in order to make every
sequence appear spontaneous and inevitable. Only on the surface does
he have affinities with naturalism; deep below, he is vibrant with
poetic undertones, pregnant with the weighted symbols of allegory,
dwelling often within the dark and mysterious region of myth. If he
sometimes overworks certain devices of style, like his notorious tendency to fall into iambics in moments of emotion, and his excessive use
of rhetorical repetition, at his best he is dazzling in verbal brilliance,
coruscating in comedy, and, if anything, exorbitant in his ingenuity
of plotting. *Bleak House, Little Dorrit,* and *Our Mutual Friend,* all
masterpieces of his maturity, are dark and tremendous symphonic
structures almost epic in magnitude and impressiveness.

But amid the torrential plenty of Dickens's creation it is almost
invidious to single out individual novels for special praise. *Pickwick*
is an inspired improvisation almost throughout, and even in the hasty
and sometimes careless work of *The Old Curiosity Shop* there are
brilliances that the toil of other writers could not achieve. "He is, by
the pure force of genius," Shaw summarized it, "one of the greatest

writers of the world. . . . There is no 'greatest book' of Dickens; all his books form one great life-work: a Bible in fact . . . all are magnificent." [61]

Few of the world's great novelists surpass him in vitality and scope. In the thousands of pages of his works he paints the thronging complexity of nineteenth-century society with a range, solidity, and panoramic inclusiveness equaled only by Balzac. He was Dostoevski's master; for *Crime and Punishment* and *The Brothers Karamazov*, though far greater books than *Barnaby Rudge* and *Martin Chuzzlewit*, are tremendously indebted to their studies of murderers and rebels against society. But with John Jasper, in 1870, Dickens was approaching those dark and tangled labyrinths of alienation that Dostoevski explored in Raskolnikov, whose very name means dissenter. And although there is a kind of twisted comedy in Dostoevski, he cannot come within measurable distance of Dickens's high-spirited and irresistible vivacity. There, indeed, even the great humorists, even Rabelais, Voltaire, and Fielding, must bow to him. "We must go back for anything like it to the very greatest comic poets, to Shakespeare or to Aristophanes." [62]

Charles Dickens, said his adoring friend James T. Fields, was "the *cheerfullest* man of his age." [63] But Fields did not see beneath the surface and did not realize that the cheerful demeanor, the courageous faith, were as much achievements as they were the sparkling gifts of temperament. The *Pickwick* sun had risen out of the darkness of the prison and the blacking warehouse, not out of the radiance of a cloudless childhood. And the resolute belief in life and in humanity that Dickens maintained was a banner that he held high in spite of all the evils he saw in society, and in spite of the gathering clouds of personal misery that shadowed his later years. Dickens carried his distresses in his heart, not upon his lips. In middle age, like his middle-aged hero Clennam, he would not be so weak and cowardly as to hold that because a happiness had not come his way or worked well for him, "therefore it was not in the great scheme, but was reducible, when found in appearance, to the basest elements. A disappointed mind he had, but a mind too firm and healthy for such unwholesome air. Leaving himself in the dark, it could rise into the light, seeing it shine on others, and hailing it." [64]

Dickens himself refused to remain in the darkness. Over and over again, though with increasing weariness and difficulty, he beat back the shadows. Out of his sympathy and indignation at men's sufferings, he built up a picture of society and its failures, of the obstacles to the harmonious fulfillment of human needs, that is unsurpassed for clarity and understanding. Out of his own life of struggle and frustration, he wrought a philosophy of dauntless and generous courage that could laugh while it fought and struck its mighty blows for mankind. He was one of the heroes of art, not merely battling the unpastured dragons of life's waste, but enriching and creating a world. When Keats was near the point of death, "Perhaps," he was heard to say, "I may be among the English poets after my death." Matthew Arnold gave the world's reply: "He is; he is with Shakespeare." [65] Of what English novelist can that be said except Charles Dickens?

CHAPTER FIVE

The Narrow Bed

THE summer and mild autumn days following Dickens's breakdown passed swiftly and quietly. It was the Indian summer of his life. During the mornings he worked in the chalet on the book his hand would leave unfinished. In the sunny afternoons he strolled among the trees and rhododendrons of Cobham Park, or ruminated in straw hat and velvet jacket along Rochester High Street, through the old gatehouse into the green Cathedral close, and thence past the quaint old houses of Minor Canon Row.[1]

His health was still uncertain, but he was in cheerful spirits. Teasing his friend Fields's mania for antiques, he pretended to have found for him a decrepit chair without a bottom, "very ugly and wormy," of which it was claimed that "on one occasion Washington declined to sit down in it." [2] He had made further improvements at Gad's Hill, each one "positively the last," and now watched with pleasure the growth of his limes and chestnuts. Indoors, there was a new staircase with a parquet floor on the first landing. October saw the beginning of a conservatory, "glass and iron," opening from both the drawing room and the dining room, "brilliant but expensive, with foundations as of an ancient Roman work of horrible solidity." [3] "You are not expected to admire," he wrote Macready, "but there *is* a conservatory building at this moment—be still my soul!" [4]

Recently, Percy Fitzgerald had married a little charmer whose pretty face and engaging prattle everyone declared to be delightfully like David Copperfield's Dora. Although Dickens had once hoped that Mary might fall in love with Fitzgerald, he was enchanted by the young bride. Forster too proclaimed himself captivated, and was her most obstreperous slave. Prevented by illness from attending one of her little dinner parties, he sent Dickens a note of mock warning: "I can't join you today. But mark you this, sir! No tampering, no poaching on *my* grounds; for I won't have it. Recollect *Codlin's the friend not Short!*" With a twinkling eye Dickens read this note aloud to his host and hostess. " 'Codlin's the friend not Short,' " he repeated in a tone of seeming wonder. "What can he mean? What do you make of it?" Fitzgerald knew quite well, as did his wife, who stood there smiling and fluttered, but both felt it awkward to admit; they could only agree "that Forster at times was perfectly 'amazing.' " Keeping up his joke of pretended ignorance, "I think," Dickens concluded, "he is a little mad." [5]

Christmas Dickens spent at Gad's Hill. His left foot was again painful, and he sat in the library all day having it poulticed; at dinner it rested bandaged on a chair.[6] But he was feeling pleased: Harry had done so well at Cambridge that the family confidently expected him to win a fellowship. Shortly after the new year, Dickens entered him at the Temple, where he was to take the first steps toward the successful career he later pursued at the bar.[7] Dickens was also looking forward excitedly to the last twelve readings, which would, in some degree at least, make up for the twenty-six canceled by his breakdown the previous spring. Partly to cut out the railway traveling he would otherwise have to do between Gad's Hill and London, and partly for Mary's sake, he rented the Milner Gibson house at 5 Hyde Park Place, just opposite the Marble Arch, from January to the 1st of June.[8] New Year's Eve he spent at Forster's, where his old friend, none too well himself, was troubled by observing that Dickens's left foot and left hand both gave him pain. Dickens, however, made light of his uncertainties of touch and tread, and read the second installment of *Edwin Drood* with such overflowing humor that Forster forgot his worry in enjoyment and enthusiastically pronounced the number "a clincher." [9]

On January 6th, as President of the Birmingham and Midland Institute, Dickens awarded the prizes and certificates won by its most successful students. He seized the occasion to reaffirm his declaration of the preceding fall that he had "very little faith in the people who govern us," but that he had "great confidence in the People whom they govern." [10] Severely shaken by the railway journey and the fatigue of these ceremonies, he returned to London for his last appearances as a reader.[11]

He began at St. James's Hall on the evening of January 11th. Throughout most of the remainder of that month he was to read twice a week, on Tuesdays and Fridays, and thereafter once a week until March 15th. Two of his performances were scheduled for afternoons, and there was a morning one given at the request of actors and actresses, who could not come later in the day.[12] Dickens's family and friends feared he might break down again under the strain, but in the face of his determination they could do nothing except see that instant help was available in case of need. Dr. Frank Beard came to every reading,[13] and he privately bespoke Charley's attendance as well. "I have had some steps put up at the side of the platform," he told him. "You must be there every night, and if you see your father falter in the least, you must run and catch him and bring him off to me, or, by Heaven, he'll die before them all." [14]

David Copperfield and the "Trial," on the opening night, went "with the greatest brilliancy." [15] But afterward Beard found that Dickens's pulse had gone from its normal 72 to 95. From that night on, it rose ominously. Even before the first "Murder" reading, on the morning of the 21st, his fermenting anticipation raised it to 90; at the end it was 112, and even fifteen minutes later had descended only to 100.[16] Dickens was so prostrated that he could not get back his breath for some time and meanwhile, as he said himself, the "express image" of a man who had lost a fight. But the pretty actresses in his audience delighted him with their rapture; he was thrilled that even those professional observers who were bent on watching how he achieved his effects were carried out of themselves.[17] Two days later, when he saw Carlyle for the last time, his arm was once more in a sling.[18]

Nevertheless, he went on, his pulse rising to 114—to 118—to 124.[19] During intermissions he had to be helped into his retiring room and laid on a sofa; fully ten minutes would pass before he could speak a rational or consecutive sentence. Then he would swallow a wineglassful of weak brandy and water and rush back on the platform. Throughout February his hand never ceased to be swollen and painful. As he wiped the readings out one by one his feverish excitement and bodily pain grew ever greater.[20]

His audiences, however, were almost hysterical with enthusiasm. A boy whose father was a friend of Dickens brought him to one of the *Pickwick* readings, where they sat in the front row, and the youngster laughed, roared, wept, and howled; "I must have been a terrible nuisance to Dickens," he said in later years, "for I was at his feet, and at least twice I remember very distinctly he looked at me, I am sure with the idea of having me removed." On their left, however, they were wedged in by a fat man who roared even louder, and he *couldn't* be removed. At the end, stepping down to speak to the father, Dickens looked quizzically at the boy, "but he gave me a friendly tap or pat of forgiveness on the head." [21]

As the suicidal ordeals drew to their close, Dickens's energies were visibly exhausted. During one of the last three readings Charley noticed that he was unable to articulate "Pickwick" correctly, "calling it 'Pickswick,' 'Picnic,' 'Peckwicks,'" and "all sorts of names except the right one, with a comical glance of surprise" at friends in the front row.[22] On the last evening of all he read the *Christmas Carol* and the "Trial." An audience of over two thousand, cramming the hall to capacity, gave him a tumultuous ovation that made the glittering chandeliers vibrate.[23] Dickens's granddaughter, little Mekitty, had been brought for the first time that night to hear him read, and she was frightened by the apparition of her "Wenerables" as a terrible and unfamiliar figure a long way off "speaking in unknown voices." And, worst of all, came "the dreadful moment when he *cried*." [24]

He had been called back to the platform at the end by thunders of applause, and looked tremulously at his audience, striving to speak, while tears rolled down his cheeks. It was the end. These clamors that had meant so much to him were sounding in his ears for the last time; this ferment of excitement which for twelve years had filled so much of his life, which had often been almost all his life, would soon be irrevocably over. With effort he restrained himself sufficiently to say the words of appreciation and love on which he had determined. His voice was controlled, but weighted with emotion.[25] "From these garish lights," he concluded, "I now vanish forevermore, with a heart-felt, grateful, respectful, affectionate farewell." [26] Mournfully he limped from the stage, only to be recalled again by repeated demonstrations. His cheeks still wet, he kissed his hand, and then walked off for the last time.[27]

All told, the paid readings had numbered 423, including 111 given under the management of Arthur Smith, 70 under Thomas Headland, and 242 under Dolby. Dickens had no exact record of his net profits under Smith and Headland, but he always estimated them at about £12,000. Under Dolby he cleared nearly £33,000. The impressive total of £45,000 represented an average of more than £100 a reading and amounted to almost half of the £93,000 that proved to be the value of his estate when he died.[28]

But the great sum was bought at more than a dear sacrifice of health; it was at the cost of life itself. In melancholy inversion of one of those legendary bards at whose singing palaces and towers rose in the enchanted air, Dickens's voice had been sinking his grave. His reckless and burning energy hardly more than veils a weariness almost indistinguishable from that which Macaulay expressed in his journal shortly before he died: "A month more of such days as I have been passing of late would make me impatient to get to my narrow little crib, like a weary factory child." [29] Despite the sparkling face Dickens still turned on the world, the warehouse child that time had so transformed was hastening to his rest.

* * * * *

Though the readings were over, his impetuosity continued, working, walking, hurrying excitedly. There were invitations to dinners, invitations to speak at public functions, an invitation to Buckingham Palace from the Queen. Not long since, Dickens had chanced to show some American Civil War photographs to Arthur Helps, the Clerk of the Privy Council, and Helps in turn had mentioned them to the Queen. At her request, Dickens had sent them for her to look at, and presently Helps brought a message that the Queen would like to thank him in person.[30] Formally responding that he would be "proud and happy to wait upon Her Majesty," Dickens also sent Helps a facetious little note pretending to believe that he was about to be made a baronet. "We will have 'Of Gad's Hill Place' attached to the title of the Baronetcy, please—on account of the divine William and Falstaff," he wrote jestingly. "With this stipulation, my blessing and forgiveness are enclosed." [31]

The meeting took place shortly after the middle of March. Court etiquette did not allow Dickens to sit down, but Victoria herself remained standing throughout the entire hour and a half of their interview, leaning over the back of a sofa. Gracious though the gesture was, she could do so with less strain than if she had been an ailing man with a swollen foot. Under like circumstances the preceding year, Carlyle had bluntly announced that he was a feeble old man and helped himself to a chair. But except in private surroundings Dickens's pride would have driven him to collapse before he would have yielded to an infirmity.

The forty-year-old widow who confronted him was as changed from the breathless girl who had delighted in dancing all night as Dickens was from the wildly spirited young writer who had roamed the terrace and Long Walk at Windsor vowing himself madly in love with her. She regretted, the Queen said politely, that she had never heard one of the readings. He too was sorry, Dickens replied, but they were now finally over. He could not give a private reading, he told her; he considered a mixed audience essential to success. The Queen agreed that it would be inconsistent for him to alter his decision, quietly adding that she knew him to be the most consistent of men. Perhaps she was remembering his firm refusal to wait upon her in his farce dress, after the performance of *The Frozen Deep*. She then made some complimentary references to her pleasure in seeing that play; they talked of his American trip, the servant problem, and the high cost of food. At the close of the interview, the Queen presented him with an autographed copy of her *Journal of Our Life in the Highlands* and asked for a set of his works. She would like, if possible, she remarked, to have them that afternoon. Dickens begged for time to have the books suitably bound, and later sent her a set in red morocco and gold.[32]

Little more than a week later Dickens was bidden to Her Majesty's next levee,[33] which he attended, making merry with Dolby beforehand over his court dress and joking about whether he should wear his cocked hat "fore and aft" or "th'wart ships." [34] Dickens sent the Queen the first number of *Edwin Drood*, which was to be published on March 31st, and offered, if she "should ever be sufficiently interested in the tale to desire to know a little more of it in advance of her subjects," to send advance copies of its further installments.[35] Soon after, Mary was presented to the Queen. Later still, in May, Dickens was invited to dinner at Lord Houghton's to meet the Prince of Wales and the King of the Belgians. He was by this time so lame again that he could not ascend the staircase to meet the company, and had to be helped immediately into the dining room.[36] All these events, and possibly a circulation of his little joke about a baronetcy, gave rise to rumors that he was to be made a member of the Privy Council, even offered a peerage. "You will probably have read before now," he wrote a correspondent, "that I am going to be everything the Queen can make me. If my authority be worth anything believe on it that I am going to be nothing but what I am, and that includes my being as long as I live,—Your faithful and heartily obliged, Charles Dickens." [37] He had already won for himself, in fact, every significant distinction he could possibly possess.

His bodily health continued to give reason for alarm. Less than a week after the last reading, he confessed to Forster that once more, walking along Oxford Street, he had found himself unable to read more than the right-hand halves of the names over the shops. [38] Other grave symptoms presented themselves, although as usual he tried to make light of them. "My uneasiness and hemorrhage, after having quite left me, as I supposed, has come back with an aggravated irritability that it has not yet displayed. You have no idea what a state I am in today from a violent rush of it; and yet it has not the slightest effect on my general health that I know of." [39]

Nevertheless, Dickens went his way undeterred. On Forster's birthday he dined with his old friend at Palace Gate, [40] and three nights later presided and spoke at the dinner of the Newsvendors' Institution. [41] On April 7th he gave a reception at Hyde Park Place for all his friends. Joachim performed on the violin, and there were songs by Cummings, the eminent tenor, and Santley, the famous baritone. [42] Dickens was everywhere, his face a little strained and worn, but genial and smiling. Toward suppertime, Fitzgerald's wife stopped him as he flitted by, saying, "Mr. Dickens, you have passed me constantly during the night and have never *once* stopped to speak to me." He threw up his hands in horror. "Good gracious! N-n-o? You *don't* tell me so? Then let us make up for it at once, and go downstairs together to supper!" At the table he was gay, chatting vivaciously, pulling paper crackers, and exclaiming over one of the favors, a green fan of tissue-paper, which she carried away as a souvenir. [43]

At the same time, Dickens went on toiling as hard as ever. The first number of Edwin Drood had "*very, very far outstripped every one of its predecessors,*" and he labored to make the numbers that should follow no less successful. [44] "For the last week," he reported, as he drew near the completion of the fifth number, "I have been most perseveringly and ding-dong-doggedly at work, making headway but slowly. The spring always has a restless influence over me; and I weary, at any season, of this London dining-out beyond expression; and I yearn for the country again." [45] As he limped to the office of *All the Year Round* one morning, with bent back and at a snail's pace, oaken staff in hand, he was seen by a son of Douglas Jerrold, who hardly recognized him, so deep were the lines in his face and so much more nearly white was his grizzled hair.[46]

Luckily, Charley had taken good hold of his work on the magazine, and was able to relieve Dickens now of all the routine that Wills had once performed. At the end of April, indeed, his father formally installed him as subeditor.[47] It seemed to Dickens that his eldest son had at last found something for which he was fitted. Though it was clear that he was not gifted as a businessman, Dickens evidently thought he had some elements of literary taste, and might do well as editor. A month and a half later, by a codicil to his will, Dickens left Charley all his share and interest in the publication.[48]

On April 27th Dickens heard with sorrow of the death of his old friend Daniel Maclise.[49] "It has been only after great difficulty, and after hardening and steeling myself to the subject by at once thinking of it and avoiding it in a strange way," he wrote Forster, "that I have been able to get any command over it or over myself." [50] Maclise's solitary ways had kept them apart for long years, but Dickens had never ceased to be fond of him. At the Royal Academy dinner on May 2nd, Dickens paid tribute to his friend's memory. "The gentlest and most modest of men, the freshest as to his generous appreciation of young aspirants, and the frankest and largest-hearted as to his peers," no artist, Dickens said, "ever went to his rest leaving a golden memory more pure from dross, or having devoted himself with a truer chivalry to the art goddess whom he worshipped." [51] Only a few weeks later, stout, good-hearted Mark Lemon died, and Dickens was at once gladdened and grieved to remember that he and Lemon had embraced affectionately over Stanfield's grave.[52]

His foot was by now a source of distress that would "yield to nothing but days of fomentation and horizontal rest." [53] "Last night," he wrote Georgina on May 11th, "I got a good night's rest under the influence of Laudanum but it hangs about me very heavily today. I have had the poultices constantly changed, hot and hot, day and night . . ." [54] On the 16th the foot was "a mere bag of pain." [55] The following evening, despite having "viciously bubbled and blistered it in all directions," [56] he was unable to go with Mary to the Queen's Ball, to which they had both been invited.[57]

Deep within his consciousness he must have known that the end was near. Receiving a young girl with literary aspirations whom Lord Lytton had sent to him, he spoke of his habits of publication while his work was still in progress. "But suppose," she said diffidently, "suppose you died before all the book was written?" "Ah-h!" he said, and paused. "That has occurred to me at times." His long, future-piercing gaze seemed to her to be penetrating golden veils. Then, looking at her kindly, he said cheerfully, "One can only work on, you know—work while it is day." [58]

Forster saw him for the last time on May 22nd. Not long before, an admirer had written Dickens from Liverpool, describing himself as a self-raised man, attributing his prosperous career to what he had learned of kindness and sympathy from Dickens's writings, and asking in gratitude that Dickens accept an enclosed check for £500. Dickens refused the gift, but replied that he would be glad to accept any small memorial in some other form. Presently there arrived a silver basket, and a silver centerpiece designed to portray Spring, Summer, and Autumn. The giver explained that he desired to connect Dickens "with none save the brighter and milder days." "I never look at it," Dickens told Forster, "that I don't think most of the Winter." The gift, Forster mournfully observed, foreshadowed that season which Dickens was never again to see.[59]

Throughout all the month of May the pace of his engagements had never slackened. Gladstone, the Prime Minister, invited him to breakfast; he dined with John Lothrop Motley and Disraeli at Lord Stanhope's.[60] He met Arthur Stanley, the Dean of Westminster, at Frederick Locker-Lampson's, and a little later dined at Stanley's with the Russells, the Clarendons, and Connop Thirlwall, the Bishop of St. David's, who had been, with Mill and Macaulay, among the three child-prodigies of the age.[61] He attended the theater with Lady Molesworth and Lord Redesdale, and was so full of droll thoughts tumbling out one after another that he kept himself and his companions "laughing at the majesty of his own absurdities"; his talk, Lord Redesdale said, "had all the sparkle of champagne." [62]

It was almost the last flare of that delight in the theater that had burned brightly throughout Dickens's entire life. Walking with a friend only a short time before, Dickens had paused in the shadow of Westminster Abbey and asked, "What do you think would be the realization of one of my most cherished day-dreams?" Without waiting for a reply, he instantly continued that it would be to "hold supreme authority" in the direction of a great theater, with "a skilled and noble company." "The pieces acted should be dealt with according to my pleasure, and touched up here and there in obedience to my own judgment; the players as well as the plays being absolutely under my command. That," he ended, laughing, and glowing at the fancy, *"that's* my day-dream!" [63]

Toward the end of May he took charge of some private theatricals being given by his London neighbors, Mr. and Mrs. Freake, at Cromwell House. Mary and Katey were among the actors and Millais painted the scenery. Dickens rehearsed the company daily, brilliantly showing them how to do all the parts, from the "old man" to the "young lover." He had meant to take a role himself but was prevented by his lameness. Though June 2nd, the night of the production, was a stifling one, he acted as stage manager, ringing all the bells, working all the lights, and between these activities sitting in the prompter's corner.[64]

Dolby had been with him at the office that very afternoon. Rising to leave, and extending his hand across the table at which they had been sitting, Dolby was shocked by the pain mirrored in his Chief's face, and noticed that his eyes were suffused with tears. Throwing off his emotion, Dickens also rose. Grasping Dolby's hand, and looking him full in the face, instead of using the words "Good day" or "Good night," as he usually did, Dickens earnestly said, "Goodbye, Dolby, old man." [65]

*   *   *   *   *

On June 3rd he was back at Gad's Hill. The country was delicious with the foliage and flowers of early summer. Dickens rejoiced in his escape from London and "the preposterous endeavour to dine at preposterous hours and preposterous places." [66] On the suggestion of an actress friend, he had sent off for a "Voltaic Band" which he hoped might give some relief to his foot.[67] He was looking forward to uninterrupted morning hours among the leaves and mirrors and fresh scents of the chalet. But coming down on Saturday to spend the week-end, Katey was heavy-hearted to see him looking so worn. Dickens, however, was talkative and cheerful.[68] The new conservatory had been completed while he was in London, and he delighted in its perfumed brightness of massed blossoms. "Well, Katey," he exclaimed gaily, "you now see POSITIVELY the last improvement at Gad's Hill"; and they all laughed at the joke against himself.[69]

On Sunday Dickens seemed refreshed on returning from a quiet afternoon walk. When dinner was over, he and Katey remained sitting in the dining room to be near the flowers in the conservatory, while they listened to Mary singing in the drawing room. At eleven o'clock Mary and Georgina retired, but Dickens and Katey sat on, with the lamps turned low, enjoying the warm, sweet-scented summer air coming in through the open windows. He and his daughter talked long and affectionately. He wished, Dickens told her, that he had been "a better father, and a better man." Later he spoke of his hopes that he might make a success of *Edwin Drood*, "if, please God, I live to finish it." Katey looked startled: "I say *if*," Dickens told her, "because you know, my dear child, I have not been strong lately." It was three o'clock, and the summer dawn was creeping into the conservatory before they went upstairs and parted at his chamber door.

It was long before Katey slept. When she arose late in the morning, he had already gone to the chalet. She had to go up to London that morning, and would be unable to return to Gad's Hill until the following Saturday. But she felt uneasy about her father. Confiding in Mary and her aunt, she drew a promise from Georgina to write the next day with news of how he was. Knowing his dislike of partings, she was going only to leave her dear love for him without any farewell. As she waited on the porch for the carriage, however, she felt an uncontrollable impulse, and went down the tunnel, through the Shrubbery to the chalet, and climbed the stairs to the upper room.

"His head was bent low down over his work, and he turned an eager and rather flushed face towards me as I entered." Usually, Dickens merely raised his cheek for a kiss, "saying a few words, perhaps, in 'the little language'" he had used when his daughters were children, "but on this morning, when he saw me," Katey remembered, "he pushed his chair back from the writing table, opened his arms, and took me into them." She hurried back to the house, saying to herself, without knowing why, "I am so glad I went—I am so glad." [70]

In the afternoon Dickens walked with the dogs to mail some letters in Rochester. Tuesday morning, Mary left for a visit to Katey in London. Dickens felt tired, and only drove in the carriage to Cobham Wood with Georgina, where he strolled about under the trees of the park. That evening he strung some Chinese lanterns in the conservatory, and sat long with Georgina enjoying their shimmering illumination on the flowers. He was glad, he told her, at having finally abandoned London for Gad's Hill. Only a few days before, he had said that he wished his name to be more and more associated with this place while he lived, and repeated a hope he had often expressed before, that he might lie in the little Cathedral graveyard at the foot of the Castle wall when he died.[71]

On the 8th of June, in violation of his usual habits, he worked all day, returning to the house only for lunch, and then going directly back to the chalet to write again. The last page that he wrote there, among the dappled sunshine and shadow of the leaves, has a picture of a brilliant morning in Rochester: "Changes of glorious light from moving boughs, songs of birds, scents from gardens, woods, and fields —or, rather, from the one great garden of the whole cultivated island in its yielding time—penetrate the Cathedral, subdue its earthy odour, and preach of the Resurrection and the Life. The cold stone tombs of centuries ago grow warm; and flecks of brightness dart into the sternest marble corners of the building, fluttering there like wings." [72] The words, so serene and still elegiac, are a fitting valedictory to the exalted, laughing, despairing, tormented, and triumphant career.

He was late leaving the chalet, but in the study before dinner he wrote a few letters.[73] In one of them he quoted Friar Laurence's warning to Romeo: "These violent delights have violent ends." [74] It was true. Looking at him across the table, Georgina was alarmed by the expression of pain on his face. "For an hour," he told her, "he had been very ill." Nevertheless he desired dinner to go on. He made a few other random and disconnected remarks. Suddenly he said he had to go to London at once. Pushing back the crimson-damasked chair in which he had been sitting, he rose, but would have fallen where he stood if Georgina had not hurried around the table to support him. She tried to help him to a sofa. His body was too heavy for her strength, however, and after a slight struggle she was obliged to lower him to the floor, where he sank heavily on his left side. "On the ground," he murmured faintly.[75]

With the aid of the servants Georgina placed him on the sofa. She at once summoned a local surgeon, and dispatched telegrams to Mary and Katey and Dr. Beard. Charley also received a telegram instructing him to bring a London physician for consultation.[76] Mary and Katey arrived late that night with Frank Beard. It was judged safer not to move him, and all night he remained unconscious on the dining-room sofa. Early next morning Charley brought the London doctor. But nothing could be done. It was a paralytic stroke; an effusion of blood on the brain left no gleam of hope.[77] Katey was sent back to London to break the news to her mother, and returned that afternoon, when Ellen Ternan also came. All day Dickens's body lay, breathing heavily, in the bright dining room opening on the scarlet geraniums, musk, and blue lobelias in the conservatory.[78] The day was mild and the windows were wide. Katey and Charley sat outside on the steps, where the scent of syringa was heavy in the air. Afterward, Charley could never bear that flower near him.[79]

Just before six o'clock Dickens's breathing grew fainter. At ten minutes past that hour, he gave a deep sigh. His eyes were closed, but a tear welled from under his right eye and trickled down his cheek. Then he was gone.[80] "Like a weary factory child," he had sunk to his narrow bed. It was just four months and two days past his fifty-eighth birthday.

Charley went to the porch, where Mary Boyle had been sitting outside all afternoon in a hired carriage, and brought her in to gaze on the face of her adored friend.[81] When Harry arrived from Cambridge it was too late to see his father alive.[82] The following day, June 10th, came John Everett Millais, who made a pencil sketch of Dickens's bandaged head. With him he brought Thomas Woolner, the sculptor, for whom Dickens had promised to pose in December when *Edwin Drood* was finished. Woolner took a death mask from which he later modeled a bust. The deep lines and wrinkles, he said, had nearly faded from the face; Dickens looked calm and dignified.[83]

The news of Dickens's death flashed over the world, overwhelming men and women everywhere, in India, in Australia, in America, with incredulous sorrow.[84] "Dickens was so full of life that it did not seem possible he could die . . . ," Longfellow wrote Forster. "I never knew an author's death to cause such general mourning. It is no exaggeration to say that this whole country is stricken with grief." [85] "My pen trembles between my fingers," said a writer in the *Moniteur des Arts,* "at the thought of all we—his family—have just lost in Charles Dickens." [86] In Genoa, Mary Cowden Clarke read the telegraphed four words in an Italian newspaper, " '*Carlo Dickens è morto,*' and the sun seemed suddenly blotted out." [87] "The well of kindness" in him, exclaimed Blanchard Jerrold, "was open to mankind, and from it generations will drink: but it was never fathomed." [88]

"It is an event world-wide," Carlyle wrote Forster: "a *unique* of talents suddenly extinct, and has 'eclipsed' (we too may say) 'the harmless gaiety of nations.' No death since 1866"—the year his own wife died—"has fallen on me with such a stroke, no Literary Man's hitherto ever did. The good, the gentle, ever friendly noble Dickens— every inch of him an Honest Man!" [89] Put aside in gentleness and generous truth were all Carlyle's temptations to depreciate his devoted friend as a mere entertainer. And as he reflected longer—that prickly, fantastically prejudiced, yet sage and tender-hearted old man—he attained an insight more profound than he had ever voiced before. Beneath Dickens's "sparkling, clear, and sunny utterance," beneath his "bright and joyful sympathy with everything around him," Carlyle perceived, there were, "deeper than all, if one has the eye to see deep enough, dark, fateful silent elements, tragical to look upon, and hiding amid dazzling radiances as of the sun, the elements of death itself." [90]

The London *Times,* Dickens's one-time enemy, took the lead in demanding that his body be buried in Westminster Abbey. "Statesmen, men of science, philanthropists, the acknowledged benefactors of their race," it said editorially, "might pass away, and yet not leave the void which will be caused by the death of Dickens. . . . Indeed, such a position is attained by not even one man in an age. It needs an extraordinary combination of intellectual and moral qualities . . . before the world will consent to enthrone a man as their unassailable and enduring favourite. This is the position which Mr. Dickens has occupied with the English and also with the American public for the third of a century. . . . Westminster Abbey is the peculiar resting place of English literary genius; and among those whose sacred dust lies there, or whose names are recorded on the walls, very few are more worthy than Charles Dickens of such a home. Fewer still, we believe, will be regarded with more honour as time passes, and his greatness grows upon us." [91]

The Dean of Westminster sent a message through Locker-Lampson, who had introduced him to Dickens, that he was "prepared to receive any communication from the family respecting the burial." [92] They had already learned that the little graveyard at the foot of the Castle was closed to further burials. So were the churches of Cobham and Shorne, where Dickens had sometimes thought he would like to lie.[93] But the family had accepted an offer from the Dean and Chapter of Rochester to lay him to rest within the Cathedral itself, and a grave had been prepared in St. Mary's Chapel when Dean Stanley's letter came into their hands.[94] Forster and Charley went up to London to tell the Dean that the terms of Dickens's will bound them to an absolutely private and unannounced funeral. These instructions made impossible any ceremony of public homage. Dean Stanley, however, assured them that Dickens's wishes should be obeyed, and they yielded to the desire of the nation.[95]

At six o'clock on the morning of June 14th a plain coffin left Gad's Hill and was brought in a special train to Charing Cross. There it was removed to a hearse without feathers or any funereal trappings. Three coaches followed it to the Abbey. The first held those four of Dickens's children who were in England, Charley, Mary, Katey, and Harry. In the second were Georgina, Dickens's sister Letitia, Charley's wife, and John Forster. In the third were Frank Beard, Charles and Wilkie Collins, and Dickens's solicitor, Frederic Ouvry.

The bell of St. Stephen's was just sounding the half-hour after nine when the procession reached the entrance to the Dean's Yard. There were few people in the street, and the public had not been admitted to the Abbey. All was still as the little cortège swept round the Broad Sanctuary and drove under the archway. Then, a moment later, the great bell began tolling. Through the western cloister door the body was conveyed along the nave into the South Transept, the Poets' Corner. Here, the night before, a grave had been dug. In the peacefulness and silence of the shadowy arches the brief words of the burial service were said. There were no choristers, but at the end the organ sounded a Dead March.[96] Last to turn away, when all was over, was a burly man tightly buttoned up in a black frock coat, who could not trust himself to speak.

Outside, the day grew sultry, fiercely glowing, but it was cool and dim beneath the vast stone vaulting. Toward evening Percy Fitzgerald came to look on all that was visible now of his friend. Already the public had somehow come to know, and a great crowd was gathered in the transept about the narrow enclosure. Gazing down, Fitzgerald saw the polished oak coffin, with the plain inscription, CHARLES DICKENS. "There was a wreath of white roses lying on the flags at his feet, a great bank of ferns at his head, rows of white and red roses down the sides." [97]

"He sleeps as he should sleep," said an elegy in *Punch*—

> *"He sleeps as he should sleep—among the great*
> *In the old Abbey: sleeps amid the few*
> *Of England's famous thousands whose high state*
> *Is to lie with her monarchs—monarchs too." [98]*

Dean Stanley had given permission for the grave to be left open a few days, and even on that first day, before the afternoon papers bore the news, it had spread throughout the metropolis, and thousands came to pay the tribute of their hearts. Flowers were thrown upon the coffin, even single blossoms that had been worn in buttonhole or bosom, until the enclosure was heaped to overflowing. At six o'clock, when the Abbey closed, there were still a thousand outside who had not yet obtained admittance.[99] For two days more, while the grave remained open, the endless processions filed past, with tears and flowers innumerable. For many months after it was closed no day passed without still other mourners coming and leaving the Abbey floor around the great block of stone that bore Dickens's name a mound of fragrant color.

At dusk on June 16th, the Abbey was closed to the public. From Dean Stanley Lord Houghton heard that the grave would not be closed until near midnight. With a lantern for his only light, he came and was the last to look upon the coffin.[100] It lay at the foot of the grave of Handel, with that of Macaulay by its side. A few feet away lay Johnson, and not far on each side in the solemn darkness were the busts of Milton and Spenser and the monuments of Dryden, Chaucer, and Shakespeare.

More than eighty years have passed since Charles Dickens died. His passionate heart has long crumbled to dust. But the world he created shines with undying life, and the hearts of men still vibrate to his indignant anger, his love, his tears, his glorious laughter, and his triumphant faith in the dignity of man.

A NOTE ON THE GENEALOGICAL CHARTS

THE genealogical charts are collated from the following sources:

1) Mr. W. J. Carlton's researches into the Barrow family, reported in the *Dickensian*, Winter, 1949–50;

2) the genealogical researches of A. T. Butler and Arthur Campling into both the paternal and maternal ancestry of Dickens, as summarized by Mr. Leslie C. Staples in the *Dickensian*, Spring and Autumn, 1949;

3) Mr. T. W. Hill's charts based on these and other sources, in the *Dickensian*, Spring, 1951;

4) genealogical information about the Barrow family personally supplied me by Mr. Reginald F. R. Barrow; and

5) information about the descendants of Dickens's children gathered and personally communicated to me by the kindness of Mr. Leslie C. Staples. The sections dealing with the newest generations are not absolutely complete; it was not always possible for Mr. Staples to question Dickens's descendants, some of whom were strangers. He apprises me, lest readers suspect there may be an error, that there are two Danbys in the charts, one the second husband of Rosemary Shuckburgh, and the other, his brother, husband of her cousin Doris.

1. PATERNAL ANCESTRY OF CHARLES DICKENS

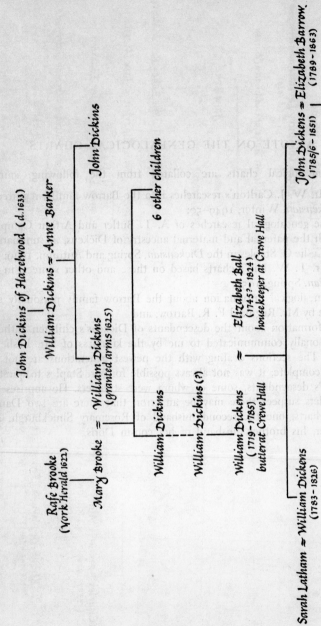

Rafe Brooke
(York Herald 1622)

Mary Brooke

John Dickins of Hazelwood (d.1633)

William Dickins = Anne Barker

William Dickins
(granted arms 1625)

John Dickins

William Dickins

William Dickins (?)

William Dickins
(1719–1785)
butler at Crewe Hall

= Elizabeth Ball
(1745?–1824)
housekeeper at Crewe Hall

6 other children

Sarah Latham = William Dickens
(1783–1826)

John Dickens = Elizabeth Barrow.
(1785/6–1851)   (1789–1863)

CHARLES DICKENS
(1812–1870)

2. MATERNAL ANCESTRY
of CHARLES DICKENS

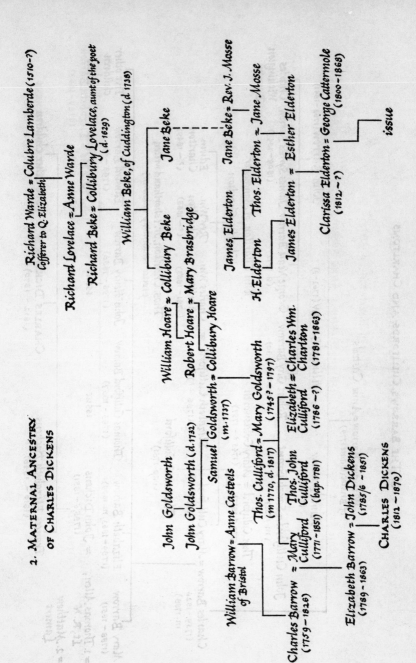

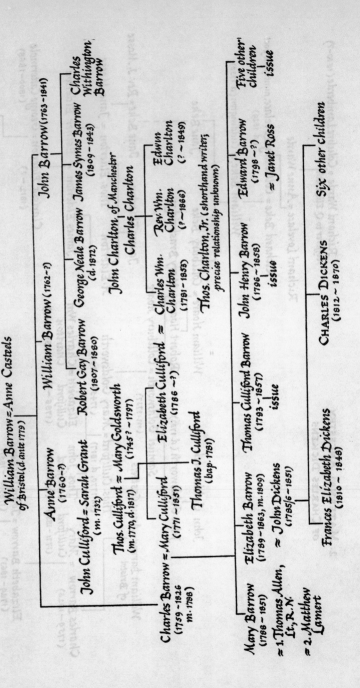

3. THE BARROWS, CULLIFORDS, AND CHARLTONS

William Barrow = Anne Castels
of Bristol (d. ante 1779)

- Anne Barrow (1760-?)
- William Barrow (1762-?)
- John Barrow (1763-1841)

John Culliford = Sarah Grant (m. 1732)

Robert Gay Barrow (1807-1880)

George Neale Barrow (d. 1872)

James Synnes Barrow (1809-1843)

Charles Withington Barrow

Thos. Culliford = Mary Goldsworth (m. 1770, d. 1817) (1745? - 1797)

John Charlton, of Manchester
Charles Charlton

Elizabeth Culliford (1786 - ?)

Charles Wm. Charlton (1791-1853) = Charles Wm. Charlton

Rev Wm. Charlton (? - 1866)

Edwin Charlton (? - 1849)

Charles Barrow = Mary Culliford (1759 - 1826) (1771 - 1851) m. 1788

Thomas J. Culliford (bap. 1781)

Thos. Charlton, Jr. (shorthand writer; precise relationship unknown)

Mary Barrow (1786 - 1851)
= 1. Thomas Allen, Lt., R.N.
= 2. Matthew Lamert

Elizabeth Barrow (1789 - 1863, m. 1809) = John Dickens (1785/6 - 1851)

Thomas Culliford Barrow (1793 - 1857) issue

John Henry Barrow (1796 - 1858) issue

Edward Barrow (1798 - ?) = Janet Ross

Five other children issue

Frances Elizabeth Dickens (1810 - 1848)

CHARLES DICKENS (1812 - 1870)

Six other children

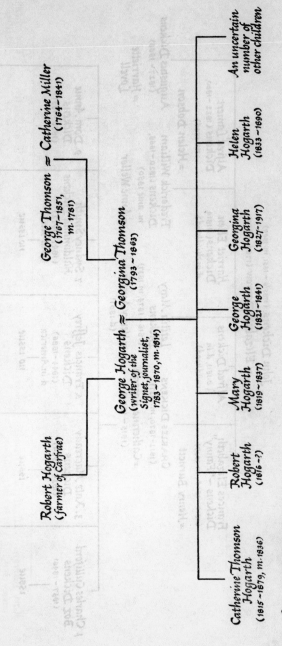

4. THE HOGARTH FAMILY

Robert Hogarth
(farmer of Carfrae)

George Thomson = Catherine Miller
(1767–1851,   (1764–1841)
m. 1781)

George Hogarth = Georgina Thomson
(writer of the   (1793–1863)
Signet, journalist,
1783–1870, m. 1814)

Catherine Thomson
Hogarth
(1815–1879, m. 1836)

=CHARLES DICKENS
(1812–1870)

Robert Hogarth
(1816–?)

Mary Hogarth
(1819–1837)

George Hogarth
(1821–1841)

Georgina Hogarth
(1827–1917)

Helen Hogarth
(1833–1890)

An uncertain
number of
other children

5. The Immediate Family of Charles Dickens

John Dickens (1785/6–1851, m. 1809)
= **Elizabeth Barrow** (1789–1863)

Frances Elizabeth Dickens – "Fanny" (1810–1848, m. 1837)
= Henry Burnett

Charles Dickens (1812–1870, m. 1837)
= Catherine Hogarth (1815–1879)

Alfred Dickens (b. 1813, d. in childhood)

Letitia Mary Dickens (1816–1874, m. 1837)
= Henry Austin (d. 1861)

Harriet Ellen Dickens (b. 1819, d. in childhood)

Frederick William Dickens (1820–1868, m. ante 1850)
= Anne Weller

Alfred Lamert Dickens (1822–1860, m. 1846)
= Helen Dobson

Augustus Dickens (1827–1866)
= Harriette Lovell

---

1. **Charles Culliford Boz Dickens** (1837–1896) — issue

2. **Mary Dickens** (1838–1896) — no issue

3. **Kate Macready Dickens** (1839–1929) — issue

4. **Walter Landor Dickens** (1841–1863) d. in India — no issue

5. **Francis Jeffrey Dickens** (1844–1886) d. in America — no issue

6. **Alfred Tennyson Dickens** (1845–1912) d. in America — issue

7. **Sydney Smith Haldimand Dickens** (1847–1872) d. at sea — no issue

8. **Henry Fielding Dickens** (1849–1933) — issue

9. **Dora Annie Dickens** (1850–1851)

10. **Edward Bulwer Lytton Dickens** (1852–1902) d. in Australia — no issue

6. CHARLES DICKENS'S DESCENDANTS (A)

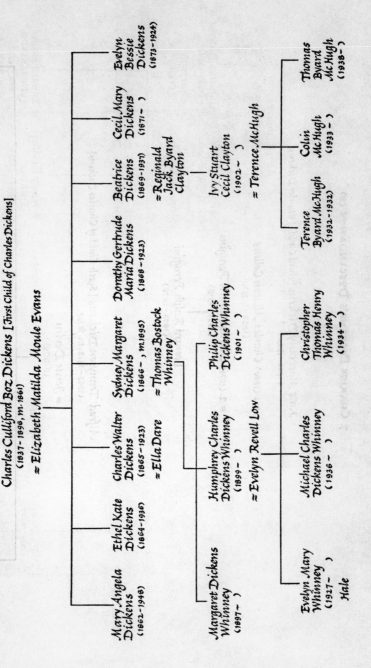

Charles Culliford Boz Dickens [First Child of Charles Dickens]
(1837–1896, m.1861)

= Elizabeth Matilda Moule Evans

Mary Angela Dickens (1862–1948)

Ethel Kate Dickens (1864–1936)

Charles Walter Dickens (1865–1923)
= Ella Dare

Sydney Margaret Dickens (1866– , m.1895)
= Thomas Bostock Whinney

Dorothy Gertrude Maria Dickens (1868–1923)

Beatrice Dickens (1869–1937)
= Reginald Jack Byard Clayton

Cecil Mary Dickens (1871–)

Evelyn Bessie Dickens (1873–1924)

Margaret Dickens Whinney (1897–)

Humphrey Charles Dickens Whinney (1899–)
= Evelyn Revell Low

Philip Charles Dickens Whinney (1901–)

Ivy Stuart Cecil Clayton (1902–)
= Terrence McHugh

Evelyn Mary Whinney (1927–)
Hale

Michael Charles Dickens Whinney (1936–)

Christopher Thomas Henry Whinney (1934–)

Terence Byard McHugh (1932–1932)

Colin McHugh (1933–)

Thomas Byard McHugh (1938–)

7. CHARLES DICKENS'S DESCENDANTS (B)

Kate Macready Dickens [Third Child of Charles Dickens]
(1839–1929)

≈ 1 (1860) Charles Allston Collins
(1828–1873)

≈ 2. (1874) Charles Edward Perugini
(1839–1918)

Leonard Ralph Perugini
(1875–1876)

Alfred Tennyson Dickens [Sixth Child of Charles Dickens]
(1845–1912, m. 1873)

= Jessie Devlin
(d. 1879)

Katherine Mary Dickens
(1874–1951)

Violet Dickens
(1876?–1952)

6 CHARLES DICKENS'S DESCENDANTS (A)

8. CHARLES DICKENS'S DESCENDANTS (c)

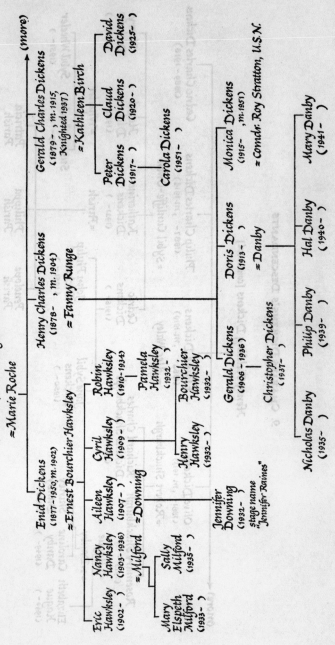

Henry Fielding Dickens [Eighth Child of Charles Dickens]
(1849–1933, m.1876, Knighted 1922)
= Marie Roche

(more)

Henry Charles Dickens
(1878– , m.1904)
= Fanny Range

Gerald Charles Dickens
(1879– , m.1915,
Knighted 1937)
= Kathleen Birch

Peter Dickens
(1917–)

Claud Dickens
(1920–)

David Dickens
(1925–)

Carola Dickens
(1951–)

Enid Dickens
(1877–1950, m.1902)
= Ernest Bourchier Hawksley

Nancy Hawksley
(1903–1936)
= Milford

Aileen Hawksley
(1907–)
= Downing

Cyril Hawksley
(1909–)

Robin Hawksley
(1910–1944)

Pamela Hawksley
(1932–)

Henry Hawksley
(1932–)

Bourchier Hawksley
(1932–)

Eric Hawksley
(1902–)

Mary Elspeth Milford
(1933–)

Sally Milford
(1935–)

Jennifer Downing
(1932–)
stage name
"Jennifer Raines"

Doris Dickens
(1913–)
= Danby

Gerald Dickens
(1906–1936)

Christopher Dickens
(1937–)

Monica Dickens
(1915– , m.1951)
= Comdr. Roy Stratton, U.S.N.

Nicholas Danby
(1935–)

Philip Danby
(1939–)

Hal Danby
(1940–)

Mary Danby
(1941–)

9. CHARLES DICKENS'S DESCENDANTS

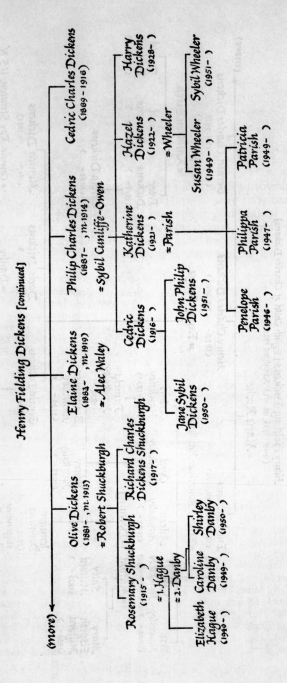

(more)

Notes

In abbreviating dates I have followed the American usage of giving month, day, and year: 1/20/56 for January 20, 1856. Dates later than the nineteenth century have the year in full: 10/27/1905. For the abbreviations used to identify quotations from or references to manuscript sources, the works of Dickens, and other printed books and articles, see the explanations in the three sections of the Bibliography.

PART SEVEN

Chapter 1 [pp. 589-606]

1. Macready, *Diaries*, 2/12/46.
2. Dickens says this, in fact, in a letter to an unknown correspondent, 2/24/46, of which I have a copy from Maurice Inman, Inc. "I have no connexion whatever with the active management of the Daily News, having subsided (as I always intended) into my old, and much better loved, pursuits."
3. *Coll. P.*, I, 39-43, "Crime and Education," *Daily News*, 2/4/46, 43-64, "Capital Punishment," *Daily News*, 3/9,13,16/46.
4. Ibid., 44-6.
5. Ibid., 47, 53-4.
6. Ibid., 58.
7. Ibid., 64.
8. Forster, 388.
9. *Let.*, I, 744, Forster, [4/?/46].
10. Ibid., Mme. De la Rue, 4/17/46.
11. Altick, Dickens to Poe, 3/19/46.
12. *Coll. P.*, II, 368-9, speech, 4/6/46.
13. Ibid., 369.
14. Ibid., 370.

15. Forster, 388.
16. *Let.*, I, 754, Jerrold, 5/26/46; Forster, 389.
17. Hunt. MS., Dickens to Mitton, "Tuesday," [5/?/46].
18. Forster, 388.
19. *Let.*, I, 754, Forster, 6/7/46.
20. Ibid.; Forster, 390.
21. Gummer, 8-9.
22. Forster, 391.
23. *Let.*, I, 755, Forster, 6/11/46.
24. Suzannet MS., Dickens to Maclise, 6/14/46.
25. *Let.*, I, 756, Forster, [6/?/46].
26. Morgan MS., Dickens to Miss Coutts, 6/25/46, incomplete in *Let.*, I, 758.
27. *Let.*, I, 757, Forster, 6/22/46.
28. Ibid., 756, [6/?/46].
29. Ibid., 757, 6/22/46.
30. Forster, 392.
31. Morgan MS., Dickens to Miss Coutts, 6/25/46. Before going to Italy Charley had first had a governess and then gone to school at St. John's Wood, where he returned as a day boarder on coming back to London. Miss Coutts had then asked Dickens to give her the pleasure of financing Charley's

education (Morgan MS., Dickens to Miss Coutts, 9/10/45). At that time, Dickens intended to send him to Marlborough, but later decided on Eton and King's College (Morgan MS., Dickens to Miss Coutts, 12/1/45, 8/30/49). In the spring, Dickens determined to wait until after the Swiss sojourn (Morgan MS., Dickens to Miss Coutts, 4/22/46).

32. Morgan MS., Dickens to Miss Coutts, 6/25/46, also in *Let.*, I, 758.
33. *Let.*, I, 757, Forster, 6/22/46.
34. Morgan MS., Dickens to Miss Coutts, 6/25/46, also in *Let.*, I, 759.
35. *Let.*, I, 760, Forster, 6/28/46. *The Life of Our Lord*, the children's version of the New Testament referred to, was completed in 1849. It was not intended for publication, and until 1937, when it at last saw print, existed in only two manuscripts, one of which had been made for the use of the Dickens children and the other given to the children of Mark Lemon. It is of very slight literary importance, but significant for its consistently Unitarian emphasis. It always refers to Joseph as Christ's father; instead of calling Jesus the Son of God the opening chapter has the angels tell the shepherds that "God will love him as his own son." No mention is made of the conception by the Holy Ghost or of Mary being a virgin. The entire stress is upon a nontheological reverence for Christ as a great spiritual teacher, not upon his divinity.
36. Ibid., 749-50, Miss Coutts, 5/26/46.
37. Ibid. The mark system which Dickens elaborated and put into practice when the Home was established was based, as he explains in this letter, upon a system devised by Captain Maconochie. There is a detailed table of marks in Dickens's autograph in the Morgan MSS., Dickens to Miss Coutts, 9/17/48. An accumulation of good marks was translated each month into a proportional sum of money credited to their earner.
38. Ibid., 751.
39. Ibid.
40. Ibid., 749-50.
41. Ibid., 752.
42. Ibid., 772, 7/25/46.
43. Ibid., 760, Forster, 6/28/46.
44. Ibid.
45. Forster, 402 fn.
46. *Let.*, I, 764, Forster, 7/5/46.
47. Ibid., 763.
48. Ibid., 757, 6/22/46.
49. Ibid., 758.
50. Ibid., 768, 7/15/46.
51. Ibid., 770, 7/25/46.
52. Ibid., 771.
53. Forster, 394-5.
54. *Let.*, I, 775-6, Forster, [8/?/46].
55. Ibid., 761-2, Chapman, 7/3/46.
56. Ibid., 593, Powell, 4/16/44.
57. *Dick.*, XLIII, 199.
58. *Let.*, I, 760-1, Chapman, 7/3/46.
59. Ibid., 768, Forster, 7/25/46.
60. Forster, 414 fn.
61. *Let.*, I, 778, Forster, 8/14/46.
62. Ibid., 781, 8/24/46.
63. Ibid., 793, 10/3/46, 796, 10/10/46.
64. Ibid., 784, Lever, 8/31/46.
65. Ibid., Mitton, 8/30/46.
66. Berg MS., Dickens to De la Rue, 8/17/46.
67. *Let.*, I, 822 fn.
68. Ibid., II, 117, Frederick Dickens, 9/3/48.
69. Forster, 396.
70. *Let.*, II, 495, Forster, [10/?/53].
71. Ibid., I, 765, 7/8/46.
72. Forster, 399.

73. *Let.*, I, 769-70, Forster, 7/25/46.
74. Ibid., 774, 8/2/46.
75. Ibid., 777, 8/11/46. But Forster, 474, gives the date as 8/14/46.
76. Ibid., 785-6, 9/6/46.
77. Ibid., 786.
78. Ibid., 776, 8/7/46.
79. Ibid., 778, 8/14/46. But Forster, 474, gives the date as 8/13/46.
80. Ibid., 777, 8/11/46. See note 75 above.
81. Ibid., 788, [9/?/46].
82. Ibid.
83. Ibid., 782-3, 8/30/46.
84. Ibid., 789-90, 9/20/46.
85. Ibid.
86. Ibid., 791, 9/26/46.
87. Ibid.
88. Ibid.
89. Ibid., 790, [9/?/46].
90. Ibid., 793, 10/3/46.
91. Ibid., 791, 9/26/46.
92. Ibid., 792, 9/30/46.
93. Ibid., 793, 10/1/46.
94. Ibid., 10/3/46.
95. Ibid., 799, 10/20/46.
96. Ibid., 798, Forster, 10/14/46. The wording of the second sentence quoted distinctly implies that the sales must have been well *over* the 30,000 Dickens had hoped, but there is no indication of how high they were.
97. Ibid., 809, 11/15/46.
98. Forster, 402.
99. *Let.*, I, 762-3, Forster, 7/5/46.
100. Ibid., 776-7, 8/9/46.
101. Suzannet MS., Dickens to Maclise, 6/14/46.
102. *Let.*, I, 778-9, Forster, [8/?/46].
103. Ibid., 797, 10/11/46.
104. Ibid., 798.
105. Ibid., 797.
106. Ibid., 802, Macready, 10/24/46.
107. Ibid., 799, Forster, 10/20/46.
108. Ibid., 802, Macready, 10/24/46.
109. Ibid., 807, Forster, 11/4/46.
110. Forster Coll., Dickens's notes, with *Dombey and Son* MS.
111. *Let.*, I, 807, Forster, 11/4/46.

Chapter 2 [pp. 607-625]

1. *Let.*, I, 810, Forster, 11/22/46.
2. Forster, 443.
3. *Let.*, I, 814, Watson, 11/27/46.
4. Ibid., 812, Forster, 11/26/46.
5. Ibid., 814, Watson, 11/27/46.
6. Ibid., 817, Forster, 11/29/46.
7. Ibid., 814, Watson, 11/27/46.
8. Ibid., 818-9, Forster, 11/30/46.
9. Ibid., 820, 12/6/46.
10. Ibid., Thompson, 12/2/46.
11. Ibid., Forster, 12/6/46.
12. Forster, 443.
13. *Let.*, I, 812, Forster, [11/?/46].
14. Ibid.
15. Forster, 445.
16. *Let.*, I, 818, Forster, 11/30/46.
17. Forster, 448-9.
18. Dexter, *Mr. and Mrs.*, 122, 12/19/46.
19. *Let.*, I, 811, Forster, 11/22/46.
20. Ibid., 809, [11/?/46].
21. Ray, II, 266, Thackeray to Edward Fitzgerald, [1/?/47].
22. Forster, 482 fn.
23. London *Times*, 1/2/47.
24. *Let.*, II, 3, Forster, 1/5/47.
25. Dexter, *Mr. and Mrs.*, 120-1, 12/19/46.
26. Ibid., 122.
27. Ibid., 124, 12/22/46.
28. *Let.*, I, 824, Forster, 12/31/46.
29. Ibid., II, 3, 1/5/47.
30. Ibid., 6, Lady Blessington, 1/24/47.
31. Ibid., 4, Miss Coutts, 1/18/47.
32. Ibid., 13, Forster, 2/10/47.
33. Forster, 482 fn.
34. Hodder, *Memories*, 277.
35. Forster, 481.
36. *Let.*, I, 795, Forster, 10/3/46.
37. Ibid., II, 6, Lady Blessington, 1/24/47.
38. Forster, 452.
39. *Let.*, II, 10, Tagart, 1/28/47.
40. Forster, 451.
41. *Let.*, II, 6, Lady Blessington, 1/24/47.
42. Forster, 452.

43. *Let.*, II, 6, Lady Blessington, 1/24/47.
44. Forster, 453.
45. *Let.*, I, 818, Forster, 11/30/46. Cf. Morgan MSS., Dickens to Miss Coutts, 9/10/45, 12/1/45, 4/22/46, 6/25/46, 8/30/49, all discussed in Part Seven, I, note 31. Charley was to be prepared for the British Army. See Morgan MS., Dickens to Miss Coutts, 12/6/49.
46. *Let.*, II, 12-3, Forster, 2/7,10/47.
47. Ibid., 16, 2/17/47.
48. Charles Dickens, Jr., *Reminiscences*, quoted by Pope-Hennessy, but there mistakenly dated as occurring in December.
49. Forster, 453.
50. *Let.*, II, 17 fn.
51. Forster, 453-4.
52. *Let.*, II, 17, Georgina Hogarth, 3/9/47.
53. Ibid., 20, Browne, 3/15/47.
54. Morgan MS., Dickens to Macready, 4/19/47.
55. Ibid., Dickens to Austin, 4/26/47.
56. *Let.*, II, 24, Robertson, 5/3/47.
57. Hunt. MS., Dickens to Macready, "Monday," [5/10/47].
58. *Let.*, II, 24, Robertson, 5/3/47.
59. Ray, II, 294 et seq., entire correspondence involving Thackeray, Forster, Dickens, and Taylor.
60. Ibid., 295, Thackeray to Forster, 6/9/47, 301, Taylor to Forster, 6/11/47.
61. Stevenson, *Showman*, 161.
62. Ray, II, 296, Forster to Thackeray, 6/9/47.
63. *Let.*, II, 29, Forster, 6/9/47.
64. Ray, II, 299, Thackeray to Dickens, 6/11/47.
65. Ibid., 303, Forster to Dickens, 6/12/47.
66. Ibid., 308, Thackeray to Mrs. Carmichael-Smyth, 7/2/47.
67. Ibid., 333, 1/7/48.
68. Ibid., 258, 12/23/46. Thackeray's

figures, of course—especially in their depreciation of his own sales—are a burlesque.
69. Ibid., 336-7, Dickens to Thackeray, 1/9/48, incomplete in *Let.*, II, 70.
70. Ibid.
71. Ibid., 369, Dickens to Thackeray, 3/30/48.
72. *Let.*, II, 29, Thompson, 6/9/47.
73. Ibid., 30, Hodgson, 6/12/47.
74. Kitton, *Pen and Pencil*, 108 fn.
75. *Let.*, II, 29, Thompson, 6/9/47.
76. Berg MS., Dickens to De la Rue, 3/24/47.
77. *Let.*, II, 34, 42, Ireland, 6/24/47, 7/11/47.
78. Forster, 456.
79. *Let.*, II, 37, Miss Power, 7/2/47.
80. Ibid., 43, 7/13/47.
81. Ibid., 44, Beard, 7/14/47.
82. Ibid., 41, Thompson, 7/9/47.
83. Hunt. MS., Dickens to Radley, 7/22/47.
84. Forster, 463.
85. Ibid., 457-8.
86. *Let.*, II, 45, Miss Kelly, 8/2/47, 46, Lemon, 8/3/47.
87. Ibid., 45, Forster, 8/3/47.
88. Forster, 458-9. The proceeds were divided between Hunt and Poole. Dickens doled out an allowance to Poole in half-year installments. See *Let.*, II, 253, Russell, 12/18/50.
89. *Let.*, II, 49, unknown correspondent, 8/11/47.
90. Ibid., Phelps, 8/29/47.
91. Ibid., 52, Forster, 9/2/47.
92. Ibid., 51, Andersen, 8/30/47.
93. Ibid., 52, Forster, 9/2/47.
94. Ward, 86.
95. Jerrold, *Dramatist*, II, 630.
96. Let., II, 52, Forster, 9/2/47.
97. Ibid., 53, 9/5/47.
98. Ibid., 54, 9/10/47.
99. Ibid., 57, 9/19/47.
100. Ibid., 7-8, Frederick Dickens, 1/28/47.
101. Ibid., 11, 2/5/47.
102. Ibid., 14, 2/12/47.

103. Ibid., 9, 1/28/47.
104. Ibid., 8.
105. Ibid., 56, 10/14/47.
106. Morgan MS., Dickens to Miss Coutts, 10/28/47, partly printed in *Let.*, II, 56.
107. Morgan MS., Dickens to Miss Coutts, 5/23/47.
108. Morgan MS., Dickens to Miss Coutts, 10/28/47. For his selection of the Matron and her assistants, see Morgan MSS., Dickens to Miss Coutts, 11/9/47, 11/20/47, 11/25/47, 11/27/47, 12/8/47, 12/9/47, 12/22/47. Various additions and replacements were made in 1848. See Morgan MSS., Dickens to Miss Coutts, 3/3/48, 5/23/48.
109. Morgan MS., Dickens to Miss Coutts, 11/3/47, partly printed in *Let.*, II, 57.
110. *Let.*, II, 61, Chapman, 11/26/47.
111. Morgan MS., Dickens to Miss Coutts, 11/3/47. See note 109 above.
112. Macready, *Diaries*, 10/18,19/47, 11/4/47.
113. *Coll. P.*, II, 375, 377, speech, 12/1/47.
114. *Let.*, II, 62, Lyttleton, 12/10/47.
115. Ibid., 63, Forster, 12/21/47.
116. Ibid., 64, Georgina Hogarth, 12/30/47.
117. Ibid., 69, Alfred Dickens, 1/1/48.
118. Ibid., 65, Forster, 12/30/47.
119. Ibid., 69, Forster, 1/1/48.
120. Forster, 468.
121. Ibid., 469; Dickens to Miss Kelly, 11/27/47, Scheuer Catalogue, No. 3, 1927.
122. *Let.*, II, 72, Lemon, 2/14/48.
123. Forster, 469.
124. *Let.*, II, 73-4, Lewes, Cruikshank, 2/28/48.
125. Ibid., 74, Forster, 2/29/48.
126. Berg MS., Dickens to De la Rue, 2/29/48.
127. *Let.*, II, 75, Macready, 3/2/48.

128. Trevelyan, *British History*, 295.
129. *Let.*, II, 74, Jebb, 2/29/48.
130. Ibid., 76, Forster, 3/25/48.
131. Ibid., 79, 82-3, Forster, 4/14?/48, 4/22/48, but inaccurate there. My quotations are from the originals in the Forster Collection.
132. Ibid., 79, Mrs. Clarke, 4/14/48.

Chapter 3 [pp. 626-643]

1. *Let.*, II, 102, Moir, 6/17/48.
2. Ibid.
3. Ibid., I, 518, Jerrold, 5/3/43.
4. *P. P.*, was written in 1836-7, but, as has often been pointed out, its internal chronology is confused and ambiguous. The first chapter states that it is supposed to begin in 1827, but in the second Mr. Jingle refers to the Revolution of July, 1830. This was later covered up by a joking footnote about "the prophetic force of Mr. Jingle's imagination." The imagined time of *P. P.* on the whole, however, is hardly distinguishable from the period in which it appeared. And the main body of events in *O. T.*, 1837-9, is almost completely current.
5. *D. and S.*, VI, 63-4.
6. Ibid.
7. Ibid., XXXIII, 474.
8. Ibid., XX, 283-4.
9. Ibid., III, 22.
10. Ibid., XXXVI, 514.
11. Ibid., II, 17.
12. Ibid., V, 60.
13. Ibid., XX, 281.
14. Driver, 469, quoting Oastler, *The Champion*, I, 151.
15. *D. and S.*, V, 53.
16. Ibid., V, 58.
17. Ibid., VI, 66.
18. Ibid., XXXVIII, 538.
19. Ibid., XLVII, 668.
20. Ibid., XLVIII, 670.
21. Ibid., XLIX, 683-4.
22. Ibid., 687-8.

23. Ibid., XXXIX, 548.
24. Ibid., XX, 279.
25. Ibid., X, 128.
26. Ibid., XXI, 296.
27. Ibid., XXVII, 389.
28. Ibid., XXXVII, 531.
29. Ibid., XL, 577.
30. Ibid., LIII, 754.
31. Ibid., XL, 578.
32. Ibid., LXI, 873.
33. Ibid., VI, 69.
34. Ibid., XXXVIII, 543-4.
35. Ibid., I, 2.
36. Ibid., 5.
37. Ibid., V, 47.
38. Ibid., XL, 569.
39. Ibid., XLV, 630.
40. Ibid., III, 30.
41. Ibid., XI, 151.
42. Ibid., XVIII, 258.
43. Ibid., XL, 563.
44. Ibid., VIII, 97.
45. Ibid., XI, 151.
46. Ibid., XXXV, 505.
47. Ibid., 506.
48. Ibid., LIX, 841.
49. Ibid., 842.
50. Ibid., 845.
51. Ibid., 846.
52. Ibid., LVIII, 814.
53. Ibid., XLVII, 650.
54. Ibid., XXX, 431.
55. Ibid., XXXIII, 474.
56. Ibid., XXXVI, 515.
57. Ibid., 517.
58. Ibid., XLIX, 687.

Chapter 4 [pp. 644-660]

1. *Let.*, II, 85, White, 5/4/48.
2. Forster, 469.
3. *Let.*, II, 79, Mrs. Cowden Clarke, 4/14/48. Mrs. Clarke had first seen Dickens at the dinner given to Macready on his retirement from the management of Covent Garden in 1839, and had first met Dickens socially in 1848 at the home of Edward Tagart, the Unitarian clergyman. Clarke,

Recollections, 93-4, 297-9; Pope-Hennessy, 107.
4. *Let.*, II, 79, to various members of the acting group.
5. Ibid., 81, Cunningham, 4/21/48.
6. Ibid., 85, 5/4/48.
7. Ibid., Lemon, 5/3/48.
8. Emerson, VII, 441.
9. Clarke, *Recollections*, 302.
10. *Let.*, II, 86, Tagart, 5/6/48.
11. Ibid., 87, Leech, 5/7/48.
12. Ibid., 88, Beard, 5/10/48.
13. Ibid., 89, Cunningham, 5/12,13/48.
14. Ibid., 105, Fletcher, 6/22/48.
15. Forster, 469. The date, however, as both Dickens's correspondence and playbills of the first night make clear, was not, as Forster mistakenly says, 4/15/48, but 5/15/48. Between the first and the second night Mrs. Cowden Clarke dined at Devonshire Terrace, 5/16/48, and afterward went with Kate to hear Jenny Lind in *La Somnambula*. Clarke, *Recollections*, 310.
16. Espinasse, 267.
17. Clarke, *Recollections*, 305.
18. *Let.*, II, 90, Cunningham, 5/18/48.
19. Ibid., 91, Lemon, 5/22/48, 92-3, Cunningham, 5/24,26/48.
20. Wright, *Life*, 192.
21. Ibid.
22. Clarke, *Recollections*, 315.
23. Ibid., 316.
24. *Let.*, II, 96-7, Fletcher, 6/10/48.
25. Ibid., 101, Dalglish, 6/16/48. They ultimately paid Alexander £75. See *Let.*, II, 116 fn., for his receipt.
26. Clarke, *Recollections*, 316.
27. *Let.*, II, 106-10, to various members of the cast, 6/30—7/11/48.
28. Ibid., 110, Lewes, 7/9/48.
29. Ibid., 101, Dalglish, 6/16/48.
30. Dickens to Anne Romer, 7/4/48, MS Division, N. Y. Pub. Lib., clipping of facsimile from a Thomas F. Madigan catalogue, 1935.

31. Clarke, *Recollections*, 322.
32. Ibid.
33. Ibid., 324.
34. Forster, 469, 469 fn.
35. Wright, *Life*, 192.
36. *Let.*, II, 110, Mrs. Clarke, 7/22/48.
37. Dickens to Anne Romer, 7/4/48. See note 30 above.
38. *Let.*, I, 146, Diary, 1/6/38.
39. Ibid., 818, Forster, 11/30/46; Forster, 444-5.
40. *Let.*, II, 107, Lemon, 6/30/48.
41. Ibid., 108-9, Forster, 7/5/48.
42. Ibid., 111, Mrs. Watson, 7/27/48.
43. Ibid., 113, Lytton, 8/4/48.
44. Ibid., 114, Mrs. Clarke, 8/5/48.
45. Ibid., 111, Mrs. Watson, 7/27/48.
46. Ibid., 113, Lytton, 8/4/48.
47. Forster, 494.
48. *Let.*, II, 114-5, Forster, 8/10/48.
49. Ibid., 115, Miss Coutts, 8/10/48.
50. Ibid., Horne.
51. Ibid.
52. Ibid., Forster.
53. Dexter, *Mr. and Mrs.*, 129-30, 9/1/48.
54. Morgan MS., Dickens to Miss Coutts, 9/2/48.
55. *Let.*, II, 118, Leech, Beard, 9/6/48.
56. Ibid., 117, Frederick Dickens, 9/3/48.
57. Ibid., 121, 9/24/48.
58. N. Y. Pub. Lib., MS Division, American Autograph Shop catalogue, September, 1938, Dickens to Frederick Dickens, 10/15/48.
59. Hunt. MS., Dickens to Mrs. Watson, 10/5/48, gives the date of return as 10/3/48.
60. *Let.*, II, 122, Forster, [9/?/48].
61. Ibid., 126, Miss Coutts, 11/1/48.
62. Ibid., 127, Roche, 11/4/48.
63. *Coll. P.*, I, 152-3, "Ignorance and Crime," *Examiner*, 4/22/48.
64. Ibid., 157-8, "Cruikshank's 'The Drunkard's Children,'" *Examiner*, 7/8/48.
65. Ibid., 176-7, "The Niger Expedition," *Examiner*, 8/19/48.

66. Ibid., 154-5, "The Chinese Junk," *Examiner*, 6/24/48. Cf. "National Contrasts," *H.W.*, XVIII, 472, 10/30/58. There is a discussion of Dickens's freedom from occidental chauvinism in Orwell, 29-31.
67. Hunt. MS., Dickens to Mrs. Watson, 10/5/48.
68. *Let.*, II, 123, Kay-Shuttleworth, 10/5/48.
69. Ibid., 128, Miss Coutts, 11/18/48.
70. Ibid., 11/15/48.
71. Ibid., 134, Bradbury, 12/1/48.
72. Ibid., 136, Beard, 12/19/48.
73. Ibid., 135, Lemon, 12/13/48.
74. Ibid., 136, Hogarth, 12/15/48.
75. *H .M.*, II, 416.
76. Ibid., I, 384.
77. Ibid., 392.
78. Ibid., 402.
79. Ibid.
80. Ibid.
81. Ibid., 403.
82. Ibid., 398.
83. Ibid., 405.
84. Ibid., 383.
85. Ibid., III, 466.
86. Ibid., II, 449-50.
87. Ibid., 452.
88. Ibid., III, 482.
89. I have already called attention in I, 3, n. 63, to the ambiguities in Forster's account of when the autobiographic fragment was written. If my suggestion of late 1845–early 1846 be accepted as probable, it would precede the first conception of *H. M.* by over a year.
90. Forster, 35.
91. Ibid., 25.
92. Ibid., 35.

Chapter 5 [pp. 661-676]

1. Forster, 527.
2. *Let.*, II, 141, Marryat, 1/3/47.
3. Forster, 529; Mary Dickens, 25.
4. Morgan MS., Dickens to Macready, 2/2/49.

5. Forster, 523.
6. Dexter, *Mr. and Mrs.*, 130-1, 1/8/49.
7. *Let.*, II, 141-2, Forster, 1/12/49.
8. Dexter, *Mr. and Mrs.*, 133, 1/9/49.
9. *Let.*, II, 142, Forster, 1/12/49.
10. Ibid., Committee of the Giles Testimonial.
11. Morgan MS., Dickens to Macready, 2/2/49.
12. Ibid.
13. *Let.*, II, 144, Burnett, 1/31/49. The grave of Fanny Burnett was in a plot belonging to the Dickens family.
14. Morgan MS., Dickens to Letitia Austin, 2/1/49.
15. *Coll. P.*, I, 193-200, "The Paradise at Tooting," *Examiner*, 1/20/49.
16. Ibid., 194.
17. Ibid., 198.
18. Ibid., 195.
19. Ibid., 197.
20. Ibid., 200.
21. Ibid., 200-3, "The Tooting Farm," *Examiner*, 1/27/49; cf. House, 99-102.
22. *Coll. P.*, I, 203-5, "The Verdict for Drouet," *Examiner*, 4/21/49.
23. Ibid., 203.
24. Forster, 496.
25. *Let.*, II, 145, Forster, [2/?/49].
26. Ibid.
27. Ibid., 146, 2/23/49.
28. Ibid., 2/26/49.
29. Forster, 524-5.
30. Ibid.
31. Ibid.
32. *Let.*, II, 150, Forster, 4/19/49.
33. Forster, 525.
34. Ray, II, 533, Thackeray to Brookfield, [5/?/49].
35. Ibid., 531, Thackeray to Mrs. Brookfield, 5/4/49.
36. Forster, 528.
37. Carlyle, *Letters to Family*, Jeannie Walsh, [5/17/49]; *Dick.*, XXXIII, 40, has Mrs. Gaskell's account of the same dinner, letter of 5/13/49.
38. Forster, 528.
39. Ibid., 530-1.
40. Ibid., 532.
41. Ibid., 536.
42. *Let.*, II, 151, Browne, 5/4/49.
43. Ibid., 152, Evans, 5/5/49.
44. Forster, 536.
45. *Let.*, II, 159, Evans, 7/4/49.
46. Ibid., 160, Forster, 7/10/49; Forster, 497.
47. *Let.*, II, 160, Leech, 7/9/49.
48. Ibid., 161-2, 7/12,13/49.
49. Ley, 304, suggests that Dickens may have met White through Macready, who produced White's successful play *The King of the Commons* in 1846. Later, White was a contributor to *H. W.*
50. Dexter, *Mr. and Mrs.*, 133, 7/16/49.
51. *Let.*, II, 163, Beard, 7/18/49, 166, Bradbury, 7/28/49.
52. Ray, II, 569, Thackeray to Mrs. Brookfield, 7/24/49.
53. *Let.*, II, 165, Forster, 7/28/49.
54. Kitton, *Pen and Pencil*, 57-8.
55. Ley, 239.
56. *Let.*, II, 166, Forster, 8/5/49.
57. Ibid., 165, 7/28/49.
58. Ibid., Forster, 598.
59. *Let.*, II, 164-5, Watson, 7/21/49
60. Forster, 542, n. 364, quoting *Examiner*, 9/18/49; *Dick.*, X, 320, printed from original Ms. in Dickens's hand.
61. *Let.*, II, 165, Forster, 7/28/49.
62. Ibid., 167, 8/10/49.
63. Forster, 500.
64. *Let.*, II, 169-70, Forster, [8/?/49]; Forster, 501.
65. Forster, 503.
66. *Let.*, II, 177, Leech, 10/5/49.
67. Ibid., 174, Forster, 9/23/49.
68. Ibid., 9/24/49.
69. Ibid., 175, 9/26/49.
70. Ibid., Evans, 9/25/49.
71. Ibid., Forster, 9/26/49.
72. Ibid., Lemon.

73. Ibid., 176, Mrs. Leech, [9/30/49].
74. Ibid., 177, 10/5/49.
75. Ibid., Forster, [10/?/49].
76. Ibid., Mrs. Leech, 10/5/49.
77. Ibid., 173, Forster, [9/?/49].
78. Ibid., 167, 8/10/49.
79. Ibid., 173, [9/?/49].
80. Maurice Inman, Inc., has given me a copy of an a.l.s. to Miss Coutts, 10/20/49, which establishes the date of Dickens's return as 10/15/49 or thereabouts.
81. *Let.*, II, 181, Chapman, 10/20/49.
82. *Dick.*, XLIV, 14-23, 193-200.
83. Yale MS., Dickens to L. Gaylord Clark, 10/22/49; cf. *Let.*, II, 181, Chapman, 10/20/49, 182, Snow, 11/1/49.
84. *Let.*, II, 191, Editor of the *Sun*, 12/14/49, 193, Ireland, 12/24/49, 201, Augustus Dickens, 1/25/50.
85. Elkins Coll., printed pamphlet with copies of Dickens to John Chapman and Company, 12/13/49, and John Chapman and Company to Dickens, 12/13/49, London *Times*, 1/10/49, news article, and Southwood Smith statement.
86. Archibald Barrow MS., Dickens to L. Gaylord Clark, 5/25/52.
87. *Coll. P.*, I, 737-8, "Public Executions," London *Times*, 11/14/49.
88. Ibid., 738-42, 11/17/42.
89. *Let.*, II, 186, Tagart, 11/20/49.
90. Forster, 545, n. 383.
91. *Let.*, III, 76, Jerrold, 11/20/58; Masson, I, 31.
92. *Let.*, II, 246, Forster, 11/15/50. This letter, and those in the two following notes, are all incorrectly dated 1850; reference to the corresponding numbers of D. C. makes it obvious that all three are 1849. See also Forster, 536.

93. Ibid. Correct date should be 11/17/49.
94. Ibid. Correct date should be 11/20/49.
95. Cf. *Coll. P.*, I, 207-16, "An American in Europe," *Examiner*, 7/21/49, a review of Henry Colman's *European Life and Manners in Familiar Letters to Friends*. American readers had resented *American Notes* for finding some flaws in their country and its institutions; with jocular irony Dickens takes Colman to task for centering his observations around an awestruck admiration for the magnificent hospitality of great country mansions and for having nothing but praise for his experiences in England.
96. *Let.*, II, 188, Forster, 11/30/49.
97. Widener MS., holograph in Dickens's hand addressed to Miss Boyle, with envelope dated 12/3/49.
98. *Let.*, II, 188, Forster, 11/30/49.
99. Ibid., 189, Mrs. Watson, 11/30/49.
100. Ibid., 191, Lawrence, 12/10/49.
101. Browne, 48.
102. Suzannet MS. copy, Mrs. Hill to Dickens, 12/18?/49.
103. Suzannet MS. copy, Dickens to Mrs. Hill, 12/18/19. The dates on these two letters show that Forster was in error in dating as 12/28/49 Dickens's note to him saying he had heard from "Miss Mowcher" "This morning."
104. *Let.*, II, 194, Cerjat, 12/29/49.
105. Ibid., Cf. *Coll. P.*, I, 79-81, "An Appeal to Fallen Women," which Dickens wrote for the Home at Shepherd's Bush in 1849.
106. *Let.*, II, 201, Forster, 1/29/50.
107. Ibid., 206, 2/20/50.
108. Ibid., 208, Miss Coutts, 3/6/50.

109. Morgan MS., Dickens to Henry Austin, 3/13/50.
110. *Let.*, II, 214, Forster, 5/7/50.
111. Ibid., 218, Macready, 6/11/50.
112. Ibid., 223, White, 7/13/50.
113. Ibid.
114. Ibid., 228, Forster, 8/20/50.
115. Ibid., 233, 9/15/50.
116. Ibid., 235, Miss Coutts, 9/22/50.
117. Ibid., 240, Forster, 11/21/50.

Chapter 6 [pp. 677-700]

1. *D. C.*, II, 15.
2. Ibid., XI, 154; cf. Forster, 26.
3. *D. C.*, XVI, 236.
4. Forster, 25.
5. *D. C.*, XIV, 212.
6. Ibid., XI, 155-6.
7. Ibid., XII, 173.
8. Forster, 552.
9. Ibid.
10. *D. C.*, XI, 158.
11. Ibid.
12. Ibid., 165; cf. Forster, 29.
13. *D. C.*, LIV, 768.
14. Ibid., 764.
15. *Let.*, I, 588, Thompson, 3/29/44.
16. *D. C.*, XIII, 183-5, passim.
17. Langton, 187.
18. *D. C.*, XIV, 211.
19. *Let.*, I, 429, Mitton, 4/4/42.
20. *D. C.*, XXXIII, 480.
21. Ibid., 484.
22. Ibid., 485.
23. Ibid., XXXV, 499.
24. Ibid.
25. Ibid., XLIII, 628.
26. Ibid., XLVIII, 688-9.
27. Ibid., 691.
28. Ibid.
29. Ibid., XLV, 655, XLVIII, 692.
30. Ibid., XLV, 656, XLVIII, 692 .
31. Ibid., preface to Charles Dickens Edition (1869), xiii.
32. Brown, 663.
33. *D. C.*, II, 13.
34. Ibid., 14.
35. Ibid., 15.
36. Ibid., 17.
37. Ibid., IV, 45.

38. Ibid., 48.
39. Ibid., 50.
40. Ibid., LIX, 828.
41. Ibid., IV, 46.
42. Ibid., IX, 128.
43. Ibid., 123.
44. Brown, 659.
45. *D. C.*, XIV, 211-2.
46. Ibid., 212.
47. Ibid., 212-3.
48. Ibid., XVII, 251.
49. Ibid., XXVII, 384-5.
50. Ibid., XXV, 370, 367.
51. Ibid., XX, 291.
52. Ibid.
53. Ibid., XXI, 307.
54. Ibid., XXII, 318.
55. Ibid., XXIX, 432-3.
56. Ibid., XXII, 335.
57. Ibid., LII, 741.
58. Ibid., XXXV, 512.
59. Ibid., XXXIX, 569-70.
60. Ibid., 570.
61. Ibid., XLIX, 705.
62. Ibid., LII, 744.
63. Ibid., XLII, 601.

Chapter 7 [pp. 701-718]

1. *Let.*, II, 128, Forster, 10/7/49.
2. Ibid.
3. Ibid., 202, [1/?/50].
4. Forster, 512.
5. Lehmann, *Dickens as Editor*, preface, xiii.
6. *Let.*, II, 216, Cunningham, 5/12/50.
7. Lehmann, *Dickens as Editor*, 19, outlining *Household Words* agreement, 3/28/50; *Let.*, II, 200, Wills, 1/22/50.
8. Ibid.
9. H. W. Office Book, information supplied by courtesy of Leslie C. Staples; *Let.*, II, 208, Wills, 3/6/50.
10. *Let.*, II, 202, Mrs. Gaskell, 1/31/50, 204, White, 2/5/50; Dickens to Mrs. Howitt, 2/19/50, quoted in Kitton, *Minor Writings*, 111.
11. Fitzgerald, *Memories*, photograph f. 125.

12. *Coll. P.*, I, 223-4, *H. W.*, "Preliminary Word," 3/30/50.
13. Ibid., 223, 225.
14. Morgan MS., Dickens to Henry Austin, 1/29/50, 3/20,21/50.
15. *Let.*, II, 205, Knight, 2/8/50.
16. Ibid., 202, Mrs. Gaskell, 1/31/50.
17. Perkins, 88.
18. Sala, *Things Seen*, I, 81-2.
19. *H. W.* Office Book, information supplied by courtesy of Leslie C. Staples.
20. Pearson, 176.
21. *H. W.*, 3/30/50, 6-12.
22. Ibid., 12-5; in *Coll. P.*, I, 227-32.
23. *Coll. P.*, I, 229.
24. Ibid., 231.
25. Ibid., 227.
26. Ibid., 228.
27. Fitzgerald, *Memories*, 135.
28. *Let.*, II, 210, Forster, 3/14/50; Forster, 513.
29. *Let.*, II, 211, Bradbury, 3/14/50.
30. *H. W.*, 4/6,13,20/50.
30a. See Morgan MSS., Dickens to Henry Austin, 1/29/50, 3/20,21/50.
31. *H. W.*, 4/6,13,20/50.
32. Ibid. Lehmann, *Dickens as Editor*, 165, shows that later the *Household Narrative* was handled by Wills. Ultimately it ceased publication because of difficulties connected with the claim of the Inland Revenue that it was a newspaper and therefore subject to the Newspaper Stamp Duty. A suit was instigated as a test case by the Committee for the Repeal of Taxes on Knowledge; Dickens appealed to the Court of Exchequer and was sustained by the Barons, but was later obliged to suspend publication. The case was an early stage in the abolition of the newspaper tax. See *Notes and Queries*, 12th Series, IX, 249; Jacob Holyoake, *Autobiography*, chapter "The Trouble with Queen Anne"; Maltus Questell Holyoake, "Memories of Charles Dickens," *Chambers's Journal*, XIV, 724, 11/13/97, 721-5.
33. *H. W. Narrative*, passim.
34. *Let.*, II, 222, Wills, 7/12/50.
35. Ibid., 250, 12/12/50.
36. Ibid., 213, 3/29/50.
37. Ibid., 228, 8/21/50.
38. Ibid., 213, 3/29/50.
39. Ibid., 216, Faraday, 5/28/50.
40. Ibid., 217, 5/31/50.
41. *H. W.*, 8/3/50, 489.
42. Ibid., 9/7/50, 565, 11/16/50, 176.
43. Ibid., e.g. 5/25/50, 8/24/50, 6/1/50, 6/15/50, 10/25/51, 3/12/53, 9/10/53, 7/9/53, 11/11/56, 5/10/51, 4/14/55.
44. Dexter, *Mr. and Mrs.*, 136-40, 6/23,24,28/50.
45. *Let.*, II, 220, Wills, 6/27/50.
46. Ibid.
47. Hunt. MS., Dickens to Mrs. Watson, 7/3/50. Incomplete and erroneously given in *Let.*, II, 220, as to Richard Watson.
48. *Let.*, II, 222, Wills, 7/12/50.
49. Ibid., a second letter of same date.
50. Lehmann, *Dickens as Editor*, 53, Wills to Dickens, 8/17/50.
51. *Let.*, II, 227, Wills, 8/16/50.
52. Ibid., 229, Wills, 8/27/50; cf. *H. W.* Office Book, Wills to Dickens, 8/17/50, in Lehmann, *Dickens as Editor*, 35-6.
53. *Let.*, II, 280; Horne, 3/18/51.
54. Ibid., 226, Browne, 8/14/50.
55. Ibid., 227, Forster, 8/15/50.
56. Ibid., Wills, 8/16/50, 227 fn.
57. Dexter, *Mr. and Mrs.*, 143, 8/21/50.
58. Ibid., 142-6, 8/20,21,26/50, 9/3/50.
59. Ibid., 143, 8/20/50.
60. Ibid., 146, 9/3/50.
61. Ibid., 147.
62. *Let.*, II, 232, Wills, 9/8/50; *H.W.*, 9/21/50.
63. *H. W.*, 9/28/50.
64. Ibid., 9/28/50, 10/5/50, 11/2,16,23/50.

65. *Let.*, II, 238, Beard, 10/1/50.
66. Ibid., 233, 9/15/50.
67. Ibid., 204-5, Frederick Dickens, 2/7/50, establishes it as probable that the marriage had taken place by this date, by adding, "Love to Anna, whom Kate is coming to see."
68. Ibid., 237, 9/26/50.
69. Ibid., 247, 11/28/50.
70. Ibid., 224, 230, Lytton, 7/26/50, 9/3/50.
71. Ibid., 250, Wills, 12/12/50.
72. Hollingshead, I, 131.
73. *Let.*, II, 518, Wills, 11/17/53.
74. *Ibid.*, 352, 10/16/51. Cocker was the author of a standard arithmetic book; Walkingame, of a *Tutor's Assistant*. See *H. W.*, V, 389.
75. *Let.*, II, 481, Wills, 8/5/53.
76. *H. W.* Office Book, passim; cf. Grubb, *Dickens's Influence*, 811-23.
77. *H. W.*, I-XIX, passim.
78. Ibid.
79. *Coll. P.*, I, 512, "To Working Men," *H. W.*, 10/7/54.
80. *H. W.*, 4/20/50, 82.
81. Ibid., 6/22/50, 297.
82. Ibid., 7/2/50, 577.
83. Ibid., 5/4/50, 130.
84. Ibid., 12/18/58, 58.
85. Ibid., 8/10/50, 460.
86. Ibid., 11/11,18/50, 292, 319.
87. Crotch, *Social Reformer*, 106.
88. *Coll. P.*, II, 384-6, speech, 2/6/50.
89. *O. T.*, preface to 1st Cheap Edition, xiv-v, March, 1850.
90. *Coll. P.*, II, 393-5, speech, 5/10/51.
91. Ibid., 395.
92. Crotch, *Social Reformer*, 106.
93. *H. W.*, 4/22/54, 224.
94. Ibid., 4/14/55, 241.
95. Ibid., 5/12/55, 337.
96. Maurice, 111.

Chapter 8 [pp. 719-739]

1. *Let.*, II, 224, Lytton, 7/27/50.
2. Pope-Hennessy, 197.
3. Macready, *Diaries*, 12/13/38.
4. *Let.*, II, 230, Lytton, 9/3/50.
5. Ibid., 233, Miss Boyle, 9/20/50.
6. Morgan MS., Dickens to Miss Boyle, 10/7/50.
7. *Let.*, II, 240, Frederick Dickens, 10/21/51; Hunt. MS., Dickens to Mrs. Watson, 10/8/50.
8. *Let.*, II, 241, Miss Boyle, 10/30/50.
9. Ibid., 240, Frederick Dickens, 10/31/50, 11/1/50.
10. Ibid., 242, Lytton, 11/3/50.
11. Communicated by Horne to Bernard Shaw, and told me by Shaw during a conversation in the summer of 1946.
12. *Let.*, II, 242, Radcliffe, 11/2/50.
13. Ibid., 249, Mrs. Watson, 12/9/50.
14. Ibid., 245, Lytton, 11/13/50.
15. Hunt. MS., Dickens to Mrs. Watson, 10/1/50; details supplied me in conversation with the late Earl of Lytton at Knebworth in the summer of 1946.
16. *Let.*, II, 243, Lytton, 11/7,9/50.
17. Ibid., 238, Leech, 10/1/50.
18. Ibid., 246, Mrs. Watson, 11/23/50. The complete casts of the Knebworth performances are recorded: *Every Man in His Humour* and *Turning the Tables* in Kitton, *Pen and Pencil*, VII, 108, 113 fn.; *Animal Magnetism* in Pemberton, 112-3.
19. *Dick.*, VII, 188.
20. Forster, 515.
21. *Let.*, II, 287, Miss Coutts, 3/31/51.
22. Lehmann, *Dickens as Editor*, 44; Kitton, *Famous Society*, 118-27; *Let.*, II, 264 fn.
23. *Let.*, II, 263, Lytton, 1/5/51.
24. Ibid., 252-3, Russell, 12/18/50.
25. Ibid., 256, 12/24/50.
26. Ibid., 255, Poole, 12/24/50.
27. Hunt. MS., Dickens to Mrs. Watson, 10/1/50.
28. *Let.*, II, 251, Mrs. Watson, 12/14/50.

29. Ibid., 263, Lytton, 1/5/51.
30. Ibid., 254, Mrs. Watson, 12/19/50.
31. Hunt. MS., Dickens to Mrs. Watson, 12/11/50.
32. Ibid., 11/28/50.
33. *Let.*, II, 251-2, Mrs. Watson, 12/14/50.
34. Hunt. MS., Dickens to Mrs. Watson, 12/7/50.
35. Ibid., Dickens to Mrs. Watson, 12/11/50; *Let.*, II, 254, Mrs. Watson, 12/19/50.
36. Hunt. MS., Dickens to Mrs. Watson, 12/7/50.
37. Ibid., 12/27/50.
38. *Let.*, II, 255-6, Mrs. Watson, 12/30/50.
39. Ibid.
40. Kitton, *Pen and Pencil*, 60.
41. *Let.*, II, 251, Mrs. Watson, 12/14/50, 264, Lytton, 1/7/51.
42. Morgan MS., Dickens to Miss Boyle, 1/15/51.
43. The colors of Miss Boyle's costumes are not fictional invention: they are established by unpublished letters of Dickens to Mary Boyle, Morgan MS., 9/24/50, and Anne Romer, 7/4/48, Thomas F. Madigan catalogue, 1935.
44. Forster, 535.
45. *Let.*, 264, Mrs. Watson, 1/24/51.
46. Ibid., 1/28/51.
47. Ibid., 261-2, Lytton, 1/5/51.
48. Ibid., 338, Miss Coutts, 8/17/51.
49. Ibid., 359, Bradbury, 11/22/51.
50. Ibid., 339, Wills, 8/13/51.
51. This statement is established by the marginal notes in Dickens's handwriting in his copy of Keightley. See also Kitton, *Life*, 199.
52. *Let.*, II, 262-3, Lytton, 1/5/51.
53. Ibid., 272, Wills, 2/10/51.
54. Frith, *Leech*, I, 206.
55. Dexter, *Mr. and Mrs.*, 150, 2/13/51.
56. *Let.*, II, 271, Leech, 2/8/51.
57. Ibid., 273-5, various letters.

58. Frith, *Autobiography*, 144.
59. *Let.*, II, 275, Macready, 2/27/51.
60. Ibid., Duke of Devonshire, 3/4/51.
61. Ibid., 277, quoting Duke of Devonshire's reply to Dickens, 3/4/51.
62. Ibid., Lytton, 3/4/51.
63. Jerrold, *Dramatist*, II, 574.
64. *Let.*, II, 272, Wills, 2/10/51; Hunt MS., Dickens to Wills, 2/13/51.
65. *Let.*, II, 278, Egg, 3/8/51.
66. Ibid., 279, Duke of Devonshire, 3/15/51.
67. Ibid., 286, Lytton, 3/23/51.
68. Ibid., 288, 3/25/51.
69. Ibid., 303, 4/28/51.
70. Ibid., 282, Miss Coutts, 3/20/51.
71. Ibid., Roberts, 3/20/51.
72. Ibid., 303, Lytton, 4/28/51.
73. Dexter, *Mr. and Mrs.*, 151, 3/26/51.
74. *Let.*, II, 270, Mrs. Leech, 2/3/51.
75. Morgan MS., Dickens to Henry Austin, 3/12/51; Hunt. MS., Dickens to Mrs. Watson, 3/9/51.
76. *Let.*, II, 278, Wilson, 3/8/51.
77. Morgan MS., Dickens to Austin, 3/12/51.
78. *Let.*, II, 278, Wilson, 3/8/51.
79. Ibid., 279, 3/11/51.
80. Ibid., 278, 3/8/51.
81. Ibid., 279, 3/11/51.
82. Dexter, *Mr. and Mrs.*, 150, 3/25/51.
83. *Let.*, II, 294, Beard, 3/31/51.
84. Dexter, *Mr. and Mrs.*, 151, 3/25/51.
85. Ibid., 152, 3/26/51.
86. *Let.*, II, 293, Forster, 3/31/51.
86a. Childhood reminiscences already quoted from Forster, e.g., 2-3, 6, 9-10, 13, 29, 34-5.
87. Forster, 538-9.
88. Ibid., 539-40; *Coll. P.*, II, 392, speech, 4/14/51.
89. *Let.*, II, 655, Lemon, 4/26/55.
90. Dexter, *Mr. and Mrs.*, 154, 4/15/51.

91. *Let.*, II, 295, Duke of Devonshire, 4/4/51, 294, Wills, 4/3/51.
92. Ibid., 298, Duke of Devonshire, 4/15/51.
93. Ibid., 300, Beard, Mitton, 4/19/51.
94. Ibid., Wills, 4/19/51.
95. Morgan MS., Dickens to Letitia Austin, 4/19/51.
96. *Let.*, II, 300, Mitton, 4/19/51.
97. Ibid., 299, Duke of Devonshire, 4/15/51. Rehearsals were resumed 4/22/51.
98. Horne, *Bygone Celebrities*, 247-62.
99. Ibid.
100. Ibid.
101. *Let.*, II, 302, Lytton, 4/28/51.
102. Ibid., 310, Beard, 5/13/51.
103. Ibid., 312, Ward, 5/21/51; Rosenbach MSS., Dickens to Joseph J. Jenkins, 5/13,21/51.
104. *Let.*, II, 291, 293, Duke of Devonshire, 3/28,30/51.
105. Ibid., 306, 5/9/51, 307, Lytton, 5/9/51.
106. Lytton MS., Charles Dickens, Jr., to Catherine Dickens, 5/11/51, commenting to his mother on the contents of a letter from Lady Lytton to his father, which Catherine had forwarded to the boy by mistake.
107. *Let.*, II, 307, Lytton, 5/9/51.
108. Ibid., 306, Duke of Devonshire, 5/9/51.
109. Ibid., 308, 5/10/51, Ward, 5/11/51.
110. Horne, *Bygone Celebrities*, 247-62; also the playbill of the performance, reproduced in Straus, f. 212. Not everybody agreed with Horne on Dickens's comparative failure as Lord Wilmot. Macaulay, for example, was delighted with his performance: see his letter to Lytton, 5/17/51, quoted in Lytton's *Life* (1913), 154.
111. Horne, *Bygone Celebrities*, 660-72.
112. *Let.*, II, 304, Lytton, 5/1/51.
113. Ibid., 286, Lytton, Forster, 3/23/51.
114. Ibid., 312, Lytton, 5/21/51, 313, Macready, 5/24/51.
115. Horne, *Bygone Celebrities*, 660-72.
116. *Let.*, II, 316-7, Duke of Devonshire, 6/1/51.
117. Ibid., 315, Wills, 5/30/51, 316, Lytton, 6/1/51.
118. Ibid., 316, Duke of Devonshire, 6/1/51.
119. Ibid., 323, Lytton, 7/4/51.
120. Ibid., 324, 7/10/51.
121. Ibid., 336, Hills, 8/9/51.
122. Ibid., 337, Wills, 8/13/51. George Augustus Sala was the son of Mme. Sala, who had played Julia Dobbs in Dickens's early farce, *The Strange Gentleman*.
123. *H. W.*, 8/23/51, 505-7.
124. Forster, 517.
125. Dexter, *Mr. and Mrs.*, 162, 11/13/51.
126. Morgan MS., Dickens to Henry Austin, 11/13/51.
127. *Dick.*, XXXVI, 77, gives both the itinerary and the dates of the tour.
128. *Let.*, II, 375, Lytton, 2/4/52.
129. Ibid., 377-8, 2/15/52.
130. Ibid., 377.
131. Horne, *Bygone Celebrities*, 660-72.
132. *Let.*, II, 391, Beadnell, 5/4/52.
133. Ibid., 372, Mrs. Gaskell, 1/27/52.
134. Horne, *Bygone Celebrities*, 660-72; Hawthorne, *Notebook*, 10/22/53.
135. *Let.*, II, 411, Duke of Devonshire, 8/27/52.
136. Ibid., 412-3, Forster, 8/29/52.
137. Morgan MS., Dickens to Miss Coutts, 9/2/52, fragment in *Let.*, II, 414. There were four thousand spectators at the last Manchester performance. The program did not include a repetition of *Not So Bad as We Seem*, but consisted of a group

of farces. See *Let.*, II, 399, Mrs. Gaskell, 7/29/52, and 414, Alfred Dickens, 8/29/52. On 9/2/52 Dickens, with Lytton and Thackeray, was among the speakers when the Queen opened the Manchester Public Library. See *Coll. P.*, II, 535, speech, 9/2/52, and *Dick.*, XXX, No. 232, Autumn, 1934.

138. *Let.*, II, 403, Miss Boyle, 7/22/52.

139. Ibid., 413, 415, Forster, 8/29/52, 9/?/52.

140. Chairman's Agenda and Minute Book of the Guild of Literature and Art, owned by Carl Pforzheimer and in the custody of the Rosenbach Company. Consulted by the generous permission of both Mr. Pforzheimer and Dr. Rosenbach.

141. Lytton, *Life* (1913), 145, quoting letter from Macaulay, 5/17/51.

PART EIGHT

Chapter 1 [pp. 743-761]

1. *Let.*, II, 359, Bradbury, 11/22/51.
2. Morgan MS., Dickens to Henry Austin, 1/22,25,30/51.
3. Ibid., 3/12/51.
4. *Let.*, II, 283, Booth, 3/20/51, 283 fn.
5. Ibid., 296, Wills, 4/7/51.
6. Ibid., 320, Hawtrey, 6/24/51, 321, Beard, 6/25/51.
7. Ibid., 326, Mrs. Watson, 7/11/51.
8. Ibid., 327.
9. Morgan MS., Dickens to Henry Austin, 7/14/51.
10. Mackenzie, *Life*, 187, notes that the three houses were built by James Perry, a former owner of the *Morning Chronicle*, on land leased from the Duke of Bedford.
11. Kitton, *Life*, 208.
12. Morgan MS., Dickens to Henry Austin, 7/14/51.
13. *Let.*, II, 331, Stone, 7/20/51.
14. Ibid., 338, Miss Coutts, 8/17/51.
15. Ibid., 340, Forster, [8/?/51].
16. Forster, 568 fn.
17. *Let.*, II, 341, Wills, 9/6/51; Hunt. MS., Dickens to Wills, 9/9/51.
18. *Let.*, II, 341-2, Austin, 9/7/51.
19. Ibid., 344, 9/21/51.
20. Morgan MS., Dickens to Henry Austin, 10/1/51.
21. *Let.*, II, 344, Austin, 9/21/51.
22. Morgan MS., Dickens to Henry Austin, 9/25/51; *Let.*, II, 345, Smith, 9/26/51.
23. Morgan MS., Dickens to Henry Austin, 10/1/51.
24. *Let.*, II, 342, Austin, 9/7/51.
25. Ibid., 341-2.
26. Morgan MS., Dickens to Henry Austin, 9/19/51. Mistakenly printed in *Let.*, II, 343, as part of a letter to Austin, 9/8/51—again through following the Georgina Hogarth-Mary Dickens text, which in this case omits several paragraphs from the actual letter of 9/8/51 and adds material from two other letters.
27. Morgan MS., Dickens to Spencer Lyttleton, 10/9/51.
28. *Let.*, II, 348, Beard, 10/6/51.
29. Ibid., 353, unknown correspondent, 10/17/51; Morgan MS., Dickens to Henry Austin, 10/17/51.
30. *Let.*, II, 354, Austin, 10/25/51.
31. Hunt. MS., Dickens to the Hon. Richard Watson, 10/31/51.
32. *Let.*, II, 359, Mrs. Gaskell, 10/25/51.
33. Morgan MS., Dickens to Henry Austin, 9/24/51, and all the detailed correspondence about the house, with Austin and others, in the Morgan Library.
34. *Let.*, II, 353, 359, Eeles, 10/22/51, 11/17/51.
35. Kitton, *Pen and Pencil*, Sup., 34-6, has a detailed list of the titles;

cf. Langton, 122-6, and Rubens, 18. Not all were devised by Dickens, however: the Forster Collection has an overlapping collection of mock titles, noted there as the inventions of Dickens, Forster, and B. W. Proctor.

36. *Let.*, II, 345, Smith, 9/26/51.
37. Ibid., 362, Wills, 12/7/51.
38. *Dick.*, XVI, 94; Wright, *Life*, 223-4.
39. Charles Dickens, Jr., 23.
40. *H. W.* The first one appeared in the number for 12/13/51, 265; the last, 5/21/53, 277.
41. *Let.*, II, 361, Mrs. Gaskell, 12/5/51.
42. Ibid., 364, 12/21/51.
43. Ritchie, *Unwritten Memoirs*, 78-84. These are not dated, but given as general memories of Dickens Christmas parties. They must, however, be about this time, for Thackeray was in America during the Christmas-New Year season of 1852–3, and in Rome during that of 1853–4. By 1854–5, Annie Thackeray would have been seventeen to eighteen and she would probably have recalled the year and thought of herself not as a little girl but as a young lady.
44. Storey, 86.
45. Ibid., 77.
46. A. T. Dickens, 640.
47. Storey, 78.
48. A. T. Dickens, 641.
49. *Let.*, II, 382, Hogarth, 3/4/52.
50. Ibid., Forster, 3/7/52.
51. Ibid., 383, Wills, 3/13/52.
52. Ibid., Howitt, 3/19/52.
53. Ibid., 416, Mrs. Gore, 9/27/52. I have corrected one slight deviation in the text (which should read "offer up prayers," not "put prayers"), from the original in the Berg Coll.
54. Hunt. MS., Dickens to Mrs. Watson, 5/6/52.
54a. Blunden, 328.

55. *Let.*, II, 383, Forster, 3/17,18/52.
56. Ibid., 382, 3/7/52.
57. *B. H.*, VI, 68-9.
58. Morgan MS., Dickens to Miss Coutts, 4/18/52, mostly in *Let.*, II, 388.
59. *Let.*, II, 394, Cerjat, 5/8/52.
60. Ibid., 391, Beadnell, 5/4/52.
61. Ibid., 396, Horne, 5/28/52, Lemon, 5/29/52, 397, Wills, 6/3/52.
62. Mass. Hist. Soc., undated clipping of an article in N. Y. *Tribune*, by "Grace Greenwood." This was a pseudonym for Sara Jane Clarke (later Mrs. L. K. Lippincott), whose *Haps and Mishaps of a Tour in Europe* was published by Ticknor, Reed, and Fields, 1854. These anecdotes, however, do not appear in her book.
63. *Let.*, II, 403, Miss Boyle, 7/22/52.
64. Ibid., 405, Knight, 8/1/52.
65. Ibid., 406, Forster, 8/1/52.
66. Ibid., 408, 8/8/52.
67. Pollock, 92-3; *Let.*, II, 418, Macready, 10/5/52. Forster, 569, is a little inaccurate in saying that Mrs. Macready's death was less than a month after D'Orsay's; the two dates were 8/4/52 and 9/18/52.
68. *Let.*, II, 408, Forster, [9/?/52].
69. Ibid., 429, Hawtrey, 11/13/52.
70. A. T. Dickens, 629.
71. *Let.*, II, 430, Miss Coutts, 11/19/52.
72. *Coll. P.*, I, 405-15, *H. W.*, 11/27/52.
73. *Let.*, II, 430, Mrs. Watson, 11/22/52.
74. Ibid., 434, Wills, 12/9/52.
75. *Coll. P.*, II, 400-6, speech, 1/6/53.
76. *Let.*, II, 460, Stanfield, 5/5/53, 461, Cunningham, 5/11/53.
77. Felton, 5/13,19,20/53, 6/5/53.
78. *Let.*, II, 463, Forster, [6/?/53].
79. Ibid.

80. Ibid., 472, Collins, 6/30/53, 464, Ward, 6/30/53.
81. Ibid., 472, Collins, 6/30/53.
82. Ibid., 463, Bradbury and Evans, 6/11/53.
83. Ibid., 464, Wills, 6/13/53.
84. Ibid., 467-8, Forster, 6/26/53.
85. Ibid., 473, Lemon, 7/3/53.
86. Ibid.
87. Ibid., 468-9, Forster, 6/26/53.
88. Ibid., 469.
89. R. P., "Our French Watering Place," 40.
90. *Let.*, II, 466, Stone, 6/23/53.
91. Ibid., 473, Lemon, 7/3/53.
92. Ibid., 488, Beard, 9/18/53.
93. Ibid., 480, Wills, 8/5/53.
94. Ibid., 483, Mrs. Watson, 8/27/53.
95. Ibid., 482, Miss Coutts, 8/27/53.
96. Forster, 564, 564 fn. The pamphlet was by W. Challinor, of Leek, Staffordshire.
97. *Coll. P.*, II, 407, speech, 5/1/53.
98. *B. H.*, preface, ix.
99. *Let.*, II, 400 fn.
100. Ibid., 445 fn. Lord Denman's articles are included in a bound volume of Modern Pamphlets in the Forster Collection.
101. Ibid., 445, Mrs. Cropper, 1/21/53.
102. Ibid., 400-1, 7/9/52, where the correspondent's name is not given. The original letter, in the Morgan Library, is addressed to the Reverend Henry Christopherson.
103. *Dick.*, XL, 141, quoting a letter by Mill, 3/20/54.

Chapter 2 [pp. 762-782]

1. *B. H.*, I, 2-3.
2. Ibid., 3.
3. Ibid., 4.
4. Ibid., III, 32-3.
5. Ibid., 20.
6. Ibid., V, 50.
7. Ibid., VIII, 99.
8. Morgan MS., Dickens to Miss Coutts, 3/4/50: "I dream of Mrs. Chisholm and her housekeeping. The dirty faces of her children are my continual companions."
9. *B. H.*, XIX, 261.
10. Ibid., 269.
11. Ibid., III, 17.
12. Ibid., XXI, 285-6.
13. Ibid., XLVII, 637-8.
14. Ibid., XIV, 199.
15. Ibid., LX, 815.
16. Ibid., V, 51-2.
17. Ibid., 52.
18. Ibid., preface, ix-x; *Let.*, II, 481, Wills, 8/7/53, 481 fn.
19. Ibid., preface, ix; cf. preceding chapter, n. 96, and Forster, 564, 564 fn.
20. *B. H.*, preface, x; *Dick.*, XI, 2.
21. *B. H.*, XXXIX, 547.
22. Ibid., 547-8.
23. Ibid., I, 3.
24. Ibid., II, 9.
25. Ibid., LVI, 758.
26. Ibid., XI, 566.
27. Ibid., 569-70.
28. Shaw, Preface to *Great Expectations*.
29. *B. H.*, XII, 159-60.
30. London *Times* Lit. Sup., 7/28/1950, 476, "John Wilson Croker as Gossip, I," by Alan Lang Strout, quoting a letter of Croker's to Lord Hertford, 1/8/28.
31. *B. H.*, XI, 561-2, 564. Could Doodle's nephews, cousins, and brothers-in-law have suggested Sir Joseph Porter's "sisters and his cousins and his aunts," in Gilbert's *Pinafore?*
32. Ibid., VIII, 104-5.
33. Ibid., 105.
34. Cazamian, 297.
35. *B. H.*, VIII, 105-6.
36. Ibid., XVI, 219.
37. Ibid., 220.
38. Ibid., XLVII, 646.
39. Ibid., XXXVII, 522.
40. Ibid., XLV, 623.
41. Ibid., LXV, 866.

42. Shaw, Preface to *Great Expectations*.
43. Ibid.
44. *B. H.*, XLVI, 624.
45. Ibid., XXXII, 453-4.

Chapter 3 [pp. 783-800]

1. *Let.*, II, 491, Mrs. Watson, 9/21/53.
2. Ibid., 486, Delane, 9/12/53, 681, Gibson, 7/18/55.
3. Dexter, *Mr. and Mrs.*, 176, 10/5/53.
4. *Let.*, II, 494, Miss Coutts, 10/8/53.
5. Dexter, *Mr. and Mrs.*, 177, 10/13/53.
6. Ibid., 180-1, 10/16/53.
7. *Let.*, II, 500, Georgina Hogarth, 10/25/53.
8. Dexter, *Mr. and Mrs.*, 186, 10/20/53.
9. *Let.*, II, 499, Miss Coutts, 10/25/53.
10. Ibid., 484, Mrs. Watson, 8/27/53.
11. Ibid., 499, Georgina Hogarth, 10/25/53.
12. Dexter, *Mr. and Mrs.*, 186-7, 10/20/53.
13. *Let.*, II, 500, Georgina Hogarth, 10/25/53.
14. Forster, 580.
15. Dexter, *Mr. and Mrs.*, 196-7, 10/28/53.
16. *Let.*, II, 508, Georgina Hogarth, 11/4/53.
17. Ibid., 510, Miss Coutts, 11/13/53.
18. Dexter, *Mr. and Mrs.*, 203, 11/4/53.
19. Ibid.
20. *Let.*, II, 510, Miss Coutts, 11/13/53.
21. Dexter, *Mr. and Mrs.*, 208-9, 11/14/53.
22. *Let.*, II, 523, Forster, 12/5/53.
23. Ibid., 507, Georgina Hogarth, 11/4/53.
24. Dexter, *Mr. and Mrs.*, 208, 11/14/53.

25. Ibid., 219, 11/21/53.
26. *Let.*, II, 516-7, Forster, [11/?/53].
27. Ibid., 516.
28. Dexter, *Mr. and Mrs.*, 216-7, 11/21/53.
29. Ibid.
30. Berg MS., Dickens to De la Rue, 12/4/53; *Let.*, II, 517-8, Wills, 11/17,21/53.
31. *Let.*, II, 521-3, Forster, 11/28/53.
32. Berg MS., Dickens to De la Rue, 11/14/53.
33. Dexter, *Mr. and Mrs.*, 194, 10/28/53.
34. Ibid., 227, 12/5/53.
35. Ibid.
36. *Let.*, II, 545, De la Rue, 3/9/54.
37. Dexter, *Mr. and Mrs.*, 201, 10/30/53, 211, 11/14/53; *Let.*, II, 535, Cerjat, 1/16/54.
38. Morgan MSS., Dickens to Miss Coutts, 9/20/52, 1/14/54.
39. *Let.*, II, 431, Mrs. Watson, 11/22/52; Morgan MS., Dickens to Henry Austin, 11/10/53.
40. *Let.*, II, 534, Cerjat, 1/16/54.
41. Ibid.
42. Ibid., 527, Lemon, 12/24/53.
43. Ibid., 533, Mrs. Watson, 1/13/54.
44. *Dick.*, XXXVI, 109; Forster, 572. The presentation was made at a dinner at the Hen and Chickens on 12/31/53.
45. E.g., *Let.*, II, 538, Forster, 1/27/54.
46. Forster, 573; *Dick.*, XXXVI, 131.
47. A. T. Dickens, 632.
48. Forster, 573; see also Ainger, II, 195-6. A. T. Dickens, 632, identifies Ainger as the small boy who played Lord Grizzle. He was later Canon Ainger, Master of the Temple and biographer of Charles Lamb.
49. *Let.*, II, 576, Mrs. Colden, 8/4/54, establishes the hotel at which she and her brother were staying.
50. Ibid., 532, 1/9/54.
51. Ibid., 531, 1/8/54.

52. *Dick.*, XLVI, 197-203, especially the tabulation on 198.
53. *Let.*, II, 602, Mrs. Watson, 11/1/54.
54. Ibid., 537, Miss Coutts, 1/23/54.
55. Ibid., 602, Mrs. Watson, 11/1/54.
56. Hodder, *Shaftesbury*, 120, Dickens to Edward Fitzgerald, 12/29/38.
57. Neff, 101, et seq.
58. The figure of speech is adapted from Chesterton, *Criticisms*, 177.
59. *Let.*, II, 537, Forster, 1/20/54.
60. Hunt. MS., Dickens to W. H. Wills, 1/25/54.
61. *Coll. P.*, I, 480, "On Strike," *H. W.*, 2/11/54.
62. *Let.*, II, 538-9, Forster, 1/29/54.
63. Ibid., 543, [2/?/54].
64. Ibid., 547, Lady Talfourd, 3/17/54; Elkins MS., Dickens to W. J. Clement, 3/17/54.
65. *Coll. P.*, I, 494, "The Late Mr. Justice Talfourd," *H. W.*, 3/25/54.
66. Fitzgerald, *Memories*, 161.
67. *Dick.*, XLVI, 200, n. 6.
68. *Let.*, II, 548, Knight, 3/17/54.
69. Morgan MS., Dickens to Henry Coles, 6/17/54.
70. *Let.*, II, 550, Wills, 4/12/54.
71. Ibid., 552, 4/18/54.
72. Ibid., 554, Mrs. Gaskell, 4/21/54.
73. Ibid., 560, Lemon, 6/2/54.
74. Ibid., 561, Collins, 6/6,7/54.
75. Ibid., 576, Mrs. Colden, 8/4/54.
76. Yates, *Recollections*, I, 256. Dickens's departure for Boulogne was 6/17/54; therefore this meeting must have taken place 6/11/54.
77. *Let.*, II, 561, Lemon, 6/14/54.
78. Ibid., 555, Collins, 4/24/54.
79. Ibid., 565, 7/12/54.
80. Forster, 595, 595 fn.
81. *Let.*, II, 564, Miss Coutts, 6/22/54.
82. Ibid.
83. Ibid., 565, Wills, 6/22/54.
84. Ibid.
85. Ibid., 565-6, Collins, 7/12/54.
86. Ibid., 566, Wills, 7/13/54.
87. Ibid., 567, Forster, 7/14/54.
88. Ibid., Carlyle, 7/13/54.
89. Ibid., 569, Wills, 717/54.

90. Ibid., 602, Mrs. Watson, 11/1/54.
91. Dexter, *Mr. and Mrs.*, 231, 7/19/54.
92. *Let.*, II, 570, Georgina Hogarth, 7/22/54.

Chapter 4 [pp. 801-819]

1. Shaw, Introduction to *Hard Times*.
2. *H. T.*, I, v, 508.
3. Ibid., II, i, 592.
3a. Ibid., 591-2.
4. Ibid., I, ix, 545.
5. Ibid., III, 499.
6. Ibid., II, 491.
7. Leavis, 231.
8. *H. T.*, III, III, 709.
9. Shaw, Introduction.
10. *H. T.*, I, i, 489.
11. Ibid.
12. Ibid., II, 490.
13. Ibid., 493-4.
14. Ibid., ix, 541.
15. Ibid., 539.
16. Ibid., III, 496.
17. Ibid., II, 491.
18. Ibid., 492.
19. Ibid., 494-5.
20. Ibid., v, 509.
21. Ruskin, XI, 7n.
22. *H. T.*, I, XI, 552.
23. Ibid., v, 510.
24. Ibid., II, I, 594.
25. Ibid., 591.
26. Ibid., IV, 616.
27. Ibid.
28. Shaw, Introduction.
29. *Coll. P.*, I, 482, "On Strike," *H. W.*, 2/11/54.
30. Ibid., 510-3, "To Working Men," *H. W.*, 10/7/54.
31. *H. T.*, II, v, 626.
32. Ibid., 627-8.
33. Ibid., III, VI, 739.
34. Ibid., II, VI, 638.
35. Ibid., I, III, 497.
36. Ibid., v, 512.
37. Ibid., II, XII, 686.
38. Ibid., I, VI, 520.
39. Ibid., 522.

40. Ibid., xv, 577.
41. Ibid., 578.
42. Ibid., 579.
43. Ibid., 580.
44. Ibid.
45. Ibid., 582.
46. Ibid.
47. Ibid.
48. Ibid., II, xii, 687.
49. Ibid., 688-9.
50. Ibid., 690.
51. Ibid., III, i, 694.
52. Ibid., vii, 752.
53. Ibid., viii, 755.
54. Ibid., 756.
55. Ibid.
56. Ibid.
57. Ibid., 758.
58. Ibid., 760.
59. Ibid.

Chapter 5 [pp. 820-839]

1. *H. T.*, I, xi, 555.
2. Ibid., II, v, 627.
3. Ibid., 626.
4. *Let.*, II, 603, Mrs. Watson, 11/1/54.
5. Ibid., 615, Cerjat, 1/3/55.
6. Ibid., 603, Mrs. Watson, 11/1/54.
7. Ibid., 572, Yates, 7/30/54, 574, Mrs. Gaskell, 7/31/54.
8. Ibid., 575, Mrs. Colden, 8/4/54.
9. Ibid., 574, Wills, 8/2/54.
10. Ibid., 580, Wills, 8/19/54.
11. Ibid., 581, 8/20/54.
12. Ibid., 583, 8/24/54.
13. Ibid., 646, Collins, 3/24/55.
14. Ibid., 598, Wills, 10/14/54.
15. Ibid., 585, Austin, 9/3/54.
16. Forster, 596 fn.
17. *Let.*, II, 585, Austin, 9/3/54.
18. Ibid., 586, Forster, [9/?/54].
19. Forster, 597, erroneously says seventeen windows; cf. *Let.*, II, 585, Austin, 9/6/54, and 586 fn.
20. *Let.*, II, 586, Forster, [9/?/54].
21. Hunt. MS., Dickens to Wills, 9/19/54; *Let.*, II, 587, Wills, 9/21/54.
22. *Let.*, II, 591, Collins, 9/26/54.

23. Ibid., 587, Wills, 9/21/54.
24. Ibid., 576, Mrs. Colden, 8/4/54.
25. Ibid., 520, Georgina Hogarth, 11/25/53.
26. Ibid., 588, Beard, 9/23/54.
27. Ibid., 592, Collins, 9/26/54.
28. Ibid., 591.
29. Hunt. MS., Dickens to Wills, 8/28/54; *Let.*, II, 582, Wills, 8/23/54, 589, Mitton, 9/23/54. Dickens's contributions to the Christmas number of *H. W.* that year were the first chapter of "The Seven Poor Travellers" and "The Story of Richard Doubledick."
30. *Let.*, II, 588-9. Beard, Mitton, 9/23/54, 592, Wills, 9/29/54, 594, 10/4/54.
31. Forster, 595 fn.
32. *Let.*, II, 594, Wills, 10/4/54.
33. Ibid., 595, Forster, 10/8/54.
34. Ibid., 615, Cerjat, 1/3/55.
35. Ibid., 596, Forster, [10/?/54].
36. Ibid., 589 fn.
37. Ibid., 589, Wills, 9/25/54; *Coll. P.*, I, 510-1, "To Working Men," *H. W.*, 10/7/54.
38. *Coll. P.*, I, 511-2.
39. *Let.*, II, 599, Miss Coutts, 10/26/54.
40. Ibid., 600.
41. Ibid., 603, Mrs. Watson, 11/1/54.
42. Ibid., 601, Macready, 11/1/54.
43. *H. W.*, 11/11/54, "A Home Question," 292-6.
44. *Let.*, II, 604, Stanfield, 11/3/54, establishes the date of the Sherborne reading.
45. *Let.*, II, 601-2, Macready, 11/1/54.
46. Ibid., 602, Mrs. Watson, 11/1/54, establishes the 12/19/54 date; *Mr. and Mrs.*, 232, 12/28/54, that of 12/28/54.
47. Dexter, *Mr. and Mrs.*, 233, 12/28/54.
48. *Let.*, II, 617, Planché, 1/7/55.
49. Van Amerongen, 14.
50. Forster, 574.

51. *Let.*, II, 610, Collins, 12/24/54.
52. Forster, 574; Straus, 251.
53. Straus, 251; Charles Dickens, Jr., 20.
54. Forster, 574.
55. Van Amerongen, 13.
56. *Let.*, II, 620, Knight, 1/30/55.
57. Ibid., 622, Forster, 2/3/55. I have been able to find no indication that this is, as Pope-Hennessy, 40, claims, a youthful composition revised at this time. On the contrary, Dickens writes Forster about it: "I have rather a bright idea . . . I think, for Household Words this morning: a fine little bit of satire: an account of an Arabic MS lately discovered very like the Arabian Nights— called the Thousand and One Humbugs."
58. *Coll. P.*, I, 574-80, *H. W.*, 4/21/55.
59. *Let.*, II, 620, Forster, [1/?/55].
60. Ibid., 622, Cunningham, 2/1/55, 624, Miss Coutts, 2/9/55.
61. Ibid., 624-5, Wills, 2/9/55.
62. Ibid., 623, Régnier, 2/3/55.
63. Ibid., 625, Maria Winter, 2/10/55.
64. Ibid.
65. Ibid., 626-7.
66. Ibid., 626.
67. Ibid., 626-7.
68. *Let.*, II, 630, Georgina Hogarth, 2/16/55, 631, Wills, 2/16/55, 631-2, Forster, [2/?/55].
69. Ibid., 634, Maria Winter, 2/22/55.
70. Ibid., 628, 2/15/55, 634, 2/22/55.
71. Ibid., 635-6, 2/24/55.
72. Ibid., 628-9, 215/55.
73. Ibid., 629.
74. Ibid., 628-9.
75. Ibid., 629.
76. Ibid.
77. Ibid., 633, 2/22/55.
78. Ibid., 634.
79. Ibid., 634-5.
80. Ibid., 633, Maria Winter,

2/22/55, which was a Thursday, naming Sunday as the date of meeting.
81. *L. D.*, I, xiii, 155-60; *Let.*, II, 785, Duke of Devonshire, 7/5/56.
82. *L. D.*, I, xiii, 156.
83. Ibid., 160-1.
84. Ibid., 155.
85. Ibid., 158.
86. Ibid., 159.
87. Forster, 49; *Let.*, II, 716, Forster, gives the date of this letter, with what authority I don't know, as December. During that month Dickens was in Paris, and had not seen Maria for months, whereas this letter speaks in the present tense, "now," of seeing her and hearing her voice.
88. The date of this dinner is established by *Let.*, II, 640, Maria Winter, 3/10/55, which speaks of Dickens catching cold from her the previous Wednesday evening.
89. Ibid., 640, Maria Winter, 3/11/55.
90. Ibid.
91. Ibid., 642, Ella Winter, 3/13/55.
92. Ibid., 648, Maria Winter, 3/29/55. On the previous Wednesday, 3/27/55, Dickens read the *Christmas Carol* to an audience of railway workers at Ashford, Kent, *Let.*, II, 613, calendar. Lemon and Wills went with him, and Thomas Beard was also invited, *Let.*, II, 645, Beard, 3/20/55.
93. Ibid., 649-50, Maria Winter, 4/3/55.
94. Ibid., 650.
95. Ibid., 670, 6/11/55.
96. Ibid., 658, Hunt, 5/4/55.
97. Ibid., 659, Miss Coutts, 5/8/55.
98. Ibid., 661, Collins, 5/11/55.
99. Ibid., 644, Morley, 3/19/55; *H. W.*, 3/31/55, "Frost-Bitten Homes," 193.
100. *Let.*, II, 655, Forster, 4/27/55.

Chapter 6 [pp. 840-862]

1. *Let.*, II, 648, Layard, 4/3/55.
2. Ibid., 661, Miss Coutts, 5/15/55.
3. Ibid.
4. Ibid., 651-2, Layard, 4/10/55.
5. Ibid., 658, 5/7/55, 662, Miss Coutts, 5/15/55.
6. Ibid., 650, Forster, 4/3/55; *Dick.*, XLII, 139, speech, 4/2/55.
7. *Coll. P.*, I, 580-7, H. W., 4/28/55.
8. Ibid., 587-94, H. W., 5/5/55.
9. H. W., 7/14/55, "Mr. Philip Stubbes," 553.
10. *Coll. P.*, I, 599-604, "Cheap Patriots," H. W., 6/9/55.
11. Ibid., 594-9, "The Toady Tree," H. W., 5/26/55.
12. *Let.*, II, 660, Collins, 5/11/55, 663, Stanfield, 5/20/55.
13. Ibid., 664, Stanfield, 5/22/55.
14. Ibid., Lemon, 5/23/55.
15. Ibid., 665, Stone, 5/24/55.
16. Charles Dickens, Jr., 20.
17. Most biographers have followed Forster, 575, in saying three performances, and give the dates 6/16, 18, and 19, but *Let.*, II, 672, 6/15/55, lists a letter to the Police Station stating that there will be a performance that evening and asking to have a constable in attendance from 7 P.M. to 12 P.M.
18. Forster, 575.
19. *Let.*, II, 672, Miss Coutts, 6/19/55.
20. Pemberton, 124-8, quoting Henry Morley's *Journal of a London Playgoer.*
21. *Let.*, II, 674, 677, Collins, 6/24/55, 7/8/55.
22. Ibid., 677, Beard, 7/6/55.
23. Morgan MS., Dickens to Macready, 6/30/55, incomplete in *Let.*, II, 675-6.
24. *Coll. P.*, II, 415-7, speech, 6/27/55.
25. Ibid., 417.
26. Ibid., 418-23.

27. *Let.*, II, 659, Miss Coutts, 5/8/55.
28. Forster, 623.
29. Hunt, MS., Dickens to Mrs. Watson, 5/21/55.
30. *Let.*, II, 666, Miss Coutts, 5/29/55.
31. Ibid., 678, Collins, 7/8/55.
32. R. P., 112, "Out of Town," H. W., 9/29/55; *Let.*, II, 680, Collins, 7/17/55.
33. *Let.*, II, 680, Collins, 7/17/55.
34. Morgan MS., Dickens to Henry Austin, 8/12/55; *Let.*, II, 681, Gibson, 7/18/55.
35. *Let.*, II, 685, Ward, 8/17/55.
36. Ibid., Forster, 8/19/55.
37. Ibid., 686, Beard, 8/23/55.
38. Ibid., 687-8, Wills, 9/11,15/55.
39. Ibid., 689, Forster, 9/16/55.
40. Ibid., 690, Mrs. Watson, 9/16/55.
41. Ibid., 694, Collins, 9/30/55.
42. Morgan MS., Dickens to Miss Coutts, 1/12/55, also in Payne-Harper, *Charity*, 75-6.
43. Morgan MS., Dickens to Miss Coutts, 3/17/55, also in Payne-Harper, *Charity*, 92.
44. *Let.*, II, 693, Wills, 9/23/55.
45. Ibid., 695, Macready, 10/4/55.
46. Ibid., 693, Wills, 9/23/55.
47. Ibid., 668 fn.
48. Ibid., 693, Wills, 9/25/55.
49. Ibid., 696, Collins, 10/14/55.
50. Ibid.
51. Ibid., 698, Wills, 10/19/55, 697, Collins, 10/14/55.
52. Ibid., 699, Wills, 10/19/55, 698, Houssaye, 10/16/55.
53. Dexter, *Mr. and Mrs.*, 234, 10/16/55.
54. *Let.*, II, 699, Wills, 10/21/55.
55. Ibid., 738, Forster, 1/30/56.
56. Ibid., 752, Macready, 3/22/56.
57. Ibid., 702, Forster, [1855].
58. Ritchie, *Dickens*, 308.
59. Delattre, 45-7.
60. Translated from *Let.*, II, 701, Wills, 10/24/55.
61. *Let.*, II, 720, Hachette, 1/2/56, 722, Forster, 1/6/56, 729,

Hachette, 1/14/56, 737,
Forster, 1/30/56.
62. Ibid., 702-3, Forster, [1855].
63. Ibid., 703.
64. Ibid., 728, 1/11/56.
65. Forster, 611.
66. Pope-Hennessy, 333.
67. Forster, 613-5.
68. Let., II, 703-4, Forster, [1855].
69. Ibid., 762, Collins, 4/22/56.
70. Ibid., 760, Forster, [4/?/56].
71. Ibid.
72. Forster, 606.
73. Let., II, 710, Forster, [11/?/55].
74. Ibid., 734, 1/20/56.
75. Ibid., 712, Morgan, [11/?/55].
76. Ibid., Forster, 12/2/55.
77. Ibid., 745, Evans, 2/12/56.
78. Dr. William Brown, the husband
of Miss Coutts's companion,
had died in October, and Dickens went to London to aid his
two friends by taking into his
own hands all the arrangements
for the funeral. Dr. Brown was
interred in St. Stephen's
Church, Westminster, the
church Miss Coutts had built
in memory of her father, Sir
Francis Burdett. Morgan MSS.,
Dickens to Miss Coutts,
10/31/55, Dickens to Mrs.
Brown, 11/3/55; Let., II, 701,
Wills, 10/28/55; Dexter, Mr.
and Mrs., 237, 11/3/55.
79. Dexter, Mr. and Mrs., 240,
12/16/55. The three stories
were "The Guest," "The
Boots," and "The Bill." The
second was later made into
one of Dickens public
readings.
80. Ibid., 242, 12/21/55.
81. Let., II, 715-6, Wills, 12/30/55.
82. Ibid., 720, 1/3/56, 720 fn.
83. Lehmann, Dickens as Editor, 193.
84. H. W., 1/19/56, "Our Wicked
Misstatements," 13-9.
85. Let., II, 721, Wills, 1/6/56.
86. Ibid., 722.
87. Sala, Things Seen, 123-6.

88. Let., II, 725, Wills, 1/10/56.
89. Ibid., 726, Miss Coutts, 1/10/56.
90. Ibid., 738, Forster, 1/30/56.
91. Ibid., 736, Miss Boyle, 1/28/56.
92. Ibid., 740-1, Georgina Hogarth,
2/8/56; Dexter, Mr. and Mrs.,
244-5, 2/5,7/56.
93. Let., II, 669-70, Wills, 6/10/55;
Lehmann, Dickens as Editor,
164-6.
94. Let., II, 707, Wills, 11/16/55.
95. Ibid., 724, 1/10/56, 741, 2/8/56.
96. Lehmann, Dickens as Editor,
196-7.
97. Let., II, 741, Georgina Hogarth,
2/8/56.
98. Ibid., 743-4, Wills, 2/12/56.
99. Pearson, 63.
100. Let., II, 750, Georgina Hogarth,
3/11/56.
101. Ibid., 752, Forster, 3/23/56.
102. Ibid., 695, Macready, 10/4/55.
103. Ibid., 700, Forster, [10/?/55].
104. Ibid., 797, 8/15/56.
105. Ibid., 747, Miss Coutts, 2/19/56.
106. Ibid., 738, Forster, 1/30/56.
107. Morgan MS., Dickens to Collins,
1/19/56, incomplete in Let.,
II, 734.
108. Let., II, 763, Collins, 4/22/56.
109. Ibid., 785, Duke of Devonshire,
7/5/56.
110. Ibid., 756, Forster, 4/7/56.
111. Ibid., 713, Collins, 12/12/55.
112. Ibid., 732, 1/19/56.
113. Ibid., 757, 4/13/56.
114. Ibid., 762, 4/22/56.
115. Ibid., 765, Forster [4/?/56].
116. Ibid., 723, Lemon, 1/7/56.
117. Dexter, Mr. and Mrs., 238,
11/3/55; Let., II, 725, Wills,
1/10/56.
118. Dexter, Mr .and Mrs., 239,
12/16/55.
119. Ibid., 249, 5/9/56.
120. Let., II, 771, Webster, 5/17/56.
121. Ibid., 769, Georgina Hogarth,
5/5/56.
122. Ibid., 569, 7/22/54.
123. Ibid., 646, Collins, 3/24/55.
124. Ibid., 764, Wills, 4/27/56.

125. Ibid., 695, Macready, 10/4/55.
126. Ibid., 620-1, Forster, [1/?/55].
127. Ibid., 765, Forster, [4/?/56].

Chapter 7 [pp. 863-882]

1. *Let.*, II, 755-6, Wills, 4/6/56.
2. Ibid., 770, Georgina Hogarth, 5/5/56.
3. Ibid., 769-70.
4. Dexter, *Mr. and Mrs.*, 249, 5/9/56.
5. *Let.*, II, 772, Georgina Hogarth, 5/9/56.
6. Ibid., 768, Collins, 4/30/56, 777, Lemon, 6/3/56.
7. Ibid., 775, Milman, 5/27/56.
8. Ibid., 779-80, Forster, [6/?/56].
9. Ibid., 781-2, Beard, 6/21/56.
10. Ibid., 780, Lemon, 6/15/56.
11. Ibid., 780-1, Beard, 6/21/56.
12. Ibid., 790, Macready, 7/8/56.
13. Morgan MS., Dickens to Miss Boyle, 7/21/56.
14. *Let.*, II, 793, Collins, 7/29/56.
15. Ibid., 791, 7/13/56.
16. Ibid., 795, Miss Coutts, 8/13/56.
17. Ibid., 789, Forster, 7/6/56.
18. Ibid., 792, Collins, 7/13/56.
19. Ibid., 798, Beard, 9/8/56.
20. Dexter, *Mr. and Mrs.*, 250-2, 8/25/56, 9/2/56.
21. *Let.*, II, 800, Wills, 9/16/56, 800 fn.
22. Ibid., 798-9, Collins, 9/12,13/56.
23. Ibid., 802, Miss Coutts, 10/3/56.
24. Ibid., 803, Mary Dickens, 10/4/56, Mrs. Watson, 10/7/56.
25. Ibid., 806, Wills, 10/15/56.
26. The original MS. of *The Frozen Deep*, with Dickens's autograph emendations, additions, and deletions, is in the Morgan Library.
27. These words were among Dickens's additions. See *Frozen Deep* MS. in Morgan Library. There is a slightly different wording of this suggestion in *Let.*, II, 799, Collins, 9/13/56, but the MS.

version is undoubtedly the form that was used in performance.
28. *Let.*, II, 803-4, Mrs. Watson, 10/7/56.
29. Ibid., 810, Collins, 11/1/56.
30. Ibid., 816, Miss Power, 12/15/56.
31. Ibid., 815, Macready, 12/13/56.
32. Ibid., 807, Forster, 10/18/56.
33. Ibid., Elwin, 10/17/56.
34. Ibid., 825, Tennent, 1/9/57.
35. Ibid., 815, Macready, 12/13/56.
36. Charles Dickens, Jr., 21.
37. *Let.*, II, 809, Collins, 10/26/56.
38. Ibid., 815, Macready, 12/13/56.
39. Kitton, *Pen and Pencil*, 119-20, Sup., 18; *Let.*, II, 812, Duke of Devonshire, 12/1/56. There was also a preliminary performance given for the servants and tradesmen and their friends on 1/5/57. Morgan MS., Dickens to Miss Coutts, 12/9/56.
40. *Let.*, II, 823, Wills, 1/4/57, 825, Milman, 1/9/57.
41. Morgan MS., Dickens to Collins, 10/26/56; *Let.*, II, 806, Collins, 10/15/56, 826, Berger, 1/17/57.
42. *Coll. P.*, II, 325, Prologue to *The Frozen Deep*, 1856.
43. The sunset effect alone took ten minutes of gradually changing lights. Morgan MS., Dickens to Mrs. Brown, 1/2/57.
44. Wright, *Life*, 248, quoting Charles Dickens, Jr.
45. *Let.*, II, 824, Wills, 1/7/57.
46. Ibid., 827, Cerjat, 1/17/57.
47. Ibid., 831, Macready, 1/28/57.
48. Ibid., 844, Carlisle, 4/15/57.
49. Ibid., 838, Paxton, 3/1/57.
50. Ibid., 845, Carlisle, 4/15/57.
51. Ibid., 835, Collins, 2/14/57.
52. Ibid., 838, 3/4/57.
53. Wright, *Life*, 243.
54. *Let.*, II, 846, Collins, 5/12/57.
55. Ibid., 848, 5/22/57.
56. Ibid., 827-8, Cerjat, 1/17/57.
57. Ibid., 828.
58. Morgan MS., Dickens to Austin, 8/12/55.

59. *Let.*, II, 699, Wills, 10/21/55.
60. Ibid., 701, 10/24/55.
61. Ibid., 751, Georgina Hogarth, 3/14/56.
62. Ibid., 743, Miss Coutts, 2/9/56.
63. Morgan MS., Dickens to Austin, 4/17/56.
64. Ibid., 2/15/57.
65. *Let.*, II, 841, Andersen, 4/3/57.
66. Ibid., 848, White, 5/22/57.
67. Ibid., 847, Collins, 5/17/57, Beard, 5/17/57.
68. Ibid., 852, Collins, 61/57.
69. Ibid., 855, Russell, 6/10/57.
70. Ibid., III, 76-7, Blanchard Jerrold, 11/26/58.
71. Ibid., II, 854, Forster, 6/10/57.
72. According to Berger, *Reminiscences*, 22, the Gallery of Illustration was offered for the purpose by the T. German Reeds, who occupied it. Mrs. Reed was the former Priscilla Horton, the "Ariel" to whom Dickens had written a poem in 1838. *Coll. P.*, II, 301.
73. *Let.*, II, 858, Forster, 6/21/57. Dickens agreed, however, to go to the Palace if the Queen *wouldn't* come to the Gallery of Illustration. Morgan MS., Dickens to Miss Coutts, 6/20/57.
74. Widener MS., schedule of rehearsals, 6/19/57.
75. *Let.*, II, 854, Forster, 6/10/57.
76. Widener MS., schedule of rehearsals, 6/19/57.
77. Ellis, *Collins*, 18 fn., quoting a reminiscence of Henry Fielding Dickens.
78. Andersen, *A Visit*, 185-6; Andersen, *Letters*, quoted by Pope-Hennessy, 372.
79. Andersen, *A Visit*, 188-90, 193.
80. *Let.*, II, 860, Miss Coutts, 7/10/57.
81. Ibid., 864, Jerdan, 7/21/57.
82. Ibid.
83. Dexter, *Letters to Lemon*, 148, quoting Georgina Hogarth's letter to Maria Winter.
84. *Let.*, II, 859, Thackeray, 7/2/57.
85. Ibid., Forster, 7/5/57.
86. Ibid., 862, Macready, 7/13/57.
87. Wright, *Life*, 251-2, illustration f. 253.
88. *Let.*, II, 864, Jerdan, 7/21/57.
89. Andersen, *Letters*, quoted by Pope-Hennessy, 377.
90. Ellis, *Collins*, 19, quoting a reminiscence of Henry Fielding Dickens; A. T. Dickens, 636.
91. Andersen, *A Visit*, 196; Andersen, *Letters*, quoted by Pope-Hennessy, 377.
92. Storey, 22.
93. *Let.*, II, 531, Landor, 1/7/54.
94. Ibid., 784, 7/5/56.
95. Ibid., 486, 9/8/53.
96. Morgan MS., Dickens to Miss Coutts, 8/22/51.
97. Ibid., 6/18/54.
98. Ibid., 7/25/52.
99. *Let.*, II, 817, Eastwick, 12/21/56.
100. Ibid., 835, Wills, 2/9/57.
101. Ibid., 862, Macready, 7/13/57.
102. Morgan MS., Dickens to Miss Coutts, 4/9/57.
103. *Let.*, II, 835 fn.
104. Morgan MS., Dickens to Miss Coutts, 4/9/57.
105. Ibid., 7/10/57.
106. *Let.*, II, 863, Yates, 7/19/57.
107. Morgan MS., Dickens to Austin, 7/21/57.
108. *Let.*, II, 853, Austin, 6/6/57.
109. Ibid., 869, Forster, [8/?/57].
110. Ibid., 870, Austin, 8/15/57.
111. Ibid., 886, Forster, 9/24/57.
112. Morgan MS., Dickens to Austin, 8/28/57.
113. *Let.*, II, 866, Collins, 8/2/57.
114. Ibid., 866-7, Mrs. Compton, 8/2/57.
115. Wright, *Life*, 242, 242-3 fn.
116. *Let.*, II, 870, Stone, 8/17/57.
117. Berger, 35.
118. Hunt. MS., Dickens to Mrs. Watson, 12/7/57.
119. Ibid.

120. Pemberton, 129, quoting Collins's preface to the play in narrative form. Wright, *Life*, 256, says there was a third Manchester performance on 8/24/57.
121. Morgan MS., Dickens to W. H. Russell, 7/7/58. The part quoted is omitted from *Let.*, III, 31.
122. *Let.*, II, 875, Austin, 9/2/57.
123. Morgan MS., Dickens to Collins, 8/29/57.
124. *Let.*, II, 881, Georgina Hogarth, 9/9/57.
125. Ibid., 880, Forster, 9/9/57.
126. Ibid., 881, Georgina Hogarth, 9/9/57.
127. R. P., "Lazy Tour," 821.
128. *Let.*, II, 883, Georgina Hogarth, 9/12/57.
129. Forster, 633-4; *Let.*, II, 885, Forster, [9/?/57], 885 fn.
130. *Let.*, II, 887-8, Forster. Here dated as September, but Forster, 640, gives it as *earlier* than 9/5/57, and it may even be late August.
131. Ibid., 888, [10/?/57].
132. Ibid., 877-8, Forster, 9/5/57.
133. Ibid.
134. Ibid., 888, [10/?/57].

Chapter 8 [pp. 883-903]

1. Shaw, Preface to *Great Expectations*.
2. Wilson, *Wound and Bow*, 56.
3. *L. D.*, I, xxiv, 293.
4. Ibid., iii, 36.
5. Ibid., ii, 23.
6. Ibid., iii, 39.
7. Ibid., xxiii, 287.
8. Ibid., 288. Wright, *Life*, 217, says Bleeding Heart Yard was Bedfordsbury, off St. Martin's Lane; but see also *H. W.*, IX, 297, 5/13/54, and 466, 7/1/54, "Tattyboy's Rents."
9. Ibid., xxi, 254-5.
10. Ibid., II, xxv, 734.
11. Ibid., preface to 1st edition, ix.
12. *Let.*, II, 766, Forster, [4/?/56].

13. *L. D.*, I, xxi, 259.
14. Ibid., 260.
15. Ibid., 259.
16. Ibid., 257.
17. Ibid., xxv, 320-1.
18. Ibid., II, vii, 528-9.
19. Ibid., I, xxv, 322.
20. Ibid., 324.
21. Ibid., xvii, 215.
22. Ibid., 212.
23. Ibid., xxxiv, 415.
24. Pearson, 220.
25. *L. D.*, I, xxxiv, 414.
26. Yates, *Recollections*, II, 25. Yates wrote "deed stupid," but I have rendered it "d——d" for clarity of meaning.
27. *L. D.*, I, ix, 103.
28. Ibid., x, 109-11.
29. *Dick.*, XLII, 35-8.
30. *H. W.*, "The Doom of English Wills," 10/5/50, 25-9, 11/2/50, 125-8.
31. Ibid., *Dick.*, XLI, 35-8.
32. *L. D.*, I, xvii, 213.
33. Ibid., xxxiv, 418-9.
34. R. P., 125-32, "A Poor Man's Tale of a Patent," *H. W.*, 10/19/50.
35. Ibid., 132.
36. *L. D.*, I, x, 125-6.
37. Cf. House, 175 fn.
38. Ibid., 187.
39. *L. D.*, I, x, 128.
40. Ibid., xix, 233.
41. Ibid., 237-8.
42. Ibid., 238.
43. Ibid., ix, 102.
44. Ibid., xxxv, 431
45. Ibid., II, v, 494.
46. Ibid., xix, 670-1.
47. Ibid., 670.
48. Ibid., 673.
49. Ibid., I, xiii, 170.

Chapter 9 [pp. 904-926]

1. Morgan MS., Dickens to Mrs. Brown, 8/28/57.
2. *Let.*, II, 888, Forster, [10/?/57].
3. Ibid., 878, Forster, 9/5/57.
4. Forster, 641-2.

5. Fielding, London *Times* Lit. Sup., 3/2/1951, quoting Dickens letter to Miss Coutts, 5/9/58.
6. Hawthorne, 379, 7/10/56.
7. Fielding, London *Times* Lit. Sup., Dickens letter to Miss Coutts, 5/9/58.
8. Berg MS., Dickens to Miss Coutts, 8/23/58.
9. Pearson, 238.
10. Morgan MS., Dickens to Miss Coutts, 1/19/54.
11. Fielding, London *Times* Lit. Sup., 3/9/1951.
12. Berg MS., Dickens to De la Rue, 10/23/57.
13. Dexter, *Mr. and Mrs.*, 274, the "violated letter," 5/25/58.
14. Wright, *Life*, 244, f. 258.
15. Hunt. MS., Dickens to Mrs. Watson, 12/7/57.
16. *Let.*, II, 621, Forster, [1/?/55].
17. R. P., "Lazy Tour," 762.
18. Hunt. MS., Dickens to Mrs. Watson, 12/7/57.
19. *Let.*, II, 890, Anne Cornelius, 10/11/57.
20. Hunt. MS., Dickens to Mrs. Watson, 12/7/57, records this occurrence as having taken place some six or eight weeks previous to the date of the letter.
21. Millar MS., Dickens to Lord Brougham, 10/18/57; Ray, IV, 61, Dickens, Thackeray, and Forster to the Friends of Lady Blessington, 12/24/57.
22. *Coll. P.*, II, 427-31, speech, 11/5/57.
23. *Let.*, III, 5, Forster, 2/2/58.
24. *Coll. P.*, II, 433, speech, 2/9/58.
25. Ibid., 434-5.
26. Ibid., 436.
27. Forster, 645.
28. *Let.*, III, 7, Marston, 2/3/58.
29. Ibid., 14, Collins, 3/21/58.
30. Ibid., 13, Forster, [3/?/58].
31. Ibid., 12, 3/20/58.
32. Forster, 646.
33. *Let.*, III, 14, Forster. Dated merely as March, 1858, but must be

after 3/26/58, when Dickens went to Edinburgh, inasmuch as this was clearly written after his return.
34. Ibid., 15, Forster. Dated merely as March, but must be still later than the preceding letter, in which he hasn't yet made up his mind about the readings, whereas in this his decision is established. Very probably, therefore, early April.
35. Ibid.
36. Numerous letters: *Let.*, II, 640-1, Smith, 3/12/55, Blackwood, 3/12/55, Cunningham, 3/12/55, 642, Reeve, 3/16/55, Dilke, 3/16/55, 655, Lemon, 4/21/55, 656, Elwin, 5/1/55, 667, Lemon, 6/6/55, 668, Pickersgill, 6/7/55, 747, Wills, 2/17/56, 840, Dilke, 3/19/57. Also article by Morley in *H. W.*, 3/8/56, "The Royal Literary Fund," 169-72.
37. Berg Coll., "The Case of the Reformers."
38. Parrish Coll., "The Royal Literary Fund: A Summary of the facts."
39. Berg Coll., "The Answer to the Summary."
40. Forster, 645, 661.
41. *Let.*, III, 17, Forster, 4/9/58.
42. Ibid., 20, Beard, 5/1/58.
43. Forster, 661. Forster and Kent, 59, both say there were sixteen readings in this series, but see *Dick.*, XXXVII, 133.
44. *Let.*, III, 20, Beard, 5/1/58.
45. Wright, *Life*, 254. Cf. Bigelow, I, 264, who makes it a brooch, and renders Ellen's name as Miss Teman.
46. *Let.*, II, 826, Berger, 1/13/57.
47. Wright, *Life*, 254.
48. Storey, 96.
48a. Morgan MS., Dickens to Miss Coutts, 10/25/53.
48b. Morgan MS., Dickens to Miss Coutts, 5/9/58.
49. Mention should be made here of a letter supposedly written 8/20/58

by Catherine Dickens's aunt, Mrs. Helen Thomson, to a Glasgow friend, Mrs. Stark, telling her a number of details about the separation. The late Ralph Straus generously allowed me to make a copy of this letter from a transcript in his possession. His own copy had been made over twenty years before from a document sent him by a correspondent. Although Mr. Straus no longer recalled who his correspondent had been and could not remember whether the document was the original or a copy, he believed it genuine. The late Walter Dexter, however, believed it a fabrication and doubted that any original existed. Although the letter was undeniably composed by someone well acquainted with the facts, Dexter in my judgment disposes conclusively of its claims to authenticity by pointing out in *Dick.*, XXXIII, 2-4, that it refers to Dickens's "violated letter" as "now going the rounds of the press." This was first published in the N. Y. *Tribune* on 8/16/58—only four days before the date of this supposed comment on it by Mrs. Thomson—and was not copied in British papers till 8/31/58. Further, there was no such address in Glasgow as "1, Vanbrugh Place, Links Leath."

To these points Dexter might have added the further psychological argument that the letter is unnecessarily detailed in explaining family relationships ("her sister Helen," "her daughter Georgina"), mentioning how many children Catherine had borne, and telling how old the youngest was at this time, considering that "Mrs. Stark" is presumably a close enough friend to receive a confidential story of the separation. Less significant, perhaps, is the fact that Catherine's name is consistently misspelled "Catharine." All told, however, these facts seem to me to preclude attaching any authority even to the missing original.

50. Dexter, *Mr. and Mrs.*, 277-8, Appendix III, Lemon to Forster, 5/14/58, saying "Mrs. Dickens thankfully accepts the proposal."

51. Ibid., 257, 280, Appendix IV, including letter of Charles Dickens, Jr., to his mother, 7/13/58.

52. *Let.*, III, 25 fn., letter of Charles Dickens, Jr., to his father, 5/10/58.

53. Storey, 96.

53a. Observe the wording of the quotation from Catherine's letter, 5/19/58, two paragraphs lower in the text, written on the same day as Dickens's refusal to discuss the subject with Miss Coutts.

54. Suzannet MS., Dickens to Miss Coutts, 5/19/58.

54a. Morgan MS., Catherine Dickens to Miss Coutts, 5/19/58.

55. Dexter, *Mr. and Mrs.*, 275-6, Appendix II, statement dated 5/29/58, and signed by Mrs. Hogarth and Helen Hogarth. Note, however, that there is some slight ambiguity about dates; this statement accompanied the "violated letter" and a note to Arthur Smith, both of which were dated 5/25/58.

56. Ray, IV, 86-7, Thackeray to Mrs. Carmichael, [5/?/58].

57. Berg MS., Dickens to Miss Coutts, 8/23/58.

58. Yates, *Recollections*, 92-6.

59. Forster, 648.

60. Morgan MS., Dickens to Macready, 6/7/58.

61. Dexter, *Mr. and Mrs.*, 257-8, 6/4/58.

62. Ibid., 271-2; H. W., 6/12/58, 601.

63. Morgan MSS., Dickens to Macready, 5/28/58, Dickens to Mary

Boyle, 5/29/58, Dickens to Mrs. Gore, 5/31/58; Let., III, 27, Tagart, 6/14/58, 29, Cerjat, 7/7/58.

64. Dexter, Mr. and Mrs., 276; Let., III, 21-2, Smith, 5/25/58.

65. Dexter, Mr. and Mrs., 273-5; Let., III, 22-3.

66. Rylands Lib., copy of Our Contemporaries, London: 1858, Blagney and Fryer, 63, quoting these comments.

67. Forster, 648.

68. Dexter, Mr. and Mrs., 258, Dickens to Ouvry, 9/5/58.

69. Storey, 94.

PART NINE

Chapter 1 [pp. 929-952]

1. Yates, Recollections, II, 96. Yates's memory, however, confused this occasion with the first professional reading on 4/29/58, when Dickens read The Cricket on the Hearth. At the first reading after the appearance of the Household Words statement, on 6/17/58, the readings were "The Poor Traveller," "The Boots," and "Mrs. Gamp."

2. Let., III, 26, Yates, 6/8/58.

3. Dexter, Mr. and Mrs., 278, Appendix III, Lemon to Forster, 5/20,21/58.

4. Let., III, 33, Evans, 7/22/58.

5. Yates, Recollections, II, 9-10.

6. Ray, IV, facsimile bet. 90-91; also Yates, Mr. Thackeray, 3-4.

7. Ray, II, 660, Thackeray to Forster, 4/3/50.

8. Thackeray often expressed this fear: e.g., Ray, III, 283, Thackeray to Sarah Baxter, 7/4-5/53, 287, Thackeray to Mrs. Carmichael-Smyth, 7/18/53, 294, Thackeray to William Bradford Reed, 7/21/53, 616, Thackeray to Mrs. Elliot and Kate

Perry, 9/10/56, IV, 80, Thackeray to Mrs. Baxter, 8/25/56, 108, Thackeray to the Baxters, 8/25/58; also Stevenson. Showman, 323, quoting a comment Thackeray made to Whitwell Elwin in October, 1856.

9. Ray, IV, 89-90, Thackeray to Yates, 6/13/58.

10. Yates, Recollections, II, 15-8; also Yates, Mr. Thackeray, 5-6.

11. Ray, IV, 91-2, Yates to Thackeray, 6/15/58; also Yates, Mr. Thackeray, 6.

12. Ray, IV, 93-4, Thackeray to the Committee of the Garrick Club, 6/19/58; also Yates, Mr. Thackeray, 6.

13. Ray, IV, 95-6, Yates to the Committee of the Garrick Club, 6/23/58; also Yates, Mr. Thackeray, 7.

14. Let., III, 32, Russell, 7/7/58; Ray, IV, 96-7, Doland to Yates, 6/26/58; Yates, Mr. Thackeray, 8.

15. Let., III, 32, Committee of the Garrick Club, 7/12/58.

16. Ray, IV, 98, n. 49, quoting this allusion from The Virginians, No. IX, Ch. 35.

17. Ibid., 109-10, n. 59, quoting from The Virginians, No. XI, Ch. 43.

18. Let., III, 32, Russell, 7/7/58.

19. Ibid., 33, Simpson, 7/23/58.

20. Yates, Mr. Thackeray, 10.

21. Ray, IV, 107, Fladgate to Thackeray, 7/27/58.

22. Yates, Mr. Thackeray, 11.

23. Ray, IV, 116-8, Dickens to Thackeray, 11/24/58; also Let., III, 74.

24. Ray, IV, 118, Thackeray to Dickens, 11/26/58.

24a. Yates, Recollections, II, 36 fn.

25. Jeaffreson, II, 265-6.

26. Ray, IV, 119-20, Thackeray to the Committee of the Garrick Club, 11/28/58.

27. Yates, Recollections, II, 32; also Yates, Mr. Thackeray, 11.

28. Ray, IV, 238, Thackeray to Elwin, 5/24/61.
29. Kent, *Dickens as Reader*, passim.
30. *Dick.*, IX, 97; cf. reading copies of the various books and stories in Berg Collection.
31. *Let.*, III, 38, Collins, 8/11/58.
32. Hunt. MS., Dickens to Georgina Hogarth, 8/5/58, incomplete and inaccurate in *Let.*, III, 35.
33. *Let.*, III, 38, Collins, 8/11/58.
34. Hunt. MS., Dickens to Georgina Hogarth, 8/5/58; see note 32 above.
35. *Let.*, III, 35-6, Mary Dickens, 8/7/58.
36. Ibid., 36, Wills, 8/9/58.
37. Ibid., 38, Collins, 8/11/58.
38. Ibid., 41, Yates, 8/25/58.
39. Ibid., 44-5, Georgina Hogarth, 8/25/58.
40. Ibid., 46, Mary Dickens, 8/28/58.
41. Ibid., 48, Georgina Hogarth, 8/29/58.
42. Ibid.
43. Morgan MS., Dickens to Mary Boyle, 9/10/58, incomplete in *Let.*, III, 52-3.
44. Hunt. MS., Dickens to Wills, 10/25/58.
45. *Let.*, III, 235, Webster, 9/9/61.
46. Ibid., 291, Yates, 4/3/62.
47. Hunt. MS., Dickens to Wills, 10/25/58.
48. *Let.*, III, 54-5, Georgina Hogarth, 9/12/58.
49. Ibid., 58-9, 9/26/58.
50. Ibid., 60, Wills, 10/2/58.
51. Payn, *Recollections*, 588. On 586, Payn inaccurately gives as 9/19/58 the date of a letter in which Dickens invited him to accompany them on this walk; the original MS. in the Boston Public Library clearly reads 9/29/58.
52. *Let.*, III, 62, Forster, 10/10/58.
53. Ibid., 70, Collins, 11/9/58.
54. Ibid., 63, Beard, 10/14/58. There were, all told, 87 readings in this series: see *Dick.*, XXXVII,

133, also Forster, 661, and Kent, *Dickens as Reader*, 60.
55. *Let.*, III, 65, Miss Coutts, 10/27/58.
56. Nisbet, 157-76.
57. *Let.*, III, 61, Forster, 10/10/58.
58. Ibid., 49, Georgina Hogarth, 8/29/58.
59. Ibid., II, 815, Frederick Dickens, 12/12/56.
60. Ibid., 824, 833, Frederick Dickens, 1/8/57, 2/5/57.
61. Ibid., III, 49, Georgina Hogarth, 8/29/58.
62. Morgan MSS., Dickens to T. J. Thompson, 10/27/58, 11/8/58. The quotation is from the second of these.
63. Morgan MS., Dickens to T. J. Thompson, 11/22/58.
64. Ibid., Dickens to T. J. Thompson, 12/27/58. The Morgan Library has one more letter, dated 1/6/59, from Dickens to Thompson on this subject, in which Dickens remarks that "it is mere beating the air" for them to discuss it. "If Mr. Weller will make no proposal on the one hand, and Frederick will make none on the other, any proposal from us will only draw us into difficulty—will only be twisted into a proposal from the fountain head—and will necessitate our personal explanation and disclaimer in the Witness Box. They must go on. We can do nothing."
65. *Let.*, III, 252, Georgina Hogarth, 11/7/61.
66. Ibid., 415, Cunningham, 2/15/65.
67. Waugh, *Hundred Years*, 111, 115-6.
68. *Let.*, III, 66, Wills, 11/3/58.
69. Ibid., 67, 11/3/58 (a second letter of same date).
70. Ibid., 71, 11/10/58.
71. Morgan MS., draft of a letter dated 12/10/58 from Forster to

Bradbury and Evans. Although transcribed in Dickens's hand, this manuscript *says* that Dickens knows nothing of its contents or of a letter dated 12/9/58, which Bradbury and Evans had written Forster. It is possible, of course, that Dickens made this copy later from one Forster showed him.

72. Fitzgerald, *Life*, 234; Fitzgerald, *Garrick Club*, 68.
73. Forster, 671.
74. Ibid., 671-2; also *Let.*, III, 90, Collins, 1/26/59.
75. *Let.*, III, 91, Forster, 1/28/59.
76. Ibid., 94-5, 2/21/59.
77. Lehman, *Dickens as Editor*, 261.
78. Fitzgerald, *Memories*, 192-4.
79. Hollingshead, I, 307, Dickens to Hollingshead, 3/3/59.
80. Fitzgerald, *Memories*, 192-4.
81. *Let.*, III, 103-4, Georgina Hogarth, 5/16/59. Mackenzie, 253, suggests that inasmuch as Bradbury and Evans, who owned only one-quarter of *Household Words*, would receive £887 out of its purchase price, Dickens positively made a profit in the acquisition of its plates and stock, but this argument ignores the fact that Dickens already owned three-quarters of these assets as well. Dickens's own estimate is therefore the correct one.
82. *Coll. P.*, I, 226-7, *H. W.*, 620, 5/28/59.
83. *Let.*, III, 100, Wills, 4/28/59.
84. Ibid., 108-9, 7/1/59.
85. Fitzgerald, *Memories*, 199.
86. Altick, 331-4, giving the text of Dickens's agreement with Thomas C. Evans.
87. *Coll. P.*, I, 226, *H. W.*, 601, 5/28/59.
88. *Let.*, III, 113, Forster, [7/?/59].
89. This calculation is based on the figures given in *Dick.*, XLVI, 197-203.

90. Fielding, *Dickens and Evans*, 123-4.
91. *Let.*, III, 108, Fields, [6/?/59].
92. Ibid., 112, Forster, [7/?/59].
93. Hird MS., Dickens to George H. Lewes, 8/14/59.
94. *Let.*, III, 115-6, Collins, 8/16/59. Around this time Dickens sold to the New York *Ledger* for £1,000 a story called "Hunted Down," which had its imaginative roots in the career of Thomas Griffiths Wainewright, the artist, critic, and poisoner whom Dickens had seen in prison years ago while visiting there with Macready. The story was published in the *Ledger*, 8/20,27/59, 9/3/59, and in *All the Year Round*, 4/4,11/60.
95. Forster, 729.
96. *Let.*, III, 95, Forster, 2/21/59.
97. Ibid., 97, Carlyle, 3/24/59.
98. Pope-Hennessy, 402.
99. *T. T. C.*, preface, vii.
100. *Let.*, III, 95, Forster, 3/11/59.
101. Yates, *Recollections*, II, 32.
102. Frith, *Autobiography*, 206.
103. Frith, *Small Talk*, 806.
104. Frith, *Autobiography*, 208-9.
105. Forster, 688-9.
106. *Dick.*, XXXVII, 133. This series of eight was overlooked in Kent's listing of the readings.
107. Frith, *Autobiography*, 209-10.
108. Wright, *Life*, 286, 288.
109. *Let.*, III, 105, Mrs. Watson, 6/5/59.
110. Ibid., 107, Mary Dickens, 6/13/59.
111. For the jaunting car, see *Let.*, III, 48, Georgina Hogarth, 8/29/58, 50, Finlay, 9/2/58, 108, 6/28/59.
112. *Let.*, III, 110, Forster, 7/9/59.
113. Barrett MS., Dickens to Miss Coutts, 4/8/60.
114. *Let.*, III, 104, Mrs. Watson, 5/31/59.

Chapter 2 [pp. 953-971]

1. *Let.*, III, 110, White, 7/7/59.
2. Ibid., 108, Finlay, 6/28/59, 112, Collins, 7/17/59, 114, Beard, 8/2/59, Fitzgerald, 8/2/59.
3. Ibid., 115-6, Collins, 8/16/59.
4. Ibid., 120, Mary and Kate Dickens, 9/2/59.
5. Morgan MS., Dickens to Miss Coutts, 9/16/59.
6. *Let.*, III, 160, Cerjat, 5/3/60.
7. Ibid.
8. Ibid., 104, Mrs. Watson, 5/31/59, 124, Gibson, 9/23/59.
9. Ibid., 122, Gibson, 9/8/59.
10. Ibid., 104-5, Mrs. Watson, 5/31/59.
11. Ibid., 122, Gibson, 9/8/59.
12. Ibid., 103, 5/16/59, 123, 9/8/59, 178, Mrs. Watson, 9/14/60.
13. Ibid., 69, Gibson, 11/6/58.
14. Ibid., 85, Lytton, 1/6/59, 103, Gibson, 5/11/59; House MS., Dickens to Lord Clarence Paget, 1/5/60.
15. *Let.*, III, 178, Mrs. Watson, 9/14/60.
16. Ibid., 179-80, Mary Dickens, 9/23/60.
17. Ibid., 153, Bewsher, 3/14/60.
18. Ibid., 134, Felton, 11/10/59.
19. Ibid., 118, Forster, 8/25/59.
20. Ibid., 126, Mrs. Hulkes, 10/16/59.
21. Ibid., 134, Felton, 11/10/59, 131, Carlyle, 10/30/59.
22. Ibid., 127, Wills, 10/16/59. Kent, *Dickens as Reader*, overlooks this group of readings.
23. Ibid., 129, Georgina Hogarth, 10/21/59, Stone, 10/19/59, 128, Yates, 10/18/59.
24. Ibid., 130, Wills, 10/26/59.
25. Ibid., 10/28/59.
26. Ibid., 4, Eliot, 1/18/58.
27. Ibid., 110-1, 7/10/59.
28. Berg MS., Dickens to George H. Lewes, 11/14/59.
29. Ibid., 11/20/59.
30. *Let.*, III, 150, Lewes, 2/13/60.
31. Ibid., 139, Mrs. Gaskell, 12/20/59.
32. Ibid., 144, Lever, 1/2/60, 146-7, 1/13/60.
33. Ibid., 151-2, 2/21/60, 152, 3/1/60.
34. Ibid., 165, 6/21/60.
35. Ibid., 159, Forster, 5/2/60.
36. Ibid., 155, Macready, 3/30/60.
37. *Coll. P.*, II, 14-7, A. Y. R., 12/24/59, "Leigh Hunt, a Remonstrance."
38. *Let.*, III, 137, Wills, 11/19/59.
39. Ibid., 138, Longmans, 11/28/59; Royal Academy MSS., Dickens to Marcus Stone, 11/26/59, Dickens to John Murray, 11/28/59.
40. Storey, 80; Mackenzie, 34.
41. *Let.*, III, 135, Helen Dickens, 11/13/59.
42. Ibid., 169, Forster, 7/29/60.
43. Ibid., 172, Mrs. Dickinson, 8/19/60.
44. Ibid., 174-5, Georgina Hogarth, 8/21/60.
45. Ibid., 192-3, 11/27/60.
46. Storey, 104. There is no information about the suitor's identity or Dickens's reasons for disapproving.
47. Ibid., 212.
48. Ibid., 104.
49. Forster, 685-6; D. N. B., XI, 366.
50. *Let.*, III, 163, Beard, 6/12/60.
51. Forster, 685-6.
52. *Let.*, III, 168, Helen Dickens, 7/19/60.
53. Ibid., 173, Mrs. Dickinson, 8/19/60.
54. Ibid., 168, Helen Dickens, 7/19/60.
55. Ibid., 173, Mrs. Dickinson, 8/19/60.
56. Storey, 106.
57. *Let.*, III, 172, Mitton, 8/19/60; Pope-Hennessy, 408.
58. *Let.*, III, 171, Anne Cornelius, 8/15/60, Mitton, 8/16/60.
59. Ibid., 176, Wills, 9/4/60; Hunt.

MS., Dickens to Ouvry, 8/19/60.

60. *Let.*, III, 174-5, Lillie, 8/21,24/60.
61. Ibid., 182, Forster, [9/?/60].
62. Hole, 77, quoting Dickens's letter, 12/20/60.
63. Storey, 107.
64. *Let.*, III, 177, Wills, 9/4/60.
65. Pearson, 281.
66. Bigelow, II, 127.
67. *Let.*, III, 180, Mary Dickens, 9/23/60.
68. R. P., U. T., I, 283.
69. *Let.*, III, 182, Forster, [9/?/60].
70. Ibid., 10/4/60.
71. Ibid., 183, 10/6/60, Lever 10/6/60.
72. Quoted in Pearson, 269.
73. *Let.*, III, 183, Lever, 10/6/60.
74. Ibid., 182, Forster, 10/4/60.
75. Ibid., 183, 10/6/60.
76. Ibid., 186, [10/?/60].
77. Quoted in Pearson, 268; also in Stevenson, *Dr. Quicksilver*, 154, 161.
78. *Let.*, III, 183-4, Lever, 10/6/60.
79. Ibid., 186-7, 10/15/60.
80. See advertisements on end pp. of A. Y. R., beginning 2/9/61, announcing that *A Day's Ride* will conclude 3/23/61.
81. See Dickens's letters to Lever, Livingston, ed., and Rollins's introduction, xiv-v; also *Let.*, III, 207, Lever, 1/25/61, 210, 2/13/61, 271, 12/28/61, 278, 1/13/62, 278, Chapman, 1/13/62 (two of this date), 282, Lever, 1/24/62, 286, 2/8/62, 305, 10/2/62, 315 11/4/62, 370, 11/5/63, 371 12/1/63; Livingston, Chapman to Dickens, 12/15/63; *Let.*, III, 373, Lever, 12/16/63, 406, 12/24/64.
82. *Let.*, III, 190, Georgina Hogarth, 11/1/60.
83. Ibid., 193, 11/27/60.
84. Ibid., 11/28/60.
85. Ibid., 208, Cerjat, 2/1/61.

86. Ibid., 196, Mary Boyle, 12/28/60.
87. Ibid., 209, Cerjat, 2/1/61.
88. Wright, *Life*, 280.
89. Forster, 687. This series of six is not listed in Kent, *Dickens as Reader*. At one of the readings Count Leo Tolstoy was an enthusiastic listener, see *Dick.*, XXVI, 106.
90. *Let.*, III, 216, Forster, 4/28/61.
91. Ibid., 217, Forster, [4/?/61].
92. Ibid., 222, Collins, 5/24/61.
93. Ibid., 224, Macready, 6/11/61.
94. Ibid., Lytton, 6/7/61, 225, 6/24/61.
95. Ibid., 225, Collins, 6/23/61.
96. Ibid., 226, Forster, 6/26/61.
97. Ibid., 225, Collins, 6/23/61.
98. Ibid., 226, Forster, 6/26/61.
99. Ibid., 231, Collins, 8/28/61.
100. Morgan MS., Dickens to Macready, 6/11/61. The paragraph quoted is omitted from *Let.*, III, 224.
101. Forster, 737 fn.
102. Ellis, *Ainsworth*, II, 264, quoting Percy Fitzgerald.

Chapter 3 [pp. 972-994]

1. *T. T. C.*, preface, vii.
2. Ibid.
3. Ibid., I, IV, 19.
4. *Let.*, III, 23, "violated letter."
5. *T. T. C.*, I, III, 12.
6. Langer, 578.
7. *Let.*, III, 117, Forster, [8/?/59].
8. *T. T. C.*, II, xv, 358.
9. Ibid., I, v, 28.
10. Ibid., II, VII, 105.
11. Ibid., VIII, 109.
12. Ibid., I, v, 28-9.
13. Ibid., II, IX, 124.
14. Ibid., XXIII, 222-3.
15. Ibid., III, v, 267-9.
16. Ibid., VI, 274-6.
17. Ibid., v, 269.
18. Ibid., VI, 272-3.
19. Ibid., II, XXI, 211-2.
20. Ibid., XXII, 214-5.
21. Ibid., 216.

22. Ibid., III, xv, 362.
23. Ibid., I, vi, 44.
24. Ibid., III, xv, 363.
25. Ibid., I, iv, 22.
26. Pearson, 267.
27. G. E., iv, 37.
28. Ibid., ii, 6.
29. Ibid., vii, 49.
30. Ibid., iv, 20.
31. Ibid., i, 3-4.
32. Ibid., xviii, 137-8.
33. Ibid., xix, 148.
34. Ibid., xxvii, 214.
35. Ibid., xviii, 140.
36. Ibid., xi, 79.
37. Ibid., xvii, 127.
38. Ibid., xxix, 228.
39. Ibid., 233.
40. Ibid., xliv, 355.
41. Ibid., xxix, 235.
42. Ibid., 241.
43. Ibid., xxxix, 316.
44. Ibid.
45. Ibid., 319.
46. Shaw, Introduction to *Great Expectations*.
47. G. E., xxxix, 319.
48. Ibid., liv, 439.
49. Ibid., 440.
50. Ibid., lviii, 471-2.
50a. Shaw, Introduction to *Great Expectations*.
51. G. E., xxxii, 261.
52. Shaw, Introduction to *Great Expectations*.
53. G. E., xxxiv, 271.
54. Jackson, *Progress of a Radical*, 196.
55. G. E., xxvi, 207.
56. Ibid., xxv, 202, 203, 204.
57. Ibid., xxxvi, 289.
58. Ibid., xxxvii, 294.
59. Ibid., xxxvi, 289.
60. *Let.*, III, 14, Collins, 3/21/58.
61. Hunt. MS., Dickens to Mrs. Watson, 12/7/57.
62. Shaw, Introduction to *Great Expectations*.
63. G. E., ix, 63-4.
64. Ibid., xxxi, 251, 252.
65. Ibid., xxx, 243.

66. Ibid., lvii, 458.
67. Milton, *Paradise Lost*, XII, 646-9.

Chapter 4 [pp. 995-1021]

1. *Let.*, III, 218, Lytton, 5/12/61, 231, 8/28/61.
2. Ibid., 234, Forster, [9/?/61].
3. Ibid., 340, Wills, 2/4/63.
4. Lehmann MS., Dickens to Frederick Lehmann, 1/6/63.
5. *Let.*, III, 370, Sawyer, 11/6/63.
6. Ibid., 349, Collins, 4/22/63.
7. Ibid., 304-5, 9/20/62.
8. Ibid., 194, Lytton, 12/4/60.
9. Ibid., 218, 5/12/61.
10. Ibid., 224, 6/7/61.
11. E. D., *Christmas Stories*, "Tom Tiddler's Ground," I, 501.
12. *Let.*, III, 234, Forster, [9/?/61].
13. Ibid., 240, 9/28/61.
14. Ibid., 241, Watkins, 9/28/61.
15. Ibid., 243, Forster, [10/?/61].
16. Morgan MSS., Dickens to Letitia Austen, 10/17/61, 11/3,6,13,15,22,25/61, 12/1,4,10,18,24/61, and various others to 6/5/64, in which Dickens announced that the grant had been made.
17. *Let.*, III, 290, James, 3/27/62.
18. Morgan MS., Dickens to Mrs. Brown, 11/3/61.
19. *Let.*, III, 249-50, Beard, 11/3/61.
20. Ibid., 320, 11/15/62.
21. Ibid., 245, Georgina Hogarth, 10/29/61.
22. Ibid., 248, Collins, 10/31/61.
23. Hunt. MS., Dickens to Georgina Hogarth, 11/1/61, incomplete in *Let.*, III, 248-9.
24. *Let.*, III, 248, Collins, 10/31/61.
25. Ibid., 256, Wills, 11/22/61.
26. Ibid., 256-7, Georgina Hogarth, 11/22/61.
27. Ibid., 259, Mary Dickens, 11/23/61.
28. Ibid., 261, Forster, [11/?/61].
29. Ibid., 259, Mary Dickens, 11/23/61.
30. Ibid., 261, Forster, [11/?/61].

31. Ibid., 264, Wills, 12/3/61.
32. Ibid., 262, 11/28/61.
33. Ibid., 276, 1/5/62.
34. Ibid., 277, Georgina Hogarth, 1/8/62.
35. Kent, *Dickens as Reader*, 64-5.
36. *Let.*, III, 267, Wills, 12/15/61.
37. Ibid., 279, Leech, 1/18/62.
38. Berg MS., Dickens to Thomas Baylis, 2/1/62, inaccurate in *Let.*, III, 284.
39. *Let.*, III, 401, Brooks, 10/16/64.
40. The residence at 16 Hyde Park Gate lasted till 6/21/62.
41. *Let.*, III, 282-3, Collins, 1/24/62.
42. Ibid., 292, Forster, [4/?/62].
43. Ibid., 289-90, Darlington, 3/23/62.
44. Ibid., 292, Forster, 4/8/62.
45. Morgan MS., Dickens to Macready, 6/2/62.
46. *Let.*, III, 301, Collins, 7/27/62.
47. H. C. Dickens MS., Dickens to Wilkie Collins, 7/20/62.
48. *Let.*, III, 304-5, Collins, 9/20/62.
49. Ibid., 306, Forster, 10/5/62.
50. Ibid., 298, 6/28/62.
51. Ibid., 312, 10/22/62.
51a. Ibid.
52. Ibid., 314-5, Beard, 11/4/62, 320, 11/15/62.
53. Ibid., 312, Forster, 10/22/62.
54. Ibid., 306, 10/5/62.
55. Ibid., 312, 10/22/62.
56. Hunt. MS., Dickens to Wills, 10/14/62.
57. *Let.*, III, 317, Letitia Austen, 11/7/62.
58. Ibid., 445, Cerjat, 11/30/65.
59. Ibid., 317, Letitia Austen, 11/7/62.
60. Ibid., 227, Forster, 7/1/61.
61. Ibid., 288-9, Cerjat, 3/16/62.
62. Ibid., 310, Collins, 10/14/62.
62a. There is no further correspondence bearing on this point, and the chapters of *No Name* that were being published in *All the Year Round* during this period show no stylistic signs of being by any hand other than that of Collins.
63. *Let.*, III, 77, Maria Winter, 11/13/58.
64. Ibid., 320, 11/17/62.
65. Ibid., Beard, 11/15/62.
66. Ibid., 328, 12/24/62.
67. Ibid., 328-9, Miss Boyle, 12/27/62.
68. Ibid., 336, Wills, 1/19/63.
69. Ibid., 340, 2/4/63.
70. Quoted in Wright, *Life*, 283.
71. Yates, *Recollections*, II, 98; cf. Bigelow, I, 264, IV, 382. It is observable that both Sala and Yates are anxious at once to assert their scandalous knowledge and to hide its nature behind the claim of a "discretion" concerned for Dickens's good name and the susceptibilities of those still living. These facts make it impossible that they could have been referring merely to his temperamental frictions with Catherine; Dickens had blazoned them to the world in his "violated letter," and Catherine, who had died in 1879, could no longer be hurt by further reference to them. Bigelow, as I have already indicated in Part Eight, Ch. 9, n. 45, was rather less discreet. He claimed (IV, 382) to have received directly from Wilkie Collins the information that Ellen Ternan had been Dickens's mistress, and although in his earlier statement (I, 264), he incorrectly spells Ellen's name "Teman" and her mother's maiden name "Jermain," his story fits in with all the other independent revelations and discoveries.

For the additional evidence, cf. nn. 74, 75, 154, below, and the passages in this chapter to which they refer—Dickens's entry in his diary for November, 1867, the blacked-out memorandum to Wills, the inquiry to the Station Master at Charing Cross about the jewelry Ellen lost in the Staplehurst accident —and, in Part Ten, Thomas Wright's information about her tenancy of Windsor cottage (Ch. 1, n. 74) and Dickens's own letter to Mrs. Frances Elliot (Ch. 1, n. 75). Much more hypothetical, of course, is the possibility pointed out in Part Ten, Ch. 2, n. 45, that the unusually large sums paid over to W. H. Wills while Dickens was in America may have been intended to provide for Ellen's financial needs during his absence, but in view of the memorandum to Wills the suggestion cannot be altogether dismissed. The diary and the memorandum by themselves, however, are conclusive: a man does not consider bringing with him on such a journey a young lady with whom his relations are other than deeply intimate. In its totality the testimony of all these quite unconnected observers and investigators, rendered unquestionable by the documents in Dickens's own hand, is as authoritative as the evidence on a matter so discreetly handled can be.

72. Storey, 128.
73. See p. 1020 of the present book, quoting Rosenbach MS., Dickens to the Station Master, Charing Cross, 6/12/65.
74. Berg. Coll., Dickens's Diary for 1867, entry opposite November calendar.
75. Berg MS., memorandum to Wills, obviously written shortly before Dickens's departure on 11/7/67, most of which is printed in Let., III, 563, but there dated as October. The two sections I have quoted, however, are not in the

printed version, and in the manuscript the first of them is heavily overlined in black ink rendering it quite illegible to the eye. The words are clearly visible, however, in an infra-red photograph of the original in my possession. It is still further significant, of course, that someone—Georgina Hogarth? Mary Dickens?—made this effort to obliterate them. The second sentence of the second notation, beginning "He knows Nelly as you do," is interlineated, clearly as an afterthought, in writing so small as to be quite inconspicuous, and must have been overlooked by the mutilator of the earlier entry about Ellen.

76. Storey, 131.
77. Ibid., 24.
78. Ibid., 128.
79. Ibid., 93.
80. Ibid., 132.
81. Ibid., 91.
82. Ibid., 132.
83. Ibid., 93.
84. Wright, Autobiography, 67. Wright also reproduces f. 66 an autograph letter from Canon Benham, reading in part: "I am very glad you are going to publish a life of Dickens. I have one curious relic of him—the pen with which he wrote a part of the last number of Edwin Drood. It was given to me by the lady concerning whom he quarrelled with his wife. This between ourselves." Ardent defenders of Dickens's conventional good name, who have not hesitated to suggest that Wright invented his entire story and disbelieved that a clergyman would so betray a confidence, should study the implications of this facsimile. The last two sentences make it clear that

Benham had previously told Wright something of the story, and the last sentence would be unnecessarily cautious if it were an entirely innocent one. Those determined not to believe a word of Wright's statements must transfer most of their distrust to Canon Benham.

85. Hunt. MS., Dickens to Georgina Hogarth, 2/1/63, inaccurate and incomplete in *Let.*, III, 338.

86. *Let.*, III, 342-3, Macready, 2/19/63.

87. Hunt. MS., Dickens to Georgina Hogarth, 2/1/63. It should be noted that the last independent clause of the sentence I have quoted was excised, with no indication of its omission, from the version included in the selection of Dickens's letters edited by Mary Dickens and Georgina Hogarth, two volumes, 1880–81, and a third, 1882.

88. Forster, 694-5; *Let.*, III, 341-2, Forster, 2/7/63; Hunt. MS., Dickens to Georgina Hogarth, 2/12/63.

89. *Let.*, III, 348, Carlyle, 4/13/63.

90. Wilson, *Carlyle*, V, 504.

91. Pike, 811, quoting from his notebook of 4/28/63.

92. Woolner, 232.

93. Wilson, *Carlyle*, V, 504, quoting a letter of Carlyle to his youngest sister, 4/29/63.

94. A. T. Dickens, 629-31.

95. *Let.*, III, 347, Macready, 3/31/63.

96. MS. memorandum for agreement, n.d., in possession of Major Philip Dickens, who generously sent me a copy; Hunt. MS., Dickens to Ouvry, 9/30/63.

97. *Let.*, III, 364, Forster, [10/?/63].

98. See my article, "Dickens, Fagin, and Mr. Riah," *Commentary*,

January, 1950, 47-50, for a further discussion of Dickens's attitude toward the Jews.

99. *Let.*, III, 357, Mrs. Davis, 7/10/63.

100. *O. M. F.*, III, ix, 586.

101. Ibid., IV, ix, 819.

102. *Let.*, III, 405, Mrs. Davis, 11/16/64.

103. Ibid., 512 fn.

104. Ibid., Mrs. Davis, 3/1/67.

105. Ibid., 350, Brookfield, 5/17/63.

106. Ibid., 370, Sawyer, 11/6/63.

107. Ibid., 340, Wills, 2/4/63.

108. Ibid., 371-2, Beadon, 12/2/63.

109. Ibid., 378, Collins, 1/24/64.

110. *Dick.*, VII, 41.

111. Morgan MS., Dickens to Macready, 2/10/64.

112. *Let.*, III, 349, Collins, 4/22/63.

113. Ibid., 362, Wills, 9/14/63. The date of Elizabeth Dickens's death is taken from a genealogical chart sent me by R. F. R. Barrow.

114. Ley, 95, says Thackeray's burial took place thirteen days later. Since this was 12/29/63, it dates the reconciliation scene as 12/16.

115. Perugini, *Thackeray and My Father*, 215.

116. Ley, 95; with slight variants in wording, the same story is given in Howe proofs, Berg. Coll.

117. Perugini, *Thackeray and My Father*, 215.

118. Ley, 179.

119. Ibid., 95.

120. *Let.*, III, 378, Collins, 1/24/64.

121. Ibid., 374, Wills, 12/20/63.

122. Ibid., 380, Stone, 2/23/64.

123. Morgan MS., Dickens to Stone, 5/5/64.

124. Ibid., 9/12/64. This letter and the two previously cited are all jumbled together in *Let.*, III, 380, the text of which was taken from the Mary Dickens-Georg-

ina Hogarth edition of Dickens's letters, 1880–81 and 1882.

125. *Let.*, III, 380, Forster, 2/25/64.
126. Ibid., 387, 5/3/64.
127. Morgan MS., Catherine Dickens to Frederic Chapman, 4/15/64.
128. *Let.*, III, 392, Mrs. Major, 6/17/64, Mrs. Nichols, 6/26/64.
129. Ibid., 30, Cerjat, 7/7/58.
130. Forster, 654.
131. Ibid.; *Let.*, III, 363, Collins, 924/63.
132. Forster, 654.
133. Ibid.; *Let.*, III, 406, Trollope, 12/11/64.
134. Hunt. MSS. contain an extensive correspondence with Dickens's solicitor Ouvry on this exchange of land: 3/1,11,13,20/62, 6/20/62, 7/29/62, 9/8,10/62, 11/2/62,1/29/63,3/1,5,17/63, 4/23/63, 5/11,14/63. See also Forster, 656.
135. *Let.*, III, 394, Forster, 7/29/64.
136. Ibid., 394-5, Mrs. Wills, 8/7/64.
137. Ibid., 401, Wills, 10/16/64, 401 fn., 415, Secretary of Garrick Club, 2/25/65, 416, 3/3/65, 417, 3/9/65.
138. Ibid., 417-8, Wills, 3/17/63.
139. Ibid., 352, Cerjat, 521/63.
140. Ibid., 402, 2/25/64.
141. Ibid., 404, Forster, [11/?/64]. Leech died 10/29/64.
142. Ibid., 416, Forster, 3/3/65.
143. Ibid., 419, Macready, 4/22/65.
144. Lehmann MSS., Dickens to Frederick Lehmann, 1/8/62, 1/6/63, 2/3,21/63.
145. *Let.*, III, 421, Layard, 5/17,18/65, and a third, n.d., on same page.
146. Ibid., 422, Forster, [5/?/65].
147. Forster, 700.
148. All the details of the accident in this and the preceding three paragraphs are in *Dick.*, XXXVIII, 148-53.
149. *Let.*, III, 425-6, Mitton, 6/13/65.
150. Ibid.

151. Ibid.
152. Fitzgerald, *Life*, I, 227, quoting a fellow passenger on the train.
153. *Let.*, III, 426, Mitton, 6/13/65.
154. Rosenbach MS., Dickens to the Station Master, Charing Cross, 6/12/65. Although Dickens does not give Ellen's surname, it is obviously beyond all likelihood that chance would have placed in the same compartment with him another lady of the same Christian name in whose behalf he would be likely to make the inquiry.
155. *Let.*, III, 429, Forster, [6/?/65].
156. Ibid., Thompson, 6/25/65.
157. Ibid., Forster, [6/?/65].
158. Ibid., 666, Cerjat, 8/26/68.
159. Dolby, 11.
160. *Let.*, III, 666, Cerjat, 8/26/68.
161. Lindsay, 386, quoting Henry Fielding Dickens; Pearson, 295.

Chapter 5 [pp. 1022-1045]

1. *O. M. F.*, III, III, 503.
2. *Let.*, I, 66, Chapman and Hall, 2/18/36.
3. Adams, H., *The Education of Henry Adams*, V, 73 (Modern Library Ed.).
4. *O. M. F.*, I, XII, 163.
5. Ibid., III, I, 475.
6. Ibid., I, II, 13.
7. Ibid., II, I, 245.
8. Ibid., III, XVII, 701.
9. Ibid., I, XI, 143.
10. Ibid., X, 127.
11. Ibid., II, 8.
12. Ibid., X, 132.
13. Ibid., 131.
14. Ibid., II, 12.
15. Ibid., IV, XVII, 920.
16. Ibid., III, XVII, 706.
17. Ibid., I, XI, 143.
18. Ibid., 144.
19. Ibid., 144-5.
20. Ibid., 157.
21. Ibid., 158.

22. Ibid., 158-9.
23. Ibid., 143-4.
24. Ibid., XVII, 233.
25. Ibid., 234.
26. Ibid., 233.
27. H. W., I, 379-84, 7/13/50.
28. H. T., II, XI, 678.
29. O. M. F., III, VIII, 571.
30. Ibid., I, XVI, 223.
31. Ibid., 223-4.
32. Ibid., III, VIII, 574.
33. Ibid., Postscript, 927.
34. Ibid., II, II, 267.
35. Ibid., 271.
36. Ibid., 268.
37. Ibid.
38. Ibid., I, 244.
39. Lindsay, 383.
40. O. M. F., IV, XVII, 922.
41. Ibid., 923.
42. Ibid., 924.
43. Ibid., 924-5.
44. Ibid., III, IX, 595.
45. Ibid., I, IV, 40.
46. Ibid., XVI, 232.
47. Ibid., II, XIII, 421.
48. Ibid., III, V, 526-7.
49. Ibid., 526.
50. Ibid., 535.
51. Ibid., IX, 599.
52. Ibid., XV, 676.
53. Ibid., 676-7.
54. Ibid., 677.
55. Ibid., IV, V, 763.
56. Young, Early Victorian England, II, 493, "Portrait of an Age."
57. O. M. F., IV, IV, 759.
58. Let., III, 304-5, Collins, 9/20/62.
59. O. M. F., II, XV, 447.
60. Ibid., 446.
61. Let., III, 4, Collins, 3/21/58.
62. O. M. F., II, XV, 446.
63. Ibid., 447.
64. Ibid., 447-8.
65. Ibid., 449.
66. Ibid., I, III, 23.
67. Pope, The Dunciad, IV, 653-7.
68. Morse, 286.
69. Ibid., 278-9.
70. Eliot, The Waste Land, I, 60-64.

PART TEN

Chapter 1 [pp. 1049-1069]

1. Fields, Memories, Diary, 8/15/67.
2. Forster, 654.
3. Let., III, 441, Forster, 1/7/65. Forster gives this date to the letter, but a copy of the Gad's Hill Gazette in the Berg Collection shows that the chalet was not actually completed till 8/19/65. It is possible, however, that the later date refers to the furnishing rather than the construction of the building.
4. Fields, Yesterdays, 240; Coll. P., I, 116-7, "On Mr. Fechter's Acting," Atlantic Monthly, August, 1869.
5. Coll P., I, 120, "On Mr. Fechter's Acting."
6. Let., III, 289, Cerjat, 3/16/62.
7. Coll. P., I, 119.
8. Let., III, 292, Beard, 4/5/62.
9. Ibid., 341, Fechter, 2/4/63.
10. Ibid., 398, fn.
11. Ibid., 453, Miss Boyle, 1/6/66.
12. Ibid., 456, Lytton, 1/17/66, 545, 9/4/67, 549, 9/13/67, 549-50, Fechter, 9/16/67, 550, Lytton, 9/16/67, 551-2, 9/17/67, 560, 10/14/67.
13. Perkins, 147.
14. Forster, 660, n. 440.
15. Ibid., 698.
16. Let., III, 341, Fechter, 2/4/63.
17. Quoted in Ley, 310.
18. Berg Coll., Gad's Hill Gazette, 8/19/65.
19. Let., III, 431, Lytton, 7/20/65.
20. Fitzgerald, Memories, 20.
21. Let., III, 439, Forster, 10/8/65.
22. Fitzgerald, Memories, 21-2.
23. Ibid., 24-5.
24. Ibid., 40.
25. Fitzgerald, Life, I, 243.
26. Ibid., 232.
27. Ibid., 245.
28. Fitzgerald, Memories, 40.
29. Let., III, 478, Wills, 7/30/66.
30. Fitzgerald, Life, I, 248.

31. Hunt. MS., Dickens to Georgina Hogarth, 7/28/64.
32. Berg Coll., *Gad's Hill Gazette*, 8/20,27/64.
33. Dolby, 49.
34. Ibid.
35. Forster, 652.
36. Dolby, 48-9.
36a. Fitzgerald, *Life*, I, 190.
37. Fields, *Memories*, Diary, 1/6/68.
38. Yates, *Recollections*, circa 105, Fitzgerald, *Life*, I, 190.
39. *Let.*, III, Mrs. Fields, 5/25/68.
40. Yates, *Recollections*, circa 105.
41. Mary Dickens, 15.
42. Ibid., 97.
43. *Let.*, III, 179, Mary Dickens, 9/23/60.
44. Langton, 133.
45. Boyle, 239.
46. Mary Dickens, 91.
47. *Let.*, III, 436, Fitzgerald, 9/23/65.
48. Ibid., 447, 11/30/65.
49. Ibid.
50. Ibid., 489, 11/6/66.
51. Ibid., 499, Cerjat, 1/1/62.
52. Forster, 655.
53. Fields, *Yesterdays*, 237.
54. Yates, *Recollections*, circa 106.
55. Forster, 80, n. 85, quoting Laman Blanchard. Ley's note points out that Blanchard's memory was in error about which house was the honeymoon residence, mistakenly identifying it as the Craddock house on the southern side of the road instead of Mrs. Nash's cottage opposite.
56. Yates, *Recollections*, circa 106.
57. Quoted by Pearson, 288.
58. Mary Dickens, 76.
59. Fields, *Yesterdays*, 227.
60. *Let.*, III, 499, Forster, 1/1/67.
61. Mary Dickens, 38.
62. Trollope, 113.
63. Fitzgerald, *Life*, I, 201.
64. *Let.*, III, 323, Forster, [12/?/62].
65. Powell, 176.
66. Mary Dickens, 28.
67. Ibid., 35.

68. Evans, 14.
69. Ibid., 12-3.
70. Fitzgerald, *Memories*, 18, Diary, 8/3/65.
71. Fitzgerald, *Life*, I, 201.
72. Ibid., 197; Dolby, 51.
73. Wright, *Life*, 309.
74. Wright, *Autobiography*, 239-41. It is possible that the entry "Turnham" in the Peckham rate-book was merely a carelessly inaccurate rendering of Ternan (like the entry "Elizabeth Raylace" for Mrs. Roylance in Dickens's boyhood days in Camden Town). "Tringham," in turn, might be a still more careless misreading of Turnham, although the statement that the woman who worked at the Lodge knew Dickens himself as "Mr. Tringham" renders this suggestion less likely than the first one.
75. *Let.*, III, 476, Mrs. Elliot, 7/5/66. Dr. Eric George Millar has pointed out to me that this date, however, must be erroneous, and that the correct date must be 7/4/67, because the letter refers to Dolby as sailing for America the following month, an event which took place 8/3/67.
76. Wright, *Life*, 310-1.
77. *Let.*, III, 459-60, Georgina Hogarth, 2/9/66.
78. Ibid., 463, Forster, [2/?/66].
79. Dolby, 3.
80. *Let.*, III, 464, Forster, 3/11/66.
81. Dolby, 7-10.
82. Payne, 139-40; for Dolby's stammer, see Hunt. MS., Dickens to Georgina Hogarth, 3/6/67.
83. Dolby, 30.
84. Ibid., 11-2.
85. Ibid., 33-4.
86. Ibid., 35.
87. Ibid., 31.
88. Ibid., 36.
89. Hunt., MS., Dickens to Georgina Hogarth, 4/17/66.

90. Ibid., 5/11/66, incomplete in *Let.*, III, 471.
91. Dolby, 37-8.
92. Ibid., 39-40.
93. *Let.*, III, 466, Mary Dickens, 4/14/66.
94. Hunt, MS., Dickens to Georgina Hogarth, 5/11/66. The part of this letter on which my statements depend is not included in *Let.*, III, 471.
95. *Let.*, III, 483, Beard, 9/6/66.
96. Ibid., Forster, [9/?/66].
97. Dolby, 41.
98. *Let.*, III, 467 fn., 480, Chappell, 8/2/66.
99. Ibid., 467, Forster, [4/?/66]. So dated by Forster, but inasmuch as the letter shows clearly that it was written near the close of the reading series, it must have been in May if not in June.
100. Ibid., 481, [8/?/66].
101. Ibid., 487, Collins, 10/4/66.
102. There are sixteen scattered issues of the *Gad's Hill Gazette* in the Berg Collection, ending with No. 31, 1/13/66. The first number in this group is No. 14, 8/6/64, and the others show that it was published between late July and late August and again between late December and early February in each year. These facts, in combination with the numbering of the sixteen issues, enable one to count back and establish the probability that No. 1 must have appeared in July, 1863.
103. *Let.*, III, 526, Taylor, 7/15/67.
104. Ibid., 537, 7/15/67.
105. Ibid., the two previously cited.
106. Ibid., 526, 5/4/67.
107. Ibid.
108. Renton, 191, quoting B. W. Procter to Forster, a letter written while Dickens was in America, 1867-8.
109. Morgan MS., Dickens to Miss Coutts, 2/12/64.

110. House MS., Dickens to the Rev. Mr. W. Brackenbury, 9/18/65.
111. Ibid.
112. *Let.*, III, 479, Georgina Hogarth, 8/1/66.
113. Ibid., 478, Lytton, 7/16/66.
114. Ibid., 445-6, Cerjat, 11/30/65.
115. Ibid., 500-1, 1/1/67.
116. Ibid., 500.
117. Hunt. MS., Dickens to Georgina Hogarth, 11/3/66.
118. Ibid., 11/6/66.
119. *Dick.*, VIII, 216, quoting an interview Stone gave to the *Morning Post*, 7/4/1912.
120. Hunt. MS., Dickens to Mrs. Watson, 11/8/66.
121. *Let.*, III, 502, Georgina Hogarth, 1/21/67.
122. Ibid., 511, Forster, 2/23/67.
123. Ibid., 502, Georgina Hogarth, 1/21/67.
124. Ibid., 503, Mary Dickens, 1/22/67.
125. Ibid., 504, Georgina Hogarth, 1/24/67.
126. Ibid., 506, Forster, 1/29/67.
127. Ibid., 509, Mary Dickens, 2/17/67.
128. Ibid., 508, Georgina Hogarth, 2/15/67.
129. Dolby, 66-7; cf. *Let.*, III, 504, Mary Dickens, 1/24/67.
130. Hunt. MS., Dickens to Georgina Hogarth, 3/6/67, incomplete in *Let.*, III, 514.
131. *Let.*, III, 525, Stanfield, 4/18/67.
132. Ibid., 515, Collins, 3/13/67.
133. Hunt. MS., Dickens to Georgina Hogarth, 3/16/67.
134. *Let.*, III, 516, Forster, 3/15/67.
135. Hunt. MS., Dickens to Georgina Hogarth, 3/17/67.
136. *Let.*, III, 529, Chorley, 6/2/67.
137. Ley, 116, 282.
138. *Let.*, III, 527, George Stanfield, 5/19/67.
139. Ibid., Georgina Hogarth, 5/10/67.
140. Ibid., 528, Forster, 5/20/67.
141. Ibid., [5/?/67].
142. Ibid.

143. G. E., XXXVIII, 309.
144. *Let.*, III, 527, Georgina Hogarth, 5/10/67, 555, Mary Dickens, 9/30/67. The sentences in the two letters are almost identical.

Chapter 2 [pp. 1070-1094]

1. *Let.*, III, 527, Forster, [5/?/67].
2. Berg Coll., Dickens's Diary for 1867, entries for April, May 19, 25, November.
3. *Let.*, III, 530 fn., quoting Wills on Dickens's letter to him, 6/6/67.
4. Forster, 709.
5. *Let.*, III, 530-1, Wills, 6/6/67.
6. Ibid., 531, Fields, 6/13/67.
7. Ibid., 535, Forster, 7/2/67.
8. Dolby, 119; MS., Division, N. Y. Pub. Lib., Dickens to Ticknor and Fields, 4/8/67.
9. Benjamin Wood was a brother of the more well-known Fernando Wood, had twice been a member of the House of Representatives, and was in 1867 a member of the New York State Senate. He was editor and owner of the New York *Daily News*. D. A. B.
10. *Let.*, III, 533, Wills, 6/28/67.
11. Ibid., 539, Fields, 7/25/67.
12. Dolby, 107.
13. Ibid., 108-10.
14. Ibid., 122-3.
15. Ibid., 124.
16. Ibid.
17. Ibid., 125.
18. Ibid., 128-9.
19. *Let.*, III, 541, Collins, 8/23/67, 546, 9/9,10/67, 553, 9/23/67.
20. Dolby, 131.
21. Ibid., 132.
22. *Let.*, III, 553-4, Wills, 9/24/67, 553-4, fn., quoting "The Case in a Nutshell" in full.
23. Dolby, 136-8.
24. *Let.*, III, 540, Georgina Hogarth, 8/2/67, Forster, 8/6/67.
25. Hunt. MS., Dickens to Georgina Hogarth, 8/10/67; *Let.*, III, 547, Bishop, 9/11/67.
26. *Let.*, III, 544 fn.
27. Ibid., 543, Dixon, 9/3/67.
28. Ibid., 544-5, Fields, 9/3/67.
29. Ibid., 544, Finlay, 9/3/67.
30. Ibid., 555, Georgina Hogarth, 9/30/67.
31. Ibid., 556, Fields, [10/?/67].
32. Hunt. MSS. contain an extensive correspondence on this farewell dinner between Dickens and its Secretary, Charles Kent, and between Kent and numerous persons invited to be present.
33. *Charles Dickens Dinner*, 1.
34. Myall, 166.
35. Hunt. MS., Dickens to Kent, 10/30/67, erroneously printed in *Let.*, III, 560, as a postscript to 10/19/67.
36. *Let.*, III, 543, Wills, 9/2/67.
37. *Charles Dickens Dinner*, 7-8; Myall, 167.
38. Myall, 168.
39. Conway, *Autobiography*, II, 128.
40. *Charles Dickens Dinner*, 14-6.
41. Conway, *Autobiography*, II, 128-9.
42. Ibid., 129.
43. *Let.*, III, 565, Mrs. Watson, 11/5/67.
44. Dexter, *Mr. and Mrs.*, 265, 11/5/67.
45. Macy Coll., Dickens's account book with Messrs. Coutts and Co., 12/29/65–5/23/68, contains a number of entries that may possibly be connected with Ellen Ternan, although it must be emphasized that the suggestion is purely hypothetical. Recalling that Dickens often referred to her as "N," we may note that there are six checks made out to "N Trust": 10/17/66, £40, 11/3/66, £15, 11/8/66, £10, 11/29/66, £35, 12/14/66, £15, and 1/14/67, £12.10. Before the eve of Dickens's departure for America there are only a few checks made

out to Wills, for sums insignificant in comparison with those drawn later: 2/12/67, £24.17, 2/19/67, £35, 5/15/67, £22. But on 11/7/67, there is one made out to "Wills Trust," £150, and during the period of Dickens's absence two more to W. H. Wills which are much larger still: 1/27/68, £1,000, and 3/2/68, £1,100. In view of Dickens's parting memorandum to Wills about Ellen, and Dickens's decision not to have her join him in America, the reader may give these payments totaling £2,250 what significance he wishes. It should be noted that in a MS. letter in the Huntington Library, Dickens instructs Georgina Hogarth, 1/10/68, about the second of these payments: "Draw a cheque for £1,100 in favor of W. H. Wills Esquire and let him have it at once. He has my instructions how to invest the money." I have found no other record to show whether an investment of such a sum was or was not made around this time.

46. *Let.*, III, 558, Henry Fielding Dickens, 10/7/67; Millar MS., Dickens to Shirley Brooks, 11/10/67, written on board the *Cuba* at Queenstown.

47. *Let.*, III, 567, Georgina Hogarth, 11/16/67.

48. Ibid., 568, Mary Dickens, 11/21/67.

49. Payne, 188, 243, quoting the New York *Tribune*, 12/2/67, and the Boston *Post*, 3/5/68.

50. Dolby, 150-5.

51. Ibid., 158-9.

52. *Let.*, III, 568, Mary Dickens, 11/21/67; Dolby, 149.

53. *Let.*, III, 568, Mary Dickens, 11/21/67; Payne, 150.

54. Dana, 86-7, quoting Longfellow's journal, 11/20/67, and a letter

from Longfellow to Forster, 11/23/67.

55. Dana MS., Dickens to Richard Henry Dana, Jr., 11/22/67; Houghton Library MS., Dickens to Samuel Gridley Howe, 11/22/67.

56. Payne, 156, quoting from Dickens's correspondence with James T. Fields.

57. Fields, *Memories*, Diary, 11/21/67.

58. Hunt. MS., Dickens to Georgina Hogarth, 11/25/67, partly in *Let.*, III, 572.

59. *Let.*, III, 571, cablegram to Wills, 11/22/67.

60. Dana, 88, quoting Longfellow's journal, 11/28/67.

61. Aldrich, *Memories*, 102-5.

62. Dana, 89.

63. *Let.*, III, 575, Charles Dickens, Jr., 11/30/67.

64. Ibid., 585, Georgina Hogarth, 12/22/67.

65. Ibid., 575, Charles Dickens, Jr., 11/30/67.

66. Ibid., 585, Georgina Hogarth, 12/22/67.

67. Ibid., 569, Wills, 11/21/67.

68. Hunt. MS., Dickens to Georgina Hogarth, 11/25/67, mostly in *Let.*, III, 572.

69. Dana, 90, quoting the N. Y. *Tribune*.

70. Dolby, 176.

71. Dana, 90-1, quoting Longfellow's journal, 12/2/67, and a letter from Longfellow to Sumner, 1/12/68.

72. Ibid., 91, quoting a letter from John Greenleaf Whittier to Celia Thaxter, 12/14/67.

73. *Let.*, III, 578, Wills, 12/3/67.

74. Ibid., Miss Boyle, 12/4/67.

75. Payne, 202, quoting the Boston *Post*, 1/4/68.

76. Hunt. MS., Dickens to Georgina Hogarth, 12/6/67, misdated as 1/4/68 in *Let.*, III, 597. The

error is pointed out in Payne, 200.

77. *Let.*, III, 602, Forster, 1/14/68.
78. Ibid., 631, Fechter, 3/8/68.
79. Ibid., 570, Wills, 11/25/67.
80. Ibid., 568, Mary Dickens, 11/21/67. The name of the chef at the Parker House is from Payne, 151.
81. *Let.*, III, 576, Mary Dickens, 12/1/67.
82. Ibid., 579, Wills, 12/6/67. Dickens estimated his profits in pounds, at the rate of $7 to the pound; and the same figure has been used in translating them back into dollars.
83. Dana, 87, quoting an unidentified newspaper clipping Longfellow enclosed with a letter to Forster, 11/23/67.
84. Dolby, 164.
85. Forster, 768.
86. Dolby, 165-6, 169, 163; cf. *Let.*, III, 579, Forster, 12/6/67.
87. *Let.*, III, 582, Forster, 12/15/67.
88. Ibid., 583, Georgina Hogarth, 12/16/67.
89. Ibid., 589, Mary Dickens 12/26/67.
90. Ibid., 581, 12/11/67.
91. Ibid., 580, Wills, 12/10/67.
92. Ibid., 581, Mary Dickens, 12/11/67.
93. Ibid., 584, Wills, 12/17/67.
94. Ibid., 581, Forster, 12/14/67.
95. *Dick.*, XVI, 202.
96. *Let.*, III, 580, Wills, 12/11/67.
97. Ibid., 582, Forster, 12/15/67.
98. Ibid., 584, Georgina Hogarth, 12/22/67.
99. Ibid., 587, Wills, 12/24/67.
100. Dolby, 202; cf. *Let.*, III, 588-9, Georgina Hogarth, 12/26/67, 602, Mary Dickens, 1/13/68.
101. *Let.*, III, 585, Forster, 12/22/67, 588, Mary Dickens, 12/26/67.
102. Ibid., 605, Charles Dickens, Jr., 1/15/68.
103. Ibid., 585, Forster, 12/22/67.

104. Ibid., Georgina Hogarth, 12/22/67.
105. Ibid., 587, Forster, 12/22/67.
106. Ibid., 589, Mary Dickens, 12/26/67, 12/27/67 postscript.
107. Ibid., 589-90, Fields, 12/29/67.
108. Ibid., 588, Wills, 12/24/67, 595, Georgina Hogarth, 1/3/68, 624, Fechter, 2/24/68.
109. Ibid., 606-7, Georgina Hogarth, 1/21/68.
110. Dana, 92, quoting Annie Longfellow.
111. Harrington, II, 640.
112. *Let.*, III, 591, Lytton. The date is here given as December, 1867, but it must have been after 1/5/68, the date of Dickens's visit to the Medical School, as established by the next reference.
113. Ibid., 599, Collins, 1/12/68, which was a Sunday, and which says that the visit took place "last Sunday."
114. Ibid., 590, Mary Dickens, 12/30/67, 591, Wills, 12/30/67.
115. Ibid., 598, Forster, 1/9/68, 600-1, Georgina Hogarth, 1/12/68.
116. Ibid., 598, Forster, 1/5/68.
117. Ibid.
118. Ibid., 606-7, Georgina Hogarth, 1/21/68.
119. Ibid., 607, Forster, 1/23/68; Dolby, 219, identifies the speaker as George W. Childs.
120. Mackenzie, 34; *Dick.*, XXXV, 145. Augustus Dickens died 10/6/66 and was buried in Graceland Cemetery, Chicago.
121. Mackenzie, 34; *Dick.*, XXXV, 145.; Macy Coll., entries in Dickens's account book with Coutts and Company, 1/11/67, £23.6.0, 4/25/67, £14.11.6, 7/16/67, £23.6, 8/5/67, £29.2, 10/15/67, £14.11.6, made out to "Mrs. Augustus Trust," and 2/13/68, £23.0.6, to "Augustus Dickens." This Augustus Dick-

ens must have been a son of
Dickens's brother.

122. Hunt. MS., Dickens to Georgina
Hogarth, 2/27/68.

123. Ibid., 3/8/68. The parts quoted
from this and the preceding letter are omitted from *Let.*, III,
626-7, 629-30.

124. *Let.*, III, 607-8, Mary Dickens,
1/23/68.

125. Payne, 204, quotes from the Boston *Transcript*, 2/3/68.

126. Ibid., 231-3; *Let.*, III, 648, 655,
Howe, 5/18/68, 6/23/68.

127. *Let.*, III, 610, Cartwright,
1/29/68.

128. Ibid., 608, Mary Dickens,
1/23/68; Dolby, 232.

129. Let., III, 614, Mary Dickens,
2/4/68.

130. Ibid., 618, Fields, 2/9/68.

131. Ibid., 614, Mary Dickens, 2/4/68.

132. Ibid., 615, Forster, 2/4/68.

133. Ibid., 617, Georgina Hogarth,
2/7/68, 619, Mary Dickens,
2/11/68.

134. Ibid., 619, Mary Dickens,
2/11/68.

135. Dolby, 246, 254.

136. Hunt. MS., Dickens to Georgina
Hogarth, 2/27/68; *Let.*, III,
622, Wills, 2/21/68.

137. Dolby, 249-52.

138. Hunt. MS., Dickens to Georgina
Hogarth, 2/27/68; cf. *Let.*, III,
627, Wills, 2/28/68.

139. Hunt. MS., Dickens to Georgina
Hogarth, 4/1/68.

140. *Let.*, III, 622-3, Wills, 2/21/68.

141. Ibid., 624, 2/25/68, 625-6, Forster, 2/25/68; Dolby, 259-60.

142. Hunt. MS., Dickens to Georgina
Hogarth, 1/29/68, incomplete
in *Let.*, III, 609.

143. Ibid.

144. Dolby, 241.

145. Hunt. MS., Dickens to Georgina
Hogarth, 1/29/68.

146. *Coll. P.*, I, 110-2, "The Great International Walking Match,"
2/29/68; Dolby, 261-4. There

are copies of the broadside in
the Berg Collection, the Morgan Library, the Library of Con-
gress, and various other collections.

147. Hunt. MS., Dickens to Georgina
Hogarth, 2/27/68, inaccurate
in *Let.*, III, 626-7.

148. *Let.*, III, 628, Mary Dickens,
3/2/68.

149. *Coll. P.*, I, 112-4, "The Great International Walking Match,"
2/29/68; Dolby, 265-9.

150. *Let.*, III, 628, Mary Dickens,
3/2/68.

151. Ibid.

152. *Coll. P.*, I, 111; Dolby, 263.

153. Payne, 229-30; Fields, *Memories*,
Diary, 3/3/68.

154. Fields, *In and Out of Doors*;
Dolby, 275.

155. Hunt. MS., Dickens to Georgina
Hogarth, 2/27/68.

156. Berg MS., Dickens to James T.
Fields, 2/27/68; *Let.*, III, 626.

157. Hunt. MS., Dickens to Georgina
Hogarth, 3/8/68, and postscript, 3/9/68. The parts noted
are omitted from *Let.*, III, 629-
30.

158. *Let.*, III, 629, Fields, 3/8/68.

159. Hunt. MS., Dickens to Georgina
Hogarth, 3/8/68. See n. 157
above.

160. *Let.*, III, 631, Georgina Hogarth,
3/12/68.

161. Ibid., 636, Ouvry, 3/21/68.

162. Ibid., 635, Mrs. Fields,
3/19/68.

163. Ibid., 636, Ouvry, 3/21/68.

164. Ibid., 639, Mary Dickens,
3/29/68.

165. Ibid., 640, Forster, 3/30/68.

166. Wiggin, 17-8.

167. Ibid., 18-9.

168. Ibid., 20-2.

169. Ibid., 28.

170. Ibid., 30.

171. *Let.*, III, 642, Mary Dickens,
4/7/68.

172. Fields, *Memories*, Diary, 4/2/68.

173. *Let.*, III, 642, Mary Dickens, 4/7/68.
174. Ibid.
175. Dolby, 319.
176. *Let.*, III, 643, Mary Dickens, 4/7/68.
177. Fields, *Memories*, Diary, 4/15/68.
178. Sweetser, 21, 24-5.
179. Dolby, 311.
180. Sweetser, 24-5; New York *World*, 4/19/68.
181. *Dick.*, VI, 181.
182. *Coll. P.*, II, 504-8, speech, 4/18/68; Dolby, 312-8.
183. *Coll. P.*, II, 506.
184. Ibid., 507.
185. Ibid., 507-8.
186. Ibid., 508.

Chapter 3 [pp. 1095-1114]

1. Fields, *Memories*, Diary, 4/21/68.
2. New York *Tribune*, 4/22/68, quoted by Dolby, 327.
3. Winter, 185.
3a. Dolby, 322.
4. Ibid., 322-3.
5. Winter, 181-2.
6. Dolby, 323, 325.
7. New York *Tribune*, 4/22/68, quoted by Dolby, 327.
8. Dolby, 328.
9. *Let.*, III, 644, Forster [4/?/68]: cf. Dolby, 331-2.
10. *Let.*, III, 568, Forster, 11/18/67; Forster, 797.
11. Forster, 797; cf. *Let.*, III, 697, Finlay, 1/1/69.
12. *Let.*, III, 644, Fields, 4/26/68.
13. Ibid., 645, 4/30/68.
14. Ibid., 646, Mrs. Watson, 5/11/68.
15. Ibid., 651, Mrs. Fields, 5/25/68.
16. Ibid.
17. Ibid.
18. Ibid.
19. Hunt. MS., Dickens to Georgina Hogarth, 4/1/68; *Let.*, III, 648, Fitzgerald, 5/18/68.
20. Fitzgerald, *Memories*, 233.
21. *Let.*, III, 654, Macready, 6/10/68; Dolby, 336.
22. *Coll. P.*, I, 115, "Explanatory Introduction to 'Religious Opinions' by the late Reverend Chauncey Hare Townshend."
23. Hunt. MS., Dickens to W. Farrer, 12/1/68.
24. Dolby, 340.
25. *Let.*, III, 647-8, Fields, 5/15/68.
26. Ibid., 649, Fechter, 5/22/68.
27. Ibid., 651, Mrs. Fields, 5/25/68; Suzannet MS., Dickens to Alfred Hermant, 6/2/68.
28. Dana, 97-8, quoting two previously unpublished letters from Dickens to Longfellow, 6/28,30/68.
29. *Let.*, III, 657, Fields, 7/7/68.
30. Dana, 99-100, quoting Alice Longfellow's journal and letters to various friends.
31. *Let.*, III, 620-1, Henry Fielding Dickens, 2/11/68.
32. Hunt. MS., Dickens to Georgina Hogarth, 6/25/68.
33. *Let.*, III, 662-3, Charles Dickens, Jr., 8/9/68.
34. Ibid., 669, Wills, 9/27/68.
35. Ibid., 664, Ouvry, 8/23/68.
36. Berg MS., Dickens to Dolby, 9/25/68.
37. *Let.*, III, 664, Ouvry, 8/23/68.
38. Sawyer, *Dickens Library*, No. 24.
39. *Let.*, III, 667-8, Edward Dickens, 9/26/68.
40. Ibid., 669, Mary Dickens, 9/26/68.
41. Ibid., Fechter, [9/?/68].
42. Ibid., 677, Forster, [10/?/68].
43. Henry Fielding Dickens, *Reminiscences*, quoted by Pearson, 282.
44. Forster, 798-9.
45. *Let.*, III, 671, Georgina Hogarth, 10/11/68, 672, Mary Dickens, 10/12/68.
46. Ibid., 671, Beard, 10/11/68.
47. Ibid., 675, Forster, 10/25/68.
48. Ibid., 676, Georgina Hogarth, 10/29/68.
49. Ibid., 675, Howison, 10/23/68.
50. Ibid., 676, Forster, 10/24/68.
51. Ibid., 674, [10/?/68].

52. Charles Dickens, Jr., 28-9.
53. Ibid.
54. Dolby, 344-5.
55. *Let.*, III, 686-7, Mrs. Fields, 12/16/68.
56. Ibid.
57. Charles Dickens, Jr., 29.
58. *Let.*, III, 680, Georgina Hogarth, 12/6/68; cf. Dolby, 353.
59. Fields, *Memories*, Diary, 1/8/68.
60. *Let.*, III, 688, Georgina Hogarth, 12/16/68.
61. Dolby, 362.
62. Ibid., 367; cf. Fitzgerald, *Life*, I, 223.
63. Dolby, 367-8.
64. Ibid., 371.
65. *Let.*, III, 704, Fields, 2/15/69.
66. Ibid., 702, Mary Dickens, 1/27/69.
67. Ibid., Forster, 1/29/69.
68. Ibid., 703, 2/15/69.
69. Forster, 801-2.
70. Inman MS., Dickens to Georgina Hogarth, 2/25/69; Hunt. MS., Dickens to Georgina Hogarth, 2/26/69; cf. *Let.*, III, 708, Forster, 3/2/69.
71. *Let.*, III, 704-5, Fields, 2/15/69.
72. Dolby, 386.
73. *Let.*, III, 678, Frith, 11/16/68.
74. Ibid., 718-9, Fields, 4/9/69.
75. Ibid., 708, Georgina Hogarth, 2/26/69; Pearson, 328.
76. Dolby, 385-7.
77. Ibid., 387-8.
78. Ibid., 388.
79. Ibid., 391, 393.
80. Forster, 803.
81. *Let.*, III, 716, Georgina Hogarth, 4/4/69.
82. Ibid., 717, Fields, 4/9/69.
83. Ibid., 719, Beard, 4/13/69.
84. Hunt. MS., Dickens to Georgina Hogarth, 4/15/69.
85. *Let.*, III, 720, Beard, 4/19/69.
86. Ibid., 721, Georgina Hogarth, 4/21/69.
87. Ibid., Forster, 4/22/69.
88. Ibid., 722, Mary Dickens, 4/22/69.
89. Dolby, 408. Dolby did "get through," but not without having to defend Dickens against some ignorant and ill-natured criticism from some of those who resented the cancellation of the Preston reading. On the way to the railway station at Blackpool, Dickens had been obliged to chase his hat, which was blown off by a gust of wind; some people who witnessed the episode said they had seen him "kicking his hat about as if he had been a boy" and refused to believe in his breakdown (Dolby, 411).
90. Forster, 804.
91. Ibid., 805, 805 fn.
92. Ibid., 805.
93. *Let.*, III, 723-4, Forster, 5/3/69; cf. Dolby, 416.
93a. Mr. Henry Charles Dickens has kindly sent me a transcript of a letter from Dickens to Frederic Ouvry, 9/27/61, which shows that Dickens had made at least two wills previous to 1869. This letter expresses dissatisfaction with a will then in existence and gives certain directions for drawing another. It outlines provisions for the repetition of "such and such legacies" in the existent will, leaves a life income to Catherine, and arranges a trust fund for the benefit of Georgina and the children. The amounts of the various bequests are evidently the same as those in the will to be superseded, but they are not named in the letter. I have no evidence of whether there were any further changes between 1861 and 1869.
94. *Let.*, III, 797, Dickens's will, 5/12/69.
95. Ibid., 797-8.
96. Ibid., 798-9.
97. Ibid., 799.

98. Morgan MS., Dickens to Macready, 7/20/69, inaccurate in *Let.*, III, 730-1.
99. Hunt. MS., Georgina Hogarth to Mrs. Fields, 6/18/72.
100. *Let.*, III, 726, Rusden, 5/18/69.
101. Ibid., 779, 5/20/70.
102. Ibid., 726, 5/18/69.
103. Ibid., 665, 8/24/68.
104. Ibid., 724, Fields, 5/5/69.
105. Dolby, 419-20, says Mr. and Mrs. George W. Childs of Philadelphia were among the group of American friends Dickens welcomed to England at this time. But Morgan MS., Dickens to George W. Childs, 11/4/68, shows that these two had arrived six months earlier. It is possible that they were still there, or had come again, but except for Dolby's statement I have found nothing to show that they were among the visitors in May and June.
106. *Let.*, III, 725, Eytinge, 5/14/69; Dolby, 419-20; Fields, *Yesterdays*, circa 202.
107. *Let.*, III, 727, Fields, 5/25/69.
108. Fields, *Yesterdays*, 220-4.
109. *Let.*, III, 732, Forster, [7/?/69].
110. Ibid., 735, 8/6/69.
111. Forster, 807 fn.
112. Hunt. MS., Dickens to James T. Fields, 10/10/69.
113. Fields, *Yesterdays*, 228.

Chapter 4 [pp. 1115-1141]

1. E. D., II, 7.
2. Ibid., XII, 129.
3. Forster, 808, quoting a letter from Longfellow, 6/12/70.
4. Chesterton, *Dickens*, 242.
5. Quoted by Wilson, *Wound and Bow*, 84.
6. E. D., II, 15.
7. Ibid., 17.
8. Ibid., X, 107.
9. Ibid., XIV, 159.
10. Ibid., IX, 94.

11. Ibid., VI, 55-6.
12. Ibid., VIII, 80.
13. Ibid., XIV, 151.
14. Ibid., XVIII, 208.
15. Forster, 808.
16. Baker, *Drood Murder Case*, 148, quoting Charles Dickens, Jr.
17. Perugini, *Edwin Drood and Dickens's Last Day*, quoted by Baker, 148.
18. London *Times*, 10/27/1905, letter of Sir Luke Fildes.
19. E. D., I, 5.
20. Ibid., III, 26.
21. For more detailed discussion of these aspects of the story, see Duffield, *John Jasper*.
22. E. D., VI, 68-9. For more detailed discussion of the mesmeric aspect, see Boyd, *New Angle*.
23. E. D., VI, 64.
24. Ibid., 69.
25. Ibid., III, 20.
26. Ibid., XIX, 212.
27. Ibid., 213.
28. Ibid., 217.
29. Forster Collection, Dickens's original MS. notes.
30. Quoted by Wilson, *Wound and Bow*, 84.
31. E. D., VIII, 70.
32. Ibid.
33. Ibid., 77.
34. Ibid., XVIII, 205.
35. Ibid., XVI, 183-4.
36. Ibid., VI, 56.
37. Pater, *The Renaissance*, 196 (Modern Library ed.).
38. Ibid., 197.
39. Quoted by Shaw, in preface to *Great Expectations*.
40. *Let.*, II, 85, Lemon, 5/3/48.
41. All except Dickens's admiration for Gluck's *Orpheus* have been noted in earlier pages; for this last, see *Let.*, III, 322, Forster, [11/?/62].
42. Kitton, *Pen and Pencil*, Supp., 50.
43. See *Coll. P.*, I, 291, "Old Lamps for New Ones," *H. W.*, 6/15/50; cf. *Let.*, III, 658, Millais, 7/19/68, 760, Fields, 1/14/70.

44. *Let.*, II, 700, Forster, [10/?/55].
45. Fields, *Yesterdays*, 237.
46. Winter, 182.
47. *H. W.*, 3/3/55, "Children of the Czar," 108-14, 4/7/55, "More Children of the Czar," 227-32, 4/21/55, "Nothing like Russia-Leather," 286-8; Stonehouse, *Catalogue*.
48. *A. Y. R.*, 7/7/60, "Natural Selection," 293 et seq.
49. Ruskin in a letter to Sir Henry Acland, 2/?/52, quoted by Amabel Williams-Ellis, *The Exquisite Tragedy*, 126.
50. Morgan MS., Dickens to Miss Coutts, 8/22/51.
51. *Let.*, III, 698, Cerjat, 1/4/69, 402, 10/25/64.
52. Chesterton, *Criticisms*, 186.
53. *Dick.*, X, 150, quoting Shaw.
54. *Coll. P.*, II, 524, speech, 9/27/69.
55. Ibid., 526-7, speech, 1/6/70.
56. Shaw, preface to *Great Expectations*.
57. Strachey, *Landmarks in French Literature*, 82-3 (Home University Library edition).
58. Forster, *Aspects of the Novel*, 93, 98-9.
59. Santanyana, *Works*, II, "Dickens," 203-4.
60. Ibid., 264-5.
61. *Dick.*, VII, 72, quoting Shaw.
62. Santanyana, *Works*, II, 266.
63. Fields, *Yesterdays*, 241.
64. *L. D.*, I, xiii, 170.
65. Arnold, *Essays in Criticism*, 1st and 2nd series, "John Keats," 341 (Home Lib. ed., A. L. Burt, n.d.).

Chapter 5 [pp. 1142-1158]

1. *Dick.*, XXXII, 19, quoting Cecil Hunt's *Autobiography*.
2. Hunt. MS., Dickens to James T. Fields, 8/3/69.
3. Forster, 656.
4. *Let.*, III, 745, Macready, 10/18/69.
5. Fitzgerald, *Life*, I, 256; Fitzgerald, *Memories*, 79.

6. Hunt. MS., Georgina Hogarth to Mrs. James T. Fields, 11/21/70.
7. *Let.*, III, 760, Fields, 1/14/60.
8. Dolby, 440; *Let.*, III, 755, Mrs. Elliot, 12/28/69.
9. Forster, 845; *Let.*, III, 760, Fields, 1/14/70.
10. *Coll. P.*, II, 526, speech, 1/6/70.
11. Dolby, 443; *Let.*, III, 759, Forster, 1/9/70.
12. Dolby, 441; Forster, 845-6.
13. Forster, 846.
14. Charles Dickens, Jr., 30.
15. *Let.*, III, 759, Fields, 1/14/70.
16. *Dick.*, XXXIX, 93; Forster, 846-7.
17. *Let.*, III, 761, Wills, 1/23/70.
18. Forster, 847.
19. *Dick.*, XXXIX, 93.
20. Dolby, 444-5.
21. Conway, *Anthony Munday*, 103-4.
22. Kitton, *Life*, 390-1, quoting Charles Dickens, Jr., from *North American Review*, May, June, 1895.
23. Dolby, 447.
24. Mary Angela Dickens, *My Grandfather*, 110.
25. Dolby, 449.
26. *Coll. P.*, II, 578, Farewell Speech, 3/15/70.
27. Dolby, 450.
28. Ibid., 450-1.
29. Trevelyan, *Macaulay*, II, 397.
30. Dolby, 453-4; Forster, 829-30, 830 fn., 831.
31. *Let.*, III, 765, Helps, 3/3/70.
32. Dolby, 455-7; Forster, 831-2; *Let.*, III, 768, Helps, 3/26/70.
33. *Let.*, III, 768, Forster, 3/26/70.
34. Dolby, 459-60.
35. *Let.*, III, 768, Helps, 3/26/70.
36. Forster, 832.
37. *Let.*, III, 780, Rusden, 5/20/70; cf. Forster, 829-30 fn.
38. Forster, 847-8.
39. *Let.*, III, 769, Forster, 3/29/70.
40. Ibid., 768, 3/26/70.
41. Forster, 848; cf. *Coll. P.*, II, 528-32, speech, 4/5/70.
42. Dolby, 461.
43. Fitzgerald, *Life*, II, 310.

44. *Let.*, III, 771, Fields, 4/18/70.
45. Ibid., 772, Kent, 4/25/70.
46. Kitton, *Life*, 453-4, quoting Blanchard Jerrold.
47. Hunt. MS., Dickens to Frederic Ouvry, 3/24/70.
48. *Let.*, III, 799-800, codicil to will, 6/2/70.
49. Forster, 848.
50. *Let.*, III, 773, Forster, 4/29/70.
51. *Coll. P.*, II, 534, speech, 5/2/70.
52. *Let.*, III, 780-1, Harry Lemon, 5/25/70.
53. Ibid., 776, Mrs. Ward, 5/11/70.
54. Ibid., Georgina Hogarth, 5/11/70.
55. Ibid., 778, Ralston, 5/16/70.
56. Ibid., Kent, 5/17/70.
57. Forster, 849.
58. Cross, *Dickens*, 397.
59. Forster, 850.
60. Ibid., 849.
61. Kitton, *Pen and Pencil*, 190, quoting Locker-Lampson's recollections.
62. *Dick.*, XXXIII, 135, quoting Lord Redesdale's *Memories*.
63. Kitton, *Pen and Pencil*, Supp., 30-1, quoting Herman Merivale's recollections; cf. Fitzgerald, *Life*, II, 314.
64. Kent, *Dickens as Reader*, 263-4.
65. Kitton, *Pen and Pencil*, Supp., 26-7, quoting Dolby's recollections.
66. *Let.*, III, 778, Forster, 5/16/70.
67. Ibid., 782-3, Mrs. Squire Bancroft, 5/31/70, Pulvermacher and Co., 6/3,8/70.
68. Perugini, *Edwin Drood*, 652.
69. Forster, 656.
70. Storey, 132; Perugini, *Edwin Drood*, 652-4.
71. Forster, 851.
72. *E. D.*, XXIII, 271.
73. Forster, 851.
74. *Let.*, III, 784, Kent, 6/8/70.
75. Forster, 851-2; Storey, 135.
76. Fitzgerald, *Life*, I, 92, quoting the telegram to Charles Dickens, Jr.; Forster, 852.
77. Forster, 852.
78. Storey, 137.
79. Mary Angela Dickens, *My Grandfather*, 105.
80. Storey, 137.
81. Pope-Hennessy, 476.
82. Forster, 852; Hunt, MS., Georgina Hogarth to Mrs. James T. Fields, 7/4/70. Harry arrived just two hours after his father's death.
83. Kitton, *Pen and Pencil*, 97-9.
84. Forster, 855.
85. Forster Coll., Henry Wadsworth Longfellow to John Forster, 6/12/70.
86. Blanchard Jerrold, *In Memoriam*, 240, quoting Ernest Filloneau.
87. Kitton, *Pen and Pencil*, 172, quoting Mrs. Cowden Clarke's *Recollections of Writers*.
88. Blanchard Jerrold, *In Memoriam*, 228.
89. Forster MS., Thomas Carlyle to John Forster, 6/11/70.
90. Ibid., 2/16/74.
91. Forster, 855 fn., quoting London *Times* editorial.
92. Kitton, *Pen and Pencil*, 190; Locker-Lampson, 327.
93. Forster, 855.
94. Ibid.; Forster Coll., newspaper clipping dated 6/14/70.
95. Forster, 855-6.
96. Ibid., 856; Forster Coll., newspaper clippings dated 6/14,15/70; Locker-Lampson, 328.
97. Fitzgerald, *Life*, II, 321.
98. *Dick.*, XXXV, 178, quoting *Punch*, 6/25/70.
99. Forster Coll., newspaper clipping, 6/15/70.
100. Reid, II, 227-9. Pope-Hennessy, 476, says the tomb was closed on Waterloo Day, June 18th, but Forster, 856, says Thursday, which was the 16th, and Reid, 229, quoting a letter from Lady Augusta Stanley to Lord Houghton, would seem to confirm Forster's statement.

Bibliography

I

All of the unpublished letters of Dickens that I quote or refer to—and possibly the letters to him or about him, the letters written by other members of his family, the texts of contracts and agreements, and other memoranda—will ultimately appear in full in a new edition of *The Letters of Charles Dickens* edited by Humphry House, an enterprise of which I have the honor to serve on the Advisory Board. As I write these notes I am also engaged in editing a selection of Dickens's letters to Miss Angela Burdett Coutts and her companion Miss Hannah Meredith (Mrs. William Brown). But meanwhile, both in courtesy to the many private collectors, dealers in autograph letters, and institutional libraries generously allowing me to quote from material in their possession and as a service to scholars interested in the authority for my statements, it is proper that I indicate the locations of all unpublished documents to which I refer. I therefore list below a key to all my manuscript sources as they are identified in the footnotes.

MANUSCRIPT KEY

Barrett	Letters in the possession of Mr. Roger W. Barrett of Kenilworth, Illinois.
Barrow	Letters in the possession of Mr. Archibald Barrow of New York.
Berg	Letters and other documents in the Henry W. and Albert A. Berg Collection of the New York Public Library.
Boston	Letters in the Boston Public Library, Boston, Massachusetts.
Dana	Letters in the collection of the late Henry Wadsworth Longfellow Dana of Cambridge, Massachusetts.
Dickens House	Letters and other documents in the collection of the Dickens House of the Dickens Fellowship, London.
H. C. Dickens	Letters in the possession of Mr. Henry Charles Dickens, O.B.E., of London.
Philip Dickens	Letters and memoranda in the possession of Major Philip Dickens of Charing, Kent.
Elkins	Letters and other documents in the collection of the late

William M. Elkins of Philadelphia, now in the Philadelphia Free Library.

Forster   Letters and other documents in the Forster Collection of the Victoria and Albert Museum, London.

Hird   Letters in the collection of Mr. Lewis A. Hird of Englewood, New Jersey.

Houghton   Letters in the Houghton Library of Harvard University.

House   Letters in the possession or custody of Mr. Humphry House of Cambridge, England.

Hunt.   Letters and other documents in the Henry E. Huntington Library and Art Gallery of San Marino, California.

Inman   Letters in the possession of Maurice Inman, Inc., of New York.

Lehmann   Letters in the possession of Mrs. R. C. Lehmann of London.

Lytton   Letters in the collection of the late Earl of Lytton of Knebworth, Hertfordshire.

Macy   Account Book in the collection of Mr. George Macy of New York.

Maggs   Letters in the possession of Maggs Brothers of London.

Millar   Letters in the collection of Dr. Eric George Millar, formerly Egerton Librarian and Keeper of Manuscripts of the British Museum, London.

Morgan   Letters and other documents in the collection of the Pierpont Morgan Library, New York.

N. Y. Pub. Lib., MS. Division   Letters in the Manuscript Division of the New York Public Library.

Parrish   Letters and other documents in the Parrish Collection of the Princeton Library.

Pforzheimer   Documents in the collection of Mr. Carl Pforzheimer of New York.

Rosenbach   Letters in the possession of Dr. A. S. W. Rosenbach of New York.

Royal Academy   Letters in the Royal Academy of Arts, London.

Rylands   Letters in the John Rylands Library, Manchester, England.

Suzannet   Letters in the collection of the late Comte Alain de Suzannet of Lausanne.

V. and A.   Letters in the Victoria and Albert Museum, London.

Widener   Letters and other documents in the Harry Elkins Widener Collection of the Harvard University Library.

Yale   Letters in the Library of Yale University.

II

Quotations from the published writings of Dickens and references to them are almost invariably identified by their locations in *The Nonesuch Dickens*, edited by Arthur Waugh, Hugh Walpole, Walter Dexter, and Thomas Hatton, and published by the Nonesuch Press in 1938. This is the most nearly complete and accurate of all editions of Dickens's work, especially noteworthy for its three huge volumes of his letters and its two volumes of collected papers containing his speeches and his contributions to periodicals. When it has been necessary to refer to letters or speeches subsequently published elsewhere, these are separately identified. Since the Nonesuch edition, however, is not readily accessible to all scholars, in quoting from the novels and stories I have not only indicated the volume and page of that edition, but the Book or Part as well as the chapter, to facilitate their being located in any edition. I have used the following abbreviations for titles:

WRITINGS BY DICKENS

A. N.	American Notes	Let., I, II,	Letters of Charles
A. Y. R.	All the Year Round	III	Dickens, vols. I, II,
B. H.	Bleak House		III.
B. of L.	The Battle of Life	L. D.	Little Dorrit
B. R.	Barnaby Rudge	M. C.	Martin Chuzzlewit
C. C.	A Christmas Carol	N. N.	Nicholas Nickleby
Chimes	The Chimes	O. C. S.	The Old Curiosity
Coll. P.,	Collected Papers, vols.		Shop
I, II	I, II	O. M. F.	Our Mutual Friend
C. on H.	The Cricket on the	O. T.	Oliver Twist
	Hearth	P. from I.	Pictures from Italy
D. C.	David Copperfield	P. P.	Pickwick Papers
D. and S.	Dombey and Son	R. P.	Reprinted Pieces
E. D.	The Mystery of Edwin	S. by B.	Sketches by Boz
	Drood	S. U. 3 H.	Sunday Under Three
G. E.	Great Expectations		Heads
H. M.	The Haunted Man	T. T. C.	A Tale of Two Cities
H. T.	Hard Times	U. C.	The Uncommercial
H. W.	Household Words		Traveller

III

I have thought it desirable to list in the bibliography of published sources both those books and articles from which I quoted or to which I made direct reference and those which provided background information even though they might not be explicitly alluded to in either text or notes. The frequent references to *The Dickensian* are indicated by the abbreviation *Dick.*, followed by volume and page numbers. References in the notes are

identified by giving the author's surname and the page, but when there
are two authors with the same surname or more than one book or article
by the same author a key part of the title is given as well.

PUBLISHED SOURCES

Ainger, Alfred: *Lectures and Essays.* Macmillan. 1905.

Aldrich, Lilian Woodman: *Crowding Memories.* Houghton Mifflin. 1920.

Allingham, William: *A Diary.* Macmillan. 1907.

Altick, Richard D.: *The Cowden Clarkes.* Oxford. 1948.
  "Dickens and America." *Pennsylvania Magazine of History and Biography.* July, 1949.

Andersen, Hans Christian: "A Visit to Charles Dickens." *Eclectic Magazine.* February, 1871.

Armour, Richard Willard: *A Biography of Bryan Waller Procter.* Meador. 1935.

Armstrong, M. F.: "Our Letter." *St. Nicholas.* May, 1877.

Aydelotte, William O.: "The England of Marx and Mill as Reflected in Fiction." *Journal of Economic History.* Supp. VIII, 1948.

Baker, Richard M.: *The Drood Murder Case.* Univ. of California. 1951.

Baldrey, A. L.: "The Life and Work of Marcus Stone." *Art Annual.* 1896.

Ballantine, William: *Some Experiences of a Barrister's Life.* Bentley. 1882.

Barham, Richard Harris: *The Life and Letters of R. H. Barham, by his Son.* Bentley. 1870.

Barrow, John Henry, Ed. *The Mirror of Parliament.* 1830–36.

Beers, Henry A.: *Nathaniel Parker Willis.* Houghton. 1885.

Berger, Francesco: *Reminiscences, Impressions, and Anecdotes.* Sampson, Low, Marston. 1913.

Bibliography of Charles Dickens, A: Author unstated. Kerslake. 1879.

Bigelow, John: *Restrospections of an Active Life.* Baker and Taylor. 1909.

Blunden, Edmund: *Leigh Hunt.* Harper. 1930.

Bourne, Henry R. Fox: *English Newspapers.* Chatto and Windus. 1887.

Boyd, Aubrey: "A New Angle on the Drood Mystery." *Washington University Studies: Humanistic Series.* October, 1921.

Boyle, Mary: *Mary Boyle, Her Book.* Sir Courtenay Boyle, Ed. Dutton. 1902.

Brampton, Henry Hawkins, Baron: *The Reminiscences of Sir Henry Hawkins, Baron Brampton.* Richard Harris, Ed. E. Arnold. 1904.

Brewer, Luther A.: *Leigh Hunt and Charles Dickens.* Privately printed. Cedar Rapids. 1932.

Broderip, Frances Freeling: *Memorials of Thomas Hood.* Ticknor and Fields. 1870.

Brookfield, Charles and Frances: *Mrs. Brookfield and Her Circle.* Scribner. 1905.

Brown, E. K.: "David Copperfield." *Yale Review*. June, 1948.

Browne, Edgar: *Phiz and Dickens*. Dodd, Mead. 1914.

Browning, Elizabeth Barrett: *Letters*. F. G. Kenyon, Ed. Smith, Elder. 1897.

Browning, Robert: *Browning's Letters to Isa Blagden*. A. Joseph Armstrong, Ed. Baylor Univ. 1923.

Byrne, Julia Clara [Mrs. W. P. Byrne]: *Gossip of the Century*. Ward and Downey. 1892.

Calhoun, Philo, and Heaney, Howell J.: *Dickens's "Christmas Carol" After a Hundred Years: A Study in Bibliographical Evidence*. Papers of the Bibliographical Society of America. Fourth Number, 1945.

Carlton, William J.: *Charles Dickens: Shorthand Writer*. Cecil Palmer. 1926.

Carlyle, Jane Welsh: *Letters and Memorials*. Harper. 1883.

Letters to Her Family. Leonard Huxley, Ed. Murray. 1924.

Cazamian, Louis: *Le roman social en Angleterre (1830–1850)*. Société Nouvelle de Librairie et d'Édition. 1904.

Chancellor, E. Beresford: *Dickens and His Times*. Richards. 1937.

The London of Dickens. Richards. 1924.

The Charles Dickens Dinner: An Authentic Record of the Public Dinner Given to Mr. Charles Dickens, at the Freemasons' Hall, London, on Saturday, November 2, 1867, Prior to His Departure for the United States. Chapman and Hall. 1867.

Chesterton, Gilbert Keith: *Charles Dickens: A Critical Study*. Dodd, Mead. 1913.

Criticisms and Appreciations. Dent. 1933.

Childs, George W.: *Recollections*, Lippincott, 1890.

Chorley, Henry F.: *Autobiography, Memoir, and Letters*. Compiled by H. G. Hewlett. Bentley. 1873.

Christian, Eleanor E.: *Recollections of Charles Dickens*. Temple Bar. April, 1888. (Amplified and varied from an earlier version, in *Englishwoman's Domestic Magazine*, X, 336, 1871.)

Christian, Mildred G.: "Carlyle's Influence upon the Social Theory of Dickens." *Trollopian*. Vol. 3, 1947.

Christie, John: *The Ancestry of Catherine Thomason Hogarth*. Hay. 1912.

Clark, Cumberland: *Charles Dickens and the Yorkshire Schools*. Privately printed. Chiswick Press. 1918.

Clark, Lewis Gaylord: "Letters from Charles Dickens to L. Gaylord Clark." *Harper's Magazine*. August, 1862.

Clark, William Andrews, Jr.: *The Library of William Andrews Clark*. Nash. 1921–23.

Clarke, Mary Cowden: *Recollections of Writers*. Scribner. 1878.

Cockburn, Henry Thomas Cockburn, Lord: *Life of Lord Jeffrey*. Black. 1852.

Coleman, John: *Fifty Years of An Actor's Life*. Hutchinson. 1904.

Collier, John Payne: *An Old Man's Diary, Forty Years Ago*. For private circulation. Richards. 1872.

Connely, Willard: *Count D'Orsay: The Dandy of Dandies*. Cassell. 1952.

Conway, Eustace: *Anthony Munday and Other Essays*. Privately printed. New York. 1927.

Conway, Moncure D.: *Autobiography*. Cassell. 1904.

Cooper, T. C.: *With Dickens in Yorkshire*. 1923.

Cooper, Thomas Parsons: *The Real Micawber*. Simkin, Marshall, Hamilton, Kent. 1920.

Corkran, Henriette: *Celebrities and I*. Hutchinson. 1902.

Cross, Constance: "Charles Dickens: A Memory." *New Liberal Review*. October, 1901.

Cross, John W.: *George Eliot's Life as Related in Her Letters and Journals*. Blackwood. 1885.

Crotch, W. Walter: *Charles Dickens: Social Reformer*. Chapman and Hall. 1913.

Crowe, Sir Joseph Archer: *Reminiscences of Thirty-Fve Years of My Life*. J. Murray. 1895.

Cruikshank, Robert J.: *Charles Dickens and Early Victorian England*. Chanticleer. 1949.

Dana, Henry Wadsworth Longfellow: "Longfellow and Dickens: The Story of a Trans-Atlantic Friendship." *Cambridge Historical Society*. Vol. 28, 1942.

Darwin, Bernard: *Dickens*. Duckworth. 1933.

The Dickens Advertiser. Macmillan. 1930.

Delattre, Floris: *Dickens et la France*. Librairie Universitaire. 1927.

Dent, H. C.: *The Life and Characters of Charles Dickens*. Wheeler. 1933.

Devey, Louisa: *Life of Rosina, Lady Lytton*. Sonnenschein, Lowrey. 1887.

Dexter, John F.: *Dickens Memento. With Introduction by Francis Phillimore* [Alice Meynell] *and Hints to Dickens Collectors by John F. Dexter*. Field and Tuer, The Leadenhall Press. [1885].

Dexter, Walter: *The England of Dickens*. Palmer. 1925.

The Kent of Dickens. Palmer. 1924.

The London of Dickens. Palmer. 1930.

Dexter, Walter, Ed: *Mr. and Mrs. Charles Dickens. His Letters to Her*. Constable. 1935.

The Unpublished Letters of Charles Dickens to Mark Lemon. Halton and Truscott. 1927.

Dexter, Walter, and Ley, J. W. T.: *The Origin of Pickwick*. Chapman and Hall. 1936.

Dickens, Alfred Tennyson: "My Father and His Friends." *Nash's Magazine*. September, 1911.

Dickens, Charles, Jr.: "Reminiscences of My Father." *Windsor Magazine*. Supplement. December, 1934.

Dickens, Henry Fielding: *Memories of My Father*. Duffield. 1929.

The Recollections of Sir Henry Dickens, K.C. Heinemann. 1934.

Dickens, Mary ["Mamey"]: *My Father as I Recall Him*. Dutton. 1900.
Dickens, Mary Angela: "A Child's Recollections of Gad's Hill." *Strand Magazine*. January, 1897.
"My Grandfather as I Knew Him." *Nash's Magazine*. October, 1911.
Dickensian, The. Published by the Dickens Fellowship. Monthly, 1905–1918; quarterly, 1919–. Vols. I-XLVII.
Dictionary of American Biography.
Dictionary of National Biography.
Dilke, Charles Wentworth, Dickens, Charles, and Forster, John: *The Case of the Reformers of the Literary Fund*. Bradbury and Evans. 1858.
[See also: *Royal Literary Fund: A Summary of the Facts . . .*]
Dods, Louis Ferdinand ["Ole Man River"]: *Beloved Ghosts*. Bale, Danielsson. 1936.
Dolby, George: *Charles Dickens as I Knew Him*. Scribner. 1912.
Downey, Edmund: *Charles Lever, His Life in His Letters*. Blackwood. 1906.
Driver, Cecil: *Tory Radical: The Life of Richard Oastler*. Oxford. 1946.
Duffield, Howard: "John Jasper, Strangler." *Bookman*. February, 1930.
Duffy, Sir Charles Gavan: *Conversations with Carlyle*. Scribner. 1892.
Dunlap, Leslie W.: "Letters of W. G. and L. G. Clark." *New York Public Library Bulletin*. June, 1938.
Eckel, John C.: *The First Editions of the Writings of Charles Dickens*. Maurice Inman. 1932.
Elkins, William M.: *The Life and Works of Charles Dickens. An Exhibition from the Collection of William M. Elkins, Esq., of Philadelphia, held at the Free Library, June-July, 1946*. [An illustrated descriptive catalogue].
Ellis, Stewart M.: *Harrison Ainsworth and His Friends*. Lane. 1911.
Wilkie Collins, Sheridan LeFanu, and Others. Constable. 1931.
Elwin, Malcolm: *Victorian Wallflowers*. Cape. 1934.
Emerson, Ralph Waldo: *Journals*. Edited by Edward Waldo Emerson and Waldo Emerson Forbes. Houghton Mifflin. 1911.
Escott, T. H. S.: *Masters of English Journalism*. Unwin. 1911.
Espinasse, Francis: *Literary Recollections and Sketches*. Hodder and Stoughton. 1893.
Evans, Thomas C.: *Of Many Men*. American News Company. 1888.
Felton, Cornelius: *Familiar Letters from Europe*. Ticknor and Fields. 1865.
Field, Kate: *Charles Albert Fechter*. Osgood. 1882.
Pen Photographs of Charles Dickens's Readings. Loring. 1868.
Fielding, K. J.: "Charles Dickens and Thomas C. Evans." *Notes and Queries*. Vol. 196, 1951.
"Dickens to Miss Burdett Coutts." London *Times* Literary Supplement. March 2, 9, 1951.
Fields, Annie A. [Mrs. James T. Fields]: *Memories of a Hostess*. M. A. DeWolfe Howe, Ed. Atlantic Monthly Press. 1922.

Fields, James T.: *In and Out of Doors with Charles Dickens*. Osgood. 1876.

Yesterdays with Author. Houghton Mifflin. 1900.

Fitzgerald, Percy: *The Garrick Club*. Stock. 1904.

John Forster by One of His Friends. Chapman and Hall. 1903.

The Life of Charles Dickens as Revealed in His Writings. Chatto and Windus. 1905.

Memories of Charles Dickens. Arrowsmith. 1913.

Fitzgerald, S. J. Adair: *Dickens and the Drama*. Chatto and Windus. 1910.

Fonblanque, Edward Barrington de: *The Life and Labours of Albany Fonblanque*. Bentley. 1874.

Forster, John: *The Life of Charles Dickens*. Edited and Annotated with an Introduction by J. W. T. Ley. Doubleday Doran. [1928].

Francis, John C.: *A Literary Chronicle of Half a Century*. Bentley. 1888.

Frith, W. P.: *John Leech: His Life and Work*. Bentley. 1891.

My Autobiography and Reminiscences. Bentley. 1889.

Frith, Walter: "Small Talk with My Father." *Cornhill Magazine*. December, 1907.

Froude, James Anthony: *Thomas Carlyle: His First Forty Years*. Harper. 1882.

Thomas Carlyle: A History of His Life in London. Scribner. 1884.

Gad's Hill Gazette: Published by Henry Fielding Dickens and Edward Bulwer Lytton Dickens at Gad's Hill. Copies in Berg Collection, New York Public Library.

Gissing, George: *The Immortal Dickens*. Palmer. 1925.

Gordan, John W.: "The Secret of Dickens' Memoranda." *A Bookman's Holiday: Notes and Studies Written and Gathered in Tribute to Harry Miller Lydenberg*. New York Public Library. 1943.

Grant, James: *The Newspaper Press*. Tinsley. 1871.

Greeley, Horace: *Recollections of a Busy Life*. J. B. Ford. 1869.

Greville, Charles C. F.: *The Greville Diaries*. P. W. Wilson, Ed. Doubleday Page. 1927.

Griffin, James: *Memories of the Past*. Hamilton, Adams. 1883.

Griffin, W. Hall, and Minchin, Harry C.: *The Life of Robert Browning*. Methuen. 1910.

Grolier Club: *The Catalogue of an Exhibition of the Works of Charles Dickens. January 23rd to March 8th* [1913]. Grolier Club. 1913.

Grubb, Gerald G.: "Dickens and the *Daily News*. The Origin of the Idea." *Booker Memorial Studies*. Univ. of North Carolina Press. 1950.

"Dickens's Editorial Methods." *Studies in Philology*. Vol. 40, 1943.

"Dickens's Influence as an Editor." *Studies in Philology*. Vol. 42, 1945.

"Dickens's Pattern of Weekly Serialization." *Journal of English Literary History*. Vol. 9, 1942.

"Dickens's Western Tour and the Cairo Legend." *Studies in Philology*. Vol. 48, 1951.

"The Editorial Policies of Charles Dickens." *PMLA*. Vol. 58, 1943.

"The Personal and Literary Relations of Dickens and Poe." *Nineteenth Century Fiction*. Vol. 5, 1950.

Gummer, Ellis N.: *Dickens' Works in Germany, 1837–1937*. Oxford. 1940.

Gwynn, Stephen, and Tuckwell, Gertrude: *The Life of Charles Wentworth Dilke*. Macmillan. 1917.

Haight, Anne Douglas: "Charles Dickens Tries to Remain Anonymous." *Colophon*. "New Graphic Series." No. 1, 1939.

Haldane, Elizabeth: *Mrs. Gaskell and Her Friends*. Hodder and Stoughton. 1930.

Hall, Samuel Carter: *A Book of Memories*. Virtue and Co. 1877.
Retrospect of a Long Life. Bentley. 1883.

Hansard: *Parliamentary Debates*. 3rd Series [1830–36].

Hare, Augustus: *The Story of My Life*. Dodd, Mead. 1896–1901.

Harrington, Thomas F.: *The Harvard Medical School*. J. G. Mumford, Ed. Boston. 1905.

Hatton, Thomas, and Cleaver, Arthur H.: *A Bibliography of the Periodical Works of Charles Dickens, Bibliographical, Analytical, and Statistical*. Redway. 1899.

Hawthorne, Nathaniel: *English Note Books*. Randell Stewart, Ed. MLA. 1941.

Hayward, Abraham: *Selections from The Correspondence of Abraham Hayward*. Scribner and Welfard. 1887.

Hayward, Arthur L.: *The Dickens Encyclopaedia*. Dutton. 1924.

Helps, Arthur: *The Correspondence of Sir Arthur Helps*. E. E. Helps, Ed. Lane. 1907.

Hodder, Edwin: *The Life of the Seventh Earl of Shaftesbury*. Cassell. 1886–7.

Hodder, George: *Memories of My Times*. Tinsley. 1870.

Hole, Samuel R.: *Memories of Dean Hole*. Macmillan. 1893.

Holland, Lady: *A Memoir of the Reverend Sydney Smith, by his daughter Lady Holland, with a selection of his letters edited by Mrs. Austin*. Longmans, Green, Reade, and Dyer. 1869.

Hollingshead, John: *My Lifetime*. Sampson, Low, Marston. 1895.

Hollister, Paul: *The Author's Wallet*. R. H. Macy. 1934.

Holyoake, Maltus Q.: "Memories of Charles Dickens." *Chambers's Journal*. Vol. 14, 1897.

Hone, Philip: *Diary of Philip Hone*. B. Tuckerman, Ed. Dodd, Mead. 1889.

Hood, Thomas: *The Letters of Thomas Hood*. Leslie A. Marchand, Ed. Rutgers. 1945.

Hopkins, Annette B. "Dickens and Mrs. Gaskell." *Huntington Library Quarterly*. August, 1946.

Horne, Richard H.: "Bygone Celebrities." *Gentlemen's Magazine*. February, May, 1871.

A New Spirit of the Age. Harper. 1844.

House, Humphry: *The Dickens World.* Oxford. 1941.

Houtchens, Caroline Washburn, and Lawrence Houston: "Contributions of Early American Journals to the Study of Charles Dickens." *Modern Language Quarterly.* Vol. 6, 1945.

Howe, Julia Ward: *Reminiscences.* Houghton Mifflin. 1899.

Howells, William Dean: *The Life in Letters of William Dean Howells.* Mildrew Howells, Ed. Doubleday. 1928.

Howitt, Mary B.: *An Autobiography.* Houghton Mifflin. 1889.

Hughes, James L.: *Dickens as an Educator.* Appleton. 1900.

Humphreys, Arthur L.: *Dickens and His First Schoolmaster.* (pamphlet, 23 pp.). Manchester. 1926.

Hunt, Leigh: *The Correspondence of Leigh Hunt. Edited by his Eldest Son.* Smith, Elder. 1862.

Huxley, Aldous: *Vulgarity in Literature.* Chatto and Windus. 1930.

Irving, Pierre M.: *The Life and Letters of Washington Irving.* Putnam. 1864.

Jackson, Joseph: *Dickens in Philadelphia.* Campbell. 1912.

Jackson, Thomas A.: *Charles Dickens: The Progress of a Radical.* International. 1938.

James, Henry: *William Wetmore Story and His Friends.* Houghton Mifflin. 1904.

Jeaffreson, John Cordy: *A Book of Recollections.* Hurst and Blackett. 1894.

Jerdan, William: *The Autobiography of William Jerdan.* Hall, Virtue. 1853.

Jerrold, Blanchard: "Charles Dickens. In Memoriam." *Gentlemen's Magazine.* July, 1870.

A Day with Charles Dickens. The Best of All Good Company. Useful Knowledge Company. June, 1871.

Jerrold, Walter: *Douglas Jerrold and Punch.* Macmillan. 1910.

Douglas Jerrold: Dramatist and Wit. Hodder and Stoughton. 1914.

Thomas Hood: His Life and Times. Alston River. 1907.

Kemble, Fanny: *Records of Later Life.* Holt. 1884.

Kent, William Charles: "Charles Dickens as a Journalist." *Time.* July 28, 1884.

Charles Dickens as a Reader. Lippincott. 1872.

Kerslake: See: *A Bibliography of Charles Dickens.*

Kiddle, Margaret: "Caroline Chisholm and Charles Dickens." *Historical Studies. Australia and New Zealand.* Vol. 3, July, 1945.

Kitton, Frederic G.: *Charles Dickens: His Life, Writings, and Personality.* T. C. and E. C. Jack. n.d.

Charles Dickens by Pen and Pencil. Sabin, Dexter. 1889–1890.

Dickens and His Illustrators. Redway. 1899.

The Dickens Country. A. and C. Black. 1905.

Dickensiana. Redway. 1886.

The Minor Writings of Charles Dickens. Elliot Stock. 1900.

The Novels of Charles Dickens. Stock. 1897.

"Phiz": A Memoir. Redway. 1882.

"The Story of a Famous Society." *Gentlemen's Magazine.* February, 1898.

Knight, Charles: *Passages of a Working Life.* Bradbury and Evans. 1864. *Passages from the Life of Charles Knight.* Putnam. 1874.

Knowles, R. B.: *The Life of James Sheridan Knowles.* Privately printed for James McHenry. 1872.

Landor, Walter Savage: *Letters and Oher Unpublished Writings.* Bentley. 1897.

Letters: Private and Public. Stephen Wheeler, Ed. Duckworth. 1899.

Langer, William L., Ed.: *Encyclopedia of World History.* Houghton Mifflin. 1948.

Langton, Robert: *The Childhood and Youth of Charles Dickens.* Hutchinson. 1891.

Latimer, Elizabeth Wormeley: "A Girl's Recollections of Charles Dickens." *Lippincott's Magazine.* September, 1893.

Layard, Austen H.: *Autobiography and Letters.* Scribner. 1903.

Layard, George Soames: *Shirley Brooks of Punch.* Pitman. 1907.

Lehmann, Rudolph C.: *Charles Dickens as Editor.* Sturgis and Walton. 1912.

Memories of Half a Century. Smith, Elder. 1908.

Lewes, Mrs. C. L.: *Dr. Southwood Smith.* Blackwood. 1908.

Lewes, George: "Dickens in Relation to Criticism." *Every Saturday.* Vol. 1, 1872.

Ley, J. W. T.: *The Dickens Circle.* Dutton. 1919.

Lindsay, Jack: *Charles Dickens: A Biographical and Critical Study.* Dakers. 1950.

Linton, Eliza Lynn: *My Literary Life.* Hodder and Stoughton. 1899.

Lippincott, Mrs. L. K. ["Grace Greenwood"]: An undated, untitled article in the New York *Tribune,* of which there is a clipping in the Massachusetts Historical Society.

Livingston, Flora V., Ed.: *Charles Dickens's Letters to Charles Lever.* With an Introduction by Hyder E. Rollins. Harvard. 1933.

Locker-Lampson, Frederic: *My Confidences.* Smith, Elder. 1896.

Longfellow, Samuel: *Henry Wadsworth Longfellow.* Houghton Mifflin. 1891.

Lunn, Hugh Kingsmill: *The Sentimental Journey.* Wishart. 1934.

Lytton, Edward, Earl of: *The Life, Letters, and Literary Remains of Edward Bulwer, Lord Lytton.* Harper. 1883.

Lytton, Victor, Earl of: *The Life of Edward Bulwer, First Lord Lytton.* Macmillan. 1913.

Mackay, Charles: *Forty Years Recollections.* Chapman and Hall. 1877. *Through the Long Day.* Allen. 1887.

Mackenzie, Robert Shelton: *The Life of Charles Dickens*. Peterson. 1870.

Macready, Sir Nevil: *Annals of an Active Life*. Hutchinson. 1924.

Macready, William Charles: *The Diaries of William Charles Macready*. William Toynbee, Ed. Chapman and Hall. 1912.

Madden, R. R.: *The Literary Life and Correspondence of Marguerite, Countess of Blessington*. Harper. 1855.

Markham, Violet: *Paxton and the Bachelor Duke*. Hodder and Stoughton. 1935.

Martin, Sir Theodore: *Helena Faucit, Lady Martin*. Blackwood. 1900.

Martineau, Harriet: *Autobiography, with Memorial by Maria Weston Chapman*. Smith, Elder. 1877.

   The Factory Controversy: Misstatements in "Household Words." Ireland. 1855.

Masson, David: *Memories of London in the Forties*. Blackwood. 1908.

Maude, Aylmer, Ed.:*Family Views of Tolstoy* [esp. Preface, p. 8, and "Tolstoy and Dickens," by Nikolay Apostolov, 71-84]. Allen and Unwin. 1926.

Maurice, Arthur Bartlett: "Dickens as an Editor." *Bookman*. Vol. 30, 1909.

Maurois, André: *Dickens*. Harper. 1935.

McCarthy, Justin H., and Robinson, Sir John: *The Daily News Jubilee*. Sampson, Low, Marston. 1896.

McCrie, Thomas: *Memoirs of Sir Andrew Agnew*. Groombridge. 1850.

Melville, Lewis: *William Makepeace Thackeray*. London. 1910.

Meynell, Alice: *Hearts of Controversy*. Scribner. 1917.

Meynell, Viola. *Alice Meynell: A Memoir*. Cape. 1929.

Meynell, Wilfrid: *A Dickens Friendship*. Privately printed. n.d.

Mill, John Stuart: *Autobiography*. Columbia. 1924.

Miller, William: *The Dickens Student and Collector*. Harvard. 1946.

Minnigerode, Meade: *The Fabulous Forties*. Garden City Press. 1924.

Mitford, Mary Russell: *The Life of Mary Russell Mitford, Told by Herself in Letters to Her Friends*. A. G. K. L'Estrange, Ed. Harper. 1870.

More, Paul Elmer: *Shelburne Essays*, Vol. 5. Putnam. 1908.

Moreland, Arthur: *Dickens in London*. Palmer. 1928.

Morse, Robert: "Our Mutual Friend." *Partisan Review*. March, 1949.

Motley, John Lothrop: *Correspondence*. George William Curtis, Ed. Harper. 1889.

Myall, Laura Hain Friswell: *In the Sixties and Seventies*. Hutchinson. 1905.

Napier, Macvey: *Selections from the Correspondence of Macvey Napier*. Edited by his son, Macvey Napier. Macmillan. 1879.

Neff, Emery E.: *Carlyle and Mill*. Columbia. 1924.

Nevill, Lady Dorothy: *Reminiscences*. Arnold. 1906.

Nicoll, Allardyce: *A History of Early Nineteenth Century Drama, 1800–1850*. Cambridge. 1930.

Nisbet, Ada B.: "Dickens Loses an Election." *Princeton Univ. Quarterly.* Vol. 2, 1950.

Notes and Queries: Eighth Series, No. VI, 226, 251. Twelfth Series, No. IX, 249.

Oberholzer, Ellis Paxson: *Literary History of Philadelphia.* Jacobs. 1906.

Orwell, George: *Dickens, Dali, and Others.* Reynal and Hitchcock. 1946.

Osborne, Charles C.: *Letters of Charles Dickens to the Baroness Burdett Coutts.* Dutton. 1932.

"Mr. Pecksniff and His Prototype." *Independent Review.* Vol. 10, 1906.

Pacey W. C. D.: "Washington Irving and Charles Dickens." *American Literature.* Vol. 16, 1945.

Paul, Howard: *Dinners with Celebrities.* Newton and Eskell. 1896.

Payn, James: "The Youth and Middle Age of Charles Dickens." (From *Chambers's Journal.*) Privately printed. 1883.

Payne, Edward F.: *Dickens Days in Boston.* Houghton Mifflin. 1927.

Payne, Edward F., and Harper, Henry H.: *The Charity of Charles Dickens.* Bibliophile Society. 1929.

The Romance of Charles Dickens and Maria Beadnell Winter. Bibliophile Society. 1929.

Pearson, Hesketh: *Dickens. His Character, Comedy, and Career.* Harper. 1949.

Peel, Lady Georgiana: *Recollections of Lady Georgiana Peel, Compiled by her Daughter, Ethel Peel.* John Lane. 1920.

Pemberton, Thomas Edgar: *Charles Dickens and the Stage.* Redway. 1888.

Perkins, Frederic B.: *Charles Dickens. A Sketch of His Life and Works.* Putnam. 1870.

Perugini, Kate Dickens: "Edwin Drood and the Last Days of Charles Dickens." *Pall Mall Magazine.* June, 1906.

"Thackeray and My Father." *Pall Mall Magazine.* August, 1911.

Perugini, Mark: *Victorian Days and Ways.* Jarrolds. 1932.

Phillips, Walter C.: *Dickens, Reade, and Collins, Sensation Novelists.* Columbia. 1919.

Planché, James R.: *Recollections and Reflections.* Sampson, Low, Marston. 1901.

Pike, James S.: "Dickens, Carlyle, and Tennyson." *Atlantic Monthly.* December, 1939.

Pollack, Juliet, Lady: *Macready as I Knew Him.* Remington. 1884.

Pope-Hennessy, Dame Una: *Charles Dickens.* Howell, Soskin. 1946.

Powell, Thomas: *The Living Authors of England.* Appleton. 1849.

Powys, John Cowper: *Visions and Revisions.* G. Arnold Shaw. 1915.

Prescott, William H.: *Correspondence of William Hickling Prescott.* Massachusetts Historical Society. 1925.

Procter, Bryan Waller: *Autobiographical Fragment.* Bell. 1877.

Pugh, Edwin: *Charles Dickens: The Apostle of the People.* New Age Press. 1908.

Putnam, George W.: "Four Months with Charles Dickens." *Atlantic Monthly*. October, November, 1870.

Quennell, Peter: *Victorian Panorama*. Scribner. 1937.

Ray, Gordon N.: *The Letters and Private Papers of William Makepeace Thackeray*. Harvard. 1945–6.

Redding, Cyrus: *Fifty Years' Recollections*. Skeet. 1858.

Redesdale, Lord: *Memories*. Dutton. 1916.

Reid, T. Wemyss: *The Life, Letters, and Friendships of Richard Monckton Milnes, First Lord Houghton*. Cassell. 1890.

Renton, Richard: *John Forster and His Friendships*. Scribner. 1913.

Richards, Laura E.: *Samuel Gridley Howe*. Appleton-Century. 1935.

Ritchie, Anne Thackeray, Lady: "Charles Dickens as I Remember Him." *Pall Mall Magazine*. March, 1912.

   From the Porch. Scribner. 1913.

   Some Unwritten Memoirs. Harper. 1895.

Roberts, Richard E.: *Samuel Rogers and His Circle*. Methuen. 1910.

Robinson, Henry Crabb: *Diary, Reminiscences, and Correspondence*. Thomas Sadlier, Ed. Macmillan. 1869.

Robinson, Kenneth: *Wilkie Collins*. Macmillan. 1952.

Robinson, Ralph M.: *Coutts': The History of a Banking House*. Murray. 1929.

Rogers, Samuel: *Recollections by Samuel Rogers*. W. Sharpe, Ed. Longmans. 1859.

Rosenbach, A. S. W.: *A Catalogue of the Writings of Charles Dickens in the Library of Harry Elkins Widener*. Privately printed. Philadelphia. 1918.

Royal Literary Fund: *A Summary of Facts . . . in answer to Allegations contained in a Pamphlet entitled 'The Case of the Reformers of the Literacy Fund.'* March 12, 1858.

Rubens, Charles: *The Dummy Library of Charles Dickens at Gad's Hill, as narrated by Charles Rubens to J. Christian Bray*. Privately printed. n.d.

Ruskin, John: *Works*, Vol. II. *Unto This Last*. Crowell. 1905.

Sadleir, Michael: *Bulwer: A Panorama*. Little, Brown. 1931.

   The Strange Life of Lady Blessington. Little, Brown. 1933.

Sala, George Augustus: *Things I Have Seen and People I Have Known*. Cassell. 1894.

Santayana, George: *Works*, Vol. II. "Dickens." Scribner. 1936.

Sawyer, Charles J.: *A Dickens Library: The Sawyer Collection*. Privately printed. 1936.

   [with "F. J. H. D."]: *Dickens vs. Barabbas. Forster Intervening*. Sawyer. 1930.

Shaw, George Bernard: Introduction to *Hard Times*. Waverley. 1912.

   Preface to *Great Expectations*. Limited Editions Club. Clarke. 1937.

Sims, George R.: *Among My Autographs*. Chatto and Windus. 1904.

Smiles, Samuel: *The Autobiography of Samuel Smiles.* Dutton. 1905.

Smith, Harry B., Ed. *The Earliest Letters of Charles Dickens (Written to His Friend Henry Kolle).* Bibliophile Society. 1910.

Smith, Harry B.: *A Sentimental Library.* Privately printed. 1936.

Snyder, J. F.: *Charles Dickens in Illinois.* Illinois State Historical Society. Vol. 3, October, 1910.

Spencer, Walter T.: *Forty Years in My Bookshop.* Houghton Mifflin. 1923.

Spielman, M. H.: *The History of "Punch."* Cassell. 1895.

Spiller, Robert E., *Americans in England.* Holt. 1936.

Stevenson, Lionel: "Dickens's Dark Novels, 1851–57." *Sewanee Review.* Summer, 1943.

   Dr. Quicksilver. The Life of Charles Lever. Chapman and Hall. 1939.

   "The Second Birth of the English Novel." *University of Toronto Quarterly.* July, 1945.

   The Showman of Vanity Fair. Scribner. 1947.

Stoddard, Richard Henry, Ed.: *Anecdote Biographies of Thackeray and Dickens.* Scribner, Armstrong. 1874.

Stonehouse, John Harrison: *Catalogue of the Libraries of Charles Dickens and William Thackeray.* Piccadilly Fountain Press. 1935.

   Green Leaves. Fountain Press. 1931.

Storey, Gladys: *Dickens and Daughter.* Muller. 1939.

Straus, Ralph: *Charles Dickens.* Cosmopolitan. 1928.

Strong, Sandford Arthur: *Critical Studies and Fragments.* Duckworth. 1905.

Sweetser, Kate D.: "Dining with Dickens at Delmonico's." *Bookman.* March. 1919.

Swinburne, Algernon C.: "Charles Dickens." *Quarterly Review.* July, 1902.

Taine, Hippolyte: *History of English Literature.* Vol. IV, Book V, Ch. 1.

Taylor, Bayard: *At Home and Abroad.* Putnam. 1862.

Taylor, Sir Henry: *Autobiography.* Longmans. 1885.

Tennyson, Hallam, 2nd Baron: *Alfred Lord Tennyson, A Memoir by his Son.* Macmillan. 1897.

Thomson, David Croul: *The Life and Labours of Hablôt Knight Browne.* Chapman and Hall. 1884.

Thorrington, James Monroe: *The Life and Times of Albert Smith.* Winston. 1934.

Ticknor, Caroline: *Glimpses of Authors.* Houghton Mifflin. 1922.

Ticknor, George: *The Life, Letters, and Journal of George Ticknor.* Osgood. 1876.

Trevelyan, George Macaulay: *British History in the Nineteenth Century.* Longmans, Green. 1922.

Trevelyan, George Otto: *The Life and Letters of Lord Macaulay.* World's Classics Edition. 1932.

Trollope, Thomas Adolphus: *What I Remember.* Bentley. 1887.

Trumble, Alfred: *In Jail with Charles Dickens*. Francis P. Harper. 1896.

Van Amerongen, J. B.: *The Actor in Dickens*. Appleton. 1927.

Van Dyke, Catherine: "A Talk with Charles Dickens's Office Boy." *Bookman*. March, 1921.

Vizetelly, Henry: *Glances Back Through Seventy Years*. Kegan Paul, Trench, Trübner. 1893.

Wagenknecht, Edward: *The Man Charles Dickens*. Houghton Mifflin. 1929.

Walford, Lucy Bethia: *Memoirs of Victorian London*. Arnold. 1912.

Ward, Henrietta M. A. [Mrs. E. M. Ward]: *Memories of Ninety Years*. Holt. 1926.

Warner, Rex: *The Cult of Power*. "On Reading Dickens." Lippincott. 1947.

Waugh, Arthur: *A Hundred Years of Publishing*. Chapman and Hall. 1930.

Waugh, Francis Gledstanes: *The Athenaeum Club and Its Associations*. Privately printed. 1897.

West, Sir Algernon: *Recollections of Sir Algernon West*. Smith, Elder. 1899.

Wiggin, Kate Douglas: *A Child's Journey with Dickens*. Houghton Mifflin. 1912.

Wilkins, William Glyde: *Charles Dickens in America*. Scribner. 1911.

Williams, Stanley T., *The Life of Washington Irving*. Oxford. 1935.

Wilson, David Alec: *Thomas Carlyle*. Paul. 1923–34.

Wilson, Edmund: *The Wound and the Bow*. "Dickens: The Two Scrooges." Houghton Mifflin. 1941.

Wilson, James Grant: *The Life and Letters of Fitz-Greene Halleck*. Appleton. 1869.

Wingfield-Stratford, Esmé: *Victorian Cycle*. Morrow. 1935.

Winter, William: *Old Friends*. Moffat, Yard. 1909.

Winterich, John T.: *An American Friend of Dickens*. Madigan. 1933.

Woollcott, Alexander: *Mr. Dickens Goes to the Play*. Putnam. 1922.

Wright, Thomas: *Autobiography*. Jenkins. 1936.

    The Life of Charles Dickens. Jenkins. 1935.

Yates, Edmund: *Celebrities at Home*. Office of "The World." 1877–9.

    Mr. Thackeray, Mr. Yates, and the Garrick Club. Privately printed. 1859.

    Recollections and Experiences. Bentley. 1884.

Young, G. M., Ed.: *Early Victorian England*. Oxford. 1934.

I have also consulted various numbers from the files of the following newspapers:

The London *Daily News*, the London *Morning Chronicle*, the London *Times*, the New York *Herald*, and the New York *Tribune*;

and have consulted various numbers of the following magazines and other periodicals:

American Literature, American Notes and Queries, the *Athenaeum,* the *Atlantic Monthly, Baldwin's Monthly, Bentley's Miscellany, Blackwood's Magazine,* the *Bookman, Chambers's Journal,* the *Cornhill Magazine,* the *Edinburgh Review, Fraser's Magazine,* the *Gentlemen's Magazine, Harper's New Monthly Magazine,* the *Independent Review,* the *Knickerbocker Magazine, Lippincott's Magazine, Macmillan's Magazine,* the *Modern Language Quarterly, Nash's Magazine,* the *New Liberal Review, Nineteenth Century Fiction* (the *Trollopian*), the *North American Review,* the *Northern Monthly, Notes and Queries,* the *Pall Mall Magazine, PMLA, Punch,* the *Quarterly Review,* the *Queen's Quarterly,* the *Sphere,* the *Strand Magazine, Studies in Philology, Temple Bar, Town Talk,* and the *Windsor Magazine.*

The sections dealing with the sales of autograph materials in all of the successive volumes of *American Book Prices Current* have been enormously valuable to me, as have been numerous auction-sales catalogues of the American Art Association, the Anderson Galleries, the Parke-Bernet Galleries, and Sotheby and Company, especially the catalogues of the Barrett, Benton, Coggeshall, Edgar, Goelet, Hatton, Morrison, Read, Smith, Suzannet, and Wells sales. I have also made profitable use of many booksellers' catalogues, including those of the Carnegie Book Shop, the City Book Auction, Goodspeed's Book Shop, Thomas F. Madigan, Maggs Brothers, Bernard Quaritch, Charles J. Sawyer, Alwin J. Scheuer, and Dr. J. Schwartz.

and have consulted various numbers of the following magazines and other periodicals:

American Literature, American Notes and Queries, the Athenaeum, the Atlantic Monthly, Baldwin's Monthly, Bentley's Miscellany, Blackwood's Magazine, the Bookman, Chambers's Journal, the Cornhill Magazine, the Edinburgh Review, Fraser's Magazine, the Gentleman's Magazine, Harper's New Monthly Magazine, the Independent Review, the Knickerbocker Magazine, Lippincott's Magazine, Macmillan's Magazine, the Modern Language Quarterly, Nash's Magazine, the New Liberal Review, Nineteenth Century Fiction (the Trollopian), the North American Review, the Northern Monthly, Notes and Queries, the Pall Mall Magazine, PMLA, Punch, the Quarterly Review, the Queen's Quarterly, the Sphere, the Strand Magazine, Studies in Philology, Temple Bar, Town Talk, and the Windsor Magazine.

The section dealing with the sales of autograph materials in all of the successive volumes of American Book Prices Current have been remarkably valuable to me, as have been numerous auction-sales catalogues of the American Art Association, the Anderson Galleries, the Parke-Bernet Galleries, and Sotheby and Company, especially the catalogues of the Barrett, Benton, Coggeshall, Edgar, Godel, Hatton, Morrison, Read, Smith, Sessanac, and Wells sales. I have also made profitable use of many booksellers' catalogues, including those of the Carnegie Book Shop, the City Book Auction, Goodspeed's Book Shop, Thomas F. Madigan, Maggs Brothers, Bernard Quaritch, Charles J. Sawyer, Alwin J. Scheuer, and Dr. J. Schwartz.

Index

Shorter writings by Dickens that appeared in *All the Year Round* and *Household Words* are all identified in the index by printing the abbreviations A.Y.R. or H.W. in parentheses after the title. Characters in his novels and stories are identified by indicating in parentheses the titles of the works in which they appear. The following abbreviations are used:

B.H.	*Bleak House*	H.T.	*Hard Times*
B.R.	*Barnaby Rudge*	L.D.	*Little Dorrit*
C.C.	*A Christmas Carol*	M.C.	*Martin Chuzzlewit*
Chimes	*The Chimes*	N.N.	*Nicholas Nickleby*
C. on H.	*The Cricket on the Hearth*	O.C.S.	*The Old Curiosity Shop*
		O.M.F.	*Our Mutual Friend*
D.C.	*David Copperfield*	O.T.	*Oliver Twist*
D. and S.	*Dombey and Son*	P.P.	*Pickwick Papers*
E.D.	*The Mystery of Edwin Drood*	S. by B.	*Sketches by Boz*
		T.T.C.	*A Tale of Two Cities*
G.E.	*Great Expectations*	U.T.	*The Uncommercial Traveller*
H.M.	*The Haunted Man*		

A

DICKENS: CHARACTERISTICS, *etc.*

birth of Henry Fielding Dickens, 662-3; signs of feeling about her in *David Copperfield*, 688-9; her clumsiness again, 721; her nervous illness, 730; his concern for her at time of Dora's death, 731-2; patronizing about her activities at Tavistock House, 749; criticizes her handwriting, 787; her jealousy of Mme. De la Rue, 789-90; superseded by Georgina in household affairs, 798, 848-9; suppressed desire for divorce, 821-2; admission to Forster of skeleton in domestic closet, 862; open avowal of uncongeniality, 880-2; Dickens confesses their uncongeniality to Miss Coutts, 905; his accumulated criticism of Kate, 905-8; he confesses to De la Rue, 909; her suggestion that they separate, 909-10; his infatuation for Ellen Ternan, 910-11; his move to a separate bedroom, 911; the gift to Ellen, 916-7; his conviction that Kate would be unhappy with anyone, 919; his bitterness at the suspicions over Ellen, 920-1; and against Kate, 922; his distress at publication of "Violated Letter," 727; longing for freedom from, 972; refusal to see Kate after separation, 1064-5; cold mention in will, 1111

Will power, 45, 54, 66, 132, 134, 139, 214, 246, 250, 255-6, 555, 644, 1087

Work habits, 192-3, 207, 221-2, 303, 306, 458, 518, 520-1, 595-7, 601-3, 622, 624, 656, 675-6, 746, 756, 796, 799-800, 845-7, 852-3, 860, 947-8, 955, 964-5, 968-9

WORKS, LISTED HERE FOR CONVENIENCE. EXCEPT FOR A SMALL NUMBER, ALL NOTED, SEE UNDER MAIN ENTRIES:

American Notes (1842)
Barnaby Rudge (1841)
Battle of Life, The (1846)
Bleak House (1852-3)

DICKENS'S WORKS:

Child's History of England, A (1853)
Chimes, The (1844)
Christmas Carol, A, (1843)
Christmas Stories (in *Household Words* and *All the Year Round*): "Doctor Marigold's Prescriptions" (1865); "Going into Society" (1858), *see* "Mr. Chops the Dwarf"; "Haunted House, The" (1859); "Holly Tree, The," with Collins (1855), *see* "Boots at the Holly Tree, The"; "Message from the Sea, A," with Collins (1860); "Mrs. Lirriper's Legacy" (1864), not discussed; "Mrs. Lirriper's Lodgings" (1863); "Mugby Junction" (1866), not discussed; "No Thoroughfare," with Collins (1867); "Perils of Certain English Prisoners, The," with Collins (1857); "Seven Poor Travellers, The" (1854), *see* "Poor Travellers, The"; "Somebody's Luggage" (1862); "Tom Tiddler's Ground" (1861); "Two Ghost Stories" (1865-6), not discussed; "Wreck of the Golden Mary, The," with Collins (1856), not discussed
Cricket on the Hearth, The (1845)
David Copperfield (1849-50)
Dombey and Son (1846-8)
"George Silverman's Explanation" (1868)
Great Expectations (1860-1)
Hard Times (1854)
Haunted Man, The (1848)
"Holiday Romance, A" (1868)
"Hunted Down" (1859)
Is She His Wife? (1837)
Lamplighter, The (1838)
Lazy Tour of Two Idle Apprentices, A, with Collins, (1857)
Life of Our Lord (written 1849, published 1934)
Little Dorrit (1855-7)
Martin Chuzzlewit (1843-4)
Master Humphrey's Clock (1840-1) (consisting mainly of *Barnaby*

converses with, his admiration for, 612; quotes, 1112; 1132

Hull, Yorkshire, 940

Hullah, John, 89; Dickens writes opera libretto for, 108, 127, 143; 151, 154, 191; through Dickens has opera produced by Macready, 211; 219-20; Dickens has Hullah arrange singing-lessons for girls in Urania Cottage, 621; 713

Hullah, Miss, 751

Humphrey Clinker (Smollett), 21, 31

Humphrey, Master (*Master Humphrey's Clock*), 296, 305

Huncamunca (*Tom Thumb*), 791

Hunchback, The (Knowles), 60, 623

Hungerford Stairs, 31-3, 36, 43, 684

Hunt, Frederic Knight, 577

Hunt, James Henry Leigh, 186; first acquaintance with Dickens, 220; comment on Dickens's animation, 254; 419, 449; Dickens's benefit performances of *Every Man in His Humour* for, 616-7; pensioned, 617; 625, 676, 713, 723; caricature of in *Bleak House*, 753; contributes to *Household Words*, 759; 838; death of, Dickens's article regretting caricature, 958; 970, 1132

Hunt, William Holman, 960-1, 1131

Hunter, Mrs. Leo (P.P.), critical discussion of, 167; 369

Huskisson, William, 36

Huxley, Aldous, 289, 322, 765

Huxley, Thomas Henry, 1065

Hyde Park Gate South, No. 16 (Dickens residence), 1000

Hyde Park Place, No. 5 (Dickens residence), 1143, 1148

Hypnotism; *see* Mesmerism

I

Iago (*Othello*), 642, 958, 1050

Ibsen, Hendrik, 1038

Idler, The (Johnson), 21

"Ignorance and Crime" (Dickens) (*Examiner*), 653-4

Illustrated London News, 840

Ilusha (*Brothers Karamazov*), 323

Imaginary book titles in Dickens's library, 749-50

Imogen (*Cymbeline*), 323

Imperialism, 1124-5

Inchbald, Mrs. Elizabeth Simpson, 21

Independent Exhibition, Paris (1855), 858-9, 1131

India, 875, 1012, 1064-5, 1124, 1154

"India Rubber" (*H.W.*), 708-9

Indian Mutiny (1857-8), 1065

Industrialism, Dickens's emerging vision of, 317-8, 326-7; his growing preoccupation with its problems, 534; 565; philosophy of, 631, 743; growth of, 794-5; the development of Dickens's analysis of, 801-2; his view of industrialism as a vast jail, 885; 1104; imperialistic developments of, 1124-5; Dickens's understanding of, 1128; his ultimate hostility to, 1134

Industrial labor, condition of in 1830's, 275; exploitation of, 326-7; in America, 372; in 1840's, 704; *Household Words* articles on, 714; Dickens's defense of, 1134

Industrial Midlands, Dickens's first sight of, 224-5; portrayed in *Old Curiosity Shop*, 328-9; 534

Industrialists, 315, 489; opposition to factory regulation, not all brutal, 631; mutilations of factory workers in accidents, 714; attitudes of, 810; future dangers to, 974-5; Dickens's ultimate judgment of, 1134

"Infant Gardens" (*H.W.*), 714

Infant Phenomenon (*N.N.*), 284

Inge, William Ralph, Dean of St. Paul's, 1130, 1132

Ingres, Jean Auguste Dominique, 1131

"Inimitable Boz," origin of epithet, 221

Innocents Abroad, The (Twain), 561

Inquisition, The, 508

Insane Asylums, 372, 380

Insolvent Debtors' Act, 35, 53

Insull, Samuel, 889

International Copyright, Dickens's interest in Talfourd's work for, 212-

W

856; 857, 865, 868; discovers that Gad's Hill is for sale, 869-70; 907, 939-40, 942, 944; becomes quarter-owner of *All the Year Round*, 945; 958, 961-2, 1004; Dickens arranges with for Ellen Ternan's care in 1867, 1006, 1076; 1010, 1014; blackballed at Garrick Club, Dickens resigns, 1015-6; 1051; friction with Forster, 1052; 1061-3; tries to dissuade Dickens from going to America, 1070; 1072, 1078; retirement from *All the Year Round*, 1098; 1100, 1149

Wills, Mrs. W. H., plays Nurse Esther in *Frozen Deep*, 863, 877; 961, 1010

Wilmot, Lord (*Not So Bad as We Seem*), 727, 729, 734, 754

Wilmott, Mr. (Macready's manager), 647

Wilson (wig-man), 608

Wilson, Edmund, quoted, 45, 167, 886; 163

Wilson, Dr. James, 730

Wilson, General Sir John, 361

Wilson, Professor John ("Christopher North"), 122, 339-40, 454

Wimbledon, Surrey, Walter Dickens in school at, 847; Alfred Tennyson Dickens at, 954; Harry and Plorn at, 995; 1009; Plorn unhappy at, leaves, 1012; Harry does well at, 1064, 1100

Windsor, 293, 359, 716, 744, 1099, 1113, 1147

Windsor Lodge, 1059

Winkle, Nathaniel (*P.P.*), 119, 136, 153; critical discussion of, 158, 161-2, 169, 171, 174; 684, 936, 989, 1004

Winter, Gilbert, 225

Winter, Henry Louis, 831, 837, 1003

Winter, Maria Beadnell (Mrs. Henry Louis Winter), Dickens's emotion at hearing from, 831-5; disillusion on meeting, 835-6; later avoidance of, 837-8; 845; caricature of in Flora Finching, 860; Dickens's last

communications with, 1003-4; 1005; *see also* Beadnell, Maria

Winter's Tale, The (Shakespeare), 323, 877

Winterbourne (Dickens residence at Bonchurch, Isle of Wight), 667, 676

Wits' Miscellany, 179

Witterterley, Mrs. (*N.N.*), 285

Witterleys, the (*N.N.*), 284

Wolverhampton, Staffordshire, 224, 317, 795, 941

Woman in White, The (Collins), 946, 953, 956, 964

Wood, Hon. Benjamin, 1071-2

Woolner, Thomas, 1009, 1154

Woolwich, Kent, 995

Wopsle, Mr. (*G.E.*), 993

Worcester, Massachusetts, 379-80, 1087, 1090

Worcester, Worcestershire, 937-8

Wordsworth, William, 167, 302

Workhouses, Dickens's hatred of, 166; his portrayal of in *Oliver Twist*, 273-7; 318, 319; dread of among the poor, 1031-2

Workingmen, callous treatment of by society, 486-7; outlook of under doctrines of political economy, 519; *Household Words* articles advocating welfare of, 714; educational advances of, 756; Dickens's consistent support of, 793-4; his satire on businessmen's view of in *Hard Times*, 810; his appeal to, 825-7; 869, 885, 1134

Workingmen's College, London, 715

World and the Stage, The (Simpson), 949

Wound and the Bow, The (Wilson), 163; quoted, 45, 167, 886

Wrayburn, Eugene (*O.M.F.*), 1023, 1025, 1033-5, 1042-5

Wren, Jenny (Fanny Cleaver) (*O.M.F.*), 685, 1014; critical discussion of, 1024, 1033-4, 1042

Wright, Richard, 577

Wright, Thomas, quoted, 332; 1008, 1059